THIRD EDITION
SUMMIT 2

TEACHER'S EDITION AND LESSON PLANNER

JOAN SASLOW
ALLEN ASCHER

Summit: English for Today's World Level 2, Third Edition
Teacher's Edition and Lesson Planner

Copyright © 2017 by Pearson Education, Inc.

All rights reserved. No part of this publication may be reproduced, stored in a retrieval system, or transmitted in any form or by any means, electronic, mechanical, photocopying, recording, or otherwise, without the prior permission of the publisher.

Pearson, 221 River Street, Hoboken, NJ 07030

Staff credits: The people who made up the Summit team representing editorial, production, design, manufacturing, and marketing are Pietro Alongi, Rhea Banker, Peter Benson, Stephanie Bullard, Jennifer Castro, Tracey Munz Cataldo, Rosa Chapinal, Aerin Csigay, Dave Dickey, Gina DiLillo, Christopher Leonowicz, Laurie Neaman, Alison Pei, Sherri Pemberton, Jennifer Raspiller, Mary Rich, Courtney Steers, Katherine Sullivan, and Paula Van Ells.

Cover credit: Tonis Pan/Shutterstock

Text composition: Electra Graphics

Photo credits: Original photography Mike Cohen. Page 2 Robert Churchill/Alamy Stock Photo; p. 3 (t) Amble Design/Shutterstock, (b) Maximinogomes/Fotolia; p. 4 (l) YUTAKA/AFLO SPORT/Newscom, (r) FRANCISCO TRUJILLO/NOTIMEX/Newscom; p. 5 (r) Alistair Berg/DigitalVision/Getty Images, (l) blvdone/Fotolia; p. 6 (tr) wavebreakmedia/Shutterstock, (b , 1-4) Shutterstock, DRB Images/LLC/Getty Images, Andersen Ross/Blend Images/Getty Images, Jupiterimages/Stockbyte/Getty Images (b, 5-8) Tracy Whiteside/Shutterstock, Djomas/Shutterstock, Juanmonino/E+/Getty Images, pressmaster/Fotolia; p. 7 YAY Media AS/Alamy Stock Photo; p. 9 (t) Juniart/Shutterstock, (r) Shutterstock; (l) Stefan Schurr/Shutterstock; p. 13 goodluz/Fotolia; p. 15 Andersen Ross/Stockbyte/Getty Images; p. 17 Kzenon/Fotolia; p. 18 petrrunjela/Fotolia; p. 19 Bits and Splits/Fotolia; p. 20 Wavebreak Media Ltd/123RF; p. 21 Zurijeta/Shutterstock; p. 22 (Machal) ROBIN TOWNSEND/EPA/Newscom, (Ka-shing) YONHAP/EPA/Newscom, (Caldicott) Paul Lovelace/REX/Newscom (human rights) tang90246/Fotolia, (smokestacks) Nickolay Khoroshkov/Shutterstock, (refugees) Photo by Antonio Masiello/NurPhoto/REX/Shutterstock, (children in line) Joseph Project - Malawi/Alamy Stock Photo, (school) BSIP/Newscom, (elderly woman and child) Kumar Sriskandan/Alamy Stock Photo; p. 23 demerzel21/Getty Images; p. 26 Drobot Dean/Fotolia; p. 27 ONOKY/Eric Audras/Brand X Pictures/Getty Images, p. 28 (l-r) BMP/Shutterstock, Vladimir Wrangel/Shutterstock, Billion Photos/Shutterstock; p. 29 bertys30/Fotolia; p. 30 (t) Imagewerks/Getty Images, (r) Shutterstock, (l) Racorn/Shutterstock; p. 32 Byron Purvis/AdMedia/Newscom; p. 33 Shariff Che'Lah/123RF; p. 34 Kook Je Newspaper/AP Images; p. 35 (Parks) World History Archive/Alamy Stock Photo, (Khan) Pardis Sabeti, (crocodile) Jeep5d/Fotolia; p. 37 (l-r) Otnaydur/Shutterstock, AVAVA/Fotolia, Andresr/Shutterstock; p. 38 (clockwise) Jade/Blend Images/Getty Images, Andresr/Shutterstock, iofoto/Shutterstock, Shutterstock, fotogenicstudio/Fotolia, nyul/Fotolia; p. 39 wavebreakmedia/Shutterstock; p. 43 wavebreakmedia/Shutterstock; p. 44 (l) Phil Date/Shutterstock, (r) Jack Hollingsworth/Stockbyte/Getty Images; p. 46 georgerudy/Fotolia; p. 47 gstockstudio/Fotolia, BillionPhotos.com/Fotolia, Mat Hayward/Fotolia, Scott Griessel/Fotolia, Cheryl Savan/Shutterstock, gstockstudio/Fotolia; p. 50 (sand) Douglas Sacha/Moment Open/Getty Images, (caution) jdoms/Fotolia, (bad cat) FotoYakov/Shutterstock, (zipper) memo_frame/Fotolia, (egg) Morrowind/Shutterstock, (corn) Patti McConville/Photographer's Choice/Getty Images, (horse) byllwill/Vetta/Getty Images,(kitten) pavelmayorov/Shutterstock; p. 51 Tom Merton/Hoxton/Getty Images; p. 52 Rouelle Umali Xinhua News Agency/Newscom; p. 53 DragonImages; p. 54 (l) DW labs Incorporated/Shutterstock, (r) east2/Fotolia; p. 55 (laptop/park) wavebreakmedia/Shutterstock, (cartoon) Cartoonresource/Shutterstock; p. 57 Tyler Olson/Fotolia; p. 64 (tl) Kurhan/Fotolia, (tr) HillCreek Pictures/UpperCut Images/Getty Images, (br) Birkholz/E+/Getty Images , (bl) EMPPhotography/E+/Getty Images; p. 66 Daisy Daisy/Fotolia; p. 68 Tetra Images/Getty Images; p. 69 nakophotography/Fotolia; p. 70 (t) Thinkstock Images/Stockbyte/Getty Images, (m) Petert2/Fotolia, (b) Digital Vision/Photodisc/Getty Images; p. 71 Robin Nelson/ZUMA Press/Newscom; p. 73 Photographyttl/Fotolia; p. 74 (A) Cosid/Shutterstock, (B) Juriah Mosin/Shutterstock, (C) Til Vogt/Shutterstock, (D) Pathdoc/Fotolia, (E) Objowl/Shutterstock; p. 75 Dave/Les Jacobs/Blend Images/Getty Images; p. 77 (t) kupicoo/E+/Getty Images, (m) kupicoo/E+/Getty Images, (b) Shutterstock (diamond) Atiketta Sangasaeng/Shutterstock; p. 80 (l) kubais/Shutterstock, (r) Steven Heap/123RF; p. 84 t_fuji/Fotolia; p. 86 SWP/Fotolia; p. 87 Digitalskillet/E+/Getty Images; p. 88 BillionPhotos.com/Fotolia, Rick Gomez/Blend Images/Getty Images, Huntstock/Getty Images, Scott Griessel/Fotolia, BillionPhotos.com/Fotolia, Istockalypse Elkor/Getty Images, Bst2012/Fotolia, Mark Bowden/123RF; p. 89 StockLite/Shutterstock; p. 90 VLADGRIN/Shutterstock; p. 91 Nomad_Soul/Fotolia; p. 92 DragonImages/Fotolia; p. 93 Indeed/Getty Images, JackF/Fotolia, Minerva Studio/Fotolia, Felix Mizioznikov/Shutterstock, Jeanette Dietl/Shutterstock, leungchopan/Fotolia; p. 94 (Einstein) akg images/Newscom, (Ramanujan) Nick Higham/Alamy Stock Photo; p. 98 Anibal/Fotolia; p. 99 Michal Krakowiak/Getty Images; p. 100 (Olsen) Carol Francavilla/AP Images, (Jobs) Terry Schmitt/UPI/Newscom, (Gates) Richard Ellis/Alamy Stock Photo; p. 101 (tl) Jun Dangoy/Fotolia, (tr) Patrick/Fotolia, (br) VictorHabbickVisions/Science Photo Library/Getty Images, (bl) Hxdyl/Fotolia; p. 102 (headset) wayne_0216/Fotolia, (finger) Mihaperosa/Fotolia, (atom) Petecek/Fotolia; p. 103 Serge Black/Fotolia; p. 104 (redwoods) Tomasz Zajda/Fotolia, (Milarch) Dusty Christensen/MCT/Newscom, (Tuy) Jeremy_Holden/Photoshot/Newscom; p. 105 Design56/Fotolia, Robraine/Shutterstock; p. 106 Epicurean/Vetta/Getty Images; p. 107 (wedding) Paylessimages/Fotolia, (baby) rSnapshotPhotos/Shutterstock, (wheelchair) Kzenon/Shutterstock; p. 110 (t) Bst2012/Fotolia, (b) XiXinXing/Shutterstock; p. 111 (park backdrop) Trofotodesign/Fotolia; p. 113 Djoronimo/Fotolia; p. 114 (t) StockLite/Shutterstock, (m) Daniel Ingold/Getty Images, (b) LDprod/Shutterstock; p. 115 (l) James Brunker/Alamy Stock Photo, (c) Natalie Behring/Newscom, (tr) Peter Muller/Cultura/Getty Images, (b) Dean Bertoncelj/Shutterstock; p. 117 Federico Rostangno/Fotolia; p. 118 (l) Dmitrimaruta/Fotolia, (r) Alen-D/Fotolia.

Illustration Credits: Aptara pp. 8, 26, 44, 56, 67, 78; Steve Attoe p. 45, 58 (b); Dusan Petricic p. 16, 57, 59; el Primo Ramon p. 10, 14, 31, 58 (t), 62, 82, 119.

Printed in the United States of America

ISBN-10: 0-13-449905-0
ISBN-13: 978-0-13449905-5
1 17

pearsonelt.com/summit3e

Impreso en los talleres de DocuMaster
(Master Copy, S.A. de C.V.)
Plásticos #84 Local 2 Ala S ur
Fracc. Industrial Alce Blanco
Naucalpan de Juárez, C.P. 53370
www.documaster.mx

CONTENTS

About the Authors. v
Learning Objectives vi
To the Teacher. x
Components xi
Using your *Summit* Teacher's Edition and Lesson Planner xii

Lesson Planner

UNIT 1	Dreams and Goals.	T2
UNIT 2	Character and Responsibility	T14
UNIT 3	Fears, Hardships, and Heroism	T26
UNIT 4	Getting Along with Others	T38
UNIT 5	Humor.	T50
UNIT 6	Troubles While Traveling.	T62
UNIT 7	Mind Over Matter.	T74
UNIT 8	Performing at Your Best	T86
UNIT 9	What Lies Ahead?	T98
UNIT 10	An Interconnected World	T110

Reference Charts. 122
GRAMMAR BOOSTER T128
PRONUNCIATION BOOSTER T143
TEST-TAKING SKILLS BOOSTER 151

Other Resources

Audioscript 161
Summit TV Teaching Notes 180
Conversation and Discussion Activator Video Scripts. 205

Contents

About the Authors v
Learning Objectives vi
To the Teacher x
Components xi
Using your Summit Teacher's Edition and Lesson Planner xii

Lesson Planner

Dreams and Goals T2
Character and Responsibility T14
Fears, Hardships, and Heroism T26
Getting Along with Others T38
Humor T50
Troubles While Traveling T62
Mind Over Matter T74
Performing at Your Best T86
What Lies Ahead? T98
An Interconnected World T110

Reference Charts 127
.... T128
.... T143
.... T151

Other Resources

Audioscript 161
Summit TV Teaching Notes 180
Conversation and Discussion Activator Video Scripts 205

ABOUT THE AUTHORS

Joan Saslow

Joan Saslow has taught in a variety of programs in South America and the United States. She is author or coauthor of a number of widely used courses, some of which are *Ready to Go*, *Workplace Plus*, *Literacy Plus*, and *Top Notch*. She is also author of *English in Context*, a series for reading science and technology. Ms. Saslow was the series director of *True Colors* and *True Voices*. She has participated in the English Language Specialist Program in the U.S. Department of State's Bureau of Educational and Cultural Affairs.

Allen Ascher

Allen Ascher has been a teacher and teacher trainer in China and the United States, as well as academic director of the intensive English program at Hunter College. Mr. Ascher has also been an ELT publisher and was responsible for publication and expansion of numerous well-known courses including *True Colors*, *NorthStar*, the *Longman TOEFL Preparation Series*, and the *Longman Academic Writing Series*. He is coauthor of *Top Notch*, and he wrote the "Teaching Speaking" module of *Teacher Development Interactive*, an online multimedia teacher-training program.

Ms. Saslow and Mr. Ascher are frequent presenters at professional conferences and have been coauthoring courses for teens, adults, and young adults since 2002.

AUTHORS' ACKNOWLEDGMENTS

The authors wish to thank Katherine Klagsbrun for developing the digital Extra Challenge Reading Activities that appear with all reading selections in *Summit 2*.

The authors are indebted to these reviewers, who provided extensive and detailed feedback and suggestions for *Summit*, as well as the hundreds of teachers who completed surveys and participated in focus groups.

Cris Asperti, CEL LEP, São Paulo, Brazil • **Diana Alicia Ávila Martínez**, CUEC, Monterrey, Mexico • **Shannon Brown**, Nagoya University of Foreign Studies, Nagoya, Japan • **Cesar Byrd**, Universidad ETAC Campus Chalco, Mexico City, Mexico • **Maria Claudia Campos de Freitas**, Metalanguage, São Paulo, Brazil • **Alvaro Del Castillo Alba**, CBA, Santa Cruz, Bolivia • **Isidro Castro Galván**, Instituto Teocalli, Monterrey, Mexico • **Melisa Celi**, Idiomas Católica, Lima, Peru • **Carlos Celis**, CEL LEP, São Paulo, Brazil • **Jussara Costa e Silva**, Prize Language School, São Paulo, Brazil • **Inara Couto**, CEL LEP, São Paulo, Brazil • **Gemma Crouch**, ICPNA Chiclayo, Peru • **Ingrid Valverde Diaz del Olmo**, ICPNA Cusco, Peru • **Jacqueline Díaz Esquivel**, PROULEX, Guadalajara, Mexico • **María Eid Ceneviva**, CBA, Cochabamba, Bolivia • **Erika Licia Esteves Silva**, Murphy English, São Paulo, Brazil • **Cristian Garay**, Idiomas Católica, Lima, Peru • **Miguel Angel Guerrero Pozos**, PROULEX, Guadalajara, Mexico • **Anderson Francisco Guimarães Maia**, Centro Cultural Brasil Estados Unidos, Belém, Brazil • **Cesar Guzmán**, CAADI Monterrey, Mexico • **César Iván Hernández Escobedo**, PROULEX, Guadalajara, Mexico • **Robert Hinton**, Nihon University, Tokyo, Japan • **Segundo Huanambal Díaz**, ICPNA Chiclayo, Peru • **Chandra Víctor Jacobs Sukahai**, Universidad de Valle de México, Monterrey, Mexico • **Yeni Jiménez Torres**, Centro Colombo Americano Bogotá, Colombia • **Simon Lees**, Nagoya University of Foreign Studies, Nagoya, Japan • **Thomas LeViness**, PROULEX, Guadalajara, Mexico • **Amy Lewis**, Waseda University, Tokyo, Japan • **Luz Libia Rey**, Centro Colombo Americano, Bogotá, Colombia • **Diego López**, Idiomas Católica, Lima, Peru • **Junior Lozano**, Idiomas Católica, Lima, Peru • **Tanja McCandie**, Nanzan University, Nagoya, Japan • **Tammy Martínez Nieves**, Universidad Autónoma de Nuevo León, Monterrey, Mexico • **María Teresa Meléndez Mantilla**, ICPNA Chiclayo, Peru • **Mónica Nomberto**, ICPNA Chiclayo, Peru • **Otilia Ojeda**, Monterrey, Mexico • **Juana Palacios**, Idiomas Católica, Lima, Peru • **Giuseppe Paldino Mayorga**, Jellyfish Learning Center, San Cristobal, Ecuador • **Henry Eduardo Pardo Lamprea**, Universidad Militar Nueva Granada, Colombia • **Dario Paredes**, Centro Colombo Americano, Bogotá, Colombia • **Teresa Noemí Parra Alarcón**, Centro Anglo Americano de Cuernavaca, S.C., Cuernavaca, Mexico • **Carlos Eduardo de la Paz Arroyo**, Centro Anglo Americano de Cuernavaca, S.C., Cuernavaca, Mexico • **José Luis Pérez Treviño**, Instituto Obispado, Monterrey, Mexico • **Evelize Maria Plácido Florian**, São Paulo, Brazil • **Armida Rivas**, Monterrey, Mexico • **Luis Rodríguez Amau**, ICPNA Chiclayo, Peru • **Fabio Ossaamn Rok Kaku**, Prize Language School, São Paulo, Brazil • **Ana María Román Villareal**, CUEC, Monterrey, Mexico • **Reynaldo Romano C.**, CBA, La Paz, Bolivia • **Francisco Rondón**, Centro Colombo Americano, Bogotá, Colombia • **Peter Russell**, Waseda University, Tokyo, Japan • **Rubena St. Louis**, Universidad Simón Bolivar, Caracas, Venezuela • **Marisol Salazar**, Centro Colombo Americano, Bogotá, Colombia • **Miguel Sierra**, Idiomas Católica, Lima, Peru • **Greg Strong**, Aoyama Gakuin University, Tokyo, Japan • **Gerald Talandis**, Toyama University, Toyama, Japan • **Stephen Thompson**, Nagoya University of Foreign Studies, Nagoya, Japan • **José Luis Urbina Hurtado**, Instituto Tecnológico de León, Mexico • **René F. Valdivia Pereyra**, CBA, Santa Cruz, Bolivia • **Magno Alejandro Vivar Hurtado**, Salesian Polytechnic University, Ecuador • **Belkis Yanes**, Caracas, Venezuela • **Holger Zamora**, ICPNA Cusco, Peru • **Maria Cristina Zanon Costa**, Metalanguage, São Paulo, Brazil • **Kathia Zegarra**, Idiomas Católica, Lima, Peru.

LEARNING OBJECTIVES

UNIT	COMMUNICATION GOALS	VOCABULARY	GRAMMAR
UNIT 1 **Dreams and Goals** PAGE 2	• Ask about someone's background • Discuss career and study plans • Compare your dreams and goals in life • Describe job qualifications	• Job applications • Collocations for career and study plans • Describing dreams and goals **Word Study:** • Collocations with <u>have</u> and <u>get</u> for qualifications	• Simultaneous and sequential past actions: review and expansion • Completed and uncompleted past actions closely related to the present **GRAMMAR BOOSTER** • Describing past actions and events: review • Stative verbs: non-action and action meanings
UNIT 2 **Character and Responsibility** PAGE 14	• Describe the consequences of lying • Express regret and take responsibility • Explore where values come from • Discuss how best to help others	• Taking or avoiding responsibility • Philanthropic work	• Adjective clauses: review and expansion • "Comment" clauses **GRAMMAR BOOSTER** • Adjective clauses: overview • Grammar for Writing: adjective clauses with quantifiers • Grammar for Writing: reduced adjective clauses
UNIT 3 **Fears, Hardships, and Heroism** PAGE 26	• Express frustration, empathy, and encouragement • Describe how fear affects you physically • Discuss overcoming handicaps and hardships • Examine the nature of heroism	• Expressing frustration, empathy, and encouragement • Physical effects of fear **Word Study:** • Using parts of speech	• Clauses with <u>no matter</u> • Using <u>so</u> … (<u>that</u>) or <u>such</u> … (<u>that</u>) to explain results **GRAMMAR BOOSTER** • Embedded questions: review and common errors • Non-count nouns made countable • Nouns used in both countable and uncountable sense
UNIT 4 **Getting Along with Others** PAGE 38	• Discuss how to overcome shortcomings • Acknowledge inconsiderate behavior • Explain how you handle anger • Explore the qualities of friendship	• Shortcomings • Expressing and controlling anger	• Adverb clauses of condition • Cleft sentences: review and expansion **GRAMMAR BOOSTER** • Grammar for Writing: more conjunctions and transitions • Cleft sentences: more on meaning and use
UNIT 5 **Humor** PAGE 50	• Discuss the health benefits of laughter • Respond to something funny • Analyze what makes us laugh • Explore the limits of humor	• Ways to respond to jokes and other funny things • Common types of jokes • Practical jokes	• Indirect speech: backshifts in tense and time expressions • Questions in indirect speech **GRAMMAR BOOSTER** • Imperatives in indirect speech • Changes to pronouns and possessives • <u>Say</u>, <u>tell</u>, and <u>ask</u> • Other reporting verbs

CONVERSATION STRATEGIES	LISTENING / PRONUNCIATION	READING	WRITING
• Use <u>Thanks for asking</u> to express appreciation for someone's interest. • Use <u>Correct me if I'm wrong, but …</u> to tentatively assert what you believe about someone or something. • Say <u>I've given it some thought and …</u> to introduce a thoughtful opinion. • Informally ask for directions by saying <u>Steer me in the right direction</u>. • Say <u>As a matter of fact</u> to present a relevant fact. • Offer assistance with <u>I'd be more than happy to</u>. • Say <u>I really appreciate it</u> to express gratitude.	**Listening Skills:** • Listen to activate vocabulary • Listen for main ideas • Listen to confirm content • Listen for supporting details • Listen to infer **PRONUNCIATION BOOSTER** • Sentence stress and intonation: review	**Texts:** • An application for employment • An article about two famous people • An article about good and bad interview behavior • A job advertisement • A résumé **Skills / strategies:** • Understand idioms and expressions • Confirm information • Apply ideas	**Task:** • Write a traditional cover letter to an employer **Skill:** • A formal cover letter
• Admit having made a mistake by apologizing with <u>I'm really sorry, but …</u> • Confirm that someone agrees to an offer with <u>if that's OK</u>. • Use <u>That's really not necessary</u> to politely turn down an offer. • Take responsibility for a mistake by saying <u>Please accept my apology</u>.	**Listening Skills:** • Listen to infer information • Listen to support an opinion • Listen for main ideas • Listen to classify • Listen to confirm content • Listen for point of view • Listen to summarize • Listen to draw conclusions **PRONUNCIATION BOOSTER** • Emphatic stress and pitch to express emotion	**Texts:** • A survey about taking or avoiding responsibility • An article about lying • A textbook article about the development of values • Dictionary entries • Short biographies **Skills / strategies:** • Understand idioms and expressions • Relate to personal experience • Classify vocabulary using context • Critical thinking	**Task:** • Write a college application essay **Skill:** • Restrictive and non-restrictive adjective clauses
• Ask <u>Is something wrong?</u> to express concern about someone's state of mind. • Ask <u>What's going on?</u> to show interest in the details of someone's problem. • Begin an explanation with <u>Well, basically</u> to characterize a problem in few words. • Say <u>Hang in there</u> to offer support to someone facing a difficulty. • Say <u>Anytime</u> to acknowledge someone's appreciation and minimize what one has done.	**Listening Skills:** • Listen to predict • Listen to activate parts of speech • Listen for details • Listen to retell a story • Listen to summarize **PRONUNCIATION BOOSTER** • Vowel reduction to /ə/	**Texts:** • A self-test about how fearful you are • Interview responses about how fear affects people physically • An article about Marlee Matlin • Profiles of three heroes **Skills / strategies:** • Understand idioms and expressions • Understand meaning from context • Summarize	**Task:** • Write a short report about a dangerous or frightening event **Skill:** • Reducing adverbial clauses
• Introduce an uncomfortable topic with <u>there's something I need to bring up</u>. • Say <u>I didn't realize that</u> to acknowledge a complaint about your behavior. • Use <u>I didn't mean to …</u> to apologize for and summarize someone's complaint. • Say <u>On the contrary</u> to assure someone that you don't feel the way they think you might. • Say <u>I can see your point</u> to acknowledge someone's point of view.	**Listening Skills:** • Listen to activate grammar • Listen to summarize the main idea • Listen to infer information • Listen to draw conclusions **PRONUNCIATION BOOSTER** • Shifting emphatic stress	**Texts:** • Profiles about people's shortcomings • Descriptions of different workshops • An article on friendship **Skills / strategies:** • Understand idioms and expressions • Understand meaning from context • Apply ideas • Relate to personal experience	**Task:** • Write a three-paragraph essay presenting a solution to a common shortcoming **Skill:** • Transitional topic sentences
• Exclaim <u>You've got to see this</u>! to urge someone to look at something. • Introduce a statement with <u>Seriously</u> to insist someone not hesitate to take your suggestion. • Say <u>That's priceless</u> to strongly praise something. • Agree informally with <u>Totally</u>.	**Listening Skills:** • Listen to activate vocabulary • Listen to summarize • Listen to take notes • Listen to apply ideas **PRONUNCIATION BOOSTER** • Intonation of sarcasm	**Texts:** • A self-test about your sense of humor • An article about the health benefits of laughter • An article about the theories of humor • Descriptions of practical jokes **Skills / strategies:** • Understand idioms and expressions • Critical thinking • Classify	**Task:** • Write a true or imaginary story **Skill:** • Writing dialogue

vii

UNIT	COMMUNICATION GOALS	VOCABULARY	GRAMMAR
UNIT 6 **Troubles While Traveling** PAGE 62	• Describe some causes of travel hassles • Express gratitude for a favor while traveling • Discuss staying safe on the Internet • Talk about lost, stolen, or damaged property	• Travel nouns **Word Study:** • Past participles as noun modifiers	• Unreal conditional sentences: continuous forms • Unreal conditional statements with <u>if it weren't for</u> … / <u>if it hadn't been for</u> … **GRAMMAR BOOSTER** • The conditional: summary and extension
UNIT 7 **Mind Over Matter** PAGE 74	• Suggest that someone is being gullible • Examine superstitions for believability • Talk about the power of suggestion • Discuss phobias	• Ways to express disbelief • Expressions with <u>mind</u> **Word Study:** • Noun and adjective forms	• Nouns: indefinite, definite, unique, and generic meaning (review and expansion) • Indirect speech: <u>it</u> + a passive reporting verb **GRAMMAR BOOSTER** • Article usage: summary • Definite article: additional uses • More non-count nouns with both a countable and an uncountable sense • Grammar for Writing: indirect speech with passive reporting verbs
UNIT 8 **Performing at Your Best** PAGE 86	• Discuss your talents and strengths • Suggest ways to boost intelligence • Explain how you produce your best work • Describe what makes someone a "genius"	• Expressions to describe talents and strengths • Adjectives that describe aspects of intelligence	• Using auxiliary <u>do</u> for emphatic stress • The subjunctive **GRAMMAR BOOSTER** • Grammar for Writing: emphatic stress • Infinitives and gerunds in place of the subjunctive
UNIT 9 **What Lies Ahead?** PAGE 98	• Discuss the feasibility of future technologies • Evaluate applications of innovative technologies • Discuss how to protect our future environment • Examine future social and demographic trends	• Innovative technologies • Ways to express a concern about consequences • Describing social and demographic trends	• The passive voice: the future, the future as seen from the past, and the future perfect • The passive voice in unreal conditional sentences **GRAMMAR BOOSTER** • Grammar for Writing: when to use the passive voice
UNIT 10 **An Interconnected World** PAGE 110	• React to news about global issues • Describe the impact of foreign imports • Discuss the pros and cons of globalization • Suggest ways to avoid culture shock	• Phrasal verbs to discuss issues and problems	• Separability of transitive phrasal verbs **GRAMMAR BOOSTER** • Phrasal verbs: expansion

Reference Charts .... page 122
Grammar Booster .... page 128
Pronunciation Booster .... page 143
Test-Taking Skills Booster .... page 151

CONVERSATION STRATEGIES	LISTENING / PRONUNCIATION	READING	WRITING
• Ask a stranger for help with I wonder if you could do me a favor. • Agree to offer assistance with How can I help? • Confirm willingness to perform a favor with I'd be happy to. • Introduce a statement of relief with It's a good thing.	**Listening Skills:** • Listen to infer • Listen to activate grammar • Listen for main ideas • Listen to confirm content • Listen to understand meaning from context • Listen for details • Listen to summarize **PRONUNCIATION BOOSTER** • Regular past participle endings • Reduction in perfect modals	**Texts:** • A travel tips contest • Interview responses about travel hassles • An article about the dangers of public Wi-Fi **Skills / strategies:** • Understand idioms and expressions • Understand meaning from context • Paraphrase • Find supporting details	**Task:** • Write an essay comparing and contrasting two means of transportation **Skill:** • A comparison and contrast essay
• Call someone's attention to an outrageous claim with Can you believe this? • Express surprise at someone's gullibility with Oh, come on. • Use That's got to be to underscore a conclusion. • Add I guess to an opinion one isn't sure about. • Express extreme agreement to another's opinion with You can say that again.	**Listening Skills:** • Listen for details • Listen to confirm content • Listen to summarize • Listen to infer **PRONUNCIATION BOOSTER** • Linking sounds	**Texts:** • A website about superstitions • An article about the placebo and nocebo effects **Skills / strategies:** • Understand idioms and expressions • Infer meaning • Draw conclusions • Critical thinking	**Task:** • Write a four-paragraph essay on superstitions **Skill:** • Subject / verb agreement: expansion
• Say Guess what? to introduce exciting news. • Use I can't make up my mind between … to signal indecision. • Use I wouldn't say … to express modesty or doubt. • Support a statement or point of view with I've been told that. • Provide support for someone's decision with I don't think you can go wrong.	**Listening Skills:** • Listen for main ideas • Listen to infer • Listen for supporting details • Listen to draw conclusions **PRONUNCIATION BOOSTER** • Emphatic stress with auxiliary verbs	**Texts:** • A quiz on emotional intelligence • An article on whether intelligence can be increased • An article on staying on target **Skills / strategies:** • Understand idioms and expressions • Apply ideas • Relate to personal experience	**Task:** • Write a three-paragraph essay about the challenges of staying focused **Skill:** • Explaining cause and result
• Use For one thing to introduce an important first argument. • Say Well, if you ask me … to offer an opinion. • Use I mean to clarify what you just said. • Say I see your point to concede the value of someone else's opinion.	**Listening Skills:** • Listen to activate vocabulary • Listen to identify point of view • Listen to confirm content • Listen to infer information • Listen to draw conclusions **PRONUNCIATION BOOSTER** • Reading aloud	**Texts:** • A survey on future predictions • An article on how people in the past envisioned the future • An article on what some people are doing to protect the environment • Dictionary entries **Skills / strategies:** • Understand idioms and expressions • Understand meaning from context • Draw conclusions	**Task:** • Write a four- or five-paragraph essay about the future **Skill:** • The thesis statement in a formal essay
• Begin a statement with Can you believe … to introduce surprising, exciting, or disturbing information. • Use But on the bright side to change a negative topic to something more positive. • Begin a statement with It just goes to show you … to emphasize a point. • Say Well, that's another story to acknowledge a positive or negative change of topic. • Begin a statement with You'd think … to express frustration with a situation.	**Listening Skills:** • Listen to activate vocabulary • Listen to summarize • Listen to confirm information • Listen to understand meaning from context • Listen to draw conclusions **PRONUNCIATION BOOSTER** • Intonation of tag questions	**Texts:** • A quiz on English in today's world • News stories about global issues and problems • People's opinions about foreign imports • An article about the pros and cons of globalization **Skills / strategies:** • Understand idioms and expressions • Understand meaning from context • Identify supporting ideas • Interpret information in a graph	**Task:** • Write a four-paragraph essay to rebut an opposing view about globalization **Skill:** • Rebutting an opposing point of view

TO THE TEACHER

What is *Summit*?

Summit is a two-level high-intermediate to advanced communicative course that develops confident, culturally fluent English speakers able to navigate the social, travel, and professional situations they will encounter as they use English in their lives. *Summit* can follow the intermediate level of any communicative series, including the four-level *Top Notch* course.

Summit delivers immediate, demonstrable results in every class session through its proven pedagogy and systematic and intensive recycling of language. Each goal- and achievement-based lesson is tightly correlated to the Can-Do Statements of the Common European Framework of Reference (CEFR). The course is fully benchmarked to the Global Scale of English (GSE).

Each level of *Summit* contains material for 60 to 90 hours of classroom instruction. Its full array of additional print and digital components can extend instruction to 120 hours if desired. Furthermore, the entire *Summit* course can be tailored to blended learning with its integrated online component, *MyEnglishLab*. *Summit* offers more ready-to-use teacher resources than any other course available today.

NEW This third edition represents a major revision of content and has a greatly increased quantity of exercises, both print and digital. Following are some key new features:

- **Conversation Activator Videos** to build communicative competence
- **Discussion Activator Videos** to increase quality and quantity of expression
- A **Test-Taking Skills Booster** (and **Extra Challenge Reading Activities**) to help students succeed in the reading and listening sections of standardized tests
- An **Understand Idioms and Expressions** section in each unit increases the authenticity of student spoken language

Award-Winning Instructional Design*

Demonstrable confirmation of progress
Every two-page lesson has a clearly stated communication goal and culminates in a guided conversation, free discussion, debate, presentation, role play, or project that achieves the goal. Idea framing and notepadding activities lead students to confident spoken expression.

Cultural fluency
Summit audio familiarizes students with a wide variety of native and non-native accents. Discussion activities reflect the topics people of diverse cultural backgrounds talk about in their social and professional lives.

Explicit vocabulary and grammar
Clear captioned illustrations and dictionary-style presentations, all with audio, take the guesswork out of meaning and ensure comprehensible pronunciation. Grammar is embedded in context and presented explicitly for form, meaning, and use. The unique "Recycle this Language" feature encourages active use of newly learned words and grammar during communication practice.

Active listening syllabus
More than 50 listening tasks at each level of *Summit* develop critical thinking and crucial listening comprehension skills such as listen for details, main ideas, confirmation of content, inference, and understand meaning from context.

Conversation and Discussion Activators
Memorable conversation models with audio provide appealing natural social language and conversation strategies essential for post-secondary learners. Rigorous Conversation Activator and Discussion Activator activities with video systematically stimulate recycling of social language, ensuring it is not forgotten. A unique Pronunciation Booster provides lessons and interactive practice, with audio, so students can improve their spoken expression.

Systematic writing skills development
Summit teaches the conventions of correct English writing so students will be prepared for standardized tests, academic study, and professional communication. Lessons cover key writing and rhetorical skills such as using parallel structure and avoiding sentence fragments, run-on sentences, and comma splices. Intensive work in paragraph and essay development ensures confident and successful writing.

Reading skills and strategies
Each unit of *Summit* builds critical thinking and key reading skills and strategies such as paraphrasing, drawing conclusions, expressing and supporting an opinion, and activating prior knowledge. Learners develop analytical skills and increase fluency while supporting their answers through speaking.

We wish you and your students enjoyment and success with *Summit*. We wrote it for you.

Joan Saslow and Allen Ascher

*Summit is the recipient of the Association of Educational Publishers' Distinguished Achievement Award.

COMPONENTS

ActiveTeach

Maximize the impact of your *Summit* lessons. Digital Student's Book pages with access to all audio and video provide an interactive classroom experience that can be used with or without an interactive whiteboard (IWB). It includes a full array of easy-to-access digital and printable features.

For class presentation . . .

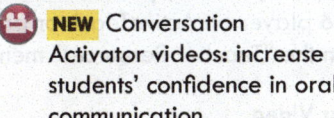
- **NEW** Conversation Activator videos: increase students' confidence in oral communication

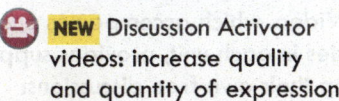
- **NEW** Discussion Activator videos: increase quality and quantity of expression

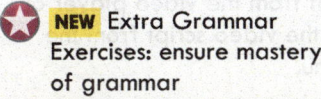
- **NEW** Extra Grammar Exercises: ensure mastery of grammar

- **NEW** Extra Challenge Reading Activities: help students succeed at standardized proficiency tests.

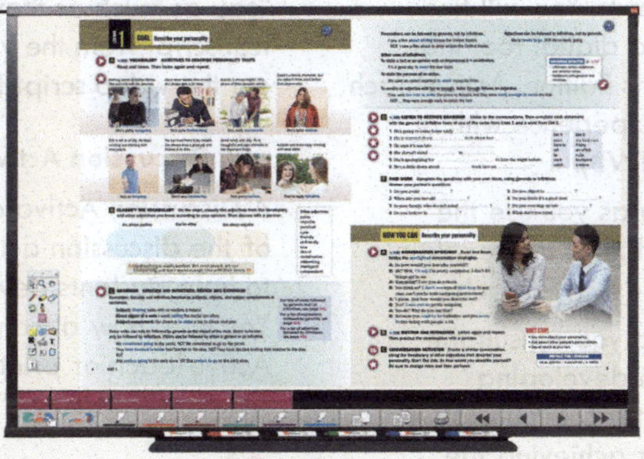

PLUS
- Interactive Whiteboard tools, including zoom, highlight, links, notes, and more.
- Clickable Audio: instant access to the complete classroom audio program
- *Summit TV* Video Program: fully-revised authentic TV documentaries as well as unscripted on-the-street interviews, featuring a variety of regional and non-native accents

For planning . . .

- A *Methods Handbook* for a communicative classroom
- Detailed timed lesson plans for each two-page lesson
- *Summit TV* teaching notes
- Complete answer keys, audio scripts, and video scripts

For extra support . . .

- Hundreds of extra printable activities, with teaching notes
- *Summit TV* activity worksheets

For assessment . . .

- Ready-made unit and review achievement tests with options to edit, add, or delete items using test generator software.

Ready-made Summit Web Projects provide authentic application of lesson language.

MyEnglishLab
An optional online learning tool

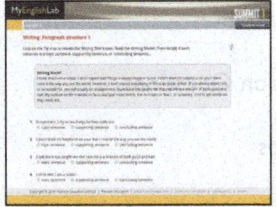

- **NEW** Immediate, meaningful feedback on wrong answers
- **NEW** Remedial grammar exercises
- **NEW** Grammar Coach videos for general reference
- Interactive practice of all material presented in the course
- Grade reports that display performance and time on task
- Auto-graded achievement tests

Teacher & Student Resources

- Teachers can access all their resources on the Pearson English Portal, including MyEnglishLab, test generator software, and all the resources from ActiveTeach. Contact your local rep for a code.
- Students can access the audio files, web projects, and interactive digital activities on the Portal.

Workbook
Lesson-by-lesson written exercises to accompany the Student's Book

Full-Course Placement Tests
Choose between printable and online versions

Classroom Audio Program

- A set of Audio CDs, as an alternative to the clickable audio in ActiveTeach
- Contains a variety of authentic regional and non-native accents to build comprehension of diverse English speakers
- **NEW** The complete audio program is available on the Pearson English Portal and the Pearson Practice English app

Teacher's Edition and Lesson Planner

- Detailed interleaved lesson plans, language and culture notes, answer keys, and more
- Also accessible as pdfs in the ActiveTeach

For more information: www.english.com/summit3e

xi

USING YOUR *SUMMIT* TEACHER'S EDITION AND LESSON PLANNER

The **Teacher's Edition and Lesson Planner** provides detailed notes for planning and presenting your lessons, plus ideas for extending them. You will find additional support in ActiveTeach, a digital tool that goes hand in hand with the Teacher's Edition. ActiveTeach provides an interactive classroom experience with or without an interactive whiteboard (IWB).

The instructions here will guide you as you use the teaching suggestions in the Lesson Plans, and explain the printable and digital resources in ActiveTeach.

In addition, the authors recommend you consult the **Methods Handbook** for support in developing effective techniques for teaching in a communicative classroom and for teaching tips for achieving the best results with the *Summit* course. You can find the **Methods Handbook** in the folder labeled "Methodology" within "Teacher Resources" on ActiveTeach. Within "Methodology", you will also find the article **"Great Ideas for Teaching with *ActiveTeach*,"** which explains numerous ways in which you can use ActiveTeach to enhance your in-class lessons.

Overview

Starting with Unit 1, each two-page lesson is designed for a period of 45 to 60 minutes. To plan a class of approximately 45 minutes, use the shorter estimated teaching times as a guide when a range is shown. To plan a class of at least 60 minutes, use the longer estimated times. Your actual teaching time may vary according to your students' needs, your program schedule, and your teaching style. Write your actual teaching time in the space provided for future reference.

Activities labeled *Option* include suggested teaching times that should be added to the lesson.

In addition, these optional digital activities referenced throughout this Teacher's Edition are available in ActiveTeach to enrich your lesson.

  More Exercises

Additional exercises are provided for each grammar presentation. The Extra Grammar Exercises can be presented as interactive digital activities, or they can be printed out and distributed as handouts from the "Printable Extension Activities" menu in "Teacher Resources."

 Conversation Activator Video

This unique video provides a dramatic demonstration of how students can be maximally productive as they create their own personalized conversations. The Conversation Activator Video encourages students to "say as much as they can." If you wish, you can show a transcript from the video player on ActiveTeach or print out the video script from the "Teacher Resources" menu.

 Discussion Activator Video

A Discussion Activator Video, which accompanies one of the discussion activities in each unit, provides support to help students develop their own free discussions. You can show a transcript from the video player on ActiveTeach or print out the video script from the "Teacher Resources" menu.

 Digital Games

A game called "Stepping Stones" provides additional review and practice of unit language. It can be opened by clicking the icon on the digital Student's Book page in ActiveTeach, or it can be accessed in "Teacher Resources" within ActiveTeach.

 Extension Activities and other resources

A multitude of optional extension activities enable you to tailor *Summit* to the needs of your class. Throughout the Lesson Planner notes, printable extension activities and other resources are referenced at the suggested point of use in the lesson. Included are:

- Conversation Activator-Speaking Booster
- Discussion-Speaking Booster
- Extra Challenge Reading Activities
- Extra Grammar Exercises
- Extra Reading Comprehension Questions
- Graphic Organizers
- Inductive Grammar Activities
- Listening Strategies
- Pronunciation Pair Work
- Reading Speed Calculator
- Reading Strategies
- Vocabulary-Building Strategies
- Writing Process Worksheets

In the Lesson Planner notes, activities with both ⭐ and 🖨 icons will appear as "pop ups" in the ActiveTeach (click on the ⭐ icon located on the Student's Book page). In addition, all activities and resources can be accessed from the "Printable Extension Activities" menu within the "Teacher Resources" tab. Other available resources within the "Teacher Resources" tab include Audio and Video Scripts, Answer Keys, "Can-Do" Self-Assessment Charts, GSE Teaching Booklets, Methodology, Oral Progress Assessment Charts, and Web Projects.

Clicking on 🔖 next to the Grammar Booster, Pronunciation Booster, and Test-Taking Skills Booster boxes on the digital Student's Book page in ActiveTeach opens the associated Booster page from the back of the Student's Book. Clicking on the 🔙 icon returns you to the lesson you were viewing.

Other Supplements

In addition to the digital and printable extras listed, *Summit* offers even more supplements. The **EXTRAS** icon which appears at the end of each unit lists additional supplementary components and materials available to support the lesson or individual units.

Supplementary components include:

Workbook Lesson-by-lesson written exercises.

MyEnglishLab An online learning tool with a multitude of features to support students and teachers, including: Grammar Coach videos, immediate and meaningful feedback on wrong answers, remedial grammar exercises, interactive practice of all material presented in the course, grade reports that display performance and time on tasks, and auto-graded achievement tests.

Summit TV The video program includes authentic documentaries (all new for the third edition), and unscripted, unrehearsed on-the-street interviews, featuring a variety of regional and non-native accents. Summit TV Activity Worksheets provide additional listening and language review and practice. Access the full video program and the worksheets from the "*Summit TV*" menu in ActiveTeach.

Assessment Ready-made unit and review achievement tests, with options to edit, add, or delete items.

Online Teacher Resources Additional teacher resources are available at **pearsonelt.com/summit3e**.

Summit Go App Students can download the entire Classroom Audio Program onto their mobile device for listening and pronunciation practice outside of class. With the Summit Go app, students can control the audio speed and access the audio transcripts.

Free Student Resources Additional student resources are available at english.com/summit3e, including Extra Practice Activities, Web Projects, and—as an alternative to the Summit Go app—the complete Summit Classroom Audio Program in downloadable mp3 files.

Full Course Placement Tests Accurately place your students into *Summit*. Available on CD or online. Includes detailed instructions for administering the test, and guidelines for scoring and placement.

Student's Book icons and ActiveTeach icons

The icons used in the Student's Book and ActiveTeach are different. Here are the corresponding icons:

	Student's Book icon	ActiveTeach icon
Conversation Activator Video	DIGITAL VIDEO	🎥
Discussion Activator Video	DIGITAL VIDEO	🎥
Conversation Activator-Speaking Booster	DIGITAL SPEAKING BOOSTER	⭐ 🖨
Discussion-Speaking Booster	DIGITAL SPEAKING BOOSTER	⭐ 🖨
Extra Challenge Reading Activity	DIGITAL EXTRA CHALLENGE	⭐ 🖨
Extra Grammar Exercises	DIGITAL MORE EXERCISES	⭐ 🖨
Inductive Grammar Activity	DIGITAL INDUCTIVE ACTIVITY	⭐ 🖨
Listening Strategies	DIGITAL STRATEGIES	⭐ 🖨
Reading Strategies	DIGITAL STRATEGIES	⭐ 🖨
Vocabulary-Building Strategies	DIGITAL STRATEGIES	⭐ 🖨
Writing Process Worksheets	DIGITAL WRITING PROCESS	⭐ 🖨
Game	DIGITAL GAMES	🎮

xiii

UNIT 1

Dreams and Goals

PREVIEW

COMMUNICATION GOALS
1 Ask about someone's background
2 Discuss career and study plans
3 Compare your dreams and goals in life
4 Describe job qualifications

A **FRAME YOUR IDEAS** Complete the first section of an application for employment, using real or invented information.

Application for Employment

PERSONAL INFORMATION

Name: [last] [middle] [first]

date of application: [/ /]

Address: [ ] City: [ ] State / province: [ ] Country: [ ] Postal code / zip code: [ ]

Contact Information: [home telephone] [cell phone] [e-mail]

Type of position sought: [ ]

Available start date: [/ /]

CURRENT EMPLOYMENT

Are you currently employed? ☐ yes ☐ no

If so, where? [ ]

How long have you worked there? [ ]

EDUCATION

	Name	Major field of study	Did you graduate?
High School			
College or University			
Other Education			

SKILLS AND / OR TRAINING: Please list skills and / or training you have had that may contribute to your ability to perform the position you seek:

📎 **PREVIOUS EMPLOYMENT HISTORY**
Please attach a list of previous positions and job responsibilities, starting with the most recent. Include the names and addresses of each company.

📎 **STATEMENT OF GOALS**
Please attach a short statement about your short-term and long-term employment goals.

To apply online, go to getajob@jobco.com

B ▶ 1:02 **VOCABULARY** **JOB APPLICATIONS** Find and circle these words and phrases in the application. Then listen and repeat.

- employment
- contact information
- position
- start date
- training
- employment history

C **ACTIVATE VOCABULARY** Look at how each word or phrase from Exercise B is used in the job application. Then on a separate sheet of paper, write a definition or synonym for each one.
See page T2 for answers.

D **PAIR WORK** What are some do's and don'ts for filling out a job application? With a partner, create a list of suggestions to help an applicant complete a job application successfully.
See page T2 for answers.

Be neat and spell all words correctly.

UNIT 1

Dreams and Goals

PREVIEW

A FRAME YOUR IDEAS

| Suggested teaching time: | 5 minutes | Your actual teaching time: |

- Have students skim the application for employment. Ask *Have you ever filled out an application like this?*
- Tell students they can fill out the form using real or invented information about themselves.
- You may wish to remind students that *last name* refers to a family name and *first name* to a given name. Some English forms request last name first for alphabetizing.
- Have students compare applications. Invite them to guess if the partner's information is real or not.

CULTURE NOTE Point out that in the United States, dates are stated month first, day second. Forms use *MM* and *DD* to suggest that all months and days be written with two digits, even the ones that only have one; for example, January would be transcribed *01*, not *1*. Where *YY* is shown, the expectation is that only the last two digits of the year need be entered. Where *YYYY* is shown, the expectation is that all four digits of the year be entered.

Challenge: [+5 minutes] On the board, write *goals*. Ask *Why might goals be valuable on a job application?* (They allow the person hiring to see immediately what type of job an applicant is looking for.) On the board, write *I am looking for a position focusing on sales, customer service, and office management.* Invite students to guess what type of a position the goal may be for. (e.g., administrative assistant) Have students experiment writing similar objectives for jobs they are or might one day be interested in. Circulate and assist as needed. Then have students share and guess the positions the goals are for.

B ▶ 1:02 VOCABULARY

| Suggested teaching time: | 5 minutes | Your actual teaching time: |

- Ask students to skim the application for the words in the exercise.
- Then have students listen and repeat the words chorally.

C ACTIVATE VOCABULARY

| Suggested teaching time: | 5 minutes | Your actual teaching time: |

- Have students work in pairs to write the definitions and synonyms. Model the first item. Point to the word *Employment* in *Application for Employment*. Ask *What is employment?* (the condition of having a job or work) Tell students they can refer to a dictionary if they need help coming up with a definition or synonyms.

- Circulate and assist as needed.
- Bring the class together and go over the answers. Compare the use of the word *employment* in *Application for Employment* and *Employment History*. (One is a noun, and one is an adjective.) Invite students to share what kinds of definitions/synonyms they came up with. For example, a word like *work* could similarly function as a noun or an adjective.

Option: [+5 minutes] For more practice, have students use the vocabulary words in sentences. They can write these down or make them up with a partner out loud.

Answers for Exercise C
Answers will vary but may include the following:
employment: the condition of having a job or work
contact information: a phone number or an email at which a person can be reached
position: job
start date: the month and day when something begins
training: skills a person has for a particular job
employment history: a list of previous positions and job responsibilities

D PAIR WORK

| Suggested teaching time: | 5 minutes | Your actual teaching time: |

- On the board, write *Do's and Don'ts*. Ask *What does this refer to?* (things you should and should not do in a particular situation) Elicit possible topics for Do's and Don'ts lists. (e.g., do's and don'ts for social media, caring for an animal, writing a business e-mail, buying a house)
- Tell students they will create a list of Do's and Don'ts for filling out a job application. Draw a chart on the board or print it out from the ActiveTeach and distribute it to students.

Do's	Don'ts

Call on a volunteer to read the sample answer and write it into the chart. Point out that the imperative *Be* is used. Elicit a *Don't* suggestion. (e.g., *Don't write information that is not true.*) Students should be encouraged to express their opinions about appropriate and inappropriate things to do or say in filling out a job application. (Possible answers: Don't make factual errors in dates and places. Don't leave information out—be complete. Be honest.)

- Accept all reasonable opinions.

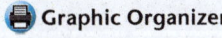 Graphic Organizer

E ▶ 1:03 SPOTLIGHT

| Suggested teaching time: | 10–15 minutes | Your actual teaching time: |

- Have students look at the photo. Where are these young women? (maybe at one of their homes) Have students read and listen to the conversation.
- To check comprehension, ask:
  How many schools did Anne apply to in the end? (ten)
  How far away is Anne willing to go to school? (100 miles)
  Why has it gotten difficult to get into culinary schools? (The food industry has become trendy.)
  How are the Culinary Center and Taste Institute different? (The CC is more demanding, and the certificate has more prestige; it guarantees an interview at a top restaurant.)

LANGUAGE NOTE *To end up doing something* refers to what you finally do. *An x-mile radius* refers to an area that covers a particular distance in all directions from a central point. *To get in* is a phrasal verb that means to succeed in entering a certain place, often used in reference to gaining admission to a school or university. *A ticket to something* is the precise thing that is needed for something. *A better bet* is a more advantageous approach to achieving something—the superlative can also be used (*the best bet*) to indicate the most advantageous approach to achieving a particular goal.

CULTURE NOTE In American English, people adhere to references to miles and almost never refer to kilometers or any other metric measures in conversation. *Within a hundred-mile radius* means within 100 miles in any direction of a circle. One hundred miles = 160 kilometers. So within a 100-mile radius means within a 160-kilometer radius.

F UNDERSTAND IDIOMS AND EXPRESSIONS

| Suggested teaching time: | 5–10 minutes | Your actual teaching time: |

- Focus on the idioms and expressions as a class. Call on volunteers to read them aloud.
- In pairs, have students locate them in context and then paraphrase the meanings.
- Have students compare answers with a partner, returning to Exercise E to check any items students don't agree on.
- Bring the class together to go over the answers.

Challenge: [+5 minutes] Divide the class into pairs and assign each pair one or two idioms/expressions from the list. Have pairs create brief dialogues around them. Invite pairs to share dialogues.

Answers for Exercise F
Answers will vary but may include the following:
1. I've done all I can do. Now I just have to wait for the answer.
2. That might be doing too much.
3. I wanted to be sure.
4. I really want ... / My first choice is ...
5. Aren't they all the same?
6. ordinary
7. Generally,... / My conclusion is ...
8. I hope you get what you want.

G THINK AND EXPLAIN

| Suggested teaching time: | 5 minutes | Your actual teaching time: |

- Have students discuss the questions in pairs. Then bring the class together to go over the answers.

LANGUAGE NOTE Focus on *Hope all your dreams come true*. Point out that in spoken English it is common to skip the subject *I* when making a statement.

Option: [+5 minutes] Invite students to share their opinions about the school application process. Ask *Is it common to apply to so many schools? Do you think Anne needed to apply to that many schools? Would you?*

SPEAKING

| Suggested teaching time: | 5 minutes | Your actual teaching time: |

- On the board, write 1, 2, 3, 4, 5. Say *You are going to rate different factors on a scale of 1 to 5, 1 being the most important, 5 being the least important.*
- Have students rate the factors individually. Then have them compare answers with a partner.
- Bring the class together and poll the class for the most important and the least important factors.

Option: [+5 minutes] Have students look at their highest-rated factors. Then, in pairs, have them discuss further what kind of job or career could encompass these factors. If a student already has such a job, invite the student to describe specifics of the factor(s) in the job.

T3 UNIT 1 PREVIEW

ENGLISH FOR TODAY'S WORLD
Understand a variety of accents.
Anne = Korean
Nina = Spanish

E ▶ 1:03 **SPOTLIGHT** Read and listen to a conversation between two friends discussing career plans. Notice the spotlighted language.

Anne: Well, I finally sent in the applications. Now **it's just wait and see**.
Nina: How many schools did you end up applying to?
Anne: Ten. That's just about every single one within a hundred-mile radius!
Nina: Don't you think **that might be a little overkill**? You shouldn't have any trouble getting in, should you?
Anne: Well, the food industry's so trendy right now, and it's gotten pretty competitive. **I didn't want to take any chances**. This has been a lifelong dream of mine.
Nina: So which one's your first choice? I've read the Taste Institute's pretty good.
Anne: Actually, at first I'd been thinking of going there, but now **I've got my heart set on** the Culinary Center. I've heard it's far superior to the TI.
Nina: The Taste Institute? Really? Aren't chef schools all **six of one, half a dozen of the other**?
Anne: I would have thought so, but it turns out they're not.
Nina: How so?
Anne: Well, the CC's training is more demanding. You've really got to work hard. And their certificate's got a lot more prestige. A CC certificate's a ticket to an interview with all the top restaurants.
Nina: And that's not true with the TI?
Anne: Apparently not. I did a lot of reading, and it seems that the TI's pretty **run-of-the-mill**— nothing wrong with it, but nothing particularly outstanding about it either. **All in all**, the CC's a better bet if I can get in.
Nina: Well, **I'll keep my fingers crossed** for you, Anne. Hope all your dreams come true.
Anne: Thanks! I appreciate that.

F **UNDERSTAND IDIOMS AND EXPRESSIONS** With a partner, paraphrase each of these expressions from Spotlight, saying each one a different way. See page T3 for answers.

1 "… it's just wait and see."
2 "… that might be a little overkill?"
3 "I didn't want to take any chances."
4 "I've got my heart set on … "
5 "… six of one, half a dozen of the other."
6 "run-of-the-mill"
7 "all in all"
8 "I'll keep my fingers crossed … "

G **THINK AND EXPLAIN** Answer the following questions. Explain your answers. Answers will vary but may include the following:

1 Why did Anne apply to so many schools? So she would be accepted to at least one school.
2 In your opinion, which of the two reasons Anne gives for preferring the Culinary Center is a better reason? Explain. You are guaranteed an interview with all top restaurants if you attend the CC. The ultimate goal is to get a job.
3 What does Nina mean when she says, "Hope all your dreams come true"? She hopes that Anne gets into the school she wants and gets a good job.

SPEAKING Which factors are the most important to you in choosing a job or career? Rate each of the following on a scale of 1 to 5, with 1 being the most important. Then compare charts with a partner, explaining your ratings to each other.

The training period for the job is short.	The job has lots of prestige.
There's not too much competition in the field.	The field is trendy right now.
The work is interesting and fun.	The job doesn't require a lot of overtime work.
The pay is good.	The field contributes something important to the world.
The people in this field are interesting.	

LESSON 1

GOAL Ask about someone's background

A ▶ 1:04 GRAMMAR SPOTLIGHT   Read about two famous people. Notice the spotlighted grammar.

Kohei Uchimura

Kohei Uchimura is considered by some to be the greatest gymnast of all time. He **began** gymnastics very early in life. When Uchimura **joined** Japan's national team at the age of eighteen in 2007, he **had** already **been practicing** gymnastics for fifteen years. And since then, he **has competed** in world-class events year after year and **has won** many prizes and honors. Uchimura trains hard and consistently beats almost all his competition. Although Uchimura **had** already **won** many competitions before the 2012 Olympics, he **had** a close call there and **fell** as he **was dismounting** from the pommel horse. In spite of this, his team **managed** to win the silver medal, so the event **went** into his "win" record anyway. Uchimura has continued to win prize after prize ever since. Uchimura is renowned for the intensity of his concentration during practice. Surprisingly, however, for a world-class athlete, he is known to be pretty relaxed and has a normal life outside of the gym. He's been married since 2012, and he and his wife **had** their first child in 2013.

Singer, songwriter, and actress Lila Downs, whose mother was from Mexico and whose father was from the United States, **grew up** in both countries. She **had learned** to sing as a child and **had performed** with traditional mariachi bands before she **had** any formal training. She **attended** the Institute of Arts in Oaxaca and **studied** classical voice at the University of Minnesota. During the time Downs **was living** in the United States, she **became** more and more interested in the diverse cultural heritage of Mexico. To help support pride in those cultures, Downs **learned** and **incorporated** a variety of indigenous Mexican languages into her songs. One of Downs's other passions is social justice, and the lyrics of some of her songs focus on the stories of workers who **migrated** from rural Mexico to the U.S. Downs has won many prizes, including a Grammy and a Latin Grammy. She and her husband **had been trying** for many years to have a baby, and in 2010, they **adopted** a son. The family travels together on Downs's international singing tours.

Lila Downs

B DISCUSSION
Is it necessary to have formal training to be an elite athlete or a world-class singer? Support your opinion with reasons and examples.

> **GRAMMAR BOOSTER** p. 128
> Describing past actions and events: review

C GRAMMAR   SIMULTANEOUS AND SEQUENTIAL PAST ACTIONS: REVIEW AND EXPANSION

Review: completed past actions: the simple past tense and the past perfect
The simple past tense describes actions completed in the past, whether or not a specific time is mentioned. Context or time expressions can indicate whether the actions were simultaneous (at the same time) or sequential (one before the other).

   When Uchimura **entered** the stadium, the gymnastics event **began**. (= simultaneous completed actions)
   Downs **studied** voice in the U.S. **in the years before** she **moved** back to Mexico. (= sequential completed actions)

> **Remember:** The present perfect can also describe completed past actions.
> Uchimura has competed in world-class events year after year.

The simple past tense and the past perfect can be used to describe two sequential completed past actions. However, in informal spoken English it's common to avoid the past perfect and use the simple past tense for both actions, especially when context clarifies the order of occurrence.

   Before Uchimura **competed** in the 2012 Olympics, he **had won** several world championships.

Review: simultaneous actions in progress: the past continuous
A statement in the past continuous describes an action that was in progress at a time—or during a period of time—in the past.

   Lila Downs **was** already **singing** while I **was looking** for my seat.

> **Remember:** To describe an action that was completed during an action in progress, use the simple past tense.
> Lila met her future husband, Paul, when [or while] she was working in Oaxaca.

Expansion: sequential continuing and completed past actions: the past perfect continuous and the simple past tense
The past perfect continuous can be used to focus on the fact that one past action was already in progress before another one occurred. (It often emphasizes the duration of the action.) Form the past perfect continuous with <u>had been</u> and a present participle. Describe the completed action with the simple past tense.

   By the time Downs **moved** to the United States with her parents, she **had been performing** with mariachis for several years.
   How long **had** Uchimura **been training** before he **was asked** to join the Japan National Team?

LESSON 1

GOAL Ask about someone's background

A ▶1:04 GRAMMAR SPOTLIGHT

Suggested teaching time:	5–10 minutes	Your actual teaching time:

- Ask students to look at the photos of the people. Call on a volunteer to read their names. Ask *Have you heard of these people? What are their professions?* If students haven't heard of Lila Downs, they can guess.
- Have students listen to the article as they read along.
- To check comprehension, ask *Where is Kohei Uchimura from?* (Japan) *How long had he been practicing gymnastics when he joined Japan's national team?* (fifteen years) *What happened in 2007?* (He joined Japan's national team.) *When did he participate in the Olympics?* (2012) *What happened at the Olympics?* (He fell.) *What is Uchimura known for?* (his concentration, but also for being relaxed and having a normal life outside the gym) *Where did Lila Downs grow up?* (in Mexico and the United States) *When did she start singing?* (when she was a child) *When did she become more interested in the diverse cultural heritage of Mexico?* (when she was living in the United States) *What kinds of languages did Downs incorporate into her songs?* (indigenous Mexican languages) *What do the lyrics of some of her songs focus on?* (social justice; stories of workers who migrated from rural Mexico to the United States)

LANGUAGE NOTE *A close call* is something bad that almost happens, but does not; *to dismount* means to get off of something like a horse or a bicycle; *a pommel horse* is a piece of equipment used in gymnastics that has two handles on top, which you hold on to when you jump or swing over it; *mariachi* is a kind of Mexican dance music; *indigenous* refers to people or things that have always been in the place where they are, rather than being brought there from another place; *social justice* refers to how wealth, opportunities, and privileges are distributed within a society.

B DISCUSSION

Suggested teaching time:	5 minutes	Your actual teaching time:

- Ask a student to read the direction line. Make sure students know that *elite* means most experienced or skilled; *world-class* means among the best in the world. Ask *Do Uchimura or Downs have formal training?* (Yes, they both do.)
- Then, in pairs, have students share if they think formal training is necessary for each job.

C GRAMMAR

Suggested teaching time:	10–15 minutes	Your actual teaching time:

- Call on a student to read the title of the grammar chart. On the board, write the words *simultaneous* and *sequential*. Elicit the meaning. (*Simultaneous* means happening at the exact same time; *sequential* means following a particular order.)

- Ask a student to read the first explanation. Focus on the first example sentence. Ask *When did the gymnastics event begin?* (when Uchimura entered the stadium) *Did Uchimura entering and the event beginning happen at the same time?* (yes) Focus on the second example sentence. Ask *Which event happened first?* (Downs studied voice.) *And second?* (She moved back to Mexico.)
- Bring students' attention to the Remember note and example sentence. Point out that the present perfect is used to show that something is part of a person's life experience. Write an additional example on the board:

  Karen has traveled to Africa.

  Ask *Is this action completed?* (yes) *Is Karen in Africa now?* (no) *Is traveling to Africa part of her life experience?* (yes) Then write:

  Karen has lived in Africa for ten years.

  Ask *Does this describe a completed past action?* (No, this action is still ongoing—Karen is still living in Africa.)
- Ask a student to read the second explanation and example sentence. Then ask a student to read the same sentence as it might be used in informal spoken English. (The simple past would be used instead of the past perfect.) Write another example on the board:

  Before I started University, I spent a year in South America.

  Ask *Which event happened first?* (spent a year in South America) Elicit the formal way to state this sentence grammatically.
- Read the head of the next section. Restate that *simultaneous* means happening at the same time. Call on a volunteer to read the explanation and example sentence. Write an additional example on the board:

  Howard was speeding and talking on his cell phone.

  Ask *Did either event happen first?* (No, they happened at the same time.)
- Call on a student to read the Remember note and example. Then write:

  Howard lost control of the car while he was speeding.

  Ask *Which happened first?* (Howard was speeding.) *What happened while he was speeding?* (He lost control of the car.)
- Finally, ask a student to read the last explanation. Write an additional example on the board:

  Before I got fired, I had already been looking for a new job.

  Ask *Which event happened first?* (I was looking for a new job.) *Which happened second?* (I got fired.) Point out that the sentence focuses on the fact that the looking for a new job was already in progress before the person got fired.

Option: 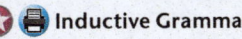 *(Teaching notes p. T128)*

⭐ 🖨 Inductive Grammar Activity

D ▶ 1:05 UNDERSTAND THE GRAMMAR

Suggested teaching time:	5 minutes	Your actual teaching time:

- Tell students they will listen to three short conversations. Instruct them to pay attention to simultaneous and sequential past actions being described.
- Have students listen to each conversation and choose the correct answer. Then have them listen again to check their answers.
- Ask students to compare answers with a partner. Then bring the class together. If necessary, play the audio again to break down the situation to support the correct answer.

⭐ 🖨 Extra Grammar Exercises

E GRAMMAR PRACTICE

Suggested teaching time:	5 minutes	Your actual teaching time:

- Hint to students that they will be deciding if the sentence describes two sequential completed past actions, or if the sentence focuses on the fact that one past action was already in progress before another one occurred.
- Have students complete the exercise. Then ask them to compare answers with a partner.
- Bring the class together. Ask *Which item focuses on an action already in progress before another one occurred?* (item 3, 4) *Which ones focus on two sequential completed actions?* (items 1, 2, 5) For each one ask *Which action happened first?* (1. My brother won the swim meet. 2. The family went to bed. 5. My friend saw Lila Downs in concert.)

NOW YOU CAN Ask about someone's background

A FRAME YOUR IDEAS

Suggested teaching time:	5 minutes	Your actual teaching time:

- Tell students to skim the questions. Explain that they will be writing down information about their background. If students aren't married or don't yet have a career, they can talk about whether they have a boyfriend, a girlfriend, or are engaged, and they can talk about what they are studying and how long they have been studying that. Be sensitive and tell students to discuss only what they feel comfortable talking about.
- Focus on the last question. On the board, write *3 periods*. Elicit what this might mean. (Possible answers: childhood, adolescence, adulthood; *OR* child, college student, working adult; *OR* before children born, raising children, after children grew up)

B DISCUSSION ACTIVATOR

Suggested teaching time:	10–15 minutes	Your actual teaching time:

🎦 Discussion Activator Video

- Divide the class into pairs and have students use the questionnaire from Frame Your Ideas to ask questions. Ask a volunteer to read the model question in the speech bubble. Encourage the pairs to provide details and examples. Tell students that they should say as much as possible.
- Circulate and listen for correct use of past tenses to describe simultaneous and sequential past actions.

For more support, play the Discussion Activator Video before students do this activity. Ask students to summarize the discussion in their own words. After each video, ask if the students in the video included sufficient details.
Note: You can print the script or you can view it on the video player on the ActiveTeach.

OPTIONAL WRITING [+15–20 minutes]

- Tell students they will compile information about their partner into a biography. Call on a student to read the model about Lisa Lee.
- First have students write down information they remember about their partner. Tell them they can look at Frame Your Ideas in their partner's book for ideas or ask additional questions. Remind students to use the past continuous to describe actions that were in progress at a time in the past.
- Refer students to the grammar on page 4 to help express simultaneous or sequential past actions correctly.
- Invite students to swap drafts of the biographies and have them confirm if all the information is correct and/or offer additional information.
- Decide if and how you want to compile the biographies. Be sure to correct mistakes with students before publishing online or compiling a notebook for display and to get students' permission to publish photos and information about them online.

Option: [+5 minutes] For further grammar practice, have students swap biography drafts and underline all the uses of the past to make sure all past actions are expressed correctly. Tell students to refer to the grammar on page 4. Circulate and assist as needed.

D ▶ 1:05 UNDERSTAND THE GRAMMAR
Listen to the conversations and circle the letter of the correct summary of the events. Listen again if necessary.

1	a They continued filming after he got on the bus.	**b** The bus arrived after the filming was finished.
2	**a** Lisa had been thinking of buying the sweater that she left on the table.	b The other girl bought the sweater before Lisa had a chance to try it on.
3	a Diane was texting and driving at the same time.	**b** Diane had stopped driving before she texted.

E GRAMMAR PRACTICE
Complete the statements with the past perfect or past perfect continuous.

1 My brother (**had already won** / had already been winning) the swim meet when the diving competition began.
2 The house was completely dark when I got home because the family (**had gone** / had been going) to bed.
3 The audience (had stood / **had been standing**) in line for hours to buy tickets when they canceled the concert.
4 The women's tennis team (**had practiced** / had been practicing) on a grass court four times before today's event started.
5 My friend (**had already seen** / had already been seeing) Lila Downs in concert, so we decided not to go.

NOW YOU CAN Ask about someone's background

A FRAME YOUR IDEAS
Complete the questionnaire about your background.

Where were you born? _____   How long have you been living at your current address? _____
Where had you been living before you moved to your current address? _____
If you are married, when did you get married? _____   Where were you living then? _____
If you have children, what are their names and ages? _____
If you have a career, what is it? _____
How long have you been studying English? _____
If you divided your life into three periods, how would you describe each one?
1. _____
2. _____
3. _____

B DISCUSSION ACTIVATOR
Get to know a classmate's background. Use the questionnaire as an interview guide. Use the simple past tense, the past perfect, the past continuous, and the past perfect continuous in your questions and answers to clarify events in the past. Say as much as you can.

> Where were you living when you got married?

OPTIONAL WRITING Write a one-page biography of your partner, using the information from your Discussion Activator. Put the biographies together in a notebook or post them on a class blog. Include pictures of the classmates.

Lisa Lee

Lisa has been living in Templeton Towers since February. Before that, she had been living with her family in Easton. She got married in January…

LESSON 2

GOAL Discuss career and study plans

A ▶ 1:06 VOCABULARY COLLOCATIONS FOR CAREER AND STUDY PLANS Read and listen. Then listen again and repeat.

decide on a course of study or a career
Jonathan decided on a career as a veterinarian because he's interested in medicine and loves animals.

take up something you're interested in
Lida is so impressed by the latest animated films that she's decided to take up computer graphics.

apply for a job or a position in a company
Gary is interested in environmental conservation, so he's applied for a job at the Wildlife Center.

apply to a school or program of study
I hope it's not too late to apply to dental school. I don't want to wait another year.

sign up for a course or an activity
Nora needs math for engineering school, but she hasn't used it since secondary school, so she's signed up for a refresher course.

"I started out in art, but **I'm switching** to graphic design."

switch to a new course of study or a career
Magdalena started out in cultural anthropology but soon switched to medicine.

be accepted to / into / by a school or a program
Only two students from our class were accepted to medical school this year.

be rejected by a school or a program
Iris couldn't believe she had been rejected by the Wright College of Music, but luckily she was accepted elsewhere.

enroll in a school or program
Matt has been accepted into flight school, but he won't enroll in the program until next year.

B ▶ 1:07 LISTEN TO ACTIVATE VOCABULARY Listen to the conversations. Then listen again. After each conversation, complete the statement with the Vocabulary. Use each collocation only once. *Answers will vary but may include the following:*

1 She has **been accepted to** engineering school.
2 She has **decided on** a career in music.
3 He has **taken up** meditation.
4 She has **been rejected by** two graduate programs.
5 He has **switched to** teaching math.
6 She has **applied for** a position in a medical lab.

C VOCABULARY PRACTICE Complete each person's statement, using the Vocabulary. There may be more than one way to answer correctly. *Answers will vary but may include the following:*

1 I've just **been accepted to** graduate school!

2 I've been an English teacher all my life, but I've decided to **switch to** teaching French!

3 It may take me years, but my lifelong dream has been to be an architect. I'm going to **enroll in** architecture school this year.

4 I retired a few years ago, but I'm bored, so I've just **applied to** law school. My kids think I'm crazy.

5 When I finish school I want to be a conductor, so I've **applied to** the music program at my university.

6 I've just had a baby, but I'm **signing up for** an evening program at the college. I want to study graphic design.

7 I want to ride a motorcycle, but my mom and dad won't even let me **sign up for** lessons!

8 I'm really a nervous person, but I've **taken up** yoga and it really helps calm me down.

LESSON 2

GOAL Discuss career and study plans

A ▶1:06 VOCABULARY

| Suggested teaching time: | 5–10 minutes | Your actual teaching time: |

- Ask a student to read the heading (Collocations for Career and Study Plans). Write *collocations* on the board. Elicit that this refers to the way in which words are used together.
- Call on a volunteer to read the sentence in the speech bubble. Focus on the phrase *switching to*. Have students find *switch to* in the list. Call on a student to read the information and example sentence. Ask students *What is another way to say this?* (to change)
- Have students read and listen to the collocations.
- Then have students listen and repeat the words chorally.
- To quiz comprehension, ask students another way to state each word. (*decide on*: choose, pick; *take up*: engage in something; *apply for*: make a request for a job or position; *apply to*: send a request to a school or company for a job or position; *sign up for*: register; *switch to*: change; *be accepted to / into / by*: get in or gain a place or position; *be rejected by*: not get in or not get a place or position; *enroll in*: officially be put on a list for a course or an activity)

LANGUAGE NOTE Point out the difference between *decide on* and *take up*. When you *decide on* something, you are making a mental decision to choose one thing over another. *Decide on* can be used with a variety of things/situations. For example, in a restaurant: *I've decided on the fish*; or larger things such as a career: *I've decided on a career as a dancer*. *Take up* means to embark on a course of action: *I've decided to take up horseback riding*.

Option: [+5 minutes] Have pairs write additional sentences using the vocabulary. Then ask volunteers to share.

LANGUAGE NOTE Point out the difference between *apply for* + a position (a job) versus *apply to* + place (a company). Make sure students understand that acceptance at a school may be necessary before one can *enroll in* or *sign up for* a course. Regarding acceptance, explain that one can be accepted to medical school or law school, which is a general statement. One can be accepted by a particular institution, for example, *I was accepted by the University of Wisconsin*. The same applies for being *rejected by* a particular institution. Also, you can use *at* to specify a particular named institution: *I was accepted at Downstate Medical College*. You cannot say *I was accepted at medical school*.

 Vocabulary-Building Strategies

B ▶1:07 LISTEN TO ACTIVATE VOCABULARY

| Suggested teaching time: | 5 minutes | Your actual teaching time: |

- Pre-listening: Have students skim the exercise items. Tell them to think about which collocations could potentially fit into the various sentences. For example, in item 1, possible collocations could be *decided on, applied to, switched to, been accepted to / rejected by, enrolled in*.
- First listening: Pause after each conversation to allow students time to choose the best collocation.
- Second listening: Have students listen again to check their work. Go over the answers as a class.

LANGUAGE NOTE Explain the following expressions from the conversations as needed. *A whiz* (conversation 1) is a person who is very skilled in a particular activity. The expression *What's come over him* (conversation 3) means what has made him suddenly act in a particular way? The expression *What's with Nina* (conversation 4) means what's the matter with her? To talk about *where one would be a year from now* (conversation 4) is a common expression to predict how one's life might change in a year. *You can't blame her* (conversation 4) means you can't be surprised she feels or is acting a certain way. *To feel down* (conversation 4) means to feel sad. *To be well suited for something* (conversation 5) means to have the right qualifications.

C VOCABULARY PRACTICE

| Suggested teaching time: | 5–10 minutes | Your actual teaching time: |

- Point out to students that more than one answer is possible. Model the first item. Ask *What are possible answers?* (applied to; been accepted into; enrolled in) Point out that considering the happy look on the man's face, it's not likely he's saying *been rejected by*.
- Have students do the exercise individually. Tell them to think carefully about which collocation fits grammatically. Encourage them to refer to Exercise A.
- In pairs, have students compare answers.
- Time permitting, call on volunteers to share what they wrote for the various items.

Option: [+5 minutes] Have students use one of the notes from the exercise as a model, but fill it in with their own information. For example, item 8 can be changed to: *I am very active. Recently I've taken up interval training. It keeps me challenged.* Have students write their own note. Then students can share with a partner or with the class.

D GRAMMAR

Suggested teaching time:	5–10 minutes	Your actual teaching time:

- Call on a volunteer to read the first explanation and example sentences.
- Ask students to read the Be careful! note and look at the example. Write the following set of sentences on the board: *She's just been offered a job. She was offered a job last month.*
  Elicit the difference. (In the first sentence there is no specific time mentioned; in the second sentence there is—last month.)
- Focus on the second explanation and example. Ask individual students *What have you been doing lately? What have you been doing recently?* Make sure students name things that are still ongoing. (Possible answers: I've been exercising a lot lately. I've been doing a lot of homework recently.) Read the Remember note with the class to review stative words, which can't be used in the present perfect continuous.
- Have students read the third explanation and example to themselves. List the adverbs on the board. Invite volunteers to suggest additional example sentences using the present perfect.

Option: GRAMMAR BOOSTER *(Teaching notes p. T128)*

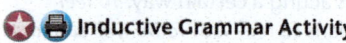 Inductive Grammar Activity

E GRAMMAR PRACTICE

Suggested teaching time:	5 minutes	Your actual teaching time:

- Tell students to look for hints in the sentences to help determine the correct verb phrase.
- Have students complete the exercise individually.
- Have them compare answers with a partner, underlining what in the sentence determines the correct answer. (1. in 2016, 2. still, 3. lately, 4. yet, 5. 9:00 sharp, 6. Lately)

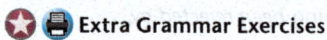 Extra Grammar Exercises

F GRAMMAR PRACTICE

Suggested teaching time:	5 minutes	Your actual teaching time:

- Ask students to work individually. Encourage them to write a variety of questions using different tenses and adverbs.
- Have students swap questions with a partner, checking for correct grammatical use. Tell students not to ask each other the questions yet.

Option: PRONUNCIATION BOOSTER *(Teaching notes p. T143)*

🖨 Pronunciation Pair Work

NOW YOU CAN Discuss career and study plans

A ▶1:08 CONVERSATION SPOTLIGHT

Suggested teaching time:	5 minutes	Your actual teaching time:

These conversation strategies are implicit in the model:
- Use *Thanks for asking* to indicate appreciation for interest.
- Use *Correct me if I'm wrong* to politely invite disagreement.
- Use *I've given it some thought* to introduce a decision.
- Use *steer me in the right direction* to invite guidance.
- Use *As a matter of fact* to add emphasis to what you are saying.
- Use *I really appreciate it* to thank someone.

- Have students look at the photo. Ask *Where do you think they are? What might they be talking about?*
- Ask students to read and listen to the conversation.
- To check comprehension, ask *What did Vanessa study before?* (biology) *What does she want to study now?* (social work) *How will the man help Vanessa?* (He will write her a recommendation.)

B ▶1:09 RHYTHM AND INTONATION

Suggested teaching time:	5 minutes	Your actual teaching time:

- Have students repeat chorally. Make sure they:
  ○ use rising intonation for *Have you decided on a career yet?* (line 1), *...but weren't you a biology major?* (line 5)
  ○ use falling intonation for *So how can I help?* (line 8)
  ○ pause after *Correct me if I'm wrong* before *but* (lines 4–5)
  ○ use emphatic stress on *As a matter of fact* (line 11)
  ○ stress *really* in *I really appreciate it* (line 13)

C CONVERSATION ACTIVATOR VIDEO

Suggested teaching time:	5 minutes	Your actual teaching time:

🖨 Conversation Activator Video

- Divide the class into pairs. Instruct students that they will use the model in Exercise A, Conversation Spotlight, to role-play their own conversation with a partner.
- Refer students to Exercise F for the questions they wrote about career or education plans. Have them also look back at the lists of idioms and expressions in Exercise E on page 3 and the Vocabulary in Exercise A on page 6.

DON'T STOP! Before students begin to activate their conversations, bring their attention to the Don't Stop! note. Tell students that they should extend or lengthen their conversations by following directions in the Don't Stop! Explain that this is an essentail part of the activity. After students have activated their conversation one time, tell pairs to change roles so each student gets a chance to play A and B. Then have students change partners and activate the conversation again.

For more support, play the Conversation Activator Video before students do this activity. After they've watched the video, ask students how the model was changed and extended by the actors. *Note:* You can print the script or you can view it on the video player on the ActiveTeach.

⭐ 🖨 Conversation Activator: Speaking Booster

D GRAMMAR COMPLETED AND UNCOMPLETED PAST ACTIONS CLOSELY RELATED TO THE PRESENT

You can use the present perfect for recently completed actions. The adverbs just, recently, and lately often accompany these statements. (Note: Lately is rarely used in affirmative statements.)

> She's **just been accepted** into a top-notch business school.
> **Have** you **looked** at the program requirements **lately**? They've **changed**.

The present perfect continuous can describe an action or event that began in the recent past (and continues in the present and is therefore uncompleted). You can use recently and lately.

> We've **been filling** out a lot of applications **recently**.

However, the following adverbs are used only with the present perfect, not the present perfect continuous, because they signal a completed action: ever, never, before, already, yet, still (with negative), so far, once, twice, (three) times.

> Have you **ever** considered applying to graduate school? I **never** have.
> I **still** haven't signed up for lifeguard training.

Be careful!
Use the simple past tense, not the present perfect, to talk about actions completed at a specific time in the past.
  She applied for a position at the Science Institute last week.
  NOT She has applied for the position at the Science Institute last week.

Remember: Don't use the present perfect continuous with these stative verbs: be, believe, hate, have (for possession), know, like, love, own, seem, understand.
  DON'T SAY I've been knowing him for a year.

GRAMMAR BOOSTER p. 128
Stative verbs: non-action and action meanings

E GRAMMAR PRACTICE Circle the correct verb phrase to complete each statement.

1. In 2016, I (have enrolled in / **enrolled in**) the computer graphics program.
2. I still (haven't been receiving / **haven't received**) an acceptance letter.
3. No one (saw / **has seen**) Mike lately.
4. We (haven't been signing up / **haven't signed up**) for the professional development course yet.
5. The class (has started / **started**) at 9:00 sharp.
6. Lately, she's (**been getting** / got) ready to apply for that new position.

F GRAMMAR PRACTICE On a separate sheet of paper, write five questions to ask someone about his or her career or education plans. Use the present perfect, the simple past tense, and appropriate adverbs.
Answers will vary but may include the following:
Where did you go to high school? When did you decide to take up architecture? Have you chosen a school yet? Have you ever considered studying abroad? Have you enrolled in online courses before?

PRONUNCIATION BOOSTER p. 143
Sentence stress and intonation: review

NOW YOU CAN Discuss career and study plans

A ▶ 1:08 CONVERSATION SPOTLIGHT Read and listen. Notice the spotlighted conversation strategies.

A: So, Vanessa, have you decided on a career yet?
B: **Thanks for asking.** Actually, I've been thinking of taking up social work.
A: Social work. That's interesting. **Correct me if I'm wrong, but** weren't you a biology major?
B: Yes, that's right. But **I've given it some thought and** decided science just isn't for me.
A: So how can I help?
B: Well, I'd like to enroll in a good graduate program. I was hoping you could **steer me in the right direction**.
A: **As a matter of fact** we have a great program right here. **I'd be more than happy to** write you a recommendation.
B: That's super! **I really appreciate it.**

B ▶ 1:09 RHYTHM AND INTONATION Listen again and repeat. Then practice the conversation with a partner.

C CONVERSATION ACTIVATOR Create a similar conversation, using the questions you wrote in Exercise F. Start like this: *So, have you decided on …* Be sure to change roles and then partners.

DON'T STOP!
• Discuss your background and interests.
• Say as much as you can.

LESSON 3

GOAL Compare your dreams and goals in life

A ▶1:10 **LISTENING WARM-UP   VOCABULARY   DESCRIBING DREAMS AND GOALS**   Read and listen to what the people are saying. Then listen again and repeat the verb phrases and adjectives.

I'm fulfilling my lifelong dream to be an archaeologist. I'm in a graduate program and expect to get my degree in three years.

I know the goal I've set is ambitious, but I don't think it's unrealistic.

My husband will be working from home for the next three years so we can share the housekeeping and childcare responsibilities 50-50.

Verb phrases	Adjectives	
fulfill a dream	ambitious	modest
set a goal	achievable	unachievable
work towards / pursue a goal	realistic	unrealistic
put [something] off		
share responsibilities		

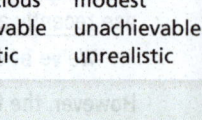

My wife put off her studies and worked to support us while I was studying. Now it's my turn to support her as she pursues her goal.

If we have a common goal and work towards it, anything's achievable. Hey, the sky's the limit for us!

B **ACTIVATE THE VOCABULARY**   Complete each statement, using a word or phrase from the Vocabulary.

1 One way a husband and wife can ....share responsibilities.... is by each one doing half of the household chores.
2 Sometimes a goal requires too much work and it becomes ....unachievable.....
3 When you finally achieve what you've wanted all your life, you have ....fulfilled a dream......
4 ....Ambitious.... is an adjective that means almost the same thing as "challenging."
5 Sometimes people ....put off....... working towards their own goals for a while in order to help a spouse pursue his or her own goals for now.
6 The first step in achieving something is to ....set a goal......

C ▶1:11 **LISTEN FOR MAIN IDEAS**   Listen. Complete each statement, choosing the correct word or phrase.
1 Dan stays home because he (lost his job / <u>wants to stay home</u>).
2 Sarah is the primary (<u>breadwinner</u> / caregiver) in the family.
3 Sarah's lifelong dream was to be (a stay-at-home mom / <u>a surgeon</u>).
4 The number of (mothers / <u>fathers</u>) who choose to stay home to take care of the children is increasing.
5 Dan and Sarah have decided to lead a (traditional / <u>nontraditional</u>) lifestyle.

D ▶1:12 **LISTEN TO CONFIRM CONTENT**   Write a checkmark next to the topics that were discussed. Write an X next to the topics that weren't. Listen again to check your answers.

- ✓ the definition of a stay-at-home dad
- ✓ the number of stay-at-home dads in the U.S.
- ✗ the kind of work Dan did before the children were born
- ✗ the ages of Dan and Sarah's children
- ✓ the sexes of Dan and Sarah's children
- ✗ the number of years it took for Sarah to complete her degree

LESSON 3

GOAL Compare your dreams and goals in life

A ▶ 1:10 LISTENING WARM-UP

| Suggested teaching time: | 5 minutes | Your actual teaching time: |

- Have students look at the two illustrations. Ask them to predict this family's situation. (It appears that the father cares for the children or helps care for the children, and the mother is a student.) Ask *Is this type of family arrangement common in your culture? How would you feel about such an arrangement?*
- Call on a volunteer to read the verb phrases. Elicit that *to put off* means to postpone. Ask another volunteer to read the pairs of adjectives.
- Have students read and listen. Then have them listen again for the verb phrases and adjectives.
- Ask students to listen and repeat the verb phrases and adjectives.

Option: [+5 minutes] Invite a volunteer to read the last line in the man's speech bubble. Write on the board, *The sky's the limit.* Elicit the meaning. Hint that the meaning is stated another way in the speech bubble. (anything is achievable) Invite students to answer this question: *Do you believe that anything is achievable? Why? Why not?*

Option: [+5 minutes] Remind students of the terms *short-term* and *long-term*, which are often used to describe goals. Ask *Do you have a short-term goal for your studies? What are your long-term goals for your career?*

 Vocabulary-Building Strategies

B ACTIVATE THE VOCABULARY

| Suggested teaching time: | 5 minutes | Your actual teaching time: |

- Have students work individually to complete each statement with the correct word from the two vocabulary lists in Exercise A. Hint that students should think about whether the missing word is a verb phrase or an adjective.
- Ask students to compare answers with a partner. Then bring the class together to go over any issues.

C ▶ 1:11 LISTEN FOR MAIN IDEAS

| Suggested teaching time: | 10–15 minutes | Your actual teaching time: |

- Pre-listening: Write *breadwinner* and *caregiver* on the board. Elicit the meanings. (The *breadwinner* is the member of a family who earns the money to support the others. The *caregiver* is the member of the family who takes care of the children.) Explain that in some families there is a primary caregiver and breadwinner, while in others the roles are more shared.
- First listening: Have students listen once while books are closed. Then ask them to do the exercise.
- Second listening: Have students listen again and check their answers.

LANGUAGE NOTE The audio includes the following terms: *a trend* is a general change in a situation or in the way people are acting—a *hot* trend is a popular trend; *a heart-to-heart talk* is a conversation in which two people sincerely say what they really feel about something; *a nest egg* is money saved to use for something specific in the future; *the whole nine yards* means everything; *to put your finger on something* means to understand something precisely.

Challenge: [+5 minutes] Have students use the five lines to help them summarize the entire TV broadcast. Invite them to fill in any gaps with additional information and details.

 Listening Strategies

D ▶ 1:12 LISTEN TO CONFIRM CONTENT

| Suggested teaching time: | 5–10 minutes | Your actual teaching time: |

- Pre-listening. Let students read the questions.
- First listening. Have students listen once and check the topics that were discussed.
- Second listening. Then have them listen again to see if they checked the correct topics.

Challenge: [+5 minutes] Invite students to write the definition of a stay-at-home dad. First have students try to see if they can remember from the audioscript. If students need hints, write on the board:

stay-at-home dad
1. out of necessity
2. by choice

(A stay-at-home dad is a father who is the daily primary caregiver of his children under age eighteen. There are two types of stay-at-home dads. There is a father who is home out of necessity, having lost his job while his wife takes a job to support the family. The other type is a father who chooses to be the primary caregiver at home).

UNIT 1 LESSON 3 T8

E LISTEN FOR SUPPORTING DETAILS

Suggested teaching time:	5 minutes	Your actual teaching time:

- **Pre-listening:** Call on students to read the questions. Invite students to write notes on the questions they feel they can answer right away.
- **First listening:** Play the audio starting from *Dan, what did your friends and family think of your plan?* Give students time to answer the questions. Ask a volunteer to read the sample answer.
- **Second listening:** Have students listen again (again starting from *Dan, what did your friends and family . . .*) to answer any outstanding questions.
- Then ask students to compare answers with a partner.

Option: [+5 minutes] On the board, write the terms *housewife* and *househusband*. Ask students to discuss why Dan probably does not like the term *househusband*. Then have them share their own reactions to these terms.

Challenge: [+5 minutes] Have pairs role-play a question from a guest in the audience and Dan's response. The guest should make a comment challenging Dan's choice, a comment supporting his choice, or just a statement about his choice. Dan's response should fit with his point of view as presented on the TV program.

F DISCUSSION

Suggested teaching time:	5 minutes	Your actual teaching time:

- Divide the class into groups of three. Have students discuss the questions in their groups. Circulate and assist as necessary. Play the audio again if students disagree on any points.
- Bring the class together and ask individual students *Could you reverse roles with a spouse if a situation required it?* Then ask *Would any man here choose to be a stay-at-home dad? Would any woman choose to be the primary breadwinner?*

NOW YOU CAN Compare your dreams and goals in life

A FRAME YOUR IDEAS

Suggested teaching time:	5 minutes	Your actual teaching time:

- On the board, write *goals* and *dreams*. Have students look at the pictures. Ask *How might these images represent goals and dreams?* (Possible answers: a dream for a high-powered job; a goal to be in a bike marathon; a dream to have a family) Ask *Do these pictures represent any of your goals or dreams?*
- Ask a volunteer to read the example answer. Point out the infinitive used to express a goal and the present perfect used to express what a person has done to achieve this goal.
- Have students work individually to complete the chart.

B DISCUSSION

Suggested teaching time:	5–10 minutes	Your actual teaching time:

- Ask a student to read the Recycle This Language box. Tell students to think of ways to use this language to discuss the information in their charts.
- Then have students share and compare goals. Tell students to also refer to the phrases on page 8 to use in their discussions.
- Bring the class together and call on each student to share which they consider their biggest dream or goal. See if any students have similar goals and dreams.

Challenge: [+5 minutes] Tell students to write a paragraph describing a life goal and the steps they have taken so far to achieve it. On the board, write:

Goal:

What I have done/have been doing to achieve it:

What I still need to do:

Remind students to use the present perfect and the present perfect continuous to discuss things they have done or have been doing to achieve the goal. When specifying a date when something was done (e.g., I graduated from college in 2012), the past tense should be used. Circulate and assist. Then collect students' work and offer feedback.

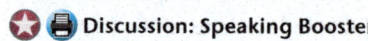 Discussion: Speaking Booster

E LISTEN FOR SUPPORTING DETAILS On a separate sheet of paper, answer each question. Explain your answers with details from what Dan said. Listen again if necessary.

1. Is Dan happy with his lifestyle choice? How do you know?
   He's happy because he's doing what he always wanted to do.
2. Why does Dan think comments about his life choices are sexist?
   Because they reflect a double standard.
3. What's Dan's opinion of women who become the primary breadwinner of the family?
   He thinks everyone should be able to set his or her own goals.
4. Why does Dan think it's good for his children to observe the roles he and Sarah have taken?
   He wants them to pursue their individual dreams and not have the dreams limited because of their sex.
5. Why would the person who sent the tweet be against his son's deciding to be a stay-at-home dad?
   Traditionally, men have been the breadwinners, and he probably thinks being a stay-at-home dad is not acceptable.
6. How do you know Dan doesn't like the terms *housewife* and *househusband*?
   These words don't cover the complexity of the job of staying at home to raise your children.
7. What's Dan's hope for the next generation?
   He hopes that the next generation won't think it's strange for a man to stay home and a woman to be the sole breadwinner.

> "He's happy because he's doing what he always wanted to do."

F DISCUSSION Discuss the following questions. Express and support your opinions.

1. Should any careers or parental / household roles be limited to people of one sex or the other? Be specific and support your opinion with reasons.
2. Why do people have a double standard for men and women? Is there any good reason to have one?
3. Will Dan and Sarah's children benefit or be harmed by their parents' reversal of roles. In what ways?
4. Are men or women naturally more ambitious in their careers? If you think they are, why do you think that is?
5. Do you think Dan and Sarah fulfilled their dreams and goals? If so, explain how.

NOW YOU CAN Compare your dreams and goals in life

A FRAME YOUR IDEAS Complete the chart with your own dreams and goals. If you need more space, continue on a separate sheet of paper.

Goals I've set	What I have done to achieve them
to get married and have three children	I've signed up for an online dating site.

	Goals I've set	What I have done to achieve them
for my family		
for my career		
other		

RECYCLE THIS LANGUAGE

- decide on
- take up
- apply for / to
- sign up for
- switch to
- be accepted to / into / by
- be rejected by
- a breadwinner
- a caregiver
- sexist
- traditional
- have a double standard

B DISCUSSION Share and compare goals with your partner. Use the Vocabulary from page 8.

LESSON 4
GOAL Describe job qualifications

A READING WARM-UP How qualified are you for the job you want—now or in the future? Explain.

B ▶ 1:13 **READING** Read the article about good and bad interview behavior. In your opinion, which suggestion is the most important?

Answers will vary but may include the following: In my opinion, the most important suggestion is not overly informal or too familiar during an interview.

JOB BUILDER

Home | About | Advice & tips | Build a career | Search

The Successful Job Interview
Charlotte Watson

OK. So you've sent in an application and a résumé for that dream job you saw advertised. The employer thinks you might be a good candidate, and you've landed an interview. You already know it's important to dress right, offer a firm handshake, and maintain eye contact, but do you know that other aspects of your behavior can make the difference between getting that job or not?

Being late to a job interview is almost always a disqualifier. Most candidates are on their best behavior for their interview, so being late is a major red flag for employers. Since punctuality is expected in any kind of work setting, arriving late makes your future employer think you'll be late for work if you get the job. If you are late for your interview, it's important to provide an airtight detailed excuse, explaining why your lateness was unavoidable. Apologize and reassure the interviewer that this isn't habitual behavior on your part.

Another thing that can get an interviewee off on the wrong foot is being overly informal or too familiar. Even though the person who interviews you might be friendly or dressed informally, don't take this as permission to be inappropriately casual. If an interviewer wants to be addressed by his or her first name, he or she will invite you to do that. If not, be sure to stick with last names and titles.

Remember that employers want to know that you are interested in the job and will be a motivated employee. A candidate who hasn't taken the time to learn something about the company or the position being offered appears unmotivated and willing to take anything that comes along. Even if you are sure you already know everything you need to know about the job or the company, prepare two or three relevant questions for the interviewer of the position. And listen with obvious interest to the answers, following up with thoughtful questions that demonstrate that you have been listening.

So before your next job interview, check out the list of do's and don'ts and follow the suggestions. They'll take you a long way towards getting that dream job!

Good morning, Ms. Bates. Please have a seat and make yourself comfortable.

Oh, thanks. I'm sorry for being late. I had written down eleven o'clock!

By the way, you don't mind if I call you Ian, do you?

Uh... no. That's OK.

Top Ten Do's and Don'ts for Your Job Interview

Do
Arrive on time.
Stay on topic when answering questions.
Ask questions.
Listen.
Be modest, yet positive about yourself.

Don't
Be too familiar.
Talk too much.
Seem desperate to get the job.
Criticize your current employer.
Brag about yourself.

C CONFIRM INFORMATION Write a checkmark for the ideas that Charlotte Watson expressed in the article. Then, for the statements that don't reflect what she said, work with a partner to clarify what she did say.

✓ 1 Employers expect employees to be punctual on the job.

☐ 2 You shouldn't ask the employer questions during a job interview because it might indicate that you don't know anything about the company. *Asking questions during the interview shows that you are really interested in the company.*

✓ 3 It's important for job candidates to express interest in the company offering the job.

☐ 4 Employers should dress informally when they interview job candidates. *Job candidates should dress nice when they have an interview.*

☐ 5 It's better not to explain why you are late for an interview. *You should offer a good explanation about why you are late for an interview.*

LESSON 4

GOAL Describe job qualifications

A READING WARM-UP

Suggested teaching time:	5 minutes	Your actual teaching time:

- Write *job qualifications* on the board. Ask *What are job qualifications?* (the experience and education you have that make you a good candidate for a job)
- Ask a volunteer to read the question in the Student's Book. Have students discuss it in pairs or small groups. If students currently have the job they want, tell them to think of another position they might want in the future.

B ▶1:13 READING

Suggested teaching time:	5–10 minutes	Your actual teaching time:

- Have students look at the website. Call on a volunteer to read the various heads—the website name, the tabs, and the article title. Ask *Which tab do you think was clicked on to get this article?* (likely *Advice & tips*)
- Ask two volunteers to role-play the conversation illustrated in cartoons on the right. Invite them to act it out as well.
- Then ask students to read the list of Do's and Don'ts at the bottom.
- As students read and listen, tell them to write *Do* and *Don't* in the margins next to the paragraphs. (paragraph 1: Do's, paragraph 2: Don'ts, paragraph 3: Don'ts, paragraph 4: Do's)
- In pairs, have students discuss the focus question. Then bring the class together and call on volunteers to share. (Possible answer: be respectful)

LANGUAGE NOTE *To land something* means to succeed in getting it; *a disqualifier* is something that disqualifies or eliminates someone from competition because something has been done wrong; *airtight* means not allowing air to come in or out—an airtight excuse is one that has no weak points; *to get off on the wrong foot* means to get an unsuccessful start (*to get off on the right foot* means the opposite).

 Reading Strategies

C CONFIRM INFORMATION

Suggested teaching time:	5–10 minutes	Your actual teaching time:

- Have students check the ideas that were expressed in the article. Then have them correct the unchecked statements to reflect ideas that were indeed expressed in the article.
- Ask students to compare answers with a partner.

🖨 Extra Reading Comprehension Questions

UNIT 1 LESSON 4 **T10**

D APPLY IDEAS

Suggested teaching time:	5 minutes	Your actual teaching time:

- In pairs, have students read Ms. Bates's comments and decide if they follow the advice in the article.
- Bring the class together and go over the answers as a class.

Challenge: [+5 minutes] Elicit from students what interview query each of the quotes might be an answer to and write these on the board. Possible questions:

1. Describe how you interact with your colleagues.
2. Tell me about yourself.
3. Tell me about your current job.
4. Do you have good presentation skills?
5. Do you have any questions for us?
6. What do you think makes you a good candidate for this job?

Invite students to role-play the questions with the answers.

As a secondary challenge, invite students to role-play again, making up appropriate answers for questions 2, 3, 4, and 6.

E DISCUSSION

Suggested teaching time:	5 minutes	Your actual teaching time:

- Call on a volunteer to read the list of Do's in the article out loud. Ask another volunteer to read the list of Don'ts. Read the model answer. On the board, write:

  If you + base form ... the interviewer could ... and might.

  Point out the use of the conditional and the modals to speculate. Tell students they will use this structure to speculate about the Don'ts.

- Then to model the Do's write:

  If you + base form ... the interviewer will ...

- Elicit the first example answer: *If you arrive on time, the interviewer will have a good first impression.*

⭐ 🖨 **Extra Challenge Reading Activities**

Answers for Exercise E

Answers will vary but may include the following:

If you arrive on time, your potential employer will see you are punctual.
If you are too familiar, the interviewer might think you don't know appropriate manners in the workplace.
If you ask questions, the interviewer will see you are serious about the job.
If you brag about yourself, the interviewer might not believe everything you say.

F ▶ 1:14 WORD STUDY

Suggested teaching time:	5 minutes	Your actual teaching time:

- Have students read and listen.
- Then have students listen and repeat the words chorally.

⭐ 🖨 **Vocabulary-Building Strategies**

G PERSONALIZE THE VOCABULARY

Suggested teaching time:	5 minutes	Your actual teaching time:

- Call on a volunteer to read the example answer.
- Then have students use the collocations to write at least four statements about their qualifications.
- Students will likely need assistance with forms that follow each collocation. Refer to this list or write it on the board:

have experience (doing something)	have training in (a field or doing something)
have experience with (equipment, a process)	get training in (a field or doing something)
have experience in (a field or doing something)	get a degree/certificate in (a field)
get (some) experience in (a field or doing something)	get certified in (a field)

Option: [+5 minutes] In pairs, have students role-play mini-interviews. On the board, write:

Interviewer: So tell me about your qualifications.

Have students take turns asking about qualifications and sharing the sentences they wrote down.

NOW YOU CAN Describe job qualifications

A FRAME YOUR IDEAS

Suggested teaching time:	5 minutes	Your actual teaching time:

- Give students a few minutes to read the job ad and the résumé. Tell students to underline qualifications in the résumé to correspond to the requirements in the job ad.
- Then, in pairs, have students use the collocations from Exercise F to make notes about Ben's qualifications.
- Bring the class together and ask *Does Ben appear to need to get any additional training or experience?* (Possible answer: No, he appears to be a qualified candidate.) *What is the next step in the application process?* (the interview)

B ROLE PLAY

Suggested teaching time:	5–10 minutes	Your actual teaching time:

- Have students work together to draft interview questions. Encourage students to not limit the questions to experience that reflects the needs of the job. Refer students to the article in Exercise B on page 10 for other ideas (e.g., questions from interviewer about an applicant's current job). Remind pairs that the interviewee also should be prepared to ask questions.
- Then have one student role-play Ben and the other the hiring manager. Remind students to keep in mind the do's and don'ts from the article on page 10.

OPTIONAL WRITING [+15–20 minutes]

- Have students draft résumés in class or at home, using Ben's model or an online template.
- In class, let students peer review. Then collect and offer feedback.

D **APPLY IDEAS** Read more things Ms. Bates said in her interview. With a partner, explain whether she followed Watson's suggestions.

1 "I'd say I'm kind of a people person and a pretty good listener. My colleagues often come to me when they need advice and support."
YES: She is being modest yet positive about herself.

2 "Correct me if I'm wrong, Ian—you're married, right?"
NO: She's being too familiar.

3 "I really can't stand my supervisor. He's not fair. If I don't get this job, I'll be very depressed!"
NO: She's criticizing her current employer *and* she seems too desperate to get the job.

4 "I make even better presentations than my boss. You would be lucky to have me in this job."
NO: She is bragging about herself.

5 "What is the biggest challenge the company sees itself facing in the next year?"
YES: She's asking questions about the company.

6 "Let me tell you what my teacher did when I was still a child. My mother was visiting and the teacher showed her my artwork, which she said was the best in the class. And since this job entails creating presentations at meetings, I thought that information would indicate that this has been a lifelong interest of mine and something that I have developed a lot of skills in."
NO: She's talking too much.

E **DISCUSSION** Explain the reason for each of the do's and dont's on the list in the article.
See page T11 for answers.

> If you criticize your current employer, the interviewer could think you're not a loyal employee and might say bad things about his or her company too.

F ▶ 1:14 **WORD STUDY** COLLOCATIONS WITH <u>HAVE</u> AND <u>GET</u> FOR QUALIFICATIONS
Read and listen to the collocations, paying attention to <u>have</u>, <u>get</u>, and the prepositions. Repeat.

have experience	get experience in
have experience with	get training in
have experience in	get a degree / certificate in
have training in	get certified in

G **PERSONALIZE THE VOCABULARY** On a separate sheet of paper, write statements about your qualifications, using at least four of the collocations.

> I've had some training in IT and gotten some experience in managing technical staff ...

NOW YOU CAN Describe job qualifications

A **FRAME YOUR IDEAS** Read the job ad and Ben Breeden's résumé. With a partner, make notes describing his qualifications for this job. Use the collocations from Word Study.

Wilton Hotel, Miami FLORIDA, USA
Seeks Assistant Manager to work at front desk and in office. Must possess good people skills and knowledge of the hotel industry. The Wilton Hotel has many guests and workers from Latin America so ability to speak Spanish and Portuguese fluently a must.

Ben Breeden
102 Shanley Avenue +1 555 776 9833
Newtown, FL 32793 ben.breeden@blue.net

Objective
To use my background and experience in a managerial position in the hotel industry

Experience
July 2016 to the present
  Corporate sales associate, Holiday House Hotel, Newtown, FL
August 2015 to June 2016
  Event planning assistant, Holiday House Hotel, Newtown, FL
September 2013 to June 2015
  Part-time salesclerk, Pennyworth's Department Store, Newtown, FL

Education
Comstock School of Hotel Management, Comstock, GA
  Certificate in Hotel Management (June 2015)
University of Central Florida, Hyperion, FL
  B.S. in Communication with major in Spanish and Portuguese (June 2014)

B **ROLE PLAY** In pairs, role-play a job interview between Ben Breeden and the hiring manager of the Wilton Hotel. Follow Charlotte Watson's suggestions.

OPTIONAL WRITING Write your own one-page résumé. Include your employment history, education and / or training. Use Breeden's résumé as a model, or select a template from an online résumé-building website.

WRITING A formal cover letter

A WRITING SKILL Study the rules.

The purpose of a cover letter is to acquaint an employer with you and to express interest in a position. If a job ad provides instructions about what to include in your cover letter, be sure to follow the directions carefully. If you don't, you may not receive a response. The letter can be sent in traditional paper form by mail, or as an e-mail.

Traditional paper form

Follow the style used for other formal letters. Use good quality paper and be neat. Proofread your letter carefully to be sure there are no spelling mistakes or typographical errors. Try to limit the letter to one page. Include your résumé on a separate sheet of paper in the same envelope.

E-mail form

Use formal e-mail style, addressing the recipient with his or her title and last name followed by a colon. Make paragraphs easy to read by separating them with a blank line space. Do not attach your cover letter to your e-mail. Make the e-mail the actual cover letter so the recipient can see the information upon opening the e-mail. Attach your résumé to your e-mail.

Here are some suggestions:

- Tell the employer why you are writing (in response to an ad, as a general expression of interest in working at that company or institution, etc.).
- Say why you think you would be a good candidate for the (or a) position; i.e., briefly state your qualifications.
- Tell the employer how to contact you for follow-up or to schedule an interview.
- Do not include too much information about your life.

WRITING MODEL

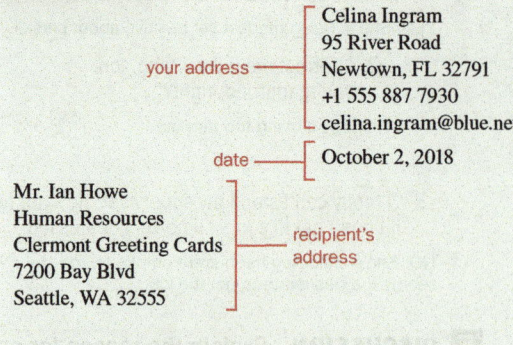

I am writing in response to your advertisement on giantjob.com for the executive administrative assistant position at the Clermont Card Company in Seattle.

I have often bought Clermont greeting cards because of their positive messages and nice graphics, which is why I would be proud to work there. In addition, I believe I would be a good candidate because of my successful experience as an administrative assistant at Pinkerton Greeting Cards.

I have attached my résumé and the names and contact information of two managers here at Pinkerton who have offered to provide a recommendation.

If you agree that my experience and other qualifications make me a good candidate, please contact me at the address or e-mail address above. As I will be moving to Seattle in two weeks, please contact me at my e-mail address after October 15.

I look forward to hearing from you.

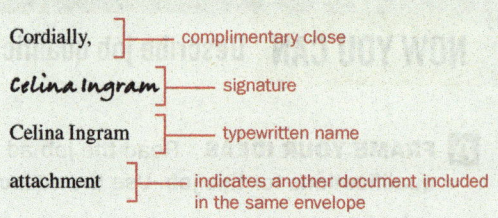

B PRACTICE Read the e-mail cover letter. On a separate sheet of paper, rewrite it, correcting errors in style and formality. See page T12 for answer.

Subject:

Hi, Bill—Just wanted u 2 know Im intersted in that great advertising copy writer job I saw listed in the want ads ☺. I think I'm the rite person 4 u. Here's why: I am 26 years old and graduated from Meecham College with a major in english. I have been working at Poco Cola in the advertising department for five years I am ready to move to a new company. My résumé is attached so you can see my qualifications. If you are interested in discussing the job, please e-mail me at the address above to set up an interview. –Jon

C APPLY THE WRITING SKILL On a separate sheet of paper, write a formal cover letter to an employer, expressing interest in a job. Create a job title that interests you and use the name of a real or a fictitious employer. Use real or invented information.

SELF-CHECK

- ☐ Does my letter have any spelling, punctuation, or typographical errors?
- ☐ Did I use formal letter writing conventions?
- ☐ Did I tell the employer the purpose of my letter?
- ☐ Did I say why I think I would be a good candidate?
- ☐ Did I tell the employer how to contact me for follow-up?

WRITING: A formal cover letter

A WRITING SKILL

Suggested teaching time:	5–10 minutes	Your actual teaching time:

- Write *cover letter* on the board and ask students what this is. (a letter that you send with your résumé to apply for employment)
- Ask a volunteer to read the introduction.
- Then have students read to themselves about the two forms of cover letters. Then bring the class together and ask *Which form(s) have you used? Which do you think is more common?* (Probably e-mail is becoming more common.) Point out that there are variations in layout of formal letters. Some people center their address at the top. Others set it to the right, as here. Some people indent paragraphs. Others set a line space above each new paragraph.
- Bring students' attention to the writing model. Have students note the parts of the cover letter. Then have them number the five paragraphs.
- Call on students to read the bulleted points under *Here are some suggestions*. After each bullet point, direct them to the paragraphs in the writing model that illustrate it. (first bullet: paragraph 1, second bullet: paragraphs 2 and 3, third bullet: paragraph 4)
- Focus on the last line of the suggestions. Ask *Why might it be wise not to include too much information?* (The person hiring likely reads through a lot of cover letters; it's good to be brief and to the point.)

Option: [+5 minutes] You may choose to distinguish for students the difference between a spelling error, which indicates a lack of knowledge of correct spelling, from a typographical error (often called a typo), which is due to careless typing or keyboarding that results in an incorrect letter or letters in a word.

Emphasize for students the importance of proofreading letters at least one time, preferably twice, because the person reading the letter can have a strong positive or negative impression of the writer based on the correctness or incorrectness of the letter.

Also remind students that they can't rely on spell check applications on electronic devices because many words have variant spellings (e.g., too, two, to; their, they're, there).

Option: [+5 minutes] Invite students to look online for various templates for formal business letters and choose a template they would like to use as a model for their own letter in Exercise C.

Challenge: [+5 minutes] Invite students to share experiences looking for work online. Ask: *Do you belong to an employment social networking site? Is your résumé posted online? Is your résumé posted online? Have employers ever contacted you about a job that you haven't directly applied for? Do you network with people online?*

B PRACTICE

Suggested teaching time:	5 minutes	Your actual teaching time:

- Ask students to skim the paragraph. Then ask *What do you think an employer would do if he or she got this e-mail?* (most likely would delete it)
- Have students rewrite the paragraph, using the writing model to help them. Tell students they can make up information such as last name, address, date. Circulate and assist as needed.
- Then have students compare cover letters with a partner.

Answer to Exercise B

Answers will vary but may include the following:

Dear Mr. Ramsay,

I am writing to let you know that I am interested in the copy-writer job I saw advertised in the [add name of publication]. I think I would be a very good candidate for the position. I am 26 years old and graduated from Meecham College with a major in English. I have been working at Poco Cola in the advertising department for five years. I have really enjoyed my time there but am now ready to try something new. My résumé is attached for your review. Please contact me at at my e-mail address. I look forward to hearing from you.

Sincerely,
Jon Roberts

C APPLY THE WRITING SKILL

Suggested teaching time:	10–15 minutes	Your actual teaching time:

- Have students think of a job title, either real or fictitious, and then take notes describing the qualifications for this job.
- Refer students to the Writing Process Worksheet in ActiveTeach for guidance with prewriting and peer feedback.
- Encourage students to use the Self-Check in the Student's Book to go over the letters they wrote.

Option: [+5 minutes] Time-permitting, students can exchange papers with a partner and offer feedback using the topics in the checklist. Encourage partners to also check for use of examples.

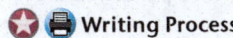 Writing Process

UNIT 1 WRITING   T12

REVIEW

 Digital Game

A ▶ 1:15

| Suggested teaching time: | 5 minutes | Your actual teaching time: |

- Call on a volunteer to read the chart headings. Then have students read and listen to all four conversations.
- Have students listen again to the first conversation and answer the questions. Do the same with the remaining conversations.
- After students complete the chart, have them compare answers with a partner.
- Then have students listen again. Stop after each conversation and have students identify the line that reveals whether the speaker is confident. (1. I don't think I'll ever really be able to outdo them [not confident]; 2. I'm starting to feel like maybe it's time to just give up ... I'm really not sure I'll ever have a house of my own [not confident]; 3. I've already applied for a loan [confident]; 4. You're probably right [confident]). In Conversation 4, point out that although at first the woman is not confident, she becomes confident after talking about her qualifications.
- Ask students if they answered most questions correctly. Replay conversations as needed.

Challenge: [+5 minutes] Using the conversations in the Listening Comprehension from Lesson 3 as models, have pairs create their own conversation about a lifelong dream. Tell students to decide if they are confident about achieving their dream. Invite pairs to present the conversations to the class. Ask the class to determine whether the speaker is confident. Have the class identify the line(s) in the conversation that revealed the level of confidence.

B

| Suggested teaching time: | 5 minutes | Your actual teaching time: |

- Have students read the sentences before filling in the prepositions.
- Ask students to complete the exercise individually. Refer them to Exercise A on page 6 and Exercise F on page 11 if they have difficulty.
- Then have them compare answers with a partner. Go over any questions as a class.

C

| Suggested teaching time: | 5 minutes | Your actual teaching time: |

- Refer students to Exercise A on page 8 if they have difficulty matching the items.
- After students complete the matching, have them compare answers with a partner.
- After students write sentences, bring the class together and invite students to share their plans and goals.

Challenge: [+5 minutes] Invite students to connect their sentences into a paragraph about goals and plans. Instruct them to think about meaning and sequence, moving sentences around and adding others as needed. Encourage students to refer to the grammar on page 4 to help them incorporate adverbial clauses where appropriate.

D

| Suggested teaching time: | 5 minutes | Your actual teaching time: |

- Call on a student to model the first item on the board:

  How long had you been working on ...

  Then have students complete the exercise.
- Bring the class together and go over the answers.

Option: **TEST-TAKING SKILLS BOOSTER** *(p. 151)*

EXTRA

- Workbook
- MyEnglishLab
- Online Student Resources (www.english.com/summit3e)
  – Classroom Audio Program
  – Extra Practice Activities
  – *Summit GO* App
  – Web Projects
- ActiveTeach
  – Assessment
  – Additional Printable Resources
    ○ Audioscripts and Answer Keys
    ○ "Can-Do" Self-Assessment Charts
    ○ Conversation and Discussion Activator Video Scripts
    ○ Oral Progress Assessment Charts
    ○ Reading Speed Calculator
  – Summit TV Video Program
    ○ Activity Worksheets
    ○ Teaching Notes
    ○ Video Scripts

REVIEW

A ▶ 1:15 Listen to the conversations. Then read the questions in the chart and listen again. Complete the chart after each conversation.

	What is his or her dream in life?	Is he or she confident about achieving his or her goal?	
1	To have the biggest collection of stamps in the world.	☐ yes	☑ no
2	To buy a house.	☐ yes	☑ no
3	To start her own business.	☑ yes	☐ no
4	To become a flight attendant.	☑ yes	☐ no

B Complete the statements with the correct prepositions.
1. She has always wanted to take ..**up**.. the piano and has enrolled ..**in**.. a program that teaches the basics of music to adults.
2. Anyone applying ..**for**.. a job in the newspaper business should have training ..**in**.. journalism.
3. He has decided ..**on**.. a career as a chef and has been accepted ..**to**.. a top-notch cooking school in Peru.
4. Her experience ..**with**.. the diplomatic service and her degree ..**in**.. international relations make her an excellent candidate for a position at the U.N.
5. After being rejected ..**by**.. two accounting firms for a summer internship, he decided to switch ..**to**.. a different major at his university.
6. Before she applied ..**to**.. law school, she signed up ..**for**.. speed reading.

C Match each word or phrase with its definition. Then, on a separate sheet of paper, use each one in a statement about your own plans and goals.

..a.. 1 achievable   **a** capable of being reached
..e.. 2 ambitious   **b** decide what one wants to do and work towards it
..b.. 3 work towards a goal   **c** divide necessary work between two or more people so neither one has to do it all
..d.. 4 put off   **d** postpone
..f.. 5 unrealistic   **e** requiring a lot of work
..c.. 6 share responsibilities   **f** unreasonably hard and thus unlikely to be achieved

D Complete each information question, using the past perfect continuous.
1. (how long / you / work on) **How long had you been working on** that project before you changed jobs?
2. (where / they / study) **Where had they been studying** before they moved to Europe?
3. (which program / she / apply for) **Which program had she been applying for** when she decided to change majors?
4. (what professor / you / study with) **What professor had you been studying with** when they closed the university?
5. (how long / they / look) **How long had they been looking** at résumés before they saw yours?

TEST-TAKING SKILLS BOOSTER p. 151

Web Project: Careers
www.english.com/summit3e

UNIT 2
Character and Responsibility

PREVIEW

COMMUNICATION GOALS
1 Describe the consequences of lying
2 Express regret and take responsibility
3 Explore where values come from
4 Discuss how best to help others

A | **FRAME YOUR IDEAS** Look at the pictures. Then answer the questions in the survey. Check what *you* would do in each situation.

Taking responsibility... or avoiding it

IS IT HARD FOR YOU TO ACCEPT RESPONSIBILITY?

What would you do if you …	A	B	C	Other
made a serious mistake at work or school?	☐	☐	☐	☐
forgot to finish an assignment at work or school?	☐	☐	☐	☐
broke or lost something you had borrowed?	☐	☐	☐	☐
were late for an appointment?	☐	☐	☐	☐
were stopped for exceeding the speed limit?	☐	☐	☐	☐
damaged someone's car while parking, but no one saw you?	☐	☐	☐	☐
hadn't kept a promise you made to a friend or relative?	☐	☐	☐	☐
forgot a friend's birthday?	☐	☐	☐	☐
were caught telling a lie?	☐	☐	☐	☐

A I would admit making a mistake. *"Sorry. It was my fault!"*

B I would shift the blame to someone or something else. *"It was the cat's fault!"*

C I would make up an excuse. *"Sorry, I'm going to be late. The traffic is just terrible!"*

B ▶ 1:16 **VOCABULARY** **TAKING OR AVOIDING RESPONSIBILITY** Listen and repeat.

- admit making a mistake
- make up an excuse
- shift the blame
- keep a promise
- tell a lie / tell the truth

C **PAIR WORK** Compare and explain your responses to the survey.

D **DISCUSSION** Are there ever good reasons *not* to be truthful? Is it ever a better idea to make up an excuse or shift the blame to someone else? Explain your answers and give examples.

14   UNIT 2

UNIT 2
Character and Responsibility

PREVIEW

A FRAME YOUR IDEAS

Suggested teaching time:	5–10 minutes	Your actual teaching time:

- Ask a student to read the title of the unit. Write *character* on the board. Elicit that character refers to the combination of qualities (such as honesty or loyalty) that are distinctive to a person.
- Have students look at the thought bubble in the cartoon. Ask *What happened here?* (The woman knocked over a vase.) Ask volunteers to read speech bubble and reaction A and then speech bubble and reaction B. Call on students to share which way they would likely react in this or a similar situation.
- Focus on the last illustration. Have a volunteer read the speech bubble. Ask *Have you ever been in this situation?* Read reaction C.
- Tell students they will choose one of these reactions—A, B, or C—in relation to different scenarios in the survey.
- Have students complete the survey individually.
- Bring the class together. Point out that many A answers mean a person tends to accept responsibility for his or her actions. Many B or C answers mean a person tends to avoid responsibility. Have students analyze their surveys.

LANGUAGE NOTE The verb *admit* or *take* can be used with *responsibility* to mean agreeing to having made a mistake or having done something wrong. *To exceed the speed limit* means to drive too fast. *To be caught telling a lie* means someone found out you weren't telling the truth.

B ▶ 1:16 VOCABULARY

Suggested teaching time:	5 minutes	Your actual teaching time:

- Have students read and listen to the vocabulary related to taking or avoiding responsibility.
- Then have students listen and repeat the phrases chorally.

Options: [+5 minutes] Call on students to share examples of each situation. Model the first item. Say: *I remember a time when I admitted to making a mistake. I had scratched my friend's car. She was pretty mad, and I had to pay for the damage.*

Invite volunteers for additional examples for item 1, or continue on to the other examples.

C PAIR WORK

Suggested teaching time:	5 minutes	Your actual teaching time:

- Have students compare answers to the survey with a partner. Have students explain their responses, mentioning specific examples if possible.
- Bring the class together and have pairs share if they have similar characteristics when it comes to taking or avoiding responsibility. Then ask volunteers *Is it hard for you to accept responsibility?*

D DISCUSSION

Suggested teaching time:	5 minutes	Your actual teaching time:

- Divide the class into groups of three, or combine pairs from Activity C into groups of four. Have students discuss the questions. Instruct one member of the group to take notes that he or she will report to the class.
- Then bring the class together and have each reporter share the group's views.

E ▶ 1:17 SPOTLIGHT

Suggested teaching time	5–10 minutes	Your actual teaching time

- Have students look at the photo. Ask *Who are these people?* (probably a father and son) *What are they doing?* (They appear to be discussing something.) *Do they seem happy?* (No, they look serious.) *What might they be talking about?* (Maybe the son did something wrong.)
- Have students read and listen to the conversation.
- To check comprehension, ask *What mistake did Jason make?* (He and his classmate Joey made fun of a classmate's drawing of a horse and hurt her feelings.) *Does he regret what he did?* (yes) *How do we know?* (He says that he wishes he had told Joey to cut it out rather than join in.) *What advice does Jason's dad give?* (to apologize and buy the girl lunch, and also to talk to the teacher) *Did Jason take responsibility for his actions?* (Yes, he did.)

LANGUAGE NOTE Point out that Jason shifts to the present tense when he's telling the story, even though he's talking about the past, an occasional but common characteristic in narrating, or telling a story in spoken language. This emphasizes certain details and makes the listener more "present."

Option: [+5 minutes] Write the following questions on the board: *Why do you think the boy came to the dad?* (Possible answers: He felt guilty. He felt bad. He wasn't sure how to make the situation right.) *Do you think the dad should have been stricter with him?* (Possible answers: No, the boy took responsibility and will likely follow his dad's advice to amend the situation. Yes, the boy should have some kind of consequence for poor behavior.)

Challenge: [+5 minutes] On the board, write:

If I were Jason, I would . . .

If I were the dad, I would . . .

Review the unreal conditional form and have students speculate in pairs what they would do if they were Jason or the dad. This form was also used in the Spotlight conversation when the dad gives Jason advice saying *If I were you* . . .

F UNDERSTANDING IDIOMS AND EXPRESSIONS 1

Suggested teaching time:	5 minutes	Your actual teaching time:

- Call on two volunteers to read the two exercise items. For item 2, make sure students understand that *to go too far* means to act in a way that is not acceptable.
- In pairs, have students find the spotlighted expressions.
- Go over the answers as a class.

Challenge: [+5 minutes] Invite students to experiment swapping the two synonymous expressions meaning allowing behavior to go too far: *I guess we just kind of let things get out of hand . . . Take responsibility for getting carried away.* Ask *Does the meaning change?* (no)

G UNDERSTANDING IDIOMS AND EXPRESSIONS 2

Suggested teaching time:	5–10 minutes	Your actual teaching time:

- Focus on the idioms and expressions as a class. Call on volunteers to read them aloud.
- Let students work individually to locate them in context to figure out the meanings. Then have students match each expression with the correct definition.
- Ask students to compare answers with a partner, returning to Exercise E to check items as necessary.
- Bring the class together to go over the answers.

Challenge: [+5 minutes] Divide the class into pairs and assign each pair one or two idioms/expressions from the list. Have them create brief dialogues around them. Invite pairs to share dialogues.

H DISCUSSION

Suggested teaching time:	5 minutes	Your actual teaching time:

- In pairs or small groups, have students discuss the questions.
- Bring the class together and discuss. Make sure students address the notion of moral responsibility (Jason's and Joey's) to treat classmates nicely and practical responsibility (Mr. Rogg's, who shouldn't have left the class unattended).

Option: [+5 minutes] Invite students to speculate:

If I were the girl . . . (Possible answer: I wouldn't have cared and would not have cried)

If I were another student in the class . . . (Possible answer: I would have stood up for the girl and made her feel better)

Challenge: [+5 minutes] Ask students to ponder if this type of situation happens only to children, or if adults also act similarly with each other. Have students discuss and offer examples.

SPEAKING PAIR WORK

Suggested teaching time:	5 minutes	Your actual teaching time:

- Call on a student to read the direction line. Ask *What does* accidentally *mean?* (not on purpose) *Did Jason accidentally hurt the girl's feelings?* (It was not accidental, even though he claims he couldn't help himself.) Point out that *accidental* means you say or do something not knowing that someone could be hurt. For example, you innocently say something tastes awful, to then find out that the person you're speaking to prepared the dish.
- Tell students the situation they discuss does not have to be one they have directly experienced. Circulate and make sure pairs talk about accidental situations and use language related to taking or avoiding responsibility.

E ▶ 1:17 **SPOTLIGHT** Read and listen to a conversation between a father and his teenage son. Notice the spotlighted language.

ENGLISH FOR TODAY'S WORLD
Understand a variety accents.
Jason = American English (regional)
Dad = American English (regional)

Jason: Dad … I think I messed up big time today.
Dad: What happened?
Jason: Well, you know how teachers always like to put up students' artwork on the walls? So Joey and I noticed this really weird drawing of a horse.
Dad: So what? You didn't like it. That's not a crime.
Jason: True. But that's not all.
Dad: Uh-oh.
Jason: See, Mr. Rogg had to step out for a bit. And Joey—you know how he's always fooling around—he starts **making fun of** the drawing, acting like he's the horse.
Dad: And I suppose the class loved that?
Jason: Totally. Everyone was cracking up. Anyway, I **couldn't help myself**. I started joking around, too, and I guess we just kind of **got carried away**.
Dad: Don't tell me the kid who drew it was in that class!
Jason: No one realized it until she got up and ran out.
Dad: Wow. Her feelings must have really been hurt.
Jason: **That's not the worst of it**. She came back with Mr. Rogg and she was crying, which made me feel awful. I could just kick myself! I wish I'd told Joey to **cut it out**.
Dad: Well, it's never too late to apologize. If I were you, I'd **own up to** what you did and tell her how bad you feel. Take responsibility for **letting things get out of hand**. Maybe later you could **make it up to her** by buying her lunch.
Jason: You're probably right.
Dad: And it wouldn't hurt to talk to Mr. Rogg afterward … just so he knows you did the right thing.

F **UNDERSTANDING IDIOMS AND EXPRESSIONS 1** Find two spotlighted expressions that mean someone allowed his or her behavior to go too far. letting things get out of hand; got carried away

G **UNDERSTANDING IDIOMS AND EXPRESSIONS 2** Complete the statements.

1 "Making fun of something" means ..d.. .
2 "Couldn't help myself" means ..e.. .
3 "That's not the worst of it" means ..f.. .
4 "Cut it out" means ..b.. .
5 "Own up to something" means ..a.. .
6 "Make it up to someone" means ..c.. .

a admit you did it and take responsibility for it.
b "Stop doing that!"
c do something nice for someone you have wronged.
d joking about it in order to criticize it.
e wasn't able to stop doing [something].
f there's even more negative information.

H **DISCUSSION** Discuss the questions. Answers will vary but may include the following:

1 Whose responsibility was it to prevent what happened in the art class—Joey's, Jason's, Mr. Rogg's, or the girl's? Explain. It was Jason and Joey's responsibility to treat their classmate nicely. It was Mr. Rogg's responsibility not to leave the class unattended.
2 In what way could Joey, Jason, Mr. Rogg, or the girl have handled the situation differently? Jason could have stopped Joey from making fun of the drawing, or at least not joined in. The girl could have been less sensitive and not run out of the room.

SPEAKING **PAIR WORK** Tell a partner about a situation in which someone's feelings were accidentally hurt. How was the situation resolved? Use the Vocabulary from page 14 and expressions from Spotlight.

LESSON 1

GOAL Describe the consequences of lying

A ▶ 1:18 **GRAMMAR SPOTLIGHT** Read the article. Notice the spotlighted grammar.

"Telling the Truth? It's Not So Easy!"

I REALLY LIKE YOUR NEW HAIRCUT.

The honest truth? We *all* tell lies. In a psychological study, 147 participants were asked to keep a diary of the lies they told over the course of a week. Researchers found that:

- Participants told lies to about 30 percent of the people **with whom they interacted**.
- There wasn't a single day **when the participants didn't tell at least one lie**.

In fact, we live in a world **where we are often punished for telling the truth and rewarded for lying**. For example, we tell our boss we got stuck in traffic instead of admitting that we overslept. Making up an excuse keeps us out of trouble.

Here's another common situation **in which we often tell lies**: we pretend to like something to avoid hurting others. For example, we say we love a friend's gift when in fact we don't like it.

Some researchers argue that lying may in fact be good for us socially because it protects the feelings of the people **with whom we interact**. Interestingly, they note that the people **whose professions require the most social contacts**—for example, store clerks, salespeople, politicians, and journalists—tell the most lies.

The truth is, everyone tells "white lies" to avoid hurting others. Sometime **when you're ready**, try keeping a diary for a week and see how long you can go without telling a single lie!

B **APPLY IDEAS** With a partner, brainstorm one or more additional situations in which people would be likely to tell a lie, according to the article. Explain why. Answers will vary but may include the following: A person blames a co-worker or the computer for a mistake to avoid getting in trouble. A person lies about skills on a résumé to ensure getting a job. A guest lies that meal is delicious when in fact it isn't to avoid hurting the host's feelings.

C **EXPRESS AND SUPPORT AN OPINION** Do you agree that "lying may in fact be good for us socially because it protects the feelings of the people with whom we interact"? Explain, using examples from your life if possible. Answers will vary but may include the following: I think lying is good for us socially. If we always spoke our mind about everything there would be a lot of unhappy people. There is no harm in telling your friend her hair looks nice, even if you don't like it. Often it's a matter of opinion.

D **PAIR WORK** How truthful are you? Write an X on the continuum. Explain your choice to your partner, giving examples from your experience.

NEVER TRUTHFUL ← SOMETIMES TRUTHFUL → ALWAYS TRUTHFUL

E **RELATE TO PERSONAL EXPERIENCE** Discuss and then make a list of times in your life when you …

- made an excuse to avoid getting in trouble.
- told a lie to avoid hurting someone else's feelings.
- were punished or got in trouble after telling the truth.
- were rewarded for telling a lie.

> **GRAMMAR BOOSTER** p. 129
> - Adjective clauses: overview
> - Adjective clauses with quantifiers

DIGITAL INDUCTIVE ACTIVITY

F **GRAMMAR** **ADJECTIVE CLAUSES: REVIEW AND EXPANSION**

Remember: An adjective clause gives more information about a noun. The relative pronouns <u>who</u>, <u>whom</u>, and <u>that</u> introduce adjective clauses about people. The relative pronouns <u>that</u> and <u>which</u> introduce adjective clauses about things.

> The participants **who kept a diary** recorded that they told lies every day. (who = the participants)
> White lies are some of the most common lies **that people tell**. (that = the most common lies)

Use <u>when</u>, <u>where</u>, and <u>whose</u> to introduce adjective clauses about time, location, and possession.

> **Time:** There has never been a time **when** some form of lying wasn't a part of everyday life.
> **Location:** There's no place in the world **where** people are completely honest all the time.
> **Possession:** People **whose** jobs require frequent social contact have the most opportunity to lie.

16 UNIT 2

LESSON 1

GOAL Describe the consequences of lying

A ▶ 1:18 GRAMMAR SPOTLIGHT

Suggested teaching time:	5 minutes	Your actual teaching time:

- Write *consequence* on the board. Elicit the meaning. (something that happens as a result of a particular action) Have a student read the lesson title. Ask *What could be a consequence of lying?* (getting in trouble, e.g., in school or with the law)
- Call on a student to read the title of the article. Ask *Do you agree that telling the truth isn't so easy?*
- As a class, look at the cartoon. Ask *Have you ever said something nice to someone when you didn't really mean it?* Call on a few volunteers to share.
- Have students listen to the article as they read along.
- To check comprehension, ask *What did the people in the psychological study do?* (They kept diaries of lies they told during one week.) *What did the study reveal?* (The participants told at least one lie every day; in a week, the participants told lies to about 30 percent of the people with whom they interacted.) *Which lies are the most common?* (pretending to like something to avoid hurting others and making up excuses to get out of trouble) *In which professions do people lie the most?* (professions that require the most social contact, such as shop assistants, salespeople, politicians, and journalists)
- Have students listen to the article again, noticing the spotlighted grammar. Ask *What do you see highlighted in the spotlighted grammar?* (adjective clauses)

B APPLY IDEAS

Suggested teaching time:	5 minutes	Your actual teaching time:

- On the board, write the following lying categories as outlined in the article:

  lying to avoid punishment
  lying to be rewarded
  lying to avoid hurting people's feelings

- In pairs, have students brainstorm examples of lies people tell that exemplify each situation. Ask *Would you tell a lie in this situation, too? Why? Why not?*

C EXPRESS AND SUPPORT AN OPINION

Suggested teaching time:	5 minutes	Your actual teaching time:

- Have students work in groups of two or three and discuss the question. Tell them to give examples to support their point of view.

Challenge: [+5 minutes] Conduct a mini debate in which half the class argues that lying is good for us socially, and the other half of the class argues that truthfulness is the best.

D PAIR WORK

Suggested teaching time:	5 minutes	Your actual teaching time:

- In pairs, have students compare where they fall on the continuum. Tell them to provide examples.
- Circulate and assist. If students don't feel comfortable talking about themselves, tell them they can talk about someone they know.
- Bring the class together and poll how many students are never truthful, sometimes truthful, and always truthful. Write the result on the board: *Our class is mostly _____ truthful!*
- Finally, ask *Do you think it's possible to always be truthful?*

E RELATE TO PERSONAL EXPERIENCE

Suggested teaching time:	5 minutes	Your actual teaching time:

- Have students think of personal experiences that reflect the various categories.
- Then bring the class together. Ask *Did anyone NOT have a personal example for any of the categories?* Determine who is the most truthful person in the class. Use information from Exercise D if necessary.

F GRAMMAR

Suggested teaching time:	5 minutes	Your actual teaching time:

- Write *adjective clause* on the board. Say *Adjective clauses are also referred to as relative clauses*, in case students have heard them called such elsewhere.
- Ask a student to read the Remember note at the beginning of the grammar chart.
- You may wish to tell students that they can use the term *relative pronouns* to refer to the following words that introduce adjective clauses: *who, whom, whose, that,* and *which*. You can also point out that in formal English, *who*, not *that*, is preferred for referring to people. Be sure students understand that *which* can never be used with people, even though *that* can.
- Focus on the two example sentences. Ask *What does the adjective clause give more information about?* (in sentence 1, the participants; in sentence 2, lies). Point out that in sentence 1, *who* functions as the subject of the adjective clause. In sentence 2, *that* functions as the object of the adjective clause.
- Call on a student to read the second explanation and the three example sentences. Ask *What nouns do the adjective clauses modify?* (time, world, people) Point out that in spoken English, *where* is sometimes used instead of *when* to introduce adjective clauses about time. On the board, write:

  There are occasions <u>when</u> / <u>where</u> telling the truth may not be a good idea.

Option: GRAMMAR BOOSTER *(Teaching notes p. T129)*

⭐ 🖨 Inductive Grammar Activity

- Ask a volunteer to read the third explanation. Then call on students to read the pairs of formal and informal sentences. Remind students that the informal example sentence in each pair can be further reduced by omitting the relative pronoun. For example, *The participants lied to many people they interacted with*. Have students reduce the other informal example. (*It's a question most people don't give a truthful answer to.*)
- Have students note the different placements of the preposition in the sentences. In informal spoken English, the preposition is often at the end of the sentence. Point out that *whom* is less and less common in informal spoken English.
- Have students read the Be careful! note to themselves. Remind students that *who* is a subject and *whom* is the object.

Option: [+5 minutes] Invite students to look back at the Grammar Spotlight and circle the relative pronouns and adverbs (*with whom, when, where, in which, with whom, whose, when*).

G UNDERSTAND THE GRAMMAR

Suggested teaching time:	5 minutes	Your actual teaching time:

- Review the categories of adjective clauses by asking *Which words are used for people?* (who, whom, that) *For things?* (that, which) *For possession?* (whose) *For location?* (where) *For time?* (when, where—in spoken English)
- Have students work with a partner to answer the questions and rewrite the sentences with adjective clauses that are objects of a preposition. Circulate and assist as needed. Remind students that in informal English, the preposition usually appears at the end of the sentence.
- Then go over the answers as a class.

⭐ 🖨 Extra Grammar Exercises

Answers for Exercise G

1. Possession: whose professions require the most social contacts
   Location: where we are often punished for telling the truth and rewarded for lying
   Time: when you're ready

2. Objects of preposition: with whom they interacted in which we often tell lies with whom we interact

   Rewritten in Informal English: Participants told lies to about 30 percent of the people they interacted with. Here's another common situation which we often tell lies in. Some researchers argue that lying may in fact be good for us socially because it protects the feelings of the people we interact with.

H GRAMMAR PRACTICE

Suggested teaching time:	5 minutes	Your actual teaching time:

- Before students do the exercise, have them scan each sentence for clues that will help them decide if the adjective clause is about people, things, possession,

location, or time. (1. *place*, location; 2. *people*, possession; 3. *people*, people; 4. *people*, people; 5. *situations*, thing; 6. *moments*, time; 7. *people*, people; *people*, people; 8. *times*, time; *times*, time; 9. *action*, thing; 10. *People*, possession)

- After students complete the exercise, have them compare answers with a partner. Circulate and assist as needed. Then go over the answers as a class.

NOW YOU CAN Describe the consequences of lying

A NOTEPADDING

Suggested teaching time:	5 minutes	Your actual teaching time:

- Call on volunteers to read the headings for the two categories. For each heading, ask *What is the adjective clause?* (in which we shouldn't tell lies, in which telling a lie is the best solution) *What noun does each adjective clause modify?* (situations, situations)
- Have students complete the exercise independently.
- Then bring the class together and have students compare their examples. Invite students to explain why they listed the specific situations and people they did.

B ACTIVATE THE GRAMMAR

Suggested teaching time:	5 minutes	Your actual teaching time:

- Have students refer to their notepads as they write the consequences of lying. Encourage students to use adjective clauses in their sentences.
- On the board, write some hints of structures they may use:

   people who
   people to whom
   people whose
   time(s) when
   place(s) where
   lies that

C DISCUSSION ACTIVATOR

Suggested teaching time:	5 minutes	Your actual teaching time:

🎬 Discussion Activator Video

- *Note:* You can print the script or you can view it on the video player on the ActiveTeach?
- Divide the class into pairs and have students use their descriptions from the Notepadding to talk about the people. Encourage the pairs to ask each other questions and provide details and examples. The goal is to say as much as they can about the people.

For more support, play the Discussion Activator Video before students do this activity. After each video, ask if the students in the video included sufficient details.

In formal English, when a relative pronoun is the object of a preposition, the preposition appears at the beginning of the clause. In informal English, the preposition usually appears at the end.

The participants lied to many of the people **with whom** they interacted. (formal)
The participants lied to many of the people **who** they interacted **with**. (informal)

It's a question **to which** most people don't give a truthful answer. (formal)
It's a question **which** most people don't give a truthful answer **to**. (informal)

Be careful!
Use whom, not who, directly after a preposition.
... **with whom** they interacted.
NOT with who they interacted.
Use which, not that, directly after a preposition.
... **to which** most people don't give a truthful answer.
NOT to that most people don't give a truthful answer.

G UNDERSTAND THE GRAMMAR With a partner, study the adjective clauses in Grammar Spotlight on page 16 and answer the questions. See page T17 for answers.
1 Which adjective clause is about possession? Which is about location? Which are about time?
2 Which three are objects of a preposition? On a separate sheet of paper, rewrite those sentences in informal English.

H GRAMMAR PRACTICE Complete the sentences with one of the relative pronouns from the box. (Do not add any prepositions.)

who	whom
which	whose
where	when

1 The workplace is the place **where** people tend to tell the most lies.
2 People **whose** lies are discovered lose the trust of their friends and colleagues.
3 The people with **whom** I work are trustworthy.
4 People **who** break their promises cannot be trusted.
5 There are situations in **which** it's impossible to tell the truth.
6 There are moments **when** being honest can cause you problems.
7 The people to **whom** I never lie are the people **who** are really close to me.
8 There are times **when** I lie to avoid getting into trouble and times **when** I lie to avoid hurting others.
9 Telling the truth is an action for **which** there is sometimes no reward.
10 The people **whose** lies were recorded said they would tell about 75 percent of those lies again.

NOW YOU CAN Describe the consequences of lying

A NOTEPADDING With a partner, write examples for each category.

Situations in which we shouldn't tell lies	Situations in which telling a lie is the best solution

B ACTIVATE THE GRAMMAR On a separate sheet of paper, describe the consequences of lying in the situations on your notepad. Use adjective clauses.

Lying to someone who is a good friend is wrong.
You could destroy the friendship that way.

C DISCUSSION ACTIVATOR Discuss the consequences of lying. Explain further by providing examples. Say as much as you can.

LESSON 2

GOAL Express regret and take responsibility

A ▶1:19 **LISTEN TO INFER INFORMATION** Listen to the conversations. Then listen again and choose the expression that best describes each person's behavior.

1 She …… the damage.
   (a) took responsibility for
   b avoided taking responsibility for

2 He …… the damage.
   a took responsibility for
   (b) avoided taking responsibility for

3 He …… .
   a admitted making a mistake
   (b) shifted the blame to someone else

4 She …… .
   (a) admitted making a mistake
   b made up an excuse

5 She …… for being late.
   a took responsibility
   (b) made up an excuse

6 She …… for losing the scarf.
   (a) took responsibility
   b made up an excuse

B ▶1:20 **LISTEN TO SUPPORT AN OPINION** Listen again. After each conversation, discuss whether you think each person did the right thing. What would *you* have done in each situation? Explain why.

> " She definitely did the right thing. She took responsibility and offered to pay for the repair. I would have done the same thing. However, if I were the man, I'm not sure I would have accepted her offer. "

C **GRAMMAR** "COMMENT" CLAUSES

An adjective clause beginning with *which* can be used to modify—or comment on— an independent clause.

He broke his sister's camera, **which made him feel terrible**.
She blamed Paul for causing the accident, **which was totally unfair**.
I had avoided taking responsibility, **which was embarrassing**, so I just made up an excuse.

Comment clauses are non-restrictive—that is, they provide additional information that is not essential to the meaning of the sentence. Use a comma before a comment clause and after it if something else follows.

Be careful!
You cannot use *that* in place of *which* in a comment clause:
She always borrows Bob's tablet, **which** really bugs him.
NOT She always borrows Bob's tablet, that really bugs him.

GRAMMAR BOOSTER p. 130
Reduced adjective clauses

D **GRAMMAR PRACTICE** Write sentences that include comment clauses with *which*.

Example: Mark is going to replace my camera. (It's really thoughtful of him.)
Mark is going to replace my camera, which is really thoughtful of him.

1 Lena insists on paying for the tickets I gave her. (It's just unnecessary.)
Lena insists on paying for the tickets I gave her, which is just unnecessary.

2 Mona never returned the book I lent her. (It really bothers me.)
Mona never returned the book I lent her, which really bothers me.

3 Apparently, replacing Nancy's ring would cost an arm and a leg. (It's just ridiculous.)
Apparently, replacing Nancy's ring would cost an arm and a leg, which is just ridiculous.

4 I offered to pay for dinner. (It was the right thing to do, in my opinion.)
I offered to pay for dinner, which was the right thing to do, in my opinion.

5 Gerry crossed the street in the middle of the block. (It's against the law and dangerous.)
Gerry crossed the street in the middle of the block, which is against the law and dangerous.

PRONUNCIATION BOOSTER p. 144
Emphatic stress and pitch to express emotion

LESSON 2

GOAL Express regret and take responsibility

A ▶ 1:19 LISTEN TO INFER INFORMATION

Suggested teaching time:	5–10 minutes	Your actual teaching time:

- Tell students to listen carefully to the attitudes and actions expressed in the six conversations.
- Then have students read the first two items in the exercise. Have them listen again to the first two conversations and complete the items with the correct expressions.
- Have students repeat the procedure with the second two items and then finally with the last two items
- Ask students to listen again to all six conversations to check their answers.
- Tell students to compare answers with a partner before you review the exercise with the class.

LANGUAGE NOTE *To cut someone off* as used in conversation 3 means to pass someone's car abruptly, without signaling or giving any warning (the expression can also mean to interrupt someone). *To buy something* means to believe something. The expression is often used in the negative: *They didn't buy my excuse.*

B ▶ 1:20 LISTEN TO SUPPORT AN OPINION

Suggested teaching time:	5 minutes	Your actual teaching time:

- Ask a volunteer to read the model answer. Focus on the last line and write it on the board:

  . . . if I were _____ I would . . .

- Stop the audio after each conversation and call on a volunteer to share if he or she thinks the person did the right thing. Model the first item: *I think the woman did the right thing. If I were the woman, I might even offer to buy the man a new bike. I would feel awful if he had problems with a bike due to my accident.*

Challenge: [+5 minutes] In pairs, invite students to choose one of the scenarios and role-play a different reaction to the situation. For example, for situation 2:

A: *What happened to the suitcase? When I lent it to you, it had two wheels.*
B: *Oh my goodness! I didn't notice. Sorry! I'll buy you a new one!*
A: *No, that's OK. Maybe you could just get the wheels repaired.*
B: *No, no. I insist. I feel horrible. Those baggage guys are way too rough with people's bags! I might actually file a complaint with the airline as well!*

C GRAMMAR

Suggested teaching time:	5–10 minutes	Your actual teaching time:

- Ask a student to read the first explanation. Focus on the first example sentence. Ask *Is the highlighted clause necessary to the meaning of the sentence?* (No, it just comments on the main clause.) Ask volunteers to read the other two example sentences. Ask the same question about each sentence: *Is the highlighted clause necessary to the meaning of the sentence?* (no) Tell students to look again at the last example sentence. Ask *How many independent clauses are there?* (two) *Which one does the highlighted comment clause comment on?* (the first one: *I had avoided taking responsibility*)
- Call on a volunteer to read the second explanation. Write the following sentences on the board to illustrate the point further:

  Maria Wells, who lives up the street from us, has three cats.
  Maria Wells has three cats.

Ask *Does the second sentence make sense without the clause?* (Yes, it does; the clause just provides additional information that is not essential to the meaning of the sentence.)

- Note that restrictive and non-restrictive clauses and their punctuation are presented and practiced in the writing lesson later in this unit. However, since the term *non-restrictive clause* has been introduced, you may want to point out that a restrictive clause—in contrast with a non-restrictive clause—is crucial to the meaning of the sentence. Write on the board:

  The woman who lives up the street from us has three cats.

Remove the clause from the sentence:

  The woman has three cats.

Ask *Do we know which woman has three cats?* (No, we do not.)

- Focus students' attention on the Be careful! note. Point out that *that* is used only in a restrictive clause. For example, write on the board, *The report that I helped write has been published.* You can point out, however, that *which* can be used in both restrictive and non-restrictive clauses. Write on the board, *The report which I helped write has been published.*

Option: GRAMMAR BOOSTER *(Teaching notes p. T130)*

⭐ 🖨 Inductive Grammar Activity

D GRAMMAR PRACTICE

Suggested teaching time:	5 minutes	Your actual teaching time:

- Point out to students that they will combine independent clauses with comment clauses. Ask a student to read the example sentence.
- Then have students complete the sentences independently. Have them compare answers with a partner. Circulate and make sure students use commas. For item 4, accept two variant answers with *in my opinion* at the end or after *which*.

⭐ 🖨 Extra Grammar Exercises

Option: PRONUNCIATION BOOSTER *(Teaching notes p. T144)*

🖨 Pronunciation Pair Work

UNIT 2 LESSON 2 T18

NOW YOU CAN Express regret and take responsibility

A ▶ 1:21 CONVERSATION SPOTLIGHT

Suggested teaching time:	5 minutes	Your actual teaching time:

These conversation strategies are implicit in the model:
- Use *I'm really sorry, but . . .* to introduce bad news.
- Say *I feel awful about it* to express regret.
- End a sentence with *if that's OK* to elicit permission or agreement.
- Use *That's really not necessary* to politely refuse a kind gesture.
- Use *please accept my apology* to formally say you're sorry about something.

- Have students read and listen to the conversation.
- To check comprehension, ask *What did the woman do?* (She broke Tim's tablet.) *How did this happen?* (She tripped and dropped it.) *Is the woman going to have the tablet fixed?* (No, it can't be fixed.) *What does she offer to do instead?* (replace the tablet)
- Finally, have students listen to the ways to express regret. Have a volunteer read Student A's second line and use another way to express regret. Note that the sentence *I'm so sorry* does not conclude with *about it*. The sentences *I feel awful / (just) terrible* can conclude with *about it*.
- Call students' attention to the conversation strategies highlighted in the model.

B ▶ 1:22 RHYTHM AND INTONATION

Suggested teaching time:	5 minutes	Your actual teaching time:

- Have students repeat chorally. Make sure they:
  ○ use emphatic stress for *that* in *How did that happen?* (line 4)
  ○ use falling intonation for *How did that happen?* (line 4)
  ○ use emphatic stress for *awful* in *I feel awful about it.* (line 6)
  ○ use rising intonation for *Are you sure it can't be fixed?* (line 7)

C NOTEPADDING

Suggested teaching time:	5 minutes	Your actual teaching time:

- Have students skim the situations in the survey in Exercise A on page 14 and check off two that have actually happened to them.

- Tell students to fill out the Notepad specifying what they said and did. As they work, list the following on board:
  freaked me out
  upset me
  I had my heart set on
  ticked me off
  I felt awful about

Encourage students to use these and similar comments with *which* in non-restrictive clauses.

D CONVERSATION ACTIVATOR

Suggested teaching time:	5–10 minutes	Your actual teaching time:

🎥 Conversation Activator Video

- *Note:* You can print the script or you can view it on the video player on the ActiveTeach.
- Divide the class into pairs. Instruct students that they will use the model in Exercise A, Conversation Spotlight, to role-play their own conversation with a partner.
- Ask volunteers to read the words under Recycle This Language. Encourage students to incorporate these words into their conversation.
- Reinforce the use of the spotlighted conversation strategies; for example, *I'm really sorry, but . . .* and *That's really not necessary*.
- Bring students' attention to the Don't Stop! note. Ask a volunteer to read the bullet points. Explain that students should continue talking after they have covered the points in the original Conversation Spotlight.
- Tell students to change roles, so each student gets a chance to play A and B.

For more support, play the Conversation Activator Video before students do this activity themselves. After the video, ask students how the model has been changed by the actors.

⭐🖨 Conversation Activator: Speaking Booster

E DISCUSSION

Suggested teaching time:	5 minutes	Your actual teaching time:

- In small groups, have students choose a situation from their notepads and share. Encourage students to discuss details they didn't discuss before in the Conversation Activator.

T19 UNIT 2 LESSON 2

NOW YOU CAN Express regret and take responsibility

A ▶ 1:21 **CONVERSATION SPOTLIGHT** Read and listen. Notice the spotlighted conversation strategies.

A: Tim, you know that tablet you lent me? Well, **I'm really sorry, but** I have some bad news. I broke it.
B: Oh, no. How did that happen?
A: Well, I tripped and dropped it, **which was completely my fault**. I feel awful about it.
B: Are you sure it can't be fixed?
A: Pretty sure. I took it to the store, and they said it wouldn't be worth it. I'm going to get you a new one, **if that's OK**.
B: **That's really not necessary**. I was just about to get a new one anyway.
A: No, I insist. It's no problem. And **please accept my apology**.

▶ 1:23 **Ways to express regret**
I feel awful (about it).
I feel (just) terrible.
I'm so sorry.

B ▶ 1:22 **RHYTHM AND INTONATION** Listen again and repeat. Then practice the conversation with a partner.

C **NOTEPADDING** Choose two situations from the survey on page 14 that have actually happened in your life. Make notes about what happened and what you said and did. Use "comment" clauses when possible.

Situation 1: *I forgot a friend's birthday, which was embarrassing.*

Situation 1:	Situation 2:
What I said:	What I said:
What I did:	What I did:

RECYCLE THIS LANGUAGE
- messed up big time
- got carried away
- let things get out of hand
- admit making a mistake
- make up an excuse
- tell the truth
- tell a lie
- shift the blame to someone else
- take responsibility
- avoid taking responsibility
- So what?
- That's not the worst of it.

D **CONVERSATION ACTIVATOR** Create a conversation similar to the one in Exercise A. Start like this: *I'm afraid I have some bad news …* Be sure to change roles and then partners.

E **DISCUSSION** Choose one of the situations you wrote about on your notepad. Tell your classmates about what happened and details about what you said and did. Then say whether or not you're satisfied with the outcome and why.

DON'T STOP!
- Continue to negotiate how you'll make up for what happened.
- Say as much as you can.

LESSON 3

GOAL Explore where values come from

A **READING WARM-UP** Where do you think people learn the difference between right and wrong? What are the most important lessons children need to learn?

B ▶ 1:24 **READING** Read the article. Which influences do you think are the most important? See page T20 for ans

THE DEVELOPMENT OF VALUES

We all live by a set of principles or beliefs that guide our actions and help us distinguish between what is morally acceptable or unacceptable. But where do our values come from? In fact, they develop throughout our lives and originate from a variety of sources. Here are some key influences:

PARENTS From earliest childhood, most of us learn a sense of right and wrong from our parents. When they tell us children's stories, we learn simple morals—life lessons about the consequences of good and bad behavior. Our parents correct us when we make mistakes. More importantly, we learn from our parents' actions. Children see everything. They observe how their parents relate to each other and handle social situations, and they always notice whether their parents are truthful or not.

PEERS From childhood through adulthood, our everyday conversations with our friends, classmates, colleagues, neighbors, and acquaintances play a role in developing our moral outlook. We are strongly affected by the views of our peers. We naturally "categorize" the people we know or who we hear about on the news—for instance, who is unfriendly, who is generous, which politicians or celebrities are honest.

RELIGION AND CULTURE Many people attribute their moral principles to their religious upbringing. Religion can provide a clear set of guidelines to live by that make it easier to distinguish between right and wrong. All the world's religions offer values that can move us away from being self-centered toward helping others. The dominant values of the group, community, or culture we grow up in are also a powerful influence on our own worldview. For example, more importance may be placed on conforming to society than on the individual, which affects the choices we make in life.

INSTITUTIONS We also pick up values from the code of ethics promoted by our school, profession, or company. Some schools take a public stand against students' bullying their classmates, which sets a clear principle for how students should behave. A corporation might establish a mission statement for all its employees to follow. In such cases, the company expects employees to make its values part of their personal values.

LIFE EVENTS Significant life events, such as the death of a loved one, a divorce, an accident, or an illness, can shape our sense of ethics. Perhaps a loved one falls gravely ill. Having to take care of a sick relative teaches us about setting priorities and the value of selflessness. A sudden financial loss may force us to re-examine and rethink what is important to us. We might be the victim of a major accident or a natural disaster. Surviving such an event teaches us about the miracle and fragility of life and helps us see—and appreciate—each day differently from the way we did before the event.

Sometimes we face an ethical dilemma in which we have to choose between two opposing values. For example, a close friend may ask us to tell a lie in order to avoid his or her getting in trouble, which presents us with a conflict. While we believe it's important to protect the ones we love, our values also may place great importance on remaining truthful. It's the combined lessons we have learned throughout our lives that help us make the right (or wrong) choices.

C **RELATE TO PERSONAL EXPERIENCE** Complete the chart. Identify one or more values you learned from each of the influences mentioned in the Reading.

Your parents
They taught me to work hard.

Your parents	Your school, profession, or company
Your peers	Your life events
Your religion or culture	Other

LESSON 3

GOAL Explore where values come from

A READING WARM-UP

| Suggested teaching time: | 5 minutes | Your actual teaching time: |

- On the board, write the word *values*. Elicit that this refers to a person's ideas about what is right and what is wrong.
- Ask a volunteer to read the questions. Call on students to answer. Then on the board list important lessons for children.

Option: [+5 minutes] If someone mentions not lying among the important lessons for children, ask *Do you think it is confusing to children when they see adults lying in certain situations?* Introduce the term *white lie*, which is a harmless lie that you tell in order to protect someone or avoid hurting feelings.

B ▶ 1:24 READING

| Suggested teaching time: | 10–15 minutes | Your actual teaching time: |

- Invite students to look at the photo of the mother and daughter and the title of the article. Have students speculate about the situation. (Maybe the girl did something wrong or wanted to do something wrong and the mother is reprimanding her.)
- As students read and listen, tell them to underline information in the article that will help them answer the focus question in the direction line (Which influences are the most important?).
- Bring the class together. Have volunteers share their answers to the focus question. (Answers will vary.)

LANGUAGE NOTE *To attribute* means to believe a situation caused something; *a code of ethics* is a set of guidelines for individuals in a school or workplace that outlines how they are expected to act; *fragility* refers to the quality of being delicate.

⭐ 🖨 Reading Strategies

Answer for Exercise B
Answers will vary but may include the following:
In my opinion, the most important influence in our lives are our parents or guardians. We learn some of the most important life lessons when we are young. The way we are corrected or not as children influences how we will act the rest of our lives.

C RELATE TO PERSONAL EXPERIENCE

| Suggested teaching time: | 10–15 minutes | Your actual teaching time: |

- Tell students that in this exercise they will give examples of values from their lives for the various categories. Ask a student to read the model answer. Then elicit additional answers from students. (Possible answers: to not take things that are not yours, to treat people kindly, to be thoughtful)
- After students complete the chart have them compare answers with a partner.
- Ask individual students *Which of the influences has / have had the most profound effect on the development of your values?*

🖨 Extra Reading Comprehension Questions

UNIT 2 LESSON 3 T20

D CLASSIFY VOCABULARY USING CONTEXT

Suggested teaching time:	5 minutes	Your actual teaching time:

- Instruct students to complete the exercise individually.
  - Have students compare answers with a partner and explain their choices. If they are not sure how to explain their answers, model item 1: *values, beliefs,* and *guidelines* are all similar because they express something we believe in or act on; *events* are something that happen, not a system of beliefs.
  - Bring the class together and elicit answers.

Challenge: [+5 minutes] Have students work in pairs to write statements that include each set of words. To help students, elicit the part of speech for each set of words. (The words in 1 through 4 are nouns, and the words in 5 are adjectives.) Possible answers:

Values, beliefs, and guidelines help us to act appropriately in certain situations.

Our peers, acquaintances, and colleagues have more of an influence on us than we realize.

A divorce, an accident, or a life event can influence how we look at the world.

Ethics, morals, and principals are developed all through life.

A young child already notices what is moral, ethical, or right.

E CRITICAL THINKING

Suggested teaching time:	5 minutes	Your actual teaching time:

- Call on volunteers to read the quotes from the article.
- Have students discuss the questions in pairs.
- Bring the class together and call on students to share.

Challenge: [+5 minutes] Divide the class into three groups. Have each group speculate about one of the following situations:

Group 1: A boy observes his mother lying all the time in various situations—big lies, little lies. That seems normal to him. How does this affect his values?

Group 2: A family's house burned down with all their belongings. Everyone is safe, but they have to start from scratch, and they will get very little insurance money. How does this affect their values?

Group 3: A woman has to choose between being loyal to a boss who cheats, or being fired. How does this affect her values?

⭐ 🖨 Extra Challenge Reading Activity

Answers for Exercise E

Answers will vary but may include the following:

1. Children usually have a deep respect for their first role-models–their parents. When they see their parents do something, they believe it must be right and mimic it.

2. A financial loss could force a person to re-evaluate one's life. Suddenly things that were taken for granted–for example a regular paycheck or a house, may no longer be available. A person can be forced to look at and appreciate life differently than before.

3. Examples of ethical dilemmas could be taking credit for something at work when we didn't earn it, keeping cash from a wallet we find on the street, or stealing ideas or words from a source when writing a research paper.

NOW YOU CAN Explore where values come from

A FRAME YOUR IDEAS

Suggested teaching time:	5–10 minutes	Your actual teaching time:

- Have students skim the chart. If students feel both their parents have or have had an equal influence on their values, they can rate them together. Instruct students to fill in *other* if they have something they want to add.
- Then have students write in the numbers.

B PAIR WORK

Suggested teaching time:	5 minutes	Your actual teaching time:

- Call on volunteers to read the model answers in quotes.
- In pairs, have students compare how they rated the influences. Remind students to provide specific examples, referring to the chart in Exercise C on page 20.
- Finally, bring the class together. Poll the number one influence in the class.

D **CLASSIFY VOCABULARY USING CONTEXT** Cross out the one word that doesn't belong with the other three in each group of words. Explain your answers, based on how the words are used in the article.

1 values   ~~events~~   beliefs   guidelines
2 peers   acquaintances   ~~celebrities~~ colleagues
3 ~~a situation~~ a divorce   an accident   a life event
4 ethics   ~~priorities~~   morals   principles
5 moral   ethical   right   ~~self-centered~~

E **CRITICAL THINKING** Read each quote from the article and discuss the questions. See page T21 for answers.

1 "[Children] observe how their parents relate to each other and handle social situations, and they always notice whether their parents are truthful or not."
How do you think children develop values from their observations?

2 "A sudden financial loss may force us to re-examine and rethink what is important to us."
In what ways could a financial loss affect our values?

3 "Sometimes we face an ethical dilemma in which we have to choose between two opposing values."
In addition to the one mentioned in the article, what are some other examples of ethical dilemmas?

NOW YOU CAN Explore where values come from

A **FRAME YOUR IDEAS** Where do you think your values mostly come from? Rank the following influences in the order of importance in your life, from 1 to 10, with 1 being the most important. Include an "other" if necessary.

my mother	my colleagues or classmates	my culture
my father	my teachers	a life event
other relatives	my school or job	other:
my friends	my religion	

B **PAIR WORK** Take turns explaining the most important influences on the development of your own values. Provide specific examples. Refer to the chart you completed in Exercise C on page 20. Ask your partner questions.

" The religious teaching I got as a child was, I think, the strongest influence on me. Those are the guidelines that help me remember the difference between right and wrong. "

" When I was just a kid, my dad got very sick and he couldn't work. We all had to help take care of my dad. My mom and my oldest sister both worked, so it was a lot harder for both of them. It made me realize how important family is. "

LESSON 4

GOAL Discuss how best to help others

A ▶ 1:25 VOCABULARY PHILANTHROPIC WORK Read and listen. Then listen again and repeat.

do•nor /ˈdoʊnər/ n. a person or organization that gives money for a specific cause or charity ALSO **do•na•tion** n. *A number of donors have chosen to make their contributions privately. They prefer not to have their names associated with their donations.*

phi•lan•thro•pist /fɪˈlænθrəpɪst/ n. a wealthy person who donates a significant amount of his or her money, time, and / or reputation to charitable causes ALSO **phi•lan•thro•py** n., **phi•lan•thro•pic** adj. *A number of celebrities have gotten deeply involved in philanthropy. As philanthropists, they have become almost as famous for their philanthropic work as for their work as actors, singers, and athletes.*

hu•man•i•tar•i•an /hyuˌmænəˈtɛriən/ n. a person who is dedicated to improving people's living conditions and treatment by others ALSO **hu•man•i•tar•i•an** adj., **hu•man•i•tar•i•an•ism** n. *Many celebrities choose to make humanitarianism an important part of their lives. In some cases, they discover that humanitarian work takes up even more of their time—that being a humanitarian can be a full-time job.*

ac•tiv•ist /ˈæktəvɪst/ n. a person who works hard for social or political change, often as a member of a social or political organization ALSO **ac•tiv•ism** n. *His activism has often gotten him into trouble. As a political activist, he comes into conflict with those who do not share his views.*

B ACTIVATE THE VOCABULARY Read the biographies. Use the Vocabulary to write a sentence about each person and his or her work. See page T22 for answers.

Graça Machel
Graça Machel, the widow of two presidents of two countries—Mozambique and South Africa—is known for her work protecting the rights of child refugees. She currently works to improve children's health.

Li Ka-shing
Hong Kong businessman Li Ka-shing is considered to be the wealthiest man in Asia. A number of universities have benefited from the numerous multi-million dollar contributions from his Li Ka-shing Foundation.

Helen Caldicott
In an effort to protect the environment for the future, Australian physician Helen Caldicott has worked for decades to oppose the use and spread of nuclear weapons and the use of nuclear power.

C LISTENING WARM-UP When someone achieves wealth and fame, do you think it's that person's responsibility to donate time and money to help others? Explain your point of view.

Answers will vary but may include the following: In my opinion, it's not necessarily a responsibility, but it is honorable when celebrities do share their wealth and make a difference in the world. By acting kindly towards others they also can inspire people who admire them to do the same.

D ▶ 1:26 LISTEN FOR MAIN IDEAS Listen to Part 1 of a report on celebrity philanthropic work. Choose the best title for it.

☐ 1 Many celebrities try to change the world.
☑ 2 Two celebrities try to make a difference.
☐ 3 Jolie and Bono are highly successful in their chosen careers.
☐ 4 Philanthropic work teaches celebrities new skills.

defending human rights

protecting the environment

improving literacy

helping refugees

fighting hunger

eliminating poverty

22 UNIT 2

LESSON 4

GOAL Discuss how best to help others

A ▶1:25 VOCABULARY

Suggested teaching time:	5 minutes	Your actual teaching time:

- With students' books closed, write *How best to help others* on the board. Call on students to share ideas. (Possible answers: raise money for charity, work with children, visit the elderly)
- Call on a student to read the topic of the exercise (*philanthropic work*). Write *philanthropy* on the board and have students repeat. Elicit that this refers to the practice of giving money and help to people who are poor or in trouble.
- Ask students *Where might you see words listed like this?* (in a dictionary) Tell students to skim the words to see if they are familiar. Have them underline the words in their various forms of speech. (1. donor, donation; 2. philanthropist, philanthropy, philanthropic; 3. humanitarian, humanitarianism; 4. activist, activism) For review, elicit that *n.* refers to noun and *adj.* refers to adjective.
- Ask students to read and listen.
- Then have them listen again and repeat.

Challenge: [+5 minutes] Elicit additional parts of speech into which these words could be formed. (Possible answers: *donate* (v); *philanthropically* (adv); *humanitarianly* (adv))

⭐ 🖨 Vocabulary-Building Strategies

B ACTIVATE THE VOCABULARY

Suggested teaching time:	5 minutes	Your actual teaching time:

- Ask students to scan the images and the names. Ask *Have you heard of these people? What do you know about them?*
- Call on volunteers to read the descriptions, or have students read them individually.
- Then have students write sentences using the Vocabulary from Exercise A. Point out that the word *activist* can be used like this: He / She is an activist for [noun]. He / She is a / an [adj] activist.
- Have students compare sentences with a partner.

Answers to Exercise B
Answers will vary but may include the following:
1. Graça Machel is a humanitarian whose work is focused on children's health.
2. Li Ka-shing has made many donations to universities.
3. Helen Caldicott is an activist who works against the spread of nuclear power.

C LISTENING WARM-UP

Suggested teaching time:	5 minutes	Your actual teaching time:

- Have students think about the question and call on volunteers to share their point of view.

- Ask *If you achieved wealth and fame, do you think you would donate time and money to help others?*

Option: [+5 minutes] Have students look at the biographies in Exercise B and choose a philanthropist whose organization or cause they would be interested in joining. Encourage students to explain why.

Challenge: [+5 minutes] In pairs, have students imagine having a significant amount of money that they are able to use for a good cause. Have them create a short description of the cause. Have pairs share with the class.

D ▶1:26 LISTEN FOR MAIN IDEAS

Suggested teaching time:	5–10 minutes	Your actual teaching time:

- Pre-listening: Ask students to look at the pictures and captions. Elicit meanings: *human rights* are rights which all people should have—it means they are treated in a fair, equal way without cruelty; *a refugee* is a person who has been forced to leave his or her country; *literacy* is the ability to read and write; *eliminate* means to completely get rid of something.
- First listening: Have students listen once, with their books closed. Then, in pairs, ask them to eliminate the topics they don't think are the main idea.
- Second listening: Have students listen again. Ask *What do you think the main idea is?* (item 2) Why? (The focus is on two celebrities that are changing the world.)

LANGUAGE NOTE Point out that when the quote from each celebrity is cited, we hear the reader of the report say *Jolie encourages people to live a life of use to others, too, saying quote "Get outside yourself . . ." unquote.* Point out that in spoken English it is common to indicate something is being quoted by sandwiching the quote in the terms *quote* and *unquote*.

Option: [+5 minutes] Have students look at the pictures at the bottom of the page again. Ask *Which of these causes are mentioned in the report?* (all of them) *Which celebrity is interested in which cause?* (Angelina Jolie: helping refugees, improving literacy, protecting the environment, human rights; Bono: fighting hunger, fighting poverty)

Challenge: [+5 minutes] Have students focus on items 1, 3, and 4. Ask *Are all these items mentioned in the article?* (yes) Have students listen again for the information. (1. over the last few decades we have seen a huge increase in celebrity philanthropy—actors, singers, and athletes—who have added to their fame by making donations of time and money to address some of the worlds' biggest problems; 3. Angelina Jolie is one of Hollywood's highest paid actors, and Bono is one of the world's most successful musicians; 4. Philanthropy can also greatly change a celebrity's life and help him or her develop new skills)

⭐ 🖨 Listening Strategies

UNIT 2 LESSON 4 T22

E ▶1:27 LISTEN TO CLASSIFY

Suggested teaching time	5 minutes	Your actual teaching time

- **Pre-listening:** Call on volunteers to read the exercise items. Have them see if they can remember from the previous listening which celebrity participates in which philanthropic activities.
- **Listening:** Have students listen and complete the exercise. If necessary, have students listen again.

Option: [+5 minutes] Write the quotes from each celebrity on the board:

"Get outside yourself. Get outside your environment. Do something for other people."

"...I want to have fun and I want to change the world. I have a chance to do both."

Ask *Which celebrity said which quote?* In pairs, have students discuss how celebrities might influence their fans to be more aware of and involved in world issues.

F ▶1:28 LISTEN TO CONFIRM CONTENT

Suggested teaching time	5 minutes	Your actual teaching time

- Have students listen again and cross out the reasons not mentioned. Point out that some topics are mentioned about celebrities in general, not specifically in relation to Bono and Angelina Jolie. Specify that students should cross out items not mentioned at all.
- Have students compare answers with a partner. Then go over the answers as a class.

Challenge: [+5 minutes] On the board, write *Which are honorable reasons for philanthropy? What do you think about celebrities who contribute philanthropically for superficial reasons?*

G ▶1:29 LISTEN FOR POINT OF VIEW

Suggested teaching time	5 minutes	Your actual teaching time

- **Pre-listening:** Have students read the three points of view.
- **First listening:** Point out to students that they will be listening to Part 2 of the report. Tell them to determine which point of view is reflected in this second part.
- **Second listening:** Then have students listen again to check that they chose the correct point of view.

Option: [+5 minutes] Ask *What is your point of view? Based on the information in both parts of the report, do you think Bono and Angelina Jolie are dedicated to their work?*

H ▶1:30 LISTEN TO SUMMARIZE

Suggested teaching time	5 minutes	Your actual teaching time

- Have students listen to Part 2 again and list criticisms they hear. Then have them listen again and fill in any information they initially missed.
- In pairs, have students compare answers.

Option: [+5 minutes] In pairs, have students write a summary. On the board, write a topic sentence for students to use: *Even though celebrity philanthropy has many benefits, there are many criticisms. For example, ...*

Answers for Exercise H

Answers will vary but may include the following: Celebrity philanthropists can be self-centered and demanding. They can spread a false impression that nothing can be done about a problem without international celebrity help. Huge donations raised by celebrities often provide increased opportunities for corruption. Some celebrity philanthropists can be motivated by their own fame. They see philanthropy as an opportunity for photo ops.

I SUPPORT AN OPINION

Suggested teaching time	5 minutes	Your actual teaching time

- Divide the class into groups of three and have them support their opinions. Tell students their response does not have to be yes or no—it can indicate that in some cases, celebrities make good philanthropists.
- Bring the class together and make some conclusions.

Challenge: [+5 minutes] Invite students to look up names of other celebrity philanthropists to see how else famous people are influencing the world. Invite students to also share stories of philanthropists who might be more self-centered than Jolie or Bono.

NOW YOU CAN Discuss how best to help others

A FRAME YOUR IDEAS

Suggested teaching time	5 minutes	Your actual teaching time

- Have students choose what they consider to be the most urgent topics and suggest possible solutions for the problems.
- Poll topics chosen to see which issues students feel most strongly about. Ask *Are there any other topics not mentioned that you think are important?*

B DISCUSSION

Suggested teaching time	5 minutes	Your actual teaching time

- Ask a student to read the model answer.
- In small groups, have students choose an issue from their notepad and suggest activities for solving the problem.

OPTIONAL WRITING [+15–20 minutes]

- Tell students to think back to details of the report in both Part 1 and Part 2 as they compile their ideas. Tell students to include specific reasons why they support their point of view.
- Offer an opportunity for peer review in class, or collect student work and provide individual feedback.

Discussion: Speaking Booster

E ▶ 1:27 **LISTEN TO CLASSIFY** Read the following philanthropic activities. Listen to Part 1 again and write J for Jolie's activities and B for Bono's, according to the report.

1. _J_ donates money to build schools.
2. _B_ organizes events to raise money.
3. _J_ works to protect wildlife.
4. _B_ gets world leaders to work together.
5. _B_ works to improve medical care.
6. _J_ works with the United Nations.

F ▶ 1:28 **LISTEN TO CONFIRM CONTENT** Listen to Part 1 again. Cross out the reasons for celebrity philanthropy that are NOT mentioned.

1. to develop new skills
2. ~~to get attention from the media~~
3. to satisfy a desire to help end human suffering
4. to show gratitude for one's success
5. ~~to increase one's fame and wealth~~
6. to change how one is seen by others
7. to address one's concerns about the future

G ▶ 1:29 **LISTEN FOR POINT OF VIEW** Now listen to Part 2. Which statement best represents the speaker's point of view? Explain your answer.

☐ 1 Celebrity philanthropists are only interested in their own fame and getting "photo ops."
☑ 2 While the criticism may have some truth, Jolie's and Bono's philanthropy has been mainly positive.
☐ 3 Despite their good work, Jolie's and Bono's philanthropy deserves a lot of criticism.

H ▶ 1:30 **LISTEN TO SUMMARIZE** Listen to Part 2 again. With a partner, write at least five criticisms of celebrity philanthropists from the report on a separate sheet of paper. See page T23 for answers.

I **SUPPORT AN OPINION** Do celebrities make good philanthropists? Explain. Use information from the report or about other celebrity philanthropists you are aware of. Answers will vary but may include the following: I think that celebrities can make good philanthropists as long as their involvement is honorable and honest. The work of people like Angelina Jolie has changed lives and has inspired others to do the same.

NOW YOU CAN Discuss how best to help others

A **FRAME YOUR IDEAS** Which three of the issues in the photos on page 22 do you think most urgently need attention? Write them on the notepad and write one activity that would help for each one.

1.	2.	3.

B **DISCUSSION** Discuss the best activities for solving one of the problems on your notepad.

> 66 I feel strongly about helping children, so I think it's crucial to provide good schools and ... 99

OPTIONAL WRITING Do rich and famous people have a responsibility to donate fame and money to help others? Write at least two paragraphs, supporting your point of view.

23

WRITING: Restrictive and non-restrictive adjective clauses

A WRITING SKILL Study the rules.

Restrictive adjective clauses

A restrictive adjective clause provides *essential information* necessary to identify the noun or pronoun it modifies. Do not use commas.

The person **who borrowed my camera yesterday** just told me she had broken it.
She replaced the camera lens **that she had broken the day before**.
The friend **whose phone I lost** insisted I didn't need to replace it.
The hotel in the town **where we stayed last weekend** offered to give us a refund.

Non-restrictive adjective clauses

A non-restrictive adjective clause provides *additional information* that is not necessary to identify the noun or pronoun it modifies. Use commas before and after, except at the end of a sentence, when the adjective clause ends with a period.

Lara, **who works in my office,** told me she broke the camera that she had borrowed.
The Aimes Hotel, **where we always get a room in July,** offered to give us a refund.
She replaced the tablet, **which made her very happy.**
My laptop, **which was always crashing when I really needed it,** finally died.

> **Be careful!**
> Use punctuation that supports your intended meaning.
> The laptop **which I bought last week** is great. (Differentiates this laptop from others: essential)
> The laptop, **which I bought last week**, is great. (An additional comment about the laptop: not essential)

B PRACTICE Read the college application essay, in which the writer describes a life lesson. Correct punctuation errors with adjective clauses. Add three commas and delete three.

What I Learned from My First Job

While working at my first job, which was at a clothing store, I had a co-worker who got me into a lot of trouble. When the manager counted the money in the cash register, it had come up short. The co-worker had taken some of the money, so she shifted the blame to me. I insisted that I wasn't responsible, but the manager, who didn't know me fired me immediately.

Ten years later, I got a phone call that really surprised me. It was from the woman, who had blamed me for taking the money. She called me to apologize for what she had done. Apparently it had been bothering her for a long time.

This incident taught me an important lesson. Sometimes, when people tell a lie, they hurt themselves more than the other person. While I had completely forgotten about the incident, it was my former co-worker, who felt badly about it for all those years.

C PRACTICE Decide if the adjective clause provides essential or additional information. Write a checkmark if the punctuation is correct. Make corrections if it is a non-restrictive clause.

☑ 1 His grandparents are the ones who taught him the most about right and wrong.
☐ 2 My cousin, who was always truthful about everything, told my aunt she was wrong.
☑ 3 I told a lie that I have regretted for more than ten years.
☐ 4 Her favorite vase, which her mother had given her, had been broken.
☐ 5 We found out that Megan was going to join us, which was great.

D APPLY THE WRITING SKILL On a separate sheet of paper, write a college application essay in which you describe an experience that taught you a life lesson or that shaped your values. Provide details by including at least three adjective clauses to add essential and additional information.

> **SELF-CHECK**
> ☐ Did I include at least three adjective clauses?
> ☐ Did I distinguish between essential and additional information?
> ☐ Did I use commas correctly in non-restrictive adjective clauses?

WRITING   Restrictive and non-restrictive adjective clauses

A   WRITING SKILL

Suggested teaching time:	5–10 minutes	Your actual teaching time:

- On the board, write *restrictive and non-restrictive adjective clauses*. Call on a volunteer to read the explanation of restrictive clauses. Write the first example sentence on the board. Then erase the clause. Ask *Does the sentence make sense without it?* (no) Point out that the clause identifies which person is being talked about and is essential to the sentence.
- Have volunteers read the remaining example sentences. After each one, ask *Is the clause necessary?* (yes)
- Focus on the non-restrictive clauses. Write the first example sentence on the board. Then erase the clause. Ask *Does the sentence make sense without it?* (yes) Review that the clause provides additional information. Point to the commas in the sentence.
- Look together at the remaining example sentences. As volunteers read, bring students' attention to the commas. Ask *how is the third example different?* (The non-restrictive clause is at the end of the sentence, so it just ends with a period.)
- Finally, tell students that either a restrictive or a non-restrictive clause may be possible, depending on your meaning. Write:

    The laptop which I bought last week is great.

- Then read the Be careful! note and the first example sentence. Point to the same sentence on the board and underline *laptop*. The implication is that the person has several laptops. The clause identifies which laptop she is talking about. Have students repeat the sentence after you, as you demonstrate that the pause in the sentence takes place at the end of the clause: *The laptop which I bought last week* [pause] *is great*.
- Then add commas to the sentence and ask *How is the clause different?* (It just provides additional information. There is no question which laptop is being talked about.) Have students reread the second example sentence in the Be careful! note. Have students repeat the sentence after you, as you demonstrate that the sentence has two pauses: *The laptop* [pause] *which I bought last week* [pause] *is great*. Compare to the previous example sentence in which the pause appears at the end of clause.

B   PRACTICE

Suggested teaching time:	5 minutes	Your actual teaching time:

- Have students read the paragraphs. Tell them first to find the incorrectly punctuated clauses. Then tell them to decide whether the clauses are restrictive or non-restrictive and to review the use of commas with each kind of clause.
- After students complete the exercise individually, have them compare answers with a partner. Ask them to explain why the information in each clause they corrected

is essential or non-essential and what punctuation, if any, is required. (Answers:
- *which was at a clothing store* is non-essential information because *first job* sufficiently identifies which job is being talked about; a comma is necessary at the beginning of the non-restrictive clause.
- *who didn't know me* is nonessential information because *the manager* sufficiently identifies the person; commas are needed to set off the non-restrictive clause.
- *that really surprised me* is essential information because it is needed to identify the phone call. Restrictive clauses are not set off by commas.
- *who had blamed me for taking the money* is essential information because it is needed to identify the woman. Restrictive clauses are not set off by commas.
- *when people tell a lie* is non-essential information because *sometimes* sufficiently references time. A comma is necessary at the beginning of the non-restrictive clause.
- *who felt badly about it for all those years* is essential information indicating who felt badly about the incident. Restrictive clauses are not set off by commas.)

C   PRACTICE

Suggested teaching time:	5 minutes	Your actual teaching time:

- Have students work individually to check off the sentences that are correct and to add commas to those that are not.
- Tell students to compare answers with a partner.
- Bring the class together and go over the answers. Ask volunteers to explain why the information in the two checked items is essential. (1. *who taught him the most about right and wrong* is essential information needed to identify *the ones*; 3. *that I have regretted for more than ten years* is essential information identifying *lie*)
- Then focus on the sentences in which information is not essential and explain why. (2. *My cousin* sufficiently identifies who is being talked about; 4. *Her favorite vase* sufficiently identifies which vase is being discussed; 5. *which was great* is a comment clause, not essential to the meaning of the sentence) Have students share where they added commas to set off these non-restrictive clauses.

D   APPLY THE WRITING SKILL

Suggested teaching time:	10–15 minutes	Your actual teaching time:

- On the board, write *Describe an experience that taught you a life lesson or that shaped your values*. Tell students to use the essay in Exercise B as a model.
- Refer students to the Writing Process Worksheet for guidance with pre-writing and peer feedback.
- Encourage students to use the Self-Check in the Student's Book to go over the essays they wrote.

⭐ 🖨 Writing Process

REVIEW

🎮 **Digital Game**

A ▶ 1:31

Suggested teaching time:	5–10 minutes	Your actual teaching time:

- Pre-listening: Have students skim the questions.
- First listening: Ask students to listen to the first conversation and then answer the two questions. Then have them listen to the second conversation and answer the second question.
- Second listening: Have students listen again to check their answers.

LANGUAGE NOTE Conversation 1: *a tough call* is a difficult decision; *be short of cash* means not to have enough cash to spare. Conversation 2: *so much for buying a new one* means that the idea of buying a new jacket is not a possible solution.

Option: [+5 minutes] Invite students to share if they would shift the blame or tell the truth in Conversation 1. Then have them say what they would do in Conversation 2.

B

Suggested teaching time:	5 minutes	Your actual teaching time:

- Tell students to consider the context of the sentences when choosing the phrases.
- Have students compare answers with a partner. Go over any questions with the whole class. Accept *tell the truth* as a possible answer for item 3.

C

Suggested teaching time:	5 minutes	Your actual teaching time:

- If necessary, refer students to the grammar box on page 16 to review adjective clauses and words used to introduce them.
- Before students do the exercise, have them scan the sentences for clues that will help them decide if the adjective clause is about people, things, possession, location, or time. (1. people, 2. people, 3. time, 4. things, 5. things, 6. things, 7. things, 8. people, 9. location) Have students also note the sentences in which pronouns are used as objects of prepositions, and remind them to use *whom* (not *who*) and *which* (not *that*) after a preposition. (1. with, 5. on, 6. about, 7. in)
- Have students compare answers with a partner.

LANGUAGE NOTE The phrase *one of* takes a singular verb. For example, in item 8, *Nora was one of those people who fails to understand . . .*

D

Suggested teaching time:	5 minutes	Your actual teaching time:

- Ask a volunteer to read the example and model answer.
- Have students make up the comment clauses individually. Then have them compare answers with a partner.
- Bring the class together and call on students to answer.

Option: **TEST-TAKING SKILLS BOOSTER** (p.152)

EXTRAS

- Workbook
- MyEnglishLab
- Online Student Resources (www.english.com/summit3e)
  - Classroom Audio Program
  - Extra Practice Activities
  - *Summit GO* App
  - Web Projects
- ActiveTeach
  - Assessment
  - Additional Printable Resources
    - Audioscripts and Answer Keys
    - "Can-Do" Self-Assessment Charts
    - Conversation and Discussion Activator Video Scripts
    - Oral Progress Assessment Charts
    - Reading Speed Calculator
  - Summit TV Video Program
    - Activity Worksheets
    - Teaching Notes
    - Video Scripts

REVIEW

A ▶ 1:31 Listen to each conversation. Then listen again and complete the statements.

Conversation 1
1 The man is thinking about …… .
   a shifting the blame   b taking responsibility   **c** telling the truth
2 The woman suggests …… .
   a shifting the blame   **b** making up an excuse   c telling the truth

Conversation 2
3 The woman has decided to …… .
   a shift the blame   b make up an excuse   **c** take responsibility

B Complete the sentences with phrases from the box. Use each phrase only once.

| shift the blame | admit making a mistake | tell the truth | make up an excuse | take responsibility |

1 If Matt makes a mistake, he tries to **shift the blame** to other people in his office so he won't get in trouble with his boss.
2 Dan forgot to prepare his report for the sales meeting, so he decided to **make up an excuse**. He told his boss that his computer deleted the file.
3 Alice borrowed Susan's umbrella, but she forgot it on the train. She wanted to take responsibility, but she didn't want to **admit making a mistake**, so she just replaced it and didn't say anything to Susan about it.
4 Jane doesn't **take responsibility** when she does something wrong. Either she makes up an excuse or she doesn't tell the truth about what happened.
5 I really believe that in some situations it's better not to **tell the truth**, especially when you are protecting someone's feelings. For example, if my grandmother spent all day cooking dinner, but it tasted terrible, I would still tell her it was delicious.

C Complete the paragraph with the relative pronouns from the box.

who / which / that / whom / where / when

Nora Richards, with **whom** (1) I worked for five years, was a person **who** (2) could never get her work done on time. I still remember the time **when** (3) she asked me to help her write a long report **which** (4) was due the next day! The report, on **which** (5) she had been working for an entire month, was needed for a business deal with a very important client. The deal, about **which** (6) Nora talked all the time (instead of writing the report), fell through, and Nora was fired. There are situations in **which** (7) you simply have to meet your deadlines. Nora was one of those people **who** (8) fails to understand that the office is a place **where** (9), as the saying says, "Actions speak louder than words."

D On a separate sheet of paper, complete each statement with your own comment clause, using **which**. Don't forget to use a comma.
Example: Some celebrity philanthropists only care about publicity, *which I think is a shame*.
1 Angelina Jolie has received many awards for her philanthropic work… .
2 Most people tell lies to avoid hurting people's feelings… .
3 My brother took responsibility for his mistake… .
4 I made up an excuse for being late to work… .

TEST-TAKING SKILLS BOOSTER p. 152

Web Project: Celebrity Philanthropists
www.english.com/summit3e

UNIT 3
Fears, Hardships, and Heroism

COMMUNICATION GOALS
1. Express frustration, empathy, and encouragement
2. Describe how fear affects you physically
3. Discuss overcoming handicaps and hardships
4. Examine the nature of heroism

PREVIEW

A **FRAME YOUR IDEAS** Take the self-test. Total your responses.

How chicken are you?

Rate the situations below, according to how scary they are to you, from 1 to 3, with 1 being not scary at all, 2 being somewhat scary, and 3 being very scary.

YOUR CHICKEN SCORE
TOTAL YOUR SCORE

16–26 You're cool and collected. Nothing freaks you out.

27–37 You're just cautious.

38–48 You're a total chicken! You're probably afraid of your own shadow.

- getting stuck in an elevator
- seeing a bee on your arm
- driving in bad weather
- eating in an unclean restaurant
- riding a horse
- smelling smoke in a building
- being a passenger in a speeding car
- taking a roller-coaster ride
- walking outside during a bad storm
- standing near the edge of a cliff
- going to the dentist
- walking down a dark street at night
- experiencing turbulence during a flight
- getting an injection from a doctor or nurse
- seeing a snake in your garden
- being in a place undergoing an epidemic

B **PAIR WORK** Compare self-tests with a partner. Are you both afraid of the same things? Which of you is more chicken?

C **GROUP WORK** How chicken is your class? Calculate the average score for each situation in your class. Which situation is the most frightening to everyone?

26 UNIT 3

UNIT 3

Fears, Hardships, and Heroism

PREVIEW

A FRAME YOUR IDEAS

| Suggested teaching time: | 5–10 minutes | Your actual teaching time: |

- On the board, write *You're chicken!* Ask *What do you think this means?* (that you're afraid or not brave enough to do something)
- Call on a student to read the title of the self-test. Elicit that it is asking *How afraid are you?* Ask a student to read the instructions.
- Have students take the test. Circulate and clarify vocabulary if needed. For example, you may need to explain that *an injection* involves putting a drug into a person's body using a needle or that *an epidemic* is many cases of a disease that happen at once.
- Then have students read the scoring information and tally their responses.

LANGUAGE NOTE In the title *How chicken are you?*, the word *chicken* is used like an adjective. It means how afraid are you? Explain that the word can also be used as a noun (e.g., in the sentence *You're a total chicken*). Point out that it is possible to use *chicken* in verb form: *to chicken out* (*I wanted to jump out of the plane, but I chickened out*).

B PAIR WORK

| Suggested teaching time: | 5 minutes | Your actual teaching time: |

- In pairs, have students compare tests and see if they are afraid of the same things.
- On the board, write *Which one of you is more chicken?* Elicit that this means which one of you is more afraid / more of a coward. Call on students to answer the question.

Option: [+5 minutes] Call on volunteers to read the situations in Exercise A. After each one, ask *Who has been in this situation?* Invite students to elaborate and specify how chicken they were. Alternatively, students can discuss the various situations in pairs or groups.

C GROUP WORK

| Suggested teaching time: | 5 minutes | Your actual teaching time: |

- Time-permitting, calculate the average score situation-by-situation. Alternatively, use a show of hands to determine the situations that were the most frightening for everyone.
- Then ask *How chicken is our class?* (Possible answers: very chicken, somewhat chicken, not chicken at all)

D ▶ 2:02 SPOTLIGHT

| Suggested teaching time: | 10–15 minutes | Your actual teaching time: |

- Have students read and listen. Check comprehension by asking *What's wrong with Michel?* (He was supposed to propose to his girlfriend but he didn't; he got scared.) *How does his girlfriend feel?* (upset) *Does Michel still want to be with her?* (yes) *What's the problem?* (He just gets nervous and panics at the thought of getting married.) *Do you think Luiz makes Michel feel better?* (yes)

E UNDERSTAND IDIOMS AND EXPRESSIONS

| Suggested teaching time: | 10–15 minutes | Your actual teaching time: |

- To model the activity, invite a volunteer to read the first idiom. Ask students to find the idiom in Exercise D. Call on another volunteer to read Michel's part where he uses the idiom. Then read the choices and elicit the answer.
- Have students work in pairs to complete the rest of the exercise. Encourage them to refer to the conversation and context to help them determine the correct answer. Circulate and assist as needed.
- Bring the class together and go over the answers.

LANGUAGE NOTE *Lovey-dovey* means overly romantic; the idiom *to chill* can also be used as *chill out*, which also means to relax instead of feeling anxious or nervous about something; an even more informal variation is *take a chill pill*, which means to calm down or relax.

Option: [+5 minutes] Have students find each idiom or expression in Exercise D and replace it with the definition from the matching expression in Exercise E. Tell students to make necessary changes in the sentence. Model the first item: *I'm just in trouble with Emilie.*

Challenge: [+5 minutes] Divide the class into pairs. Assign each pair one of the idioms or expressions. Have pairs prepare short role plays consisting of 4–5 exchanges, demonstrating correct use of the idiom or expression.

SPEAKING SUMMARIZE AND PERSONALIZE

| Suggested teaching time: | 10 minutes | Your actual teaching time: |

- Divide the class into pairs. For students who may need guidance, write on the board:

who: (Michel)

problem: (He has cold feet about getting married.)

resolution: (I would wait a little while.)

- Then add the word *speculation* to the list on the board and have pairs discuss what might happen next. (Possible answer: He will propose a little later.) Encourage students to present various scenarios.
- Finally, have students discuss the two types of fear and have them share which one scares them more. Tell students to provide examples.

Challenge: [+5 minutes] On the board, write *How to overcome fear*. Have students work in pairs to discuss different ways to overcome fear. (Possible answers: face your fear, breathe deeply, try to control your imagination) Bring the class together and ask *Do you think fears of physical harm can be overcome in the same ways as emotional fears?* (Possible answers: Perhaps it depends on how imminent the danger is, for example, getting stuck in an elevator versus seeing a fire in a building.)

D ▶ 2:02 **SPOTLIGHT** Read and listen to two friends discuss a problem. Notice the spotlighted language.

Luiz: Hey, Michel. Anything wrong? You look like you've lost your best friend.
Michel: No. Nothing like that. I'm just in hot water with Emilie.
Luiz: Emilie? But the two of you were so lovey-dovey when I saw you at the restaurant on Sunday. What's up?
Michel: Well, Sunday was her birthday, and we'd been planning to get engaged on her birthday, but I guess I got cold feet. I just don't think I'm ready to make that kind of commitment yet. In any case, she's really upset. She feels like I pulled the rug out from under her.
Luiz: Well, I can imagine that must have been really disappointing for her. Don't you feel like you're in love anymore? Or is there someone else?
Michel: No. Definitely not. I love her with all my heart, but no matter how much I tell myself she's the only one for me, I just can't take the plunge. I don't know what's wrong with me. Maybe it's some kind of psychological problem.
Luiz: I wouldn't jump to that conclusion. Marriage is a big deal, Michel. And it's forever. Most people find that scary.
Michel: I think that's what freaks me out about it. Every time I think of proposing, I panic. I feel so guilty that I don't even want to see her right now.
Luiz: Well, it's not the end of the world. Sounds like you just have a minor case of the jitters.
Michel: You think so?
Luiz: Mark my words. She'll wait for you. Just chill for a while until you're ready, OK?

ENGLISH FOR TODAY'S WORLD
Understand a variety of accents.
Luiz = Portuguese
Michel = French

E **UNDERSTAND IDIOMS AND EXPRESSIONS** Choose the best way to complete each statement.

1. If you're "in hot water," you're ....
   a in trouble **b** excited

2. When you "get cold feet," you ....
   a decide to do something as you had planned
   b decide not to do something as you had planned

3. If Emilie feels like Michel "pulled the rug out from under her," she feels that ....
   a he didn't do what he had promised
   b he was disappointed with her

4. If you do something "with all your heart," you do it ....
   a unwillingly **b** with 100% commitment

5. When Michel said "I just can't take the plunge," he meant he ....
   a couldn't go through with proposing
   b didn't want to marry her

6. When Luiz says "I wouldn't jump to that conclusion," he's suggesting that Michel's reasoning is probably ....
   a right **b** not right

7. Something that's "a big deal" is ....
   a full of advantages **b** of great importance

8. If something "freaks you out," it ....
   a scares you **b** excites you

9. If something "isn't the end of the world," it's ....
   a not a big deal **b** not good

10. When Luiz says "Sounds like you just have a minor case of the jitters," he means ....
    a Michel is just nervous
    b Michel should take his doubt seriously

11. When you say "Mark my words," you want someone to ....
    a remember your prediction later
    b wait for you later

12. When Luiz tells Michel to "just chill," he's suggesting that Michel ....
    a do something right away
    b wait

SPEAKING **SUMMARIZE AND PERSONALIZE** First, summarize Michel's problem and say what you would do in his situation. Speculate about what will happen next. Then, discuss what scares you more: fears of physical harm such as the ones in the self-test, or emotional fears such as the ones Michel is experiencing. Explain your reasons, using examples from your life.

LESSON 1

GOAL Express frustration, empathy, and encouragement

A ▶ 2:03 **VOCABULARY** EXPRESSING FRUSTRATION, EMPATHY, AND ENCOURAGEMENT
Read and listen. Then listen again and repeat.

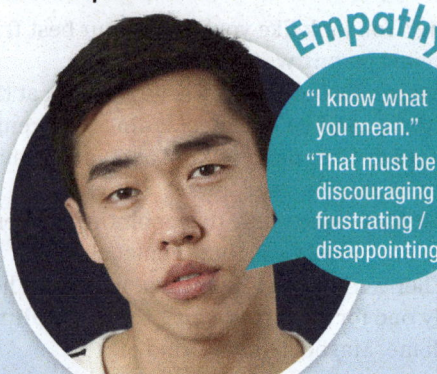

Frustration
"I give up!"
"I'm fed up!"
"I've had it!"
"I just can't take it any more!"

Empathy
"I know what you mean."
"That must be discouraging / frustrating / disappointing."

Encouragement
"Don't let it get you down."
"Don't give up!"
"Hang in there!"

B ▶ 2:04 **LISTEN TO PREDICT** Listen to the conversations. Then choose what the other person will probably say next.

1 ⓐ That must be frustrating.   b I just can't take it anymore.
2 a I give up!   ⓑ I know what you mean.
3 a I've had it!   ⓑ Well, don't give up.
4 a I'm really fed up!   ⓑ Don't let it get you down.
5 ⓐ Hang in there.   b I just can't take it any more!

C **GRAMMAR** CLAUSES WITH NO MATTER

Use <u>no matter</u> + a noun clause beginning with a question word to express frustration (that no amount of anything, for example *effort*, can make something change). Use a comma before or after clauses with <u>no matter</u>.

No matter how careful I am, I always forget something!
No matter what they said, he didn't believe them.
No matter what time we check in, we always have to wait for a room.
No one answers, **no matter when we call**.
They can't understand her, **no matter how slowly she speaks**.

> **GRAMMAR BOOSTER** p. 131
> Embedded questions: review and common errors

Be careful!
Use normal, not inverted, word order in the noun clause and don't use an auxiliary verb.
No matter **who you ask**, no one can give you directions.
NOT No matter ~~who do you ask~~, ...

D **GRAMMAR PRACTICE** Mark correct sentences with a checkmark. Mark incorrect sentences with an X. Correct the incorrect sentences.

[X] 1 No matter how much do I encourage my sister, she won't take a plane anywhere.
No matter how much I encourage my sister, she won't take a plane anywhere.

[X] 2 Eric couldn't find his folder, no matter how hard did he look.
Eric couldn't find his folder, no matter how hard he looked.

[✓] 3 No matter how late Phil stays up, he still gets up for his exercise class.

[X] 4 They were unable to find a gas station, no matter how many people did they ask.
They were unable to find a gas station, no matter how many people they asked.

[✓] 5 No matter how many cups of coffee I drink, I sleep like a baby.

[X] 6 No matter when do I go to bed, I always get up tired.
No matter when I go to bed, I always get up tired.

28 UNIT 3

LESSON 1

GOAL Express frustration, empathy, and encouragement

A ▶ 2:03 VOCABULARY

| Suggested teaching time: | 5 minutes | Your actual teaching time: |

- With students' books closed, write these three lines on the board:
  1. I give up!
  2. I know what you mean.
  3. Hang in there.

  Then write *empathy, encouragement, frustration* on the board. Ask students to match each word to the correct line. (1. frustration, 2. empathy, 3. encouragement)

- With students' books open, have students look at other expressions of each emotion. Elicit or explain that *empathy* refers to the ability to understand other people's feelings or problems; *frustration* refers to being upset or impatient because you cannot change a situation in order to get something you want or need; *encouragement* refers to giving someone courage and confidence to help them overcome a problem.

- Focus on *empathy* and the line *That must be discouraging / frustrating / disappointing*. Explain that the three participial adjectives are close in meaning but have slight differences. You may wish to point out that *discouraging* means causing a loss of confidence or enthusiasm; *frustrating* means causing annoyance or upset (particularly when something stands in the way of one's progress); *disappointing* means failing to fulfil one's hopes or expectations.

LANGUAGE NOTE *To be fed up* means to be annoyed by something and want it to change; *have had it* or *have had it (up to here) with* is used to indicate that you are no longer willing to tolerate something; *can't take something* means you can't tolerate an unpleasant situation; *to get someone down* means to get a person very sad; *to hang in there* means to not give up.

⭐ 🖨 Vocabulary-Building Strategies

B ▶ 2:04 LISTEN TO PREDICT

| Suggested teaching time: | 5–10 minutes | Your actual teaching time: |

- Tell students they will listen to conversations and decide if they elicit expressions of frustration, empathy, or encouragement from the other speaker.

- Model the first item. Play the audio. Then ask *What will the second woman say next?* (That must be frustrating.) *What is she expressing?* (empathy)

- Have students listen and answer the questions individually. If necessary, have students listen again.

- Bring the class together and go over any questions. For each item ask *What is being expressed—frustration, empathy, or encouragement?* (1. empathy, 2. empathy, 3. encouragement, 4. encouragement, 5. encouragement)

C GRAMMAR

| Suggested teaching time: | 5–10 minutes | Your actual teaching time: |

- Write on the board *No matter how careful I am, I always forget something*. Ask *What's another way of saying this?* (Possible answer: It doesn't matter how careful I am. I always forget something.) Write students' suggestions on the board.

- Ask a student to read the explanation and first example sentence. Point to the restatements on the board.

- Call on volunteers to read the remaining example sentences and then say them in a different way. For each item *No matter* can be restated as *It doesn't matter* + the question word.

- Focus on the last example sentence and point out that *how* is an intensifier combined with an adjective or adverb.

- Ask a volunteer to read the Be careful! note. Provide another example on the board: *No matter when does she go to bed, she's still tired in the morning*. Have students correct it. (No matter when she goes to bed . . .)

- Finally, ask *Can the clauses introduced by* no matter *stand alone?* (No. They are dependent clauses and need to be attached to an independent clause.) Have students notice the unhighlighted independent clause in the example sentences. Point out that a clause introduced by *no matter* can appear before or after the independent clause. Invite volunteers to try to reverse the order of the clauses in the example sentences. Ask *Does the meaning change?* (no)

LANGUAGE NOTE Point out that we commonly express frustration using *no matter what*, which is a shortened version of *No matter what [I do, she says, happens, etc.]*. For example, *No matter what, she gets here on time*.

Option: [+5 minutes] Have students look back to Exercise D, Spotlight on page 27, and find one example of a sentence with *no matter*. (...no matter how much I tell myself she's the only one for me, I just can't take the plunge.) Ask pairs to restate the sentence with *It doesn't matter...* (how much I tell myself she's the only one for me, I just can't take the plunge). Answers may vary. Call on volunteers to share.

Option: GRAMMAR BOOSTER *(Teaching notes p. T131)*

⭐ 🖨 Inductive Grammar Activity

D GRAMMAR PRACTICE

| Suggested teaching time: | 5 minutes | Your actual teaching time: |

- Focus on the example sentence. Ask *Which is the independent clause?* (she won't take a plane anywhere) Then focus on the *no matter* clause and ask *What is the problem?* (It uses inverted word order.) Tell students they will rewrite each sentence per the model if there is a mistake. They will write a checkmark if the sentence is correct.

- After students complete the exercise individually, have them check answers with a partner. Circulate and assist as needed.

⭐ 🖨 Extra Grammar Exercises

UNIT 3 LESSON 1 T28

E PAIR WORK

Suggested teaching time:	5 minutes	Your actual teaching time:

- Have students look through the exercise. Ask *Which items will need independent clauses?* (1 and 2) *Which ones will need dependent no matter clauses?* (3 and 4)
- Model item 1. Ask the class *What can the main clause be in this sentence?* Tell students to think up what any amount of effort to eat less cannot change (Possible answers: gaining weight; inability to lose weight) Then ask *What should the first sentence express: frustration, empathy, or encouragement?* (frustration) *What could the last sentence express: frustration, empathy, or encouragement?* (empathy or encouragement)
- Have students fill in the blanks in all the items on their own. Then have them role-play the dialogues with a partner, one person reading A and the other person reading B. Tell them to alternate roles.

Option: [+5 minutes] Pairs can choose role plays to read to the class. Alternatively, they can make up their own scenarios to read to the class.

Option: PRONUNCIATION BOOSTER *(Teaching notes p. T145)*

🖨 Pronunciation Pair Work

NOW YOU CAN Express frustration, empathy, and encouragement

A ▶ 2:05 CONVERSATION SPOTLIGHT

Suggested teaching time:	5 minutes	Your actual teaching time:

These conversation strategies are implicit in the model:
- Use *Is something wrong?* to notice a problem.
- Use *What's going on?* to find out what's happening.
- Use *Well, basically* to introduce a situation.
- Use *Hang in there* to express encouragement.
- Use *Anytime* to respond to a thank you.

- Have students look at the photo. Ask *What emotion does the woman on the right appear to be feeling?* (She looks worried or upset about something.) *What is the other woman doing?* (telling a friend about something)
- Have students read and listen to the conversation.
- To check comprehension, ask *Why is Nina upset?* (She's been having a bit of trouble at work.) *What kind of trouble?* (Her boss doesn't give her credit for her work.) *What does she say to express her frustration?* (I'm feeling really fed up.) *What words of encouragement does her friend give her?* (Hang in there . . .)

LANGUAGE NOTE In the second exchange, the woman says *I've been having a bit of trouble at work.* Remind students that some stative verbs, such as *have*, have active forms that do not indicate possession (e.g., *have dinner*). These can be used in the continuous aspect.

B ▶ 2:06 RHYTHM AND INTONATION

Suggested teaching time:	5 minutes	Your actual teaching time:

- Have students repeat chorally. Make sure they:
  ◦ use rising intonation for *Is something wrong?* (line 1) and *OK* (line 11).
  ◦ stress *sorry* in *I'm sorry to hear that.* (line 5)
  ◦ use falling intonation for *What's going on?* (line 5)
  ◦ pause after *Well* and *basically* (line 6)
  ◦ use emphatic stress on *Actually* (line 3) and *Anytime* (last line)
  ◦ use an encouraging tone for *Hang in there.* (line 10)

C NOTEPADDING

Suggested teaching time:	5 minutes	Your actual teaching time:

- Ask a student to read the list of problem topics. Have another volunteer read the example sentence.
- Tell students to fill in the notepad with *no matter* statements. Tell students to use a variety of question words (*how, what, when, where*). Circulate and assist as needed. If students don't feel comfortable sharing private information about money, health, or relationships, tell them they can make up statements or write about other people.

Option: [+5 minutes] Time-permitting, students can compare statements with a partner. Then bring the class together and ask *Did any pairs have similar problems?*

D CONVERSATION ACTIVATOR

Suggested teaching time:	5–10 minutes	Your actual teaching time:

🎬 Conversation Activator Video

Note: You can print the script or you can view it on the video player on the ActiveTeach.

- Divide the class into pairs. Instruct students that they will use the model in Exercise A, Conversation Spotlight, to role-play their own conversation with a partner.
- Refer students back to the Vocabulary in Exercise A to express frustration, empathy, and encouragement.
- Ask a volunteer to read the words under Recycle This Language. Encourage students to incorporate these words into their conversation.
- Reinforce the use of the spotlighted conversation strategies. For example, *Is something wrong; I'm sorry to hear that; Hang in there.*
- Bring students' attention to the Don't Stop! note. Ask a volunteer to read the bullet points. Explain that students should continue talking after they have covered the points in the original Conversation Spotlight.
- Tell students to change roles, so each student gets a chance to play A and B.

For more support, play the Conversation Activator Video before students do this activity themselves. After the video, ask students how the model has been changed by the actors.

⭐🖨 Conversation Activator: Speaking Booster

E PAIR WORK Complete the conversations with your own ideas, using the Vocabulary from page 28. Then read your conversations with a partner.

1 A: ....! No matter how little I eat, ...
   B: ....
2 A: ....! No matter what I tell my supervisor at work, ...
   B: ....
3 A: ....! I can't find my keys, ...
   B: ....
4 A: ....! Mary is always late, ...
   B: ....

PRONUNCIATION BOOSTER	p. 145
Vowel reduction to /ə/	

NOW YOU CAN Express frustration, empathy, and encouragement

A ▶ 2:05 CONVERSATION SPOTLIGHT Read and listen. Notice the spotlighted conversation strategies.

A: Hey, Nina. You look upset. **Is something wrong**?
B: Actually, I've been having a bit of trouble at work.
A: I'm sorry to hear that. **What's going on**?
B: **Well, basically**, no matter how well I do something, my boss never gives me credit.
A: That must be frustrating.
B: It is. I'm feeling really fed up.
A: I totally understand. **Hang in there**, though, OK?
B: Thanks for the encouragement! I appreciate it.
A: **Anytime.**

B ▶ 2:06 RHYTHM AND INTONATION Listen again and repeat. Then practice the conversation with a partner.

C NOTEPADDING Write statements on the notepad describing problems. Use no matter.

D CONVERSATION ACTIVATOR Create a conversation similar to the one in Exercise A. Start like this: *You look upset. Is something wrong?* Use one of the problems from your notepad. Be sure to change roles and then partners.

DON'T STOP!
- Ask for more details about the problem.
- Offer specific advice.
- Say as much as you can.

RECYCLE THIS LANGUAGE
- No way!
- Don't freak out.
- Just chill.
- It's not the end of the world.
- Wish me luck!
- Mark my words.

with a relationship: with my boyfriend. No matter how many times I ask him, he won't be friendly to my friends.

at home:

at work:

at school:

with money:

with a relationship:

with my health:

LESSON 2

GOAL Describe how fear affects you physically

A ▶ 2:07 **GRAMMAR SPOTLIGHT** Read how fear affects people physically. Notice the spotlighted grammar.

Q: What happens to you when you get really scared? What situations usually cause this reaction?

The worst thing for me is that I get sweaty palms and my hands shake. The first time I met my fiancée's parents, we were at a nice restaurant and my hands were shaking **so badly that** I avoided even picking up my glass. I was afraid they would think I had some kind of disease. I wish I could control this, but I can't. It's so embarrassing!

Kenji Yaegashi, 28 Nagoya, Japan

I get **such terrible palpitations that** it feels like my heart's going to jump right out of my chest. And when things are really bad, I can actually lose my voice. Fortunately, this only happens when I'm really panicked, like the time I was on a flight and the landing gear got stuck. I tried to pretend I was cool and collected, but the truth is I was terrified.

Having to speak English on the phone! I know it's crazy because I speak pretty well. But there's just something about it that makes me panic. It's **so bad that** when I know I have to make a call in English, I get **such awful butterflies in my stomach that** I think I'm going to get sick. Silly, I know, but true. But actually, once I start talking the butterflies go away.

Isil Farat, 24 Izmir, Turkey

Jorge Pardo, 32 Cuenca, Ecuador

B **RELATE TO PERSONAL EXPERIENCE** Which situation described in the Grammar Spotlight do you identify with most? Explain, providing examples from your own life.

GRAMMAR BOOSTER p. 132
Count and non-count nouns:
• Non-count nouns made countable
• Nouns used in countable and uncountable sense

DIGITAL INDUCTIVE ACTIVITY

C **GRAMMAR** USING SO ... (THAT) OR SUCH ... (THAT) TO EXPLAIN RESULTS

Use <u>so</u> to intensify an adjective or an adverb to explain the result of an extreme situation. <u>That</u> is optional. Don't use a comma.

extreme situation	result
It was **so stormy**	(that) I was afraid to get on the plane.
She left **so quickly**	(that) she forgot her umbrella.

If the adjective is followed directly by a noun, use <u>such</u>, not <u>so</u>.
   I was wearing **such uncomfortable shoes (that)** I could hardly walk.
   I made **such salty soup (that)** no one could eat it.
   She had **such a bad accident (that)** she never drove again.

If the noun is preceded by <u>many</u>, <u>much</u>, <u>few</u>, or <u>little</u>, use <u>so</u>.
   There will be **so many people** there **(that)** we won't be able to find each other.
   There was **so much lightning (that)** all the passengers on the plane were terrified.
   We ate **so few meals** out last month **(that)** we saved a lot of money.
   There's **so little ice** on the road **(that)** I think it's safe to drive.

Be careful!
Always use <u>a</u> or <u>an</u> with a singular count noun following <u>such</u>.
   She had **such a bad accident** that she never drove again.
   NOT She had ~~so bad accident~~ that she never drove again.

Remember: Use <u>many</u> and <u>few</u> with count nouns. Use <u>much</u> and <u>little</u> with non-count nouns.
   He had **so many tickets** that he lost his driver's license.
   NOT He had ~~so much tickets~~ that he lost his driver's license.

30 UNIT 3

LESSON 2

GOAL Describe how fear affects you physically

A ▶ 2:07 GRAMMAR SPOTLIGHT

Suggested teaching time:	10 minutes	Your actual teaching time:

- Ask students to look at the photos of the three people. Call on volunteers to read the names, ages, and cities where they live. Tell students that they will read how fear affects these people physically.
- Have students listen to the article as they read along.
- To check comprehension, ask *What happens to Kenji when he's scared?* (He gets sweaty palms and his hands shake.) *What is an example of a situation that can cause this?* (meeting his fiancée's parents) *What happens to Jorge?* (He gets terrible palpitations; sometimes he loses his voice.) *What type of situation can cause this?* (being stuck on a flight due to mechanical problems) *What happens to Isil?* (She gets awful butterflies in her stomach.) *What situation can cause this?* (having to speak English on the phone)
- Have students listen to the article again, noticing the spotlighted grammar. Ask *What form do you recognize in the spotlighted grammar?* (so / such . . . that)

LANGUAGE NOTE If you *have palpitations*, your heart beats quickly in an irregular way. *To have butterflies* is another way to say feel nervous.

B RELATE TO PERSONAL EXPERIENCE

Suggested teaching time:	5 minutes	Your actual teaching time:

- Review the causes for physical reactions to fear mentioned in the article. (meeting fiancée's parents, being stuck on a flight, having to speak English on the phone) Tell students they will discuss which situation they can relate to the most.
- Have students discuss the question in pairs. Encourage them to provide examples from their lives.

C GRAMMAR

Suggested teaching time:	5–10 minutes	Your actual teaching time:

- Have a student read the first explanation and example sentences. To check comprehension, ask *What happened as a result of it being so stormy?* (I was afraid to get on the plane.) *What happened as a result of her leaving so quickly?* (She forgot her umbrella.)
- Ask a volunteer read the second explanation and example sentences. To check comprehension, ask *What happened as a result of my wearing such uncomfortable shoes?* (I couldn't walk.) *What happened as a result of my making such salty soup?* (No one could eat it.) *What happened as a result of her having such a bad accident?* (She never drove again.) Tell students to read the Be careful! note to themselves.

- Focus on the last explanation and example sentences. To check comprehension, ask *What will happen as a result of there being so many people there?* (We won't be able to find each other.) *What happened as a result of there being so much lightning?* (The passengers on the plane were terrified.) *What happened as a result of us eating so few meals out last month?* (We saved a lot of money.) *What is the result of there being so little ice on the road?* (It is safe to drive.)
- Have students underline the noun in each phrase with *so*. (people, lightning, meals, ice) Ask *Which are count nouns?* (people, meals) *Which are non-count nouns?* (lightning, ice) Ask a student to read the Remember note. Point out that in the example sentences *many* and *few* are used with count nouns, *much* and *little* with non-count nouns.

Option: [+5 minutes] Have students look at the Grammar Spotlight in Exercise A on page 30. Instruct them to find examples with *so / such . . . that*. Ask *What was Kenji's extreme situation?* (His hands were shaking so badly.) *What was the result?* (He avoided picking up his glass.) *What is Jorge's extreme situation?* (He gets such terrible palpitations.) *What is the result?* (It feels like his heart is going to jump right out of his chest.) *What is Isil's extreme situation?* (She gets such awful butterflies in her stomach.) *What is the result?* (She thinks she's going to get sick.)

Challenge: [+5 minutes] Instruct students to look at each example in the Grammar Spotlight. Ask *Which words intensify an adjective or an adverb?* (so badly that; so bad that) *Why is such used with* awful butterflies *and* terrible palpitations? (because the adjective is followed directly by a noun)

Option: GRAMMAR BOOSTER (Teaching notes p. T132)

⭐ 🖨 Inductive Grammar Activity

UNIT 3 LESSON 2 **T30**

D GRAMMAR PRACTICE

Suggested teaching time:	5–10 minutes	Your actual teaching time:

- Focus on the model item. Ask *Why is* so *used in the sentence?* (It intensifies the adjective—*terrible*.)
- Instruct students to first identify which word or phrase will be intensified in each sentence. (2. many accidents, 3. late, 4. awful, 5. bad, 6. stormy day). Then have students decide whether *so / such . . . that* will be used to intensify, and instruct them to connect the sentences.

⭐ 🖨 Extra Grammar Exercises

E GRAMMAR PRACTICE

Suggested teaching time:	5 minutes	Your actual teaching time:

- Have students scan the exercise and underline all the count nouns (1. flights, 3. people, 4. seats) and circle all the non-count nouns (2. trouble, 3. time).
- Tell students to complete the exercise. Instruct them to think about meaning as they decide between *much / little* (non-count) and *many / few* (count)
- Have students compare answers with a partner.

F ▶ 2:08 VOCABULARY

Suggested teaching time:	5 minutes	Your actual teaching time:

- To warm up, focus students' attention on the cartoons. Ask students what each person is doing. (1. giving a speech, 2. traveling through turbulence, 3. meeting someone, 4. getting ready to jump from a plane)
- Have students read and listen about the physical effects of fear.
- Then have students listen and repeat the words chorally.
- Focus on the details in the images that illustrate the physical effects. Ask *What is happening in the first picture?* (The man's hands are shaking.) *The second?* (The "Thump! Thump!" indicates that the woman's heart is beating quickly.) *The third?* (The man's hands are wet with sweat.) *The fourth?* (The man's stomach feels nervous.)

LANGUAGE NOTE *To get butterflies in one's stomach* is also used for excitement about an extremely positive situation, such as when one is in love. For example: *She got butterflies in her stomach each time she saw her fiancé.*

⭐ 🖨 Vocabulary-Building Strategies

G ACTIVATE THE VOCABULARY

Suggested teaching time:	5 minutes	Your actual teaching time:

- Read the direction line. Tell students they will be referring to the Grammar Spotlight on page 30.
- On the board, write:
  1. Which physical effect(s) of fear did the person experience?
  2. What caused the physical effect(s) of fear?

To model, focus on Jorge Pardo. Ask a student to reread the quote and then elicit answers to questions on the board. (1. He got such terrible palpitations that it felt like his heart was going to jump right out of his chest. He lost his voice. 2. He became panicked on a flight when the landing gear got stuck.) Point out the use of the grammar *such . . . that*.

- Having gathered the information, ask a volunteer to paraphrase the situation that caused the physical effect of fear to happen. Encourage the student to restate the paraphrase in a way that used the *so / such . . . that* structure if possible. However, it is more important that students use the Vocabulary in their paraphrases.
- Have students work in pairs to paraphrase the other two people's situations and effects of fear. Circulate and assist as needed.

NOW YOU CAN Describe how fear affects you physically

A NOTEPADDING

Suggested teaching time:	5 minutes	Your actual teaching time:

- Call on a volunteer to read the prompts on the notepad.
- Have students take notes about the situation. Refer students to the Vocabulary in Exercise F on page 31 and the grammar in Exercise C on page 30.

B DISCUSSION ACTIVATOR

Suggested teaching time:	5–10 minutes	Your actual teaching time:

😀 Discussion Activator Video

Note: You can print the script or you can view it on the video player on the ActiveTeach.

- Divide the class into pairs and have students use their descriptions from the notepadding to talk about the people.
- Focus on the Recycle This Language box. Elicit an example for *No matter . . .* in the context of physical effects of fear. (Possible answer: No matter what I did, I couldn't calm down.)
- Encourage students to ask a lot of follow-up questions to increase the interest of the stories. These will also help make students' optional writing exercise more productive. If students will be doing the optional writing below, encourage them to take notes during the discussion so they can write their partner's story.

For more support, play the Discussion Activator Video before students do this activity. After each video, ask if the students in the video included sufficient details.

OPTIONAL WRITING [+15–20 minutes]

- Let students work in the same pairs as in Exercise B, Discussion Activator. Tell them to gather any notes they took during the discussion. Alternatively, students can swap books and write down ideas from the notepad in Exercise A.
- Instruct students to use *so / such . . . that* and *no matter . . .* and vocabulary for physical effects of fear in their descriptions. Review sequencing words if needed.

D GRAMMAR PRACTICE On a separate sheet of paper, combine the statements, using <u>so</u> … (that) or <u>such</u> … (that).

> The fire was so terrible that the building was totally destroyed.

1. The fire was terrible. The building was totally destroyed.
2. There are usually many accidents. We don't travel on holiday weekends.
   There are usually so many accidents that we don't travel on holiday weekends.
3. The games end late. We prefer to watch them on TV.
   The games end so late that we prefer to watch them on TV.
4. The insects are awful after dark. Most people prefer to stay inside in the evening.
   The insects are so awful after dark that most people prefer to stay inside in the evening.
5. Traffic in this region has become a bad problem. Lots of people are taking public transportation.
   Traffic in this region has become such a bad problem that lots of people are taking public transportation.
6. It was a stormy day. We postponed our picnic.
   It was such a stormy day that we postponed our picnic.

E GRAMMAR PRACTICE Complete each statement with <u>much</u>, <u>little</u>, <u>many</u>, or <u>few</u>.

1. They cancelled so ...**many**... flights that we won't be able to get there tonight.
2. There's always so ...**much**... trouble when the weather is bad that we don't travel in winter.
3. So ...**few**... people ate at that restaurant that they had to close it.
4. There were so ...**few**... seats left on the train that my friends and I couldn't sit together.
5. There was so ...**little**... time to get to the shelter that we just stayed in our basement.

F ▶ 2:08 VOCABULARY PHYSICAL EFFECTS OF FEAR Read and listen. Then listen again and repeat.

| My hands shake. | I get palpitations. | I get sweaty palms. | I get butterflies in my stomach. |

G ACTIVATE THE VOCABULARY Find and underline the Vocabulary and other physical effects of fear in the Grammar Spotlight. Paraphrase the situation that caused the physical effect for each of the three people, using the Vocabulary in your description.

> *Jorge Pardo was so scared that he got palpitations and he lost his voice.*

Kenji Yaegachi had sweaty palms and his hands shook.
Isil Farat got a jumpy feeling in her stomach and she thought she would throw up.

NOW YOU CAN Describe how fear affects you physically

A NOTEPADDING Choose a time when you were so scared that it affected you physically. Write notes about it on the notepad. Use the grammar and Vocabulary from page 30.

B DISCUSSION ACTIVATOR Discuss the situations on your notepads. Tell each other your stories, asking for more information and details. Idea: Tell the class about what happened to your partner. Say as much as you can.

RECYCLE THIS LANGUAGE
- No matter …
- Did you freak out?
- It wasn't the end of the world.

What I was afraid of:

How it affected me physically:

Write one statement with so or such … (that).

What finally happened?

OPTIONAL WRITING Write your partner's story. Use sequencing expressions (<u>first</u>, <u>next</u>, <u>after that</u>, etc.) to clarify the order of events in his or her story.

LESSON 3

GOAL Discuss overcoming handicaps and hardships

A **READING WARM-UP** What are some physical handicaps people face? What are some other hardships that might limit people's ability to succeed?

B ▶ 2:09 **READING** Read about Marlee Matlin. If you had to choose one adjective to describe her, what would it be?
Answers will vary but may include the following:
An adjective that could describe Marlee Matlin is *inspirational*.

THE COURAGE TO BE WHO SHE IS

Marlee Matlin, the only deaf performer ever to win the Oscar for Best Actress in a Leading Role, is also known worldwide as a stage and TV actor, an author, and as a spokesperson for people with hearing disabilities. Through her work and her books she has devoted her life to encouraging children and adults with hearing loss to live normal lives with normal expectations.

Born with normal hearing, Marlee suffered permanent hearing loss at 18 months from an illness with a high fever. As she approached school age, her parents were advised to send her to a specialized boarding school far from home. However, her parents felt that Marlee would be deprived of the parental contact and love essential to normal development if she didn't live at home. So instead, they put her in a public mainstream school that had both hearing and deaf students, which built her confidence to participate in activities with hearing students. At school, Marlee learned sign language, though she was encouraged to use her voice, too.

Throughout her childhood, Marlee's parents did everything they could to give her the same life she would have had if she had had normal hearing. Her family even helped Marlee develop a sense of humor about herself so she wouldn't be ashamed of her handicap. When others wondered about the strange way she pronounced some words (because she had learned to say them without ever having *heard* them), her brother would say she had an accent because she was from a foreign country, which made both of them laugh.

At seven, her parents enrolled her in a summer camp with both hearing and deaf children, and there she learned to use her hands to "sign" the lyrics of songs as the other children sang. Her campmates loved this, and their applause gave Marlee her first taste of the joy of performing.

To encourage her, when Marlee returned home from camp, her mother enrolled her in an afterschool children's theater program (now called the International Center on Deafness and the Arts, or ICODA), where children prepared some performances in sign language and others in spoken English.

Matlin continued performing when she was in college. At one performance, the popular TV actor Henry Winkler was in the audience. Matlin approached him and said she wanted to be a famous actor like him. Winkler, who suffers from dyslexia (a reading disorder that causes difficulty in reading despite normal intelligence), empathized with Matlin and encouraged her, telling her she could be anything she wanted and not to let anything stand in her way. Winkler became a longtime mentor and friend to Matlin, helping her as she pursued her acting career.

Matlin's life hasn't been without controversy or criticism. When presenting an Oscar, she spoke the nominees' names instead of signing them, causing some deaf people to complain she was suggesting *they* should speak instead of signing. To comfort Matlin, African-American actor Whoopi Goldberg told her that once she had worn blue contact lenses just for fun and was criticized for trying to "appear white." Goldberg told Matlin not to worry about what others say and just be herself.

Matlin has never let her handicap stand in her way and has continued to surpass the expectations the public has of people who can't hear. When she competed in TV's *Dancing with the Stars*, people were incredulous: How could she dance if she couldn't hear the music?

The key to Matlin's success may, in part, lie in the support and help others have given her—support that has enabled Matlin to be who she is, no matter what others may believe or say.

Marlee Matlin has never let her handicap stand in her way.

LESSON 3

GOAL Discuss overcoming handicaps and hardships

A READING WARM-UP

Suggested teaching time:	5 minutes	Your actual teaching time:

- Ask a volunteer to read the questions. On the board, write *physical handicaps*. Elicit examples. Then discuss other hardships that people are faced with and have to overcome in life.
- Invite students to mention people they know or have read about who have battled a handicap or hardship, or ask them to mention their own story.

B ▶ 2:09 READING

Suggested teaching time:	10–15 minutes	Your actual teaching time:

- Have students look at the picture. Ask *Do you know who this woman is?* Focus on the title "The Courage to Be Who She Is." Encourage students to deduce from the lesson title and warm-up that she likely has overcome some handicap or hardship. Invite students to guess what it might be.
- As students read and listen, tell them to underline information in the article that will help them answer the focus question in the direction line (If you had to choose one adjective to describe her, what would it be?).
- Bring the class together. Have volunteers share their answers to the focus question. (Possible answers: inspirational, courageous)

LANGUAGE NOTE Focus on the word *empathized*. Point out that in the unit the word has been used as a noun, *empathy*. Elicit additional parts of speech (*empathetic* [adj], *empathetically* [adv]). *To surpass expectations* means to be or perform better than was anticipated; *incredulous* means unable to believe something.

⭐ 🖨 Reading Strategies

UNIT 3 LESSON 3   T32

C UNDERSTAND MEANING FROM CONTEXT

Suggested teaching time:	5–10 minutes	Your actual teaching time:

- Before doing the exercise, have students number the paragraphs in the article, assigning number 1 to the one in purple shading down to number 8.
- If students need help finding words and phrases, give them hints: The term for item 1 is in paragraph 1, item 2 in paragraph 2, item 3 in paragraph 3, and item 4 in paragraph 5.
- Then, in pairs, have students write sentences with the terms. Encourage students to write sentences about unrelated information so they don't simply copy the sentences from the article.

Option: [+5 minutes] Have students reread paragraph 7. Invite students to speculate how Matlin was able to dance even though she couldn't hear the music. Invite students to look up videos online of her dancing in this competition. Have them write a response to the performance.

🖨 Extra Reading Comprehension Questions

D SUMMARIZE

Suggested teaching time:	10–15 minutes	Your actual teaching time:

- Have students skim the list of people and institutions that contributed to Matlin's success. Call on volunteers to share any information they remember from the first reading. Then have them write the summaries. Tell students that each summary should be a short statement in their own words, capturing the main idea.
- For a less advanced class you may choose to hint where in the article the various information can be found—her parents, paragraphs 2–4; her brother, paragraph 3; her school, paragraph 2; her summer camp, paragraph 4; Henry Winkler, paragraph 5; Whoopi Goldberg, paragraph 6.

Challenge: [+5 minutes] Invite students to speculate how Matlin's life might have been different had her parents opted to send her to a specialized boarding school far from home. On the board, write:

> *Which of the influences on the list would have been eliminated from her life?*

(probably all of them!)

> *Do you think the influences she received in life outweigh the ones she may have gotten at a specialized school?*
>
> *What challenges do you think Matlin's parents faced along the way?*

(possibly some prejudice; some resistance mainstreaming their daughter; supporting their daughter through frustrations and unequal treatment)

> *Do you think Matlin or Matlin's parents showed courage?*

(probably both)

> *Which choice do you think you would have made for your child?*

Have students discuss with a partner or in small groups. For the last question, focus on the fact that Matlin's parents made this choice 50 years ago. Elicit progress made in the past 50 years for people with disabilities.

E DISCUSSION

Suggested teaching time:	5 minutes	Your actual teaching time:

- Divide the class into groups of three. Have students discuss the questions in their groups. Circulate and assist as needed.
- Bring the class together and have groups share ideas.

⭐ 🖨 Extra Challenge Reading Activity

NOW YOU CAN Discuss overcoming handicaps and hardships

A FRAME YOUR IDEAS

Suggested teaching time:	5 minutes	Your actual teaching time:

- Have students choose a person or character to focus on. Encourage students to think of people in their own lives, celebrities, or even fictional characters from movies, TV shows, books, etc. Elicit factors that can help a person overcome a handicap. (Possible answers: hard work, persistence, positive outlook)
- Ask students to fill in the notepad.

B DISCUSSION

Suggested teaching time:	5 minutes	Your actual teaching time:

- In pairs, have students compare people from their notepads.
- Bring the class together. Focus on the factors that helped individuals overcome their handicaps. Analyze for recurring factors.

⭐ 🖨 Discussion: Speaking Booster

T33 UNIT 3 LESSON 3

C **UNDERSTAND MEANING FROM CONTEXT** Match the words and phrases from the article with these definitions. Then, with a partner, write sentences using the terms.

1 a person who represents and speaks for a group of people spokesperson
2 a system of communication using hand gestures sign language
3 a physical or mental disability or a condition that can limit a person's ability to function normally handicap
4 an advisor from whom someone receives support and encouragement mentor
5 strong differences of opinion, especially between groups of people conflicts

mentor
spokesperson
handicap
conflicts
sign language

D **SUMMARIZE** In the chart, summarize how these people and institutions contributed to Matlin's development and success. Then compare summaries with your classmates.

	Ways in which they helped Matlin
Her parents	They enrolled her in a school with both hearing and deaf children; they sent her to a camp to learn sign language.
Her school	The school taught her sign language and encouraged her to speak, too.
Her brother	Her brother helped her not to be embarrassed when people asked why she pronounced words differently.
Her summer camp	Her camp helped her discover her love of performing.
Henry Winkler	He told her she could do whatever she wanted. He helped her with her acting career.
Whoopi Goldberg	She told her stories about when she was criticized; She told her just to be herself and not listen to criticism.

E **DISCUSSION** Discuss the following questions. Answers will vary but may include the following:

1 How do you think a person can learn to speak without ever hearing others speak?
A deaf person might rely on watching lips and feeling the throat of a speaker to understand how the muscles move when a word is formed.
2 In your opinion, what are some general factors that contribute to the success of people who have handicaps or other problems that could limit their success in life?
I think it is perseverance, hard work, and a positive attitude that contribute to success of people faced with handicaps and other problems.

NOW YOU CAN Discuss overcoming handicaps and hardships

A **FRAME YOUR IDEAS** Choose a historical figure, a fictional character, or someone you know who overcame or has overcome a handicap or other hardship. Write discussion notes.

IDEAS: Some types of hardships
- a physical or mental handicap
- racial, ethnic, or sexual discrimination
- a natural disaster
- political instability or war
- poverty, lack of education or family support

Name:
Summary of handicap or hardship:

Factors that helped him or her overcome it:

Achievements:

B **DISCUSSION** Compare information. What similarities do the people share? Explain.

She has overcome her handicap by playing tennis in a wheelchair.

LESSON 4

GOAL Examine the nature of heroism

A ▶ 2:10 **LISTENING WARM-UP WORD STUDY USING PARTS OF SPEECH** Study the forms of these words related to bravery and heroism, according to the part of speech. (Check meaning of any unfamiliar words in a dictionary.) Read and listen. Then listen again and repeat.

adjective	adverb	noun
brave	bravely	bravery
confident	confidently	confidence
courageous	courageously	courage
fearless	fearlessly	fearlessness
heroic	heroically	heroism
willing	willingly	willingness

B ▶ 2:11 **LISTEN TO ACTIVATE PARTS OF SPEECH** Listen to a TV news magazine story. Use a word from the Word Study chart in the correct part of speech to complete each statement. Some items have more than one possible answer.

1 Seol's decision to go back to the plane wreckage was extremely **courageous**.

2 Although aware that the airplane could explode at any moment, Seol **bravely** returned to the plane again and again to rescue wounded passengers.

3 Seol's **willingness** to risk his life to save others was extraordinary.

4 The story suggests that anyone, even an apparently ordinary person, is capable of **heroic** acts.

5 Most people don't have the **courage** to act in the way Seol Ik Soo did.

Rescue personnel look for victims in the wreckage of an airliner.

C ▶ 2:12 **LISTEN FOR DETAILS** Listen to the story again. Complete each statement.

1 Seol carried …… passengers out of the plane.
 a three **b** more than three

2 During the rescue, Seol felt as if the passengers were very …… .
 a heavy **b** light

3 Seol used a …… to make bandages.
 a belt **b** shirt

4 …… he took passengers out of the plane, he realized that there was blood on his face.
 a Before **b** After

5 Before the crash, …… thought of Seol as a hero.
 a no one had ever b everyone had always

LESSON 4

GOAL Examine the nature of heroism

A ▶ 2:10 LISTENING WARM-UP

Suggested teaching time:	5–10 minutes	Your actual teaching time:

- To introduce the topic, write *adjective, adverb, noun* on the board. Review each part of speech as needed:
  - A noun names a person place, thing, or abstract idea. Nouns can be concrete (people, places, and things) or abstract (ideas, emotions, feelings, or qualities you cannot touch).
  - An adjective describes a noun.
  - An adverb describes a verb, an adjective, or another adverb.
- After students listen and read, have them focus on the nouns. Ask *Are these nouns concrete or abstract?* (abstract)
- Clarify the meaning of any unfamiliar words or have students look them up. Then ask *What do these words have in common?* (Possible answers: They are related to bravery and heroism. They can be used to discuss difficult or challenging experiences.)
- Have students listen and read again.

LANGUAGE NOTE *Brave* means dealing with danger or difficult situations with courage and confidence; *confident* means believing that you or someone else can do something well; *courageous* means being able to control fear in dangerous or difficult situations; *fearless* means not being afraid; *heroic* means being very brave or courageous; *willing* means being happy, ready, and able to do something.

Option: [+5 minutes] Tell students to close their books. Write the following sentences on the board. Then call on volunteers to identify the part of speech of each underlined word.

1. The volunteers were praised for their <u>heroic</u> actions during the emergency.
2. We have <u>confidence</u> that Jane will pass her entrance exam.
3. The woman <u>courageously</u> faced the challenges presented her.
4. The <u>brave</u> climbers survived the snowstorm.
5. Her <u>willingness</u> to fight the illness impressed all of us.
6. The firefighter <u>fearlessly</u> entered the building.

(Answers: 1. adjective, 2. noun, 3. adverb, 4. adjective, 5. noun, 6. adverb)

⭐ 🖨 Vocabulary-Building Strategies

B ▶ 2:11 LISTEN TO ACTIVATE PARTS OF SPEECH

Suggested teaching time:	5 minutes	Your actual teaching time:

- Have students look at the photo. Tell students they are going to hear about a man's heroic act after a plane crash.
- Pre-listening: Have students look at the sentences and decide if each missing word should be a noun, an adjective, or an adverb. (1. adjective, 2. adverb, 3. noun, 4. adjective, 5. noun)
- Listening: Have students listen to the news report and complete the sentences. If an answer is an adjective or adverb, tell students to circle the word it modifies.
- Bring the class together and go over the answers. Accept any logical answers, as long as they are stated in the correct part of speech.

Challenge: [+5 minutes] Have students restate each sentence, using a different part of speech for the missing word. This can be done in pairs or groups or as a class. (Possible answers:
1. Seol courageously went back to the plane wreckage.
2. Seol was fearless and returned to the plane to rescue other passengers. 3. Seol willingly risked his life to save others. 4. Apparently even an ordinary person can act heroically. 5. Most people aren't confident enough to act the way Seol did.)

⭐ 🖨 Listening Strategies

C ▶ 2:12 LISTEN FOR DETAILS

Suggested teaching time:	5 minutes	Your actual teaching time:

- Pre-listening: Have students read through the exercise items. If they think they know some answers, tell them to circle them with a pencil.
- Listening: Tell students to listen to the magazine story again and complete the exercise. If necessary, let students listen again to check their answers.

UNIT 3 LESSON 4 T34

D ▶ 2:13 LISTEN TO RETELL A STORY

| Suggested teaching time: | 5 minutes | Your actual teaching time: |

- **Listening:** Have students listen to the news report and take notes of important details.
- Instruct students to write their paragraphs retelling the story. Encourage them to use many details. Remind them to use at least three of the words from the word study chart in Exercise A on page 34. If necessary, let students listen again to check their information and add any details they may have overlooked.
- Have pairs exchange summaries. Circulate while students work and answer any questions.
- Bring the class together and have students listen for words from Exercise A.

Option: [+5 minutes] Encourage interested students to learn more about Seol Ik Soo and report their findings to the class.

Challenge: [+5 minutes] On the board, write:
1. How would you have acted in Seol's situation?
2. Do you think you would have done what Seol did?
3. What makes a person act heroically?
4. Where does this kind of courage come from?

Have students write a paragraph summarizing their answers. Then bring the class together and have students share.

Answers for Exercise D

Answers will vary but may include the following:

The news report is about a courageous young man Seol Ik Soo. He survived a plane crash, but rather than just save his own life, he bravely put himself in danger to save other people's lives. He fearlessly returned to the sight of the crash and carried people to safety. He was willing to risk his life to help others. Although described by his friends as an ordinary man, he proved to be a hero.

NOW YOU CAN Examine the nature of heroism

A NOTEPADDING

| Suggested teaching time: | 5 minutes | Your actual teaching time: |

- On the board, write *hero*. Have students brainstorm things that come to mind when they see this word. (Possible answers: courage, bravery, willingness to risk one's life). Write students' responses on the board.
- Ask a student to read the Recycle This Language box. Encourage students to use the phrases in their definitions.
- Have pairs complete their definition. Then bring the class together and have students share. Discuss any significant differences in definitions. Refer to the list of responses on the board and the phrases in Recycle This Language as applicable.

LANGUAGE NOTE A hero is a person who is admired for doing something good. Though *hero* is used both for a man or woman, the word traditionally refers to a man. The word *heroine* is used for a woman. The expression *freak out* means to be in an irrational emotional state, for example as a result of anger or excitement. You may want to point out that *freak out* is informal, but not offensive.

B DISCUSSION

| Suggested teaching time: | 10–15 minutes | Your actual teaching time: |

- To preview, have students look at the photos and ask volunteers to read the captions.
- Have students read the profiles individually. As they work, create a three-column chart on the board. Write each person's name at the top of a column.
- Divide the class into groups and tell students to copy the chart. Have students discuss ways each person is a hero, writing adjectives in the chart.
- Bring the class together and call on students to fill in the chart on the board.
- Finally, have students look back at their notepad and decide which person's behavior comes closest to the description they wrote in Exercise A.

C DEBATE

| Suggested teaching time: | 10–15 minutes | Your actual teaching time: |

- Write the names of the three heroes on the board:

    Rosa Parks   Dr. Khan   Alicia Sorohan

    Have each student choose which person they think is the most heroic and write a few notes explaining why.
- Divide the class into groups, making sure a variety of the heroes are represented in each group. Tell students to argue why they think their chosen person is the most heroic.
- Circulate as groups work. Listen to students' arguments. Then tell groups to decide who made the strongest case. Assist as needed.

Option: [+5 minutes] Ask students to write a paragraph summarizing arguments in favor of their hero. Collect and provide written feedback.

D ▶ 2:13 **LISTEN TO RETELL A STORY** Listen to the story again. Retell the story in writing, including the important details and using at least three of the words from the Word Study chart. Exchange stories with a partner and suggest details your partner may have left out. See page T35 for answers.

NOW YOU CAN Examine the nature of heroism

A **NOTEPADDING** Frame your ideas. With a partner, discuss and write your own description of the behavior that makes someone a hero. Use words from the Word Study chart and other phrases.

A hero is someone who …

RECYCLE THIS LANGUAGE
- hangs in there
- doesn't give up
- doesn't freak out
- No matter what happens

B **DISCUSSION** Read the three profiles. Which person's behavior comes closest to the description you wrote in Exercise A. Explain and discuss with a partner.

DAILY NEWS
ROSA PARKS

In 1955, Rosa Parks got on a city bus in Montgomery, a city in the southern U.S., and sat down in a seat near the front. In those days, buses in Montgomery were racially segregated, and the front 10 seats were permanently reserved for white passengers. The driver told her to move to the back, but Parks refused. The driver then called the police, and she was arrested and taken to jail. Rosa Parks's act of defiance took great courage because of the brutality and injustice African Americans faced at that time in the South of the U.S. Her arrest became a rallying point, and the African-American community organized a bus boycott that lasted 381 days, during which no African American rode a city bus in Montgomery. Parks's action had a powerful economic impact on the bus company, which was forced to change its policy. Ultimately through the efforts of the community, racial segregation of public buses was made illegal.

Rosa Parks on the Montgomery bus.

Dr. Sheikh Umar Khan

In 2014, an Ebola epidemic raged in three African countries—Guinea, Liberia, and Sierra Leone. This frightening viral disease, for which there was no prevention or treatment, typically killed a devastating 60% to 90% of those infected. Dr. Sheikh Umar Khan, already hailed as a medical hero in his native Sierra Leone for having saved hundreds of lives during 10 years of battling Lassa fever, a disease similar to Ebola, rushed in to care for more than 100 Ebola patients. Dr. Khan knew better than anyone else that the people at greatest risk were health care workers. In spite of taking precautions, Dr. Khan and three of the nurses who worked with him died of the virus within three days of each other.

Dr. Sheikh Umar Khan

Alicia Sorohan

On October 11, while camping in Queensland, Australia, Alicia Sorohan awoke to the sound of someone screaming. Rushing out of her tent, she came across her friend Mike Kerr in the mouth of a 4.2-meter saltwater crocodile. The 60-year-old grandmother immediately jumped on the back of the giant crocodile, which dropped Kerr and attacked her, biting her in the face and arm. When shot and killed by another member of the group, the crocodile had Sorohan's arm in its mouth and was dragging her into the water. Sorohan and Kerr both survived the incident though both had serious injuries. Family members of the victims, in shock after the horrible attack, said that Sorohan's speedy response had been astonishing. "She deserves an award of some kind," said Wayne Clancy, her son-in-law.

a giant saltwater crocodile

C **DEBATE** From pages 34 and 35, choose the person you consider to be the most heroic. Meet with two or three other classmates, each of whom has chosen someone different. Have a debate about which of the persons is the most heroic. Decide among yourselves or among the other students in the class who won the debate.

WRITING   Reducing adverbial clauses

A **WRITING SKILL**   Study the rules.

Reducing adverbial clauses to adverbial phrases

Adverbial clauses can be reduced to adverbial phrases when the subject of the independent clause and the adverbial clause are the same. Reduced adverbial phrases are more common in writing than in speaking.

Adverbial clauses	→	Reduced to adverbial phrases
When I fell off my bike, I hurt my back.	→	**Falling off my bike**, I hurt my back.
When we were eating, we got a call.	→	**When eating** (or **Eating**), we got a call.
We saw a bear **while we were hiking**.	→	We saw a bear **while hiking**.
Before I left, I sent my parents a letter.	→	**Before leaving**, I sent my parents a letter.
After I had shared my news, I felt better.	→	**After having shared my news**, I felt better.

Be careful!
When the subjects of the adverbial clause and the independent clause are different, the clause can't be reduced.
Before **she** saw the crocodile, **it** attacked.
DON'T SAY Before seeing the crocodile, it attacked.

Punctuation
Use a comma after a clause or phrase when it comes first.
Before I left, I sent my parents a letter. / I sent my parents a letter **before I left.**

B **PRACTICE**   Read the short news report to the right of a frightening event. Underline the reduced adverbial phrases and, on a separate sheet of paper, rewrite the sentences with them, changing the phrases to clauses. See page T36 for answers.

C **PRACTICE**   On a separate sheet of paper, rewrite each of the following sentences, reducing adverbial clauses to adverbial phrases when possible. If the sentence can't be reduced, explain why not.

1 When she was waking up, Alicia Sorohan heard a scream. *Waking up, Alicia Sorohan heard a scream.*
2 While Dr. Khan was trying to save his patients, several nurses on his staff came down with Ebola. *Clause can't be reduced. The subjects of the two clauses are different.*
3 When she refused to move to the back seats on the bus, Rosa Parks was arrested. *Refusing to move to the back seats, Rosa Park was arrested.*
4 Before she went to the drama program, Marlee Matlin hadn't ever performed in a play. *Before going to the drama program, Marlin Matlin hadn't ever performed in a play.*
5 Seol realized that he was covered in blood after he had exited the plane several times. *After having exited from the plane several times, Seol realized that he was covered in blood.*

WRITING MODEL

May 5—While camping yesterday, the Evans family was surprised by some frightening neighbors: a bear cub and its mother. Twin 5-year-olds Paul and Marcy were delighted because the young animal reminded them of the cute creatures in their picture books and on TV. Their father, on the other hand, wasn't as charmed because he knew that approaching a bear cub was dangerous since an adult bear is usually nearby.

  Luckily for the family, Mr. Evans was already awake and getting breakfast ready when he heard the bear. As he posted later on Facebook: "While getting the milk out of our camping bag, I heard a rustling noise behind me. I turned around and saw a bear cub trying to open the garbage can. I knew I had to think fast."

  Hearing his kids coming out of the tent, Mr. Evans quickly pushed them back inside to prevent them from approaching the bear to play with it. At that moment, a large adult female, probably the cub's mother, came by and led the cub away. The Evanses' camping day continued peacefully after that.

D **APPLY THE WRITING SKILL**   Write a short report about a dangerous or frightening event, using the Writing Model for support. Write at least two paragraphs and tell the story in the order that the events occurred. The event can be real or fictional. Use at least three adverbial clauses and phrases to clarify time relationships.

SELF-CHECK
☐ Did I write two or more paragraphs?
☐ Does my report tell the story in the order that the events occurred?
☐ Did I use at least three adverbial clauses or reduced adverbial phrases to clarify time relationships?

WRITING Reducing adverbial clauses

A WRITING SKILL

Suggested teaching time:	5–10 minutes	Your actual teaching time:

- Write *clause* and *phrase* on the board. Elicit that a clause is a group of words that contains a subject and verb. A phrase is a group of words.
- Call on a volunteer to read the first explanation. Have students read the example sentences to themselves. Ask *How are the adverbial phrases different from the adverbial clauses?* (When an adverbial clause is reduced to an adverbial phrase, there is no subject and the form of the verb changes.)
- Write the first example sentence on the board and circle the subject in each clause. Point out that when the subjects are the same, the clause can be reduced to a phrase. Read the Be careful! note to illustrate that when subjects of the two clauses are different, they cannot be reduced. Write another example on the board: *My sister called me while I was sleeping.* Ask *Can we reduce this sentence?* (no) *Why not?* (The subjects differ: *my sister, I.*) Illustrate what would happen if the sentence were reduced: *My sister called me while sleeping.* This doesn't make sense.
- Ask a student to read the note about punctuation. Have students focus on each example sentence and notice how when the clause or phrase is at the beginning of the sentence, a comma follows. When it's at the end of a sentence, there is no comma.

Option: [+5 minutes] If necessary, review the meaning of dependent and independent clauses. Remind students that adverbial clauses are dependent clauses that contain a subject and verb. They are always connected to an independent clause. If an adverbial clause is used alone, it is a sentence fragment and considered an error in writing. Adverbial clauses clarify time relationships and often answer the questions *When?* or *How?* You may wish to review some of the words that commonly introduce adverbial time clauses: *when, whenever, while, before, after, until,* etc.

B PRACTICE

Suggested teaching time:	5 minutes	Your actual teaching time:

- Hint to students that there is one reduced adverbial clause in each paragraph. Ask *What do you need to remember about the subjects of each clause when you change the phrases to clauses?* (The subject in the adverbial clause has to be the same as that in the independent clause.) Remind students that they don't have to repeat each subject—they can use pronouns.
- Have students rewrite the sentences. Then have them compare answers with a partner. (Possible answers: paragraph 1, While they were camping yesterday, the Evans family was surprised by…; paragraph 2, While I was getting the milk out of our camping bag, I heard a…; paragraph 3, When he heard his kids coming out of the tent, Mr. Evans quickly pushed them back inside to…)

Answers for Exercise B

Phrases changed to clauses:
While the Evans family was camping yesterday, they were surprised by some frightening neighbors: a bear cub and its mother.
While I was getting milk out of our camping bag, I heard a rustling noise behind me.
When Mr. Evans heard his kids coming out of the tent, he quickly pushed them back inside to prevent them from approaching the bear to play with it.

C PRACTICE

Suggested teaching time:	5–10 minutes	Your actual teaching time:

- Have students look at the sentences and underline the subject of each clause. (1. she, Alicia Sorohan; 2. Dr Khan, several nurses; 3. she, Rosa Parks; 4. she, Marlee Matlin; 5. Seol, he) Then have them identify which clauses can be reduced and reduce them.
- Tell students to compare answers with a partner. Then go over any answers as a class. For item 1, accept two ways to reduce: *When waking up* and *Waking up*.

D APPLY THE WRITING SKILL

Suggested teaching time:	5–10 minutes	Your actual teaching time:

- Tell students they will write a report about a dangerous or frightening event. Refer them to the essay in Exercise B as a model.
- Refer students to the Writing Process Worksheet in ActiveTeach for guidance with pre-writing and peer feedback.
- Encourage students to use the Self-Check in the Student's Book to go over the reports they wrote.

Option: [+5 minutes] Time-permitting, students can exchange papers with a partner and offer feedback using the topics in the Self-Check list. Encourage partners to also check for examples.

⭐ 🖨 Writing Process

REVIEW

🎮 **Digital Game**

A ▶ 2:14

| Suggested teaching time: | 5 minutes | Your actual teaching time: |

- To introduce the topic, review different problems people might have, such as health problems, career problems, or family problems. Elicit a sentence with *no matter* to illustrate one of the problems students name. For example, *No matter what I do, I can't lose any weight.*
- Have students listen to the descriptions of the three problems.
- Then have them look at the names and photos. Have students reread the task before they listen again and complete the exercise. If necessary, allow students to listen again to review each person's problem and make sure their summary sentences are applicable.
- Go over the *no matter* sentences as a class. Have students compare the different responses they provided. Accept answers with the clauses both before and after the independent clause.
- Then ask *What type of problem does Felix Tan have?* (a work or career problem) *Robert Reston?* (a health problem) *Eva Garcia?* (a personal or family problem) *Which problem do you think is the most serious? The least serious? Why?*

Option: [+5 minutes] Tell pairs to create a brief description of a problem, following the models in the listening comprehension in Lesson 4. Have students read them to the class and invite students to summarize each person's frustration with a sentence beginning with *No matter*.

B

| Suggested teaching time: | 5 minutes | Your actual teaching time: |

- Have students look at the word or phrase following each blank. Tell students to think which question word best fits in the sentence to express a frustration. Then have them fill in the blanks. Point out that more than one answer may be possible.
- Ask students to compare answers in pairs.

C

| Suggested teaching time: | 5 minutes | Your actual teaching time: |

- Have students underline the word after the multiple choices and identify the part of speech. (1. *loud*, adjective; 2. *candy*, noun; 3. *bad turbulence*, adjective followed by a noun; 4. *many brands*, quantifier followed by a noun; 5. *good time*, adjective followed by a noun; 6. *quickly*, adverb) Then have them complete the exercise.
- Circulate and assist as needed. If necessary, remind students that *so* intensifies an adjective or an adverb; *such* is used when an adjective is followed directly by a noun; and if a noun is preceded by *many, much, few,* or *little* then *so* is used.
- Go over the answers as a class.

D

| Suggested teaching time: | 5 minutes | Your actual teaching time: |

- Have students complete the exercise. Refer them to Exercise A on page 34 if they need to review vocabulary.
- Go over the answers as a class.

E

| Suggested teaching time: | 5 minutes | Your actual teaching time: |

- Write *frustration, empathy, encouragement* on the board. Focus on item 1 in the Student's Book. Have students identify each statement using one of the words on the board. (I'm fed up, frustration; Hang in there, encouragement) Then call on two volunteers to read the model answer. Point out how more detail is added to both the expression of frustration and encouragement.
- Have students work individually to write the conversations. Then have them share their answers with a partner. Encourage pairs to role-play the various scenarios.
- Bring the class together and invite volunteers to role-play.

Option: **TEST-TAKING SKILLS BOOSTER** (p. 153)

EXTRA

- Workbook
- MyEnglishLab
- Online Student Resources (www.english.com/summit3e)
  – Classroom Audio Program
  – Extra Practice Activities
  – *Summit* GO App
  – Web Projects
- ActiveTeach
  – Assessment
  – Additional Printable Resources
    ○ Audioscripts and Answer Keys
    ○ "Can-Do" Self-Assessment Charts
    ○ Conversation and Discussion Activator Video Scripts
    ○ Oral Progress Assessment Charts
    ○ Reading Speed Calculator
  – Summit TV Video Program
    ○ Activity Worksheets
    ○ Teaching Notes
    ○ Video Scripts

REVIEW

A ▶ 2:14 Listen to each person. Then listen again to summarize each person's reason for being frustrated. Write statements with **no matter**.

Felix Tan
No matter how many times Felix tells his boss he needs more time to finish the project, his boss ignores him.

Robert Reston
No matter what he tries to do to lower his blood pressure, it stays high.

Eva García
No matter how many stores she goes to, she can't find the perfect gift for her husband's 30th birthday.

B Complete each statement with **no matter** and **who, whom, when, what time, what, where,** or **how**.
1. I always get up at seven in the morning, **no matter [what time/when]** I go to bed.
2. My daughter won't go to bed early, **no matter how** many times I tell her to.
3. **No matter what** the weather is like, we're going!
4. **No matter how** few calories you eat, it's hard to lose weight.
5. No one knew which gate the train was leaving from, **no matter [who/whom]** we asked.
6. **No matter where** you leave from, the trip still takes two hours.

C Complete each statement with the correct word.
1. The thunder was (**so**/ such) loud that we couldn't sleep.
2. The kids ate (**so much**/ such many) candy that they got sick.
3. There was (so /**such**) bad turbulence that the passengers couldn't leave their seats.
4. The store has (**so many**/ so much) brands of painkillers that I don't know which to buy.
5. Lyn is having (so /**such a**) good time at the party that she doesn't want to go home.
6. He learned Italian (**so**/ such) quickly that he took the exam after only two months.

D Replace each underlined word with a word that has a similar meaning and the correct part of speech.
1. Many people don't think they are <u>courageous</u> until they are faced with an emergency.
   a fearlessly   **b brave**   c heroism
2. Few people are <u>fearless</u> enough to fight an adult bear.
   a courageous   b confidence   c willing
3. <u>Bravery</u>, especially in dangerous situations, is a rare quality.
   a Courageous   **b Heroism**   c Heroically

E On a separate sheet of paper, create a two-line conversation for each pair of expressions. Use **no matter** and your own ideas.
1. I'm fed up. / Hang in there.
2. I just can't take it anymore. / Don't let it get you down.
3. I've had it. / That must be discouraging.
4. I give up. / Don't let it get you down.
5. I'm fed up. / I know what you mean.

A: I'm fed up. No matter how much exercise I do, I still look like a weakling!
B: Hang in there. It takes time to see results.

TEST-TAKING SKILLS BOOSTER p. 153

Web Project: Heroes
www.english.com/summit3e

UNIT 4

Getting Along with Others

COMMUNICATION GOALS
1. Discuss how to overcome shortcomings
2. Acknowledge inconsiderate behavior
3. Explain how you handle anger
4. Explore the qualities of friendship

PREVIEW

A **FRAME YOUR IDEAS** Read about some common shortcomings. Rate each person according to the scale:

A = Sounds just like me!
B = Sounds a bit like me.
C = Doesn't sound like me at all!

What's your biggest shortcoming?

Martin ☐
"I wish I weren't so disorganized. My bedroom's always a mess. I can't remember where I've put anything. The way I'm doing things is just not working for me."

Lena ☐
"You know what my problem is? I'm a procrastinator! I'm always putting things off and waiting till the last minute to do things. Then I go into a panic worrying about whether or not I'll be able to finish on time."

Ricardo ☐
"I admit I'm a bit oversensitive. I tend to overreact to things people say to me—I think I'm being criticized when people are just trying to help. It really doesn't take much to get me upset about stuff."

Paul ☐
"I'm sure I'm too hot-tempered. I get angry way too easily. It doesn't take much to set me off. But I've been trying to change that."

Sophie ☐
"I know I'm too negative. I'm always focusing on the bad rather than the good. And I'm way too critical of others. My husband, though, is just the opposite!"

Jean ☐
"My husband says I'm too controlling—and he's probably right. I complain when he doesn't do things *my* way. I'm sure it drives him crazy!"

Trevor ☐
"My biggest shortcoming is that I'm a perfectionist. No matter what I do, I'm not satisfied. I just don't think it's good enough. My attitude really gets in my way."

B ▶ 2:15 **VOCABULARY** **SHORTCOMINGS** Listen and repeat.

be disorganized
be a procrastinator
be oversensitive
be hot-tempered
be negative
be controlling
be a perfectionist

C **PAIR WORK** Tell your partner how you are—or aren't—like the people in Exercise A. What are your biggest shortcomings?

> ❝ One of my biggest shortcomings is that I'm a perfectionist. I'd like to invite friends for dinner at my house, but I never do—because I don't think I cook well enough. ❞

D **DISCUSSION** Discuss these questions.

1. Do any of the people above sound like someone you know? In what ways?
2. Can you think of any other common shortcomings people have? What are they?

UNIT 4
Getting Along with Others

PREVIEW

A FRAME YOUR IDEAS

Suggested teaching time:	10–15 minutes	Your actual teaching time:

- To warm up, write the word *shortcoming* on the board. Elicit that a shortcoming is a fault or weakness that makes someone or something less successful or effective than may be desired. Invite students to brainstorm different shortcomings on the board. Students can list adjectives or nouns. (Possible answers: lazy, perfectionist, mean, disorganized)
- Tell students that they will read about common shortcomings individually. Bring students' attention to the ratings on the right and read them. Tell students they will rate each person's comment A, B, or C.

B ▶ 2:15 VOCABULARY

Suggested teaching time:	5 minutes	Your actual teaching time:

- Have students look at the list of shortcomings. Ask *Which of these words are nouns?* Hint to students that nouns have *a* before them. (procrastinator, perfectionist) *Which of these words are adjectives?* (disorganized, hot-tempered, controlling, negative, oversensitive)
- Have students listen.
- Then have them listen and repeat.

Option: [+5 minutes] Ask students to look back at the quotes to help them write definitions for each shortcoming in the vocabulary list.

- disorganized: not arranged in order, a mess
- a procrastinator: a person who puts things off and waits till the last minute to do things
- oversensitive: tending to overreact to things people say
- hot-tempered: getting angry much too easily
- negative: always focusing on the bad
- controlling: wanting other people to always do things one's own way
- a perfectionist: never satisfied, nothing is good enough

C PAIR WORK

Suggested teaching time:	5 minutes	Your actual teaching time:

- Ask a student to read the sample answer. Ask *Who is this person like?* (Trevor) Ask *Who rated Trevor with an A or a B?* Invite students to share stories of how they are perfectionists.
- In pairs, have students discuss how they compare and contrast with the people in Exercise A.

Option: [+5 minutes] Poll the class. Tell students to raise their hand for the shortcoming or shortcomings they rated A in the quiz (Just like me!). Ask *Who here is disorganized like Martin? A procrastinator like Lena? Oversensitive like Ricardo? Too hot-tempered like Paul? Too negative like Sophie? Too controlling like Jean? A perfectionist like Trevor?* On the board, write the shortcomings and numbers of students who raised their hand for each one.

D DISCUSSION

Suggested teaching time:	5 minutes	Your actual teaching time:

- Have students discuss the questions in small groups.
- Bring the class together. On the board, write *shortcomings* and have students come to the board to list words they came up with.

Challenge: [+5 minutes] Bring students' attention to the first line in Martin's quote. On the board write, *He wishes he were . . .* Have students complete the sentence about Martin. (more organized) Then in pairs, have students think up ways to complete the sentence for the various people. Encourage students to look up words that mean the opposite—not just write the negative form of the words. (Possible answers: Lena wishes she organized her time better. Ricardo wishes he were tougher. Paul wishes he could let things go more easily. Sophie wishes she were more positive. Jean wishes she were more laid back. Trevor wishes he weren't so hard on himself.)

E ▶ 2:16 SPOTLIGHT

Suggested teaching time:	10–15 minutes	Your actual teaching time:

- Ask students to look at the photo. Read the direction line and explain that these people are two colleagues at a workplace.
- Have students read and listen to the conversation.
- To check comprehension, ask: *What are Mike and Jaya talking about?* (how their colleague Sam got angry at Rob at a status meeting) *Who at this workplace is a procrastinator?* (Rob) *What was Rob's reaction to Sam's outburst?* (He took it well.) *Why does Mike think that Sam had his outburst?* (because he's been under pressure from his boss) *How does Sam's behavior affect the workplace?* (Negatively; people never know what to expect from him, and this creates an awkward feeling.)

Challenge: [+5 minutes] Focus on Jaya's second line: *That's awful! You know, even if Rob starts things late, he always finishes on time. I don't see what the big deal is.* On the board, write *Do you think it is OK to be a procrastinator at work, as long as you finish on time? Why? Why not? How does procrastination affect other people in a workplace or a team?* Have students discuss in groups.

F UNDERSTAND IDIOMS AND EXPRESSIONS

Suggested teaching time:	5–10 minutes	Your actual teaching time:

- Give students a few minutes to focus on the highlighted expressions in the conversation and think about each one in context.
- To model the activity, invite a volunteer to read the first idiom. Ask students to find the idiom in Exercise E. Call on another volunteer to read Mike's part where he uses the idiom. Then read the choices and elicit the answer.
- Have students work in pairs to complete the rest of the exercise. Encourage them to refer to the conversation to help them determine the correct answer. Circulate and assist as needed.

LANGUAGE NOTE *To make an example out of someone* means to bring attention to bad results of incorrect behavior; *to go overboard* means to do or say something that is too extreme for a particular situation; *hot-tempered* means having a tendency to get angry easily.

Option: [+5 minutes] Have students role-play the conversation in pairs. Then have them role-play it again, replacing the expressions with the meanings from the exercise. Remind students to make necessary changes. For example: *Sam lost his cool again at the status meeting!* → *Sam got angry again at the status meeting!*

Challenge: [+5 minutes] Divide the class into pairs and assign each pair several idioms or expressions. Have students create short dialogues using the idioms or expressions correctly.

G THINK AND EXPLAIN

Suggested teaching time:	5 minutes	Your actual teaching time:

- Have students discuss the questions in pairs. Then bring the class together to go over the answers.
- Focus on the last question. Call on students for their answers. Then ask *If you were Rob, would you have been upset? Why? Why not?* (Possible answers: Yes, I would have. I hate it when people make a big issue out of something small. / No, I wouldn't have. I am pretty easy-going.)

Challenge: [+5 minutes] Divide students into groups of 4 or 5 and ask them to role-play the status meeting. Write necessary roles on the board: *Sam, Rob, Mike, Employee(s)*. Have groups reread the conversation in Exercise E and choose roles. Remind students that Sam has to get angry at Rob, who is procrastinating on a project. Rob is an easy-going individual, unaffected by Sam's overboard behavior. Mike, and the other employee(s) (depending how many people are in the group), just observe, seeming uncomfortable, clearly affected by the unpleasant exchange. Invite groups to present the role-play to the class.

SPEAKING GROUP WORK

Suggested teaching time:	5 minutes	Your actual teaching time:

- Ask a volunteer to read the model answer. Ask *Do you agree that being hot-tempered causes the most problems?*
- In groups, have students look at the list of shortcomings listed in Exercise B on page 38. Have students share which shortcomings they think cause the most problems.

Option: [+5 minutes] In pairs, have students rank the shortcomings from least to most problematic. Tell students to support their ideas with experiences from their lives and the lives of people they know. Then have pairs share their rankings.

Challenge: [+5 minutes] Invite students to imagine that rather than being laid back and taking Mike's behavior pretty well, Rob is an overly sensitive individual. How might the status meeting have turned out differently? Call on volunteers to speculate. (Possible answers: If Rob were overly sensitive, he likely would have become offended or argued back, Sam could have gotten more enraged and he could have fired Rob.)

E ▶ 2:16 **SPOTLIGHT** Read and listen to a conversation between two colleagues. Notice the spotlighted language.

> **ENGLISH FOR TODAY'S WORLD**
> Understand a variety of accents.
> Mike = American English (standard)
> Jaya = Hindi

Mike: Wait till you hear this ... Sam lost his cool again at the status meeting!
Jaya: Oh, please. He's always angry about something. So what set him off this time?
Mike: You know how Rob always waits till the last minute to do the sales report? Well, Sam made a big issue out of it. When Rob tried to defend himself, Sam told him off—in front of *everyone*.
Jaya: That's awful! You know, even if Rob starts things late, he always finishes on time. I don't see what the big deal is.
Mike: But you know Sam. If there's anything he hates, it's procrastination. I'm sure he wanted to make an example out of Rob.
Jaya: Well, it sounds like he went overboard. He could have just brought it up privately with Rob after the meeting.
Mike: Good point. But, all things considered, Rob took it pretty well. He knows Sam's just hot-tempered.
Jaya: If only he'd just stop and think first before having one of his outbursts! Instead, everyone always has to walk on eggshells wondering who's going to be next.
Mike: I agree. Between you and me, I think Sam's been under a lot of pressure lately from *his* boss. But that's no excuse to take it out on someone else.
Jaya: That's right. It must have been hard for everyone at the meeting to just pick up the pieces afterwards and go on as if nothing had happened. I'll bet it was really awkward.
Mike: Totally. But it's Sam who should feel awkward. What bothers me the most is that he has no clue how he affects other people.

F **UNDERSTAND IDIOMS AND EXPRESSIONS** Find these expressions in Spotlight. Complete each statement.

1 If you "lose your cool," you ....
   (a) get angry   **b** are worried

2 If something "sets you off," it ....
   (a) makes you angry   **b** relaxes you

3 If someone "makes a big issue out of" something, he or she ...... it.
   a enjoys talking about
   (b) calls too much attention to

4 If you "tell someone off," you are expressing your ...... to that person about his or her behavior.
   (a) anger   **b** appreciation

5 If something bothers you and you "bring it up" with someone, you want to ....
   (a) discuss it   **b** avoid discussing it

6 If someone gets angry at you and you "take it well," you are ...... by it.
   (a) not very affected **b** very affected

7 If you "walk on eggshells," you ...... make someone angry.
   a try to   **(b)** are careful not to

8 If you feel stressed and "take it out on" a friend, you might need to apologize to that person for ....
   a being stressed   **(b)** acting angry

9 If you try to "pick up the pieces" after an argument, you try to ....
   (a) re-establish a friendly atmosphere
   b understand someone's point of view

G **THINK AND EXPLAIN** With a partner, discuss the questions and explain your answers. *Answers will vary but may include the following:*

1 Why does Jaya think the other people at the meeting must have felt uncomfortable?
   Jaya has witnessed Sam's outbreaks before. She imagines that after seeing Sam yell at Rob, it could not have been easy to have
2 Why do you think Rob wasn't upset about the situation? the meeting continue normally.
   Rob seems very easygoing. He knows that Sam is hot-tempered, so he didn't take the attack personally.

SPEAKING **GROUP WORK** Which of the shortcomings from page 38 do you think cause the greatest problems for people? Discuss the consequences.

> ❝ In my opinion, being hot-tempered causes the most problems. Once you've gone overboard, it's hard to pick up the pieces. ❞

LESSON 1

GOAL Discuss how to overcome shortcomings

A ▶ 2:17 **GRAMMAR SPOTLIGHT** Read about the workshops. Notice the spotlighted grammar.

SELF-HELP FOR THE SELF-CRITICAL
Practical workshops to help you reach your goals!

1 GET ORGANIZED NOW
Tired of being so disorganized? Is it hard to find things **even if you've filed them away properly**? Have papers been piling up on your desk **whether or not you've had time to go through them**? Take the bull by the horns and discover how getting organized can help you increase your productivity today.

2 STOP TRYING TO CONTROL OTHERS
Do you drive people crazy by constantly supervising what they are doing? Does this sound like you: "**Only if things are done my way** will things get done right!" Let's face it—something's got to change. **Otherwise**, no one's ever going to want to work with you! Letting go of control is easier than you think.

3 END NEGATIVE THINKING NOW
Is your negative attitude interfering with your goals in life? Achieving your goals will be possible **only if you make a decision to change your outlook today**. This workshop will move you from the negative to the positive on a journey that will change your life.

4 SAY GOOD-BYE TO PROCRASTINATION
Have you been putting off till tomorrow what you could have done today? **Unless you're the type who says "I'll never change,"** you too can learn to stop procrastinating today. Learn easy strategies for using your time more efficiently than ever.

B PAIR WORK Do you think people can really overcome their shortcomings? Why or why not? Which of the workshops would you personally find the most useful? Explain.

C GRAMMAR ADVERB CLAUSES OF CONDITION

Use <u>even if</u> or <u>whether or not</u> in an adverb clause to express the fact that no matter what the condition, there is no way to affect or change an event or situation.

Even if I have plenty of time to finish a project, I still wait till the last minute to begin.
(= No matter what, I wait till the last minute.)
She would have been late for the meeting **even if she had set her alarm**.
(= No matter what, she would have been late.)
Whether or not anyone says anything to her about it, Kyla's desk is always a disorganized mess.
(= No matter what, her desk is always a mess.)
We would have been uncomfortable at the meeting **whether or not he had lost his cool**.
(= No matter what, we would have been uncomfortable.)

Use <u>only if</u> to express the fact that a certain condition is necessary in order for something to happen or to be true. If the adverb clause comes first, invert the subject and verb (or auxiliary) in the independent clause and do not use a comma.

Nina will be happy at her job **only if she learns to say no to her boss**. OR
Only if Nina learns to say no to her boss **will she** be happy at her job.

Use <u>unless</u> to express the consequence of an action or lack of action. (Note: <u>unless</u> = <u>if</u> ... <u>not</u>)
Unless he writes himself a note, he'll forget to pay his bills.
(= If he doesn't write himself a note, he will forget to pay his bills.)
We told him we wouldn't come to the meeting **unless he apologized for his outburst**.
(= We told him we wouldn't come to the meeting if he didn't apologize.)

Note: You can also use the transition word <u>Otherwise</u> at the beginning of a sentence to express the consequences of an action or a lack of action.
He needs to write himself a note. **Otherwise**, he'll forget to pay his bills.
I always set my alarm for 7:00 A.M. on weekdays. **Otherwise**, I'm late for school.

> **Remember:** The unreal conditional with <u>if only</u> expresses a wish for a particular condition (or a strong regret).
> **If only I were more organized**, I'd get a lot more done.
> (= I wish I were OR I regret that I'm not)

GRAMMAR BOOSTER p. 133
More conjunctions and transitions

LESSON 1

GOAL Discuss how to overcome shortcomings

A ▶ 2:17 GRAMMAR SPOTLIGHT

| Suggested teaching time: | 5 minutes | Your actual teaching time: |

- Write the prefix *self-* on the board. Elicit that this means relating to yourself. Have students look at the title of the article. Ask *What do you think self-help is?* (using your own efforts to deal with problems) *What do you think self-critical is?* (the ability to criticize oneself objectively)
- Focus on the line *Practical workshops to help you reach your goals!* Make sure students understand that a workshop is a meeting at which people try to improve their skills by discussing experiences and doing practical exercises. Have students skim the workshop titles and identify which shortcomings they address (1. being disorganized, 2. being too controlling, 3. being negative, 4. procrastinating)
- Have students listen to the article as they read along.
- Ask *Have you ever participated in a self-help workshop? Any other kind of workshop?* (Possible answers: business, writing, meditation) Invite students to share.

LANGUAGE NOTE Note that *self-critical* is an adjective; however, in the title of the article *the self-critical* is a noun, categorizing a group of people—people who are critical of themselves. *To take the bull by the horns* means to bravely and directly address a difficulty or a problem; *let's face it* means let's face the truth—it is used when saying something that might be difficult for a person to accept; *don't put off till tomorrow what you could do today* is a popular quote about avoiding procrastination.

B PAIR WORK

| Suggested teaching time: | 5 minutes | Your actual teaching time: |

- In pairs, have students discuss the questions.
- Bring the class together and ask *Do you think people can overcome shortcomings? Why? Why not?* (Possible answers: Yes, you can train yourself to be more organized or to plan your time better and not put things off. / I think some shortcomings you can't change. If you're negative, you can't become positive. It's in your genetic makeup.)

Option: [+5 minutes] Ask *What other workshops do you think you could benefit from? What type of workshop do you feel qualified to lead?* To help students provide more complete answers, ask *Are you particularly well organized or even-tempered? Do you have a positive outlook on life? Do you think you could help other people improve in those areas?*

C GRAMMAR

| Suggested teaching time: | 5–10 minutes | Your actual teaching time: |

- Tell students they will learn about three different types of adverb clauses of condition.
- Draw the chart below on the board. Don't write the text yet. Ask a volunteer to read the first explanation and example sentences. Point out how the clause can appear at the beginning or the end of the sentence. Then fill in the first row of the chart.

1.	even if . . . whether or not	no matter what the condition, there is no way to affect or change it
2.	only if	a certain condition is necessary for something to happen
3.	unless Otherwise . . .	consequence of an action or inaction (if not)

- Call on another volunteer to read the second explanation and example sentences. Bring students' attention to how the word order changes in the result clause when *only if* appears at the beginning of the sentence. Then fill in the second row of the chart on the board.
- Focus on the Remember note to differentiate clauses with *if only* as opposed to *only if* clauses.
- Have a student read the explanation about *unless* and the example sentences. Then fill in the third row of the chart on the board.
- Finally, read the note about *Otherwise* and add *Otherwise* to the explanation in 3, as demonstrated above.
- Leave the chart on the board for students to refer to while practicing the grammar in Exercises D and E on page 41.

Option: [+5 minutes] In pairs, have students look at the Grammar Spotlight at the top of page 40. Tell students to focus on each sentence and analyze it against the information in the chart. Model the first item: *In the first workshop, both examples indicate something is true, no matter what the condition.* Then have students analyze the rest. (For the second workshop, the sentence with *only if* indicates that a certain condition is necessary for something to happen; the sentence with *Otherwise* indicates the consequence of an action. For the third workshop, the sentence with *only if* indicates that a certain condition is necessary for something to happen. For the fourth workshop, the sentence with *unless* indicates the consequence of an action.)

⭐ 🖨 Inductive Grammar Activity

Option: GRAMMAR BOOSTER *(Teaching notes p. T133)*

D UNDERSTAND THE GRAMMAR

Suggested teaching time:	10–15 minutes	Your actual teaching time:

- If available, have students look at the chart from the grammar presentation on the board. Tell them that they can refer to it to help them complete the exercise.
- Model item 1. Ask *Which category does this sentence fit under?* (3) Ask *What is the consequence of not putting a reminder on the smart phone?* (I find it difficult to remember appointments.)
- Have students work in pairs to complete the exercise. Then bring the class together and go over the answers. If students have any problems, pose questions based on the information in the chart:
  2. Which sentence—a or b—indicates no matter what the condition? (a)
  3. Is a certain condition necessary for something to happen? (yes) Which sentence specifies a condition? (a)
  4. Which sentence—a or b—indicates no matter what the condition? (a)
  5. Which sentence—a or b—indicates a consequence of an action? (a)

⭐ 🖨 **Extra Grammar Exercises**

Option: PRONUNCIATION BOOSTER *(Teacher's notes p T145)*

🖨 **Pronunciation Pair Work**

E GRAMMAR PRACTICE

Suggested teaching time:	5 minutes	Your actual teaching time:

- Students can complete the exercise individually or in pairs.
- If they need guidance, tell them they can look up each answer choice on the chart to help them decide the correct answer. Circulate and assist as needed. Ask the following questions for each item as indicated: 1. Which word or phrase indicates no matter what the condition? (whether or not) 2. Which word or phrase indicates consequence of an action or inaction? (Unless) 3. Which word or phrase indicates that a certain condition is necessary for something to happen? (only if) 4. Which word or phrase indicates no matter what the condition? (even if) 5. Which word or phrase indicates consequence of an action? (Unless) 6. Which word or phrase indicates that a certain condition is necessary for something to happen? (Only if)
- Bring the class together and go over the answers.

NOW YOU CAN Discuss how to overcome shortcomings

A NOTEPADDING

Suggested teaching time:	5 minutes	Your actual teaching time:

- Ask a volunteer to read the model answer.
- Have students work individually to fill in the notepad, looking at page 38, choosing three shortcomings, and providing suggestions to overcome them.

B DISCUSSION ACTIVATOR

Suggested teaching time:	10–15 minutes	Your actual teaching time:

🎬 **Discussion Activator Video**

Note: You can print the script or you can view it on the video player on the ActiveTeach.

- Ask a student to read the model answer. Divide the class into pairs and have students use information from Exercise A, Notepadding, to give advice about shortcomings. Write the following words and phrases on the board to help students incorporate adverb clause conditions into the advice:

   Even if you . . .
   Whether or not . . .
   Only if . . .
   Unless
   . . . Otherwise

- If students need more guidance, rewrite the chart provided in the grammar presentation on the board or print it out from the ActiveTeach to help students:

1.	even if . . . whether or not	no matter what the condition, there is no way to affect or change it
2.	only if	a certain condition is necessary for something to happen
3.	unless Otherwise . . .	consequence of an action or inaction (if not)

Encourage the pairs to ask each other questions and provide details and examples. The goal is to say as much as you can about them.

For more support, play the Discussion Activator Video before students do this activity. After each video, ask if the students in the video included sufficient details.

🖨 **Graphic Organizer**

D UNDERSTAND THE GRAMMAR Choose the statement with the same meaning.

1 I find it difficult to remember my appointments unless I put a reminder on my smart phone.
   a) If I don't put a reminder on my smart phone, I find it difficult to remember my appointments.
   b) If I don't put a reminder on my smart phone, I don't find it difficult to remember my appointments.

2 Even if she tries not to be controlling, her friends still think she is.
   a) Her friends find her to be controlling, no matter what she does.
   b) Her friends find her to be controlling unless she tries not to be.

3 Only if he takes a workshop about procrastination will Martin stop putting things off.
   a) Unless Martin takes a workshop, he won't stop putting things off.
   b) Whether or not Martin takes a workshop, he won't stop putting things off.

4 Whether or not you apologize, some people always have a hard time picking up the pieces after you tell them off.
   a) It's always difficult to pick up the pieces after being told off, even if you receive an apology.
   b) It's never difficult to pick up the pieces after being told off if you receive an apology.

5 You should try not to overreact when your manager criticizes your work. Otherwise, you might lose your job.
   a) Unless you try to stop overreacting to your manager's criticisms, you might lose your job.
   b) No matter how you react to your manager's criticisms, you might lose your job.

E GRAMMAR PRACTICE Circle the correct way to complete each statement.

1 (**Whether or not**/ Unless) Bob is oversensitive, his friends still like him.
2 (Only if /**Unless**) Sal overreacts again at the meeting, I won't mention his negative attitude.
3 Katia loses her cool with her kids (**only if**/ if only) she's had a bad day at work.
4 Carl's colleagues enjoy working with him (**even if**/ unless) he's a bit hot-tempered.
5 (If only /**Unless**) she really goes overboard, I don't care that much if my wife tells me off.
6 (**Only if**/ Even if) she puts something off to the last minute does Stacey worry about what her boss will think.

> **PRONUNCIATION BOOSTER** p. 145
> Shifting emphatic stress

NOW YOU CAN Discuss how to overcome shortcomings

A NOTEPADDING Look at page 38 again and choose three of the people's shortcomings. On your notepad, suggest how to overcome each shortcoming.

What is the shortcoming?	Your suggestions for how to overcome it
1. Ricardo is oversensitive.	try not to overreact remember that most people just want to be helpful

What is the shortcoming?	Your suggestions for how to overcome it
1.	
2.	
3.	

B DISCUSSION ACTIVATOR Discuss the shortcomings on your notepads and other ways you think someone could overcome them. Use adverb clauses of condition. Say as much as you can.

> 66 Whether or not you have a good reason to be angry, you should try not to take it out on someone else. 99

LESSON 2

GOAL Acknowledge inconsiderate behavior

A GRAMMAR CLEFT SENTENCES: REVIEW AND EXPANSION

Cleft sentences with What

Remember: A cleft sentence emphasizes an action or a result. You can form a cleft sentence using a noun clause with **What** as the subject + a form of **be**. Be sure the form of **be** agrees with its complement.

> **What bothers me is** getting interrupted when I'm speaking.
> **What surprised me were** the many "thank you" e-mails I received.

Cleft sentences with **What** often have a subject complement that is a noun clause. If so, always use a singular form of **be**.

> What bothered me the most **was** (that) you didn't even apologize.
> What was surprising **was** (that) she had completely cleaned up her desk.
> What I mean **is** (that) I wish I hadn't lost my cool.
> What I'm trying to say **is** (that) I'm really sorry.

> **GRAMMAR BOOSTER** p. 134
> Cleft sentences: more on meaning and use

Cleft sentences with It

A cleft sentence with the impersonal **It** emphasizes a noun or noun phrase. Use a noun clause with **who** or **that**.

> Valerie decided to have a talk with her boss. → **It was Valerie who** decided to have a talk with her boss.
> Jack's outbursts make people uncomfortable. → **It's Jack's outbursts that** make people uncomfortable.

B NOTICE THE GRAMMAR Look at Spotlight on page 39.
Find and underline two types of cleft sentences in the last paragraph.
But it's Sam who should feel awkward. What bothers me the most is that he has no clue how he affects other people.

C ▶ 2:18 LISTEN TO ACTIVATE GRAMMAR Listen to the conversations.
Then listen again and complete each statement.

1 It was her …… that he wanted to bring up.
   ⓐ missing the meeting   b not finishing the project

2 What bothered him was that Simon …… .
   ⓐ lost his cool   b refused to apologize

3 It was his …… that made her decide to talk with him.
   a apologizing for his mistake   ⓑ interrupting her meeting

4 What's surprising to him is that the two women …… .
   a are such good friends   ⓑ had such a bad argument

5 It was his …… that upset her.
   ⓐ constant criticism   b refusing to listen to her

D GRAMMAR PRACTICE Combine each pair of sentences by writing a cleft sentence with **What** and a noun clause subject complement.

Example: People tell me I'm too controlling. That has always surprised me.
What has always surprised me is that people tell me I'm too controlling.

1 My boss always criticizes me. That makes me kind of angry.
   What makes me kind of angry is that my boss always criticizes me.

2 Most people tell lies to protect the ones they love. That fascinates me.
   What fascinates me is that most people tell lies to protect the ones they love.

3 Gary actually has a hard time saying no to people. That's surprising.
   What's surprising is that Gary actually has a hard time saying no to people.

LESSON 2

GOAL Acknowledge inconsiderate behavior

A GRAMMAR

Suggested teaching time:	5–10 minutes	Your actual teaching time:

- Ask a student to read the Remember note. Have students demonstrate that they know which part of each example sentence is the complement (getting interrupted when I'm speaking; the many "thank you" e-mails I received).
- Elicit the meaning of the first two examples from students. (What bothers me is getting interrupted when I'm speaking. = Getting interrupted when I'm speaking bothers me. / What surprised me were the many "thank you" e-mails I received. = The many "thank you" e-mails I received surprised me.)
- Call on a volunteer to read the explanation following the Remember note examples. Ask *What is the subject complement in each sentence?* Elicit the sentences as non-clefts. (That you didn't even apologize bothered me the most. That she had completely cleaned up her desk was surprising. That I wish I hadn't lost my cool is what I mean. That I'm really sorry is what I'm trying to say.)
- Ask a student to read the last explanation and example sentences. Study them side-by-side with the class. Reiterate that cleft sentences with *It* call attention to a noun or noun phrase. For example, who or what did, caused, or intended something. Point out that *It* in this situation is similar in meaning to calling attention with *In fact*. On the board write *In fact, Paul did it.* = *It was Paul who did it.*

Challenge: [+5 minutes] You may choose to mention another use of cleft sentences. When the main verb is other than *say, mean,* etc., we can precede *that* with *the fact*. For example, *What bothered me the most was the fact that you didn't even apologize.* This makes it clear why we don't use a plural form of *be*—because the complement is a singular noun, *the fact*.

Option: GRAMMAR BOOSTER *(Teaching notes p. T134)*

⭐ 🖨 Inductive Grammar Activity

B NOTICE THE GRAMMAR

Suggested teaching time:	5 minutes	Your actual teaching time:

- If students need hints finding the two examples, tell them that both appear in the last exchange of the Spotlight.
- Elicit the non-cleft direct sentence format. Write both forms on the board for comparison:

  1. *It's Sam who should feel awkward.*
     Sam should feel awkward.
  2. *What bothers me is that he has no clue how he affects other people.*
     That he has no clue how he affects other people is what bothers me.

Ask *How are these sentences different?* (1. In the first sentence, the emphasis is on the noun or noun phrase. 2. In the second sentence, the emphasis is on the action or a result.)

⭐ 🖨 Extra Grammar Exercises

C ▶ 2:18 LISTEN TO ACTIVATE GRAMMAR

Suggested teaching time:	5–10 minutes	Your actual teaching time:

- Have students listen to the conversations.
- Then have them listen again and complete each statement.
- Call on students to say each statement aloud.

LANGUAGE NOTE *It was my bad* is a common way to say *It was my mistake* in informal spoken English. *To barge in* means to enter somewhere rudely, or to rudely interrupt someone.

Option: [+5 minutes] Have students skim the completed sentences and identify cleft sentences with *What* (items 2 and 4); and with *It* (1, 3, and 5). Elicit the direct sentence format for each item:

1. He wanted to bring up her missing the meeting.
2. That Simon lost his cool bothered him.
3. His interrupting her meeting made her decide to talk to him.
4. That the two women had such a bad argument was surprising to him.
5. His constant criticism upset her.

Ask *How are these sentences different?* (In items 1, 3, and 5 the emphasis is no longer on the noun or noun phrase; In items 2 and 4 the emphasis is no longer on the action or a result.)

D GRAMMAR PRACTICE

Suggested teaching time:	5 minutes	Your actual teaching time:

- Focus on the model. Ask *What is the subject in the cleft sentence?* (What has always surprised me) *What is the complement?* (that people tell me I'm too controlling) *What form of be is used?* (is)
- Have students complete the exercise individually. Circulate and assist as needed. Make sure *What* becomes the subject in the sentence students write for each exercise item. Guide students to change the first sentence in each item into a noun clause with *that*. Make sure *That* from the second sentence in each exercise item is dropped.

UNIT 4 LESSON 2 T42

E GRAMMAR PRACTICE

| Suggested teaching time: | 5 minutes | Your actual teaching time: |

- Focus on the example. Ask *What does It's emphasize?* (the way she talks to people) Ask *What must follow?* (a noun clause with *that*)
- Have students complete the exercise individually. Circulate and assist as needed. Make sure students introduce the underlined noun phrase with *It's*. Guide them to change the second part of the sentences into a noun clause with *that*.

Challenge: [+5 minutes] Call on students to change the cleft sentences with *It's* to cleft sentences with *What*. Remind students that the emphasis will be on the result. Focus on the example sentence *It's the way she talks to people that's so offensive.* On the board, write *What's . . .* and call on a student to complete the sentence. (. . . so offensive is the way she talks to people.) Call on volunteers to restate the remaining sentences, or have students write them. For items 1 and 3, where names are mentioned, tell students to first use the person's name in the sentence and then the pronoun. (1. What prevents Nancy from accepting any suggestions is her negative attitude. 2. What can give you some ideas for getting more organized is the final workshop. 3. What makes me want to avoid Bill is his being so hot tempered. 4. What hurt my feelings was the way you spoke to me this morning. 5. What was so surprising was his lying about what happened.)

NOW YOU CAN Acknowledge inconsiderate behavior

A ▶ 2:19 CONVERSATION SPOTLIGHT

| Suggested teaching time: | 5 minutes | Your actual teaching time: |

> These conversation strategies are implicit in the model:
> - Use *there's something I need to bring up* to gently introduce an issue you want to discuss with someone.
> - Use *I didn't realize that* to indicate ignorance on a topic.
> - Use *I didn't mean to* to follow up an apology.
> - Use *On the contrary, I can see your point* to insist that you appreciate an observation having been made about something.

- Have students read and listen to the conversation.
- To check comprehension, ask *What inconsiderate behavior is Scott addressing?* (Nancy interrupted him during a meeting.) *What is Nancy's response to Scott's observation?* (She apologizes.) *Why does Scott apologize for bringing the issue up?* (He doesn't want to make a big deal out of it.) *How does the conversation end?* (Nancy thanks Scott.)

B ▶ 2:20 RHYTHM AND INTONATION

| Suggested teaching time: | 5 minutes | Your actual teaching time: |

- Have students repeat chorally. Make sure they:
  ○ stress *something* in *There's something I need to bring up.* (line 1)
  ○ use falling intonation for *What's wrong?* (line 2)
  ○ use emphatic stress on *I didn't realize that!* (line 7)
  ○ stress *so* in *I'm so sorry.* (line 7)

C CONVERSATION ACTIVATOR

| Suggested teaching time: | 10–15 minutes | Your actual teaching time: |

😀 **Conversation Activator Video**

Note: You can print the script or you can view it on the video player on the ActiveTeach.

- Divide the class into pairs. Instruct students that they will use the model in Exercise A, Conversation Spotlight, to role-play their own conversation with a partner.
- Ask a volunteer to read the words in the Some possible problems box. Encourage students to use this list to help them choose a topic.
- Reinforce the use of the spotlighted conversation strategies. For example, *I didn't realize that; I didn't mean to; I can see your point.*
- Bring students' attention to the Don't Stop! note. Ask a volunteer to read the bullet points. Explain that students should continue talking after they have covered the points in the original Conversation Spotlight.
- Tell students to change roles, so each student gets a chance to play A and B.

For more support, play the Conversation Activator Video before students do this activity themselves. After the video, ask students how the model has been changed by the actors.

⭐🖨 **Conversation Activator: Speaking Booster**

4 My manager and I get along really well. That's nice.
   What's nice is that my manager and I get along really well.

5 It's been great working with you. That's what I've always wanted to tell you.
   What I've always wanted to tell you is that it's been great working with you.

6 I wish you would try to control your anger. That's what I mean.
   What I mean is that I wish you would try to control your anger.

E GRAMMAR PRACTICE Write cleft sentences with It, emphasizing the underlined noun phrase.

Example: The way she talks to people is so offensive.
   It's the way she talks to people that's so offensive.

1 Nancy's negative attitude prevents her from accepting any suggestions.
   It's Nancy's negative attitude that prevents her from accepting any suggestions.

2 The final workshop can give you some ideas for getting more organized.
   It's the final workshop that can give you some ideas for getting more organized.

3 Bill's being so hot-tempered makes me want to avoid him.
   It's Bill's being so hot-tempered that makes me want to avoid him.

4 The way you spoke to me this morning hurt my feelings.
   It's the way you spoke to me this morning that hurt my feelings.

5 His lying about what happened was so surprising.
   It's his lying about what happened that was so surprising.

NOW YOU CAN   Acknowledge inconsiderate behavior

A ▶ 2:19 CONVERSATION SPOTLIGHT Read and listen. Notice the spotlighted conversation strategies.

A: Nancy, there's something I need to bring up.
B: Of course, Scott. What's wrong?
A: Well, the other day at the meeting, I was in the middle of making a point and you interrupted me. What really bothered me was that you didn't even let me finish my thought.
B: I didn't realize that! I'm so sorry. I didn't mean to be rude.
A: Well, I don't want to make an issue out of it, but it's been bugging me. I hope you don't mind my pointing it out.
B: On the contrary. I can see your point. Thanks for saying something.

B ▶ 2:20 RHYTHM AND INTONATION Listen again and repeat. Then practice the conversation with a partner.

C CONVERSATION ACTIVATOR Create a similar conversation, acknowledging someone's criticism. Start like this: *There's something I need to bring up.* Be sure to change roles and then partners.

Some possible problems
being late
missing a meeting
losing one's cool
being too critical
not apologizing

DON'T STOP!
- Explain the problem in greater detail and how you felt about it.
- Offer to make up for it.
- Say as much as you can.

LESSON 3

GOAL Explain how you handle anger

A ▶ 2:21 **LISTENING WARM-UP** **VOCABULARY** **EXPRESSING AND CONTROLLING ANGER**
Read and listen. Then listen again and repeat.

"I lost my temper."

- lose one's temper
- have a fit
- hit the roof
- go ballistic
- blow one's top

got really angry

"When I'm angry about something, I prefer to just hold it in."

hold it in / **keep it inside** avoid expressing your feelings

"When I lose my cool, I take a deep breath and try to calm down."

calm down become quieter and more relaxed

"When someone tells me off, I just let it go."

let it go / **shrug it off** decide not to be bothered by something

"Running helps me let off steam when I'm feeling angry about something."

let off steam get rid of your anger in a way that does not harm anyone; for example, by doing something active

"When I'm upset about something, venting about it with a friend usually calms me down."

vent talk with someone you trust in order to express your anger at someone else

B **PERSONALIZE THE VOCABULARY** Use the expressions to tell about a time when you controlled your anger or lost control of it. What do you usually do to let off steam? Is there someone in particular who you can vent to when you're angry?

C ▶ 2:22 **LISTEN TO SUMMARIZE THE MAIN IDEA** Listen to the interviews. On a separate sheet of paper, write a summary in one or two sentences about the purpose of the interview.
See page T44 for answers.

D ▶ 2:23 **LISTEN TO INFER INFORMATION** Listen again and check the correct statements.

	Joseph would …	Celina would …
1 If he or she were angry with his or her boss …	☐ make an issue out of it. ☐ say what's on his mind. ☑ hold his feelings in.	☐ let off steam. ☑ say what's on her mind. ☐ hold her feelings in.
2 If he or she were angry with a friend or colleague …	☐ take it out on someone else. ☑ probably just shrug it off. ☐ probably lose his temper.	☐ take it out on someone else. ☐ probably just shrug it off. ☑ probably not hold it in.
3 If he or she were angry with a complete stranger …	☑ probably let it go. ☐ probably lose his temper. ☐ take it out on someone else.	☐ probably let it go. ☑ probably say what's on her mind. ☐ take it out on someone else.

44 UNIT 4

LESSON 3

GOAL Explain how you handle anger

A ▶ 2:21 LISTENING WARM-UP

Suggested teaching time:	10–15 minutes	Your actual teaching time:

- To introduce the topic, ask *What makes you angry? How do you handle your anger?* On the board, write the answers students give to the latter question.
- Call on volunteers to read the quotes and related expressions picture by picture.
- Clarify the meaning of any expressions with additional examples. Point out that the expressions *hold it in, keep it inside, let it go,* and *shrug it off* always use the singular *it,* even when referring to something plural. For example, *He said some pretty insulting things to me, but I just decided to let it* [referring to *some pretty insulting things*] *go.*
- Then have students read and listen to the expressions.
- Have them listen again and repeat.
- Refer to student answers on the board from the beginning of this exercise. Ask *Which ways of handling anger are listed both on the board and in the vocabulary lesson on the Student's Book page?*

LANGUAGE NOTE *Hot-tempered* means having a tendency to get angry easily; *to lose one's cool* means to suddenly become very angry; *to tell someone off* means to attack him or her verbally; *to lose one's temper* means to suddenly become very angry that you cannot control yourself; *to have / throw a fit* means to be very angry or shocked; *to hit the roof* means to suddenly become very angry; *to go ballistic* means to suddenly become irrationally angry—the word *ballistic* refers to a missile launching; *to blow one's top* means to lose one's temper.

Option: [+5 minutes] Have students read the quotes again. Then ask volunteers which one they would be likely to say themselves. On the board, write:

Which do you think is the best / worst way to handle anger? Why?

Do you think we can control how we handle anger?

Have students discuss in pairs or small groups. Then bring the class together and have students share.

⭐ 🖨 Vocabulary-Building Strategies

B PERSONALIZE THE VOCABULARY

Suggested teaching time:	5 minutes	Your actual teaching time:

- In pairs or small groups, have students talk about experiences they have had controlling their anger or losing control of it. Tell students to refer to the Vocabulary in Exercise A to help as they answer the questions. Circulate and listen for correct use.
- Bring the class together and have students share stories. After each story, ask the class *Do you think there are other ways people might react in this situation? How would you react?*

Option: [+5 minutes] Ask *Do you think you can retrain yourself to handle anger differently? Or is this just the way you are?*

⭐ 🖨 Listening Strategies

C ▶ 2:22 LISTEN TO SUMMARIZE THE MAIN IDEA

Suggested teaching time:	10–15 minutes	Your actual teaching time:

- Pre-listening: Explain that students will listen to the interview once. Tell them to listen for the main idea.
- Have students listen. If necessary, let them listen again to the interviewer's introduction (*Good evening and welcome...*). Have them briefly summarize the purpose of the interview. Then have students compare answers with a partner.

Option: [+5 minutes] Ask *Do you think the purpose of the interview is achieved? Was it a successful discussion of cultural differences in how people express anger?*

Answer to Exercise C

Answers will vary but may include the following:

The purpose of the interview is to demonstrate how people from different cultures express anger. It demonstrates how in Chinese culture people are less inclined to lose their cool publicly, while in Argentina don't usually hold things in.

D ▶ 2:23 LISTEN TO INFER INFORMATION

Suggested teaching time:	5 minutes	Your actual teaching time:

- Pre-listening: Refer students to the Vocabulary in Exercise A to review the meanings of the expressions related to anger.
- First listening: Have students listen to the interview with their books closed.
- Second listening: Ask students to read the chart. Review any expressions as needed. Have them listen to the interview again and complete the exercise. Allow students to listen again to check their answers.
- Go over the answers as a class.
- Then ask *What did you learn about the way people in Taiwan express anger?* (Possible answers: don't express anger publicly; not likely to express anger at an authority figure; for the most part people tend to let things go; outbursts of anger not likely; road rage, however, might set someone off) *What did you learn about the way people in Argentina express anger?* (Possible answers: express anger publicly, don't hold things in, will challenge an authority figure or argue with a friend or stranger)

LANGUAGE NOTE *Road rage* refers to aggressive and often violent behavior that is sometimes displayed by one driver toward other driver(s) on the roadway.

UNIT 4 LESSON 3 T44

NOW YOU CAN Explain how you handle anger

A FRAME YOUR IDEAS

Suggested teaching time:	10–15 minutes	Your actual teaching time:

- Ask a volunteer to read the first situation. Then read the question in the heading, *How would you handle your anger?* Elicit an answer and write it on the board. Make sure the student uses *would* + base form of verb. (Possible answer: I would probably hold it in.) Elicit additional answers from students.
- Call on volunteers to read the remaining situations. Depending on the available time and the needs of your class, you may want to assign three or four situations for pairs to discuss or have pairs choose themselves.
- Then have pairs do the activity. Point out that students can also respond *I wouldn't mind* to any of these situations.
- Bring the class together and call on students to describe how they would handle their anger in each situation. Model the first item on the board if necessary. For example, *If a friend arrived really late to meet me for a movie, I would probably say something, but I wouldn't get mad.*
- Then ask individual students *Which situation would make you the angriest? Why? Which situation would bother you the least? Why?*

B DISCUSSION

Suggested teaching time:	5 minutes	Your actual teaching time:

- Ask a student to read the expressions in the Recycle This Language box. Review meaning as needed.
- In groups or as a class, have students answer the question and explain their behavior. Encourage them to use expressions from the Recycle This Language box.

Option: [+5 minutes] On the board, write *Are there times you don't express your anger?* Review expressions for not expressing anger (*hold it back, keep it in, let it go, shrug it off*). Have students give specific examples of situations in which they don't express anger and explain why. Invite other students to respond. For example, *I couldn't hold back if someone insulted me like that. I would blow my top!*

Option: [+5 minutes] Have students use their answers to the following questions as a basis for class discussion: *Do you know someone who gets angry often? How does this person behave when angry? How does getting angry often affect his or her life? Do you think people who get angry often are generally less happy than people who seldom get angry? What do you think is the best advice for a perpetually angry person?*

Challenge: [+5 minutes] Have students return to the catalogue of self-help workshops on page 40. Model a workshop description:

> *Learn to let it go!*
> *Are you angry all the time? Are you having problems getting along at work? Do you lose your temper with your kids a lot? Learn how to handle difficult situations without losing your cool. Our workshop will teach you tips on how to calm down, shrug things off, and let off steam.*

In pairs, have students make up a description for a workshop that would help people deal with anger. Encourage students to use the Vocabulary from Exercise A on page 44.

OPTIONAL WRITING [+15-20 minutes]

- In class or for homework, have students write their stories about getting angry. Encourage them to use the Vocabulary on page 33 and the expressions from the Recycle This Language box at the right.
- Collect students' work and provide feedback. Alternatively, students can exchange papers and review each other's work. If you choose the latter, encourage students to respond with how they would react if they were in such a situation, practicing conditional forms.

⭐ 🖨 **Discussion: Speaking Booster**

NOW YOU CAN Explain how you handle anger

A FRAME YOUR IDEAS Discuss each situation with a partner. How similar is your behavior to your partner's? Describe how you would express or control your anger. Use the Vocabulary in your discussion.

Situation	How would you handle your anger?
1 A friend arrives really late to meet you for a movie.	
2 You tell a friend something in confidence and he or she doesn't keep it a secret.	
3 A classmate or colleague says bad things about you to people you know.	
4 Someone tells you off in front of a group of other people.	
5 Another driver cuts you off while you are driving.	
6 Someone borrows something from you and doesn't return it.	
7 Your next-door neighbor always plays very loud music and has noisy late-night parties.	
8 (your own idea)	

B DISCUSSION Do you act the same way when you get angry with someone you know as you do with a stranger? Explain.

OPTIONAL WRITING Write a true story about something that made you angry. What happened? How did you respond? Use the Vocabulary.

RECYCLE THIS LANGUAGE
- lose one's cool
- set someone off
- make a big issue out of something
- tell someone off
- take it out on someone
- mess up big time
- take it [well / badly]
- Even if ...
- Whether or not ...
- Only if ...
- Unless ...
- Otherwise, ...

45

LESSON 4

GOAL Explore the qualities of friendship

A **READING WARM-UP** How do friendships among men differ from friendships among women? How are they similar?

B ▶ 2:24 **READING** Read the article. Which qualities of friendship do you think are the most important?
See page T46 for answers.

FRIENDS THROUGH THICK AND THIN

What makes friendships stand the test of time? We interviewed 100 men and women, and here is what they had to say:

1. Friends share the good times
You build great memories together. There's nothing like having a friend around to enjoy the best moments of your life with you—graduation, your first rock concert, watching the World Cup, your wedding, and so on. You probably share a similar sense of humor and you can count on your friends to laugh at your jokes—even when they're dumb jokes. Most importantly, good friends aren't jealous of your successes. On the contrary, they cheer you on, which contributes to your achievement. Good friends want only the best for you. Otherwise, what's the point?

2. Friends are there when times are tough
Like the song says, friendship is "like a bridge over troubled water." You can always count on your friends' support when you really need a helping hand. You shouldn't even have to ask. When you're feeling down or are upset about something, friends know what makes you tick—whether or not you want to talk about it. They are thoughtful when it comes to your well-being, and they will accommodate your needs, particularly when you need it the most.

3. Friends don't judge each other
We need our friends to be dependable—through thick and thin. Your friends accept you as you are, and they don't constantly try to change you. And they roll with the punches. They get it that inside you're a good person with flaws, and that those shortcomings are part of who you are. They know you make mistakes, and they forgive you for them, knowing you'll try to do better next time. And even when someone lets you have it when you make a mistake, friends still stick up for you, because friends are patient even when you're being difficult. Even if you and your friends disagree, you respect each other's opinions.

4. Friends are trustworthy
You need your friends to be totally loyal. Above all, you need to know that your secrets are safe with them. If there's a problem between you, a friend will come to you first and not gossip about you with others. We can always count on our friends to be honest with us when others aren't. We can trust them to stick by us no matter what. Friends don't keep things bottled up inside—if there's a problem, they work things out and move on.

Are there differences between what men and women expect in their friends? Among our interviewees, husbands claimed to understand what made their wives' female friendships tick, but many wives admitted that they wondered what in the world their husbands and their male friends saw in each other. According to the women, the quality of interaction between women friends was crucial to the longevity of their friendships. They valued being able to talk about their problems and feelings. However, for the men, it was mutual acceptance—being able to simply hang out together with no judgment. One man offered this view, "Female friends prefer to face each other, while male friends do things side by side." Nevertheless, it shouldn't be all that surprising that the men and women generally agreed that *all* truly good friends stick by each other through thick and thin.

C **UNDERSTAND MEANING FROM CONTEXT** Find the words and expressions in the article. Use the context of the article to complete each statement.

1 When a friendship can "stand the test of time," it …… as people change and get older.
   (a) continues
   b becomes more difficult

2 When you "count on people" to do something, you …… .
   a worry whether they will do it
   (b) feel sure they will do it

3 When someone "cheers you on," he or she is …… of your efforts.
   (a) supportive
   b critical

4 When "times are tough," things are …… .
   a going well
   (b) difficult

5 When you know what "makes someone tick," you understand …… .
   (a) how he or she thinks and responds to things
   b that he or she likes you

6 When people are friends "through thick and thin," their friendship …… .
   (a) can survive good times and bad times
   b may be in trouble

7 When someone "lets you have it," he or she …… .
   (a) is being very critical
   b is being very supportive

LESSON 4

GOAL Explore the qualities of friendship

A READING WARM-UP

| Suggested teaching time: | 5 minutes | Your actual teaching time: |

- On the board, write *friendships among men versus friendships among women*. Invite students to brainstorm ideas in pairs about how friendships among men differ from friendships among women and how they are similar.
- Then bring the class together and have students write their ideas on the board. (Possible answers: Female friendships are more emotional. Men don't need to spend as much time together. Female friendships have more drama.)
- Invite students to respond to the opinions on the board, especially if they disagree about something. Tell students to back up ideas with examples from their lives or the lives of people they know / have heard about.

B ▶ 2:24 READING

| Suggested teaching time: | 10–15 minutes | Your actual teaching time: |

- Ask a volunteer to read the title of the article aloud. Focus on the idiom *through thick and thin*. Elicit that this means in spite of problems or difficulties. The title FRIENDS THROUGH THICK AND THIN refers to people who remain friends no matter what.
- As students read and listen, tell them to underline information in the article that will help them answer the focus question in the direction line (Which qualities of friendship do you think are the most important?).
- Bring the class together. Have volunteers share their answers to the focus question. Poll the class by asking *Which quality of friendship do you think is the most important?* Invite students to share why the particular quality they mention is most important. (Possible answers: For me trustworthiness is key. I need to know I can trust someone to be his or her friend.)
- Focus on the next-to-last line of the article (One man offered this view, "Female friends prefer to face each other, while male friends do things side by side."). Ask *What do you think he means by this statement?* (Possible answer: Women focus on interaction in their friendships like chatting and sharing feelings, while men focus on shared action like watching a game, playing golf, and so on.) Invite students to share whether they agree with the man's statement.

LANGUAGE NOTE *To stand the test of time* means to remain strong or popular, or continue to work well after a long period of time; *to count on someone* means to rely on them.

CULTURE NOTE The song *A Bridge over Troubled Water* was released in 1970 by the American musical duo Simon and Garfunkel. It is about a friend providing comfort. The song became a huge hit, gaining popularity around the world.

Option: [+5 minutes] Have students write down the name of their closest friend at the top of the article. Then tell them to read the article again and underline any sentences that apply to this friend. For example, if they share a sense of humor, the student should underline that line in the first paragraph. When students finish, have them tell a partner about this friend, referring to the lines in the Student's Book. They can also say additional things about this friend.

Challenge: [+5 minutes] Invite students to look up the song and lyrics to *A Bridge over Troubled Water* online. Have them read and analyze the words. Ask *Are any of the qualities of friendship from the reading addressed in the words of the song?*

Answers for Activity B.

Answers will vary but may include the following:
In my opinion, a friend must be trustworthy and dependable.

⭐ 🖨 Reading Strategies

C UNDERSTAND MEANING FROM CONTEXT

| Suggested teaching time: | 5–10 minutes | Your actual teaching time: |

- Before doing the exercise, have students number the paragraphs in the article, 1 through 5.
- Have students work individually or in pairs to complete the exercise. Encourage them to utilize context to help determine the meanings.
- Circulate and assist as needed. If students need help finding the words and expressions, give them hints: the term for item 1 is in the subhead under the title of the article, item 2 is in paragraph 1, item 3 is in paragraph 1, item 4 is in the title over paragraph 2, item 5 is in paragraph 2, item 6 is in paragraph 3, item 7 is in paragraph 3.

Option: [+5 minutes] Have students reread the headings in the article. Ask *What is the most important quality to you personally in a friendship?* Ask students to rate any of the qualities and information mentioned in the article. Call on students to share.

Challenge: [+5 minutes] On the board, write *How tolerant are you?* Invite students to think back to difficulties they have faced in friendships and discuss how they have resolved them. Ask *Are you forgiving? Can you let things go and move on? Or if you've been wronged by a friend, do you stop being friends with the person?*

🖨 Extra Reading Comprehension Questions

D APPLY IDEAS

Suggested teaching time:	5 minutes	Your actual teaching time:

- Ask a volunteer to read the first situation and the model answer. Point out to students that they will be providing answers based on information in the article.
- Have students discuss the situations in pairs.
- Circulate and assist as needed. If students need help locating information in the article that corresponds with the situations, provide hints. The information in item 2 is in paragraph 1; item 3 is in paragraph 2; item 4 is in paragraph 3; item 5 is in paragraph 3; item 6 is in paragraph 4.

Option: [+5 minutes] Invite students to share if they agree with the information from the article in Exercise B. Ask *Would your close friend respond in the same way? Would you respond that way to a friend?* Invite students to revisit the situations applying their own personal experience.

Answers for Exercise D

Answers will vary but may include the following:
2. Friends often share a similar sense of humor, so a friend would likely laugh even at a really dumb joke.
3. A friend knows what makes you tick and would probably know what to do to make you feel better.
4. A friend knows you are not perfect and would probably forgive you if you lost your temper.
5. A friend is loyal and would stick up for you and stick by you no matter what.
6. Friends don't keep things bottled up inside; if you have a disagreement with a friend, you would work things out and move on.

E RELATE TO PERSONAL EXPERIENCE

Suggested teaching time:	5 minutes	Your actual teaching time:

- Ask a student to read the heading of each part of the article in Exercise B. Write these four qualities on the board:

  Friends . . .
  . . . share good times.
  . . . are there when times are tough.
  . . . don't judge each other.
  . . . are trustworthy.

In pairs, have students illustrate these qualities via examples of personal friendships. If students get stuck, have them skim the paragraph under each heading for ideas.

- Bring the class together and have pairs share.

Option: [+5 minutes] Ask *Do you think all four qualities are necessary in a friendship? Is it possible to have a solid friendship without any of these? Are there any other qualities you think are crucial to a friendship?*

⭐ 🖨 Extra Challenge Reading Activity

NOW YOU CAN Explore the qualities of friendship

A FRAME YOUR IDEAS

Suggested teaching time:	10–15 minutes	Your actual teaching time:

- Explain that similarly to the Preview, at the beginning of this unit, where students rated people's comments on shortcomings, here, students will rate comments people make about friends. Bring students' attention to the purple ratings on the right and read them. Tell students they will rate each person's comment A, B, or C.
- Have pairs compare ratings. Circulate and ask *Do you have a lot of A ratings? B? C?*

Challenge: [+5 minutes] Have students work in pairs or groups. Focus on A and B answers and invite students to say how they would react in each situation. Model item 1. (Possible answer: If a friend got engaged, I'd be thrilled for her happy event. Even if I were a little jealous, I would never say anything about it to her or anyone else.)

B DISCUSSION

Suggested teaching time:	5 minutes	Your actual teaching time:

- Bring students' attention to the ratings at the bottom of the page. Have students rate their friends and then rate themselves as a friend.
- In groups or pairs, have students explain their answers with examples.

Option: [+5 minutes] Ask *Do you have a lot of friends? How many close friends do you have? Do you think it's possible to be a good friend to a lot of people?*

8 When someone "sticks up for you," he or she …… .
   (a) defends you against criticism
   b criticizes you honestly
9 When friends "stick by you," they …… .
   (a) are always loyal to you
   b tell you off
10 When someone "keeps things bottled up inside," he or she …… to talk about uncomfortable feelings such as anger.
   a is willing
   (b) isn't willing

D APPLY IDEAS Discuss what a good friend would do in response to each situation, waccording to the information in the article. Explain your answers. See page T47 for answers.

1 You get a new job at twice your current salary.

> "It says a true friend cheers you on when times are good. So I think a good friend would be happy for me and want to celebrate."

2 You tell your friend a really dumb joke.

3 You're unhappy about something, but you haven't told anyone about it yet.
4 You lose your temper with your friend.
5 A colleague criticizes you when you're not around.
6 You and your friend have a disagreement.

E RELATE TO PERSONAL EXPERIENCE Work in pairs. Using the four qualities of a good friendship in the article as examples, share personal examples of your friendships that illustrate each quality.

NOW YOU CAN Explore the qualities of friendship

A FRAME YOUR IDEAS Read each statement and write A, B, or C. Then, with a partner, compare and explain your responses.

> "That's not the kind of friend I am. Remember what the article said? Good friends aren't jealous of your successes."

A = That's not the kind of friend I am.
B = Sometimes I'm a bit like that.
C = I have to admit that sounds a lot like me.

"My friend Carla just got engaged last week. I can't figure it out. I'm so much more popular than she is."

"My friend Trevor is really feeling down right now because he split up with his girlfriend. He's kind of getting on my nerves. I wish he'd just stop talking about it."

"Laura's a good friend, but I think her clothes are really out of style. It's kind of embarrassing to be seen with her. She'd be so much prettier if she took my suggestions."

"I was really disappointed when my friend Tom didn't invite me over to watch the World Cup. I guess I just won't invite him anywhere either."

"My friend Harriet told me about the problems she's been having with her husband. I only told my neighbor Cynthia about it, but no one else."

"My friend Nick is always late for everything. Today was the last straw—if he can't change his habits, he can go find *another* friend."

B DISCUSSION How would you rate your friendships in general? All things considered, in what ways would you say you're a good friend to *your* friends? Explain your answers and give examples.

How I'd generally rate my friends
poor   average   excellent

How I'd rate myself as a friend
poor   average   excellent

47

WRITING Transitional topic sentences

A WRITING SKILL Study the rules.

Remember: Transition words and subordinating conjunctions link ideas within and between sentences.

They can also be used in a paragraph's topic sentence to connect the paragraph to the one that precedes it.

The following words and phrases can be used as transitions to announce the content of a new paragraph:

To add information

Furthermore, it's very convenient.
Moreover, it's very convenient.
More importantly, it's very convenient.

To contrast information

Even though it's convenient, it's not for everyone.
Although it's convenient, it's not for everyone.
Despite the fact that it's convenient, it's not for everyone.
Nevertheless, it's not for everyone.
On the other hand, it's not for everyone.
However, it's not for everyone.

WRITING MODEL

For an effective solution to procrastination, I suggest using the daily calendar on your smartphone. It can be used to break up the steps essential to completing a larger task into smaller tasks. That way it is easier to keep things moving forward. It also allows you to check off the smaller tasks as they are finished, which motivates you by providing a feeling of accomplishment.

Furthermore, using a smartphone calendar is not really all that difficult. You can use the calendar that's already installed, or you can download an app for that purpose. Instructions are easily available online, and they are usually very clear.

Nevertheless, using a smartphone calendar does take some getting used to. It may require some time to learn how to use it, but the calendar will make your work easier. Without a calendar, it is far too easy to simply forget about what needs to be done. With one, it is easy to keep track of your progress. If your teacher or manager asks questions, you have a record you can refer to. This increases your confidence. I believe the calendar is one of the best ways to convert procrastination into effective organization.

B PRACTICE Rewrite these transitional topic sentences from the Writing Model, using other words and phrases to announce the content of the new paragraph. (Note: You may have to make other changes in the sentence.) Answers will vary but may include the following:

Furthermore, using a smartphone calendar is not really all that difficult.

1. More importantly, using a smartphone calendar is not really all that difficult.
2. Moreover, using a smartphone calendar is not really all that difficult.

Nevertheless, using a smartphone calendar does take some getting used to.

3. Even though it's not difficult, using a smartphone calendar does take some getting used to.
4. Although it's easy, using a smartphone calendar does take some getting used to.
5. Despite the fact that it's not difficult, using a smartphone calendar takes some getting used to.
6. On the other hand, using a smartphone calendar does take some getting used to.
7. However, using a smartphone calendar does take some getting used to.

C APPLY THE WRITING SKILL Write a three-paragraph essay presenting a solution to a common shortcoming. In paragraph one, introduce the solution. Use transitional topic sentences to link the content of the second and third paragraphs.

SELF-CHECK

☐ Does the first paragraph have a topic sentence?
☐ Do the paragraphs that follow have transitional topic sentences?
☐ Does each transitional topic sentence clearly link to previous content?

WRITING Transitional topic sentences

A WRITING SKILL

Suggested teaching time:	5–10 minutes	Your actual teaching time:

- On the board, write *transitional topic sentences*. Explain that this phrase refers to sentences that connect one paragraph to another. Call on a volunteer to read the Remember note.
- Have students study the example sentences for adding information. Make sure that students notice each sentence conveys the same information.
- Have students study the example sentences for contrasting information. Make sure that students notice that the first three sentences convey the same information and the last three sentences convey the same information.

B PRACTICE

Suggested teaching time:	5 minutes	Your actual teaching time:

- Have students rewrite the transitional topic sentences individually. Circulate and make sure students make any necessary changes.
- Have students compare answers with a partner.

Challenge: [+5 minutes] For more practice, on the board, write *Exercise requires physical effort, but it can be beneficial for controlling anger.* Elicit different ways to say this sentence using the various words and phrases from the writing skill examples. Students can write or say the sentences. (Possible answers:

  Although exercise requires physical effort, it can help control anger.

  Despite the fact that exercise can help control anger, it does require physical effort.

  Exercise can help control anger. Nevertheless, it does require physical effort.

  Exercise does require physical effort. On the other hand, it can help control anger.

  Exercise requires physical effort. However, it does help control anger.)

  Then invite students to add their own information to the idea restated several times above. (Possible answer

  Furthermore, it releases endorphins and can make you feel better altogether.

  Moreover, it helps you get in shape, which can put you in a better mood.

  More importantly, exercise keeps you balanced.)

C APPLY THE WRITING SKILL

Suggested teaching time:	10–15 minutes	Your actual teaching time:

- On the board, write *common shortcomings*. Ask *What shortcoming is addressed in the writing model?* (procrastination) Elicit other shortcomings, referring students to the Vocabulary on page 38 if needed. Ask students to share which shortcoming they would like to write about.
- Refer students to the Writing Process Worksheet in ActiveTeach for guidance with pre-writing and peer feedback.
- Encourage students to use the Self-Check in the Student's Book to go over the essays they wrote.

Option: [+5 minutes] Time-permitting, students can exchange papers with a partner and offer feedback using the topics in the Self-Check list. Encourage partners to also check for examples.

⭐ 🖨 Writing Process

UNIT 4 WRITING T48

REVIEW

🎮 Digital Game

A ▶ 2:25

Suggested teaching time:	5–10 minutes	Your actual teaching time:

- With Student's Books closed, have students listen to the shortcomings the three people describe.
- Then have students read the chart and listen to the three speakers again. Tell students to complete the chart.
- Have pairs compare charts. If necessary, allow students to listen again to check their work.
- To check comprehension, ask *Which two speakers found solutions to their problems at workshops?* (speakers 1 and 3) *Did the workshops help both of them?* (yes) *How did Speaker 2 deal with her problem?* (She asked her friend for help.) *Does Speaker 2 think she may have problems in the future?* (She says she doesn't know, but that she might need to ask her friend for help again.)

Option: [+5 minutes] Following the model in the Student's Book, write a chart on the board. Have students talk about problems and solutions from their own lives and tell the class whether the solutions worked. While students share, have volunteers fill in the information on the board, or have students write in their own charts.

B

Suggested teaching time:	5 minutes	Your actual teaching time:

- Call on a volunteer to read the list of phrases (a–e) on the right. If necessary, refer students to page 38 to review Vocabulary related to shortcomings.
- Have students complete the exercise individually and then compare answers with a partner.

C

Suggested teaching time:	5 minutes	Your actual teaching time:

- Have students review the expressions related to anger on page 44.
- Tell students to think of specific situations in which they could use each of the three expressions. Then have them complete the activity.
- Ask *Do you often hold your feelings in? Do you ever tell someone off? Do you ever lose your temper?*

D

Suggested teaching time:	5 minutes	Your actual teaching time:

- Tell students that the exercise covers the various adverbial clauses of condition. Refer them to the grammar information on page 40 if they need to review.
- Have students match the sentence parts. Then ask them to compare answers with a partner.
- Go over any questions as a class.

E

Suggested teaching time:	5 minutes	Your actual teaching time:

- To warm up, call on a volunteer to read item 1, both the original sentence and the model cleft sentence. Write the sentences on the board. Point out how in the cleft sentence with *What* the emphasis is on the result—*so offensive. What* is the subject of the sentence.
- In the rest of the sentences, tell students to circle the part of the sentence that *What* will introduce. Circulate and assist as needed. (2. changes negative thinking, 3. causes people to put things off, 4. makes people feel like they're walking on eggshells, 5. makes her so successful)
- Have students rewrite the statements as cleft sentences with *What*.
- Tell students to compare answers with a partner. Discuss any issues as a class.

Option: TEST-TAKING SKILLS BOOSTER (p. 154)

EXTRA

- Workbook
- MyEnglishLab
- Online Student Resources (www.english.com/summit3e)
  - Classroom Audio Program
  - Extra Practice Activities
  - *Summit GO* App
  - Web Projects
- ActiveTeach
  - Assessment
  - Additional Printable Resources
    - Audioscripts and Answer Keys
    - "Can-Do" Self-Assessment Charts
    - Conversation and Discussion Activator Video Scripts
    - Oral Progress Assessment Charts
    - Reading Speed Calculator
  - Summit TV Video Program
    - Activity Worksheets
    - Teaching Notes
    - Video Scripts

REVIEW

A ▶ 2:25 Listen to three people describe their shortcomings. Then listen again and complete the chart. Listen a third time if necessary to check your answers.

	What is the shortcoming?	What solution did the person find?	Did it work?
1	Trying to do everything himself	Allowing colleagues to share responsibilities	Yes
2	Being very disorganized	A friend helped her get organized	Yes
3	Problem with temper	An anger management course	Yes

B Complete each statement with one of the lettered choices. (You will not use all the choices.)

1 Claire overreacts and takes things personally when her friends make suggestions. She ..d...
2 Bob is always losing his cool over things that aren't important. He ..e...
3 Laura usually misses her deadlines because she doesn't get started on her assignments right away. She ..c...
4 Nick is always worrying about every little detail. He hates making mistakes. He ..a...

a is a perfectionist.
b is negative.
c tends to procrastinate.
d is oversensitive.
e is hot-tempered.

C Complete each statement about the situations in which people express or control their anger.

1 People sometimes hold their feelings in when ....
....
2 People usually only tell someone off when ....
....
3 Most people lose their tempers only when ....
....

D Complete each statement logically and correctly with one of the lettered choices.

1 Even if I know a project is important, ..d...
2 Unless I know that a project is not important, ..b...
3 Only if I know that a project is not important ..c...
4 If only I had known that the project was important, ..e...
5 I wish I'd known that the project was so important. ..a...

a Otherwise, I wouldn't have waited till the last minute to get started.
b I never wait till the last minute to get started.
c will I wait till the last minute to get started.
d I still wait till the last minute to get started.
e I wouldn't have waited till the last minute to get started.

E On a separate sheet of paper, rewrite each sentence as a cleft sentence with **What**. Follow the example.

1 It's the way she criticizes new employees that's so offensive.

> What's so offensive is the way she criticizes new employees.

2 It's maintaining a positive attitude that changes negative thinking. *What changes negative thinking is maintaining a positive attitude.*
3 It's fear of failure that causes people to put things off. *What causes people to put things off is fear of failure.*
4 It's his being so hot-tempered that makes people feel like they're walking on eggshells. *What makes people feel like they're walking on eggshells is his being so hot-tempered.*
5 It's her ability to organize that makes her so successful. *What makes her so successful is her ability to organize.*

TEST-TAKING SKILLS BOOSTER p. 154

Web Project: Anger Management
www.english.com/summit3e

UNIT 5
Humor

PREVIEW

COMMUNICATION GOALS
1 Discuss the health benefits of laughter
2 Respond to something funny
3 Analyze what makes us laugh
4 Explore the limits of humor

A FRAME YOUR IDEAS Take the humor self-test to analyze your sense of humor.

HUMOR SELF-TEST

Rate how funny you think each images is, from 1 to 5, with 1 being not funny at all and 5 being extremely funny.

1. YOUR RATING: 1 2 3 4 5 NOT FUNNY VERY FUNNY
2. YOUR RATING: 1 2 3 4 5 NOT FUNNY VERY FUNNY
3. YOUR RATING: 1 2 3 4 5 NOT FUNNY VERY FUNNY
4. YOUR RATING: 1 2 3 4 5 NOT FUNNY VERY FUNNY
5. YOUR RATING: 1 2 3 4 5 NOT FUNNY VERY FUNNY
6. YOUR RATING: 1 2 3 4 5 NOT FUNNY VERY FUNNY
7. YOUR RATING: 1 2 3 4 5 NOT FUNNY VERY FUNNY
8. YOUR RATING: 1 2 3 4 5 NOT FUNNY VERY FUNNY

CAUTION CHILDREN TEXTING

ID NO. 1278 DATE 20150315 BAD CAT

B PAIR WORK Discuss your funniest and least funny choices with a partner. Explain why you find some of the images funny and other ones not funny. Do you have the same sense of humor?

> "I don't like the picture of the boy with the head to his side. I find it kind of scary—even a bit creepy. I gave it a 1."

C DISCUSSION Do a class survey. Which image did your classmates find the funniest? Which did they find the least funny? What were the reasons?

50 UNIT 5

UNIT 5

Humor

PREVIEW

A FRAME YOUR IDEAS

| Suggested teaching time: | 5 minutes | Your actual teaching time: |

- Tell students they will take a humor self-test. Call on a student to read the subheading. Bring students' attention to the ratings (1 to 5) next by each picture. Tell students they will rate how funny they think each picture is.
- Give students a few minutes to complete the ratings.

B PAIR WORK

| Suggested teaching time: | 5–10 minutes | Your actual teaching time: |

- Call on a student to read the model answer. Have students compare tests in pairs and make similar comments. Tell them to focus on their funniest and least funny choices.
- Circulate and ask why students find particular images funny or not funny.
- Bring the class together and ask *Do you and your partner have a similar sense of humor?*

C DISCUSSION

| Suggested teaching time: | 5 minutes | Your actual teaching time: |

- Bring the class together. Write the numbers 1 through 8 vertically on the board. Ask *What rating did you give image [1]?* Repeat the question for each item and list all ratings on the board.
- As a class, deduce the funniest and least funny images. Analyze and ask *Was there a majority? Do people in this class have a similar idea of what's funny and what is not?*

UNIT 5 PREVIEW T50

D ▶ 3:02 SPOTLIGHT

Suggested teaching time:	10 minutes	Your actual teaching time:

- Read the directions and let students know that they will hear about an embarrassing social situation.
- Have students read and listen to the conversation.
- To check comprehension, ask *What is Sylvie's background?* (She's French.) *What embarrassing social situation did she find herself in?* (She told a joke that she thought was funny but that ended up insulting people.)

LANGUAGE NOTE *Mortified*, in this context, means extremely embarrassed and ashamed, and it can also mean extremely offended; *don't quote me on that* is an expression you use when you don't want something referenced back to you—here David doesn't want it repeated that he said Americans are intimidated by the French; *we can't get enough of something* means that we really like something very much and desire a lot of it; *to surmise* is to guess something is true; *thicker-skinned* means not as easily insulted by other people's criticisms or insults.

Option: [+5 minutes] Ask *Have you ever made a fool of yourself like Sylvie?* Invite students to share. Tell students they can also tell about how other people they know have made fools of themselves.

Challenge: [+5 minutes] Ask individual students *Do you think you're thick-skinned?* On the board, write *Do people in your culture get offended easily? Are people able to laugh at themselves?* In groups, have students discuss how thick-skinned people are in their culture(s).

E UNDERSTAND IDIOMS AND EXPRESSIONS

Suggested teaching time:	10 minutes	Your actual teaching time:

- Focus on the idioms and expressions highlighted in Exercise D. Call on volunteers to read them aloud.
- In pairs, have students study each highlighted idiom and expression in context to figure out the meaning. Then have them complete each item with the correct idiom or expression.
- Go over the answers as a class.

Challenge: [+5 minutes] Divide the class into pairs and assign each pair one or two of the target idioms or expressions from Exercise D. Have students create brief dialogues around them. Invite pairs to share dialogues.

F THINK AND EXPLAIN

Suggested teaching time:	5–10 minutes	Your actual teaching time:

- Have students discuss the questions in pairs. Then bring the class together to go over the answers.
- Focus on the second question. Invite students to share their answers. Then ask *Do you think the joke Sylvie told was politically incorrect? Would it have insulted you if you were an American?*

Option: [+5 minutes] Have students focus on Sylvie's third exchange and ask a volunteer to read it. Ask *Do you think she is insulting Americans in this sentence?* (Possible answer: Yes, she is. She is saying that the group of Americans she was with were sophisticated—even eating French food—thereby implying that other Americans are *not* sophisticated.)

LANGUAGE NOTE Point out that the term *politically correct* is often abbreviated as *PC*. You could say *It's not very PC to say that*. The opposite of *politically correct* is often stated as *politically incorrect*.

SPEAKING Pair work

Suggested teaching time:	5–10 minutes	Your actual teaching time:

- Ask a volunteer to read the model answer. Ask *Do you agree with this comment about ethnic jokes?*
- Have students check the things they find funny and write at least one of their own ideas. Then have them discuss in pairs.
- Bring the class together and have students share what they wrote under Your own idea.

D ▶ 3:02 **SPOTLIGHT** Read and listen to a conversation about an embarrassing social situation. Notice the spotlighted language.

> **ENGLISH FOR TODAY'S WORLD**
> Understand a variety of accents.
> Sylvie = French
> David = American English (standard)

Sylvie: Oh, David, I can't tell you how mortified I am.
David: What on earth happened?
Sylvie: So, last night I told this funny joke French people tell about Americans: How do you know someone's an American? He asks for ketchup for his peanut butter sandwich. Well, it went over like a lead balloon. *No one laughed.* I made a total fool of myself.
David: Oh, Sylvie! That must have been awful!
Sylvie: The thing is I don't know why they took it personally. The joke wasn't about *them*! They were pretty sophisticated. We were even eating French food!
David: Well, you couldn't have known this, but it's definitely uncool to make fun of a particular nationality, an ethnic group, a religion … It just isn't done.
Sylvie: You mean you guys are that politically correct?
David: You could say that. And the fact that you're French probably didn't help. We Americans can get a bit intimidated by the French, but don't quote me on that.
Sylvie: I don't get it. Why are people here so sensitive? In France, we can't get enough jokes about ourselves.
David: I'm surmising the French are thicker-skinned than Americans …
Sylvie: You can say that again. Ethnic jokes—even ones about ourselves—are just par for the course there. You know, I don't think I can ever face those people again.
David: You know what, Sylvie? We Americans make jokes about ourselves, too. It's just less funny when it comes from an outsider. Don't take it so hard.
Sylvie: Easier said than done!

E **UNDERSTAND IDIOMS AND EXPRESSIONS** Complete the statements with spotlighted language.

1. If you want to say that someone's advice isn't easy to follow, you can say "Easier said than done."
2. Another way to say that no one liked your joke is "It went over like a lead balloon."
3. When you want to say you just don't understand something, you can say "I don't get it."
4. When you want to suggest that something isn't at all unusual, you can say it's "par for the course."
5. When you want to suggest that most people consider something rude or inappropriate, you can say "It just isn't done."
6. If you do something stupid or silly that causes other people to laugh at you, you feel embarrassed and say "I made a total fool of myself."
7. If you want to suggest that someone is reacting too strongly to something, you can tell him or her "Don't take it so hard."

F **THINK AND EXPLAIN** Can a joke about your own nationality or ethnic group ever be funny? Or are those jokes always "politically incorrect" or even offensive? Explain.

SPEAKING **PAIR WORK** Check the things you find funny. Discuss why certain things make people laugh. What other things make you laugh?

☐ Cute video clips about animals and babies	☐ People embarrassing themselves by using the wrong word or expression
☐ Physical "slapstick" humor in TV shows and movies	☐ Stories or pictures of people making fools of themselves
☐ Jokes making fun of men or jokes making fun of women	☐ Your own idea:

> ❝ Even though some ethnic jokes can be funny, I think we probably shouldn't tell them. They can end up insulting people. ❞

LESSON 1

GOAL Discuss the health benefits of laughter

A ▶ 3:03 **GRAMMAR SPOTLIGHT** Read the article about the health benefits of laughter. Notice the spotlighted grammar.

A laughter therapy group

LAUGH YOUR WAY TO HEALTH?

CAN SOMETHING AS SIMPLE AS LAUGHTER CURE DISEASE?

The concept is actually not new. Sixteenth-century humanist educator Richard Mulcaster **said** that because laughter **produced** warmth in the body, it **might be** a good remedy for colds. Other scientists of his time **noted** that laughter **increased** the rate of breathing, **boosted** muscle tone, and **exercised** the body's internal organs. They **claimed** that those effects **were** beneficial to people suffering from colds too. So although many physicians and medical researchers had long **thought** that laughter **could be** helpful, scientific studies had been inconclusive. Then, in his classic 1956 book *The Stress of Life*, Hungarian scientist Hans Selye **wrote**, based on extensive research, that he **had proved** that biological stress **has** negative effects on health. This laid the foundation for the theory that the absence of stress could have positive effects.

Later, in 1976, American editor Norman Cousins—a non-scientist—**reported** in the *New England Journal of Medicine* that laughter **had helped** cure him of a painful life-threatening chronic disease. His article captured the attention of the medical profession and some doctors began considering using laughter as therapy. Then in his 1979 bestseller, *Anatomy of an Illness*, Cousins **wrote** that he **had been** so sick that the only thing he could do was lie in bed. Cousins **theorized** that, based on Selye's research, because the stress of negative emotions **could cause** illness, positive emotions **should be able to exert** a healing effect. So he spent his time watching funny movies and he asked his friends to tell him lots of funny jokes.

Although no one **can state** definitively that laughter **cured** Norman Cousins, the concept of laughter therapy has gained popular acceptance, notably in Madan Kataria's laughter yoga movement practiced by thousands of people worldwide. In this popular activity, large groups of people sit together and force themselves to laugh until the laughter becomes contagious and real.

B **CRITICAL THINKING** Do you think it's possible that Norman Cousins was cured by laughter? Can you think of any other explanation for his recovery? In what ways do you think positive and negative emotions can affect our health? See page T52 for answers.

C **GRAMMAR** **INDIRECT SPEECH: BACKSHIFTS IN TENSE AND TIME EXPRESSIONS**

In indirect speech, when the reporting verb is in a past form, the verb form in the noun clause (the indirect speech) usually "shifts back" to preserve meaning. Compare the verb forms in direct and indirect speech.

Some common reporting verbs

admit	insist	theorize
claim	note	think
complain	report	write
continue	state	

Direct speech	Indirect speech
Dr. Ames wrote, "Negative emotions **are** harmful and **cause** illness."	Dr. Ames wrote (that) negative emotions **were** harmful and **caused** illness.
He continued, "But Cousins **hasn't proved** anything."	He continued (that) Cousins **hadn't proved** anything.
Cousins said, "Laughter **cured** me."	Cousins said (that) laughter **had cured** him.
We wrote, "He **isn't practicing** laughter yoga."	We wrote (that) he **wasn't practicing** laughter yoga.
She claimed, "We **were telling** the truth."	She claimed (that) they **had been telling** the truth.
Doctors admitted, "We**'ve learned** from Cousins's article.	Doctors admitted (that) they **had learned** from Cousins's article.
He told her, "I**'ll check** to see how you**'re feeling** later."	He told her (that) he **would check** to see how she **was feeling** later.
Pam told us, "I **can't understand** what **happened**."	Pam told us (that) she **couldn't understand** what **had happened**.
He told me, "You **have to see** this funny movie."	He told me (that) I **had to see** that funny movie.
The nurse told the little girl, "You **must rest**."	The nurse told the little girl (that) she **had to rest**.

52 UNIT 5

LESSON 1

GOAL Discuss the health benefits of laughter

A ▶ 3:03 GRAMMAR SPOTLIGHT

Suggested teaching time:	5–10 minutes	Your actual teaching time:

- Ask a student to read the lesson title. Ask *What do you think are some health benefits of laughter?* (Possible answers: lower stress, less anger)
- On the board, write *Laugh your way to health.* Ask *What do you think this means?* (Possible answer: Laughter can make you healthy.) *Do you agree or disagree? Explain.*
- Have students listen to the article as they read along. Clarify vocabulary as needed.
- To check comprehension, ask: *How far back in time do theories on the health benefits of laughter go?* (to the sixteenth century) *What did the 1956 book* The Stress of Life *prove?* (the negative effects of stress on health) *What did Norman Cousins report in 1976?* (that laughter helped him cure a painful, life-threatening disease) *What did Cousins theorize about positive emotions?* (that they should exert a healing effect—the same way that biological stress has negative effects on health) *What is the status of laughter therapy today?* (It's gained popular acceptance.)

B CRITICAL THINKING

Suggested teaching time:	5 minutes	Your actual teaching time:

- In pairs, have students think about the questions. Tell them to return to the article and then discuss.
- Bring the class together and ask *Do you think laughter can heal?* Invite students to summarize their views.

Option: [+5 minutes] Ask *Do you think you could laugh if you had a life-threatening illness? Why? Why not?* Invite students to share stories about people they know or have heard about who have used laughter therapy to fight an illness. Ask *Do you think a positive attitude can help a person fighting an illness?*

Answers to Exercise B
Answers will vary but may include the following:
In my opinion, Norman Cousins was cured by laughter. I believe that positive emotions can have a healing effect. If Cousins consciously focused time on laughing to get better, it could very well be that it was what changed his prognosis. Positive emotions instill peace and calm which could do wonders for one's entire being. Negative emotions on the contrary can cause anxiety and stress.

C GRAMMAR

Suggested teaching time:	10–15 minutes	Your actual teaching time:

- On the board, write 1. *The doctor said, "There is no cure for your illness."* Ask *Is this direct or indirect speech?* (direct) *How do you know?* (There are quotation marks around the doctor's statement.) Then write the statement in indirect speech on the board: 2. *The doctor said that there was no cure for my illness.* Encourage students to identify the changes in the sentence. (no quotation marks, *that* added, *is* changed to *was*, *your* changed to *my*)
- Ask a volunteer to read the first explanation in the grammar note. Then point to the sentence on the board and indicate the shift refers to the verb changing from present to past. Bring students' attention to the list of common reporting verbs to the right of the grammar explanation on the Student's Book page.
- Call on students to read the ten pairs of example sentences in the chart—first the sentence in direct speech and then the sentence in indirect speech. After each student reads, have him or her point out how the verbs change from direct to indirect speech. After the last pair of sentences is read, ask *How does a verb in the imperative change from direct speech to indirect speech?* (*to* is added in front of the base form)
- Be sure to point out to students the change in subject pronouns and that occurs for meaning in the indirect speech. Example sentences 5 to 10 illustrate such changes. The optional grammar booster reviews this topic.
- Remind students a comma is not used after a reporting verb in indirect speech.
- Explain that in the last example, *must* can't be backshifted. The past of *must* is *had to*.
- ⭐ 🖨 Inductive Grammar Activity

UNIT 5 LESSON 1 T52

- Focus on the Exceptions explanation at the top of the page. Ask a volunteer to read the first explanation. Point out that the first example *Tom just called. He said that the director is (OR was) leaving*, conveys two of the characteristics for an optional tense change—it is something that was just said and it's also something that's still true. Tell students to read the other two example sentences to themselves.
- Ask a student to read the next explanation. Write on the board, *The teacher said, "You should really study hard."* Elicit the corresponding reported speech. (The teacher said I should really study hard.) Note that the verb doesn't backshift.
- Finally, tell students to read how expressions of time and place backshift in indirect speech.
- Point out that changes in expressions of time depend on when the reporter is reporting the statement. A change is made only if the time of the original statement is distant from the reporting of it. Write the following examples on the board:

    I'll call the doctor tomorrow. → *She said she'd call the doctor tomorrow.*
    → *She said she'd call the doctor the next day / on Wednesday.*

- Next, explain that the changes in expressions of place depend on where the reporter is when reporting the statement. A change is made only if the reporter is in a different place from where the original speaker was. Write the following examples on the board:

    I put the book here. → *He said he had put the book here.*
    → *He said he had put the book there / on the desk.*

- Mention that changes in demonstrative adjectives also depend on the reporter's point of view and what the reporter wishes to express. Write on the board:

    I've read this book twice. → *She said she had read this book twice.*
    → *She said she had read that / Cousins's book twice.*

Option: [+5 minutes] Invite students to look back at the article in Exercise A on page 52. Ask *Are the highlighted words examples of direct or indirect speech?* (indirect; there are no quotes) Tell students to circle all the reporting verbs (*said, noted, claimed, thought, wrote, reported, wrote, theorized, can state*).

D GRAMMAR PRACTICE

Suggested teaching time:	5 minutes	Your actual teaching time:

- Before students write the sentences in indirect speech, have them skim the items and think about changes that they will need to make.
- Remind students to make appropriate shifts in verb forms, pronouns, and expressions of time and place.
- Bring the class together and go over the answers. Point out that for item 1, either *me* or *us* is correct.

Option: GRAMMAR BOOSTER *(Teaching notes p. T135)*

⭐ 🖨 Extra Grammar Exercises

E PAIR WORK

Suggested teaching time:	5 minutes	Your actual teaching time:

- Tell students that they will orally change the sentences in this exercise to indirect speech.
- Remind students to make appropriate shifts in verb forms, pronouns, and expressions of time and place.
- Bring the class together and go over the answers.

F GRAMMAR PRACTICE

Suggested teaching time:	5 minutes	Your actual teaching time:

- Point out to students that in this exercise they will be changing indirect speech to direct speech. Elicit the answer to item 1 and write it on the board: *Ellen said, "I read an article about laughter yoga in the New Yorker magazine."*
- Have students write the remaining sentences individually. Remind students to make appropriate shifts in verb forms, pronouns, and expressions of time and place.
- Go over the answers as a class.

NOW YOU CAN Discuss the health benefits of laughter

A NOTEPADDING

Suggested teaching time:	5 minutes	Your actual teaching time:

- Have students work individually to complete the statements using information from the article on page 52.
- Tell them to compare answers with a partner.

Option: [+5 minutes] Write a summary of the article using the statements on the notepad.

B DISCUSSION ACTIVATOR

Suggested teaching time:	5–10 minutes	Your actual teaching time:

🎮 Discussion Activator Video

- Divide the class into pairs and have students use the information from the notepadding exercise to discuss laughter therapy with a partner. Encourage students in each pair to ask each other questions and provide details and examples. Tell students that they should say as much as possible.

For more support, play the Discussion Activator Video before students do this activity. After each video, ask if the students in the video included sufficient details. *Note:* You can print the script or you can view it on the video player on the ActiveTeach.

Exceptions

When a reporting verb is in the simple past tense, backshifting is optional when the statement refers to something just said, something that's still true, or a scientific or general truth.

Tom just called. He said that the director **is** (OR **was**) leaving. [something just said]
Ann told me that she **needs** (OR **needed**) to renew her passport. [something still true]
He noted that the Earth **is** (OR **was**) the fifth largest planet in the solar system. [a scientific or general truth]

Do not make changes to present or perfect forms of the modals <u>should</u>, <u>could</u>, <u>may</u>, <u>might</u>, <u>would</u>, and <u>ought to</u> when converting to indirect speech.

Expressions of time and place: backshifts in indirect speech

now	→ **then**	this year	→ **that year**	
today	→ **that day**	last week	→ **the week before**	
tomorrow	→ **the next day**	next month	→ **the following month**	
yesterday	→ **the day before**	here	→ **there**	

Mark told me, "Judy was here yesterday." → Mark told me Judy had been **there the day before.**

> **GRAMMAR BOOSTER** p. 135
> Indirect speech: review and expansion
> - Imperatives in indirect speech
> - Changes to pronouns and possessives
> - <u>Say</u>, <u>tell</u>, and <u>ask</u>
> - Other reporting verbs

D **GRAMMAR PRACTICE** On a separate sheet of paper, rewrite the sentences in indirect speech. If the sentence can be written both with and without backshifting, write it both ways.

1 Ms. Barr stated, "I want you to finish your essays for the next class."
  Ms. Barr stated that she wanted / wants us to finish our essays for the next class.
2 Last week I told my husband, "This has been the best vacation we've ever taken."
  Last week I told my husband that that had been the best vacation we had ever taken.
3 My friend Amy said, "I have never seen such exciting paintings before."
  My friend Amy said that she had never seen such exciting paintings before.
4 In his lecture, Dr. White explained, "The earth rotates around the sun."
  In his lecture, Dr. White explained that the earth rotates around the sun./ rotated around the sun.

E **PAIR WORK** With a partner, take turns restating each of the following in indirect speech.

1 Pain researchers reported, "Laughter may help some patients."
  Pain researchers reported that laughter may help some patients.
2 They said, "Our new study will begin here next week."
  They said that their new study would begin there next week.
3 The doctors said, "We've recommended laughter yoga to cure his pain."
  The doctors said that they had recommended laughter yoga to cure his pain.
4 The patient told everyone, "I definitely feel better from the laughter yoga."
  The patient told everyone that he/she definitely felt better from the laughter yoga.

F **GRAMMAR PRACTICE** On a separate sheet of paper, write what the people actually said, using direct speech.

1 Ellen told me she had read an article about laughter yoga in the New Yorker magazine.
  Ellen told me, "I read an article about laughter yoga in the New Yorker magazine."
2 She claimed she believed laughter yoga could be helpful.
  She claimed, "I believe laughter yoga can be helpful."
3 I said I never would have known that.
  I said, "I never would have known that."
4 The nurse told me that she had been using laughter therapy with certain patients.
  The nurse told me, "I have been using laughter therapy with certain patients."

NOW YOU CAN Discuss the health benefits of laughter

A **NOTEPADDING** Complete the statements, based on the article. Then use that information as support in the Discussion Activator.

Richard Mulcaster and other scientists have said that

Much later, Hans Selye wrote that

Norman Cousins claimed that

B **DISCUSSION ACTIVATOR** Do you believe laughter can be "good medicine"? How could you apply the ideas in the article to help heal a sick friend or family member? If you were very sick, how might you use laughter therapy to get better? Support your opinion with ideas from the article, using indirect speech if you are reporting what someone said. Say as much as you can.

LESSON 2

GOAL Respond to something funny

A ▶ 3:04 **VOCABULARY** WAYS TO RESPOND TO JOKES AND OTHER FUNNY THINGS
Read and listen. Then listen again and repeat.

If you think it's funny:
- That's so funny!
- That's hilarious!
- That's hysterical!
- That's too much!

If you don't understand what's funny about it:
- I don't get it.
- That went over my head.

ALSO: That's ridiculous / silly / offensive*

*Be careful! These can be rude and hurt the joke-teller's feelings.

B ▶ 3:05 **LISTEN TO ACTIVATE VOCABULARY** Listen to six conversations. After each one, check Yes or No to indicate whether the listener thought it was funny. Then listen again and write your *own* response to each joke, using the Vocabulary.

Did the listener think it was funny?			
	Yes	No	Your *own* response to the joke
1	☐	☑	
2	☐	☑	Answers will vary.
3	☑	☐	
4	☐	☑	
5	☐	☑	
6	☑	☐	

C **PAIR WORK** Did you both get all the jokes? If there's a joke your partner didn't get (or didn't like), try to explain why it was funny to you. Tell your partner which joke you thought was the funniest, and why.

D **RELATE TO PERSONAL EXPERIENCE** Tell your partner about something funny you saw on TV or in a movie, or a joke or funny story you heard from a friend or family member. Respond to your partner, using the Vocabulary.

E **GRAMMAR** QUESTIONS IN INDIRECT SPEECH
Indirect questions are a kind of embedded question—a question that is included in a noun clause.
Indirect yes / no questions begin with if or whether (or whether or not).

He asked, "Did you find that joke funny?" → He asked **if I had found the joke funny.** OR He asked **whether or not I had found the joke funny.**

My boss asked me, "Were you able to finish the project yesterday?" → My boss asked **if (or whether) I had been able to finish the project the day before.**

54 UNIT 5

LESSON 2

GOAL Respond to something funny

A ▶3:04 VOCABULARY

| Suggested teaching time: | 5–10 minutes | Your actual teaching time: |

- Have students look at the pictures and describe the man and the woman. (Possible answers: The woman is laughing. The man is confused.) Call on volunteers to read each caption and the speech bubbles.
- Have students read and listen to ways to respond to jokes and other funny things.
- Then have students listen and repeat the words chorally.
- Focus on the Also note and the asterisk follow-up.

LANGUAGE NOTE Point out that *hilarious* and *hysterical* both mean extremely funny.

CULTURE NOTE It can be considered impolite to tell someone directly that you thought a joke was ridiculous. Such a comment may be acceptable when talking to a good friend who wouldn't be offended. However, you would not make such a comment to a person of authority such as a boss or professor. On the contrary, you would probably laugh at any joke such an authority figure told, even if you didn't think it was funny.

B ▶3:05 LISTEN TO ACTIVATE VOCABULARY

| Suggested teaching time: | 5 minutes | Your actual teaching time: |

- Pre-listening: Have students look at the chart to help them understand that they will be listening to six conversations in which people tell jokes.
- First listening: Have students listen for the jokes, checking after each one whether the listener liked the joke. If necessary, stop the audio after each joke.
- Second listening: Have students listen to the jokes again and write their own response. Stop after each joke to give students time to write what they think. Refer students to the Vocabulary in Exercise A for ways to respond to jokes. If necessary, allow students to listen again.
- In pairs, have students compare answers and responses.

CULTURE NOTE *Knock-knock* jokes are a popular form of juvenile humor in English. The jokes are based on puns and plays on English words. For example, the knock-knock joke in Exercise B uses the word *orange* to mean *aren't you* because they are similar in sound.

Option: [+5 minutes] Have students listen again. Tell students to listen for expressions at the end of each conversation that indicate whether the people liked the jokes. Have students write the expressions. (1. *Maybe it went over my head*; 2. *No offense, mate, but I think that's silly*; 3. *That's too much*; 4. *Uh, that's really offensive*; 5. *That's pretty silly*; 6. *Now that's funny.*) Invite students to share if they agree with any of the people.

Challenge: [+5 minutes] In pairs or small groups, have students discuss the following questions:

What makes a joke funny? Offensive?
Do you enjoy telling jokes? Why or why not?
What kind of person is good at telling jokes?

Bring the class together and share views.

C PAIR WORK

| Suggested teaching time: | 5 minutes | Your actual teaching time: |

- In pairs, have students discuss the questions.
- Bring the class together and have students share. Ask *Had you heard any of these jokes before? Which jokes did you not get? Which ones did you find silly? Were any offensive to you?*
- Vote on the funniest joke.

D RELATE TO PERSONAL EXPERIENCE

| Suggested teaching time: | 5 minutes | Your actual teaching time: |

- Have students share jokes or funny stories with a partner. Tell students to respond with expressions from the Vocabulary in Exercise A on page 54.
- Bring the class together and ask each student to retell the joke his or her partner told him or her. Remind students to use indirect speech if they are retelling a story. Tell them to share if they thought the joke or story was funny. After each one, ask *Did you find the story funny? Why? Why not?*

E GRAMMAR

| Suggested teaching time: | 5–10 minutes | Your actual teaching time: |

- To quiz comprehension of questions in indirect speech, write on the board, *Did you find the joke funny?*
- Then write: *The teacher asked me...*

Elicit the end of the sentence and write it on the board: *if I (had) found the joke funny / whether or not / I (had) found the joke funny*

- Ask a volunteer to read the first explanation. Point out that the *if / whether (or not)* structure is used for *yes / no* questions. Read the first example sentence while pointing to the same on the board. Then ask a student to read the next example sentence.

⭐ 🖨 Inductive Grammar Activity

- Focus on the next explanation and example sentence.
- Then bring students' attention to the Remember note.
- To quiz students' understanding, write the following on the board:

    "Where in Europe did you travel?" Sylvia asked.
    "What's so funny?" asked Luke.

    Elicit the indirect forms. (Sylvia asked where in Europe I had traveled. Luke asked what was so funny. / Luke asked what is so funny.) Point out that, as with statements, shifting tense depends on how close to a given time one is speaking.
- Remind students to change pronouns, verb forms, and time expressions as necessary when changing from direct to indirect speech. Have them point out those changes in the examples:

    find → had found
    you → I
    were you able → I had been able
    yesterday → the day before

F GRAMMAR PRACTICE

Suggested teaching time:	5 minutes	Your actual teaching time:

- Have students skim the exercise items. Ask *Which are yes / no questions?* (1, 3, and 4) *Which are information questions?* (5) *Is there a statement?* (yes; item 2)
- Instruct students to rewrite each item in indirect speech.
- Have students compare answers with a partner. Then bring the class together to go over any questions.

⭐ 🖨 **Extra Grammar Exercises**

Option: PRONUNCIATION BOOSTER *(Teaching notes p. T146)*

🖨 **Pronunciation Pair Work**

NOW YOU CAN Respond to something funny

A ▶ 3:06 CONVERSATION SPOTLIGHT

Suggested teaching time:	5 minutes	Your actual teaching time:

> These conversation strategies are implicit in the model:
> - Use *you've got to see this* to indicate excitement and / or urgency to share something.
> - Use *Seriously,* to stress urgency for something.
> - Use *that's priceless* to express amusement.
> - Use *Totally* to voice agreement.

- Have students read and listen to the conversation.
- To check comprehension, ask *What does the woman want to show her friend Melanie?* (a funny video of a baby laughing) *What is making the baby laugh?* (A guy keeps tearing pieces of paper.) *Does Melanie agree it's funny?* (Yes; she says it's priceless.) *Why does Melanie say Forward me the link?* (She probably wants to share the video with other people.) *Do you think you would find this video funny?*

B ▶ 3:07 RHYTHM AND INTONATION

Suggested teaching time:	5 minutes	Your actual teaching time:

- Have students repeat chorally. Make sure they:
  - use emphatic stress on *got* in *you've got to see this* (line 1) and *priceless* in *Oh, that's priceless!* (line 8)
  - use falling intonation for *What is it?* (line 3)
  - use rising intonation for *OK?* (line 9)
  - stress *Seriously* (line 6) and *Totally* (line 10).

C CONVERSATION ACTIVATOR

Suggested teaching time:	5–10 minutes	Your actual teaching time:

🎬 **Conversation Activator Video**

- Divide the class into pairs. Instruct students that they will use the model in Exercise A, Conversation Spotlight, to role-play their own conversation with a partner.
- Encourage students to use their own jokes, cartoons, video clips, etc., or they can use the cartoon at the bottom of the page or the funny images from page 50.
- Encourage students to incorporate words and phrases from the Vocabulary on page 54.
- Reinforce the use of the spotlighted conversation strategies. For example, *you've got to see this* and *that's priceless*.
- Bring students' attention to the Don't Stop! note. Ask a volunteer to read the bullet points. Explain that students should continue talking after they have covered the points in the original Conversation Spotlight.
- Tell students to change roles, so each student gets a chance to play A and B.

For more support, play the Conversation Activator Video before students do this activity themselves. After the video, ask students how the model has been changed by the actors. *Note:* You can print the script or you can view it on the video player on the ActiveTeach.

⭐ 🖨 **Conversation Activator: Speaking Booster**

Indirect information questions begin with a question word.

She asked, "How did you respond to that offensive joke?" → She asked **how I had responded to that offensive joke.**

People often ask Nora, "How many years have you been studying English?" → People often ask Nora **how many years she has been studying English.**

> **Remember:** Embedded questions always have statement (not inverted) word order. Do not use do, does, or did.
> My friend asked what movie I wanted to see. NOT My friend asked what movie did I want to see.

F **GRAMMAR PRACTICE** On a separate sheet of paper, rewrite each sentence in indirect speech. Make all necessary backshifts and changes to pronouns and time expressions.

1 The teacher asked her students, "Can you tell me what the joke is about?"
   The teacher asked her students if they could tell her what the joke was about.
2 Barry sometimes asks himself, "How would I react if someone told an offensive joke?"
   Barry sometimes asked himself how he would react if someone told him an offensive joke.
3 Lisa asked her boyfriend, "Should you have laughed at that offensive joke?"
   Lisa asked her boyfriend if he should have laughed at that offensive joke.
4 Dan asked his wife, "Have you finished reading that book of jokes?"
   Dan asked his wife if she had finished reading that book of jokes.
5 Vivian asked me, "Which is the best website for funny animal videos?"
   Vivian asked me what the best website for funny animal videos was / is.

PRONUNCIATION BOOSTER p. 146
Intonation of sarcasm

NOW YOU CAN Respond to something funny

A ▶ 3:06 **CONVERSATION SPOTLIGHT** Read and listen. Notice the spotlighted conversation strategies.

A: Oh, Melanie, **you've got to see this**! I just can't tell you how hilarious it is.
B: What is it?
A: Here. It's this video. Some guy keeps tearing pieces of paper and his baby's laughing hysterically. **Seriously**, come over here and look!
B: Oh, **that's priceless**! Forward me the link, OK?
A: **Totally**.

B ▶ 3:07 **RHYTHM AND INTONATION** Listen again and repeat. Then practice the conversation with a partner.

C **CONVERSATION ACTIVATOR** Bring a cartoon, photo, or video clip to class. Or use the cartoon below or something from page 50. Use it to create a similar conversation. Start like this: *You've got to see this …* Be sure to change roles and then partners.

DON'T STOP!
• Talk about other cartoons, videos, or video clips you've seen.
• Say why you think they're funny.
• Say as much as you can.

"It could be that it's not plugged in, but that would be too easy."

LESSON 3

GOAL Analyze what makes us laugh

A **READING WARM-UP** Who are your favorite comedians and comic actors? Why do they make you laugh?

B ▶ 3:08 **READING** Read the article about why people laugh. Provide your own examples to illustrate each theory.

THEORIES OF HUMOR

People of all ages and from all cultures laugh. Although there are many factors that make something funny, three theories are often cited.

THE SUPERIORITY THEORY

The Superiority Theory holds that we tend to find people's small misfortunes and verbal or behavioral mistakes funny. Two examples of the kind of misfortunes often depicted in funny movies and comedy routines are people falling down or bumping into things. Similarly, hearing someone mispronounce a word or use the wrong word makes us laugh, as do the ridiculous mistakes that result from automatic spell check programs. According to this theory, the reason why we laugh at the misfortunes or mistakes of others is that they make us feel superior (and happy that the mistakes and misfortunes are theirs, not ours!).

THE INCONGRUITY THEORY

The Incongruity Theory suggests that humor arises from unexpected, inappropriate, or illogical situations—such as the one about the man who says his brother thinks he's a chicken:

> A man goes to a psychiatrist and says, "Doctor, I'm worried about my brother. He thinks he's a chicken." "That IS serious," says the doctor. "Why don't you put him in a mental hospital?" So the man says, "I would, but I need the eggs."

According to the Incongruity Theory, a joke becomes funny when we anticipate that one thing will happen or be said, but something else does instead. When the joke goes in the unexpected direction, we experience two sets of incompatible thoughts and emotions—the ones we had as we were listening and the ones revealed at the end. This incongruity makes us laugh.

THE RELIEF THEORY

According to the Relief Theory, humor is the feeling of relief that comes from the removal of tension. When tension is high, we need a release, and laughter is a way to cleanse our system of the built-up tension. This theory holds that there are certain things we feel tense about, such as bodily functions, physical attractions, and shame about how we look. It is believed that the large number of jokes about those subjects come from our need to laugh about them and thus relieve or reduce our tension about them.

Regardless of the theory, in order to be able to appreciate a situation or joke as funny, some detachment is always necessary; that is, we have to feel uninvolved with the situation. For example, we can often laugh at our own past mistakes because, with the passage of time, we have become detached. Conversely, if the joke or situation is too familiar or realistic, it may "hit too close to home" and evoke sadness instead of laughter. To understand a joke—to "get it"—we might also need some knowledge of cultural, economic, political, and social issues, without which some jokes are impossible to understand. Although humor is universal, there is no universal joke.

C **CLASSIFY** Complete the chart, checking the theory you think best explains why people laugh. (You may choose more than one.) Explain your choices.

PEOPLE OFTEN LAUGH WHEN THEY …	THE SUPERIORITY THEORY	THE INCONGRUITY THEORY	THE RELIEF THEORY
discover the strange noise they heard downstairs was only the cat.			✓
see someone slip and fall down.	✓		
see someone wearing inappropriate clothes to an event.		✓	
arrive at a party where someone is wearing the same outfit.	✓		
see a little girl wearing her mother's high heels.		✓	
see someone make an embarrassing social mistake.	✓		

LESSON 3

GOAL Analyze what makes us laugh

A READING WARM-UP

| Suggested teaching time: | 5 minutes | Your actual teaching time: |

- Discuss the warm-up questions as a class. Write on the board names of comedians and actors that students mention. Ask other students *Do you think they're funny too? Why? Why not?*

B ▶ 3:08 READING

| Suggested teaching time: | 10–15 minutes | Your actual teaching time: |

- On the board, write *What makes us laugh?* Invite students to brainstorm ideas and write them on the board. (Possible answers: funny video clips, silly jokes, animals dressed in clothes)
- As students read and listen, tell them to think about why people laugh.
- To check comprehension, ask:
    What is the Superiority Theory? (We laugh at people who are at a disadvantage or who suffer a small misfortune.)
    According to the Superiority Theory, why do we laugh at these people? (It makes us feel happy or better than they are.)
    What is the Incongruity Theory? (Humor arises from unexpected, inappropriate, or illogical situations.)
    What is the Relief Theory? (Humor is the feeling of relief that comes from the release of tension.)
    According to the Relief Theory, what does humor help people do? (cope with stressful situations)
    What is necessary to appreciate a situation or joke as funny? (some detachment)
    What else may be necessary to understand a joke? (knowledge of cultural, economic, political, and social issues)
- On the board, write:
    the Superiority Theory
    the Incongruity Theory
    the Relief Theory

In pairs, have students focus on the second sentence in the direction line and discuss their own examples to illustrate each theory. Then bring the class together and call on volunteers to share.

Option: [+5 minutes] Ask students to recall the last time they laughed very hard. On the board, write *What made you laugh? Which theory would this situation fit under?* Give students a few minutes to think about the questions and then have them share their situations and theories with the class.

Challenge: [+5 minutes] Have students think about the three theories and then determine in which situations they laugh the most. Have students write a paragraph explaining which theory best explains what makes them laugh. If a combination of theories or a different theory offers the best explanation, have students write about that. Have students read their paragraphs to the class.

⭐ 🖨 Reading Strategies

C CLASSIFY

| Suggested teaching time: | 10 minutes | Your actual teaching time: |

- Have students do the exercise individually. Then have them discuss their answers with a partner. The topics should stimulate discussion. Ask students to support their answers. For instance, for the item "arrive at a party where someone is wearing the same outfit" could be the Incongruity Theory because one wouldn't expect that to happen.
- Bring the class together and elicit other situations that make people laugh. Have students use one or more of the three theories to explain why. Invite other students to respond if they think the situations are funny.

Option: [+5 minutes] Ask individual students *Which situations in the chart have happened to you? Did you find them funny? Why? Why not?*

🖨 Extra Reading Comprehension Questions

D ▶ 3:09 LISTEN TO APPLY IDEAS

Suggested teaching time:	10–15 minutes	Your actual teaching time:

- **Pre-listening:** Have students look at the illustrations. Ask *Based on the illustrations, what will the jokes be about?* (1. a lawyer and a client, 2. people and their dogs, 3. playing golf)
- **Listening:** Have students listen to the jokes once. Then have them listen again.
- Invite students to respond to the jokes. Start by calling on volunteers to read the model answers. Then let students say what they thought about the jokes.
- Refer students to the article on page 56 to review the theories about what makes jokes funny. Then have groups discuss which theory best explains the humor of each joke.
- Bring the class together and have students discuss, providing reasons for their opinions.

LANGUAGE NOTE In joke 1, the phrase *awfully steep* means very expensive; in joke 2, *he tips the kids* means he gives the kid a tip, that is, a small amount of additional money for a job; in joke 3, *a driving range* is an area where golfers practice.

Challenge: [+5 minutes] In pairs, have students retell one of the jokes. If necessary, have students listen again. Circulate and listen as students tell the jokes. Then bring the class together and ask *Do you think it is difficult to tell a joke?* Introduce the term *punchline* and write the word on the board. Elicit that this is the final part of a joke that provides *the* funny element. Ask *What is the punchline to joke 1?* (Now what's your final question?) *Joke 2?* (My dog told me.); *Joke 3?* (Do you think I could borrow your son for a few minutes?) Invite students to share if they think telling jokes is difficult or easy, providing personal examples.

⭐ 🖨 Extra Challenge Reading Activity

NOW YOU CAN Analyze what makes us laugh

E ▶ 3:10 DISCUSSION

Suggested teaching time:	10–15 minutes	Your actual teaching time:

- Ask students to skim the types of jokes on the right and write checkmarks next to ones they find funny.
- Have students read and listen.
- Divide the class into groups of three or four and have students discuss the types of jokes using theories from the article, and other reasons and ideas to determine why people find them funny.

Option: [+5 minutes] Ask *Do you think any of the jokes on the list have potential to be offensive?* (Possible answers: dirty, ethnic, sexist, political) Invite students to share situations where such a joke offended. Also invite students to share if they were telling or listening to the joke.

Challenge: [+5 minutes] Ask *Have we heard any jokes in the unit so far that would fall into the categories listed here?* (verbal jokes: the lawyer joke from exercise above and the knock-knock joke from the listening from Exercise B on page 54; ethnic joke: the ketchup and peanut butter joke from Exercise D on page 51)

⭐ 🖨 Discussion: Speaking Booster

⭐ 🖨 Vocabulary-Building Strategies

OPTIONAL WRITING [+15–20 minutes]

- Have students draft their jokes and analyses in class or at home.
- In class let students peer review. Then collect and offer feedback.

D ▶ 3:09 **LISTEN TO APPLY IDEAS** Listen to three jokes. Write the theory you think each joke exemplifies. Then discuss with a partner to see if you agreed or disagreed. Provide reasons for your opinion and listen again if necessary to settle differences of opinion.

Joke 1 — The superiority theory

Joke 2 — The incongruity theory

Joke 3 — The incongruity theory

NOW YOU CAN Analyze what makes us laugh

DISCUSSION Read the list of common types of jokes to the right and try to explain why people find each kind funny or offensive. Use the theories, other reasons, and your own ideas for support.

OPTIONAL WRITING On a separate sheet of paper, write a joke you like. Then write at least two paragraphs analyzing why you and other people find it funny.

▶ 3:10 **Common types of jokes**

a dirty joke*	a joke about sex or with sexual content
an ethnic joke*	a joke about people of a particular ethnic background
a sexist joke*	a joke about men or women
a political joke*	a joke about a political candidate, party, opinion, or government official
a verbal joke	a joke that uses language in such a way that the language itself becomes funny

*Dirty jokes, ethnic jokes, and sexist jokes can be offensive to many people. Political jokes are sometimes inappropriate.

LESSON 4

GOAL Explore the limits of humor

A ▶ 3:11 **LISTENING WARM-UP   VOCABULARY   PRACTICAL JOKES**
Read and listen. Then listen again and repeat.

a practical joke

Don't take it personally!

be the butt of a joke   be the person on whom a trick, or "practical joke," is played; be the object of ridicule

can take a joke / be a good sport   be able to laugh at a practical joke, even when one is the butt of it, without getting insulted or taking it too personally

be in bad (or **poor**) **taste**   be offensive or extremely cruel

cross the line   go beyond funny into something mean, hurtful, offensive, or cruel

B ▶ 3:12 **LISTEN TO ACTIVATE VOCABULARY**   Listen to a description of a practical joke a doctor played on another doctor. Complete each statement about the practical joke you heard described.

1 Dr. Adams ....
   a played a practical joke on another doctor
   b was the butt of another doctor's joke

2 The woman thinks her father's joke ....
   a was in pretty good taste
   b may have crossed the line

3 In the end, the younger doctor proved that ....
   a he could take being the butt of a practical joke
   b the joke was in pretty poor taste

4 We can conclude that the man thinks that ....
   a the joke crossed the line
   b the younger doctor was a pretty good sport

C ▶ 3:13 **LISTEN TO SUMMARIZE**   Listen again and write a summary of the story, using indirect speech. Then compare summaries with a partner. Use the example as a way to start:
See page T58 for answers.

66 The woman described a practical joke her father had once played on someone. One day ... 99

D ▶ 3:14 **LISTEN TO TAKE NOTES**   Listen to people who were the butt of practical jokes. Then listen again to complete the chart. Use the Vocabulary. Listen again if necessary. *Answers will vary but may include the following:*

Speaker	What was the joke?	How did the person react?
1	A woman got a new car and parked it in a lot. Her friends left a fake note from someone saying she had scratched her car.	She didn't think it was really funny to be the butt of a joke.
2	The woman's friend tricked her into doing something at work that could have gotten her fired.	She thought it crossed the line; she was angry. It was in very bad taste.
3	The man's co-worker sent a message to his computer that surprised him.	He thought it was funny.

E **DISCUSSION**   Which, if any, of the jokes in Exercise D crossed the line? Explain your opinion. Then compare how you would have reacted with the way each speaker reacted.

LESSON 4

GOAL Explore the limits of humor

A ▶ 3:11 LISTENING WARM-UP

Suggested teaching time:	5 minutes	Your actual teaching time:

- Have students look at the cartoon. Ask *What just happened?* (The man on the left placed a pail of water over the door; when the man on the right entered, it tipped over and spilled on him.) Ask *What does he mean when he says* Don't take it personally? (Possible answer: that he was just joking)
- Have students read and listen to the vocabulary related to practical jokes.
- Then have students listen again and repeat.
- To confirm comprehension, ask *Who's the butt of the joke?* (the man on the right) *Does he look like he's being a good sport?* (no) *Do you think the joke is in poor taste? Do you think it crosses the line?*
- Write *practical joke* on the board. As a class, come up with a definition and write it on the board. (Possible definition: a trick you play on someone that usually causes embarrassment or discomfort to the person)

LANGUAGE NOTE Point out that when you *play* a joke on someone, the joke is an action, but when you *tell* a joke, the joke has a verbal meaning.

⭐ 🖨 Vocabulary-Building Strategies

B ▶ 3:12 LISTEN TO ACTIVATE VOCABULARY

Suggested teaching time:	10–15 minutes	Your actual teaching time:

- Pre-listening: Tell students they will listen to a practical joke played by one doctor on another. Ask students to read the exercise items to help guide the listening.
- Listening: Have students listen once.
- Ask students to complete the exercise individually. Then bring the class together to go over the answers. Focus on item 2. If necessary, play the beginning of the description again so that students can follow exactly what the woman said: "My dad was famous for playing jokes on people. Usually they were in pretty good taste, but this one may have crossed the line."
- In item 3 focus on answer a. Refer to the vocabulary and point out that the two expressions—*be the butt of a joke* and *can take a joke*—are combined here.

⭐ 🖨 Listening Strategies

C ▶ 3:13 LISTEN TO SUMMARIZE

Suggested teaching time:	5 minutes	Your actual teaching time:

- Have students listen to the description of the practical joke again. Tell them they will summarize the joke, using indirect speech.
- Circulate while students are working on their summaries. Note any errors in indirect speech. Then bring the class together and call on students to share their summaries. Go over any common errors in retelling the joke.

LANGUAGE NOTE You may want to call students' attention to the fact that the woman describing the practical joke shifts from the simple past to the simple present in the middle of the joke. Speakers of English often shift naturally to the present when narrating a story, especially a funny or dramatic one. Note that the audio starts with the line *I've got a good one*. Point out that this is a typical way to introduce a joke.

Answers to Exercise C
Answers will vary but may include the following:
One day ... at a hospital, the chief of staff asked a security guard to help play a practical joke on Dr. Adams, a young colleague who was visiting for a conference. The chief asked the guard to stop Dr. Adams and accuse him of impersonating a doctor. The guard did this, and also said he was going to call the police! The chief was watching the whole time and finally walked up to them and explained everything.

D ▶ 3:14 LISTEN TO TAKE NOTES

Suggested teaching time:	5 minutes	Your actual teaching time:

- Pre-listening: Have students look at the chart. Tell them they will summarize each joke they hear and note how the person reacted.
- First listening: Have students listen to the three speakers without taking notes. Clarify vocabulary as needed.
- Second listening: Have students listen again and take notes in the chart.

LANGUAGE NOTE *To get even with someone* is to do something equally unpleasant or harmful to the person who did something to you first; *to show someone the ropes* is to explain to someone how things are done, as in an office; *it dawned on me* means it became clear to me; *ticked off* means annoyed; *to freak* is an informal term meaning to suddenly become angry or upset; *laugh one's head off* is an idiom meaning laugh really hard; *a jerk* is an informal term for a stupid, rude, or annoying person.

E DISCUSSION

Suggested teaching time:	5 minutes	Your actual teaching time:

- On the board, write *Did the joke cross the line?*
- Divide the class into groups. Have them apply the question on the board to each joke. Tell students to refer to their notes from Exercise D to recall details of the joke. Then tell students to compare how they would have reacted in each situation.
- Circulate and assist as needed.

NOW YOU CAN Explore the limits of humor

A FRAME YOUR IDEAS

Suggested teaching time:	5–10 minutes	Your actual teaching time:

- Ask a volunteer to read the scorecard.
- Then have pairs read and rate the practical jokes.

B PAIR WORK

Suggested teaching time:	5 minutes	Your actual teaching time:

- Divide the class into pairs and have students share their ratings.
- Then have them discuss the questions, noting how they would have responded if the joke had been played on them. Circulate and make sure students respond to each joke individually.

C DISCUSSION

Suggested teaching time:	5–10 minutes	Your actual teaching time:

- Ask a student to read the expressions in the Recycle This Language box. Then divide the class into groups of three.
- Have students discuss the questions.
- Then bring the class together and call on groups to summarize their ideas. Elicit examples of practical jokes.
- Finally, write *practical joker* on the board. Elicit that this is a person who likes to play practical jokes. Ask *Is anyone here a practical joker? Do you think most practical jokers also like to have practical jokes played on them?* (Possible answer: Possibly, since they are able to appreciate them)

T59 UNIT 5 LESSON 4

NOW YOU CAN Explore the limits of humor

A FRAME YOUR IDEAS Read the practical jokes and rate each one, using the scorecard.

SCORECARD

X = I don't get it.
1 = It crosses the line.
2 = It's silly.
3 = It's kind of funny.
4 = It's hilarious!

A RATING: ☐
Someone in your family leaves a very real-looking toy snake in a drawer with your clothes. You open the drawer and are about to put your hand in when you suddenly see the snake.

B RATING: ☐
You start getting lots of calls from people who want to buy your house, even though you have no intention of selling. It turns out a friend had secretly created an online real estate ad offering your house at a very cheap price.

C RATING: ☐
A colleague tells you that another colleague is going to get married. When you see her, you congratulate her happily. She has no idea what you're talking about.

D RATING: ☐
Someone in your family offers you a cup of coffee or tea. When you take the first sip, it tastes so bad you can hardly swallow it. You realize it has salt in it instead of sugar.

E RATING: ☐
You're invited to a friend's costume party. When you arrive at the party, everyone is nicely dressed in regular clothes, and you are dressed in a chicken costume.

B PAIR WORK Compare your ratings on the practical jokes. Do you agree? Then, for each joke, compare how you would have responded if <u>you</u> had been the butt of the joke. Would you have been a good sport? Or would you have been offended?

RECYCLE THIS LANGUAGE
- It was so [hysterical / hilarious]!
- It was [too much / too funny]!
- I didn't get it.
- What was so funny about it?
- It went over my head.
- Seriously.
- That just isn't done.
- It was kind of [ridiculous / offensive / silly].

C DISCUSSION
1 When do you think a practical joke crosses the line?
2 Have you ever played a practical joke on someone else? What was the joke and what happened? Use the Vocabulary from page 58.
3 What is your opinion of practical jokes in the workplace? Are they ever acceptable? Explain.

WRITING Writing dialogue

A WRITING SKILL Study the rules.

Paragraphing a story with dialogue
With direct speech, begin a new paragraph each time you introduce a new speaker. Remember that paragraphs should be indented or should have a space above them so the reader can see where new paragraphs begin. See one paragraphing style in the Writing Model.

Punctuation of direct speech
- When the reporting verb comes before a quotation, put a comma after the reporting verb. Put the end punctuation inside the quotation marks.

  Mr. Mann said, "That's not at all funny."

- When the reporting verb comes after a quotation, put a comma, question mark, or an exclamation point at the end of the quoted sentence, inside the quotation marks. Put the speaker's name before or after the reporting verb.

  "Please don't do anything cruel," Ms. Kane said.
  "Didn't anyone object to that mean practical joke?" asked Carlson.

- A reporting verb can also come between two parts of a quotation. Put quotation marks around each part of the quotation. Don't begin the second part of the quotation with a capital letter unless it begins a new sentence.

  "Melanie and Elaine," Mr. Sargent said, "please apologize for hurting Morgan."

- If the reporting verb comes between complete sentences, put a period after the reporting verb. Begin the new sentence with a capital letter.

  "Peter, please apologize to Morgan," continued Mr. Sargent. "You participated in that mean practical joke too."

WRITING MODEL
About a year ago, my grandmother was walking down the street, stopping from time to time to look in shop windows. At one store, she stopped to admire a dress in the window. Just as she turned to enter the store, a businessman walking very fast and, not looking where he was going, bumped into her, knocking her down.

"Oh, I'm so sorry!" said the man. "Are you OK?"

My grandmother was too stunned to reply. But then after a moment she said she was fine.

"Look!" she heard someone say from across the street. "An old woman just fell down!"

She quickly sat up and looked around with great concern and said, "Where?"

When she told us this story, we all laughed. But, it really wasn't that funny, and it could have been serious.

B PRACTICE On a separate sheet of paper, rewrite the sentences, correcting the errors in punctuation and capitalization. See page T60 for answers.

1 Norman Cousins said, "That he had cured himself with laughter."
2 "The Superiority Theory" our professor explained. "Is exemplified by finding people's errors funny."
3 "The joke was really cruel," said Claire. "they shouldn't have played it."
4 "Does that example illustrate the Incongruity Theory" asked John?
5 "I learned about all kinds of humor in my psychology class", said my sister.

C PRACTICE On a separate sheet of paper, write the following indirect speech statements in direct speech, using correct punctuation for dialogue. See page T60 for answers.

1 Dr. Summers stated that positive emotions can have a direct effect on emotional and physical health.
2 A psychologist told me many people believed that Norman Cousins's book popularized the idea that laughter therapy could be helpful in treating illness.
3 She said that practical jokes come from our need to feel superior to others.
4 Ms. Barton insisted that traditional medicine is more effective than laughter therapy.
5 Our professor asked whether there is any scientific evidence that laughter can treat illness.

D APPLY THE WRITING SKILL Write a true or imaginary story telling what happened and what people said, using dialogue. Use the Writing Model for support.

SELF-CHECK
☐ Did I use direct speech in my story?
☐ Did I punctuate direct speech correctly?
☐ Did I correctly paragraph the dialogue?

WRITING Writing dialogue

A WRITING SKILL

Suggested teaching time:	5–10 minutes	Your actual teaching time:

- Write *dialogue* on the board. Elicit that dialogue is conversation that takes place in a book, play, or film. Ask *Is dialogue direct or indirect speech?* (direct speech) Point out that when writing a story, you can use a combination of direct and indirect speech.
- Ask a volunteer to read the section on paragraphing a story with dialogue. Ask *Which paragraphing style is used in the writing model?* (indenting)
- To review direct and indirect speech, have students read the writing model individually. Tell them to notice the punctuation in sentences that include dialogue. Point out that a change in speaker may be indicated by starting a new paragraph, as in the writing model.
- Have volunteers read the four punctuation rules and example sentences. Stop after each example and ask students to write additional examples on the board.
- To test student understanding of punctuation rules for direct speech, write the following sentences on the board and have students fill in the punctuation and add capital letters where necessary:
  - Tom said laughter therapy helped me a lot
  - That practical joke crossed the line Jen cried angrily
  - Ethnic jokes and sexist jokes the supervisor stated are not acceptable here.
  - Henri loves to play jokes Lily explained he is also a good sport when a joke is played on him

(Answers: Tom said, "Laughter therapy helped me a lot."
"That practical joke crossed the line," Jen cried angrily.
"Ethnic and sexist jokes," the supervisor stated, "are not acceptable here."
"Henri loves to play jokes," Lily explained. "He is also a good sport when a joke is played on him.")

> Point out to students that it's not necessary to capitalize the first word of the reporting verb that follows the quote, even if the quotation ended with final punctuation such as a question mark or an exclamation mark. Auto capitalization usually capitalizes (incorrectly) in this instance.

Challenge: [+5 minutes] Have students look at examples of dialogue in a book or a short story and find the various examples of punctuation described above.

B PRACTICE

Suggested teaching time:	5 minutes	Your actual teaching time:

- Have students complete the exercise individually. Then have them compare answers with a partner. Point out that some items have more than one mistake.
- Go over the answers as a class. Write the sentences on the board and invite volunteers to make the corrections. Refer to the rules in Exercise A as needed.

Answers to Exercise B

1. Norman Cousins said that he had cured himself with laughter. / Norman Cousins said, "I cured myself with laughter."
2. "The Superiority Theory," our professor explained, "is exemplified by finding people's mistakes funny."
3. "The joke was really cruel," said Claire. "They shouldn't have played it."
4. "Does that example illustrate The Incongruity Theory?" asked John.
5. "I learned about all kinds of humor in my psychology class," said my sister.

C PRACTICE

Suggested teaching time:	5 minutes	Your actual teaching time:

- Have students skim the exercise items. Ask *Which ones are statements?* (items 1 through 4) *Which are questions?* (item 5) *What type of question is embedded in item 5—a Yes / No or an information question?*
- Tell students to write the sentences in direct speech.
- Go over the answers as a class. Have students come to the board and write the direct statements and question on the board.

Answers to Exercise C

1. Dr. Summers stated, "Positive emotions can have a direct effect on emotional and physical health."
2. A psychologist told me, "Many people believe that Norman Cousins's book popularized the idea that laughter can be helpful in treating illness."
3. She said, "Practical jokes come from our need to feel superior to others."
4. Ms. Barton insisted, "Traditional medicine is more effective than laughter therapy."
5. Our professor asked, "Is there any scientific evidence that laughter can treat illness?"

D APPLY THE WRITING SKILL

Suggested teaching time:	10–15 minutes	Your actual teaching time:

- On the board, write *a funny story*. Tell students they will use a combination of direct and indirect speech to retell or make up a funny story. Make sure they specify what happened and what different people said.
- Refer students to the Writing Process Worksheet in ActiveTeach for guidance with pre-writing and peer feedback.
- Encourage students to use the Self-Check in the Student's Book to go over the stories they wrote.

Option: [+5 minutes] Time-permitting, students can exchange papers with a partner and offer feedback using the topics in the Self-Check list. Encourage partners to also check for examples.

Writing Process

REVIEW

🎮 **Digital Game**

A ▶ 3:15

| Suggested teaching time: | 5–10 minutes | Your actual teaching time: |

- **Pre-listening:** Ask students to scan the answers to make sure they are familiar with all the terms. If necessary, review that *the butt of a joke* is the person on whom the trick or practical joke is played. Refer students to page 57 if they need to recall common types of jokes.
- **First listening:** Ask students to listen to each joke. Stop after each one to let students answer the question.
- **Second listening:** Have students listen again to check their answers.
- Go over the answers as a class.

B

| Suggested teaching time: | 5 minutes | Your actual teaching time: |

- Refer students to the Vocabulary on page 54 for ways to respond to a joke.
- Before students do the exercise individually, point out that more than one answer may be possible.
- Have pairs compare answers.

Answers to Exercise B
Answers will vary but may include the following:
1. I don't get it.
2. That's offensive.
3. That's hilarious!
4. That crosses the line.

C

| Suggested teaching time: | 5 minutes | Your actual teaching time: |

- Before students rewrite the sentences, remind them not to use a comma after the reporting verb in indirect speech. Also tell students to make appropriate shifts in tense, pronouns, and expressions of time and place.

Answers to Exercise C
1. Mary asked me if I got the joke.
2. The students insisted that they hadn't played any practical jokes in the gym.
3. My father admitted that 25 years of practicing medicine had taught him that laughter can be the best medicine.
4. Jess told her friends that she would tell them about a joke that she had told during her job interview the day before if they promised not to tell anyone.
5. Anne said that she can't / couldn't understand British humor.
6. She said she may not have enough familiarity with British culture to understand all the pop culture references.
7. The people at the party asked who was going to tell the first joke.

- Have students compare answers with a partner. Then go over any questions. Tell students that in item 3 it is not incorrect to omit *that* (*My father admitted that . . .*). However, because of the change in subject from the expected *he* to *twenty-five years of practicing medicine*, the use of *that* makes the sentence clearer.

D

| Suggested teaching time: | 5 minutes | Your actual teaching time: |

- If students need to review common types of jokes, refer them to page 57.
- After students complete the exercise, have them compare answers with a partner.

Option: TEST-TAKING SKILLS BOOSTER (p. 155)

EXTRA

- Workbook
- MyEnglishLab
- Online Student Resources (www.english.com/summit3e)
   – Classroom Audio Program
   – Extra Practice Activities
   – *Summit GO* App
   – Web Projects
- ActiveTeach
   – Assessment
   – Additional Printable Resources
      ○ Audioscripts and Answer Keys
      ○ "Can-Do" Self-Assessment Charts
      ○ Conversation and Discussion Activator Video Scripts
      ○ Oral Progress Assessment Charts
      ○ Reading Speed Calculator
   – Summit TV Video Program
      ○ Activity Worksheets
      ○ Teaching Notes
      ○ Video Scripts

REVIEW

A ▶ 3:15 Listen to three examples of jokes. After each one, complete the statement about it. Listen again if necessary.

1 The butt of the joke is ……… .
   (a) John   b the manager   c Mark
2 The joke is funny because ……… .
   a we feel superior to the man   (b) we are surprised at his response   c we feel relief from tension
3 This joke is an example of ……… .
   (a) a verbal joke   b an ethnic joke   c a dirty joke

B Write the response you would give in each situation, using vocabulary from Unit 5 or your own response.

1 Someone tells you a joke you don't understand.
   You: ………………………………………………………………
   ………………………………………………………………………

3 You hear a joke that you find very funny.
   You: ………………………………………………………………
   ………………………………………………………………………

2 Someone tells an insulting ethnic joke and you want to say something about it.
   You: ………………………………………………………………
   ………………………………………………………………………

4 You have a friend who wants to play a practical joke on someone, but you think it's cruel.
   You: ………………………………………………………………
   ………………………………………………………………………

C On a separate sheet of paper, rewrite the following, changing the direct speech into indirect speech. See page T61 for answers.

1 Mary asked me, "Did you get that joke?"
2 The students insisted, "We didn't play any practical jokes in the gym."
3 My father admitted, "Twenty-five years of practicing medicine have taught me that laughter can be the best medicine."
4 Jess told her friends, "I'll tell you about a joke I told during my job interview yesterday if you promise not to tell anyone."
5 "I can't understand British humor," said Anne.
6 She said, "I may not have enough familiarity with British culture to understand all the pop culture references."
7 The people at the party asked, "Who's going to tell the first joke?"

D Complete each statement about kinds of jokes.

1 A(n) *dirty* ……………………… joke is a joke that's about sex.
2 A joke that's insulting to all men or to all women is a(n) *sexist* ……………………… joke.
3 A joke that's insulting to all people of a certain nationality is a(n) *ethnic* ……………………… joke.
4 A joke that makes fun of a candidate for election is a(n) *political* ……………………… joke.
5 A joke that plays a trick on someone to make him or her the butt of the joke is a(n) *practical* ……………………… joke.

TEST-TAKING SKILLS BOOSTER p. 155

Web Project: Laughter Therapy
www.english.com/summit3e

UNIT 6
Troubles While Traveling

PREVIEW

COMMUNICATION GOALS
1. Describe some causes of travel hassles
2. Express gratitude for a favor while traveling
3. Discuss staying safe on the Internet
4. Talk about lost, stolen, or damaged property

A **FRAME YOUR IDEAS** Read about the online contest. On a separate sheet of paper, write your own tips for the common travel hassles.

THE PRACTICAL TRAVELER

HATE TRAVEL HASSLES? ENTER THE TRAVEL TIPS CONTEST!

CONTEST DIRECTIONS: Click on a pull-down menu to enter your own tip for dealing with a specific travel hassle. When you have finished entering all your tips, click on the link to our secure server to submit your tips. Contest winner will be announced on July 15. All decisions final.

CONTEST DEADLINE: July 1

Click here for a full list of prizes for the finalists.

No limit on number of submissions. Enter as many times as you want!

AIR TRAVEL
- Inedible or no food on flights
- Unexpected checked baggage fees
- Carry-on luggage fees
- Insufficient room in overhead bins
- Overbooked flights
- Missed connections
- Lost luggage
- Long lines at check-in and security screening
- Items confiscated by security

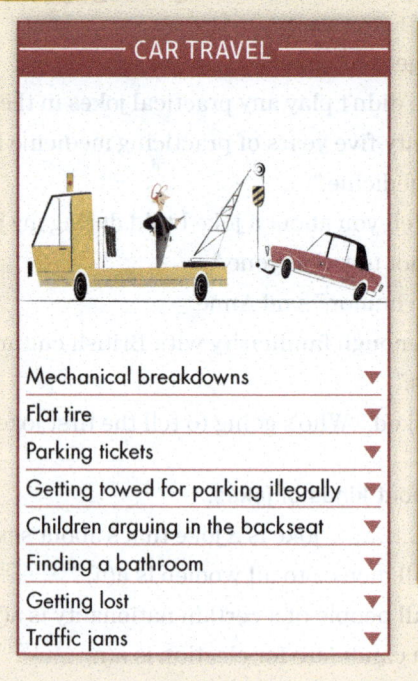

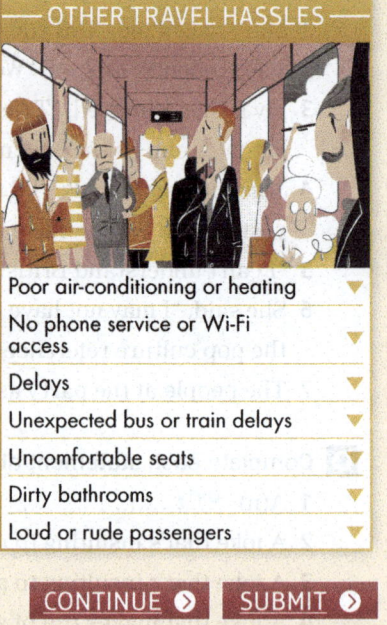

CAR TRAVEL
- Mechanical breakdowns
- Flat tire
- Parking tickets
- Getting towed for parking illegally
- Children arguing in the backseat
- Finding a bathroom
- Getting lost
- Traffic jams

OTHER TRAVEL HASSLES
- Poor air-conditioning or heating
- No phone service or Wi-Fi access
- Delays
- Unexpected bus or train delays
- Uncomfortable seats
- Dirty bathrooms
- Loud or rude passengers

CONTINUE **SUBMIT**

B ▶ 3:16 **VOCABULARY** **TRAVEL NOUNS** Find and circle these words and phrases in the contest. Listen and repeat. Then, with a partner, explain the meaning of each one. See page T62 for answers.

- checked baggage fees
- carry-on luggage
- an overhead bin
- a missed connection
- security screening
- a breakdown
- a flat tire
- a parking ticket

C **DISCUSSION** Share your tips. Decide which tips you think are good enough to win the contest.

62 UNIT 6

UNIT 6
Troubles While Traveling

PREVIEW

A FRAME YOUR IDEAS

Suggested teaching time:	5–10 minutes	Your actual teaching time:

- Write *contest* on the board. Ask *Do you like to participate in contests?* Tell students they will participate in a contest where they will give travel tips.

- As a class, look at the website as it appears in the book. Call on volunteers to read the text in the top section. Ask *What is a practical traveler?* (An effective traveler; a practical traveler is likely to be effective in a given situation.) Elicit that *travel hassles* are annoyances during travels; things that cause problems.

- Ask a volunteer to read the contest directions. Point to the categories of travel: air, car, other. Explain that in each section there are different topics (e.g., inedible food on flight). You click on a topic, you can enter a tip to be considered for the contest. Ask *What tip could you suggest that is related to inedible food or no food on flights?* (Possible answer: Pack snacks or sandwiches for your flight.) Tell students to skim the topics. These will be discussed in more detail in Exercise B, Vocabulary.

- Bring students' attention to the red box on the right. Ask a student to read the information. Ask *What do you think the prizes might be?* (Possible answers: luggage, travel books, plane tickets) *Would you participate in such a contest? How many times would you submit an entry? Have you ever won such a contest?*

B ▶ 3:16 VOCABULARY

Suggested teaching time:	5 minutes	Your actual teaching time:

- Have students look at the list of travel hassles. If necessary, explain that *woes* are problems or troubles. In pairs, have students explain the meanings of the words and phrases, referring to the website to help them with context. Invite them to share stories if they have experienced any of these issues and woes.

- Have students listen.

- Then have them listen and repeat.

LANGUAGE NOTE *Luggage* and *baggage* are often used interchangeably in the context of transportation. However, *baggage* is a more general or "official" term, referring to all the kinds of passengers' suitcases, bags, etc., carried in various types of transportation, while *luggage* refers to what one buys at the store to hold one's belongings or used for one's personal suitcases, duffel bags, etc. Some examples of interchangeable use: checked baggage / luggage; a baggage / luggage check.

Answers to Exercise B
Answers will vary but may include the following:
checked baggage fees: extra money you have to pay for baggage that you check in, often the case when bags are over the weight limit or oversize
carry-on luggage: luggage that you don't check in but take with you on the plane
an overhead bin: the compartment above the seats on a plane where passengers store carry-on luggage
a missed connection: when a traveler doesn't make it in time to a connecting flight
security screening: the process of checking passengers at the airport to make sure they don't present any risks
a breakdown: when the mechanism of a car or other vehicle stops working
a flat tire: when a tire has insufficient air in it
a parking ticket: a penalty imposed for not parking a car according to regulations

Option: [+5 minutes] Invite students to share stories of the hassles on the website that are not listed in the vocabulary list.

Option: [+5 minutes] For further vocabulary practice, encourage students to use the words and phrases in sentences. Have students work in pairs to write these sentences or just say them to each other. (Possible answers: This airline doesn't have checked baggage fees. You are permitted one carry-on luggage item. Please put all carry-on items in the overhead bin. I missed my connection in New York, so I got on a flight the next day. Security screening requires taking shoes off. We called the tow truck after the mechanical breakdown. We got a flat tire on our road trip. The parking ticket cost me $50. We got towed for parking in a fire zone.)

C DISCUSSION

Suggested teaching time:	5 minutes	Your actual teaching time:

- You may wish to have students write actual tips for any (or all) of the hassles, as if they were entering this contest. Alternatively, you could have a discussion, with students offering and discussing their tips.

- Have students work in pairs or small groups. Elicit a travel tip and model it on the board. For example, for the category *mechanical breakdowns* under Car Travel: *Take your car for an oil change and a full checkup before going on a trip. You should also check to make sure your car has had all scheduled maintenance.*

- Circulate and assist as needed. Tell students they can give tips in the imperative (e.g., *Take your car*) or give advice (*You should . . .*).

- Bring the class together and call on volunteers to share tips. Then have students vote on which ones are good enough to win the contest.

D ▶ 3:17 SPOTLIGHT

Suggested teaching time:	10 minutes	Your actual teaching time:

- Ask students to look at the photo. Ask *What travel hassle does this man seem to be experiencing?* (Possible answer: Maybe he lost something like a passport, or his luggage didn't arrive.)
- Have students read and listen to the conversation.
- To check comprehension, ask: *Why is Edison stressed?* (He's missing his folder with his passport and boarding pass.) *Is it likely he left it in the limo? Why or why not?* (No, he remembers looking back at the seat of the limo to see if he forgot something.) *Where is it probably?* (at the hotel) *What does he have to do?* (go back and get it) *Will Yuji wait for him?* (no) *Will Edison make it to the dinner?* (maybe, if he catches a later flight)

LANGUAGE NOTE *Limo* is short for *limousine*, which is a car driven by someone who is paid to drive; some limousines can be large, expensive, and comfortable. *Cab* is another word for *taxi*, a car that you pay to take you somewhere. Point out that Edison takes an airport limo from the hotel—which has the sole purpose of taking hotel guests to and from the airport; but later he grabs, or takes, a cab to go back to the hotel. *To split* means to leave a place quickly. The noun *hassle* can be both countable and uncountable: You can go through a hassle, or something can be too much hassle. *Hassle* can also be used as a verb to mean to annoy someone, especially when asking someone to do something many times. *Hassled*, the adjective form, means stressed or under pressure.

E UNDERSTAND IDIOMS AND EXPRESSIONS

Suggested teaching time:	5–10 minutes	Your actual teaching time:

- Focus on the idioms and expressions as a class. Call on volunteers to read them aloud.
- Let students work individually to locate them in context to figure out the meanings. Then have students match each expression with the correct definition.
- Ask students to compare answers with a partner, returning to Exercise D to confirm their answers.
- Bring the class together to go over the answers.

Challenge: [+5 minutes] Divide the class into pairs and assign each pair one or two idioms / expressions from the list. Have them create brief dialogues around them. Invite pairs to share dialogues.

F THINK AND EXPLAIN

Suggested teaching time:	5 minutes	Your actual teaching time:

- Have students discuss the questions in pairs. Then bring the class together to go over the answers.
- Invite students to share their speculations about what else could have happened to Edison's folder. (Possible answer: It's possible that Edison packed his folder in his luggage.)

Option: [+5 minutes] Invite students to further discuss Edison's situation in pairs. Write these questions on the board:

How would you describe Edison's stress level? (He is upset and stressed. Yuji urges him not to freak out.)

What will result from the mishap with his folder? (He has to go back to the hotel. He will miss his flight and will have to catch another one. He may be late for his meeting.)

What should he do before he goes to the hotel? (Call to see if the folder is there—if it isn't, he might check his bags more carefully and find it there.)

Bring the class together and have students share how they would handle such a situation.

SPEAKING

Suggested teaching time:	10–15 minutes	Your actual teaching time:

- Have students work individually to check the hassles they have experienced and then write some details. Explain that they can say where or when it happened and how they resolved the problem.
- Ask students to discuss with a partner.
- Bring the class together and poll the class to see which are the most common problems.

Option: [+5 minutes] After experiencing a hassle, we anticipate that it can happen again and hopefully we can prepare for it. Have students share how they have approached travel differently over time to avoid hassles. Model an answer: *One time, when I was traveling to Europe, my bag got lost. I never saw it again. The airline offered to reimburse me for everything in the bag, but I couldn't remember all the things I'd put in it. Since then, I always keep a list of all the items I pack in each suitcase. Of course, I've never lost my luggage again. But I am prepared!*

T63 UNIT 6 PREVIEW

D ▶ 3:17 **SPOTLIGHT** Read and listen to two friends talking about a travel hassle on a business trip. Notice the spotlighted language.

ENGLISH FOR TODAY'S WORLD
Understand a variety of accents.
Edison = Portuguese
Yuji = Japanese

Edison: Oh, no. My folder's missing! It had my passport and my boarding pass in it.
Yuji: Uh-oh! Try to think. When did you see it last? Was it at the hotel?
Edison: Let's see … **I'm drawing a blank.** Oh! I remember now. I'd just finished printing out the boarding pass when the front desk called to say the airport limo was waiting downstairs. So I got my stuff together and split.
Yuji: Do you think you could have left the folder in the room or at the front desk when you checked out? Or what about in the limo?
Edison: Well, I distinctly remember looking back at the seat of the limo before I slammed the door, just to check that I hadn't left anything, and I hadn't. It's got to be in the hotel.
Yuji: Well, don't freak out. **It's a safe bet** they'll find it in the hotel.
Edison: You know, if I hadn't been rushing for the limo, this wouldn't have happened. **The way I see it**, I have no choice but to go back to the hotel. I'll grab a cab outside. You go on. You need to catch that plane.
Yuji: OK.
Edison: But if that folder isn't at the hotel, **I'm toast**. If it weren't for my stupid mistake, I wouldn't be going through this hassle. What'll happen if I miss the dinner?
Yuji: Well, **you'll cross that bridge when you come to it**. But hey, **no sweat**. If the folder's there, you can be back in time to make the four o'clock. We can meet up later. The dinner's not till seven.
Edison: OK. **I'm off**. Keep your fingers crossed!

E **UNDERSTAND IDIOMS AND EXPRESSIONS** Match the expressions from Spotlight with the statement or phrase that has a similar meaning.

1 I'm drawing a blank. e
2 It's a safe bet. b
3 the way I see it g
4 I'm toast. c
5 You'll cross that bridge when you come to it. d
6 No sweat. a
7 I'm off. f

a Don't worry about it.
b It's very probable.
c I'm in big trouble.
d You can worry about that later.
e I can't remember.
f I'm leaving right now.
g in my opinion

F **THINK AND EXPLAIN** What do you think the outcome of the situation will be? What are Edison's options if the folder isn't found in his room or at the front desk? Explain. Answers will vary but may include the following: Edison might find his folder back at the hotel. If he does not find it, he will need to go to the nearest Embassy to issue a replacement passport.

SPEAKING Check hassles you've experienced and write details about when and where they happened. Then discuss with a partner.

My Experiences	Details
☐ I lost my passport.	
☐ I missed a plane / bus / train.	
☐ I missed a connecting flight.	
☐ My luggage was delayed or lost.	
☐ My car got towed.	
☐ I was in a vehicle that broke down.	
☐ I got a parking ticket.	
☐ My cosmetics were confiscated at security.	
☐ Other	

LESSON 1

GOAL Describe some causes of travel hassles

A ▶ 3:18 **GRAMMAR SPOTLIGHT** Read the interviews about travel hassles. Notice the spotlighted grammar.

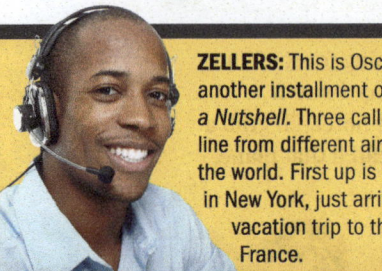

ZELLERS: This is Oscar Zellers with another installment of *Nightmares in a Nutshell*. Three callers are on the line from different airports around the world. First up is Isabela Wilson in New York, just arrived from a vacation trip to the south of France.

ZELLERS: Ms. Wilson, I understand you had your perfume taken from you when you went through security.

❶ WILSON: Unfortunately, yes. I got to the airport late and had to take my bag through security. But I'd forgotten the *expensive* French perfume I'd packed in that bag. It's not as if I don't know you can't take liquids through security. **If I'd been thinking** clearly, **I would have arrived** early enough to check my bag. Can you believe it was confiscated?!

ZELLERS: Next up is James Robillard in Montreal. He arrived in Brazil yesterday with an expired business visa and was put on a return flight back to Montreal. How unfortunate, Mr. Robillard!

❷ ROBILLARD: You can say that again! But frankly I'm pretty annoyed that the agent here in Montreal who checked me in didn't notice the expired visa. **If she'd been paying** better attention—instead of worrying about how much my baggage weighed!—**she would have noticed** it. She simply **couldn't have been looking for** the expiration date on the visa. She took a quick glance and saw that my passport was valid, but that was it.

ZELLERS: And last but not least, let's talk to Alice Yang. Ms. Yang started out in Shanghai and flew to Los Angeles, where she connected with her flight to San Salvador. But Ms. Yang's checked luggage wasn't transferred to the San Salvador flight. What bad luck, Ms. Yang!

❸ YANG: It sure was. And I've only got one day here in El Salvador. Tomorrow I'm departing for Bolivia, then the next day, Ecuador, then Peru! My bags may never catch up with me. You know, if **I were traveling** on a weekday, or if I had another day here, it **wouldn't be** such a problem since I could go shopping, but today is Sunday and most stores are closed. Take it from me. If you **have to change** planes, don't even think of checking your bag. Better safe than sorry!

B **DISCUSSION** Whose situation would be the most frustrating for you? Explain.

C **GRAMMAR** **UNREAL CONDITIONAL SENTENCES: CONTINUOUS FORMS**
Use continuous verb forms in unreal conditional sentences to express actions in progress.

Present unreal conditional sentences
You can use <u>were</u> (or <u>weren't</u>) + a present participle in the <u>if</u> clause. You can use <u>would be</u> (or <u>wouldn't be</u>) + a present participle in the result clause. Note: The verb forms should reflect what you want to express. You don't have to use continuous forms in both clauses.

If I **were walking** in traffic, I **wouldn't be talking** on my cell phone.
[continuous forms in both clauses]
If he walked there, he **would be going** through the most dangerous section of town.
[continuous form only in the result clause]

Past unreal conditional sentences
You can use <u>had been</u> (or <u>hadn't been</u>) + a present participle in the <u>if</u> clause. You can use <u>would have been</u> (or <u>wouldn't have been</u>) + a present participle in the result clause. You don't have to use continuous forms in both clauses.

If he'**d been using** his webcam during the conference call, he **would have been wearing** a tie.
[continuous forms in both clauses]
If I **hadn't been checking** my messages, I wouldn't have known the flight was delayed. [continuous form only in the <u>if</u> clause]

Sequence of tenses
The traditional sequence of tenses in all past unreal conditional sentences (past perfect in the <u>if</u> clause and <u>would have</u> + a past participle in the result clause) can change to express time. Compare the following sentences.

past unreal condition	present or past result
If I'**d gone** to India last year,	I **wouldn't be flying** there right now.
If I'**d gone** to India last year,	I **would have seen** the Taj Mahal.

Remember:
Conditional sentences usually have two clauses: an <u>if</u> (or "condition") clause and a result clause. The clauses in conditional sentences can be reversed.

Real (or "factual") conditionals describe the results of real conditions. Unreal conditionals describe the results of unreal conditions.

Be careful! Don't use <u>would</u> in the <u>if</u> clause in any unreal conditional sentence.
If I were watching TV, I would be watching the news.
NOT If I would be watching TV, …

GRAMMAR BOOSTER p. 137
The conditional: summary and extension

LESSON 1

GOAL Describe some causes of travel hassles

A ▶ 3:18 GRAMMAR SPOTLIGHT

Suggested teaching time:	5–10 minutes	Your actual teaching time:

- Ask a student to read the direction line. Then tell students to look at the pictures. Invite students to describe these people's emotions. (annoyed, stressed, worried) On the board, write the adjective *hassled* and elicit that it means under pressure or stressed.
- Before students read and listen, ask a volunteer to read the first line of the interview. Write this phrase on the board: *Nightmares in a Nutshell*. Ask *What is a nightmare?* (a frightening dream) The word *nightmare* is often used to describe a difficult, unpleasant, or frightening experience or situation. Then focus on the expression *in a nutshell*. Whereas *nutshell* is the hard outer part of a nut, the expression *in a nutshell* is used when you are stating the main facts about something in a short way. Elicit that *nightmare in a nutshell* refers to short summaries of unpleasant situations—in this instance, related to travel.
- Have students listen to the article as they read along.
- To check comprehension, ask *What was Ms. Wilson's hassle?* (Her expensive French perfume was taken from her since you can't take liquids through security.) *Did she know that liquids are not permitted?* (yes) *What was James Robillard's hassle?* (He arrived in Brazil with an expired Visa and had to travel back to Montreal.) *Who does he blame for the oversight?* (the agent in Montreal) *Why does he think the agent missed the fact that his visa was expired?* (She was too busy checking the weight of his items.) *What was Alice Yang's hassle?* (Her luggage didn't travel with her when she connected flights.) *Why does she mention shopping as solving her problem, if stores were open?* (She could buy things she needs.)

LANGUAGE NOTE *It's not as if* is an informal way to indicate that of course something is true; *to confiscate* means to officially take something away from someone; *You can say that again* is a popular colloquial expression used to indicate complete agreement; *catch up with* means to reach someone in front of you by going faster

B DISCUSSION

Suggested teaching time:	5 minutes	Your actual teaching time:

- As a class, rate the travel hassles—with 1 being not so bad and 3 being the worst.
- Then invite volunteers to answer the question. Have them share how they would react in the various situations.

C GRAMMAR

Suggested teaching time:	10–15 minutes	Your actual teaching time:

- To review conditional sentences, write on the board:

  <u>real (factual) conditionals</u>
  If you boil water, it turns to steam.

  <u>unreal conditionals</u>
  If he spoke English, he would get this job.

  If our friends had been in the restaurant, we would have asked them for a ride home.

- Read the Remember note and point to the two clauses in the first sentence on the board. Reiterate that the *if* clause is the condition clause. Under a certain condition—water boiling—it turns to steam. Next to that sentence write *Water turns to steam if you boil it.* Ask *Does this mean the same thing?* (Yes; the clauses can be reversed.) Point out that when the *if* clause comes second, there is no comma.
- Point to the two sets of example sentences. Explain that real or factual conditions state general truths. Unreal conditionals, on the other hand, focus on imaginary conditions. Point to the first example sentence on the board under *unreal conditionals*. Ask *Does he speak English?* (no) *Will he get the job?* (no) *What would happen in an imaginary scenario in which he did speak English?* (He would get the job.) Review that this is a present unreal conditional. Then focus on the next example sentence and say *This is a past unreal conditional.* Underline the verbs in each clause (*had been / would have asked*). Ask *Were their friends in the restaurant?* (no) *Did they ask their friends for a ride?* (no) *What would have happened in an imaginary scenario if they had been in the restaurant?* (They would have asked their friends for a ride.)
- Bring students' attention to the grammar box and continuous forms in unreal conditionals. Focus on the first example sentence. Ask *Am I walking in traffic?* (no) *What would happen in an imaginary scenario if I were walking in traffic?* (I wouldn't be talking on my cell phone.) Next, look at the second example sentence. Ask *Is he going to walk there?* (no) *What would happen in an imaginary scenario if he did walk there?* (He would be going through the most dangerous section of town.)
- Ask a student to read the explanation of past unreal conditional sentences. Then focus on the first example sentence. Ask *Had he been using his webcam during the conference call?* (no) *What would have happened in an imaginary scenario if he had been using his webcam?* (He would have been wearing a tie. / He would have worn a tie.) Then draw students' attention to the next example sentence. Ask *Was I checking my messages?* (yes) *What would not have happened in an imaginary scenario if I had not been checking my messages?* (I would not have known the flight was delayed.)
- Finally, look at the last section on sequence of tenses. Ask a student to read the explanation, and have students compare the two sentences with the same *if* clause. Point out how the first result clause focuses on the present and the other on the past.
- Read the Be careful! note and example sentence, and point out that it applies to all unreal conditional sentences—present or past.

★ 🖨 Inductive Grammar Activity

Option: GRAMMAR BOOSTER *(Teaching notes p. T137)*

UNIT 6 LESSON 1   T64

D UNDERSTAND THE GRAMMAR

Suggested teaching time:	5 minutes	Your actual teaching time:

- Have students do the exercise individually. Remind them that these are unreal conditional sentences and that the *if* clauses present imaginary scenarios.
- Then have them compare answers with a partner. Circulate as students work. If necessary, guide them with questions: 1. *Was the reservation made for the right date?* (no) *What is the result of that?* (I am waiting for a standby seat now.) 2. *Was my sister watching her bags?* (no) *What was the result of that?* (They got stolen.) 3. *Was I streaming a movie?* (yes) *What happened as a result of that?* (I missed the announcement.)
- Then, in pairs, have students make statements with *should have*. Ask a student to read the model answer for item 1.

⭐ 🖨 Extra Grammar Exercises

E GRAMMAR PRACTICE

Suggested teaching time:	5 minutes	Your actual teaching time:

- Ask students to complete the exercise individually. If they need help, hint that in each item at least one clause has the continuous form. One item has both.
- Have students compare answers with a partner. Then go over any questions as a class. If necessary, guide students with questions, item by item:

1. *What would happen in an imaginary situation if you were at the hotel now?* (You would be sleeping.)
2. *What would have happened in an imaginary situation if you had packed more carefully?* (You wouldn't be paying high fees.)
3. *What could have happened in an imaginary situation if they had been watching the departure board?* (They could have taken the three-o'clock flight.)
4. *What would Karina be doing in an imaginary situation if her shoes weren't sitting in her lost luggage?* (She would be wearing them.)
5. *What would have happened in an imaginary situation if they had not been speeding?* (They wouldn't have gotten a ticket.)

LANGUAGE NOTE In item 2, the adjective *exorbitant* is used exclusively to describe an unreasonably high amount of money, such as prices or fees. Stress is on the second syllable.

Option: [+5 minutes] For more practice, have students identify which statements are present unreal conditional (items 1, 2, and 4) and which are past unreal conditional (items 3 and 5).

F PAIR WORK

Suggested teaching time:	5 minutes	Your actual teaching time:

- Ask students to skim the exercise items and identify if each sentence is a present unreal or past unreal conditional. (1. present, 2. past, 3. present, 4. present, 5. past) Then have them fill in the blanks. Point out that students can complete the sentences however they want, but they must use a continuous verb phrase.
- Circulate as students work. If they get stuck suggest possible answers (e.g., 2. I hadn't been driving, 3. it weren't raining, 4. would be cooking dinner, 5. you hadn't been talking during the traffic report on the radio).

NOW YOU CAN Discuss some causes of travel hassles

A NOTEPADDING

Suggested teaching time:	5 minutes	Your actual teaching time:

- Call on a volunteer to read the model answers.
- Students can look at Exercise A on page 62 for ideas about dealing with travel hassles. Tell them to write their descriptions of what happened along with ideas about how the problems could have been avoided.

B DISCUSSION ACTIVATOR

Suggested teaching time:	5–10 minutes	Your actual teaching time:

🎬 Discussion Activator Video

- Divide the class into pairs and have students use their notes of what happened and how it could have been avoided from Exercise A, Notepadding, to make unreal conditional statements. Ask a student to read the model answer. Encourage the pairs to ask each other questions and provide details and examples. The goal is for them to say as much as they can about the situations.

For more support, play the Discussion Activator Video before students do this activity. After each video, ask if the students in the video included sufficient details. *Note:* You can print the script or you can view it on the video player on the ActiveTeach.

D UNDERSTAND THE GRAMMAR Choose the sentence that best explains the meaning of each quotation. Then, with a partner, make a statement with <u>should have</u> to indicate what could have prevented the problem.

> *I should have made the reservation for the right date.*

1. "If the reservation had been made for the right date, I wouldn't be waiting for a standby seat now."
   a. The reservation was made for the right date, so I won't have to wait for a standby seat.
   b. The reservation was made for the wrong date, so I'm waiting for a standby seat now.
   c. The reservation wasn't made for the right date, so I don't have to wait for a standby seat.
   I should have made the reservation for the right date.

2. "If my sister had been watching her bags, they wouldn't have gotten stolen."
   a. My sister wasn't watching her bags, so they got stolen.
   b. My sister isn't watching, so they might get stolen.
   c. My sister was watching her bags, so they didn't get stolen.
   My sister should have been watching her bags.

3. "I wouldn't have missed the announcement if I hadn't been streaming a movie."
   a. I was streaming a movie, and it caused me to miss the announcement.
   b. I wasn't streaming a movie, so I didn't miss the announcement.
   c. I wasn't streaming a movie, but I missed the announcement anyway.
   I shouldn't have been streaming a movie.

E GRAMMAR PRACTICE Circle the correct verb phrase to complete each statement.

1. If you (would be / **were**) at the hotel now, you (**would be** / would have been) sleeping.
2. If we (**had** / would have) packed more carefully, we (**wouldn't be** / wouldn't have been) paying these exorbitant overweight baggage fees!
3. They could (take / **have taken**) the three o'clock flight if they (would have been / **had been**) watching the departure board.
4. Karina (**would be** / would have been) wearing her most comfortable shoes on the tour today if they (wouldn't have been / **weren't**) sitting in her lost luggage right now.
5. If they (**hadn't** / wouldn't have) been speeding, they wouldn't (get / **have gotten**) that ticket.

F PAIR WORK With a partner, take turns completing the unreal conditional sentences, using continuous verb forms. Answers will vary but may include the following:

1. If it were Monday, I *would be walking to work right now* .
2. I would have been late to class if *I hadn't caught the bus* .
3. We would be watching the game now if *our TV hadn't broken* .
4. If I were at home, I *would be reading a book* .
5. There's no way I would have missed the train if *he had woken me up* .

NOW YOU CAN Describe some causes of travel hassles

A NOTEPADDING Write two travel hassles you or someone you know has faced. Write a statement with <u>should have</u> about how you could have avoided the hassle. Use the chart on page 63 for ideas.

What happened?	How could it have been avoided?
My brother's car got towed last May in New York.	He should have been paying attention to the signs.

What happened?	How could it have been avoided?

B DISCUSSION ACTIVATOR Discuss the travel hassles you experienced. Make at least one statement in the unreal conditional about how you could have avoided the hassle. Say as much as you can.

> *If I hadn't been listening to a podcast, I wouldn't have missed the flight announcement.*

LESSON 2

GOAL Express gratitude for a favor while traveling

A GRAMMAR   UNREAL CONDITIONAL STATEMENTS WITH IF IT WEREN'T FOR … / IF IT HADN'T BEEN FOR …

Make a present or past unreal conditional statement with **if it weren't for** / **if it hadn't been for** + an object to state an outcome that would occur or would have occurred under other circumstances. It's common to use this structure to express regret or relief.

Regret

"**If it weren't for** the traffic, we **would be** at the airport by now."
(= Under other circumstances, we would be at the airport by now, but unfortunately the traffic caused us not to be. We regret this.)

"**If it hadn't been for** my bad grades in science, I **would have studied** medicine."
(= Under other circumstances, I would have studied medicine. Unfortunately, my bad grades in science prevented that. I regret this.)

Relief

"**If it weren't for** this five-hour nonstop flight, the entire trip **would take** ten hours."
(= Under other circumstances, the trip would take ten hours. Fortunately, this nonstop flight caused the trip to be shortened by five hours. I'm relieved about this.)

"**If it hadn't been for** your help this morning, we **would have missed** the train."
(= Under other circumstances, we would have missed the train. Fortunately, your help prevented our missing the train. We're relieved about this.)

Remember: You can also express strong regret with **If only**. **If only** can be followed by **were** or the past perfect.
If only there weren't so much traffic, we would be at the airport by now.
If only I had had better grades in science, I would have studied medicine.

If it hadn't been for my GPS, I would have gotten hopelessly lost!

B FIND THE GRAMMAR   Find and underline a statement using **If it weren't for** or **If it hadn't been for** and the unreal conditional in Spotlight on page 63. Is it expressing regret or relief?   You know, if I hadn't been rushing for the limo, this wouldn't have happened. (regret)
If it weren't for my stupid mistake, I wouldn't be going through this hassle. (regret)

C ▶ 3:19 UNDERSTAND THE GRAMMAR   Listen to the conversations and infer whether the speakers are expressing regret or relief in each conditional statement.

1 relief
2 relief
3 regret
4 relief
5 regret
6 regret

D ▶ 3:20 LISTEN TO ACTIVATE GRAMMAR   Listen again. Complete the paraphrase of what happened, according to what you hear. Use **if it weren't for** or **if it hadn't been for**.

1 He might still be waiting for the bus _if it hadn't been for_ Ben.
2 _If it hadn't been for_ the fact that they saw the other car, they might have had an accident.
3 Millie would love to go on the tour _if it weren't for_ her cold.
4 They might still be in line _if it weren't for_ the fact that she speaks Spanish.
5 They wouldn't be late for the play _if it weren't for_ the flat tire.
6 _If it hadn't been for_ her thoughtlessness, she thinks they wouldn't have divorced.

E GRAMMAR PRACTICE   On a separate sheet of paper, rewrite each statement, using **if it weren't for** or **if it hadn't been for**.

1 Without this cold, I would go to the museum with you tomorrow.
   If it weren't for this cold, I would go to the museum with you tomorrow. / I would go to the museum if it weren't for this cold.
2 I would have totally missed our appointment without the hotel wake-up call. *If it hadn't been for the hotel wake-up call, I would have totally missed our appointment. / I would have totally missed our appointment if it hadn't been for the hotel wake-up call.*
3 Without that announcement, we would have gone to the wrong departure gate. *If it hadn't been for that announcement, we would have gone to the wrong departure gate. / We would have gone to the wrong departure gate if it hadn't been for the announcement.*
4 We would have arrived two hours early without the airline's text message. *If it hadn't been for the airline's text message, we would have arrived two hours early. / We would have arrived two hours early if it hadn't been for the airline's text message.*
5 Without the flight attendant's help with this heavy bag, I would have gotten a backache trying to put it in the overhead bin. *If it weren't for the flight attendant's help with this heavy bag, I would have have gotten a backache trying to put it in the overhead bin. / I would have gotten a backache trying to put this heavy bag in the overhead bin if it weren't for the flight attendant's help with it.*

LESSON 2

GOAL Express gratitude for a favor while traveling

A GRAMMAR

Suggested teaching time:	5–10 minutes	Your actual teaching time:

- Tell students they will analyze another use of present and past unreal conditionals. On the board, write

  If it weren't for . . .

  If it hadn't been for . . .

- Ask a volunteer to read the explanation in the Student's Book. Then tell students to read the pairs of example sentences under Regret and Relief to themselves. If necessary, clarify that *regret* refers to the sadness that you feel about something because you wish it had not happened. *Relief* is a feeling of comfort when something frightening, worrying, or painful has ended or did not happen.
- Elicit an example sentence for each *if* clause on the board. Tell students to look carefully for which prompt is present unreal (the first) and which is past unreal (the second). Students can come to the board, or you can fill in the information. (Possible answers: If it weren't for the weather, we'd play some tennis. If it hadn't been for your advice to leave early, we would have missed our flights.) Point to each of the students' statements and ask *Does it express relief or regret?* (For the possible answers, the first one expresses regret, and the second one expresses relief.)
- Focus students' attention on the Remember note and example sentences. Ask *Which one is in the present unreal?* (the first) *The past unreal?* (the second) If students wonder about the double *had* point out that this is the correct way of putting the verb *have* in the past perfect. Remind students that *if only* is used to express regret, not relief.

⭐ 🖨 **Inductive Grammar Activity**

B FIND THE GRAMMAR

Suggested teaching time:	5 minutes	Your actual teaching time:

- Write *If it weren't for* and *If I hadn't been rushing* on the board. Tell students to turn to Exercise D, Spotlight, on page 63 and find conditional sentences that start like the phrases on the board. Have students decide if each sentence expresses relief or regret.
- Call on volunteers for answers.
- Then ask a volunteer to restate each sentence using *If only*. (Possible answers: If only I hadn't made a stupid mistake, I wouldn't be going through this hassle. If only I hadn't been rushing for the limo, this wouldn't have happened.)

⭐ 🖨 **Extra Grammar Exercises**

C ▶ 3:19 UNDERSTAND THE GRAMMAR

Suggested teaching time:	5 minutes	Your actual teaching time:

- Pre-listening: Review that *regret* refers to the sadness that you feel about something because you wish it had not happened. *Relief* is a feeling of comfort when something frightening, worrying, or painful has ended or did not happen.

- Listening: Have students listen to each conversation and after each one write *regret* or *relief*. Stop the audio if necessary after each conversation. Then have students listen again to check their answers.
- Students can compare answers in pairs, or go over the answers as a class.

LANGUAGE NOTE *Drenched* means covered in a lot of water or other liquid; *a close one* refers to something that almost happened; *to patch things up* means to end an argument and stay friendly.

Option: [+5 minutes] To extend the listening comprehension practice of this exercise, ask students to summarize the reason for each instance of regret or relief. Have them listen again to complete this task. (Possible answers: 1. The man is relieved because Ben picked him up while he was standing in the rain. 2. The man is relieved that they didn't have an accident. 3. Millie regrets she can't go, but she has a bad cold. 4. The man is relieved that the woman knows how to speak Spanish; otherwise, their wait would have been much longer. 5. The woman regrets the flat tire because it made them miss the play. 6. Joanne regrets not giving her husband more attention; if she had, they might still be married.)

D ▶ 3:20 LISTEN TO ACTIVATE GRAMMAR

Suggested teaching time:	5–10 minutes	Your actual teaching time:

- Tell students that their answers will depend on the present or past unreal conditionals they hear in the audio.
- Ask students to listen and write in the correct tenses. Then have them listen again.
- Let pairs go over answers. If necessary, play the audio again, and go over any questions as a class.

Challenge: [+5 minutes] Invite students to listen to the regret statements (3, 5, 6) one more time and write them down. Then, in pairs, have students rewrite them with *if only*. (3. If only I didn't have this cold, I'd accept that invitation. 5. If only we didn't have this flat tire, we'd be arriving now. 6. If only I hadn't been so thoughtless, Jeremy and I would still be married now.)

E GRAMMAR PRACTICE

Suggested teaching time:	5 minutes	Your actual teaching time:

- Read the direction line. Ask *Which structure do we use for present unreal?* (If it weren't for) *for the past unreal?* (If it hadn't been for) Tell students to read through the five statements and decide which ones will require the present unreal conditional (item 1) and which ones will require the past unreal conditional (items 2–5).
- Have students rewrite the sentences.
- Tell students to compare answers in pairs. Then go over any questions as a class.

Option: [+5 minutes] Invite students to interpret whether each statement expresses relief or regret. (1. regret, 2–5 relief)

UNIT 6 LESSON 2 T66

F GRAMMAR PRACTICE

Suggested teaching time:	5 minutes	Your actual teaching time:

- Elicit which statements will require the present unreal conditional (1 and 3) and which ones need the past unreal conditional (2 and 4).
- Ask students to write their statements. Circulate and assist.
- Have pairs compare their answers and determine if the statements express regret or relief.
- Bring the class together to share their answers.

Option: [+5 minutes] Ask students to restate regret statements using *if only*.

NOW YOU CAN Express gratitude for a favor while traveling

A ▶ 3:21 CONVERSATION SPOTLIGHT

Suggested teaching time:	5 minutes	Your actual teaching time:

> These conversation strategies are implicit in the model:
> - Use *I wonder if you could do me a favor* to politely ask someone to do something for you.
> - Use *How can I help* to voice willingness or eagerness to help someone.
> - Use *I'd be happy to* to agree to do something.
> - Use *It's a good thing* to introduce a good result.

- Have students look at the illustration. Ask *Where are the women?* (at the airport) *How do we know?* (The sign is pointing to Gate 2A) *What are they holding?* (probably tickets and boarding passes.)
- Have students read and listen to the conversation.
- To check comprehension, ask *What does the first woman ask the second woman?* (to keep her place in line) *Why?* (She left her phone at the counter.) *Does she return quickly?* (yes) *What does the woman holding her space say about the phone?* (that it's a good thing it was still there) *Why is the woman with the phone grateful?* (because she didn't lose her place in line)
- Write *Would you mind . . .* on the board. Then call on students to complete the statement using the captions to the illustrations.

Option: [+5 minutes] Ask *What example of an unreal conditional statement do you see in the Conversation Spotlight?* (the last line—And if hadn't been for you, I would have lost my place in line) *Does the line express regret or relief?* (relief) *Is it present or past unreal conditional?* (past)

B ▶ 3:22 RHYTHM AND INTONATION

Suggested teaching time:	5 minutes	Your actual teaching time:

- Have students repeat chorally. Make sure they:
  - use falling intonation for *I wonder if you could do me a favor* (line 1) and *How can I help?* (line 2)
  - use emphatic stress on *happy* in *I'd be happy to* (line 5), on *fast* in *That was fast,* (line 7), and *you* in *And if it hadn't been for you . . .* (line 9)

C CONVERSATION ACTIVATOR

Suggested teaching time:	5–10 minutes	Your actual teaching time:

🎬 Conversation Activator Video

- Divide the class into pairs. Instruct students that they will use the model in Exercise A, Conversation Spotlight, to role-play their own conversation with a partner.
- Refer students to the examples of favors next to the Conversation Spotlight in Exercise A.
- Reinforce the use of the spotlighted conversation strategies. For example, *I wonder if you could do me a favor; How can I help; I'd be happy to*.
- Tell students to end the conversation with an unreal conditional statement starting *If it weren't for you . . .* to express gratitude.
- Ask a volunteer to read the words under Recycle This Language. Encourage students to incorporate these words into their conversation.
- Bring students' attention to the Don't Stop! note. Ask a volunteer to read the bullet points. Explain that students should continue talking after they have covered the points in the original Conversation Spotlight.
- Tell students to change roles, so each student gets a chance to play A and B.

For more support, play the Conversation Activator Video before students do this activity themselves. After the video, ask students how the model has been changed by the actors. *Note:* You can print the script or you can view it on the video player on the ActiveTeach.

⭐🖨 Conversation Activator: Speaking Booster

F **GRAMMAR PRACTICE** First complete the statements with true information, using **if it weren't for** or **if it hadn't been for**. Then take turns reading your information with a partner.

Answers will vary but may include the following:

1. I wouldn't speak English this well *if it weren't for the semester I spent in London*.
2. I would [or wouldn't] have traveled outside of my country *if it hadn't been for the political*.
3. I would [or wouldn't] be a great athlete *if it weren't for supportive family*.
4. I would [or wouldn't] have gone out last night *if it hadn't been for the snow*.

NOW YOU CAN Express gratitude for a favor while traveling

A ▶ 3:21 **CONVERSATION SPOTLIGHT**
Read and listen. Notice the spotlighted conversation strategies.
A: Excuse me. **I wonder if you could do me a favor**.
B: No problem. **How can I help**?
A: I think I left my phone at the counter. Would you mind keeping my place in line?
B: Not at all. **I'd be happy to**.
A: Thanks. I'll be right back.
…
B: Well, that was fast! **It's a good thing** your phone was still there.
A: And if it hadn't been for you, I would have lost my place in line. Thanks!

B ▶ 3:22 **RHYTHM AND INTONATION**
Listen again and repeat. Then practice the conversation with a partner.

C **CONVERSATION ACTIVATOR**
Create a similar conversation, using one of the pictures or another idea. Start like this: *Excuse me. I wonder if you could do me a favor…* Be sure to change roles and then partners.

DON'T STOP!
- Explain why you need help.
- Explain the possible consequences of not getting help.
- Continue the conversation with small talk.
- Say as much as you can.

RECYCLE THIS LANGUAGE
- No sweat.
- I'm off.
- Wish me luck!
- Don't freak out.
- Anytime.

… giving me a hand with this bag?
… keeping an eye on my things?
… grabbing that bag off the carousel?
… pointing me in the right direction?

TO GATE 2A

LESSON 3

GOAL Discuss staying safe on the Internet

A **READING WARM-UP** Do you use public Wi-Fi away from home? Why or why not?

B ▶ 3:23 **READING** Read about problems with public Wi-Fi. What surprised you the most?
Answers will vary but may include the following:
I was surprised at how important it is to use fully encrypted sites when using public Wi-Fi.

USING PUBLIC WI-FI NETWORKS

So it's your first trip away from home, and you've got your smartphone, your tablet, or laptop with you, and you plan to keep up with everything and stay in touch while you're away. You're thinking, "No sweat. There are Wi-Fi hotspots everywhere, and it's free. Well, before you lull yourself into a false sense of security, consider the downside of all that free Wi-Fi.

If you connect to a public Wi-Fi network and send information through websites or mobile apps, it might be accessed by someone else who can, for example, use your credit information to make online purchases. OK. That's not the end of the world, you say, because an unusual buying pattern usually trips a "fraud alert" at the credit card company. They'll contact you, and you'll confirm you didn't make the purchase. The card will be canceled, limiting or preventing any damage, so no harm done.

But here's a downside: An imposter could use your e-mail account to impersonate you and scam people in your contact lists. In addition, a hacker could test your username and password to try to gain access to other websites—including sites that store your financial information.

Worst case scenario? Someone could actually steal your financial identity and pose as you to clean out your bank accounts, removing all your hard-earned money. Repairing a stolen identity can take a long time and cause a lot of hassle. Identity theft is no joke. Prevent it at all costs.

So beware: If you send e-mail, share digital photos and videos, use social networks, or bank online, you're sending personal information over the Internet. How to protect yourself? Think encryption. Encryption scrambles the information you send over the Internet into a code so it's unintelligible and therefore not accessible to others. If you're on a public wireless hotspot, send personal information only to sites that are fully encrypted, and avoid using any mobile apps that require personal or financial information.

And don't just assume a Wi-Fi hotspot is secure either. Most *don't* encrypt the information you send over the Internet and aren't secure. In fact, if a network doesn't require a WPA or WPA2 password, it's probably not secure, and your personal information, private documents, contacts, family photos, and even your log-in credentials (your username and password) for any site you enter could be up for grabs.

HOW TO TELL IF A WEBSITE IS ENCRYPTED

To determine if a website is encrypted, look for "https" at the start of the web address (the "s" is for "secure"). Some websites use encryption only on the sign-in page, but if any part of your session isn't encrypted, your entire account could be vulnerable. Look for "https" on every page you visit, not just when you sign in.

TIPS FOR USING WI-FI SECURELY

▶ Log in or send personal information only to websites you know are fully encrypted. If you find yourself on an unencrypted page, log out right away.

▶ Don't stay permanently signed in to an account. When you've finished using an account, log out.

▶ Do not use the same password on different websites. It could give someone who gains access to one of your accounts access to many of your accounts.

▶ For more control over when and how your device uses public Wi-Fi, consider changing your settings so your device doesn't connect automatically.

C **UNDERSTAND MEANING FROM CONTEXT** Match each definition with a word or phrase from the article.

..d.. 1 a person who fraudulently claims to be someone else
..f.. 2 the location on a website where you identify yourself in order to enter
..e.. 3 a general term for the username and password you use to identify yourself
..g.. 4 the disadvantage of something
..a.. 5 a warning that someone else might be using your credit card
..c.. 6 pretend to be someone else
..h.. 7 a place where one can access the Internet, usually for free
..b.. 8 the use of someone's financial information in order to steal

a a fraud alert
b identity theft
c impersonate
d an imposter
e log-in credentials
f a sign-in page
g downside
h a wireless hotspot

LESSON 3

GOAL Discuss staying safe on the Internet

A READING WARM-UP

Suggested teaching time:	5 minutes	Your actual teaching time:

- Ask a student to read the questions. Poll the class. Invite students to share why they do or do not use Wi-Fi away from home.

B ▶ 3:23 READING

Suggested teaching time:	10–15 minutes	Your actual teaching time:

- Have students look at the picture. Ask *Where are these people?* (It looks like a café where there is public Wi-Fi.) *Do you ever take a computer or other device to a café or other public place?*
- As students read and listen, tell them to underline information in the article that will help them answer the focus question in the direction line.
- Together as a class, have volunteers share their answers to the focus question.

LANGUAGE NOTE *To lull* means to be made to feel safe so that one is surprised when something bad happens; *to trip* means to activate; *an imposter* is a person who pretends to be someone else to fool people; *a worst-case scenario* is the most unpleasant thing that could happen.

⭐ 🖨 Reading Strategies

C UNDERSTAND MEANING FROM CONTEXT

Suggested teaching time:	5–10 minutes	Your actual teaching time:

- Have students work in pairs to match the terms to their meanings. For items students are not sure about, tell them to find the words and phrases in the reading and look at words that come before and after to help understand the meaning.
- Circulate and assist as needed.
- Bring the class together and go over the answers.

Option: [+5 minutes] In pairs, have students practice using the terms in their own sentences. Tell them to make statements about their own lives. For example, *I change my log-in credentials pretty often. This keeps my account safe.*

🖨 Extra Reading Comprehension Questions

UNIT 6 LESSON 3 **T68**

D PARAPHRASE

| Suggested teaching time: | 10–15 minutes | Your actual teaching time: |

- Review that *to paraphrase* is to express briefly or differently something that someone else has said or written. Stress the importance of using one's own words.
- First have students scan the article for the specific lines and underline them. (1. paragraph 2; 2. the violet introductory paragraph; 3. paragraph 4; 4. paragraph 5; 5. box at upper right) Tell students they will refer to context if needed.
- Ask a volunteer to read the first line and model paraphrase. Then have students paraphrase the rest of the items. Circulate and assist as needed. Students can work in pairs if they get stuck.
- Bring the class together and invite students to share their paraphrases. Comment and help students improve them. Make sure students sufficiently change the statements and don't copy any of them word for word.

Challenge: [+5 minutes] Invite students to paraphrase the violet introductory paragraph. (Possible answer: Imagine this... You're traveling for the first time. You have your electronic device, and you plan to stay connected with everyone and everything back home. You think to yourself, "This will be easy—free Wi-Fi hotspots are all over the place." Don't get too comfortable just yet. There are many dangers to keep mind!)

E FIND SUPPORTING DETAILS

| Suggested teaching time: | 5 minutes | Your actual teaching time: |

- Have students work in pairs to discuss and answer the questions.
- Circulate and help students locate answers if they need help (answers to items 1 and 2 are in the box titled "How to Tell if a Website Is Encrypted;" the answer to item 3 is in the box titled "Tips for Using Wi-fi Securely;" the answer to item 4 is in paragraph 2; and the answer to item 5 is in paragraph 1).

⭐ 🖨 Extra Challenge Reading Activity

NOW YOU CAN Discuss staying safe on the Internet

A FRAME YOUR IDEAS

| Suggested teaching time: | 5 minutes | Your actual teaching time: |

- Have volunteers read the statements out loud.
- Give students a few minutes to check their answers in the chart.

B GROUP WORK

| Suggested teaching time: | 5 minutes | Your actual teaching time: |

- Invite a volunteer to read the model answer. Ask *Does anyone in this class do this?*
- Divide the class into small groups and have students compare their answers in the chart. If students answer *Always* or *Sometimes* for the last two items, invite them to explain how they do this.
- Finally, invite volunteers to the board to write the additional things they do to stay secure on the Internet.

Challenge: [+5 minutes] Have students reread the model answer. Invite students to work in pairs to come up with a system for scrambling passwords. Tell them it should be something that makes the password easy to remember. Then invite students to share if they write down passwords anywhere (e.g., on a piece of paper, in a password vault on the computer).

D PARAPHRASE On a separate sheet of paper, paraphrase each of the following statements from the article. *Answers will vary but may include the following:*

1. "An imposter could use your e-mail account to impersonate you and scam people in your contact lists." — *A person could pretend to be you and trick people in your contact lists.*
2. "Before you lull yourself into a false sense of security, consider the downside of all that free Wi-Fi." — *It's a mistake to believe that free Wi-Fi is secure.*
3. "Encryption scrambles the information you send over the Internet into a code so it's unintelligible and therefore not accessible to others." — *Your information is mixed up so that other people can't read it.*
4. "If a network doesn't require a WPA or WPA2 password, it's probably not secure, and your personal information, private documents, contacts, family photos, and even your login credentials … could be up for grabs." — *Networks that don't require a WPA or WPA2 password are probably not secure and can put your personal data at risk.*
5. "To determine if a website is encrypted, look for "https" at the start of the web address (the 's' is for 'secure')." — *To see if a website can protect your information, look for "https" at the beginning of the web address.*

E FIND SUPPORTING DETAILS With a partner, discuss and answer the questions. Support your answers with information from the article.

1. What should you look for when sending information to a website when you're using a public Wi-Fi network?
You should look for "https" at the start of the web address to check if the site is encrypted.
2. How can you know whether a Wi-Fi network is secure?
The "s" in "https" indicates that the site is secure. You should look for the "https" on every page you visit, not just where you sign in.
3. What should you do after concluding your online banking when on a public Wi-Fi network?
You should log out right away after concluding online banking while on a public Wi-Fi network.
4. What could happen if a hacker gained access to your contact list?
If a hacker gained access to your contact list, he could impersonate you and scam people.
5. What might happen if a credit card company discerns purchases on your card that are not ones you typically make? *An unusual spending pattern usually results in a fraud alert by the credit card company.*

DIGITAL EXTRA CHALLENGE

NOW YOU CAN Discuss staying safe on the Internet

A FRAME YOUR IDEAS Complete the chart with what you do to stay secure on the Internet—at home or away.

	Always	Sometimes	Never
I use public Wi-Fi hotspots.	☐	☐	☐
I check to see if a website is encrypted.	☐	☐	☐
I use different passwords on different sites.	☐	☐	☐
I set my mobile device to automatically connect to nearby Wi-Fi.	☐	☐	☐
I protect myself against credit card fraud.	☐	☐	☐
I actively prevent my identity from being stolen.	☐	☐	☐

B GROUP WORK Compare your answers in a small group. Discuss which practices you were familiar with and which were new to you. Then add at least one other thing you do to keep yourself secure on the Internet.

❝ I change all my passwords once a week. I have a system for scrambling them that makes it easy for me to remember them. ❞

LESSON 4

GOAL Talk about lost, stolen, or damaged property

A ▶3:24 **LISTENING WARM-UP   WORD STUDY   PAST PARTICIPLES AS NOUN MODIFIERS**
The past participles of transitive verbs can function as noun modifiers. They can precede or follow the noun they modify. Read and listen. Then listen again and repeat.

"My tire was **damaged**. I took my **damaged** tire to the garage."

"My purse was **stolen** at a store. I found the **stolen** purse (without my wallet!) at the back of the store."

"My passport was **lost**. Luckily, the police found the **lost** passport."

B **WORD STUDY PRACTICE 1** Choose five more past participles of transitive verbs from the chart on page 122. Write a sentence with each one, using the examples in Exercise A as a model.

C **WORD STUDY PRACTICE 2** On a separate sheet of paper, rewrite each sentence that contains an underlined object pronoun, using a participial adjective as a noun modifier.

1 When Julie took her skirt out of the closet, she saw that it was stained. She took <u>it</u> to the cleaners.   *She took the stained skirt to the cleaners.*
2 While we were at the train station, I found a pair of sunglasses that were lost. I gave <u>them</u> to the Lost and Found.   *I gave the pair of lost sunglasses to the Lost and Found.*
3 After walking up the steps to the pyramid, I noticed that the heel of my shoe was broken. The guy in the shoe repair stand fixed <u>it</u> in less than ten minutes.   *The guy in the shoe repair stand fixed the broken heel of my shoe in less than ten minutes.*
4 We reported that our hotel room had been burglarized. The front desk sent someone to look at <u>it</u>.   *The front desk sent someone to look at our burglarized hotel room.*
5 The repair shop sells bargain suitcases that are damaged. It's a good deal because you can pay to have <u>them</u> repaired cheaply.   *It's a good deal because you can pay to have the damaged bargain suitcases repaired cheaply.*

PRONUNCIATION BOOSTER   p. 147
• Regular past participle endings
• Reduction in perfect modals

D ▶3:25 **LISTEN FOR MAIN IDEAS** Listen to Part 1 of a radio report. Write a checkmark next to the statement that best expresses its main idea.

☐ Put your name on your luggage to avoid loss or delay.
☑ Know what to do to avoid luggage loss or delay.
☐ Don't check bags that can be carried onto the plane.

Keep your copy of the luggage check in case your bag is lost or delayed.

E ▶3:26 **LISTEN TO CONFIRM CONTENT** Listen again. Write a checkmark next to the tips Tina Traveler gave listeners. Write an X next to any tips on the list she didn't give.

☑ 1 Put your address on your luggage inside and out.
☒ 2 Request reimbursement for toiletries if your baggage is delayed.
☑ 3 File a claim with your airline if your bags are lost.
☑ 4 Provide sales receipts to prove what you paid for the clothes in your lost luggage.
☒ 5 Don't put your prescription medicines in your checked bag.
☑ 6 Keep luggage checks for checked baggage in case you have to make a claim.

70   UNIT 6

LESSON 4

GOAL Talk about lost, stolen, or damaged property

A ▶ 3:24 LISTENING WARM-UP

Suggested teaching time:	5 minutes	Your actual teaching time:

- Read the explanation of past participles as noun modifiers. Call on volunteers to read the sentences in the speech bubbles. Point out how in the first sentence of each pair, the noun modifier follows the noun it modifies; in the second sentence of each pair, the noun modifier precedes the nouns it modifies. Students may ask whether these sentences are in passive voice. The sentences in the speech bubbles do appear to be the same structure as passive voice sentences, but some are what is referred to as stative passives. Stative passives describe a condition rather than an action. Examples of stative passives are: *I am married to Edward. She isn't interested in learning to drive.* Stative passives aren't followed by a *by* phrase because there is no action. (Any actions occurred previously.)
- Have students read and listen to the list of words.
- Then have them listen again and repeat.

Option: [+5 minutes] You may choose to review that transitive verbs are verbs that take a direct object (in comparison with intransitive verbs like *go, arrive,* and *sit* that do not take a direct object). Then elicit the base verb form of the past participles used as noun modifiers in the speech bubbles, and write them on the board: *damage, steal, lose.* Ask students to suggest sentences with direct objects. (Possible answers: I damaged my tire. Someone stole my purse. I lost my passport.)

⭐ 🖨 Vocabulary-Building Strategies

B WORD STUDY PRACTICE 1

Suggested teaching time:	5 minutes	Your actual teaching time:

- Have students work in pairs to make a list of five or more transitive verbs. If students are not sure, tell them to ask themselves *Can the word take a direct object?* If it can, it is a transitive verb. (Possible answers: read, eat, want, kick, write, clean)
- Combine pairs into groups of four. Have them swap lists and check that the verbs can take direct objects.
- Ask pairs to use the verbs from their lists as noun modifiers in sentences, following the models in the speech bubbles in Exercise A.

C WORD STUDY PRACTICE 2

Suggested teaching time:	5 minutes	Your actual teaching time:

- Have students read the first sentence in item 1. Ask *What is the noun modifier in the first sentence?* (stained) *Does it follow or precede the noun it modifies?* (follows) Then focus on the second sentence. Ask *What does the underlined it refer to?* (the skirt) *What noun modifier can be used to describe the skirt?* (stained) Call on a volunteer to read the model answer.
- Ask students to do the remaining items individually or in pairs. Circulate as students work. If necessary, guide students: 2. *What does* them *refer to?* (sunglasses) *What is the noun modifier?* (lost) 3. *What does it refer to?* (shoe) *What is the noun modifier?* (broken) 4. *What does it refer to?* (hotel room) *What is the noun modifier?* (burglarized) 5. *What does* them *refer to?* (bargain suitcases) *What is the noun modifier?* (damaged) For item 5, you may need to point out the compound noun "bargain suitcases."

Option: PRONUNCIATION BOOSTER *(Teaching notes p. T147)*

🖨 Pronunciation Pair Work

D ▶ 3:25 LISTEN FOR MAIN IDEAS

Suggested teaching time:	5–10 minutes	Your actual teaching time:

- Pre-listening: Have students look at the two photos. Ask *What do you think happened to the woman?* (Her luggage never arrived.) *How does she feel?* (Possible answers: frustrated, annoyed, upset) *Have you ever been in this situation?* Focus on the photo of the suitcase. Ask *Why are destination labels on luggage important?* (They show the destination to which you are traveling.) *Do you usually check the destination on the label to make sure the bag will travel to the same place that you are traveling?*
- Ask *Based on the photos, can you predict the main idea of the report?* Have students check in pencil.
- Listening: Ask students to listen once. If necessary, have them listen again.
- Have students check the main idea and then discuss it with the class. Then ask *Did you guess correctly? Are the other statements mentioned in the report?* (Yes, both are, but they are details, not the main idea.)

⭐ 🖨 Listening Strategies

E ▶ 3:26 LISTEN TO CONFIRM CONTENT

Suggested teaching time:	5 minutes	Your actual teaching time:

- Pre-listening: First have students read the tips and check the ones they believe were mentioned.
- Listening: Ask students to listen once and then complete the exercise. If necessary, have students listen again.
- Go over the answers as a class.

Challenge: [+5 minutes] On the board, write *5 tips to prevent loss of airline luggage.* Tell students that the reporter ends the report with five tips to prevent luggage loss. Students will write these the best they can remember. If necessary, students can listen again. Then bring the class together to go over the answers. Write the tips on the board as students list them. (1. Put your name on the outside and inside of every bag, and put an itinerary inside the bag. 2. Don't check in late and avoid tight connections. 3. Don't put expensive things like computers and cameras in checked bags, as these won't be reimbursed. 4. Keep an itemized list of what you have in each bag. 5. Make sure the destination the airline puts on your bag is actually your destination.)

Then, in pairs or small groups, have students discuss which of these things they actually do. Ask *Will you incorporate any of these tips into your travels after reading this article?*

UNIT 6 LESSON 4   T70

F ▶ 3:27 LISTEN TO UNDERSTAND MEANING FROM CONTEXT

Suggested teaching time:	5–10 minutes	Your actual teaching time:

- Call on a volunteer to read the words in the box. Then have students work individually to complete the exercise.
- Play the audio and have students listen for the specific words in context to check that they completed the statements correctly.
- Have students compare answers with a partner.

G ▶ 3:28 LISTEN FOR DETAILS

Suggested teaching time:	5 minutes	Your actual teaching time:

- Pre-listening: Invite students to look at the photo. Ask *What do you think an unclaimed baggage center is? Do you think it is a store?*
- First listening: With students' books closed, have students listen to the report. Then let students look at the questions individually and answer as many of them as they can.
- Second listening: Have students listen again and answer any questions they did not answer before.
- Go over the answers as a class. Focus on item 3. Ask *How do we know there is only one store?* (The report says it's a one-of-a-kind store in the United States.) Make sure students understand *one-of-a-kind* means unique; the only one. Point out that this adjective can be applied to describe people, places, or things. Elicit other examples. (Possible answers: one-of-a-kind cake, hotel, friend, island)

H DISCUSSION

Suggested teaching time:	5 minutes	Your actual teaching time:

- Divide the class into groups of two or three and discuss shopping in the Unclaimed Baggage Center.
- Then bring the class together and poll who would shop at the store. Ask *What type of items would you buy?*

Option: [+5 minutes] Ask *Do you think people should have access to their belongings even after a claim has been settled? For example, if a piece of luggage that was thought to be lost was eventually found.*

NOW YOU CAN Talk about lost, stolen, or damaged property

A NOTEPADDING

Suggested teaching time:	5 minutes	Your actual teaching time:

- Call on volunteers to read the headings and the model answer.
- Ask students to write their own answer. If students haven't had a personal experience of this sort, ask them if they know anyone who has. Tell them they can write about another person's experience or one they have heard of.

B DISCUSSION

Suggested teaching time:	5 minutes	Your actual teaching time:

- Call on a student to read the model answer. Review that the expression *to be toast* means to be in trouble.
- Then have students discuss in pairs or small groups. Refer them to the vocabulary list in Exercise F and the word study in Exercise A.

⭐ 🖨 Discussion: Speaking Booster

OPTIONAL WRITING [+15–20 minutes]

- Have students write the story they notepadded about and discussed in Exercises A and B. Remind them to use the vocabulary list in Exercise F and other vocabulary from this unit. Encourage them to apply what they learned in the word study in Exercise A. For example: *My suitcase wasn't lost, but it was badly damaged. The wheels were broken, and it was stained.*
- Offer an opportunity for peer review in class, or collect student work and provide individual feedback.

T71 UNIT 6 PREVIEW

F ▶ 3:27 **LISTEN TO UNDERSTAND MEANING FROM CONTEXT**
Listen again and complete each statement with one of these words or phrases from Tina Traveler's advice.

a claim	luggage checks
a connecting flight	receipts
depreciated	reimburse
an itinerary	toiletries

1. Cosmetics are an example of <u>toiletries</u>.
2. The list of places and dates of your travel is <u>an itinerary</u>.
3. A value lower than the price you paid because the item isn't new is its <u>depreciated</u> value.
4. If you take two flights to get somewhere, the second one is called <u>a connecting flight</u>.
5. Slips of paper showing the destination of your checked luggage are <u>luggage checks</u>.
6. Slips of paper showing what you paid for something you bought are <u>receipts</u>.
7. A form that records loss, delay, or damage to property is <u>a claim</u>.
8. If the airline pays you money to compensate you for a damaged bag, they <u>reimburse</u> you.

G ▶ 3:28 **LISTEN FOR DETAILS** Listen to Part 2 of Tina Traveler's report. Then answer the questions. Listen again if necessary.

1. What is the Unclaimed Baggage Center? <u>It's a store where they sell unclaimed luggage from airlines.</u>
2. What's the difference between the Unclaimed Baggage Center and a Lost and Found office? <u>The items in the UBC have been paid for by the airlines through settled claims.</u>
3. How many stores does the Center have? <u>One.</u>
4. Where does the Unclaimed Baggage Center get its merchandise? <u>It gets it from airlines when baggage is unclaimed.</u>
5. How does it decide what to buy and what not to buy? <u>They only take things which the airlines have settled and paid claims on.</u>
6. What does the center do before selling merchandise? <u>It cleans it, clears out data, and prices it.</u>
7. What does it do with merchandise it can't sell? <u>It donates it to charity or recycles it.</u>

H **DISCUSSION** Would you shop at the Unclaimed Baggage Center? Explain why or why not.

NOW YOU CAN Talk about lost, stolen, or damaged property

A **NOTEPADDING** Write notes about a time your property was lost, stolen, or damaged when you were traveling. Use words and phrases from Exercise F in your description if possible.

| when / where / what?: | 2016 / Orlando USA / guitar |
| brief summary and outcome: | The airline made me check my guitar. It wasn't transferred to my connecting flight in Panama. It was found and delivered to our hotel the next day. |

| when / where / what?: | |
| brief summary and outcome: | |

B **DISCUSSION** Discuss the events you wrote about on your notepad. Discuss what happened to your property and what the final outcome was. Respond to your partner.

> *I freaked out when I didn't see the guitar case on the carousel. If it hadn't been for the baggage check, I would have been toast!*

> *It's a good thing you saved that check!*

OPTIONAL WRITING Write about the event you discussed. Include as many details as possible. Use the words and phrases from Exercise F and other vocabulary from this unit.

WRITING A comparison and contrast essay

A WRITING SKILL Study the rules.

Choose one of these formats for organizing your supporting paragraphs when you want to compare and contrast places, objects, people, ideas, etc., in an essay. (Be sure to include expressions of comparison and contrast.)

Introductory paragraph
Begin with an introductory paragraph that says what you are going to compare and contrast.

WRITING MODEL

(Introductory paragraph)
Public and private transportation have both advantages and disadvantages, so it is fortunate to have options. To make a choice, you can take into account convenience, cost, destination, and the needs and tastes of the people you are traveling with. Other factors to consider are the length of the trip and (if it is important to you) the environmental impact of the means of transportation you choose.

Supporting paragraphs
Choose Format A or B to present and support your ideas.

Format A: Discuss the similarities in one paragraph and the differences in another.

(Format A)
Public and private transportation provide clear advantages for most people. They are similar in certain ways: Both are convenient and cut travel time, allowing people to travel farther to work or school. And with the exception of a bicycle, all vehicles used in public and private transportation are capable of providing a level of comfort available with modern technology, such as air-conditioning and heating.
On the other hand, public and private transportation are different in more ways than they are similar. Cars and bicycles offer a level of privacy and convenience not available in public transportation. You can make your own schedule, take a detour, and not have to pay fares or deal with people you don't want to be with. However, it is only with public transportation that you can move around, relax, and not have to pay attention to traffic or weather conditions.

OR

Format B: Alternatively, you can focus on one specific aspect of the topic in each paragraph, and discuss the similarities and differences within each paragraph.

(Format B)
Regarding scheduling, private and public transportation are very different. When you travel by car, you can make your own schedule and stop when and where you want. Nevertheless, when you travel by bus or train you know exactly when you'll arrive, making planning easy.
In terms of comfort, private transportation has the clear advantage. Public transportation may be crowded and …

Concluding paragraph
Summarize your main ideas in a concluding paragraph.

(Concluding paragraph)
Most people choose to use a mix of private and public transportation, depending on circumstances. However, if I could choose only one means of transportation, I'd go with the car. It has its disadvantages, but I like to travel alone or only with my family and to be able to make my own schedule. All in all, I'd say I'm a car person.

B APPLY THE WRITING SKILL
On a separate sheet of paper, write an essay comparing and contrasting two means of transportation. Include the paragraph types and formats shown in Exercise A. Use expressions of comparison and contrast.

Expressions to introduce comparisons and contrasts:

Comparisons	Contrasts
Similarly,	While / Whereas …
Likewise,	Unlike …
By the same token,	Nonetheless,
In similar fashion,	Nevertheless,
… as well	In contrast,
… don't either	On the other hand,
	However,

SELF-CHECK

☐ Did I use expressions of comparison and contrast?

☐ Does my essay have an introductory and a concluding paragraph?

☐ Do the supporting paragraphs follow one of the formats illustrated above?

WRITING A comparison and contrast essay

A WRITING SKILL

Suggested teaching time:	10–15 minutes	Your actual teaching time:

- Tell the class they are going to learn how to write a comparison and contrast essay. Write on the board:

    similarities   differences

    Ask *What does it mean to compare and contrast?* (compare = describe similarities; contrast = describe differences)

- Read the introduction under Writing Skill. Reiterate that there are two ways to organize a comparison and contrast essay.

- Focus students' attention on the left column. Call on a student to read aloud the information about the introductory paragraph. Then ask students to silently read the introductory paragraph in the example on the right. Ask *What is the writer going to compare in his essay?* (public and private transportation) *What will the essay describe about these two means of transportation?* (similarities and differences)

- Read the information about supporting paragraphs. Call on a volunteer to read about format A. Then ask students to silently read the example for format A on the right. Ask *What does the first paragraph discuss?* (similarities of private and public transportation) *What does the second paragraph discuss?* (differences of private and public transportation)

- Call on a student to read about format B. Then ask students to silently read the example for format B on the right. Ask *What does the first paragraph discuss?* (scheduling regarding each type of transportation) *What does the second paragraph discuss* (comfort regarding each type of transportation)

- Call on a student to read about the concluding paragraph. Then ask students to silently read the example of a conclusion on the right.

LANGUAGE NOTE *Compare* generally means to describe both similarities and differences. In formal essay writing, the genre of writing called compare and contrast uses *to compare* to mean to show similarities.

B APPLY THE WRITING SKILL

Suggested teaching time:	10–15 minutes	Your actual teaching time:

- Focus on the expressions to introduce comparisons and contrasts. Ask *What are some expressions we use to compare things?* (similarly, likewise, as well, doesn't either) *How about contrast?* (while, whereas, unlike, in contrast, on the other hand)

- Ask students to find and underline some of these expressions in the examples for format A and format B (A: On the other Hand; however B: Nevertheless)

- Have students think of two means of transportation they want to compare and then take notes regarding their similarities and differences. Students might want to explore hassles of the two modes of transportation as part of comparing them.

- Refer students to the Writing Process Worksheet in ActiveTeach for guidance with pre-writing and peer feedback.

- Encourage students to use the Self-Check in the Student's Book to go over the essays they wrote.

Option: [+5 minutes] Time permitting, students can exchange papers with a partner and offer feedback using the topics in the Self-Check list. Encourage partners to also check for examples.

⭐🖨 Writing Process

REVIEW

🎮 Digital Game

A ▶ 3:29

Suggested teaching time:	10–15 minutes	Your actual teaching time:

- First listening: Have students listen once.
- Second listening: Have them listen again and plan their summaries. To help students organize information, on the board, write:

  Where:

  What happened:

  How resolved:

  If necessary, have students listen again.

- Circulate as students work. If necessary, help students use the guide on the board. (1. security checkpoint, shampoo and aftershave confiscated, not resolved—not reimbursed; 2. outside airport, airport bus ran over suitcase, will file a claim—bought a new bag in meantime; 3. at airport arrivals, suitcase damaged, will file a claim)
- Call on volunteers to share summaries.

B

Suggested teaching time:	5 minutes	Your actual teaching time:

- Gives students a few minutes to read the statements and decide if they describe present or past unreal conditionals. (1, 4, and 5 are present; 2 and 3 are past)
- After students complete the exercise, have them compare answers with a partner.

Option: [+5 minutes] Ask *Do the exercise items show regret or relief?* (They all show regret.) Invite students to restate the items using *If only*. (1. If only the security line weren't so long, I would get a cup of coffee. 2. If only my first flight hadn't been delayed, my checked bags wouldn't have missed the connection. 3. If only there hadn't been all the broken glass on the road, we wouldn't have had a flat tire. 4. If only there were no storm, Martin would be here. 5. If only my leg weren't broken, I would be skiing right now.)

C

Suggested teaching time:	5 minutes	Your actual teaching time:

- Have students make the corrections. Refer them to the Vocabulary in Exercise B on page 62 if they need help.
- Let students compare answers with a partner.

D

Suggested teaching time:	5 minutes	Your actual teaching time:

- If students need to review any terms, refer them to Exercise D, Spotlight, on page 63. Then have them complete the exercise.
- Go over the answers as a class.

Option: `TEST-TAKING SKILLS BOOSTER` (p. 156)

EXTRA

- Workbook
- MyEnglishLab
- Online Student Resources (www.english.com/summit3e)
  - Classroom Audio Program
  - Extra Practice Activities
  - *Summit GO* App
  - Web Projects
- ActiveTeach
  - Assessment
  - Additional Printable Resources
    - Audioscripts and Answer Keys
    - "Can-Do" Self-Assessment Charts
    - Conversation and Discussion Activator Video Scripts
    - Oral Progress Assessment Charts
    - Reading Speed Calculator
  - Summit TV Video Program
    - Activity Worksheets
    - Teaching Notes
    - Video Scripts

REVIEW

A ▶ 3:29 Listen to three conversations. On the notepad, summarize what happened in each conversation.

	Conversation Summary
1	The airlines confiscates a passenger's shampoo and aftershave due to the size of the containers.
2	A man's suitcase was crushed under the airport bus. He got a new one and switched his clothing. He will file a claim.
3	A woman's bag was damaged in transport. She will file a claim. She has the sales receipt for the bag.

B Choose the correct verb phrase to complete each statement.
1. If it weren't for this long security line, I (will / **would**) get a cup of coffee.
2. If it hadn't been for the delay in my first flight, my checked bags (wouldn't miss / **wouldn't have missed**) the connection.
3. We wouldn't have had a flat tire if it (weren't / **hadn't been**) for all the broken glass on the road.
4. Martin would be here if it (**weren't** / wouldn't be) for this storm.
5. If it (**weren't** / wouldn't be) for my broken leg, I would be skiing right now.

C Replace the words or phrases that are crossed out in each statement with ones that make sense.
1. The compartment over your airline seat where you can place your suitcase is the ~~carousel~~. **overhead compartment**
2. Before you can board an airplane, you have to go through ~~a missed connection~~. **check in**
3. If you park in an illegal space, you might get a ~~flat tire~~ or, even worse, your car might get ~~a breakdown~~. **ticket, towed**
4. A ~~checked~~ bag is one that you take on board with you when you get on a flight. **carry-on**

D Choose the correct idiom or expression.
1. If you can't remember something you're sure you should be able to, you can say, "……"
   a. I'm toast. **(b)** I'm drawing a blank.
2. When you want to indicate you're about to leave, you can say, "……"
   (a) I'm off. b. I'll cross that bridge when I come to it.
3. If you want to reassure someone that a task won't be hard at all, you can say, "……"
   (a) No sweat. b. It's a good thing.
4. When you think something terrible is definitely going to happen, you can say, "……"
   a. I'm off. **(b)** I'm toast.
5. When you're sure you've concluded something correctly, you can say, "……"
   a. I'm drawing a blank. **(b)** It's a safe bet.

TEST-TAKING SKILLS BOOSTER p. 156

Web Project: Travel Nightmares
www.english.com/summit3e

UNIT 7

Mind Over Matter

PREVIEW

COMMUNICATION GOALS
1 Suggest that someone is being gullible
2 Examine superstitions for believability
3 Talk about the power of suggestion
4 Discuss phobias

A FRAME YOUR IDEAS Play the Illusion Game with a partner. Look at each image carefully for at least a minute. Do you both see the same thing?

The ILLUSION GAME

An illusion is something likely to be wrongly interpreted. Write an explanation of what the eye sees in each picture. Then compare your explanations with the ones below.

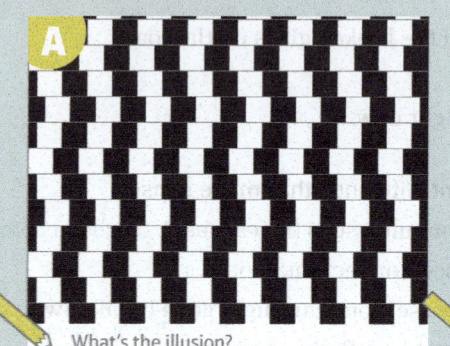

A What's the illusion?

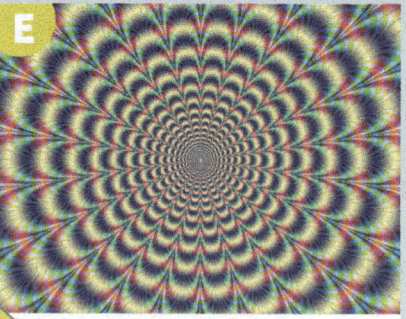

B What's the illusion?

C What's the illusion?

D What's the illusion?

E What's the illusion?

EXPLANATIONS **A** The horizontal lines appear to be sloping, creating uneven rows. But the lines actually are parallel. **B** We can see either two people or three objects that look like vases or chess pieces. **C** There are two zebras, but we only see one head. Depending on how we look at the image, the head appears to belong to the zebra on the left or to the one on the right. **D** We see half a man's face. Depending on how we look at it, he either appears to be looking out at us or in profile looking to the right. **E** The image appears to be moving, but it isn't.

B DISCUSSION What other things are we likely to misinterpret visually? What might cause us to misinterpret them?

> *Sometimes on a dark night, we might think we're seeing monsters, but in reality they're only trees. That illusion is caused by our imagination and our natural fear of the dark.*

UNIT 7

Mind Over Matter

PREVIEW

A FRAME YOUR IDEAS

| Suggested teaching time: | 10–15 minutes | Your actual teaching time: |

- Focus on the illusion game. Ask a volunteer to read the title and subhead. Elicit that an illusion is something that the mind interprets differently than it is in reality.
- Tell students to look at the first item for about a minute. Call on volunteers to share what they see. Then read the upside down explanation. Ask *Does everyone see the illusion?*
- Ask students to write what they see for the remaining images. Then have them compare answers with a partner. Tell students to look at the upside down explanations.

B DISCUSSION

| Suggested teaching time: | 5 minutes | Your actual teaching time: |

- Read the discussion questions to the class. Ask a volunteer to read the model answer.
- Have students respond providing experiences from their lives. If students get stuck, hint that maybe lack of sleep or stress can have an effect on how we interpret things visually.

UNIT 7 PREVIEW   T74

C ▶ 4:02 SPOTLIGHT

Suggested teaching time:	10–15 minutes	Your actual teaching time:

- Ask students to look at the photo. Ask *Where do you think the woman is?* (She may be at work.) *What do you think she is doing?* (She's looking at and speaking with someone.)
- Have students read and listen to the conversation.
- Ask *What is Vicky's problem?* (It seems to her that her staff is talking about her or has some secret they are hiding from her.) *Have you ever gotten such an impression? If yes, were you right? Or did it just seem to you that people were talking about you? Was Vicky's hunch an illusion?* (No, it was not; they actually were talking about her.)

LANGUAGE NOTE *To huddle together* means to group together and stay close to one another.

The phrasal verb *shut up*, meaning stop talking, is rude when used as an imperative but isn't when used to describe someone's actions; in this context, it means the people become quiet or stop talking. *Paranoid* refers to an unreasonable fear that someone is trying to harm you or treat you poorly. *To gossip* means to engage in talking about other people and their private affairs.

D UNDERSTAND IDIOMS AND EXPRESSIONS

Suggested teaching time:	10–15 minutes	Your actual teaching time:

- As a class, focus on the highlighted idioms and expressions in Exercise C, Spotlight. Call on volunteers to read them aloud.
- Let students work individually to match each expression with another that has a similar meaning.
- Ask students to compare answers with a partner, referring to the context in Exercise C to check any items.
- Bring the class together to go over the answers.

Option: [+5 minutes] Have students role-play the conversation in pairs. Then have them role-play it again, replacing the expressions with the meanings from the exercise.

Challenge: [+5 minutes] Divide the class into pairs and assign each pair one or two idioms / expressions from the list. Have students create brief dialogues around them. Invite pairs to share dialogues.

E THINK AND EXPLAIN

Suggested teaching time:	5 minutes	Your actual teaching time:

- Have students discuss the questions in pairs. Then bring the class together to go over the answers.
- Focus on the last question. If students are not sure, tell them to read Tom's last exchange. Ask *What does his saying "There's definitely something going on" suggest?* (that he knows why they are huddling, but he can't reveal why)
- Then ask *If it were your birthday, and you saw people huddling and whispering, might you conclude they are planning something for you?*

Option: [+5 minutes] Invite students to share similar scenarios where they felt paranoid that people were talking about them. If students have never felt that way, ask *Do you think some personalities are more prone to feeling paranoid or insecure than others? Do you think some people just don't notice or care if someone might be talking about them?* Invite students to share stories from their lives or lives of people they know.

SPEAKING

Suggested teaching time:	5 minutes	Your actual teaching time:

- On the board, write *seeing is believing*. Elicit that this expression means that a person will believe something is true only after seeing it for him or herself.
- Have students read and rank the perceptions.
- In small groups, have students explain their order and provide examples for the ranked items in the chart.

C ▶ 4:02 **SPOTLIGHT** Read and listen to a conversation between two colleagues. Notice the spotlighted language.

ENGLISH FOR TODAY'S WORLD
Understand a variety of accents.
Vicky = British English
Tom = American English (standard)

Vicky: Tom, do you have a minute?
Tom: Sure, Vicky. Come on in and have a seat. **What's on your mind**?
Vicky: You know, **I may be imagining things**, but I have the distinct impression that my staff's either talking about me or has some kind of secret they don't want me to know about.
Tom: What gives you that impression?
Vicky: Well, for instance, for the last few days every time I get back from lunch, Bill and Emma and Ron are all huddled together in Emma's cubicle and talking, and the minute they realize I'm there, they shut up. I mean, that's not normal, is it? It makes me think they're talking about me behind my back.
Tom: Well, **if I were in your shoes**, I wouldn't automatically assume that.
Vicky: I sound paranoid, don't I? I mean, it sounds crazy to think it has something to do with *me*, right?
Tom: Not necessarily. Their behavior *does* seem to suggest they don't want you to know what they're talking about. **Keep in mind** that there may be a totally innocent explanation. Have you considered the possibility that maybe one of them's got a job offer, or that they're just gossiping? Hey! Who knows? Maybe they're gossiping about *me*!
Vicky: I suppose you're right.
Tom: **Don't get me wrong**. There's definitely something going on, but I wouldn't jump to any conclusions. *[phone rings]* I've got to take this. Just a sec ... Well, as a matter of fact, she happens to be in my office right now. Why don't you all just walk over here, OK? ... **The cat's out of the bag**, Vicky. We all know today's your birthday and we've been planning a little surprise celebration. The gang's got a cake and a little present for you. They're on their way over now.
Vicky: Oh, Tom. I feel like such an idiot!

D **UNDERSTAND IDIOMS AND EXPRESSIONS** Find a spotlighted expression that expresses a similar meaning.

1 Please don't misunderstand me. *Don't get me wrong.*
2 It's possible that what I'm thinking is an illusion. *I may be imagining things.*
3 Faced with the same situation as you, *If I were in your shoes ...*
4 It's not a secret anymore. *The cat's out of the bag.*
5 Tell me what you're thinking about. *What's on your mind?*
6 Don't forget ... *Keep in mind.*

E **THINK AND EXPLAIN** Answer the questions with a partner. Explain your answers with information from Spotlight.

1 What makes Vicky think that her staff is talking about her behind her back? *For a few days, she has noticed her staff huddling together talking, but when she approaches they would shut up.*
2 Why is Vicky afraid that she sounds paranoid? *She feels it's crazy to think they could be talking about her.*
3 What does Tom mean when he says "there may be a totally innocent explanation"? *There may be an explanation other than her staff talking badly about her or keeping a secret from her.*
4 Did Tom know what Vicky's staff had been discussing? *Yes. Otherwise, he probably wouldn't have said, "There's definitely something going on."*

SPEAKING It is said that "seeing is believing," but can we trust our perceptions completely? Rank the following in order of reliability from 1 to 6, with 1 being the most reliable. Provide examples.

☐ A news photograph on the Internet	☐ A claim made in an advertisement
☐ A story told by a friend	☐ Statistics cited by a politician
☐ A video documentary	☐ A witness's story about a miracle

LESSON 1

GOAL Suggest that someone is being gullible

A GRAMMAR NOUNS: INDEFINITE, DEFINITE, UNIQUE, AND GENERIC MEANING (REVIEW AND EXPANSION)

A noun (or noun phrase) is *indefinite* when it doesn't refer to a specific person, place, thing, or idea. Use the indefinite articles (a / an) with indefinite singular count nouns. Indefinite non-count nouns (for example, music, love) have no article.

   You can buy **a smart watch** if you like having everything at a glance. [indefinite, not a specific smart watch]

A noun (or noun phrase) is *definite* when it refers to a specific person, place, thing, or idea. An indefinite noun already mentioned becomes definite when mentioned a second time. Use the definite article (the) with definite singular and plural count nouns and with definite non-count nouns.

   The wool they used to make **the sweaters** in this store comes from Canada.
   [definite, specific wool and sweaters]
   I saw a movie last night. **The movie** was a documentary. [definite, second mention]

A count or non-count noun can represent a person, place, or thing that is *unique*; in other words, there's only one. Use the.

   The president has named two new foreign ministers.
   Some people claim climate change has no effect on **the environment**.

Remember: Non-count nouns name things you cannot count. They are neither singular nor plural, but they always use a singular verb. Common categories of non-count nouns are abstract ideas, sports and activities, illnesses, academic subjects, and foods.

Count nouns can be used in a *generic* sense to represent all members of a class or group of people, places, or things. When using nouns in a generic sense, use a singular count noun with a / an or the, or use a plural count noun without an article. There is no difference in meaning.

   A cat is
   The cat is } a popular domestic pet in many countries of the world.
   Cats are

GRAMMAR BOOSTER p. 138
- Article usage: summary
- Definite article: additional uses
- More non-count nouns with both a countable and an uncountable sense

B UNDERSTAND THE GRAMMAR Read each statement and choose the phrase that describes the underlined word or phrase.

1 Morning snow makes highways dangerous.
   a refers to morning snow in general
   b refers to the snow that fell this morning

2 I think animated movies are boring.
   a refers to all animated movies
   b refers to some animated movies

3 The present they sent me was very expensive.
   a refers to a present as a member of a class
   b refers to a specific present I was sent

4 Some cultures regard the shark as a sign of luck.
   a refers to a specific shark we know about
   b refers to sharks as a class or group

5 The queen will address Parliament this week.
   a refers to a specific queen
   b refers to queens generically

6 A queen can address Parliament.
   a refers to a specific queen
   b refers to queens generically

C GRAMMAR PRACTICE Complete the statements about product claims. Insert a, an, or the before a noun or noun phrase where necessary. Write X if the noun shouldn't have an article.

1 ...**A**... British company claims to have invented ...**a**... machine that allows ...**X**... people to talk with their pets. ...**The**... company says ...**the**... machine, called the PetCom, will be available later in ...**the**... year.

2 It's well known that ...**X**... carrots are a good source of ...**X**... vitamins. In fact, ...**X**... research has determined that drinking ...**a**... glass of carrot juice every day can add ...**X**... years to your life.

3 ...**The**... WeightAway diet plan promises to help you lose ...**X**... weight fast. ...**The**... company guarantees that people following ...**the**... plan can lose up to 10 kilograms per week.

4 Last week, the news reported that thousands of people had sent ...**X**... money to ...**an**... organization advertising a shampoo that ...**the**... organization claimed would grow ...**X**... hair overnight.

UNIT 7

LESSON 1

GOAL Suggest that someone is being gullible

A GRAMMAR

Suggested teaching time:	10–15 minutes	Your actual teaching time:

- Have a volunteer read the first explanation about indefinite nouns in the grammar box. Read the example sentence and ask *Is the reference to a specific smart watch?* (no) *Is smart watch a count or non-count noun?* (count) Elicit an example of an indefinite non-count noun used in a sentence. For example, *I don't understand art.* To review non-count nouns, ask a student to read the Remember note on the right.

- Read the second explanation about definite nouns and the example sentences. Ask *Why is the used in the example sentences?* (*The wool* refers to a specific thing. *The sweaters* refer to specific things. *The movie* is second mention.)

- Call on a student to read the third explanation about uniqueness and the example sentences. Suggest or elicit other examples of nouns that represent something unique, such as the moon or the Internet.

- Have a volunteer read the fourth explanation about generic use and the examples. Point out that each example has the same meaning. On the board, write *Tigers are dangerous creatures.* Have a student express the same meaning using *the tiger* and *a tiger*. (The tiger / A tiger is a dangerous creature.)

Option: GRAMMAR BOOSTER *(Teaching notes p. T138)*

⭐🖨 Inductive Grammar Activity

B UNDERSTAND THE GRAMMAR

Suggested teaching time:	5 minutes	Your actual teaching time:

- Ask students to complete the exercise, referring to the grammar chart as needed.

- Have pairs compare answers. Then go over the answers as a class. On the board, write *indefinite, definite, unique, generic* and call on volunteers to identify what type of noun each item is. (1. indefinite, 2. indefinite / generic, 3. definite, 4. generic, 5. definite / unique, 6. indefinite / generic)

Challenge: [+5 minutes] Invite students to change each sentence or write a new one so as to illustrate the alternate answer. Tell students to make any other necessary changes in the sentence. Elicit and model the first item on the board. Ask *How can we change the sentence to demonstrate specific snow?* (add *the*) Write on the board *The morning snow is making the highways dangerous.* Then have students write the remaining sentences. (2. I think the animated movies we rented were boring. 3. Presents can be very expensive. 4. We observed the shark at the aquarium. 5. Queens address Parliament. 5. Queen Elizabeth can address Parliament.)

⭐🖨 Extra Grammar Exercises

C GRAMMAR PRACTICE

Suggested teaching time:	5 minutes	Your actual teaching time:

- Have students read the exercise items individually and insert missing articles where needed.

- On the board, write *Is the noun indefinite? definite? unique? generic?* Prompt students with questions if they need help completing the exercise. Circulate and assist as needed.

- Bring the class together to go over the answers. Have students explain the decision for each sentence. (1. A British company, indefinite; a machine, indefinite; people, generic; the year, definite; 2. carrots, generic; vitamins, generic; research, indefinite; a glass of carrot juice, indefinite; years, indefinite; 3. The Weight Away diet plan, definite; weight, indefinite; The company, definite; the plan, definite, ; 4. Money, indefinite; an organization, indefinite; the organization, definite, second mention)

NOW YOU CAN Suggest that someone is being gullible

A ▶ 4:03 CONVERSATION SPOTLIGHT

Suggested teaching time:	10–15 minutes	Your actual teaching time:

These conversation strategies are implicit in the model:
- Use *Can you believe this* to demonstrate disbelief.
- Use *Oh, come on* to voice that you don't believe something someone is saying.
- Use *That's got to be* to voice conviction on a topic.
- Use *I guess* to indicate speculation.
- Use *You can say that again* to indicate emphatic agreement.

- Have students look at the photo. Ask *What do you think the man and woman are laughing at?*
- Ask students to read and listen to the conversation.
- To check comprehension, ask *Do either the man or the woman believe the ad?* (They do not.) *What does the line* You don't buy that *mean?* (You don't believe that.) *When do we use* that's got to be? (to voice certainty) *What does* gullible *mean?* (quick to believe something) *What does it mean* to fall for something? (to be tricked into believing what other people say) *According to the conversation, are there people who fall for such ads?* (yes) *Why do they fall for them?* (They want them to be true, for example, a person wanting to lose weight wants to believe that it's possible to lose all belly fat in a week.) *What does the expression* wishful thinking *mean?* (It's when a person believes that something can and will happen, when in reality it's not likely.)
- Then focus on the ways to express disbelief. Have students listen and repeat. Time permitting, students can practice the expressions by role-playing exchanges 3 and 4, replacing line 4 with the two other ways to express disbelief.

B ▶ 4:04 RHYTHM AND INTONATION

Suggested teaching time:	5 minutes	Your actual teaching time:

- Have students repeat chorally. Make sure they:
  ◦ use rising intonation for *Can you believe this?* (line 1) and *You don't buy that, do you?* (line 5)
  ◦ use falling intonation for *What?* (line 2) and *Why do they fall for stuff like that?* (line 8)
  ◦ use stress on *Guaranteed!* (line 4)
  ◦ use incredulous tone for *Oh, come on.* (line 5)
  ◦ use emphatic stress on *got* in *That's got to be . . .* (line 6) and *that* in *You can say that again.* (last line)
  ◦ pause before *I guess* (line 9) and use speculative tone

C CONVERSATION ACTIVATOR

Suggested teaching time:	10–15 minutes	Your actual teaching time:

Conversation Activator Video

- Call on volunteers to read the ads and the three book covers. Elicit the suspicious claims. (Dirt will change into diamonds. Diamonds have been found in Mars rocks. Drinking vinegar will cure depression.)
- Focus students' attention on the e-mail and give them a few minutes to read it. Clarify vocabulary as needed: *humility* is modesty, not thinking a person is very important; *heir to a throne* is the person who will become the kind or queen when the existing king or queen dies; *to disparage* means to criticize someone and see him or her as unimportant. Ask *What does the letter claim?* (that a temporary loan will return a lot of money) Then ask *Have any of you ever gotten an e-mail like that? Did you believe it? Did you respond to it?*
- Divide the class into pairs. Instruct students that they will use the model in Exercise A, Conversation Spotlight, to role-play their own conversation with a partner.
- Reinforce the use of the spotlighted conversation strategies. For example, *Can you believe this? Oh, come on. That's got to be a total scam.* Encourage students to experiment using the different ways to express disbelief presented in Exercise A.
- Bring students' attention to the Don't Stop! note. Ask a volunteer to read the bullet points. Explain that students should continue talking after they have covered the points in the original Conversation Spotlight.
- Tell students to change roles, so each student gets a chance to play A and B.

For more support, play the Conversation Activator Video before students do this activity themselves. After the video, ask students how the model has been changed by the actors. *Note:* You can print the script or you can view it on the video player on the ActiveTeach.

Conversation Activator: Speaking Booster

NOW YOU CAN   Suggest that someone is being gullible

A ▶ 4:03 **CONVERSATION SPOTLIGHT**   Read and listen. Notice the spotlighted conversation strategies.

A: **Can you believe this**?
B: What?
A: This ad. It says, "Don't eat these three foods and lose all belly fat in one week! Guaranteed."
B: **Oh, come on**. You don't buy that, do you? **That's got to be** a total scam.
A: Of course it is. But people are gullible.
B: Why do they fall for stuff like that?
A: Wishful thinking, **I guess**. They believe what they want to be true.
B: **You can say that again**.

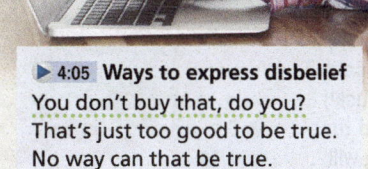

▶ 4:05 **Ways to express disbelief**
You don't buy that, do you?
That's just too good to be true.
No way can that be true.

B ▶ 4:04 **RHYTHM AND INTONATION**   Listen again and repeat. Then practice the conversation with a partner.

C **CONVERSATION ACTIVATOR**   Create a similar conversation, using the scams below. Start like this: *Can you believe this?* … Be sure to change roles and then partners.

DON'T STOP!
- Explain why the message or ad is a scam.
- Speculate about why people might fall for it.
- Talk about other scams you've seen or heard about.
- Say as much as you can.

Extraordinary Space Age Investment Opportunity

Diamonds discovered in Mars rocks, just waiting to be mined!
Invest $1,000, receive at least $100,000 return on your investment

Act quickly. Spaceships leaving soon. Visit our website for more information
www.marsdiamonds.com

Suddenly Happy
The Vinegar Diet Cure
Feeling Blue? Drink vinegar to cure depression in one short week

RICH QUICK
Using revolutionary 4-D printing technology, turn your garden dirt into genuine diamonds in just one month. No need to wait millennia!

From: Prince Montegue
Subject: Urgent Reply Needed

Most esteemed Sir:
Happy New Year!
With due respect and humility, I write to you. I know this message will come to you as a surprise. I am the next heir to the throne in Sylvania, the Crown Prince Montegue. I am hoping that you will not disparage or betray my confident trust in your excellency after I propose to you for the mutual benefit of our families an investment in my government. I can assure you that the Treasury only needs a temporary loan and that if you deposit ONE MILLION U.S. DOLLARS into our national bank [account numbers below] I will personally deposit via electronic transfer TEN MILLION DOLLARS into your personal account in 60 days' time.

LESSON 2

GOAL Examine superstitions for believability

A ▶ 4:06 **GRAMMAR SPOTLIGHT** Read about some superstitions. Notice the spotlighted grammar.

Superstitious.com

A selection of superstitions from far and wide, then and now.

Good Luck

In some countries it's said that a frog brings good luck into the house it enters. (In others, however, it's said that this brings bad luck!) In Korea it's believed that dreaming about a pig will bring good luck because pigs symbolize wealth. Read more

Bad luck

In some cultures in the 18th century, when a worker died on the job, his shoes were brought to his house and placed on the table. Ever since, it's been held that putting shoes on a table is bad luck. There are other theories about the origin of this superstition, but they are all associated with bad luck and death. Read more

Weddings

In some cultures, it's thought that if the groom drops the wedding ring during the ceremony, the marriage is doomed. And in others, it's said that after the wedding, the spouse who goes to sleep first will be the first to die. Read more

Babies

In the past it was said that the sex of a baby could be predicted by suspending a wedding ring by a string over the palm of a pregnant woman. If the ring swung in a circle, the baby would be a girl. If it moved in a straight line, it would be a boy. Read more

Animals

It has been claimed that a dog eating grass brings rain and that rats leaving a ship signifies the ship will sink. Read more

Numbers

It's estimated that more than 80% of U.S. high-rise buildings don't have a 13th floor. This is because the number 13 is considered unlucky and building owners are afraid that few people would be willing to rent an apartment, hotel room, or office on the 13th floor. Read more

See more ▼

B **GROUP WORK** Are you familiar with any of the superstitions on superstitious.com? Do you know any other superstitions for the same categories? Compare information with your classmates.

C **GRAMMAR** INDIRECT SPEECH: IT + A PASSIVE REPORTING VERB

To report a generalized statement or belief, use it + a passive reporting verb + a noun clause. As in indirect speech, the verb in the noun clause reflects the tense of the reporting verb.

It is said that spilling salt brings bad luck.
It was widely believed that the storm would be terrible.
Before the election, it had been asserted that very few people would come out to vote.
It might be thought that the offer is a scam.
It used to be believed that changing bed sheets on a Friday would bring bad dreams.

Common reporting verbs
assert   feel
believe   hold
claim   say
estimate   think

Remember: You can also report generalized statements and beliefs with people or they:
People [or They] say spilling salt brings bad luck.

GRAMMAR BOOSTER p. 140
Indirect speech with passive reporting verbs

78 UNIT 7

LESSON 2

GOAL Examine superstitions for believability

A ▶ 4:06 GRAMMAR SPOTLIGHT

Suggested teaching time:	5–10 minutes	Your actual teaching time:

- On the board, write *superstitions* and elicit that this refers to believing that certain actions, objects, and circumstances can be lucky or unlucky, and they influence how events happen. Ask *Is anyone here superstitious?* If yes, invite students to share a couple of superstitions.
- Have students listen to the article as they read along.
- To check comprehension, ask *What does a frog in a house indicate?* (good or bad luck, depends in what country) *Why do people in Korea enjoy dreams about pigs?* (Pigs symbolize wealth.) *Are shoes on a table associated with good or bad luck?* (bad luck) *What does the groom dropping a wedding band during a wedding symbolize?* (bad luck) *What is the superstition about the spouse that falls asleep first after a wedding?* (He or she will die first.) *What does swinging a wedding band over the palm of a pregnant woman reveal?* (if she will have a boy or a girl) *Why shouldn't passengers mind rats on a ship?* (If the rats left, the ship would sink.) *Would you stay in hotel room number 13, or rent apartment number 13?*

B GROUP WORK

Suggested teaching time:	5 minutes	Your actual teaching time:

- Divide the class into groups of three. Invite students to discuss the superstitions. Then ask them to suggest additional ones for the various categories. Tell students they can look up additional superstitions online if they don't know any themselves.
- Bring the class together and have students share. Note similar superstitions, and invite students to give details for more unusual superstitions.

Option: [+5 minutes] Tell students to imagine that they can click on Read More in any of the categories. In pairs, have them suggest other superstitions for one of the categories.

Challenge: [+5 minutes] Have students look at the web page and the bar with See More under the numbers category. Invite students to work in pairs to speculate what other categories would appear if they clicked on that button. (Possible answers: sports, travel, food) Have students choose one or two categories and write up short descriptions like the ones on the home page. Circulate and assist. Then bring the class together and write all the additional categories on the board. Tell students that for more ideas for categories of superstitions they can glance forward to Exercise A, Now You Can, on page 79.

C GRAMMAR

Suggested teaching time:	5–10 minutes	Your actual teaching time:

- Ask a student to read the explanation. Write the first example sentence on the board. Ask *What is the reporting verb?* (is said) *What is the verb in the noun clause?* (brings) Reiterate that like in reported speech, the verb in the noun clause reflects the tense of the reporting verb. Remind students that in some cases *that* is optional in spoken language.
- Ask students to identify the tense of each reporting verb in the remaining examples. (*was widely believed*, simple past passive; *had been asserted*, past perfect passive; *might be thought*, present modal passive; *used to be believed*, past passive with *used to*) Then tell them to notice the verb in each noun clause. You may wish to point out that for the fourth example sentence, the past form *was* is also possible depending on the speaker's point of view.
- Have a volunteer read the list of common reporting verbs. Elicit that *hold* as a reporting verb means to have a particular opinion or belief.
- Call on a volunteer to read the Remember note. Ask students to restate the example sentences using *People [they]* (say, believe, etc.). Remind students to be careful of the tenses (Possible answers: People say that spilling salt brings bad luck. People believed that the storm would be terrible. Before the election, they had asserted that very few people would come out to vote. People might think the offer is a scam, but I don't agree. People used to believe that changing bed sheets on a Friday would bring bad dreams.)

Challenge: [+5 minutes] Have students look at the spotlighted grammar in Exercise A. For each sentence, ask *What tense is the reporting verb?* (*it's said*, simple present passive; *it's said*, simple present passive; *it is believed*, simple present passive; *it's been held*, present perfect passive; *it's thought*, simple present passive; *it's said*, simple present passive; *it was said*, simple past passive; *it has been claimed*, present perfect passive; *it's estimated that*, simple present passive)

Option: GRAMMAR BOOSTER (Teaching notes p. T140)

⭐ 🖨 Inductive Grammar Activity

D GRAMMAR PRACTICE

Suggested teaching time:	5 minutes	Your actual teaching time:

- Have students underline the subject and verb in each statement. (2. People believe, 3. They say, 4. They say, 5. Some people hold, 6. They estimate)
- Ask students to complete the exercise individually. Then have them compare answers with a partner.

⭐ 🖨 **Extra Grammar Exercises**

E PAIR WORK

Suggested teaching time:	5 minutes	Your actual teaching time:

- Ask *Has anyone ever heard of any of these superstitions?*
- Call on a volunteer to read the model answer. Invite students to respond as well.
- In pairs, have students discuss each superstition, commenting if it makes sense to them or not.
- Bring the class together and have pairs share.

Option: PRONUNCIATION BOOSTER (Teaching notes p. T148)

🖨 **Pronunciation Pair Work**

F GRAMMAR PRACTICE

Suggested teaching time:	5 minutes	Your actual teaching time:

- Have students skim each exercise item and note the subject and verb they underlined. Ask *What tense were these verbs?* (all in the simple present) Tell student they will change the simple present verbs to past with *used to*, making necessary changes to the verb in the noun clause.
- Focus on the model answer. Note how with *used to* as part of the reporting verb *used to be claimed*, the *will bring* changed to *would bring*. To review past with *used to* ask *Is it still claimed that a pregnant woman at a funeral will bring bad luck?* (No, this was true in the past, but isn't any more.)
- Circulate as students work and assist as needed. Be aware that items 3 and 5 both have a conditional sentence following the reporting verb, so two verbs will need to change in 3 (hear, could expect) and three verbs will need to change in 5 (turned, had been cut, would have).
- Go over the answers as a class.

Answers to Exercise F

1. It used to be claimed that a pregnant woman at a funeral would bring bad luck.
2. It used to be believed that lightning would never strike a house where a fire was burning.
3. It used to be said that if you heard thunder and the sound came from your right side, then you could expect good luck.
4. It used to be said that letting the first rain in May touch your face brought you luck throughout the year.
5. It used to be held by some people that if you turned bread upside down after a slice had been cut from it, you would have bad luck.
6. It used to be estimated that more than 50% of people in North American wouldn't rent an apartment on the 13th floor.

T79 UNIT 7 LESSON 2

NOW YOU CAN Examine superstitions for believability

A NOTEPADDING

Suggested teaching time:	5 minutes	Your actual teaching time:

- Students will choose three other students and ask them to name a superstition they know and indicate if they or someone they know believe it. Tell students to write the information on the notepad following the model.
- Ask a volunteer to read the ideas for categories of superstitions.

B DISCUSSION ACTIVATOR

Suggested teaching time:	10–15 minutes	Your actual teaching time:

🎬 **Discussion Activator Video**

- Ask a student to read the expressions in the Recycle This Language box. Review meaning as needed.
- Divide the class into pairs and have students use the notes they gathered in Exercise A, Notepadding, to talk about superstitions. Tell students to refer to specific people who named the various superstitions and whether or not they believe them. Encourage students to use indirect speech with *it* and passive reporting words. For example, *In Bob's culture, it is believed that walking under a ladder will bring bad luck.*
- Tell pairs to ask each other questions and provide details and examples. The goal is to say as much as they can about them.

For more support, play the Discussion Activator Video before students do this activity. After each video, ask if the students in the video included sufficient details. *Note:* You can print the script or you can view it on the video player on the ActiveTeach.

D **GRAMMAR PRACTICE** Replace the subject and active verb in each statement with it + a passive reporting verb. Make necessary changes to the verb in the noun clause.

1 ~~They claim~~ *It is claimed* that a pregnant woman at a funeral will bring bad luck.
2 ~~People believe~~ *It is believed* that lightning will never strike a house where a fire is burning.
3 ~~They say~~ *It is said* if you hear thunder and the sound comes from your right side, then you can expect good luck.
4 ~~They say~~ *It is said* that letting the first rain in May touch your face brings you luck throughout the year.
5 ~~Some people hold~~ *It is held by some people* that if you turn bread upside down after a slice has been cut from it, you will have bad luck.
6 ~~They estimate~~ *It is estimated* that more than 50% of people in North America won't rent an apartment on the 13th floor.

PRONUNCIATION BOOSTER p. 148
Linking sounds

E **PAIR WORK** With a partner, discuss the six superstitions from Exercise D. Discuss whether you believe in any of them, and if so, why.

> "I totally disagree with the one about the pregnant woman at the funeral. I think a lot of superstitions about women are just sexist."

F **GRAMMAR PRACTICE** On a separate sheet of paper, rewrite each passive statement in Exercise D, beginning with **It used to be**. Make necessary changes to the verb in the noun clause. Answers on page T79.

> 1 It used to be claimed that a pregnant woman at a funeral would bring bad luck.

NOW YOU CAN Examine superstitions for believability

A **NOTEPADDING** Ask three classmates about superstitions they have heard about or believe. Write the information on the notepad. Find out if they (or anyone they know) believe in them.

name: Ryan
superstition: If you break a mirror, you'll have seven years of bad luck.

name:
superstition:

name:
superstition:

name:
superstition:

Some ideas for categories of superstitions
- foods / drinks
- good luck / bad luck
- brides and grooms
- particular months, days, or dates
- particular numbers
- dreams
- death
- your own idea: ....

B **DISCUSSION ACTIVATOR** Talk about the superstitions you listed on your notepad. Discuss why you or others believe (or don't believe) in them. Agree and disagree about the superstitions. Say as much as you can.

RECYCLE THIS LANGUAGE
- I think it's possible.
- I agree / disagree.
- People believe what they want to believe.
- Oh, come on!
- No way can that be true.
- That's just wishful thinking.
- Why do people fall for stuff like that?
- Some people are just gullible.

LESSON 3

GOAL Talk about the power of suggestion

A **READING WARM-UP** Do you think that your thoughts and beliefs can affect your health or the condition of your body? In what way?

B ▶ 4:07 **READING** Read the article about placebos and nocebos. What do they have in common? See page T80 for a

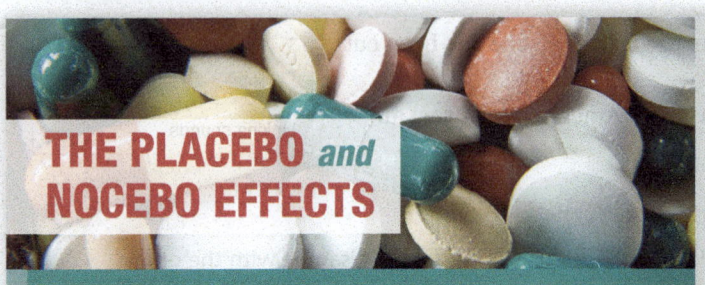

THE PLACEBO and NOCEBO EFFECTS

Two of the most fascinating examples of the power of suggestion in medicine are the *placebo effect* and the *nocebo effect*. These two opposite phenomena are two sides of the same coin. And while the placebo effect has been widely known for many years, the nocebo effect has been largely overlooked until recently and thus less well understood.

The word *placebo* refers to a fake medication (one that contains no active ingredients) or a medical procedure that patients believe will help them and then, as a result of that expectation, it does. In one well-known study, three groups of patients who were told they needed knee surgery underwent one of three procedures. One group had the usual standard surgery. In a second group, the knee was opened surgically but the interior was only washed. In the third group, the doctor made three tiny cuts in the skin, but didn't perform any surgery inside the knee at all. All patients believed they had had the standard surgery. At the end of a year, the patients who had had no surgery reported the same good results as those who had had the surgery.

It has been shown repeatedly that certain factors increase the effectiveness of placebos. If a pill, for example, looks like a genuine medicine, the person taking it is likely to believe it contains medicine. It has also been found that patients think larger pills contain larger doses of medicine, and thus must be more effective. Similarly, it has been demonstrated that taking two pills has a greater therapeutic effect than taking only one. Another important determiner of placebo effectiveness is the doctor-patient relationship. If the patient trusts the doctor administering the "medication," he or she is more likely to be helped or cured by it.

The nocebo effect is also based on the power of suggestion or expectation. If a patient has been told that a medication is likely to cause an adverse reaction (such as dizziness or headache), he or she is more likely to experience one. This has been demonstrated both in experiments and in actual medical practice. One dramatic non-medical experiment is often cited as an example of the nocebo effect: When given a non-alcoholic beverage that subjects were told was beer, they believed and acted as if they were drunk. They slurred their speech, acted silly, and even fell and hurt themselves. Simply believing a substance will make one drunk can result in drunkenness.

What are the implications of the placebo and nocebo effects for medical practice? Placebos can be used in research to help evaluate the effectiveness of real medications. If two groups of patients are treated with either a placebo or a real medication and both achieve the same result, it is clear that the medication lacks real effectiveness. Also, it is well known that some patients ask doctors for medications that are ineffective and potentially harmful (such as antibiotics for a common cold). Doctors can prescribe such patients a placebo, knowing that it may be effective and will cause no harm.

The nocebo effect, on the other hand, can present doctors with an ethical dilemma. Adverse reactions to particular medications are typically experienced by a very small percentage of patients. Doctors wonder if they should inform patients of these potential adverse reactions since they know they are very unlikely to occur. The power of suggestion of the nocebo effect could interfere with the more likely positive effects of a necessary medication, depriving patients of an effective treatment.

In conclusion, although we believe the body and the mind are separate, the existence of the placebo and nocebo effects suggests that the distinction between the two might be more complicated than we as yet understand. All humans are probably somewhat susceptible to the power of suggestion.

C **INFER MEANING** Choose the correct word or phrase to complete each statement.

1 Something that has escaped notice has been (investigated / **overlooked**).
2 The opposite of a placebo is a (fake / **genuine**) medicine.
3 (A placebo / **An adverse reaction**) is a harmful effect caused by taking a medication.
4 The false expectation that a substance is beer has been demonstrated to cause (**silly behavior** / an adverse reaction).
5 Antibiotics are an (effective / **ineffective**) medication for colds.

UNIT 7

LESSON 3

GOAL Talk about the power of suggestion

A READING WARM-UP

Suggested teaching time:	5 minutes	Your actual teaching time:

- Write *power of suggestion* on the board. Elicit that this refers to the notion that our expectations about something influence how we act or proceed with decisions in our life. Elicit or provide examples: *A student or an employee who gets consistent positive reinforcement might succeed at his undertaking. Along the same lines, on the contrary, a person who has no support or, even worse, is disheartened to believe he cannot succeed, may very well fail.*
- Ask a volunteer to read the warm-up questions. Invite students to share ideas and respond if they disagree about anything. Elicit personal examples.

B ▶ 4:07 READING

Suggested teaching time:	10–15 minutes	Your actual teaching time:

- Call on a student to read the title of the article and the introduction in green. Ask *What is the placebo effect?* (It's a fake treatment given to a person instead of real medication, without informing him or her that it is not real; due to the power of suggestion, such a medication might help the person.) Ask *Has anyone ever heard the term* nocebo? If not, point to the introduction which states that it's the opposite of placebo. Have students predict what this could mean. (a treatment that should not have any negative effect on a person, but due to the power of suggestion it harms them)
- As students read and listen, tell them to underline information in the article that will help them answer the focus question in the direction line.

- Bring the class together. Have volunteers share their answers to the focus question. Poll the class *Have you ever experienced the placebo or nocebo effect? For example, have you felt sick after taking a medication because the precautions said you might?*
- Focus on the second full paragraph. Ask *Do you think you could be fooled by a convincingly real-looking placebo pill from a trusted doctor? Do you think there is an ethical question involved with whether a doctor should be permitted to administer placebos?*

LANGUAGE NOTE The term *placebo* comes from Latin meaning "I shall please"; *nocebo* in Latin means "I will harm." Clarify that *placebo effect* and *nocebo effect* refer to the power of suggestion for each; however, *placebo* is also used to refer to the harmless pill or other treatment given to a sick person instead of medicine, without telling him or her it is not real.

Answer to Exercise B
Answer will vary but may include the following:
Both *placebo* and *nocebo* are examples of the power of suggestion in medicine.

⭐ 🖨 Reading Strategies

C INFER MEANING

Suggested teaching time:	5–10 minutes	Your actual teaching time:

- Have students complete the exercise, referring to the article to help them. For a less advanced class, guide students to paragraphs where the information is found.

🖨 Extra Reading Comprehension Questions

D DRAW CONCLUSIONS

Suggested teaching time:	5–10 minutes	Your actual teaching time:

- Have students complete the exercise individually. Then ask them to compare answers with a partner.
- If necessary, guide students to the paragraphs where the answers can be found (1. paragraph 2; 2. paragraph 3; 3. paragraph 5; 4. paragraph 5; 5. paragraph 6)
- Go over the answers as a class.

E CRITICAL THINKING

Suggested teaching time:	5 minutes	Your actual teaching time:

- Have students discuss the questions in pairs. Then bring the class together to go over the answers.
- Focus on the last question and review that *gullibility* refers to being too quick to believe what people tell you. Ask *Do you think the power of suggestion dealing with medication and medical procedures is in the same category as believing an advertisement or a superstition? Or does the power of suggestion go deeper psychologically when it comes to one's health?*

⭐ 🖨 **Extra Challenge Reading Activity**

Answers for Exercise E

Answers will vary but may include the following:

1. The pros of telling a patient potential adverse reactions to a medication is that he/she will be prepared if they were to appear. The cons are that he/she might develop them in anticipation.
2. Placebo and nocebo are "two sides of the same coin" because both are examples of the power of suggestion: placebo is a fake medication that works because patients believe it will; nocebo is a real medication that causes adverse side-effects because the patient believes it will.
3. In my opinion, anyone can be susceptible to the placebo and nocebo effect. As the article suggests, the relationship between the body and mind is quite complex. The power of suggestion can affect anyone.

NOW YOU CAN Talk about the power of suggestion

A NOTEPADDING

Suggested teaching time:	5 minutes	Your actual teaching time:

- Read the direction line, and ask a volunteer to read the sample answer. Have students look at the ideas on the right. To warm up, ask *How might the power of suggestion apply to sexism?* (Possible answer: A girl does not think she has the ability to get a college degree because in her culture women are limited in education and focused on learning how to run a household and raise a family.)
- Encourage students to list two to three ideas on their notepads. Circulate and assist as needed.

B DISCUSSION

Suggested teaching time:	10 minutes	Your actual teaching time:

- Ask a student to read the model answer. Poll the class by asking *Who here is influenced by others' beliefs? Who here isn't really influenced by what everyone else thinks?*
- Call on a volunteer to read the expressions in the Recycle This Language box. Point out how the last four expressions challenge or question what a person is saying. Encourage students to use the various expressions in their discussion.
- Divide the class into groups of three and have them share the ideas they outlined on their notepads. Circulate as students work and jot down on the board topics you hear them discuss.
- Then bring the class together and ask individual students *For which topic do you think the power of suggestion is the strongest? Why?*

⭐ 🖨 Discussion: Speaking Booster

OPTIONAL WRITING [+15–20 minutes]

- Have students write an essay about the topics they notepadded about and discussed in Exercises A and B. Help guide organization by writing the following on the board:

    Introduction

    Body: Describe 2 to 3 ways people are susceptible to the power of suggestion.

    Explain why it is hard to avoid being influenced by the power of suggestion.

    Conclusion

- Offer an opportunity for peer review in class, or collect student work and provide individual feedback.

D DRAW CONCLUSIONS
Complete each statement, based on the information in the article.

1. The factor that doesn't contribute to the placebo effect is ..b... .
   a the appearance of the medication
   b scientific research
   c trust in the doctor
   d the expectation that it will work

2. The knee surgery experiment demonstrates …… .
   a the power of suggestion that surgery was performed
   b the value of washing the interior of the knee
   c the need for procedures in surgery
   d the harmful effects of fake procedures

3. The drunkenness experiment is an example of …… .
   a the placebo effect
   b the nocebo effect
   c an ethical dilemma
   d the harmful effects of beer

4. …… is one beneficial use of placebos.
   a The scientific evaluation of the effectiveness of new medications
   b The improvement of the doctor-patient relationship
   c Causing harmful adverse reactions
   d Reducing the cost of antibiotics

5. Under normal circumstances, adverse reactions to medications occur in …… .
   a most patients
   b only a few patients
   c the sickest patients
   d the common cold

E CRITICAL THINKING
Discuss the following questions. See page T81 for answers.

1. What are the pros and cons of telling a patient about potential adverse reactions to a medication?
2. In what way are the placebo effect and the nocebo effect "two sides of the same coin"?
3. In your opinion, are only gullible people susceptible to the placebo and nocebo effect? Explain.

NOW YOU CAN Talk about the power of suggestion

A NOTEPADDING Make a list of ways people are susceptible to the power of suggestion. Write what creates the suggestion and how it makes people behave or think.

shampoo ads: seeing a beautiful model's hair makes people want to buy the shampoo

Some ideas
- advertisements
- celebrity behavior
- expert opinions
- superstitions
- sexism
- racism

B DISCUSSION With a partner, discuss the information on your notepads, providing specific examples to support your opinions.

❝ I think sometimes we just believe what others believe. We think if everyone believes something, it must be right. ❞

RECYCLE THIS LANGUAGE	
· illusion	· What gives you that impression?
· scam	· I wouldn't jump to that conclusion.
· wishful thinking	· Not necessarily.
· claims	· Don't get me wrong.

OPTIONAL WRITING Write an essay of at least two paragraphs, describing two or three ways in which people are susceptible to the power of suggestion. Try to explain why it's hard to avoid being influenced by messages in the environment and by wishful thinking.

LESSON 4

GOAL Discuss phobias

A ▶ 4:08 LISTENING WARM-UP VOCABULARY EXPRESSIONS WITH MIND
Read and listen. Then listen again and repeat.

make up one's mind
He's afraid of bees and spiders, but he can't make up his mind which are scarier.

change one's mind
She was planning to see the dentist, but it was too scary, so she changed her mind.

put (something) out of one's mind
She's terrified of flying, but she's trying to put any thought of accidents out of her mind.

be all in one's mind
He's afraid there's a monster under the bed. His mom says it's all in his mind.

be out of one's mind
Getting in the elevator would give him palpitations. But they think he's out of his mind to walk down thirty flights of stairs.

B ACTIVATE VOCABULARY Complete each definition with the correct form of an expression from the Vocabulary.
1 When you *put something out of your mind*, you try not to let it worry or bother you.
2 When you *make up your mind* to do something, you decide to do it no matter what happens.
3 When something is not real and a person is imagining it, you can tell the person, "*it's all in your mind*."
4 When you *change your mind*, you change your opinion or decision about something.
5 If people believe you *are out of your mind*, they think you're behaving in a way that is crazy or foolish.

C ▶ 4:09 LISTEN FOR DETAILS Listen to an interview. Then complete each statement, based on the interview.
1 Many people think phobias are …… because phobias are irrational.
 a scary **(b)** funny c enormous
2 People who don't suffer from phobias find them difficult to …… .
 a treat b overcome **(c)** understand
3 Phobias create both mental and …… symptoms.
 a economic **(b)** physical c irrational
4 People with phobias can't …… them.
 (a) control b cure c confront
5 The fight-or-flight response is a set of uncomfortable physical …… .
 a fears b anxieties **(c)** symptoms
6 Exposure therapy and counter-conditioning are two effective …… .
 (a) treatments b symptoms c responses

LESSON 4

GOAL Discuss phobias

A ▶ 4:08 LISTENING WARM-UP

Suggested teaching time:	10 minutes	Your actual teaching time:

- Write *phobias* on the board. Elicit that a phobia is a strong and unreasonable fear of something. Invite students to list different fears on the board. (Possible answers: heights, spiders, water). Ask *Do you or someone you know have any of these phobias?*
- Ask students to look at the cartoons in pairs and read the expressions and example sentences.
- Have students read and listen to the expressions.
- Then have them listen and repeat.
- Invite students to paraphrase the expressions. (1. decide, 2. decided not to go, 3. not to think about something, 4. isn't real / is imaginary, 5. is crazy)

Point out to students that even though the expressions with *mind* are presented in reference to phobias, they can be used with other topics.
For example: I can't make up my mind which dress to wear. It's all in your mind; Mike is not angry with you.

⭐ 🖨 Vocabulary-Building Strategies

B ACTIVATE VOCABULARY

Suggested teaching time:	5–10 minutes	Your actual teaching time:

- Have students complete the exercise individually.
- Then have them compare answers with a partner.

Option: [+5 minutes] Have students create short dialogues using one or two expressions with *mind*. Then have pairs perform for the class.

C ▶ 4:09 LISTEN FOR DETAILS

Suggested teaching time:	5–10 minutes	Your actual teaching time:

- Pre-listening: Invite students to preview the exercise items. If they feel they can answer any of the multiple choice items, tell them they can pencil in the answers. Based on the items in the exercise, ask students what they think the interview will be about. (phobias)
- Write *It's All in Your Mind* on the board. Point out that this is the name of a radio / tv program students will be listening to. Review that the name of the program indicates that something is not real.
- First listening: Have students listen to the interview. Then have them do the exercise.
- Second listening: Have students listen again to go over their answers.
- Go over the answers with the class.

⭐ 🖨 Listening Strategies

UNIT 7 LESSON 4   **T82**

D ▶4:10 LISTEN TO CONFIRM CONTENT

| Suggested teaching time: | 5–10 minutes | Your actual teaching time: |

- Ask students to read the topics. Invite them to check topics they recall being discussed in the interview.
- Have students listen and make sure they checked all covered topics. You can hint that two topics will not be checked.
- Have students compare answers and then summarize what exactly was said about each topic. If students need to listen again for this step, play the audio one last time.
- Bring the class together and fill in any other gaps.

Option: [+5 minutes] Students can use the information in the exercise to write a summary of the interview. If necessary, let students listen again for any missing information. Students can work independently or in pairs.

Challenge: [+5 minutes] Ask *What does Dr. Nordlinger say can be done to help people with phobias?* If students don't remember, remind them that he mentions two treatments. Write these on the board: cognitive behavior therapy (CBT) and counter-conditioning. Have students listen to the last section of the audio, starting with the line *So, Dr. Nordlinger. Tell us. Can people with phobias be helped?* Ask students *If you had to overcome a phobia, which therapy would you choose? Could you tolerate being exposed to your fear repeatedly (CBT), or would you prefer to be taught relaxation techniques to help you replace the symptoms related to fight or flight?*

E ▶4:11 WORD STUDY

| Suggested teaching time: | 5 minutes | Your actual teaching time: |

- Have students read through the list of words to themselves. Ask *Do you or anyone you know have these fears? Have you ever heard any of these official terms? Which two were mentioned in the listening above?* (arachnophobia and claustrophobia)
- Tell students to look at the model answer to see that a person who suffers from acrophobia is an acrophobe; the adjective form used to describe someone who is afraid of heights is acrophobic. Tell students to underline phobe in the first word and phobic in the other word. Explain that the other fears will follow the same spelling pattern.
- After students complete the exercise, have them listen and repeat.

NOW YOU CAN Discuss Phobias

A NOTEPADDING

| Suggested teaching time: | 5 minutes | Your actual teaching time: |

- Write *phobia* on the board and review that the word *phobia* is stronger than the word *fear*. A phobia is a strong, unreasonable fear of something. Then bring students' attention to the heads on the notepad. Focus on *Just afraid, or phobic?* to illustrate that the word *phobic* is stronger.
- Tell students they will list a couple of fears, and then determine how strong each fear is and if they would categorize it as a phobia. Ask a student to read the model answer and what happens to the person afraid of bees. Then elicit a milder fear. (Possible answers: I have a fear of taking tests. I get nervous, and I am afraid I will forget all the material, but usually I do fine.)
- Give students a couple of minutes to complete the notepad. Tell them that if they would prefer not to write about themselves, they can write about people they know.

B PAIR WORK

| Suggested teaching time: | 5 minutes | Your actual teaching time: |

- Before students discuss in pairs, bring students' attention to the Recycle This Language box. Call on two volunteers to role-play the model exchange.
- Then divide the class into pairs and have students talk about the fears and phobias written on their notepads. Assure students they don't have to use the "official" phobia names. The purpose of this exercise is to discuss fears and phobias.

C DISCUSSION

| Suggested teaching time: | 5 minutes | Your actual teaching time: |

- Bring the class together and call on students to write on the board the fears they spoke about. Look at the board and identify the recurrent fears.
- Focus on the most common fears and invite students to share how those fears affect their lives. Ask *Would either of the therapies discussed in the listening (cognitive behavior therapy or counter-conditioning) be a good solution to overcoming these fears?*

D ▶ 4:10 LISTEN TO CONFIRM CONTENT
Listen to the interview again. Write a checkmark next to the topics that were discussed in the interview and an X next to the ones that weren't. Then with a partner, summarize what was said about each topic that you checked.

- ☑ The number of people worldwide who suffer from phobias
- ☒ The way to avoid developing a phobia
- ☑ Some kinds of phobias that exist
- ☒ The danger of a rapid heartbeat
- ☑ The reason why people make jokes about phobias
- ☑ The physical responses to extreme fear
- ☑ Two popular treatments for phobias

E ▶ 4:11 WORD STUDY   NOUN AND ADJECTIVE FORMS
Read the noun and adjective forms that name and describe a person who suffers from acrophobia. Use the same spelling pattern to complete the chart for the other phobias. Then listen and repeat.

Phobia	Noun	Adjective
acrophobia [heights]	acrophobe	acrophobic
agoraphobia [open spaces]	agoraphobe	agoraphobic
arachnophobia [spiders]	arachnophobe	arachnophobic
aerophobia [flying]	aerophobe	aerophobic
claustrophobia [enclosed spaces]	claustrophobe	claustrophobic
ophidiophobia [snakes]	ophidiophobe	ophidiophobic
xenophobia [foreigners]	xenophobe	xenophobic

NOW YOU CAN   Discuss phobias

A NOTEPADDING
On the notepad, write some things you are afraid of. Look at the list of phobias in Word Study for ideas. Do you think your fears are just run-of-the-mill fears, or could you have real phobias?

Fear	Just afraid, or phobic?	What happens?
bees	I'm really phobic!	I get sweaty palms and palpitations. I go inside immediately!
Fear	Just afraid, or phobic?	What happens?

B PAIR WORK
Compare notes with a partner. Ask your partner questions about his or her fears, their effects on him or her, and why he or she is frightened of the thing. Listen and offer advice.

"How come you're so afraid of snakes? Have you ever seen one?"

"Actually, no, I haven't. But snakes really freak me out. I think I'm just afraid, not phobic."

"Well, maybe it would help to read about snakes to find out which are dangerous. Most are actually harmless."

C DISCUSSION
Discuss the most common fears in your class and how the fears affect your classmates in their everyday and professional lives. Provide examples.

RECYCLE THIS LANGUAGE
- ___ gives me physical symptoms.
- My hands shake.
- I get palpitations.
- I lose my voice.
- I get sweaty palms.
- I get butterflies in my stomach.
- Don't freak out.
- Chill.
- Hang in there.
- I know what you mean.

83

WRITING Subject / verb agreement: expansion

A **WRITING SKILL** Study the rules.

When the subject and verb are separated by other words, the subject and verb must still agree.

Beliefs in a supernatural event **are** common in many cultures.
The smart thing to do when someone tells you something is unlucky **is** to just listen.

When two subjects are connected with and in a sentence, the verb must be plural.

A black cat and **a broken mirror are** symbols of bad luck in several cultures.

When verbs occur in a sequence, all the verbs must agree with the subject.

My sister **believes** in ghosts, **avoids** the number 13, and **wears** a lucky charm on a chain around her neck.

When the subject is an indefinite pronoun like each, everyone, anyone, somebody, or no one, use a singular verb.

Nobody I know **worries** about the evil eye.

When the subject is all, some, or none and refers to a singular count noun or a non-count noun, use a singular verb. Otherwise use a plural verb.

If salt is spilled by accident, **some is** immediately thrown over the shoulder.
Some superstitions are old-fashioned, but **some are** not.

Remember: Subjects and verbs must always agree in number.

A superstition is a belief many people think is irrational.

Many people believe certain things can bring good luck.

B **PRACTICE** Read the paragraph and rewrite it on a separate sheet of paper, correcting the errors in subject-verb agreement.

ERROR CORRECTION

One common superstition in Western countries concern the number 13. Because they are considered unlucky, many situations involving the number 13 is frequently avoided. For example, in the past, the thirteenth floor of tall apartment buildings were often labeled "fourteen." While that is rare today, there are still many people who are uncomfortable renting an apartment on the thirteenth floor. In addition, there is a general belief that Friday the thirteenth brings bad luck, increases the chance of mishaps, and ~~make~~ it more difficult to get things done effectively.

concerr
are
was
mak

DIGITAL WRITING PROCESS

C **APPLY THE WRITING SKILL** On a separate sheet of paper, write a four-paragraph essay. In your first paragraph, introduce the topic of superstitions in general, explaining what they are and why people might believe them. Then write one paragraph each about two superstitions. Include a concluding paragraph and be sure each paragraph has a topic sentence. Be sure all your verbs and subjects agree in number.

SELF-CHECK

- ☐ Did I introduce the topic of superstitions in general in my first paragraph?
- ☐ Did my second and third paragraphs each describe a superstition?
- ☐ Did all my paragraphs include topic sentences?
- ☐ Did all my subjects and verbs agree?

In some cultures, black cats are considered to be unlucky.

WRITING Subject / verb agreement: expansion

A WRITING SKILL

Suggested teaching time:	10–15 minutes	Your actual teaching time:

- On the board, write *Horseshoes are a symbol of good luck*. Ask *What is the subject?* (horseshoes) *What is the verb?* (are) *Do the subject and verb agree?* (yes)
- Then write the following incorrect sentence:

    Superstitions about the horseshoe has been passed down for many generations.

- Ask *What is the subject?* (superstitions) *What is the verb?* (has been passed down) *Do the subject and verb agree?* (no) Correct the mistake. (have been passed down instead of has been passed down)
- Read the Remember note. Ask a volunteer to read the example sentences.
- Have volunteers read each rule and example sentence. Stop after each example sentence and ask these questions:

    Rule 1: *What are the subject and verb in the first sentence?* (S = beliefs; V = are) *What words separate them?* (in a supernatural event) *What are the subject and verb in the second sentence?* (S = The smart thing to do; V = is) *What words separate them?* (when someone tells you something is unlucky)

    Rule 2: *What is the subject in this sentence?* (There are two subjects: a black cat, a broken mirror.)

    Rule 3: *What is the subject in this sentence?* (my sister) *What are the verbs?* (believes, avoids, wears)

    Rule 4: *What is the subject in this sentence?* (Nobody)

    Rule 5: *In the first example sentence, what noun does some refer to?* (salt) *In the second example sentence, what noun does some refer to?* (superstitions)

B PRACTICE

Suggested teaching time:	5 minutes	Your actual teaching time:

- Ask students to work individually to correct the errors in subject / verb agreement. Tell them to refer to the rules in Exercise A for help.
- Have students compare the errors they found and explain the corrections they made. Then bring the class together and go over the answers.

C APPLY THE WRITING SKILL

Suggested teaching time:	10–15 minutes	Your actual teaching time:

- Tell students they will write a four-paragraph essay about superstitions. Ask a student to read the direction line. Draft an outline as the student reads it:

    Introduction
    Body: Superstition 1
                 Superstition 2
    Conclusion

- Refer students to the Writing Process Worksheet in ActiveTeach for guidance with the pre-writing and peer feedback.
- Encourage students to use the Self-Check in the Student's Book to go over the essays they wrote.

Option: [+5 minutes] Time-permitting, students can exchange papers with a partner and offer feedback using the topics in the Self-Check list. Encourage partners to also check for examples.

⭐ 🖨 Writing Process

REVIEW

🎮 **Digital Game**

A ▶ 4:12

Suggested teaching time:	5–10 minutes	Your actual teaching time:

- To review the terms *believable*, *unlikely*, and *ridiculous*, have students give examples of each type of claim. (Possible answers: believable—a rigorous exercise and diet routine that can help you lose ten pounds in one month; unlikely—a course that can teach you to draw in seven days; ridiculous—a business plan that guarantees a yearly salary of a million dollars)
- Have students listen to the conversations and decide if the claims are believable, unlikely, or ridiculous. Instruct them to check the appropriate boxes in the chart.
- Have students listen again. Stop after each conversation and have students complete the chart.
- Bring the class together and go over the chart. If students have questions, replay the conversations as needed.

Option: [+5 minutes] Tell students to listen again and identify the lines that helped them decide the type of claim. (conversation 1: Ridiculous. That sounds too good to be true. That's such an obvious get-rich-quick scam. Conversation 2: Believable. Actually, it's very possible. A group of students learned the basics of Russian in just one week, in a sleep-learning lab. Conversation 3: Unlikely. I don't know. I find that kind of hard to believe. . . . it just doesn't seem likely that anyone could do that.) Go over the lines as a class

B

Suggested teaching time:	5 minutes	Your actual teaching time:

- After students correct the errors individually, have them compare answers with a partner.
- Then bring the class together and have students explain each correction. (*an object*—indefinite singular count noun; *a gift*—indefinite singular count noun; *good luck*—indefinite non-count noun; *rabbit's feet*—generic use; *good fortune*—indefinite non-count noun; *a / the rabbit / rabbits* and *a / the hare / hares*—generic use; *people*—generic use)

Option: [+5 minutes] Have students write a paragraph describing a lucky charm that they have or that someone they know has. Tell them to be careful of article usage. Then collect students' work and give individual feedback.

C

Suggested teaching time:	5 minutes	Your actual teaching time:

- Tell students to skim the statements and decide if the reporting verb will be in the present or past passive. (1, 3, and 4 are present; 2 and 5 are past)
- Then have students complete the exercise.
- Go over the answers as a class.

D

Suggested teaching time:	5 minutes	Your actual teaching time:

- Encourage students to look at the context of the sentences when completing them. If students have difficulty, refer them to page 82 to review expressions with *mind*.
- Have students compare answers with a partner. Go over any questions.
- To check comprehension, have students paraphrase the expressions with *mind*. (1. remember, 2. decided, 3. decided not to [get married], 4. forget about it / not worry about it)

Challenge: [+5 minutes] Have students use expressions with *mind* to make comments about the claims in Exercise A (listening comprehension). For example, *You are out of your mind if you send money somewhere and just hope to get rich quick.*

Option: **TEST-TAKING SKILLS BOOSTER** (p. 157)

EXTRA

- Workbook
- MyEnglishLab
- Online Student Resources (www.english.com/summit3e)
  – Classroom Audio Program
  – Extra Practice Activities
  – *Summit GO* App
  – Web Projects
- ActiveTeach
  – Assessment
  – Additional Printable Resources
    ○ Audioscripts and Answer Keys
    ○ "Can-Do" Self-Assessment Charts
    ○ Conversation and Discussion Activator Video Scripts
    ○ Oral Progress Assessment Charts
    ○ Reading Speed Calculator
  – Summit TV Video Program
    ○ Activity Worksheets
    ○ Teaching Notes
    ○ Video Scripts

REVIEW

A ▶ 4:12 Listen to the conversations. After each conversation, summarize the claim that the people are talking about. Then listen again. After each conversation, decide whether the people find the claim believable, unlikely, or ridiculous.

	What is the claim?	believable	unlikely	ridiculous
1	You can get rick in two weeks by sending $10 to a person on a list	○	○	✓
2	You can learn a language while you sleep.	✓	○	○
3	You can learn to read a 200-page book in an hour.	○	✓	○

B Correct the errors in article usage.

A lucky charm is ~~the~~ *an* object that some people carry because they think it will bring ~~the~~ good luck. My lucky charm is a rabbit's foot that I received as *a* gift on my birthday. I don't really know if it has ever brought me ~~a~~ good luck, but I always carry it in my pocket. Since medieval times, ~~the~~ rabbits' feet have been said to bring ~~a~~ good fortune because people believed that witches were capable of turning themselves into rabbits or hares when they were being chased. Both rabbits and hares are very fast animals, so witches stood a good chance of escaping if they turned into rabbits or hares. Since then, ~~the~~ people have carried ~~a~~ rabbits' feet as ~~a~~ good luck charm*s*. They believe the rabbit's foot /feet will protect them.

C Rewrite each sentence, using a present or past passive form of the reporting verb, depending on the information in the sentence.

1. (estimate) Ten percent of people worldwide suffer from some sort of phobia.
   It is estimated that ten percent of people worldwide suffer from some sort of phobia.
2. (believe) The mind and body were completely separate, but now we know otherwise.
   It was believed that the mind and body were completely separate, but now we know otherwise.
3. (say) If a bee enters your home, you will soon have a visitor.
   It is said that if a bee enters your home, you will soon have a visitor.
4. (claim) If you say good-bye to a friend on a bridge, you'll never see that friend again.
   It is claimed that if you say good-bye to a friend on a bridge, you'll never see that friend again.
5. (think) The house was damaged by lightning before the fire, but that turned out not to be true.
   It was thought that the house had been damaged by lightning before the fire, but that turned out not to be true.

D Choose the correct expression to complete each sentence.

1. If you have a fear of spiders, you should …… that spiders are very easy to kill.
   a make up your mind   **b** keep in mind
2. Though he was hesitant at first, in the end he …… to seek help for his problem.
   a was out of his mind   **b** made up his mind
3. She made the decision to get married, but a month before the wedding, she …… .
   a changed her mind   b kept it in mind
4. People who have a phobia find it very difficult to …… .
   a make up their mind   b put it out of their mind

TEST-TAKING SKILLS BOOSTER p. 157

Web Project: Phobias
www.english.com/summit3e

UNIT 8

Performing at Your Best

PREVIEW

COMMUNICATION GOALS
1 Discuss your talents and strengths
2 Suggest ways to boost intelligence
3 Explain how you produce your best work
4 Describe what makes someone a "genius"

A FRAME YOUR IDEAS Take the EQ quiz.

HOW EMOTIONALLY INTELLIGENT ARE YOU?

The concept of emotional intelligence, developed by psychologist Daniel Goleman, is described as the ability to understand one's own emotions and those of others and use them to motivate actions and achieve goals. According to Goleman, one's emotional intelligence quotient (EQ) can be high even if one's standard intelligence test score (IQ) is low. Take the quiz to calculate your EQ. Check each statement that is true for you. Be as honest as you can!

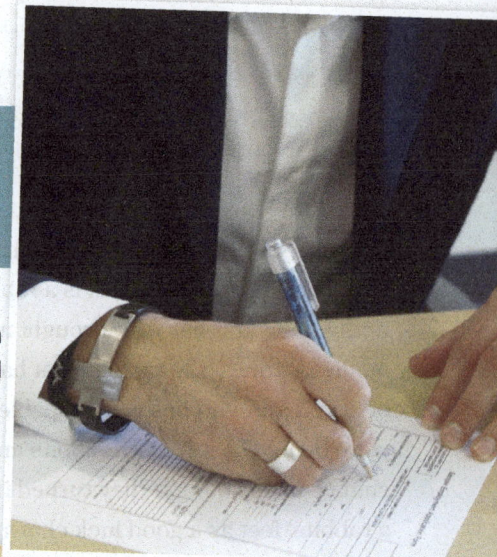

- ○ When I feel down, I try to focus on positive things.
- ○ I like learning about new things.
- ○ I'm not the kind of person who overreacts to things.
- ○ I find it easy to admit when I've made a mistake.
- ○ I see mistakes as opportunities to learn.
- ○ Most people agree that I have a good sense of humor.
- ○ When I'm upset about something, I usually know exactly what's bothering me.
- ○ Understanding the way other people feel or think is important to me.
- ○ When people criticize me, I use it as an opportunity to improve myself.
- ○ I don't mind talking with others about uncomfortable topics.
- ○ I find it fairly easy to get along with people I don't like.
- ○ I have a good awareness of how my own behavior affects others.
- ○ I don't mind conflicts or disagreements.
- ○ I'm good at helping people who disagree with each other to reach a solution.
- ○ It's easy to motivate myself to do things I don't really want to do.
- ○ Before making an important decision, I usually ask other people for advice.
- ○ I always think about the ethical consequences of the decisions I make.
- ○ I have a clear idea of what my strengths and weaknesses are.
- ○ I feel satisfied with my accomplishments, even if I haven't received any praise.
- ○ I generally feel good about who I am, even though there may be things I'd like to change.

SCORE How many statements did you check?
17–20 = you have a very high EQ
13–16 = you have an above-average EQ
9–12 = you have an average EQ
5–8 = you have a below-average EQ
1–4 = you have a very low EQ

B PAIR WORK Compare scores with a partner. Do you each feel that your score accurately measures your emotional intelligence? Explain.

C DISCUSSION According to Goleman, emotional intelligence is more important for an employee's success than either technical skills or IQ. Based on the quiz, in what ways does EQ seem to measure intelligence differently from IQ? Why might an EQ score be useful for an employer to know? Answers will vary but may include the follo
Whereas IQ measures cognitive ability, EQ measures a person's ability to understand emotions. Based on the quiz, the EQ appears to assess interpersonal skills which can be very important when employing someone. For certain jobs how a person interacts with other people, how sensitive he or she is, how he or she reacts in certain situations could be more important than cognitive intelligence.

UNIT 8
Performing at Your Best

PREVIEW

A FRAME YOUR IDEAS

Suggested teaching time:	10–15 minutes	Your actual teaching time:

- On the board, write *emotionally intelligent*. Call on students to guess what this means. Then ask a student to read the first sentence of the quiz introduction.
- Focus on the title of the quiz "How Emotionally Intelligent Are You?" and invite students to answer the question. If necessary, hint that they can say *very, somewhat, a little,* or *not at all*. Tell students that the quiz will help them determine their emotional intelligence.
- Read the remainder of the quiz introduction and instruct students to take the quiz. Circulate and clarify vocabulary as needed. You may need to explain that *ethical consequences of decisions* refer to applying the principles of what is right and wrong when choosing how to act in a certain situation.
- Then have students read the scoring information and total their responses.

B PAIR WORK

Suggested teaching time:	5 minutes	Your actual teaching time:

- In pairs, have students compare scores and see which items they each checked. Then have them say if they feel the scores are accurate.
- Bring the class together and invite students to share their EQ scores. Then ask *Who disagreed with their score? Do you feel your emotional intelligence is higher than you scored? Why? Give examples.*

Challenge: [+5 minutes] In pairs or small groups, invite students to add three questions they feel should be a part of the quiz. Then combine groups and have students answer the questions and comment.

C DISCUSSION

Suggested teaching time:	5 minutes	Your actual teaching time:

- Ask a student to read the first sentence of the direction line. Ask individual students *Do you agree?*
- Then have students compare how EQ seems to measure intelligence differently than typical intelligence tests. If students are unfamiliar with intelligence test formats, invite them to look these up online.

Option: [+5 minutes] Write on the board, *Do you think that there are some jobs that require more IQ and others that require more EQ? Explain.* In groups, have students discuss the question.

D ▶ 4:13 SPOTLIGHT

| Suggested teaching time: | 10–15 minutes | Your actual teaching time: |

- Have students read and listen. Check comprehension by asking *What is Claire studying?* (engineering) *At what point in her studies is she?* (She's almost finished.) *Why is her father concerned?* (She wants to get a part-time job taking care of cats.) *Why is Tony worried?* (He is afraid this job will affect her grades.) *What does Faye mean when she says Can I be frank?* (She means straightforward and honest.) *Why does Faye speculate that Claire wants to work with animals?* (This might lessen the stress of her schoolwork.) *Do you agree that a job can lessen the stress of schoolwork? What kind of job could you imagine for yourself that would do this?*

Challenge: [+5 minutes] Ask students *How many children does Tony have?* (three) *Does he have sons or daughters or both?* (daughters) *How do we know?* (In the first line Faye asks Tony about his youngest daughter. In the last exchange, Tony mentions three kids. *Youngest* is superlative suggesting that there are two others—and since Faye specifies *youngest daughter*, we can deduce Tony has three daughters.)

E UNDERSTAND IDIOMS AND EXPRESSIONS

| Suggested teaching time: | 5–10 minutes | Your actual teaching time: |

- Focus on the idioms and expressions as a class. Call on volunteers to read them aloud.
- Let students work individually to locate them in context to figure out the meanings. Then have students match each expression with the correct definition.
- Ask students to compare answers with a partner, returning to Exercise D to check items as necessary.
- Bring the class together to go over the answers.

Challenge: [+5 minutes] Divide the class into pairs and assign each pair one or two idioms / expressions from the list. Have them create brief dialogues around them. Invite pairs to share dialogues.

F PERSONALIZE IDIOMS AND EXPRESSIONS

| Suggested teaching time: | 5 minutes | Your actual teaching time: |

- Call on a volunteer to read the example answer. Elicit the idioms and expressions used. (gut feeling; in one ear and out the other)
- Then have students recount an instance when they were concerned about someone and gave someone advice.

Challenge: [+5 minutes] Invite pairs to keep discussing the instances when they were concerned about someone, using the conversation in Exercise D, Spotlight, as a guide.

SPEAKING

| Suggested teaching time: | 5 minutes | Your actual teaching time: |

- Create a chart on the board for students to copy or print it out from the ActiveTeach and distribute it to students.

Emotional Intelligence		
Tony	Claire	Faye

- Tell students they will analyze the emotional intelligence of the three characters from the conversation in Exercise D, Spotlight. Call on a student to read the first sample response. Ask *What does the person suggest about Claire's emotional intelligence?* (that she might not have a very high emotional intelligence) Write *doesn't ask for people's advice when making a decision* in the chart under Claire.
- Ask a student to read the second sample answer. *What does the person suggest about Faye's emotional intelligence?* (that she might have high emotional intelligence) Add *good listener; good at helping people reach agreement* in the chart under Faye.
- In pairs, have students continue discussing the people and filling in the chart. Then bring the class together and have pairs share. Finally, decide who has the highest and who has the lowest emotional intelligence.

Option: [+5 minutes] Ask *Do you think Claire has a higher IQ or EQ? Why?*

🖨 Graphic Organizer

D ▶ 4:13 **SPOTLIGHT** Read and listen to a conversation in which someone expresses concern about a family member. Notice the spotlighted language.

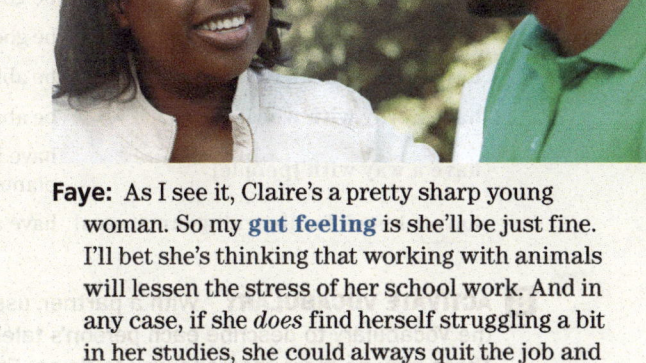

ENGLISH FOR TODAY'S WORLD
Understand a variety of accents.
Faye = Jamaican
Tony = American English (regional)

Faye: Tony, how's your youngest daughter doing?
Tony: Claire? Here's the thing ... She's just a year away from finishing her engineering degree. And, **out of the blue**, she decides to take a part-time job at an animal shelter, taking care of cats!
Faye: Well, that's not surprising. Claire's very responsible. And she's always had a way with animals. I assume she's doing it to help pay for college?
Tony: That's what she said. But in my view she really needs to **put her nose to the grindstone** and focus on her studies right now. Engineering is a tough subject.
Faye: So you're worried it'll affect her grades?
Tony: Exactly. This is her final year. **It's now or never**.
Faye: Have you tried talking with her? Maybe she'll see your point and reconsider.
Tony: Are you kidding? With Claire, everything I say **goes in one ear and out the other**.
Faye: Well, if you don't mind, I'll tell you what I think. Can I be frank?
Tony: Please.

Faye: As I see it, Claire's a pretty sharp young woman. So my **gut feeling** is she'll be just fine. I'll bet she's thinking that working with animals will lessen the stress of her school work. And in any case, if she *does* find herself struggling a bit in her studies, she could always quit the job and concentrate on catching up. I think you should stop worrying about her.
Tony: **I can't help it** ... She's my baby girl. But you're probably right. Of my three kids, she's the one I least need to worry about. She's always been very focused on achieving her goals.

E **UNDERSTAND IDIOMS AND EXPRESSIONS** Match the statement parts to define the idioms and expressions from Spotlight.

1 When you do something "out of the blue," ..d..
2 When you "put your nose to the grindstone," ..f..
3 When you say "It's now or never," ..a..
4 When something "goes in one ear and out the other," ..c..
5 When you have a "gut feeling," ..e..
6 When you say "I can't help it," ..b..

a it's the last opportunity to do something
b you're unable to stop doing something
c someone isn't listening
d you do it suddenly without warning
e you have a strong sense about something
f you're working hard

F **PERSONALIZE IDIOMS AND EXPRESSIONS**
Use two or more idioms from Ex. E to tell a partner about a time when you were concerned about someone or gave someone advice.

66 My sister wasn't sure what to study, but I had a gut feeling she would like mathematics. So I recommended that she take a course. Unfortunately, my advice went in one ear and out the other ... 99

SPEAKING Use the EQ quiz to analyze the emotional intelligence of the three characters in Spotlight: Tony, Claire, and Faye. Explain your thinking.

66 Claire doesn't seem to want to listen to her father's advice. However, according to the quiz, a part of being emotionally intelligent is asking for other people's advice before making important decisions. 99

66 I think Faye's a good listener. She seems pretty good at helping people who disagree with each other to reach a solution. 99

LESSON 1

GOAL Discuss your talents and strengths

A ▶ 4:14 VOCABULARY EXPRESSIONS TO DESCRIBE TALENTS AND STRENGTHS
Read and listen. Then listen again and repeat.

be good with one's hands	have the ability to use one's hands to make or do things
be mechanically inclined	be able to understand how machines work
have a head for figures	be good at mathematical calculations
have an ear for music	be good at recognizing, remembering, and imitating musical sounds
have an eye for detail	be good at seeing or paying attention to things that others don't usually notice
have a good intuitive sense	be able to draw conclusions based on feelings rather than facts
have a way with words	be able to express one's ideas and opinions well
have a way with [people]	have a special ability to work well with someone or something, for example, plants, children, or animals
have a knack for [learning languages]	have a natural skill or ability to do something well

B ACTIVATE VOCABULARY
With a partner, use the expressions in the Vocabulary to describe each person's talents and strengths. There may be more than one way to do so. Explain your reasons.

" Clearly Adela has a knack for learning languages! "

Answers on page T88.

Adela Petran can speak nine languages, including her native Romanian. "It's really not difficult at all," she says.

Miguel Asturias began writing poetry when he was 12. Even though he is still a teen, his teachers have encouraged him to enter his poems in competitions.

Kim Jin-ho was able to solve university math problems at the age of ten. He now teaches math. He argues, "Math's only hard if you think it's going to be hard."

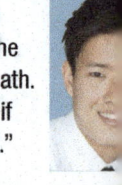

Aiko Kato began playing the violin at the age of three. Today she plays with the Nagoya Philharmonic Orchestra.

Leilah Zaman has been successful at making and selling her own line of women's clothing for five years now. She does all the sewing herself.

As a kid, **Felipe Morais** liked to take electronic devices apart to figure out how they worked. By the age of 16, he knew he wanted to study engineering.

Blair O'Connor works as an editor. Her job is to check manuscripts for errors and correct them before they get published.

Salesman **Bob Pryor** is a good listener. He pays attention to his customers' needs and can anticipate what they want before they even know it.

C PERSONALIZE
Use the Vocabulary to describe five or six people you know.

" My brother Gene, who is a family doctor, has a really good intuitive sense. He can tell what's bothering his patients even when they can't. "

D GRAMMAR USING AUXILIARY DO FOR EMPHATIC STRESS
To add emphatic stress to an affirmative statement in the simple present or past tense, use <u>do</u> or <u>did</u> before the base form of the verb.

Even if I don't have a head for figures, I **do** have a way with words.
He **did** like most of his colleagues, but he didn't like his boss.

Be careful!
Use a base form after a form of the auxiliary <u>do</u>.

She has an eye for detail. → She **does have** an eye for detail. NOT She <s>does has</s> …
He liked his job. → He **did like** his job. NOT He <s>did liked</s> …

▶ 4:15 Listen to emphatic stress on the auxiliary <u>do</u>. Then listen and repeat.
I do have an ear for music.
She does have an ear for music.
He did like his colleagues.

GRAMMAR BOOSTER p. 140
Emphatic stress

88 UNIT 8

LESSON 1

GOAL Discuss your talents and strengths

A ▶ 4:14 VOCABULARY

Suggested teaching time:	5 minutes	Your actual teaching time:

- With their books closed, ask individual students *What are your talents and strengths?* Write students' answers on the board. Then have students open their books, skim the vocabulary, and note expressions they are less familiar with.
- Have students read and listen. Then look at the expressions as a class and answer any questions students might have. Have students look at the board. Ask *Did you write any of these expressions when describing your talents and strengths? Which of the talents from the list do you have?*
- Have students read and listen again.

LANGUAGE NOTE The expression *to have a knack for* (learning languages) is also often used with nouns alone, for example *have a knack for languages / math / science.*

⭐ 🖨 Vocabulary-Building Strategies

B ACTIVATE VOCABULARY

Suggested teaching time:	5–10 minutes	Your actual teaching time:

- In pairs, have students read about each person's talents and strengths and use expressions from Exercise A to describe them. Point out that more than one answer may be possible.
- Circulate and assist as needed.
- Bring the class together and go over the answers.

Answers to Exercise B
1. Adela has a knack for languages.
2. Miguel has a way with words.
3. Kim has a head for figures.
4. Aiko has an ear for music.
5. Leilah has an eye for detail and is good with her hands.
6. Felipe is mechanically inclined and is good with his hands.
7. Blair has an eye for detail and a way with words.
8. Bob has a way with people.

C PERSONALIZE

Suggested teaching time:	5 minutes	Your actual teaching time:

- To warm up, ask *Do you know anyone who is like any of these people?*
- Call on a volunteer to read the model answer.
- Then, in pairs or small groups, have students use the vocabulary from Exercise A to discuss people they know.

D GRAMMAR

Suggested teaching time:	5–10 minutes	Your actual teaching time:

- Call on students to read the first explanation and example sentences. Ask *Could you state these sentences without the highlighted* do *and* don't? (yes) *How would the sentences differ?* (There would be no emphatic stress in the revised sentences.)
- Point out how in the first example sentence, the emphatic *do* is in the second part of the sentence. In the second example sentence, the emphatic *did* appears in the first part of the sentence. Point out, however, that emphatic stress can be used in any type of statement—not only complex or compound statements as in the examples.
- Bring students' attention to the sentences on the right. Point out that emphatic stress is often used in simple sentences to contradict what someone just said. For example, write:

  A: You have no ear for music.
  B: I do have an ear for music.

In the second statement, the person is insisting that something is true. Emphatic stress can also be used just to make statements like *I do like ice cream* and *I do enjoy action movies.*

- Have students listen to the sentences, paying attention to the auxiliary *do*. Then have them listen and repeat.
- Finally, ask students to read the Be careful! note.

Challenge: [+5 minutes] Tell students to find an example of *do* for emphatic stress in the conversation in Exercise D, Spotlight, on page 87 (*if she* does *find herself struggling a bit in her studies . . .*). Ask *What tense is the emphatic* do? (simple present; part of a conditional sentence)

Option: GRAMMAR BOOSTER (Teaching notes p. T140)

⭐ 🖨 Inductive Grammar Activity

UNIT 8 LESSON 1 T88

E GRAMMAR PRACTICE

Suggested teaching time:	5 minutes	Your actual teaching time:

- Ask a volunteer to read the two sentences in item 1. Call on another student to read the model answer. Ask the class *How does the emphatic stress in the model answer change the tone of the sentence?* (Possible answer: It puts a more positive focus on what he *is* able to make.)
- Have students work individually to rewrite the sentences. Tell them to pay attention to whether the underlined verb is in the present (1, 2, 3, and 5) or in the past (4 and 6).
- Have students compare answers with a partner.

⭐ 🖨 **Extra Grammar Exercises**

F PAIR WORK

Suggested teaching time:	5 minutes	Your actual teaching time:

- Have students write their statements individually. Tell them to refer to the vocabulary on page 88 and / or write other strengths and weaknesses.
- In pairs, have them take turns reading the statements to each other.

Option: PRONUNCIATION BOOSTER *(Teaching notes p. T148)*

🖨 **Pronunciation Pair Work**

NOW YOU CAN Discuss your talents and strengths

A ▶4:16 CONVERSATION SPOTLIGHT

Suggested teaching time:	5 minutes	Your actual teaching time:

These conversation strategies are implicit in the model:
- Use *Guess what?* to introduce a topic or share new information.
- Use *I can't make up my mind between* to show indecision.
- Use *I wouldn't say . . .* to voice disagreement.
- Use *I've also been told that* + expression of talent to indicate how people see you.
- Use *I don't think you can go wrong* to indicate that any decision will be correct.

- Have students look at the photo and speculate about the two people. Ask *Where do you think they are? What might they be talking about?*
- Ask students to read and listen to the conversation.
- To check comprehension, ask *What is the woman's news?* (She has decided to sign up for an online course.) *What subjects is she deciding between?* (engineering and psychology) *How does she compare her strengths and weaknesses?* (She says she wouldn't say she's mechanically inclined, but she does have lots of ability in math. She also says she's been told she has a good intuitive sense.) *What does the man think would be a good decision for her?* (either choice) *What advice does he give her?* (that she can always switch subjects)

B ▶4:17 RHYTHM AND INTONATION

Suggested teaching time:	5 minutes	Your actual teaching time:

- Have students repeat chorally. Make sure they:
  - use enthusiastic tone for *Guess what?* (line 1)
  - use falling intonation for *What are you going to be studying?* (line 3) and *Which subject do you think you have the most talent for?* (line 6)
  - pause after *Well* (line 8) and after *Besides* (line 14)
  - stress *wouldn't* in *Well, I wouldn't say* (line 8) and *Either* (line 13)
  - use emphatic stress for *do* in *I do have lots of ability in math* (line 9)

C CONVERSATION ACTIVATOR

Suggested teaching time:	5 minutes	Your actual teaching time:

🎬 **Conversation Activator Video**

- Divide the class into pairs. Instruct students that they will use the model in Exercise A, Conversation Spotlight, to role-play their own conversation with a partner.
- Refer students back the list of expressions to describe talents or strengths in Exercise A on page 88.
- Ask a volunteer to read the words in the Recycle This Language box. Encourage students to incorporate these words into their conversation.
- Reinforce the use of the spotlighted conversation strategies. For example, *I can't make up my mind between; I wouldn't say; I've also been told that . . .*
- Bring students' attention to the Don't Stop! note. Ask a volunteer to read the bullet points. Explain that students should continue talking after they have covered the points in the original Conversation Spotlight.
- Tell students to change roles, so each student gets a chance to play A and B.

For more support, play the Conversation Activator Video before students do this activity themselves. After the video, ask students how the model has been changed by the actors. *Note:* You can print the script or you can view it on the video player on the ActiveTeach.

⭐ 🖨 **Conversation Activator: Speaking Booster**

T89 UNIT 8 LESSON 1

E **GRAMMAR PRACTICE** On a separate sheet of paper, rewrite each item, using *do* or *did* for emphatic stress.

1. Sam isn't a great cook. However, he makes great desserts.
   Sam isn't a great cook. However, he does make great desserts.
2. You're absolutely right! I put things off way too often.
   You're absolutely right! I do put things off way too often.
3. She may not sing very well, but she knows how to dance.
   She may not sing very well, but she does know how to dance.
4. We made total fools of ourselves, but we got everyone to laugh.
   We made total fools of ourselves, but we did get everyone to laugh.
5. He's never lived abroad, but he has a knack for languages.
   He never lived abroad, but he does have a knack for languages.
6. Her decision to quit her job really happened out of the blue.
   Her decision to quit her job really did happen out of the blue.

> Sam isn't a great cook. However, he does make great desserts.

PRONUNCIATION BOOSTER p. 148
Emphatic stress with auxiliary verbs

F **PAIR WORK** On a separate sheet of paper, write five statements comparing your talents and strengths with your weaknesses, using the auxiliary *do* for emphatic stress. With a partner, take turns reading your statements aloud.

> " I don't have an eye for detail, but I *do* have a strong intuitive sense. "

NOW YOU CAN Discuss your talents and strengths

A ▶ 4:16 **CONVERSATION SPOTLIGHT** Read and listen. Notice the spotlighted conversation strategies.

A: Guess what? I've decided to sign up for an online course.
B: Fantastic! What are you going to be studying?
A: I'm not sure yet. I can't make up my mind between engineering and psychology.
B: Which subject do you think you have the most talent for?
A: Well, I wouldn't say I'm mechanically inclined, but I do have lots of ability in math.
B: Then maybe engineering would be a good fit.
A: Maybe. But I've also been told that I have a good intuitive sense.
B: I don't think you can go wrong. Either choice sounds great. Besides, you could always switch subjects down the road if you want.

B ▶ 4:17 **RHYTHM AND INTONATION** Listen again and repeat. Then practice the conversation with a partner.

C **CONVERSATION ACTIVATOR** Role-play a similar conversation in which you discuss your talents and strengths. Use the Vocabulary and emphatic stress with the auxiliary *do*. Start like this: *Guess what?* Be sure to change roles and then partners.
OPTION: Tell your classmates about your partner's talents and strengths.

DON'T STOP!
- Provide more details about your talents and strengths.
- Provide more details about what you would like to be able to do.
- Talk about the talents and strengths of people you know.
- Say as much as you can.

RECYCLE THIS LANGUAGE
- I'm [good at / not so good at] ___ .
- I wish I [were / weren't] ___ .
- I wish I [had / hadn't] ___ .
- If only I [could / would] ___ .
- My gut feeling is ___ .
- It's now or never.

LESSON 2

GOAL Suggest ways to boost intelligence

A ▶ 4:18 **GRAMMAR SPOTLIGHT** Read the article and notice the spotlighted grammar.

CAN INTELLIGENCE BE INCREASED?

In a general sense, intelligence can be defined as the ability to learn, understand, and apply knowledge or skills. In order to maximize these abilities, many argue that it's essential **that the brain not be allowed** to get lazy. Anything from reading more to doing puzzles regularly to learning a new language may in fact improve our thinking skills, capacity to remember, and general knowledge.

IQ (intelligence quotient) has long been used as a measure of intelligence based on general knowledge, mathematical and verbal ability, logic, and memory. While many experts insist **that IQ test scores not be seen** as changeable, others have pointed out that IQ tests provide an incomplete and inadequate measure of real intelligence. To some degree, they measure how one's level of academic achievement can be predicted, but do not measure creativity or "street smarts"—the ability to cope with everyday life. And they do not measure one's potential for growth.

Some experts suggest **that other aspects of intelligence be considered** as well—emotional intelligence being one example. Harvard University's Howard Gardner proposed **that psychologists and educators recognize** the following distinct areas of intelligence: *linguistic* and *mathematical* (which are currently measured to some degree by IQ tests), *interpersonal*—how successfully we interact with others—and *intrapersonal*—how we understand ourselves (both of which are measured by EQ tests). He also proposed measuring *visual-spatial* intelligence—the ability to use and understand visual information in charts, diagrams, and art. And finally Gardner recommended **that two other aspects of intelligence be included**: *musical* (the ability to make sense of sounds) and *physical* (the intelligence that dancers and athletes show through movement). Gardner considers each of these intelligences to be areas of human potential—in other words, they can be developed and increased.

B **DISCUSSION** Describe people you know who exhibit some of the types of intelligence proposed by Gardner.

C **GRAMMAR** **THE SUBJUNCTIVE**

Use the subjunctive form of a verb in a noun clause that follows a verb or adjective of urgency, obligation, or advisability. The subjunctive form of the verb is the same as the base form and doesn't change, no matter what the subject of the clause is. Use <u>not</u> before the verb for the negative.

She insisted (that) we **be** at the office at three o'clock.
I'm proposing (that) you **not apply** for that job until you've passed your driving test.
It's important (that) he **complete** the presentation in less than thirty minutes.

The passive form of the subjunctive is <u>be</u> + the past participle.

They suggested that my mother **not be given** an EQ test.

The continuous form of the subjunctive is <u>be</u> + the present participle.

It's crucial that they **be waiting** outside the room after the interview.

Urgency, obligation, and advisability	
Verbs	Adjectives
demand	critical
insist	crucial
propose	desirable
recommend	essential
request	important
suggest	necessary
urge	

90 UNIT 8

LESSON 2

GOAL Suggest ways to boost intelligence

A ▶ 4:18 GRAMMAR SPOTLIGHT

Suggested teaching time:	10–15 minutes	Your actual teaching time:

- Have students look at the graphic of the boy and the gears in the head. Invite students to identify the various images. (Possible answers: library, book, book bag, math book, paper, telescope, apple, computer) Ask students to speculate what the images and arrows represent. (Possible answer: how intelligence is made up of various components) Ask *Do you think all the images in the graphic fall under the umbrella of intelligence? Which of the graphics represent your strengths? What images would you add to the graphic?*
- Have students listen to the article as they read along.
- To check comprehension, ask *How does the article define intelligence?* (the ability to learn, understand, and apply knowledge or skills) *What can help the brain not get lazy?* (reading more, doing puzzles, learning a new language) *What does the IQ test measure?* (general knowledge, mathematical and verbal ability, logic, and memory) *What does the IQ test fail to test?* (creativity, street smarts, the ability to cope with everyday life, the potential for growth) *Do you agree with the seven aspects of intelligence? Would you add any others?*

LANGUAGE NOTE The word *intelligence* in its general sense is ordinarily a non-count noun. As used in Gardner's work about multiple intelligences, the plural was coined to indicate a diverse number of types of intelligence.

Option: [+5 minutes] On the board, write *What activities would you choose to keep your brain from getting lazy?* Have students discuss in pairs and make lists. Then bring the class together and have students share. Invite students to respond to suggestions. Then ask *Do you think technology contributes to making our brains lazy?*

B DISCUSSION

Suggested teaching time:	5 minutes	Your actual teaching time:

- Have students work in pairs to talk about people they know and the intelligences they possess.
- Bring the class together and have students share. Ask *Which intelligences do you think are important to have?*

Option: [+5 minutes] Focus on the title of the article. Ask *Do you think it's possible to increase intelligence?* In pairs, have students brainstorm ways the seven intelligences can be increased. On the board, write *Which intelligences would you like to develop more in yourself?* Have students discuss in pairs.

Challenge: [+5 minutes] Invite students to speculate how the various intelligences proposed by Gardner can be tested. Then ask *Do you think it's important to test intelligences?*

C GRAMMAR

Suggested teaching time:	10–15 minutes	Your actual teaching time:

- Have students read the first sentence of the explanation. Bring students' attention to the list of verbs and adjectives of urgency, obligation, and advisability on the side.
- Ask a volunteer to read the rest of the explanation and give students a few minutes to read the example sentences. Ask *Which sentences use verbs of urgency, obligation, advisability?* (the first two) *Which sentence uses an adjective?* (the third)
- Focus on the form of the highlighted verb in each sentence. Point out that it does not change no matter what the subject. Ask students to notice *not* before the verb in the second sentence. If appropriate for your class, explain in more detail that the action in a noun clause following verbs and adjectives of urgency, obligation, or advisability is uncertain to occur. It is often referred to as a mood rather than a tense and is contrasted with the indicative, which is a statement of reality. We don't use the subjunctive when the noun clause expresses a simple fact.
- Call on volunteers to read the second explanation and example sentence. On the board, write:

  I demand that I _____ (give) my money back
  It is crucial that the letters _____ (sent) today.

  Ask students to fill in the blanks with passive subjunctive forms (be given, be sent). Elicit additional sentences.
- Ask students to read the third explanation and example sentence. Point out that the continuous form is not often used in spoken English, but it is grammatically correct.

UNIT 8 LESSON 2 T90

- Read the Note and ask volunteers to read the example sentences. After each sentence, ask *What is the time frame of the entire sentence?* (the first is simple past; the second is simple past; the third is future; the fourth is past perfect) *What form do you need to use in the noun clause?* (the same subjunctive form for all the sentences)
- Call on a volunteer to read the Be careful! note and example sentences. Ask *Is* agree *in the first sentence a verb of urgency, obligation, or advisability?* (no) Explain that for that reason the simple present indicative is used instead of the subjunctive. On the board, write *Scientists insist that intelligence testing incorporate emotional intelligence.* Ask *Why is the subjunctive used in this sentence?* (*Insist* is a verb of urgency.) Then draw students' attention to the second example sentence. Ask *Is* interesting *an adjective of urgency, obligation or advisability?* (no) Again point out that for that reason the subjunctive is not used.

Challenge: [+5 minutes] Have students look at the spotlighted grammar in Exercise A. For each of the five sentences ask *What is the verb or adjective of urgency, obligation, or advisability? Is the sentence active or passive?* (1. *essential*, passive; 2. *insist*, passive; 3. *suggest*, passive; 4. *proposed*, active; 5. *recommended*, passive) Invite students to work in pairs to change each passive sentence to active to practice the subjunctive form. Tell students to use the subject *we* in the noun clauses of the passive sentences. (1. . . . it's essential that we not allow the brain to get lazy . . .; 2. . . . many experts insist that we not see IQ tests as changeable; 3. Some experts suggest that we consider other aspects of intelligence as well; 5. . . . Gardner recommended that we include two other aspects of intelligence . . .) Go over the answers as a class. Then, as a class, focus on the active sentence and elicit the passive form. (. . . Gardner proposed that the following distinct areas of intelligence be recognized by psychologists and educators . . .)

Option: GRAMMAR BOOSTER *(Teaching notes p. T141)*

⭐ 🖨 **Inductive Grammar Activity**

D GRAMMAR PRACTICE

Suggested teaching time:	5 minutes	Your actual teaching time:

- To preview, have students identify which sentences have a verb or adjective of urgency, obligation, or advisability in the main clause. (all but 1, 3, and 7) Then have them complete the exercise.
- Have students compare answers with a partner.

Option: [+5 minutes] Have students locate the one passive subjunctive sentence in the exercise. (5) Tell them to change it to the active using the subject *I*. (Martin demanded that I train the new assistant . . .) Next tell students to identify the sentence in the continuous form of the subjunctive. (10)

Challenge: [+5 minutes] Have students look at the three non-subjunctive sentences. (1, 3, and 7) In pairs, have them rewrite the sentences using verbs or adjectives of urgency, obligation, or advisability. Tell them to change each sentence as necessary. (Possible answers: 1. Jack and Shira insist that their daughter be at the top of her class.

3. He suggests that intuitive intelligence be taught in schools. 7. I urge that he be offered the job based on his talents and abilities.)

⭐ 🖨 **Extra Grammar Exercises**

E PAIR WORK

Suggested teaching time:	5 minutes	Your actual teaching time:

- Have students work in pairs to complete the statements in their own way.
- Bring the class together and ask *Did anyone make any passive statements?* Have students share. Then call on volunteers to complete one of the statements in the continuous subjunctive. (Possible answer: I think it's crucial that every parent be monitoring their children's use of technology.)

NOW YOU CAN Suggest ways to boost intelligence

A NOTEPADDING

Suggested teaching time:	5 minutes	Your actual teaching time:

- Have students return to the article and read aloud the intelligences mentioned there. List these on the board: *linguistic, mathematical, interpersonal, intrapersonal, visual spatial, musical, physical.* Focus on the box with some ideas for ways the various intelligences might be boosted. Invite students to share and then write in their own ideas.
- Tell students to focus on one or more intelligence and fill out the notepad with suggestions for ways it or they might be increased.

B DISCUSSION ACTIVATOR

Suggested teaching time:	5–10 minutes	Your actual teaching time:

🎬 **Discussion Activator Video**

- Divide the class into pairs and have students use their descriptions from Exercise A, Notepadding, to talk about boosting intelligences. Encourage the pairs to ask each other questions and provide details and examples. The goal is for students to say as much as they can about the intelligences.

For more support, play the Discussion Activator Video before students do this activity. After each video, ask if the students in the video included sufficient details. *Note:* You can print the script or you can view it on the video player on the ActiveTeach.

Note: The subjunctive in the noun clause doesn't change, no matter what the time frame of the entire sentence is.

It was essential (that) the theory **explain** (NOT ~~explained~~) how intelligence would be boosted.

The psychologist recommended (that) all her patients **be given** (NOT ~~were given~~) a standardized test of intelligence.

I will request (that) people **not be admitted** (NOT ~~will not be admitted~~) to the lecture unless they are already enrolled in the course.

They had insisted that no one **be texting** (NOT ~~were texting~~) during the meeting.

Be careful!
If a noun clause doesn't follow a verb or adjective of urgency, obligation, or advisability, don't use the subjunctive.
Scientists agree that EQ testing **is** a useful tool.
It is interesting that Gardner **identified** other kinds of intelligence.

GRAMMAR BOOSTER p. 141
Infinitives and gerunds in place of the subjunctive

D GRAMMAR PRACTICE Decide whether to use the subjunctive and circle the correct form. Explain each answer.

1. Jack and Shira were convinced that their daughter Sue (was / be) a genius.
2. It would be critical that every potential employee (take / took) an EQ test.
3. Everyone knows that intuitive intelligence (isn't / not be) learned in school.
4. It was important that Shelly (become / becomes) more aware of her colleague's emotions.
5. Martin demanded that the new assistant (be / was) trained to deal with customers more effectively.
6. It's crucial that she (doesn't accept / not accept) her employer's opinion about her test scores.
7. I had hoped that he (would be / be) offered the job based on his talents and abilities.
8. Jake proposed that he (didn't continue / not continue) searching for the website until after lunch.
9. Our manager insisted that no one (is / be) late for the conference call.
10. It's essential that you (be sitting / are sitting) in front of your computer at 3:00.
11. It's important that Bryce (improve / improves) his interpersonal intelligence.

You only use the subjunctive if the noun clause comes after a verb or adjective of urgency, obligation, or advisability.

If you don't have a head for figures, it's essential that you get lots of practice.

E PAIR WORK With a partner, take turns completing these statements in your own way, using the subjunctive.

1. On the first day of class, it's important that a teacher ...
2. I suggest that a visitor to our city ...
3. I would recommend that the government ...
4. I think it's crucial that every parent ...
5. When I take a taxi, I insist that the driver ...

NOW YOU CAN Suggest ways to boost intelligence

A NOTEPADDING Choose one or more of the intelligences mentioned in Grammar Spotlight. On your notepad, list suggestions for exercising the brain and boosting those intelligences.

Your suggestions
mathematical intelligence: do math puzzles, keep track of your personal finances

Your suggestions

Some ideas
- take a class
- play digital games
- eat brain-healthy foods
- get lots of sleep
- listen to audio lectures
- your own idea: ___

B DISCUSSION ACTIVATOR In a small group, share the ideas from your notes. Suggest and discuss ways to boost intelligence. Use the subjunctive in noun clauses after verbs or adjectives of urgency, obligation, or advisability. Say as much as you can.

I suggest you do math puzzles regularly to exercise your brain. It's important, though, that they be fun. Otherwise, you won't keep doing them.

LESSON 3

GOAL Explain how you produce your best work

A **READING WARM-UP** Why do you think people often have problems staying on task when they have to do something? When does that happen to *you*?

B ▶ 4:19 **READING** Read the article. What do you think the title "Stay on Target" means?
"To stay on target" means to stay focused.

STAY ON TARGET

You've got work to do, but you just can't seem to get your brain going. You stare at that blank piece of paper in front of you but can't get your thoughts organized. Your mind wanders to the argument you had with your spouse, the leftovers in the fridge … Then, just as your ideas finally start to come together, the phone rings, and you're back to square one. Sound familiar? The ability to devote all of one's attention to a single task is the key to achievement in any occupation. On the other hand, being unable to concentrate can keep you from producing your best work. The following tips can help you stay focused:

Stay organized. Let's face it—it's not easy to keep focused if your desk looks like it just got hit by a tornado. Efficiency coach Selma Wilson suggests you spend a few moments a day cleaning up your workspace and reducing the time you normally spend searching for mislaid memos or your flash drive.

Develop a routine. Studies show that following a systematic pattern of behavior can make it easier to devote your undivided attention to a task. For example, if you're a student and you have trouble preparing for exams, it's critical that you establish a study ritual. Start and finish at the same time each day. Work at the same desk or in your favorite chair. If music helps you focus, choose a piece of music and play it during every study session.

Make a list. Each morning, write down all the tasks you need to accomplish that day and cross off each item as you complete it. This visual reminder will not only keep you focused on your goals but will also give you a sense of progress and achievement.

Challenge yourself. When faced with a boring, routine task that seems to drag on forever, it's easy to lose concentration and make careless mistakes. According to writer Mihaly Csikszentmihalyi, one of the best ways to engage your attention on a dull task is to make it harder. For example, turn the task into a game by giving yourself a time limit. The increased challenge stimulates blood flow and activity in the brain, making it easier for you to focus on the job at hand.

Reserve some "do not disturb" time. If interruptions from family, friends, or co-workers prevent you from getting your work done, set aside a certain period of your schedule each day when you are unavailable. Let others know that they shouldn't disturb you during this time. Close the door to your office or find an area where you're less likely to be interrupted by colleagues, such as a conference room or a quiet coffee shop with Wi-Fi.

Go offline. While the Internet is an invaluable tool for getting and sharing information, it can be a real concentration killer. If all those quick clicks to "just check the news" are interfering with your productivity, Wilson recommends you make it a point to stay offline while you're working. And if you find your focus constantly broken by incoming e-mail and instant messages, do resist the urge to read and reply to them as they arrive. Instead, set aside certain times of the day for your e-mail—and keep working.

Take a breather. Taking short breaks can help you clear your mind and refocus on the next job. Stand up for a moment and take a short walk in the hallway or just close your eyes, relax your muscles, and breathe deeply.

The next time you have an important project that requires your full concentration, see if any of these strategies can make a difference for you.

LESSON 3

GOAL Explain how you produce your best work

A READING WARM-UP

Suggested teaching time:	5 minutes	Your actual teaching time:

- To warm up, write on the board *stay on task*. Ask *What does this mean?* (to remain focused on what has to be done)
- Then ask students to brainstorm why people often have problems staying on task. (Possible answers: having distractions like technology, being tired, being bored) Write students' answers on the board. Then have volunteers share which of the items on the board apply to them. Invite them to share other examples of times when they can't stay on task.

B ▶ 4:19 READING

Suggested teaching time:	15–20 minutes	Your actual teaching time:

- Have a volunteer read the title of the article. Point to the graphic to the right of the title and ask *What is this?* (a target, or a round shield at which you can shoot an arrow or a bullet)
- Ask a student to read the focus question. Elicit the answer. (*To stay on target* means to stay focused.) Write the expression *stay on task* on the board and explain that this means the same thing.
- Call on a volunteer to read the introduction. Take a poll by asking *How many of you have been in this situation?* Then ask *How do you feel when you can't concentrate? How does this affect your work?*
- Ask students to skim the list of highlighted tips. Then have them read and listen to the article. Clarify vocabulary as needed.
- To check comprehension of the article, ask: *What are the benefits of a clean workspace?* (It helps you stay organized, and you spend less time looking for misplaced things.) *Why is it a good idea to develop a routine?* (It helps you devote your undivided attention to a task.) *What's helpful about making a list?* (The visual reminder helps keep you focused and gives you a sense of progress and achievement.) *What does an increased challenge do to the brain?* (It stimulates blood flow and activity in the brain, making it easier to focus on your job.) *What should you do if you're constantly interrupted during your workday?* (You should reserve some "do not disturb" time.) *Why should you work offline?* (to avoid distractions such as incoming e-mail and checking the news) *Why are breaks important while you work?* (They help you to clear your mind and focus on the next job.)

⭐ 🖨 Reading Strategies

LANGUAGE NOTE *Get your brain going* means start thinking; *you're back to square one* means you're back to where you started.

Option: [+5 minutes] Have pairs role-play a conversation between employee Bill French and his supervisor Ms. Adams. Bill has been having difficulty concentrating, and his job performance has been suffering. Have Ms. Adams discuss this problem with him, ask questions, and give advice. Tell students they can use tips from the article. Invite students to role-play their conversations for the class.

Option: [+5 minutes] Ask students to work in pairs to develop additional tips for staying on target. Then combine pairs into groups of four and have them share.

UNIT 8 LESSON 3 T92

C APPLY IDEAS

Suggested teaching time:	10–15 minutes	Your actual teaching time:

- Call on volunteers to read about focus problems the various people tend to have or have had and the solutions they have implemented to stay on target.
- Bring the class together and have students match tips from the article with each person's situation. Make sure students explain their reasoning.

Challenge: [+5 minutes] Have students work independently to write a description of a problem they have with staying on target. Tell them to use the descriptions in the book as models. Then bring the class together and have students read their problem and ask the class for advice. Tell students to refer to the tips in the article as well as their own experience.

Challenge: [+5 minutes] Invite students to skim the people's problems for two examples of the subjunctive taught in the grammar on pages 90–91. If students have difficulty, hint that the examples appear in Kyoko's and Marina's descriptions (Kyoko: *When a colleague suggests she begin every paragraph with the letter S, the words start flowing smoothly;* Marina: *Her kids know that it's crucial that they not knock on the door or call her unless it's an emergency*). Analyze how in Kyoko's example *that* is omitted.

Answers for Exercise C

Answers will vary but may include the following:

Kyoko: Challenge Yourself
Tatiana: Take a Breather
Emilio: Develop a Routine
Claudio: Go offline
Marina: Reserve some "Do not disturb" time
Jae Jin: Stay organized

🖨 Extra Reading Comprehension Questions

D RELATE TO PERSONAL EXPERIENCE

Suggested teaching time:	5 minutes	Your actual teaching time:

- After students discuss the questions in groups, bring the class together and have students share answers.
- Then ask *What other tips would you recommend to a person who has difficulty staying on target?*

⭐🖨 Extra Challenge Reading Activity

NOW YOU CAN Explain how you produce your best work

A NOTEPADDING

Suggested teaching time:	5 minutes	Your actual teaching time:

- Have a volunteer read the list of distractions in the box. Ask *Which distractions are the biggest problem for you?* Invite students to give specific examples. (Possible answers: I live on a busy street, so there is always traffic noise outside. I worry about things, so often while working I start thinking and worrying about something unrelated.)
- Ask a student to read the model answers. Point to the second sentence and remind students to use gerunds after prepositions.
- After students complete their lists, have pairs discuss the distractions and the strategies they use to stay focused.

Option: [+5 minutes] Have students look at the smartphone and the various icons. In pairs, have them interpret what each represents. (Possible answers: music, photographs, texting, shopping, games, e-mail) Then have students share which items distract them most. On the board, write *Do you think shutting off your smartphone is a solution to staying focused?*

B DISCUSSION

Suggested teaching time:	5–10 minutes	Your actual teaching time:

- Read the direction line and have a volunteer read the model answer.
- On the board, write:

  I work best when ...

- Then invite students to share techniques for overcoming distractions and staying focused.
- Take a poll to find out the most common distractions and the most successful strategies for staying focused.

⭐🖨 Discussion: Speaking Booster

C **APPLY IDEAS** Which tip from the article has each person applied? Explain your choices. See page T93 for answers.

KYOKO is having trouble getting started writing an article about a topic that doesn't inspire her. When a colleague suggests she begin every paragraph with the letter S, the words start flowing smoothly.

TATANIA has to study for two important university exams tomorrow. She studies intensely but takes regular fifteen-minute breaks to relax. Before starting to study for the second exam, she takes a long walk in the park.

EMILIO is a classical singer. At every concert, just before going on stage, he always does the same thing. He slowly drinks half a cup of tea with honey and he texts his daughter just to say hello. Then he feels ready to go on.

CLAUDIO has decided to decrease distractions by setting up a separate e-mail account for his friends and family so they don't mix with his office e-mails. He makes it a strict rule to check the account for messages only during lunch or after hours.

MARINA has two young teens and works at home. From 12:00 to 3:00 each day, she keeps the door to her home office closed and turns her smartphone off. Her kids know that it's crucial that they not knock on the door or call her unless it's an emergency.

JAE JIN is responsible for five major projects, and by the end of the day, his work area is always a mess, covered with memos and files. Before leaving the office each day, he makes a point of taking five minutes to organize all the papers on his desk.

D **RELATE TO PERSONAL EXPERIENCE** With a partner, discuss which of the tips in the article seem the most useful and explain your reasons. If you have ever tried any of them, describe the results.

NOW YOU CAN Explain how you produce your best work

A **NOTEPADDING** On your notepad, list the distractions that cause you to lose focus when you are working on a task. What strategies do you use to stay focused?

I lose focus when …	I stay focused by …
I'm interrupted by phone calls.	not answering calls.

I lose focus when …	I stay focused by …

Some distractions
- noise
- phone calls
- interruptions
- worries
- aches and pains
- room temperature
- hunger
- boredom

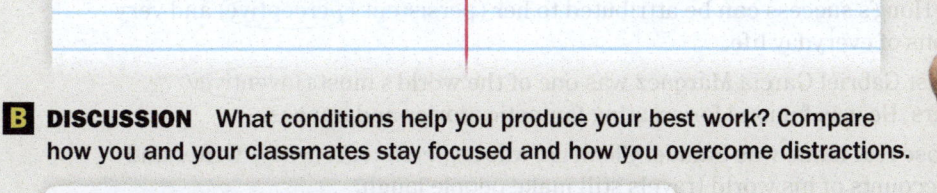

B **DISCUSSION** What conditions help you produce your best work? Compare how you and your classmates stay focused and how you overcome distractions.

"I work best when it's very quiet. If I'm reading, I can't concentrate when I get interrupted. So I just close the door to let people know they shouldn't disturb me."

LESSON 4

GOAL Describe what makes someone a "genius"

A **LISTENING WARM-UP** **DISCUSSION** In your opinion, is there a difference between describing someone as intelligent and calling him or her a genius? Explain.

B ▶ 4:20 **LISTEN FOR MAIN IDEAS** Listen to Part 1 of a lecture on human intelligence. Choose the speaker's main point.

1 Everyone with a high IQ is a genius.
② Not everyone agrees about how to define genius.
3 A genius is someone with an IQ score over 145.

C ▶ 4:21 **LISTEN TO INFER** Listen to Part 1 again and pay attention to the opposing arguments. Check the one statement that best supports the argument that a high IQ score doesn't determine whether one is a genius.

☐ Albert Einstein had an IQ of 160 and had many impressive achievements.
☐ Most average people have an IQ score that can range from about 85 to 115.
☐ Most people agree that the composer Beethoven was probably a genius.
☐ The 1,500 gifted children in Terman's study had IQs of 140 or more.
☑ None of the people with high IQs in Terman's research had any notable achievements.

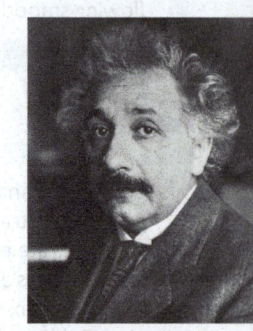

Albert Einstein, physicist and Nobel Prize winner

D ▶ 4:22 **LISTEN FOR SUPPORTING DETAILS** Now listen to Part 2 of the lecture. Write at least two arguments the lecturer mentions to support each theory.

in favor of a genetic theory	in favor of an environmental theory
1 Talented families exist	1 All the ancestors of a genius should be also geniuses, but this is not true.
2 Ramanujan came from a very poor environment	2 Even though identical twins may have the same genes, they don't necessarily have the same talents or abilities.

Srinivasa Ramanujan, mathematician

E ▶ 4:23 **VOCABULARY** **ADJECTIVES THAT DESCRIBE ASPECTS OF INTELLIGENCE** Read and listen. Then listen again and repeat.

talented	having a natural ability to do something very well
perceptive / observant	good at noticing what people are thinking or feeling
inventive / imaginative	good at thinking of new and interesting ideas; creative
witty	able to use humor intelligently; good at using words for others' enjoyment
curious / inquisitive	having the desire to learn about new things
open-minded	willing to consider new ideas; not close-minded
persistent	willing to continue trying something in spite of difficulty

F **VOCABULARY PRACTICE** Choose the best adjective to complete each description.

1 Comedian Helen Hong's success can be attributed to her (persistent /**perceptive**) and very funny observations of everyday life.
2 Colombian novelist Gabriel García Márquez was one of the world's most (**inventive**/ inquisitive) writers. He was famous for creating fantastic stories and images.
3 Mark Twain, whose real name was Samuel Clemens, was a (persistent /**witty**) writer and storyteller. His accounts of his world travels still make people laugh.

LESSON 4

GOAL Describe what makes someone "a genius"

A LISTENING WARM-UP

Suggested teaching time:	5 minutes	Your actual teaching time:

- Have students think about the question in the direction line. Then call on volunteers to share their point of view.
- Ask *Do you know anyone who you think is a genius?*

Option: [+5 minutes] Invite students to look up the word *genius* and the word *intelligent* in a dictionary. Have them share definitions and discuss how the two words differ.

B ▶ 4:20 LISTEN FOR MAIN IDEAS

Suggested teaching time:	5–10 minutes	Your actual teaching time:

- Pre-listening: Have students look at the two pictures on the side of the page. Ask *Do you recognize either of these people? Have you heard of these people before?* Tell students that they are going to hear a lecture given by a university professor in a psychology department.
- First listening: Have students listen to the lecture with their books closed. Then ask *What is the general topic of the lecture?* (defining what genius is)
- Second listening: Have students open their books. Call on a volunteer to read the three statements. Have students listen again for the main point of the lecture.
- To check comprehension, ask *What is one definition of a genius?* (a person with a high IQ) *What is the IQ range of an average person?* (85 to 115) *What IQ score does a genius have?* (over 145) *What was Albert Einstein's IQ?* (160) *How did Terman's experiment support the idea that not every person with a high IQ is a genius?* (His experiment showed that a gifted person can have a high IQ without being outstanding in any particular way.)
- Then ask *In your opinion, what makes a person a genius?*

⭐ 🖨 Listening Strategies

C ▶ 4:21 LISTEN TO INFER

Suggested teaching time:	5 minutes	Your actual teaching time:

- Pre-listening: Read the direction line aloud. Ask *What is the opposing argument in the lecture?* (that a high IQ doesn't mean a person is a genius) Have students read through the statements. Tell them they can pencil in the answer if they think they know it.
- Listening: Ask students to listen and then check the statement that best supports the argument that a high IQ score does NOT determine if one is a genius.
- Go over the answer as a class. If students check any statements other than the last, elicit why they do not support the argument.

D ▶ 4:22 LISTEN FOR SUPPORTING DETAILS

Suggested teaching time:	5–10 minutes	Your actual teaching time:

- Pre-listening: Have students look at the chart heads. Ask them to predict what part 2 of the lecture will be about (the genetic and environmental theory, probably as related to genius—which was discussed in part 1).
- First listening: Have students listen and write at least two arguments that support each theory.
- Second listening: Have students listen again and fill in any additional information. Have pairs compare answers.
- Bring the class together and ask *Based on the support provided in this lecture, which theory do you think is more accurate? Why? What other arguments could you make to support either theory?*

E ▶ 4:23 VOCABULARY

Suggested teaching time:	5 minutes	Your actual teaching time:

- Have students read and listen for adjectives that describe traits of intelligence.
- Then have students listen and repeat the adjectives chorally.

⭐ 🖨 Vocabulary-Building Strategies

F VOCABULARY PRACTICE

Suggested teaching time:	5 minutes	Your actual teaching time:

- Have students work individually or in pairs to complete each statement. Tell them to underline the context in each sentence that helps them determine the answer. (1. *observations of everyday life*, 2. *creating fantastic stories and images*, 3. *still make people laugh*, 4. *consider questions about chimp behavior that had never been explained before*, 5. *excellent imaginative movies*)
- Go over the answers as a class.

Challenge: [+5 minutes] Invite students to create a sentence for the alternate word in each item (Possible answers: 1. A good writer is persistent and works through any writer's blocks. 2. Max is an inquisitive scientist, always seeking new ways of looking at objects. 3. I couldn't get my story published, but I was persistent until I found an interested editor. 4. You need to be an inventive story writer these days; nobody wants to read anything that is too similar to something written before. 5. Max is a persistent producer; he works tirelessly on every aspect of a film project from beginning to end.)

G PERSONALIZE THE VOCABULARY

Suggested teaching time:	5 minutes	Your actual teaching time:

- In pairs or small groups, have students use adjectives from Exercise E to describe people they know or have heard about. Circulate and listen for correct use.
- Bring the class together and have students share.

Option: [+5 minutes] Ask *Which of these words have people used to describe you? Which of these words would you use to describe yourself?* Write lists of students under words mentioned. Ask *Do you feel comfortable identifying your own traits of intelligence? Is it considered immodest in your culture?*

NOW YOU CAN Describe what makes someone a "genius"

A NOTEPADDING

Suggested teaching time:	5–10 minutes	Your actual teaching time:

- To warm up, write *genius* on the board and invite students to describe what they think makes a person a genius. Write students' ideas on the board. If anyone disagrees with a comment, invite the person to voice his or her opinion.
- Tell students they will each think of a person they consider extremely intelligent—it could be a person from history or a person in students' lives. Explain that they will take notes about his or her abilities and traits of intelligence.
- Ask students to read the model notepad. Point out the note format and tell students they will write the same way on their notepads.
- Focus on the third question. Refer students to Exercise D on page 94 to review the two theories. Then ask a student to read the fourth question here in Exercise A, Notepadding. Invite students to provide their definition of genius when answering the question. For example, *My uncle Morris is extremely intelligent, but I'm not sure I would call him a genius. I think a genius is a person who applies his or her knowledge to invent something amazing. My uncle Morris hasn't done anything special like Einstein or Beethoven!*
- Circulate as students work. Assist as needed, referring students to the vocabulary in Exercise E on page 94.

B DISCUSSION

Suggested teaching time:	5 minutes	Your actual teaching time:

- Ask a student to look at the words in the Recycle This Language box. Ask *What part of speech are these words—nouns? verbs? adjectives?* (adjectives) Review the meaning of any of the words as needed. Invite students to also refer to the adjectives in Exercise E on page 94 when describing their person.
- Divide the class into pairs and have students use their notes from Exercise A, Notepadding, to talk about the extremely intelligent person.

OPTIONAL WRITING [+15–20 minutes]

Suggested teaching time:	5–10 minutes	Your actual teaching time:

- Have students write about their person in class or at home.
- In class, let students peer review. Then collect and offer feedback.

4 Jane Goodall is known for her ground-breaking work studying chimpanzees. Her (**inquisitive** / inventive) mind helped her consider questions about chimp behavior that had never been explained before.

5 Korean film director Bong Joon-ho has been praised as one of the most (**talented** / persistent) artists in recent years for his excellent imaginative movies.

G **PERSONALIZE THE VOCABULARY** With a partner, use each adjective to describe a person you know or have heard or read about.

> "I'd call my nephew Sam very imaginative. He's only eight years old, but he entertains us with fantastic stories all the time."

> "I think the Chinese pianist Yuja Wang is really talented. Her interpretations of pieces by classical composers are very perceptive. I always feel like I'm hearing something new when she plays."

NOW YOU CAN Describe what makes someone a "genius"

A **NOTEPADDING** Identify someone—famous or not—who you would consider to be extremely intelligent or even a genius. In what ways would you describe aspects of this person's intelligence? Write notes about the person on your notepad. Use the Vocabulary from this lesson and from page 88.

> **Who is it?** my uncle Morris
> **List his or her abilities and traits of intelligence:**
> – really sharp, has an incredible head for figures and a way with words
> – a little eccentric, extremely perceptive

Who is it?

List his or her abilities and traits of intelligence:

Do you think this person's intelligence came from the environment or his or her genes? Why?

Would you call this person a genius? Why or why not?

RECYCLE THIS LANGUAGE		
• difficult	• energetic	• outgoing
• easygoing	• gifted	• passionate
• eccentric	• hardworking	• serious
• egotistical	• moody	• sharp

B **DISCUSSION** With a partner, discuss the person you wrote about on your notepad. Explain where, in your opinion, the person got his or her intelligence from, providing examples from the person's background and environment.

OPTIONAL WRITING Write about the person you discussed. Support your view that this person has above-average intelligence with examples.

WRITING Explaining cause and result

A **WRITING SKILL** Study the rules.

In formal writing, connecting words and phrases are commonly used to clarify relationships between ideas. Use the following to focus on causes or results.

Causes
Use one of these phrases to focus on a cause.

Due to ___ ,   Because of ___ ,
As a result of ___ ,   As a consequence of ___ ,

―― cause ――
As a result of a high workload, our work area may get messy.

―― cause ――
It may be difficult to stay on task **due to constant interruptions by colleagues.**

Results
Begin a sentence with one of these words or phrases to focus on a result.

As a result,   Consequently,
As a consequence,   Therefore,

―― result ――
Colleagues may constantly interrupt your work. **Consequently,** it may be difficult to stay focused.

B **PRACTICE** In the Writing Model, underline five sentences with connecting words or phrases that clarify causes and results. Then, on a separate sheet of paper, rewrite each sentence twice, using a different connecting word or phrase.
See page T96 for answers.

C **APPLY THE WRITING SKILL** Write a three-paragraph essay about the challenges of staying focused while trying to complete a task. Use the "outline" below as a guide. Be sure to include connecting words and phrases to signal causes and results.

Paragraph 1
Describe the things that make staying focused difficult. Summarize the causes.

Paragraph 2
Describe the results of not being able to stay focused.

Paragraph 3
Suggest some ways one might overcome the challenges and become more focused on completing a task.

WRITING MODEL

When trying to focus on a task, you may discover there are numerous distractions that can keep you from completing your work. You may find it difficult to stay focused due to your staying up late the night before. As a consequence of frequent interruptions by colleagues, you may feel like you are always starting the task all over again. Anything can distract you from a task, and the results can be harmful.

Not being able to stay focused can affect your work in negative ways. You may not be able to produce a report for your manager by the time he or she expects it. Consequently, your manager may wonder whether or not he or she can count on you to deliver what you have promised. Your colleagues may depend on you to finish a task, but you are unable to do it. As a result, you risk your reputation at work.

If you are having difficulty completing a task, it is important that you take actions that help you stay on target. Because of frequent interruptions, you may have to close your office door or ask your colleagues not to disturb you. If you are suffering from a lack of sleep, you may have to take a break and grab a cup of coffee before you start. As long as you make an effort, you should be able to get back on target.

SELF-CHECK
☐ Did my paragraphs follow the content and sequence suggested in Exercise C?
☐ Did I use connecting phrases to focus on causes?
☐ Did I introduce sentences with connecting words or phrases to focus on results?

WRITING Explaining cause and result

A WRITING SKILL

Suggested teaching time:	10 minutes	Your actual teaching time:

- On the board, write:
  1. As a result of hard work, I do well in school.
  2. I work hard. As a result, I do well in school.

Ask *Which sentence focuses on the cause?* (1) *Which sentence focuses on the result?* (2) Leave the sentences on the board.

- Call on a student to read the introduction. Then focus on the example sentence under Causes. Read it four times, using the different connecting words. Do the same for the example sentence under Results.
- Bring students' attention to *As a result of* _____ (cause) versus *As a result* (result), as well as *As a consequence of* _____ (cause) which are followed by a noun, versus *Consequently/As a consequence* (result) which is followed by an independent clause.

B PRACTICE

Suggested teaching time:	5–10 minutes	Your actual teaching time:

- Have students read the writing model in pairs. Have them underline the sentences with connecting words or phrases that clarify causes or results.
- Have students work individually to rewrite each sentence twice using a different connecting word or phrase.
- Bring the class together and call on students to provide different ways to rewrite each sentence.

Answers to Exercise B

Answers will vary, but may include the following:

1. Because of / As a result of your staying up late at night, you may find it difficult to stay focused.
2. Due to / As a result of frequent interruptions by colleagues, you may feel like you are always starting the task all over again.
3. Therefore, / As a result, your manager may wonder whether or not she can count on you to deliver what you have promised.
4. Consequently, / Therefore, you risk your reputation at work.
5. Due to / As a result of frequent interruptions, you may have to close your office door or ask your colleagues not to disturb you.

C APPLY THE WRITING SKILL

Suggested teaching time:	10–15 minutes	Your actual teaching time:

- On the board, write *challenges to staying focused while trying to complete a task*. Call on students to read the parts of the outline and then have students skim the corresponding paragraphs in the model.
- Tell students they will write their own essays following the models.
- Refer students to the Writing Process Worksheet in ActiveTeach for guidance with pre-writing and peer feedback.
- Encourage students to use the Self-Check in the Student's Book to go over the essays they wrote.

Option: [+5 minutes] Time permitting, students can exchange papers with a partner and offer feedback using the topics in the Self-Check list. Encourage partners to also check for examples.

⭐ 🖨 Writing Process

REVIEW

🎮 **Digital Game**

A ▶ 4:24

| Suggested teaching time: | 10–15 minutes | Your actual teaching time: |

- Have students listen to what a teacher tells parents about their children. After the teacher discusses each child, have students check the correct statement. Have students listen again to check their answers.
- Bring the class together and go over the answers.
- Have students skim the answers they checked. Ask *Do the statements focus on strengths or weaknesses?* (strengths)

Option: [+5 minutes] Have students listen again. Stop after the teacher discusses each child, and have students write down the weaknesses the teacher mentions about the student. Point out that for one student the teacher does not mention any weaknesses. (Liza: struggling in French and Italian, no knack for languages; Ben: needs to pay more attention to his academic subjects, especially math and science; Stella: weakness is music; Steven: is a bit shy and is having trouble making friends and working with his classmates; Sophie: no weaknesses; Dan: often works too quickly and doesn't pay attention to the little things; Karen: has difficulty communicating her ideas, and her written work is weak; Sam: doesn't work well with the other students, needs to develop more social skills) Go over the weaknesses as a class.

LANGUAGE NOTE A *flair* is a natural talent. This word has the same meaning as *knack*.

B

| Suggested teaching time: | 5 minutes | Your actual teaching time: |

- As students do the exercise, tell them to recall verbs and adjectives of urgency, obligation, and advisability that introduce clauses with the subjunctive. Refer students to pages 90–91 if needed.
- Have pairs compare answers. Then bring the class together and answer any outstanding questions.

C

| Suggested teaching time: | 5 minutes | Your actual teaching time: |

- If students need to review adjectives that describes traits of intelligence, refer them to the Vocabulary on page 94.
- After students complete the exercise, have them compare answers with a partner.

Option: TEST-TAKING SKILLS BOOSTER (p. 158)

EXTRA

- Workbook
- MyEnglishLab
- Online Student Resources (www.english.com/summit3e)
  - Classroom Audio Program
  - Extra Practice Activities
  - *Summit GO* App
  - Web Projects
- ActiveTeach
  - Assessment
  - Additional Printable Resources
    ○ Audioscripts and Answer Keys
    ○ "Can-Do" Self-Assessment Charts
    ○ Conversation and Discussion Activator Video Scripts
    ○ Oral Progress Assessment Charts
    ○ Reading Speed Calculator
  - Summit TV Video Program
    ○ Activity Worksheets
    ○ Teaching Notes
    ○ Video Scripts

REVIEW

A ▶ 4:24 Listen to a teacher talking to parents about their children. After each conversation, check the statement that best describes each child's talents and abilities. Listen again if necessary.

1. Liza
   - ☐ has a head for figures.
   - ☑ has a way with words.
   - ☐ has a knack for languages.

2. Ben
   - ☐ is mechanically inclined.
   - ☐ has a good intuitive sense.
   - ☑ is good with his hands.

3. Stella
   - ☑ has a knack for languages.
   - ☐ has an ear for music.
   - ☐ has a way with words.

4. Steven
   - ☐ has a good intuitive sense.
   - ☐ has a way with people.
   - ☑ has a head for figures.

5. Sophie
   - ☑ has an ear for music.
   - ☐ has a way with words.
   - ☐ has a knack for languages.

6. Dan
   - ☐ has an eye for detail.
   - ☐ has a good intuitive sense.
   - ☑ is mechanically inclined.

7. Karen
   - ☐ has a way with words.
   - ☑ has an eye for detail.
   - ☐ is good with her hands.

8. Sam
   - ☐ has a head for figures.
   - ☑ has a good intuitive sense.
   - ☐ has a way with people.

B Find and correct the six errors in using the subjunctive.

Dr. Howard Gardner believes that genius is determined by the environment. Therefore, he recommends that children ~~are~~ *be* provided with greater educational opportunities in order to develop their talents. Other psychologists, however, think that genius is inherited. According to them, if a child is born with talent, it is crucial that he or she ~~receives~~ special attention.

According to Dr. Gardner, people have different kinds of intelligence, and there are different ways of learning suitable for each intelligence type. Consequently, he proposes that a teacher ~~uses~~ learning strategies that are best suited to a particular student's type of intelligence. For example, Gardner suggests that a student ~~studies~~ *study* alone if he or she has intrapersonal intelligence. If, on the other hand, the learner has interpersonal intelligence, it is important that the student ~~works~~ in a team.

Because characteristics such as motivation and emotional control are considered important in the workplace, more and more employers insist that a job applicant ~~takes~~ an EQ test to help the manager make hiring decisions.

C Write the correct letter to complete each definition.

1. A person who is witty ..e.. .
2. A person who is inquisitive ..d.. .
3. A person who is inventive ..f.. .
4. A person who is very perceptive ..c.. .
5. A person who is really sharp ..g.. .
6. A person who is open-minded ..b.. .
7. A person who is persistent ..a.. .

a keeps trying, even when things are tough
b is probably comfortable with people who disagree with his or her opinions
c is comfortable relying on gut feelings to make decisions
d enjoys learning about new things
e entertains friends with funny and intelligent stories
f has a talent for creating new ideas
g is smart and quick at figuring things out

TEST-TAKING SKILLS BOOSTER p. 158

Web Project: Emotional Intelligence
www.english.com/summit3e

UNIT 9

What Lies Ahead?

PREVIEW

COMMUNICATION GOALS
1. Discuss the feasibility of future technologies
2. Evaluate applications of innovative technologi[es]
3. Discuss how to protect our future environmen[t]
4. Examine future social and demographic trend[s]

A FRAME YOUR IDEAS Complete the survey.

WILL IT COME TRUE?

Which of the following predictions do you think will come true by the end of the 21st century? Which are just too wild to come true? Check your responses on a scale of probability from unlikely to definitely. Add your own predictions if you have any.

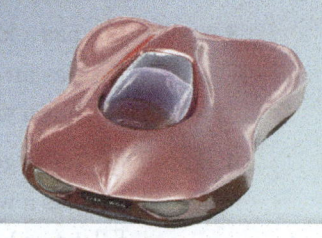

MEDICINE AND HEALTH

1. The majority of surgeries will be performed by robots.
   UNLIKELY   POSSIBLY   LIKELY   DEFINITELY

2. Scientists will have discovered effective cures for cancer and heart disease.
   UNLIKELY   POSSIBLY   LIKELY   DEFINITELY

3. Eyeglasses will have become obsolete.
   UNLIKELY   POSSIBLY   LIKELY   DEFINITELY

4. Most people will live to be over 100 years old.
   UNLIKELY   POSSIBLY   LIKELY   DEFINITELY

5. Your prediction:
   _____

TRANSPORTATION

1. Petroleum will no longer be used as an energy source.
   UNLIKELY   POSSIBLY   LIKELY   DEFINITELY

2. Most vehicles will not require a driver.
   UNLIKELY   POSSIBLY   LIKELY   DEFINITELY

3. Commercial space travel will be available to anyone who can afford it.
   UNLIKELY   POSSIBLY   LIKELY   DEFINITELY

4. Digital technology will have replaced the traditional paper passport.
   UNLIKELY   POSSIBLY   LIKELY   DEFINITELY

5. Your prediction:
   _____

HOME AND WORK

1. People will be living on another planet.
   UNLIKELY   POSSIBLY   LIKELY   DEFINITELY

2. Agricultural work will no longer require human workers.
   UNLIKELY   POSSIBLY   LIKELY   DEFINITELY

3. The majority of homes will have a robot to do household chores.
   UNLIKELY   POSSIBLY   LIKELY   DEFINITELY

4. Most people will work and make a living from their own homes.
   UNLIKELY   POSSIBLY   LIKELY   DEFINITELY

5. Your prediction:
   _____

B PAIR WORK Compare your responses and explain the reasons for your answers. What made you decide whether a prediction in the survey was just too wild or whether it might actually come true?

UNIT 9

What Lies Ahead?

PREVIEW

A FRAME YOUR IDEAS

Suggested teaching time:	15–20 minutes	Your actual teaching time:

- Focus students' attention on the title of the unit, "What Lies Ahead?" Ask *What does this mean?* (What is going to happen in the future?)
- Tell students to look at the photos and identify what they see. (Possible answers: a flying car, a futuristic house) Call on a student to read the question on the left—*Will it come true?* Point to the flying car. Ask students *Will this come true?* Point to the house and ask the same question.
- Call on a volunteer to read the introduction to the survey. Then ask a volunteer to read the heads. Have students complete the survey. Clarify vocabulary as needed.

B PAIR WORK

Suggested teaching time:	5 minutes	Your actual teaching time:

- Ask students to compare answers to the survey with a partner. Have them explain their responses.
- Bring the class together and have pairs share if they have similar visions for the future.
- Call on volunteers to share some of their own predictions for the various categories.

Option: [+5 minutes] On the board, write *What will life be like in 2025?* Ask *Do you recall making predictions about the future when you were younger? Which predictions came true?*

Challenge: [+5 minutes] Ask students to notice the categories of the quiz—medicine and health, transportation, home and work. Have students work in pairs to think up other categories they could add to the survey. (Possible answers: school, food, communication) Then have students write a prediction for each category. Finally, combine pairs into groups of four and let them rate each other's predictions as in Exercise A.

UNIT 9 PREVIEW   T98

C ▶ 5:02 SPOTLIGHT

Suggested teaching time:	10–15 minutes	Your actual teaching time:

- Have students look at the illustration. Ask *What technology is this?* (It's a drone.) Write the word *drone* on the board. Elicit that this is a pilotless aircraft that is operated by radio. Ask *Have you ever seen a drone? Where are drones used?* (They are commonly used in situations where it would be dangerous for pilots to fly. They also cover the news, put out wildfires, and take incredible pictures of nature.) Then focus on the illustration again. Ask *What is this drone being used for?* (to deliver packages)
- Have students read and listen to the conversation.
- To check comprehension, ask *What is Nate's attitude towards drones?* (He's not excited by them.) *What problems does he foresee with them?* (that they will crash into each other and cause accidents) *Does Lena have the same view as Nate?* (At first she doesn't seem to agree with him, but then she recalls a story about drones crashing into cars and people, and she starts to see the various problems.) *Why might drones flying around during take-offs and landings be a problem for pilots?* (They could distract and cause accidents.)

LANGUAGE NOTE Focus students' attention on *Is that cool or what?* in the second line. Point out that adding *or what* to an adjective or description invites agreement. For example, *Is the food great or what? Am I smart or what?* Invite students to think up additional examples. Point out that the expression *the bad outweighs the good* can also be written in reverse—*the good outweighs the bad*—to point out that there are more good qualities to something than bad ones.

Option: [+5 minutes] Invite students to brainstorm positive tasks drones perform. (Possible answers: They cover the news, take incredible pictures of nature, and replace humans in dangerous situations such as piloting planes through war zones, exploring disaster areas, and applying pesticides in agriculture.)

D UNDERSTAND IDIOMS AND EXPRESSIONS

Suggested teaching time:	5–10 minutes	Your actual teaching time:

- Focus on the idioms and expressions as a class. Call on volunteers to read them aloud.
- Let students work individually to locate them in context to figure out the meanings. Then have students match each expression with the correct explanation.
- Ask students to compare answers with a partner, returning to Exercise C to check items as necessary.
- Bring the class together to go over the answers.

Challenge: [+5 minutes] Divide the class into pairs and assign each pair one or two idioms / expressions from the list. Have them create brief dialogues around them. Invite pairs to share dialogues.

E DISCUSSION

Suggested teaching time:	5 minutes	Your actual teaching time:

- In pairs or small groups, have students discuss the current and future uses of drones and also summarize Nate's concerns.
- Bring the class together and discuss.

Option: [+5 minutes] Invite students to hold a debate in favor of and against drones. Divide the class in half and assign one group the argument for and the other the argument against. Give students time to brainstorm ideas. Then have each side present an argument and defend it. Decide which group makes the stronger argument.

Challenge: [+5 minutes] Have students work in groups of three. Tell them to role-play the conversation from Exercise A, Spotlight, but incorporate a third speaker. This person, unlike Nate and Lena, should be in favor of drones. Have students decide where to weave in the third person's arguments and then practice. Bring the class together and have groups share. If necessary, brainstorm positive aspects of drones: They are used to cover the news, put out wildfires, take incredible pictures of nature, replace humans in dangerous situations, etc.

Answers for Exercise E

Answers will vary but may include the following:

1. Currently drones are used in situations where it is dangerous for pilots to fly, for example to war zones or to put out wildfires. They also cover the news and take incredible pictures of nature. In the future drones will likely be used in new areas of environmental protection and conservation, archeological discoveries, humanitarian work, and farming.
2. Nate is concerned that with thousands of drones flying around, they might crash into each other, and people are going to get hurt. Also he worries about drone interference with take offs and landing of planes. In my opinion, Nate's concerns are valid, but I think once drones become that widespread, necessary measures will be taken to keep them under control.

SPEAKING

Suggested teaching time:	5 minutes	Your actual teaching time:

- Focus on the expression *open a can of worms*. Review by asking *Why does Nate think widespread use of drones opens a can of worms?* (Possible answer: He is not confident they would work well. They would crash. Accidents would happen.)
- Call on a student to read the model answer. Ask *Do you agree?* Invite students to indicate which other predictions on page 98 would open a can of worms.
- Then tell students they will make additional comments about the predictions using idioms and expressions from Exercise D. Call on a student to read the second model answer.
- Bring the class together and have students share their answers.

C ▶ 5:02 **SPOTLIGHT** Read and listen to a conversation about the uses for a new technology. Notice the spotlighted language.

ENGLISH FOR TODAY'S WORLD
Understand a variety of accents.
Lena = German
Nate = American English (standard)

Lena: I just read that packages are going to be delivered to people's homes using drones. Is that cool or what?
Nate: Well, it's shocking how much they seem to **be catching on**. You never know where you're going to see them next.
Lena: That's true.
Nate: Unfortunately, no matter how you look at it, it's just going to **open a can of worms**.
Lena: Really? In what way?
Nate: I just think the more drones, the more unintended consequences.
Lena: Sorry. I don't get it. Drones seem pretty harmless to me.
Nate: Well, think about it. Imagine thousands of drones flying all over the place. Who's going to make sure they don't crash into each other? **Before you know it**, somebody's going to get hurt.
Lena: **Come to think of it**, I read last week that some have already crashed into cars … and even people!
Nate: And from what I understand, that**'s just scratching the surface**. It gets worse. Pilots have been reporting sightings of drones during takeoffs and landings.
Lena: Wow! That's no joke!
Nate: Exactly. At some point there's going to be a collision—**it isn't a question of if but when**.
Lena: Well, this is definitely a case in which **the bad outweighs the good**.

D **UNDERSTAND IDIOMS AND EXPRESSIONS** Find these idioms and expressions in Spotlight. Complete each explanation by writing the correct letter.

..e.. 1 Say something "is catching on" to …
..g.. 2 Say "It'll open a can of worms" to …
..c.. 3 Say "Before you know it" to …
..a.. 4 Say "Come to think of it" to …
..b.. 5 Say "It's just scratching the surface" to …
..f.. 6 Say "It isn't a question of if but when" to …
..d.. 7 Say "The bad outweighs the good" to …

a indicate you suddenly realize or remember something.
b suggest that it provides only a small piece of the total picture.
c suggest that something is going to happen soon.
d suggest that there are more disadvantages than advantages.
e indicate that something is becoming popular.
f state that something is certain to happen.
g express concern about possible problems in the future.

E **DISCUSSION** See page T99 for answers.

1 What are some current uses for drones you're familiar with? What are some possible uses in the future? Use your own ideas.
2 Summarize Nate's concerns about the consequences of an increased use of drone technology. Do you agree with his concerns, or do you think drones are harmless? Explain your views.

SPEAKING Which of the predictions from page 98 do you think would open a can of worms? Use expressions from Spotlight. Explain your reasons.

❝ I'd worry that digital passports might open a can of worms. Before you know it, criminals or terrorists would be stealing people's identities. ❞

❝ If robots do household chores, people will get lazy! Let's face it … the bad outweighs the good. ❞

LESSON 1

GOAL Discuss the feasibility of future technologies

A ▶ 5:03 **GRAMMAR SPOTLIGHT** Read the article and notice the spotlighted grammar.

ENVISIONING THE FUTURE

In the 1960s, only large institutions, such as banks, corporations, and the military, had computers. They were expensive, slow, and very large—requiring a special air-conditioned room—and access to them was limited to only a few people. In the 1970s, computer prices came down and then small businesses began to use them. Nevertheless, in 1977, the CEO and founder of Digital Equipment, Kenneth Olsen, predicted that computers **would never be used** in the home.

> Computers **are never going to be used** in the home.
> — Kenneth Olsen

In the early 1980s, Steve Jobs and Bill Gates introduced the personal computer—the Macintosh and the IBM PC, respectively—which made computing at home possible. In 1983, Jobs gave a speech about the future, in which he predicted that, for most people, a great deal of time **would be spent** interacting with personal computers. He also predicted that, within ten years, computers in the office and at home **would be connected** so people would be able to use them to communicate.

> In the future, a great amount of our time **is going to be spent** interacting with our personal computers. And in ten years, home and office computers **will have been connected** to each other so people can use them to communicate and keep in touch.
> — Steve Jobs

In 1999, Gates predicted that small devices **would be carried** around by everyone so that they could get instant information and stay in touch with others. He also claimed that, by the early 21st century, Internet communities **would have been formed**, based on one's interests or to connect with friends and family.

> Small devices **will be carried** around by everyone to get information and stay in touch. And in the early 21st century, Internet communities **will have been formed**.
> — Bill Gates

B **DISCUSSION** Which of the twentieth century predictions about computers have come true? In what ways? See page T100 for answers.

PRONUNCIATION BOOSTER p. 149
Reading aloud

C **GRAMMAR** THE PASSIVE VOICE: THE FUTURE, THE FUTURE AS SEEN FROM THE PAST, AND THE FUTURE PERFECT

Passive voice statements about the future: will be (or be going to be) + a past participle

In the future, appliances **will be linked** to each other and to the Internet as well.
In coming years, our lives **are going to be made** easier by new home technologies.

Passive voice statements about the future as seen from the past: would be (or was / were going to be) + a past participle

Jobs and Gates predicted that computers **would be used** by millions of people at home.
Olsen thought that computers **were** never **going to be purchased** for use at home.

Passive voice statements in the future perfect: will have been (or be going to have been) + a past participle

By 2050, commercial airplanes **will have been redesigned** to be much quieter.
In a few decades, the TV set **is going to have been made** obsolete.

Note: The passive voice is often used when discussing science and technology.

Use a *by* phrase when it's important to name the agent (the performer of the action).

Our lives will be improved **by technology**.

GRAMMAR BOOSTER p. 141
When to use the passive voice

100 UNIT 9

LESSON 1

GOAL Discuss the feasibility of future technologies

A ▶ 5:03 GRAMMAR SPOTLIGHT

Suggested teaching time:	10–15 minutes	Your actual teaching time:

- Focus on the title of the article. Ask *What does it mean to envision something?* (to mentally picture something that may happen in the future) To illustrate the use of this expression, ask *When you were a child, did you envision that people would be walking around in the present day with smartphones in their pockets?*
- Have students scan the photos of the three men. Ask students to identify them, referring to the names in the captions as needed.
- Have students listen to the article as they read along.
- To check comprehension, ask *What did Kenneth Olsen predict about computers in 1977?* (that they would never be used in the home) *What predictions did Steve Jobs make about personal computers in 1983?* (that a lot of time would be spent interacting with personal computers; he also predicted that they would be used to communicate) *What did Bill Gates predict in 1999 about small devices?* (that they would be carried around by everyone so that people could get instant information and stay in touch with others) *What did he predict about Internet communities?* (that they would be formed based on one's interests or to connect with friends and family)
- Have students listen to the article again, noticing the spotlighted grammar. Ask *Does the highlighted grammar talk about the present, the past, or the future?* (the future)

Option: [+5 minutes] Ask *Are you surprised by the preciseness of Jobs' and Gates's predictions? Why do you think Kenneth Olsen was doubtful about computers being used in the home?* (It was still such a new concept that he couldn't envision it.) *What predictions can we make today about computers and technology?* Invite students to respond if they think the predictions their classmates suggest will come true and why.

B DISCUSSION

Suggested teaching time:	5 minutes	Your actual teaching time:

- In pairs or small groups, have students discuss the questions. If students need guidance, ask more specifically *What Internet communities exist that allow people to connect with friends and family?* (social networks). Ask *Do you think Bill Gates envisioned how intricate these communities would be?* (probably not)
- Bring the class together and invite students to share their answers to the questions.

Challenge: [+5 minutes] Invite students to imagine that they are in the audience listening to Jobs' 1983 speech. In pairs, have them discuss how they would respond. Ask *Do you think you would have believed him? Would you have been doubtful?*

Answers for Exercise B
Jobs's prediction that for most people a lot of time would be spent interacting with personal computer came true, as did his prediction that computers would be connected so people would use them communicate. In the past decades, computers have become an integral part of our lives, and we rely on the Internet for communication.
Gates's prediction that small computer devices will be carried around came true with the smart phone. He also foresaw the creation of Internet communities based on one's interests and to connect with friends and family. Indeed, social networks and a whole array of online communities have evolved.

Option: PRONUNCIATION BOOSTER *(Teaching notes p. T149)*

🖨 Pronunciation Pair Work

C GRAMMAR

Suggested teaching time:	5–10 minutes	Your actual teaching time:

- Write the following two sentences on the board:

  In the future, our minds will be read by computers.
  In the future, computers will read our minds.

  Elicit the difference between these two sentences. (The first is in the passive voice. The second is in the active voice.) Explain that this grammar section focuses on the passive voice to talk about the future, the future as seen from the past, and the future perfect.

- Remind students about the difference between the future and the future perfect. The future with *will* or *be going to* expresses future time. For example, *Every student in the world will be connected to the Internet.* The future perfect expresses the idea that one event will happen before another event or a time in the future. For example, *By 2050, every student in the world will have been connected to the Internet.*

- Then call on a volunteer to read the first rule about the future and the example sentences. Elicit additional sentences. Repeat the procedure for the next two rules (the future as seen from the past and the future perfect). Point out that the future as seen from the past often appears as indirect speech, as in the example sentences. Ask students to change the example sentences to direct speech. (Computers will be used . . . ; Computers are never going to be purchased for use at home.)

- Ask *Which passive forms are used in the article in Exercise A?* (future as seen from the past: *would never be used, would be spent, would be connected, would be carried, would have been formed*; future: *are never going to be used, is going to be spent; will be carried*; future perfect: *will have been connected, will have been formed*)

- Call on a student to read the Note. Elicit additional example sentences with an agent. For example, *In 2100, homes will be cleaned by robots.*

Option: [+5 minutes] Have students look at the Grammar Spotlight in Exercise C on page 99. Instruct them to find one passive voice statement about the future. (. . . *packages are going to be delivered to people's homes using drones* [line 1]) Hint to students that there are several active statements about the future; only one is in the passive.

Option: GRAMMAR BOOSTER *(Teaching notes p. T141)*

⭐🖨 Inductive Grammar Activity

UNIT 9 LESSON 1   T100

D GRAMMAR PRACTICE

Suggested teaching time:	5 minutes	Your actual teaching time:

- Have students read the predictions for a possible moon habitat to themselves and then complete the exercise independently.
- Bring the class together to go over the answers. For each sentence, ask *Who is performing the action in the sentence?* (1. rockets, 2. the construction materials, 3. the Sun, 4. technicians, 5. more than one country) *Is the agent important to the meaning of the sentence?* (yes)

Challenge: [+5 minutes] On the board, write *Workplace of the Future*. Have pairs write four passive sentences describing an office of the future. For example, *All administrative tasks will be done automatically by a computer robot.* Bring the class together and have students share their ideas.

⭐ 🖨 Extra Grammar Exercises

Answers to Exercise D

- Lightweight building materials will be transported from Earth by rockets.
- The inhabitants will be protected from radiation and solar winds by the construction materials.
- Power for electricity will be supplied by the Sun.
- The Moon's natural resources will be mined by technicians using robots.
- The costs will be shared by more than one country.

E GRAMMAR PRACTICE

Suggested teaching time:	10–15 minutes	Your actual teaching time:

- If necessary, look at the first item together as a class. Ask a volunteer to read the first prediction. Elicit the statement in the future perfect. Then call on students to state possible downsides to the prediction.
- After students complete the exercise individually, have them compare answers with a partner. Remind students that we say *the good outweighs the bad* to state that there are more advantages, and we say *the bad outweighs the good* to state that there are more disadvantages.

LANGUAGE NOTE *To have money to burn* means to be wealthy. *Wealthy* is an adjective meaning rich; *the wealthy* is a noun referring to wealthy people.

NOW YOU CAN Discuss the feasibility of future technologies

A NOTEPADDING

Suggested teaching time:	5 minutes	Your actual teaching time:

- Write *wild predictions* on the board. Review that in this context *wild* means to be beyond anything someone could have imagined. To illustrate the meaning, say that for Kenneth Olsen it was a wild prediction that computers would one day be used in the home. He didn't believe that this could happen.
- Ask students to glance at the chart. Ask *In which columns will you use the future perfect?* (the second two columns)
- Have students complete the exercise independently. Time permitting, encourage students to write a couple of sentences or jot down some notes to describe the predictions. Encourage students to use both passive voice of *will* and passive voice of *being going to* when making statements in the first column.

B DISCUSSION ACTIVATOR

Suggested teaching time:	5 minutes	Your actual teaching time:

🎬 Discussion Activator Video

- Divide the class into pairs and have students use their descriptions from Exercise A, Notepadding, to talk about the predictions with a partner. Encourage the pairs to ask each other questions and provide details and examples. The goal is for students to say as much as they can about the predictions.

For more support, play the Discussion Activator Video before students do this activity. After each video, ask if the students in the video included sufficient details. *Note:* You can print the script or you can view it on the video player on the ActiveTeach.

D **GRAMMAR PRACTICE** Look at the predictions for a possible moon habitat. On a separate sheet of paper, change the statements from active to passive voice.
See page T101 for answers.

A Moon Habitat of the Future
- Rockets will transport lightweight building materials from Earth.
- The construction materials will protect inhabitants from radiation and solar winds.
- The Sun will supply power for electricity.
- Technicians will use robots to mine the Moon's natural resources.
- More than one country will share the costs.

E **GRAMMAR PRACTICE** Read the predictions and complete the statements, putting each prediction into the future perfect in the passive voice. Then, with a partner, discuss the possible downsides to each prediction—or whether you think the good outweighs the bad. Explain your views.

Prediction 1: High-speed maglev trains will replace air travel as the preferred means of transportation.
Maglev trains, which use magnets and can travel at up to 580 kilometers per hour, are already preferred over air travel for many key European routes such as London-Paris. Will they replace even more routes? Some say it's not a question of if, but when.

By the end of the 21st century, air travel will have been replaced by high-speed maglev trains as the preferred means of transportation.

Prediction 2: Alternative methods of identification will replace passports for international travel.
Customs agencies will require cards with electronic chips that can be easily swiped, or perhaps they will rely on fingerprints to identify travelers. No matter how you look at it, stamping a passport is a thing of the past.

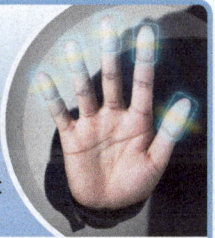

By the second half of the 21st century, passports for international travel will have been replaced by alternative methods of identification.

Prediction 3: Drone technology will make airplane pilots obsolete. Would you fly on a pilotless plane? You may not have a choice. Once drones have become widely accepted, who needs pilots?

By 2075, air pilots will have been made obsolete by drone technology.

Prediction 4: A private company will construct a space hotel with a spectacular view of the Earth.
Got money to burn? How about a vacation in outer space? After decades of experience maintaining the International Space Station, a space hotel is the next logical step. Only the wealthy will be able to afford it. But what a view!

By the year 2100, a space hotel with a spectacular view of the Earth will have been constructed by a private company.

NOW YOU CAN Discuss the feasibility of future technologies

A **NOTEPADDING** On your notepad, write at least three wild predictions about the future, using the passive voice of <u>will</u> or <u>be going to</u> or the future perfect.

In the future	By 2050	By the end of the century

B **DISCUSSION ACTIVATOR** What future technologies do you think will catch on? Are you optimistic or pessimistic about the use of science and technology in the future? Why? Use the predictions on your notepad. Say as much as you can.

101

LESSON 2

GOAL Evaluate applications of innovative technologies

A ▶ 5:04 **VOCABULARY INNOVATIVE TECHNOLOGIES**
Read and listen. Then listen again and repeat.

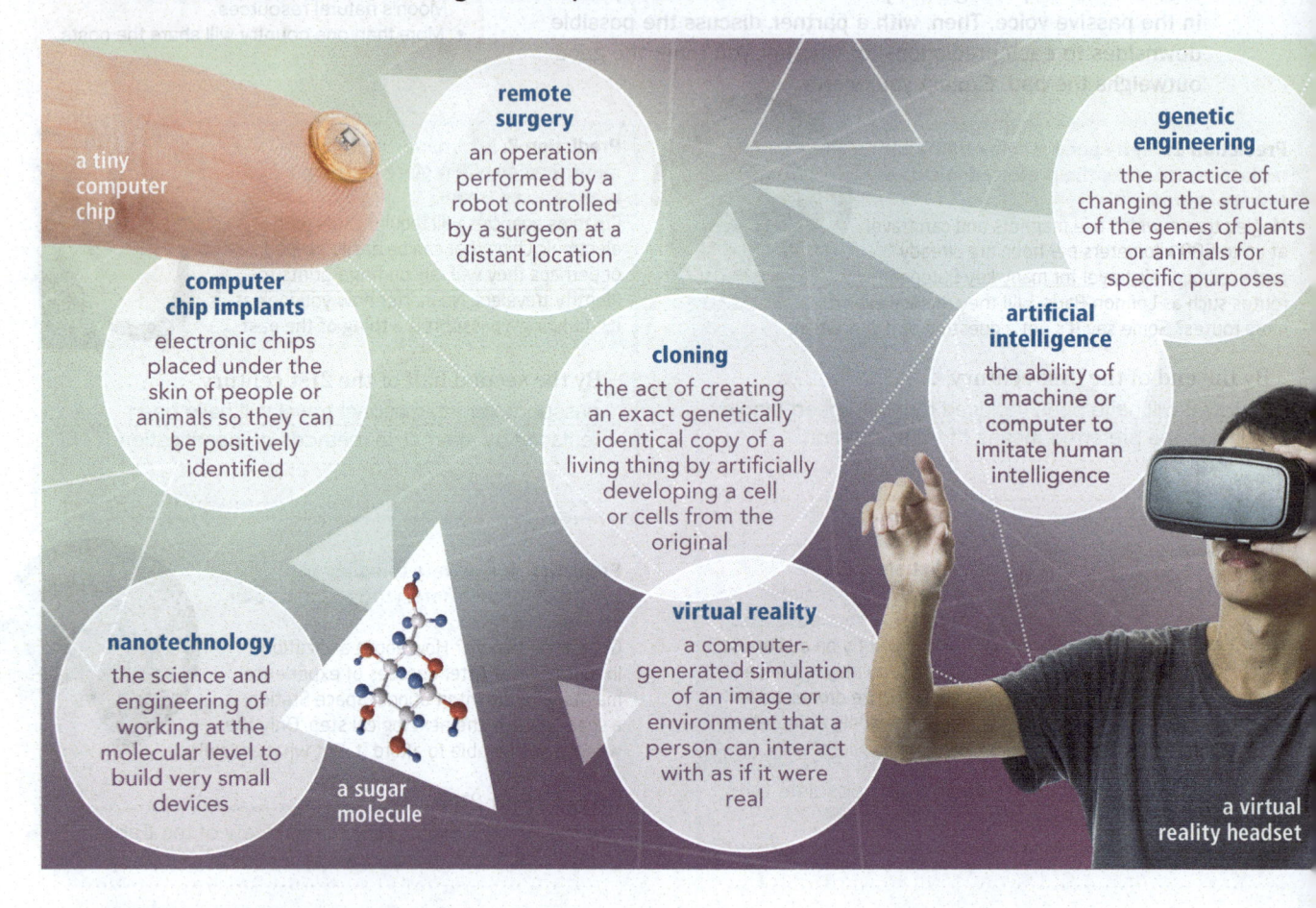

a tiny computer chip

remote surgery an operation performed by a robot controlled by a surgeon at a distant location

genetic engineering the practice of changing the structure of the genes of plants or animals for specific purposes

computer chip implants electronic chips placed under the skin of people or animals so they can be positively identified

cloning the act of creating an exact genetically identical copy of a living thing by artificially developing a cell or cells from the original

artificial intelligence the ability of a machine or computer to imitate human intelligence

nanotechnology the science and engineering of working at the molecular level to build very small devices

a sugar molecule

virtual reality a computer-generated simulation of an image or environment that a person can interact with as if it were real

a virtual reality headset

B ▶ 5:05 **LISTEN TO ACTIVATE VOCABULARY** Listen to conversations about applications of innovative technologies. After each, write the technology they're discussing, using the Vocabulary. Listen again and describe how the technology is being used.

	Innovative technology	How it's being used
1	cloning	to create an identical genetic copy of that person
2	computer chip implants	to put a tracking device under your skin to prevent identity theft
3	genetic engineering	to put the genes of fish into tomatoes
4	remote surgery	to operate on a patient in Tokyo by a doctor in Los Angeles
5	artificial intelligence	to decide what move a computer will make next in a chess game
6	virtual reality	to feel like you are walking on Mars
7	nanotechnology	to introduce tiny capsules into your arteries to deliver medicine

C ▶ 5:06 **LISTEN TO IDENTIFY POINT OF VIEW** Listen again. Circle whether the speaker is for or against each technology. Then, with a partner, explain each answer.

1 He's (**for**/ against) it.
2 She's (for /**against**) it.
3 She's (**for**/ against) it.
4 She's (for /**against**) it.
5 She's (**for**/ against) it.
6 He's (**for**/ against) it.
7 They're (**for**/ against) it.

102 UNIT 9

LESSON 2

GOAL Evaluate applications of innovative technologies

A ▶ 5:04 VOCABULARY

Suggested teaching time:	5–10 minutes	Your actual teaching time:

- Ask students to skim the innovative technologies.
- Have them read and listen to the words. Then ask them to listen and repeat the words chorally.
- Ask students to read the descriptions with a partner and discuss which technologies they are in favor of and which ones they don't support.
- Bring the class together and invite students to share ideas.

Challenge: [+5 minutes] On the board, write *How do you envision the future?* Ask students to predict which of the technologies in this exercise will be integrated into our lives. Encourage students to use the passive future forms presented in the previous lesson.

⭐ 🖨 Vocabulary-Building Strategies

B ▶ 5:05 LISTEN TO ACTIVATE VOCABULARY

Suggested teaching time:	5–10 minutes	Your actual teaching time:

- Pre-listening: Have students scan the technologies in the vocabulary in Exercise A. Point out that they will listen to conversations about each of these technologies, but the terms will not be mentioned; students will have to infer what is being talked about.
- First listening: Allow time for students to write the name of each technology discussed.
- Second listening: Have students listen again and write how the technology is being used.

LANGUAGE NOTE In conversation 1, *the good far outweighs the bad* incorporates *far* into an expression already seen in the unit; *far* here means a lot—there are a lot more advantages than disadvantages. In conversation 2, *to get a hold of* means to obtain something; *to pass oneself off as someone* means to succeed in pretending to be someone else. In conversation 3, *to be questionable* means not likely to be good; *fishy* means bad or dishonest—this is also a play on words since the two people have been discussing genetically engineering a tomato with a fish.

C ▶ 5:06 LISTEN TO IDENTIFY POINT OF VIEW

Suggested teaching time:	5 minutes	Your actual teaching time:

- Pre-listening: Explain that the focus of this listening will be to see if someone is for or against each technology. Point out the pronouns in the exercise items, and tell students to pay attention to which speaker's point of view is being asked about.
- Listening: Have students listen and complete the answers. Allow students to listen again if needed.
- Go over the answers as a class.

Option: [+5 minutes] In pairs, invite students to discuss if they agree with the person or people in the audio. Encourage students to explain why.

D GRAMMAR

Suggested teaching time:	5 minutes	Your actual teaching time:

- For review, on the board, write *If people used mass transit more, they would save a lot of energy.* Ask *Do people use mass transit more?* (no) *Do they save a lot of energy?* (no) *Is the solution to saving a lot of energy using mass transit?* (yes) Elicit that the sentence on the board uses the unreal conditional.

- Point out that the passive voice can be used in conditional statements—either in one or both clauses. Then write *If mass transit were used more, a lot of energy would be saved.* Remind students that in the present unreal conditional, *was* is not considered grammatically correct in the *if* clause. In the same way in the passive, *were* is used, not *was*—even if the subject is singular. Point out that it is also possible for one of the clauses to be in the passive. For example, *If people used mass transit more, a lot of energy would be saved.*

- Have volunteers read the example sentences in the grammar chart.

⭐ 🖨 Inductive Grammar Activity

E GRAMMAR PRACTICE

Suggested teaching time:	5 minutes	Your actual teaching time:

- Make sure students understand that this exercise requires two steps: First, students have to change each true statement to an *if* clause; then students have to write a result clause.

- Instruct students to skim the true statements and decide whether the *if* clause will be in the present or the past unreal conditional. (present unreal conditional: 1, 2, 3; past unreal conditional: 4, 5, 6, 7) Ask a volunteer to read the true statement for item 1. Then focus on the model answer. Point out how in the *if* clause the sentence is not negative; rather, it is positive. If necessary, say *Operations aren't performed by robots. If operations were performed . . . such and such would happen.*

- Then have students complete the exercise individually. Remind students to use the passive in the *if* clause. Circulate and assist as needed. Watch for correct use of the past perfect in the *if* clauses in items 4–7.

⭐ 🖨 Extra Grammar Exercises

F PAIR WORK

Suggested teaching time:	5 minutes	Your actual teaching time:

- In pairs, have students compare the opinions they wrote in the result clauses in Exercise E.

- Bring the class together and call on students to respond to individual items.

NOW YOU CAN Evaluate applications of innovative technologies

A ▶ 5:07 CONVERSATION SPOTLIGHT

Suggested teaching time:	5 minutes	Your actual teaching time:

These conversation strategies are implicit in the model:
- Use *For one thing,* to name the first thing on a list.
- Use *Well, if you ask me,* to voice your opinion.
- Use *I mean* to indicate you will be explaining yourself.
- Use *I see your point* to signal understanding someone's point of view.

- Have students look at the photo and identify which innovation it illustrates (cloning). Ask *Do you think such a prospect is exciting or disturbing?*

- Ask students to read and listen to the conversation.

B ▶ 5:08 RHYTHM AND INTONATION

Suggested teaching time:	5 minutes	Your actual teaching time:

- Have students repeat chorally. Make sure they:
  ○ use emphatic stress on *one* in *For one thing* (line 2)
  ○ pause after *Well* and use falling intonation for *If you ask me . . .* (line 4)
  ○ use rising intonation for *Really?* (line 5)
  ○ stress *I see your point* and use a disagreeing tone with *but people have always worried . . .* (lines 9 and 10)

C Notepadding

Suggested teaching time:	5 minutes	Your actual teaching time:

- Ask a student to read the example text.

- Have students fill in the notepad with technologies and applications. Refer them to Exercise A on page 102 as necessary.

D Conversation activator

Suggested teaching time:	5 minutes	Your actual teaching time:

🎬 Conversation Activator Video

- Divide the class into pairs. Instruct students that they will use the model in Exercise A, Conversation Spotlight, to role-play their own conversation with a partner.

- Refer students back to the idioms and expressions on page 99.

- Reinforce the use of the spotlighted conversation strategies. For example, *For one thing; Well if you ask me . . . ; I see your point . . .*

- Bring students' attention to the Don't Stop! note. Ask a volunteer to read the bullet points. Explain that students should continue talking after they have covered the points in the original Conversation Spotlight.

- Tell students to change roles, so each student gets a chance to play A and B.

For more support, play the Conversation Activator Video before students do this activity themselves. After the video, ask students how the model has been changed by the actors. *Note:* You can print the script or you can view it on the video player on the ActiveTeach.

⭐ 🖨 Conversation Activator: Speaking Booster

D GRAMMAR THE PASSIVE VOICE IN UNREAL CONDITIONAL SENTENCES

The present unreal conditional

If effective cancer-fighting drugs **were developed** through genetic engineering, that technology **might be** more widely **accepted**.

Note: The passive voice can be used in one or both clauses in an unreal conditional sentence.

The past unreal conditional

If antibiotics **had been discovered** earlier, the death toll from pneumonia might have been lower.
If the computer chip **hadn't been developed**, smartphones and tablets **would** never **have been invented**.

E GRAMMAR PRACTICE
Read the true statements. Then, on a separate sheet of paper, write unreal conditional statements with your own opinions, using the passive voice in <u>if</u> clauses.

Answers will vary but may include the following:

Example: Operations aren't always performed by robots.

If operations were always performed by robots, there would never be any surgical errors.

1. Chips aren't implanted in our bodies at birth.
   If chips were implanted in our bodies at birth, it would be more difficult to steal our identities.
2. Genetic engineering isn't prohibited.
   If genetic engineering were prohibited, our food would be much safer.
3. Human cloning isn't permitted.
   If human cloning were permitted, we might have doubles walking around.
4. The airplane was invented in the early 1900s.
   If the airplane hadn't been invented in the early 1900s, modern travel would be different.
5. The dinosaur was made extinct.
   If dinosaurs hadn't been made extinct, the world would not have evolved to where we are today.
6. Written language was developed thousands of years ago.
   If written language had not been developed thousands of years ago, people would have had to rely on oral communication.
7. Electricity was discovered in the seventeenth century.
   If electricity hadn't been discovered in the seventeenth century, other related discoveries would not have been made.

F PAIR WORK
Compare the seven opinions you wrote for Exercise E with a partner. Explain your opinions, providing examples.

NOW YOU CAN Evaluate applications of innovative technologies

A ▶ 5:07 CONVERSATION SPOTLIGHT
Read and listen. Notice the **spotlighted** conversation strategies.

A: I've been thinking about it and this human cloning sounds like a good thing to me. **For one thing**, couples who weren't able to have kids would finally be able to.
B: **Well, if you ask me**, I think it's pretty scary.
A: Really? What makes you say that?
B: It's a slippery slope. **I mean**, before you know it, someone's going to use it for something bad, like making designer babies.
A: **I see your point.** But people have always worried about new things.

▶ 5:09 **Ways to express a concern about consequences**
It's a slippery slope.
It's like opening a can of worms.
It's like playing with fire.
It's like opening Pandora's box.

B ▶ 5:08 RHYTHM AND INTONATION
Listen again and repeat. Then practice the conversation with a partner.

C NOTEPADDING
On your notepad, write an innovative technology that exists in the present and one you'd like to see in the future. Write one important application or use of each technology.

Present technology	Application
genetic engineering	create disease-resistant seeds

Present technology	Application

Future technology	Application

D CONVERSATION ACTIVATOR
Create a conversation similar to the one in Exercise A, using one of the innovative technologies on your notepad. Start like this: *I've been thinking about it and ___ sounds ___ to me.* Be sure to change roles and then partners.

DON'T STOP!
- Provide more reasons you are for or against a particular technology.
- Evaluate applications of other technologies.
- Say as much as you can.

103

LESSON 3

GOAL Discuss how to protect our future environment

A READING WARM-UP What threats today will affect the environment of the future?

B ▶ 5:10 **READING** Read the article. What environmental threats does it address? See page T104 for answer.

ORDINARY PEOPLE WITH BIG IDEAS—
PRACTICAL STRATEGIES TO PROTECT THE EARTH

All around the globe, there are quiet hard-working people doing what it takes to protect our environment. They are changing minds and attitudes and demonstrating that ordinary people can make a difference.

HERE ARE TWO INSPIRING STORIES.

▲ California's huge redwoods

REVERSING GLOBAL WARMING ONE TREE AT A TIME

Old-growth forests play a key role in keeping the earth's atmosphere clean. In these forests, most trees are over 100 years old—many even 1,000 years or more. Unfortunately, after centuries of logging, development, pollution, and disease, about 98% of these forests have been destroyed, contributing to global warming. However, David Milarch and Leslie Lee, co-founders of a U.S. environmental group called Archangel Ancient Tree Archive, are doing something to turn things around.

Tree experts told him it couldn't be done, but Milarch and his sons, Jared and Jake, have been cloning trees from among more than sixty of the world's best-known, oldest, and largest species, creating exact copies of these ancient trees. These include California's huge redwoods and sequoias (some are 2,000 to 3,000 years old!), Ireland's imposing ancient oaks, and Lebanon's historic cedars.

Milarch and Lee want people to buy their cloned trees and plant them—millions of them. The trees then can produce oxygen, which is good for the environment; absorb carbon, which is bad for the environment; and in some cases even be used in the manufacture of much-needed medications. Eventually Milarch hopes to clone over 200 different species and return some of the old-growth forests we have lost through human activity. "I'm a workaholic. I work 16 hours a day, 365 days a year," says Milarch. When asked how he wants to be remembered, he says, "He caused us to stop and think and take action."

◀ David Milarch

PROTECTING WILDLIFE BY CHANGING MINDS

Cambodia is experiencing a rise in population and unregulated development, which has been destructive for the environment. More and more inexperienced farmers are taking up agriculture near the edges of Cambodia's forests. Unfortunately for Cambodia's wild Asian elephants, this has caused a conflict with humans. As elephants search for food, they have destroyed farms. In turn, poor and uneducated farmers have killed the elephants to protect their livelihoods. By the early years of this century, the population of elephants had fallen dramatically from about 2,000 to 500.

Tuy Sereivathana (known as Vathana) grew up in the countryside, where he learned to respect both nature and the elephants. After choosing to study forestry, he committed himself to conservation of Cambodia's natural resources. Eventually, working for the country's national parks, he focused his attention on understanding the problems the Cambodian farmers were facing.

Vathana realized that the farmers needed to know more about the elephants' migration patterns and how to apply practical solutions for protecting their farms. He helped them build electric fences. He taught them how to use hot chili peppers and other native plants that elephants don't like in order to discourage the animals from eating their crops. He convinced the farmers to organize themselves to guard their farms at night, using fireworks and other loud noises to scare the elephants off. He also helped them improve their farming techniques so they would not have to go farther into the elephants' habitat.

Vathana worked to establish community schools to increase literacy and provide wildlife conservation education. And he helped redevelop the cultural pride Cambodians have long had in their elephants. The farmers are now the elephants' greatest protectors. Vathana is now known as "Uncle Elephant." There has not been a single killing of a wild Asian elephant since 2005.

Tuy Sereivathana ▶

LESSON 3

GOAL Discuss how to protect our future environment

A READING WARM-UP

| Suggested teaching time: | 5 minutes | Your actual teaching time: |

- Ask a volunteer to read the question. On the board, write *threats*. Elicit that a threat is the possibility of something very bad happening. Ask students for examples of threats to the environment.
- Poll the class by asking *Who here thinks or worries about the environment of the future?* Also invite students to share if they do anything to preserve the environment.

B ▶ 5:10 READING

| Suggested teaching time: | 15–20 minutes | Your actual teaching time: |

- Have students look at the photographs. Ask *Have you seen or heard of California's huge redwoods? Have you heard of David Milarch or Tuy Sereivathana?* If yes, invite students to share what they know. Focus on the title "Ordinary People with Big Ideas." Call on a volunteer to read the paragraph on the right. Ask *Do you know any such ordinary people? Are you one of them?*
- As students read and listen, tell them to underline information in the article that will help them answer the focus question in the direction line. (What environmental threats does it address?)
- Have volunteers share their answers to the focus question.
- To check comprehension of the piece on David Milarch and trees, ask *What is an old growth forest?* (forests whose trees are over 100 years old) *What has destroyed these forests?* (logging, development, pollution, and disease) *How are David Milarch and his team helping?* (They are cloning ancient trees.) *Which trees are they cloning?* (redwoods, sequoias, oaks, and cedars) *What do the trees do that's good?* (They produce oxygen, absorb carbon, and are sometimes used in the manufacture of much-needed medications.)
- To check comprehension of the piece on Tuy Sereivathana (Vathana), ask *What problem have Cambodia's wild Asian elephants been facing?* (A conflict with humans; in search for food, elephants destroy farms; in turn, poor uneducated farmers kill them.) *What role has Tuy Sereivathana played?* (He has focused his energies on understanding the problems of Cambodian farmers.) *How has he helped educate them?* (He has taught them to apply practical solutions to protecting farms—he helped them build electric fences, he taught them to use hot chili peppers and other native plants that elephants don't like to keep them from eating crops, and he convinced them to guard the farms at night using fireworks and other loud noises to scare the elephants off.) *What has Vathana done for education?* (He has established schools to educate Cambodians and revive their pride in elephants.) *What is Vathana's nickname?* (Uncle Elephant) *When is the last time a wild Asian elephant was killed?* (2005)

Challenge: [+5 minutes] Invite students to explore how exactly an ancient tree is cloned. Students can work individually or in pairs to research the process and present it to the class. Have students discuss the comment *Tree experts told them it couldn't be done.* Tell students to see if they can find out how Milarch and his team proved experts wrong.

⭐ 🖨 Reading Strategies

Answers for Exercise B

The first part of the reading addresses the threat to California's huge redwoods. David Milarch and Leslie Lee, co-founders of a US environmental group called Archangel Ancient Tree Archive, are turning to cloning these ancient trees.
The second part of the reading addresses the threat to Cambodia's wild Asian elephants. Tuy Sereivathana has committed himself to educating farmers who were killing elephants that were destroying farms.

C UNDERSTAND MEANING FROM CONTEXT

| Suggested teaching time: | 10–15 minutes | Your actual teaching time: |

- Have students work individually or in pairs to match the terms to their meanings. For items they are not sure about, tell them to find each term in the reading and look at words that come before and after to help understand the meaning.
- If students need help finding words and phrases, give them hints. (The term for item 1 is in "Reversing Global Warming," paragraph 1. The terms for items 2 and 3 are in "Reversing Global Warming," paragraph 2. The terms for item 4 and 5 are in "Protecting Wildlife," paragraph 1. The term for item 6 is in "Protecting Wildlife," paragraph 3.)

LANGUAGE NOTE Point out that *to turn things around* means to cause a negative situation to go in a positive direction. It is also possible to say *things turn around*. For example, *I've had some problems at work lately, but things will turn around soon.*

Option: [+5 minutes] In pairs, have students practice using the terms in their own sentences. Tell them to try to make statements about protecting the environment. For example, *Conserving water last month dramatically decreased our water bill.*

🖨 Extra Reading Comprehension Questions

D DRAW CONCLUSIONS

| Suggested teaching time: | 5 minutes | Your actual teaching time: |

- Have students return to the article to read about the topic in each question. Point out that they may not find the specific answer in the article, but they can make a judgment after considering information read in the article.
- If students need help locating sections of the article, for item 1, direct them to paragraph 1 in "Reversing Global Warming"; for item 2, direct them to paragraph 3 of "Reversing Global Warming"; for item 3, direct them to paragraph 3 of "Protecting Wildlife"; and for item 4, direct them to paragraph 4 of "Protecting Wildlife."
- Have students share their conclusions with the class.

⭐🖨 Extra Challenge Reading Activity

Answers for Exercise D

1. Old growth forests play a key role in keeping the earth's atmosphere clean.
2. The trees then can produce oxygen, which is good for the environment; absorb carbon, which is bad for the environment; and in some cases even be used in the manufacture of much-needed medications.
3. Vathana has taught the farmers practical tips to protect their farms from elephants as well as improve their farming techniques so they would not have to go farther into the elephants' habitat.
4. By teaching wildlife conservation in Cambodian schools Vathana has redeveloped the cultural pride Cambodians have had in their elephants. He is inspiring future generations to be the elephants' protectors.

NOW YOU CAN Discuss how to protect our future environment

A FRAME YOUR IDEAS

| Suggested teaching time: | 5–10 minutes | Your actual teaching time: |

- Have students look at the green and yellow arrow symbol. Elicit that this is the universal recycling symbol. Note that it is recognized all over the world. Point to the light bulbs. Ask *What kind of light bulbs are these?* (LED) *Do you use such light bulbs? Why? Why not?*
- Focus on the term *environmentally conscious* and elicit that this means showing concern for the environment. Tell students to skim the three categories and questions. Clarify vocabulary as needed.
- Explain that the item they write for each category doesn't have to be a huge contribution to preserving the environment. If students need ideas, possible answers are not littering, filling the dishwasher completely before running it, and using leftover food to feed a dog or other animal.

Option: [+5 minutes] Focus on the first item under To Preserve Water. Elicit why placing a brick in a toilet's reservoir tank conserves water. If students don't know about this, have them look it up online and discuss (the brick displaces some of the water, so you get the same flush pressure, but less water is used with each flush). Invite students to look up additional tips online related to how to preserve water. Students can work in pairs or small groups. This can be done at school or for homework.

B PRESENTATION

| Suggested teaching time: | 5 minutes | Your actual teaching time: |

- On the board, write *action plan*. Elicit that this is a list of steps that need to be taken to achieve a goal. Ask *What is the purpose of an action plan?* (to identify what is needed to reach each goal on the action plan, suggest a timeline, etc.)
- In groups, have students choose one of the topics, or to ensure all the topics are covered, assign groups different topics. Draw the following chart on the board for students to help organize their ideas or print it out from the ActiveTeach and distribute it to students.

What	How	Who	When

- Have students create an action plan of how to achieve the various goals.
- Guide students as needed to decide *what* needs to be done, *how* this will be achieved, *who* will perform what task, and *when* will different tasks be achieved.
- Then have groups present their plans to the class.

🖨 Graphic Organizer

C **UNDERSTAND MEANING FROM CONTEXT** Find the underlined words and phrases in the article. Then complete each statement. Explain your answers.

1 If you turn things around, it means you are making something ....
   a worse **(b) better** c stay the same
2 Redwoods, sequoias, oaks, and cedars are types of ....
   a clones **(b) trees** c medications
3 When trees absorb carbon, it is actually ....
   (a) good for the environment b bad for the environment c causing global warming
4 Unregulated development is ....
   a good for the environment **(b) bad for the environment** c good for farmers
5 If something falls dramatically, it means it ....
   a hasn't changed b has changed a little **(c) has changed a lot**
6 A native plant is one that has ...... another place.
   a been brought in from **(b) not been brought in from** c been cloned at

D **DRAW CONCLUSIONS** In small groups, discuss the following questions. Find information in the article to support your answers. See page T105 for answers.

1 What do old-growth forests do that's beneficial to this planet?
2 Why does Milarch focus specifically on cloning ancient tree species?
3 What were the benefits of Vathana's decision to work closely with the farmers?
4 What might be a long-term benefit of teaching wildlife conservation in Cambodian schools?

NOW YOU CAN Discuss how to protect our future environment

A **FRAME YOUR IDEAS** Complete the questionnaire and compare answers with a partner. Which of you appears to be the more environmentally conscious?

HOW ENVIRONMENTALLY CONSCIOUS ARE YOU?
Check off the things that you do—and add some more.

TO REDUCE POLLUTION
- ☐ I use energy-efficient appliances.
- ☐ I use energy-efficient compact fluorescent light bulbs or LED bulbs instead of incandescent bulbs.
- ☐ I walk as often as I can or take public transportation instead of driving.
- ☐ And I ...

TO PRESERVE WATER
- ☐ I place a brick in the toilet's reservoir tank.
- ☐ I take showers instead of baths whenever I can.
- ☐ I turn off the water while I brush my teeth or shave.
- ☐ And I ...

TO AVOID WASTING FOOD
- ☐ I use leftovers to create new meals.
- ☐ I compost food to use in the garden.
- ☐ I only buy as much food as I need.
- ☐ And I ...

B **PRESENTATION** In a small group, choose one of the three categories in the questionnaire. Develop an action plan and present it to your class.

LESSON 4

GOAL Examine future social and demographic trends

A ▶ 5:11 **LISTENING WARM-UP** **VOCABULARY** **DESCRIBING SOCIAL AND DEMOGRAPHIC TRENDS**
Read and listen. Then listen again and repeat.

dem·o·graph·ic /ˈdɛməˈɡræfɪk/ ◀ n. **1 demographics** [plural] information about the people who live in a particular area, such as how many people there are or what types of people there are: *the changing demographics of Southern California* **2** [singular] a part of the population that is considered as a group, especially for the purpose of advertising or trying to sell goods: *Cable television is focused on the 18 to 49 demographic (= people who are 18 to 49 years old).*

rate /reɪt/ n. [C] **1** the number of times something happens, or the number of examples of something within a certain period: **[+ of]** *The rate of new HIV infections has risen again.* | **at a rate of** sth *Refugees were crossing the border at a rate of 1,000 a day.* | *The unemployment rate rose to 6.5% in February.* | *The city still has a high crime rate.*

sta·tis·tic / stəˈtɪstɪk / n. **1 statistics** [plural] a collection of numbers which represents facts or measurements: *official crime statistics* **2** [singular] a single number which represents a fact or measurement: *a depressing statistic.* | **a statistic that** *I read a statistic that over 10,000 Americans a day turn 50.*

trend / trɛnd / n. [C] a general tendency in the way a situation is changing or developing: *Social and economic trends affect everyone.* | **[+ in]** *The researchers studied trends in drug use among teenagers.* | **[+ toward]** *There is a worldwide trend toward smaller families.* | *Davis is hoping to* **reverse the trend** *of rising taxes (= make a trend go in the opposite direction).* | **a current / recent / present trend** *If current trends continue, tourism will increase by 10%.* | *There is a growing trend in the country toward buying organic foods.*

Excerpted from *Longman Advanced American Dictionary*

B **APPLY THE VOCABULARY** Write whether each example is **a demographic**, **a statistic**, **a rate**, or **a trend**. Explain your choices.

1. An increasing number of customers are choosing to stream movies at home rather than go to a theater to see them. ......**a trend**......
2. The social media site *Pinterest* is used by more women than men. ......**a demographic**......
3. The number of births per family is lower in wealthier developed countries. ......**a rate**......
4. Fifteen percent of seniors in the U.S. are living in poverty. ......**a statistic**......

C ▶ 5:12 **LISTEN TO ACTIVATE VOCABULARY** Listen to people discussing demographic trends. Write the number of the conversation next to the rate (or rates) they are discussing. (One rate is not discussed at all.) Then circle whether the rate is rising or falling. Listen again to check your work.

▶ 5:13 **Listen and repeat.**
literacy = ability to read and write
fertility = ability to reproduce
mortality = death

3	crime rate	(**rising**/ falling)	2	literacy rate	(**rising** / falling)
4	birthrate	(rising /**falling**)	1	fertility rate	(rising /**falling**)
	mortality rate	(rising / falling)	4	divorce rate	(**rising**/ falling)

D ▶ 5:14 **LISTEN TO CONFIRM CONTENT**
Now listen to a lecture predicting world population trends. Read the list of subjects. Then listen again and check the subjects that were mentioned.

- ☐ a decrease in world population
- ☐ unemployment rates
- ☑ life expectancy
- ☐ marriage trends
- ☐ divorce rates
- ☑ fertility rates
- ☑ mortality rates
- ☐ literacy rates

LESSON 4

GOAL Examine future social and demographic trends

A ▶ 5:11 LISTENING WARM-UP

Suggested teaching time:	5–10 minutes	Your actual teaching time:

- Ask students to scan the words and note those they don't know.
- Have students listen and repeat. Then ask *What part of speech is each dictionary entry?* (noun) *Which two dictionary entries provide the plural form?* (statistics, demographics) *What is the plural form of the word* rate? (rates) *Of the word* trend? (trends)

LANGUAGE NOTE You may wish to point out that the term *demographics* is often used more broadly to denote the statistical characteristics of any human population (e.g., by age or income). Note also that *demographic* is also used as an adjective (e.g., describing demographic trends).

⭐ 🖨 Vocabulary-Building Strategies

B APPLY THE VOCABULARY

Suggested teaching time:	5 minutes	Your actual teaching time:

- If necessary, model item 1. Then have students complete the exercise.
- Have students compare answers with a partner. Then go over the answers as a class.

Option: [+5 minutes] In pairs or small groups, invite students to think up additional examples for each of the four terms.

C ▶ 5:12 LISTEN TO ACTIVATE VOCABULARY

Suggested teaching time:	10–15 minutes	Your actual teaching time:

- Pre-listening: Have students scan the chart for the various rates discussed in the conversations. Tell students they will identify the rate(s) discussed and then indicate if each rate is rising or falling.
- Focus on the six terms in the box and help students with pronunciation, if necessary. Point out that *birthrate* is the number of births in a country or other specific community over a specific period of time and shows actual population growth. *Fertility rate* is the number of births per family and implies potential population growth. Ask students to listen to the terms and repeat.
- Listening: Have students listen to each conversation and then write the information in the chart. Allow students to listen again to confirm their answers.
- Have students compare answers with a partner. To further check comprehension, ask *In conversation 1, why is the fertility rate falling?* (The country has changed from a mostly rural farm economy to a mostly urban technological one. Farm families need a lot of children to help out, but children are just an added expense for urban families.) *In conversation 2, how quickly is the literacy rate rising?* (It's going up at a rate of 2% a year.) *In conversation 3, why is the crime rate rising?* (The percentage of young men in the population has risen over 100% in just one year.) *In conversation 4, what is the danger of a rising divorce rate and a falling birthrate?* (There won't be enough people around to keep things going.)

LANGUAGE NOTE An *assault* is a physical attack; *steep* means extremely high; *go to the dogs* means deteriorate; *decline* means fall; *keep up* means continue; *lose the gloom and doom* means stop being so pessimistic.

Option: [+5 minutes] Invite students to look up statistics in their country for each of the social trends mentioned in the conversation. Then bring the class together and discuss, comparing their information to the statistics discussed in the conversation.

⭐ 🖨 Listening Strategies

D ▶ 5:13 LISTEN TO CONFIRM CONTENT

Suggested teaching time:	10–15 minutes	Your actual teaching time:

- Pre-listening: Ask a volunteer to read the subjects listed in the box. Tell students that they will listen to a lecture about world population trends. Ask *Which of these subjects do you think will be included in the lecture? Why?*
- First listening: Have students close their books and listen to the lecture.
- Second listening: Ask students to listen again with their books open and check the subjects they heard discussed.
- Ask students if they predicted correctly which topics would be included. Then ask *Why do you think a decrease in world population was not discussed?* (A decrease in population is not likely.)

E ▶ 5:15 LISTEN TO INFER INFORMATION

Suggested teaching time:	5 minutes	Your actual teaching time:

- **Pre-listening:** Before students listen, tell them to skim the statements and see if they can answer any of the questions based on information from the last listening. Tell them they can pencil in the answers.
- **First listening:** Have students listen. If they have difficulty keeping up with the lecture, stop the audio after each paragraph to let them complete the statements. Note that the answer to item 1 is in the first paragraph, to item 2 is in the second paragraph, to item 3 in the third, and to items 4 and 5 in the fourth.
- **Second listening:** Have students listen again to check their work. Then have them compare statements with a partner.
- Bring the class together to go over the questions. If necessary, focus on item 2. On the board, write *By 2050, the United Nations report predicts that China will have been surpassed by India as the world's most populous country.* Have students identify the future perfect passive in the sentence. Make sure students understand that *surpass* means to be greater than something else. Ask *Which country, India or China, will have the highest population?* (India) *Which country will have the second highest population?* (China)

Challenge: **[+5 minutes]** Ask *Was your country mentioned in the lecture?* Invite students to work independently or pair up with other people from the same country and find specific statistics predicting population trends. Then bring the class together and see where each student's country fits in with the predictions from the lecture.

F SUPPORT AN OPINION

Suggested teaching time:	5 minutes	Your actual teaching time:

- To review, ask *According to the lecture, what challenges do the demographic trends present?* (need for more funding for education, increase in healthcare resources, more food production) Elicit additional ideas. (Possible answers: poverty, immigration)
- Then invite students to share what about future world demographics concerns them most.

NOW YOU CAN Examine future social and demographic trends

A NOTEPADDING

Suggested teaching time:	5 minutes	Your actual teaching time:

- Have students look at the photos at the bottom of the page. Ask *What trends do you think the pictures illustrate?* (marriage trends, birth trends, mortality) *What are the birth trends in your country?*
- Call on a volunteer to read the list of social trends. Invite students to suggest other topics, and write these on the board for reference.
- Ask a student to read the comment about marriage and divorce trends. Then have students write independently about trends that concern them. Have pairs compare answers and note any similarities.

B DISCUSSION

Suggested teaching time:	5 minutes	Your actual teaching time:

- Bring the class together and have students form small groups with others who chose the same topic.
- Circulate as groups discuss the problems, challenges, and possible solutions for their topic. Assist as needed.

OPTIONAL WRITING **[+15–20 minutes]**

- Write the following tips on the board:

  Paragraph 1: Explain the problem and give examples.

  Paragraph 2: Explain challenges that will occur as a result of the trend.

  Paragraph 3: Suggest solutions to the trends.

- Then have students write independently about the trend their group discussed in Exercise B.
- If time permits, have students exchange papers with a partner or read their paragraphs to the class. Alternatively, collect student assignments and give individual feedback.

⭐ 🖨 **Discussion: Speaking Booster**

E ▶ 5:15 **LISTEN TO INFER INFORMATION** Read the statements. Then listen to the lecture again. Circle the word or phrase that best completes each statement, according to the information presented in the lecture.

1 According to the U.N. report, if the world's fertility and infant mortality rates don't decrease, the world's population will increase by (less than / **more than** / approximately) 30% by 2040.
2 By 2050, the country with the second highest population in the world will be (**China** / India / the U.S.).
3 By 2050, populations in Japan, Russia, and Germany will be (higher / **lower** / the same).
4 Worldwide, the number of older people will be (the same as / **lower than** / higher than) the number of younger people.
5 In 2050, the total number of children in the continent of Africa will be (**lower than** / higher than / the same as) the total number in the rest of the world.

F **SUPPORT AN OPINION** Which of the statistics about future world demographics concern you the most? Explain your reasons.

NOW YOU CAN Examine future social and demographic trends

A **NOTEPADDING** With a partner, examine some social and demographic trends in your country that concern you. Write them on your notepad. Decide which of the trends present the greatest challenges.

Marriage and divorce: *Fewer and fewer people are getting married.*

Marriage and divorce:
Government and politics:
The news media:
Education:
Family life:
Seniors:
Other:

B **DISCUSSION** Discuss with your partner some possible solutions to meet the challenges you identified in Exercise A. Then present your ideas to your class and invite your classmates to share their own ideas.

OPTIONAL WRITING On a separate sheet of paper, write three paragraphs about one of the trends you discussed. In the first paragraph, explain the problem and give examples. In the second paragraph, explain the challenges. In the third, suggest some solutions.

WRITING: The thesis statement in a formal essay

A WRITING SKILL Study the rules.

A formal essay should include a thesis statement somewhere in the introductory paragraph. The thesis statement presents an argument or point of view. The supporting paragraphs should be organized to provide reasons, facts, or examples to support your thesis. The outline on the left indicates an effective way to organize a formal essay to support a thesis.

To write a thesis statement …
- Narrow the topic to one or two main ideas.
- Make sure it expresses your point of view.

I. Introductory paragraph (with a thesis statement)
Your introduction should include a thesis statement—a sentence that presents your argument. The remaining sentences should suggest what specific topics the essay will include.

II. Supporting paragraphs (with supporting examples)
Each supporting paragraph should include a topic sentence that supports your thesis statement, followed by supporting examples.

III. Concluding paragraph (with a summary)
Your conclusion should summarize the main points of the entire essay and restate your thesis.

WRITING MODEL

In twenty years, cars will probably all be power[ed] by alternative energy sources, and they will be equipped with new technologies that take over many of the responsibilities of driving. There are good reasons to be optimistic about these predictions since car manufacturers are already moving in this direction. Undoubtedly, new technological advances will make these developments almost certain to become reality.

Many experts predict that most cars of the future will be powered by electricity. Unlike today's electric cars, which have limitations that keep them from being as popular as gas-powered vehicles, electric cars in the future will be much easier to maintain. For example, …

Advances in computing will also make human drivers obsolete. Cars of the future will have advanced technological features, some of which are being applied today, that do the thinking for the driver. First of all, cars will all be able to park themselves. In addition, …

Based on the direction the car industry is heading today, we can confidently predict some of the key advances we will see in the cars of the future. The industry is already offering both electric and hybrid vehicles, and it has introduced some "driverless" features, so we can expect much more development in those two areas.

B PRACTICE Essay tests often suggest topics in the form of a question. On a separate sheet of paper, write a thesis statement for each topic. Be sure to apply the guidelines above.

Answers will vary b[ut] include the followin[g]

1. How can we end poverty?
   Poverty can only be ended if the government makes that one of its highest priorities.
2. Are hospitals and medical care getting too expensive?
   Hospitals and medical care are becoming so expensive that more and more people cannot afford basic care.
3. How are fast-food restaurants changing the way people eat?
   Fast food restaurants have made eating a solitary experience.
4. What are the best ways to avoid becoming a crime victim?
   There are several tips that can help one avoid being the victim of crime.
5. Do video games affect young people in negative ways?
   Contrary to popular belief, research shows that there are many social and intellectual benefits to video games.
6. What are the best places to go on vacation?
   The best places to go on vacation are places where you can rest your body and mind.

C APPLY THE WRITING SKILL

Write a four- or five-paragraph essay on one of the suggested topics. State your argument in the introduction with a thesis statement. Support your argument with two or three supporting paragraphs. In your conclusion, restate your argument and summarize the main points.

Suggested topics
- Transportation in the future
- Communication in the future
- Health care in the future
- Education in the future
- The future of the earth
- Your own idea: ....

SELF-CHECK
☐ Does my thesis statement clearly state my argument?
☐ Does each of my supporting paragraphs have a topic sentence that supports my point of view?
☐ Does my conclusion summarize my main points and restate my thesis?

WRITING: The thesis statement in a formal essay

A WRITING SKILL

Suggested teaching time:	10–15 minutes	Your actual teaching time:

- Call on a volunteer to read the introduction to this skill. Tell students that an essay allows a writer to express his or her point of view.
- Allow students time to look at the outline and read the writing model. Then ask *What is the thesis statement?* (In twenty years . . .) *What is the topic sentence in the second paragraph?* (Many experts predict . . .) *What is the topic sentence in the third paragraph?* (Advances in computing . . .) *Does the conclusion restate the thesis?* (yes)
- Focus on the To write a thesis statement box and the highlighted thesis statement in the writing model. Ask *What two ideas is the topic narrowed to?* (Cars will be powered by alternative energy sources. They will be equipped with new technologies.)

Option: [+5 minutes] Have students work in pairs to fill in more supporting examples in the two supporting paragraphs, by continuing writing after *For example* in paragraph 2 and *In addition* in paragraph 3. Tell students that they can use their imagination as they make predictions about cars of the future.

B PRACTICE

Suggested teaching time:	5 minutes	Your actual teaching time:

- Go over the bulleted tips in the To write a thesis statement box in Exercise A. Ask a student to read the question and example thesis statement. Ask *How was the topic of ending poverty narrowed?* (The writer states that the government needs to make it a high priority.) Elicit additional thesis statements. (Possible answer: We can end poverty by providing quality education.) Write students' statements on the board, correcting and narrowing examples as needed.
- Have students write the thesis statements individually. Circulate and assist as needed.
- Ask pairs to compare their statements. Then bring the class together and have students share.

C APPLY THE WRITING SKILL

Suggested teaching time:	10–15 minutes	Your actual teaching time:

- Ask a student to read the suggested topics. Call on volunteers to share additional topic ideas.
- Focus on one and elicit a thesis statement. For example, for the topic *Education in the future*, the thesis statement could be *In the future, all university education will be conducted online.*
- Refer students to the Writing Process Worksheet in ActiveTeach for guidance with pre-writing and peer feedback.
- Encourage students to use the Self-Check in the Student's Book to go over the essays they wrote.

Option: [+5 minutes] Time permitting, students can exchange papers with a partner and offer feedback based on the topics in the Self-Check list. Encourage partners to also check for examples.

⭐ 🖨 Writing Process

UNIT 9 WRITING T108

REVIEW

🎮 **Digital Game**

A ▶ 5:16

| Suggested teaching time: | 5–10 minutes | Your actual teaching time: |

- **Pre-listening:** Have students review the technologies mentioned on page 102. Then have them listen to the conversations. Point out that they will have to identify each technology being discussed, as well as identify each person's opinion. For less advanced classes, you may want to put a word bank on the board: *genetic engineering, remote surgery, artificial intelligence, computer chip implants.*
- **First listening:** Have students listen and focus on identifying the technologies.
- **Second listening:** Have them listen again and circle the word or phrase that reflects each person's opinion.
- Go over the answers as a class.

Option: [+5 minutes] In pairs, have students discuss if they have the same opinion as each speaker. If not, have them explain why not.

B

| Suggested teaching time: | 5 minutes | Your actual teaching time: |

- Have students review the idioms and expressions in Exercise D on page 99 as needed.
- Call on a volunteer to read the model answer. Elicit other examples of things students think will catch on. Then have them complete the exercise.
- Ask students to compare answers with a partner.

C

| Suggested teaching time: | 5 minutes | Your actual teaching time: |

- Before students do the exercise, have them review the vocabulary from Lesson 4.
- As students complete the paragraph, tell them to note whether each noun is singular or plural in order to make sure that the noun agrees with the verb in each sentence.
- Have pairs compare answers.

D

| Suggested teaching time: | 5 minutes | Your actual teaching time: |

- After students rewrite the sentences, have them compare answers with a partner.
- Bring the class together and go over any outstanding queries. Then ask *In which sentences was the* by *phrase necessary? Why?*

Option: **TEST-TAKING SKILLS BOOSTER** (p. 159)

EXTRA

- Workbook
- MyEnglishLab
- Online Student Resources (www.english.com/summit3e)
  - Classroom Audio Program
  - Extra Practice Activities
  - *Summit GO* App
  - Web Projects
- ActiveTeach
  - Assessment
  - Additional Printable Resources
    ○ Audioscripts and Answer Keys
    ○ "Can-Do" Self-Assessment Charts
    ○ Conversation and Discussion Activator Video Scripts
    ○ Oral Progress Assessment Charts
    ○ Reading Speed Calculator
  - Summit TV Video Program
    ○ Activity Worksheets
    ○ Teaching Notes
    ○ Video Scripts

REVIEW

A ▶ 5:16 Listen to the conversations. Complete each statement with the technology the people are referring to and circle the word or phrase that reflects each person's opinion.

1 He's (skeptical /(excited)) about artificial intelligence .
2 She ((doesn't think)/ thinks) remote surgery is a great idea.
3 He's ((skeptical)/ excited) about computer chip implants .
4 He's (bothered /(not bothered)) by genetic engineering .

B Write statements, using the underlined idioms in your statements.
Answers will vary but may include the following:

> I'm certain that home delivery of restaurant meals using drones will catch on someday.

1 something you think is going to catch on in the future
I think drone deliveries will definitely catch on in the future.

2 something that would be like opening a can of worms
Renovating our basement opened a can of worms; there were problems behind every wall we removed.

3 a situation in which someone turned things around
Mark did poorly his first year of university, but he turned things around and is graduating now with top honors.

C Complete the paragraph with words and phrases from the list. Make any necessary changes.

| trend | statistics | mortality rate | birthrate | population growth | demographic |

Statistics (1) indicate that there are over 6 billion people in the world, with an increase of a million people each year. This population growth (2) is not a result of an increased birthrate (3). In fact, the worldwide trend (4) is for women to have fewer children. This increase in population is mainly the result of a decrease in the child mortality rate (5) with more children living to adulthood. People are living much longer lives. When the first humans walked the earth, the average person lived only to the age of twenty. Today, the senior demographic (6) is rapidly increasing in size, especially in developing countries.

D Rewrite each of the following sentences in the passive voice. Do not include a by phrase.

1 In two years, engineers will have designed a new factory.
In two years, a new factory will have been designed.

2 Engineers are going to equip the factory with air filters.
The factory is going to be equipped with air filters.

3 Workers will recycle paper, metal, and plastic.
Paper, metal, and plastic will be recycled.

4 They're going to treat waste before they release it into rivers.
Waste is going to be treated before it is released into rivers.

5 New technologies are going to reduce energy demands by 50 percent.
Energy demands are going to be reduced by 50 percent.

6 Pipes will collect rainwater, and they will transport it to tanks.
Rainwater will be collected and transported to tanks.

7 Pipes will also carry excess heat from one building to another.
Excess heat will also be carried from one building to another.

TEST-TAKING SKILLS BOOSTER p. 159

Web Project: Animal Conservation
www.english.com/summit3e

UNIT 10
An Interconnected World

PREVIEW

COMMUNICATION GOALS
1. React to news about global issues
2. Describe the impact of foreign imports
3. Discuss the pros and cons of globalization
4. Suggest ways to avoid culture shock

A FRAME YOUR IDEAS Complete the quiz.

GET THE FACTS!

Test your knowledge about English in today's world.

1. English is NOT an official language in ....
   - [ ] Canada
   - [ ] the U.S. or the U.K.
   - [ ] South Africa
   - [ ] Nigeria

2. There are approximately ...... people in the world who can speak English.
   - [ ] 1.5 million
   - [ ] 10 million
   - [ ] 1 billion
   - [ ] 1.5 billion

3. Approximately ...... of the world's population are native speakers of English.
   - [ ] 5%
   - [ ] 10%
   - [ ] 20%
   - [ ] 30%

4. There are about ...... million people who speak English as a foreign language.
   - [ ] 6
   - [ ] 10
   - [ ] 70
   - [ ] 700

5. ...... is the country with the most English speakers.
   - [ ] China
   - [ ] the U.S.
   - [ ] the U.K.
   - [ ] India

6. Approximately ...... million children are studying English in China.
   - [ ] 1
   - [ ] 10
   - [ ] 100
   - [ ] 500

7. In France, there are approximately ...... post-secondary degree programs offered in English.
   - [ ] 20
   - [ ] 100
   - [ ] 300
   - [ ] 700

8. Approximately ...... of the information stored in the world's computers is in English.
   - [ ] 10%
   - [ ] 30%
   - [ ] 50%
   - [ ] 80%

9. Approximately ...... new words are added to the English language each year.
   - [ ] 10
   - [ ] 100
   - [ ] 400
   - [ ] 4,000

ANSWERS: 1. Neither the U.S. nor the U.K. has an official language. English is the main language in those countries by history and tradition. Both English and French are official languages in Canada. South Africa has 11 official languages, including English. Nigeria has only one—English. **2.** According to some estimates, 1.5 billion people in the world speak English—that's one out of every six people, and the number is growing. **3.** There are about 380 million native speakers of English, a little over 5% of the world's population. **4.** There are anywhere from 700 million to one billion people who have learned—or are currently learning—English in addition to their own language. **5.** The U.S. has the most English speakers, native and non-native, at 298 million. Ranking highest after that are India (125 million), Pakistan (92 million), Nigeria (82 million), and the U.K. (64 million). But there are more English speakers in Asia than in the U.S., U.K., and Canada combined. **6.** 100 million children are learning English in China. That's more than the population of the U.K. **7.** French universities offer 700 degree programs in English. France attracts more foreign university students than any other non-English-speaking country. **8.** Eighty percent of the world's digitally stored information is in English, but the proportion of information stored in other languages is growing. **9.** Four thousand new words are added yearly, making English the language with the largest vocabulary in the world.

B PAIR WORK Did any of the answers surprise you? Explain why or why not.

UNIT 10

An Interconnected World

PREVIEW

A FRAME YOUR IDEAS

Suggested teaching time:	10–15 minutes	Your actual teaching time:

- Have students scan the quiz. Ask *What does this quiz test?* (knowledge about English in today's world) Without allowing them to read the quiz questions, ask students *What do you know about English in today's world?* (Possible answers: English is a global language. English is used widely in technical communication.)

- Tell students to complete the quiz. Then have them compare answers with a partner, referring to the answer key for any answers they don't agree on.

B PAIR WORK

Suggested teaching time:	5 minutes	Your actual teaching time:

- In pairs, have students discuss any answers that surprised them.

- Bring the class together and have them calculate how many answers they had right. Ask *Were you surprised at how you performed on the quiz?*

UNIT 10 PREVIEW T110

C ▶ 5:17 SPOTLIGHT

Suggested teaching time:	10–15 minutes	Your actual teaching time:

- Have students look at the photo and read and listen to the conversation.
- Elicit that a master's degree is an academic degree that a person can pursue at a college or university after completing a bachelor's degree.
- To check comprehension of the conversation, ask *Where is Hyo thinking about going for a master's degree?* (Los Angeles or London) *Where does Paul recommend he study?* (in Paris) *Why hasn't Hyo considered Paris?* (He assumed all coursework would be in French.) *Why is the engineering program in Paris offered in English?* (to attract foreign students) *Where is Paul from?* (Paris) *How do we know?* (He refers to Paris as his hometown.)
- You can tell students that the Ecole Centrale d'Electronique (ECE) was founded in 1919 and is a privately owned French Grande Ecole located in the heart of Paris. From its inception, ECE Paris has been committed to educating students in science and technology at the undergraduate and graduate levels.

D UNDERSTAND IDIOMS AND EXPRESSIONS 1

Suggested teaching time:	5 minutes	Your actual teaching time:

- Focus students' attention on the idioms and expressions in quotation marks. Call on volunteers to read them aloud.
- In pairs, have students complete the exercise.
- Bring the class together to go over the answers.

LANGUAGE NOTE Point out that in addition to the expression *sitting on the fence*, it is also common to say *to be on the fence about something*, meaning to be undecided.

E UNDERSTAND IDIOMS AND EXPRESSIONS 2

Suggested teaching time:	5 minutes	Your actual teaching time:

- Focus on the a, b, c choices and ask a student to read them. Explain that each expression in the exercise will be matched to an explanation of how it is used.
- Bring the class together to go over the answers. Have volunteers read the full exchange in which the idiom occurs to illustrate emphasizing a problem, offering an explanation, or expressing surprise. If needed, model putting stress on *bad* in *it's bad enough . . .* and using falling intonation for *How do you like that*.

Option: [+5 minutes] Read the following scenarios to the class and call on volunteers to make responding statements using idioms and expressions from Exercise C, Spotlight. (Possible answers: 1. How do you like your new job? / I hate it. I feel like a fish out of water there! 2. Why don't you speak Spanish with your kids? / It's a losing battle. They always answer me in English. 3. Did you hear I won the lottery? / You're pulling my leg, right? 4. Richard took the job after they offered him a higher salary. / Money talks. 5. I can't find my keys. / Seriously? It's bad enough that you lost your wallet. Now your keys? 6. Have you decided which phone you want? / Not yet. I'm still sitting on the fence. 7. I ran into my friend from high school while studying abroad! / How do you like that!)

Challenge: [+5 minutes] Divide the class into pairs and assign each pair one or two of the highlighted idioms / expressions from Exercise C, Spotlight. Have them create brief dialogues around them. Invite pairs to share dialogues.

F THINK AND EXPLAIN

Suggested teaching time:	5 minutes	Your actual teaching time:

- Have students discuss the questions in pairs.
- Then bring the class together to go over the answers.

Answers to Exercise F

Answers will vary but may include the following:
1. Paul suggests that Hyo study in Paris since that is his hometown, and ECE Paris has a top notch engineering program. A benefit would be picking up some French while he lived there.
2. When Hyo says money talks, he means that in order to continue attracting students from abroad, the university had to accommodate their language needs.

SPEAKING

Suggested teaching time:	5–10 minutes	Your actual teaching time:

- Call on volunteers to read the opinions. Clarify vocabulary as needed.
- Have pairs discuss the questions and explain the answers.

Option: [+5 minutes] Invite students to choose one of the opinions and write a paragraph rebutting the argument. For example, for the first quote, one could argue that it's not necessary to know English perfectly to be proficient. Point out that many people think they need to work on their accent to sound like a native speaker, but arguments have been made that having an accent makes you unique. The important thing is speaking correctly.

C ▶ 5:17 **SPOTLIGHT** Read and listen to a conversation about someone's plans. Notice the spotlighted language.

ENGLISH FOR TODAY'S WORLD
Understand a variety of accents.
Paul = French
Hyo = Korean

Paul: Are you still thinking about going overseas for a master's program?
Hyo: Actually, I've been checking out engineering programs in both Los Angeles and London. But I guess I'm still **on the fence**—I haven't made up my mind which I prefer.
Paul: Well, why don't you check out ECE Paris? They have a top-notch engineering program.
Hyo: Are you serious? **It's bad enough that** I wouldn't be able to handle the coursework in French. But between the culture shock and not being able to use my English there, I'd feel like **a fish out of water**.
Paul: Well, believe it or not, they're offering their engineering program in English.
Hyo: In Paris? You**'re pulling my leg**, right?
Paul: No way! I kid you not.
Hyo: No offense, Paul, but isn't France like the *last* place you'd expect anyone to be offering classes in English? I heard the French government actually tried to keep all university instruction in French.
Paul: That was probably true some years ago, but I guess they decided it was **a losing battle**. Apparently universities *had* to offer classes in English in order to continue attracting students from abroad—like you!
Hyo: **How do you like that!** I guess **money talks** …
Paul: At any rate, I'm sure you'd fall in love with my hometown. And besides, you could pick up some French while you're there.

D **UNDERSTAND IDIOMS AND EXPRESSIONS 1** Circle the correct word or phrase to complete each explanation.
1 If you're "on the fence," you haven't (**made a decision** / changed your plans).
2 If you feel like "a fish out of water," everything seems (exciting / **unfamiliar**) to you.
3 If someone "pulls your leg," he or she is (being serious / **only kidding**).
4 If something is "a losing battle," it's probably best to (**give up** / keep trying).

E **UNDERSTAND IDIOMS AND EXPRESSIONS 2** Complete each statement with the correct lettered explanation.
1 When Hyo says "It's bad enough that … ," he's …a… a emphasizing a problem.
2 When Hyo says "How do you like that!" he's …c… b offering an explanation.
3 When Hyo says "Money talks," he's …b… c expressing surprise.

F **THINK AND EXPLAIN** With a partner, discuss the questions and explain your answers. See page T111 for answers.
1 Why does Paul suggest that Hyo study in Paris? What would be the benefits?
2 What explanation is Hyo offering when he says, "I guess money talks … "?

SPEAKING Read the opinions. Explain why you agree or disagree. Discuss how you think you will use English in your own lives.

If you want to be considered proficient in English, you should never make mistakes, and you should sound like a native speaker.

These days, speaking English is like knowing how to use a computer— you need both skills for a better job.

The most important goal in learning English is to be able to function socially and communicate successfully.

I think the only real reason to learn English is to travel or work overseas. If those aren't your plans, it's not particularly useful.

LESSON 1

GOAL React to news about global issues

A ▶ 5:18 VOCABULARY PHRASAL VERBS* TO DISCUSS ISSUES AND PROBLEMS
Read and listen. Then listen again and repeat.

bring about make something happen; to cause to occur or exist	**lay off** end the employment of workers due to economic conditions
We need to agree about what the problems are if we expect to bring about changes.	The company recently announced they were laying off two hundred employees.
carry out achieve or accomplish a plan or project	**put up with** accept a bad situation or person without complaining
It's time the president carried out her promise to vaccinate all school-age children.	For many years, people in small villages have put up with inadequate roads.
come down with become sick with a particular illness	**run out of** use up all of something and not have any more of it
More than a million people have come down with the mosquito-borne virus.	If we're not careful, we'll run out of oil before alternative energy sources have been found.
come up with think of something such as an idea or a plan	**wipe out** end or destroy something completely so it no longer exists
Municipal governments need to come up with a new approach to reduce homelessness.	Ten years ago, few people could read or write in this country, but now illiteracy has been nearly wiped out.
go without live without something you need or usually have	
No one should have to go without clean drinking water.	

*Remember: Phrasal verbs contain a verb and one or more particles that together have their own meaning. Particles are most commonly prepositions and adverbs.

B ▶ 5:19 LISTEN TO ACTIVATE VOCABULARY
Listen to the conversations about global issues. After each conversation, complete the statement.

Conversation 1 The refugees will …… .
- **(a) go without food soon**
- b come down with something
- c carry out a plan

Conversation 2 Lots of people have been …… .
- a putting up with vaccinations
- **(b) coming down with the disease**
- c coming up with a plan

Conversation 3 The government hasn't …… .
- **(a) carried out the president's plan yet**
- b run out of supplies
- c laid off anyone

C VOCABULARY PRACTICE 1 Circle the correct phrasal verb to complete each sentence.

1. Because of increased availability of the flu vaccine this year, very few people have (come up with / **come down with**) the disease.
2. Many believe that it is essential to (carry out / **wipe out**) terrorist organizations.
3. A decrease in donations to humanitarian organizations will force thousands to (**go without** / put up with) the food they need to survive.
4. The oil company claims it will have to (bring about / **lay off**) one-third of its workforce on three continents.
5. Attempts to help the earthquake survivors were successful until the United Nations relief agencies (**ran out of** / laid off) supplies.
6. Change was (**brought about** / run out of) through the work of volunteers.
7. City residents will have to (**put up with** / lay off) the presence of foreign military troops.
8. Hopefully someone will (put up with / **come up with**) a plan to reverse global warming.
9. The actress's volunteer work is helping human rights groups (wipe out / **carry out**) their mission to help war refugees settle into their new lives overseas.

LESSON 1

GOAL React to news about global issues

A ▶5:18 VOCABULARY

Suggested teaching time:	5 minutes	Your actual teaching time:

- Have students skim the vocabulary and note phrasal verbs they are less familiar with.
- After students listen and repeat, bring the class together and answer any questions about the definitions. Read the Remember note. Point out that the following phrasal verbs are separable: *lay off, wipe out, carry out, bring about*. The rest of the phrasal verbs in the vocabulary list are inseparable. If necessary, refer students to the appendices (pages A3 and A4), for complete lists of separable and inseparable phrasal verbs.
- Have pairs use the phrasal verbs to create additional sentences about global issues. Assist as needed.
- Have students listen and repeat.

⭐ 🖨 Vocabulary-Building Strategies

B ▶5:19 LISTEN TO ACTIVATE VOCABULARY

Suggested teaching time:	10–15 minutes	Your actual teaching time:

- Have students skim the statements. Then have them listen to the conversations. Stop after each one to allow students to answer the question.
- Go over the answers as a class. Allow students to listen again to identify the statement that supports the answer. (1. I heard that relief groups are running out of food; 2. Have you heard about the polio epidemic in Afghanistan? 3. The president has come up with a plan. But the liberals and conservatives haven't been able to agree on how to pay for it.)

Challenge: [+5 minutes] Have students listen to each conversation again while looking at the list of phrasal verbs in the vocabulary items on page 112. Tell them to check phrasal verbs they hear and indicate in which conversation: 1, 2, or 3. (conversation 1: running out of food, come up with; conversation 2: wiped out; conversation 3: laid off, come up with)

C VOCABULARY PRACTICE 1

Suggested teaching time:	5 minutes	Your actual teaching time:

- Have students work individually to complete each sentence. Tell them to refer to the Vocabulary in Exercise A if they are not sure.
- Ask students to compare answers with a partner. Circulate and assist as needed.

Challenge: [+5 minutes] Invite students to write a statement using the alternate answer. Tell students to try to connect the statement to the topic of the original sentence. For example, for item 1, *The medical community has come up with a better way to calculate how much of a vaccine is needed.*

D VOCABULARY PRACTICE 2

Suggested teaching time:	5–10 minutes	Your actual teaching time:

- Ask students *What does UN stand for?* (United Nations)
- Have students do the exercise individually. If necessary, refer them to the Vocabulary on page 112 to review phrasal verbs. Have students compare answers with a partner.

CULTURE NOTE The United Nations (also called the UN) is a global organization that includes most of the countries in the world. Set up in 1945, following World War II, it promotes international peace and security as well as economic development. Its headquarters are in New York City.

NOW YOU CAN React to news about global issues

A ▶ 5:20 CONVERSATION SPOTLIGHT

Suggested teaching time:	5 minutes	Your actual teaching time:

These conversation strategies are implicit in the model:
- Use *Can you believe* to introduce something incredulous.
- Use *But on the bright side* to emphasize the positive aspects of a situation.
- Use *It just goes to show you* when illustrating proof of something.
- Use *That's another story* to point out another side of an argument.
- Use *You'd think* when it is surprising something isn't otherwise.

- Have students look at the photo and speculate what the woman is talking about. Ask *Do you think it's a light-hearted topic?* (No, she looks pretty serious.)
- Ask students to read and listen to the conversation.
- To check comprehension, ask *What has just happened in Northern Africa?* (a drought) *What is the bright side of the horrendous situation?* (People have been donating tons of money for relief,) *What can we infer about social media and this tragedy?* (that money is being raised via social media) *What second problem does the woman mention?* (corruption)

B ▶ 5:21 RHYTHM AND INTONATION

Suggested teaching time:	5 minutes	Your actual teaching time:

- Have students repeat chorally. Make sure they:
  ○ use rising intonation for *Can you believe what's been happening in Northern Africa?* (line 1); *You mean the drought?* (line 2); *It makes you feel hopeless, doesn't it?* (line 7)
  ○ use emphatic stress on *believe* in *Can you believe* (line 1)
  ○ stress *that* in *Well, that's another story* (line 7) and *think* in *You'd think* (line 8)

C CONVERSATION ACTIVATOR

Suggested teaching time:	5 minutes	Your actual teaching time:

Conversation Activator Video

- Have students read the newspaper clippings. Point out how the conversation in Exercise A, Conversation Spotlight, reflects the information in the first clipping.
- Divide the class into pairs. Instruct students that they will use the model in Exercise A, Conversation Spotlight, to role-play their own conversation with a partner. They can refer to the newspaper clippings or use current stories they are familiar with as well.
- Refer students to the list of phrasal verbs to discuss issues and problems in Exercise A on page 112.
- Ask a volunteer to read the words in the Recycle This Language box. Encourage students to incorporate these words into their conversation.
- Reinforce the use of the spotlighted conversation strategies. For example, *Can you believe; But on the bright side; You'd think*.
- Bring students' attention to the Don't Stop! note. Ask a volunteer to read the bulleted points. Explain that students should continue talking after they have covered the points in the original Conversation Spotlight.
- Tell students to change roles, so each student gets a chance to play A and B.

For more support, play the Conversation Activator Video before students do this activity themselves. After the video, ask students how the model has been changed by the actors. *Note:* You can print the script or you can view it on the video player on the ActiveTeach.

Conversation Activator: Speaking Booster

Option: PRONUNCIATION BOOSTER *(Teaching notes p. T150)*

Pronunciation Pair Work

T113   UNIT 10 LESSON 1

D VOCABULARY PRACTICE 2
Complete the article, using the appropriate forms of the phrasal verbs.

UN HUNGER RELIEF

The UN World Food Program (WFP) is the world's largest humanitarian organization dealing with the issue of hunger and how to (1) **wipe out** malnutrition, especially among children. Its goal is to (2) **bring about** improvements in food production and to (3) **carry out** its plans to provide food assistance to millions of people in seventy-five countries around the world. Whenever people are forced to (4) **go without** food because of droughts or war, the WFP tries to help. Under these famine conditions, people are unable to feed their families and they are forced to (5) **put up with** being hungry on a daily basis. Making the situation worse, many of its malnourished victims are more vulnerable due to weakened immune systems and may (6) **come down with** contagious diseases. It is the WFP's responsibility to make sure that relief groups do not (7) **run out of** essential emergency supplies. In the 1990s, the WFP (8) **came up with** a successful money-saving idea for responding more quickly to emergencies using small teams of experts to assess the situation before committing full-scale resources.

NOW YOU CAN React to news about global issues

A ▶ 5:20 CONVERSATION SPOTLIGHT
Read and listen. Notice the spotlighted conversation strategies.

A: Can you believe what's been happening in Northern Africa?
B: You mean the drought? It's just horrendous.
A: Awful. But on the bright side, people have been donating tons of money for relief. I find that really inspiring.
B: Totally. It just goes to show you how powerful social media can be.
A: But on the other hand, it's appalling how much corruption there is.
B: Well, that's another story … It makes you feel hopeless, doesn't it?
A: Yeah. You'd think someone could do something to stop it.

B ▶ 5:21 RHYTHM AND INTONATION
Listen again and repeat. Then practice the conversation with a partner.

C CONVERSATION ACTIVATOR
Create a similar conversation, using one of these news stories. Start like this: *Can you believe …?* Be sure to change roles and then partners.

DON'T STOP!
- Describe the news in more detail.
- Say more about your response to the news.
- Say as much as you can.

RECYCLE THIS LANGUAGE
- It's a slippery slope. / It's like opening a can of worms.
- The good outweighs the bad.
- Before you know it, …
- Don't get me wrong.
- What [bothers / concerns] me is …

PRONUNCIATION BOOSTER p. 150
Intonation of tag questions

Celebrities Raise Millions for Famine Victims
The North African drought has forced four million people to go without adequate food and water. Some of the world's best-known celebrities have come up with a plan to use social media to raise money for humanitarian efforts.

TERRORIST ATTACK ATTRACTS INTERNATIONAL ACTIVISM
After hearing about the bombing in Beirut that left forty dead, Colombian businesswoman Leticia Gómez decided to use her connections to carry out a campaign to help the families of the victims. Gómez lost her husband to a bombing in Bogotá in the eighties and knows firsthand how devastating terrorism can be.

STEPS TAKEN TO AVOID EPIDEMIC IN THE PHILIPPINES
Hundreds have come down with an unknown illness in Mindanao, causing authorities to restrict both domestic and international travel. Doctors Without Borders has agreed to send a team to investigate.

China Carries Out Conference Recommendations
The government has come up with a long-term plan for reducing factory emissions in China, where urban residents have had to put up with high levels of pollution with its resulting health consequences.

LESSON 2

GOAL Describe the impact of foreign imports

A ▶ 5:22 **GRAMMAR SPOTLIGHT** Read the people's opinions and notice the spotlighted grammar.

"I do a lot of business travel, and it's amazing how you **run into** so many foreign things—for example, a Starbucks coffee shop from the U.S. in Bogotá, Colombia. Hello! Colombia already *has* great coffee! Recently I **came across** the Japanese clothing chain UNIQLO in New York. Almost everywhere you go now, you can **count on** being able to find a restaurant that serves Indian, Thai, Japanese, or Mexican food. In any city, people can **take up** tai chi from China, yoga from India, or capoeira from Brazil. Seems like every place is becoming the same."

Gina Falcone, U.S.

"Every time my kids **turn** their tablets or smartphones **on**, I worry. I'm concerned about the influence foreign games and websites will have on them. I don't particularly **care for** some of the values they teach. But my kids are crazy about their gadgets. If I were to ask my kids to **give** them **up**, I'd never hear the end of it! They can't imagine **going without** them. I've been trying to **talk** them **into** doing other things, but it's a bit of a losing battle, I'm afraid. I guess I just have to learn to **put up with** their devices."

Mehmet Demirkahn, Turkey

"Nowadays you see foreign brands everywhere you look. Before you **throw** the packaging from a food item **away**, read the label—it might say it comes from the U.S. or Mexico. **Try** a blouse **on** at the store—nine times out of ten, it'll have come from China, Vietnam, or Bangladesh. Or **try** some new product **out** at the electronics store and there's a good chance it's imported from Korea. Some people worry that imports will **wipe out** our own local products. But the way I see it, we can enjoy foreign things and still value and appreciate our own."

Sophia Freitas, Brazil

B **ACTIVATE PRIOR KNOWLEDGE** Would people in your country express opinions similar to the ones in the Grammar Spotlight? Explain.

> **GRAMMAR BOOSTER** p. 142
> Phrasal verbs: expansion

C **GRAMMAR** SEPARABILITY OF TRANSITIVE PHRASAL VERBS

Remember: Transitive verbs are verbs that can have direct objects. Transitive *phrasal verbs* can be separable or inseparable.

Separable

A direct object noun can generally come after or before the particle of a separable phrasal verb.

  Check out their website. OR **Check** their website **out**.

However, a direct object pronoun must come before the particle.

  Check it **out**. NOT Check out it.

Inseparable

A direct object noun or pronoun always comes after the particle of an inseparable phrasal verb.

  They **cater to** younger customers. NOT They cater younger customers to.
  I **ran into** her at the park. NOT I ran her into the park.

Be careful! Some phrasal verbs are always separated. The particle never comes directly after the verb.

  I **talked** them **into** contributing money. NOT I talked into them contributing money.

Separable
bring about	give up	wipe out	turn on / off
carry out	lay off	try on	throw away
figure out	pick up	try out	
find out	take up		

Inseparable
care for	come down with	put up with
cater to	count on	run into
come across	go after	run out of
come up with	go without	

Always separated

do (sth.) over   start (sth.) over   talk (s.o.) into (sth.)

For a complete list with definitions, see pp. 124–126.

UNIT 10

LESSON 2

GOAL Describe the impact of foreign imports

A ▶ 5:22 GRAMMAR SPOTLIGHT

Suggested teaching time:	5–10 minutes	Your actual teaching time:

- To warm up, elicit that foreign imports are products brought from one country into another so that they can be sold there. Point out that the focus in the lesson will be on the impact or influence foreign imports have on our lives.
- Ask students to look at the photos of the people. Call on a volunteer to read their names and where they are from.
- Have students listen to the opinions as they read along.
- To check comprehension, ask *Why does Gina think it's strange that there is a Starbucks in Bogotá?* (Because Colombia is known for its own great coffee; it's ironic to her that an American brand would be available there.) *Is Gina's final comment positive or negative?* (Negative; by saying everything is becoming the same, she is criticizing how no place is truly unique any more.) *What is Mehmet's problem?* (He doesn't like foreign games and websites for his kids.) *Why not?* (He doesn't care for the values they teach.) *What three categories of items does Sophia mention that have foreign labels?* (food, clothes, electronics) *Does she think foreign imports have a negative impact?* (No; she thinks we can enjoy both foreign things and our own.)

CULTURE NOTE *Hello!* As used in Gina's quote is a popular colloquial way to suggest something is obvious.

B ACTIVATE PRIOR KNOWLEDGE

Suggested teaching time:	5 minutes	Your actual teaching time:

- In pairs, have students discuss with whom people in their country might agree. Circulate and assist. If students need more direction, ask specifically *Is the view in your country that all cities in the world are starting to look the same? Is there concern over influence of foreign games on children in your country? Do people in your culture see value in having imported items in addition to their own products?*
- Bring the class together and have students share.

C GRAMMAR

Suggested teaching time:	10–15 minutes	Your actual teaching time:

- To review, ask a volunteer to read the Remember note. Write these examples on the board:

    Could you please <u>turn down</u> the TV? (transitive: can take a direct object)

    Have they <u>checked in</u> yet? (intransitive: doesn't take a direct object)

- Explain that a transitive verb needs a direct object to complete its meaning.
- Focus on separable phrasal verbs. Have a volunteer read the statement about direct object nouns and the example sentence. Ask *What is the direct object noun in this sentence?* (website) Point out that the direct object noun can appear before or after the particle.
- Then have a volunteer read the next explanation about direct object pronouns and the example sentence. Make sure students understand that when the direct object of a separable phrasal verb is a pronoun, it must come before the particle.
- Tell students to skim the list of separable phrasal verbs in the box. Elicit additional example sentences. Make sure students place the direct object noun or pronoun correctly.
- Focus on inseparable phrasal verbs. Have students read the statement and the example sentence to themselves. Ask *What is the direct object in the sentence?* (customers) Help students notice that the direct object must appear after the particle.
- Tell students to skim the list of inseparable phrasal verbs in the box. Elicit additional example sentences, making sure students place the direct object after the particle.
- Finally, have students read the Be careful! note and the example sentence. Then elicit additional example sentences, making sure students place the direct object noun or pronoun before the particle.

Option: GRAMMAR BOOSTER *(Teaching notes p. T142)*

⭐ 🖨 **Inductive Grammar Activity**

D UNDERSTAND THE GRAMMAR

Suggested teaching time:	5 minutes	Your actual teaching time:

- Create a chart on the or print it out from the ActiveTeach and distribute it to students.

	Phrasal Verbs	
Separable	Inseparable	Always separated

- Call on students to fill it in with phrasal verbs from Exercise A, Grammar Spotlight, on page 114.
- Then have students work individually to change the sentences with separable phrasal verbs to the opposite format.
- Bring the class together to go over the answers.

Answers to Exercise D

<u>Separable</u>: take up, turn on, give up, throw away, try on, try out, wipe out

In any city, people can **take** tai chi **up** from China, yoga from India, or capoeira from Brazil.

Every time my **kids turn** on their tablets or smartphones, I worry.

If I were to ask my kids to **give up** their gadgets, I'd never hear the end of it.

Before you **throw away** the packaging from a food item, read the label—it might say it comes from the U.S. or Mexico.

Try on a blouse at the store—nine times out of ten, it'll have come from China, Vietnam, or Bangladesh.

Or try out some new product at the electronics store and there's a good chance it's imported from Korea.

Some people worry that imports will **wipe** our local products **out**.

⭐ 🖨 Extra Grammar Exercises

🖨 Graphic Organizer

E GRAMMAR PRACTICE

Suggested teaching time:	5 minutes	Your actual teaching time:

- Before students do the exercise, have them skim the phrasal verbs and determine if they are separable or inseparable. (separable: 1, 5, and 6; inseparable: 1, 2, 3, and 4) Remind students that with separable phrasal verbs, the direct object pronoun must come before the particle. Tell students to use the correct verb form in each sentence.
- Have students complete the exercise individually and then compare answers with a partner.
- Bring the class together and go over the answers.

Challenge: [+5 minutes] Ask *Which item has an additional phrasal verb within the sentence?* (3, laid off) *Is lay off usually a separable or inseparable verb?* (separable) *Is it separable here?* (no) Explain that in the passive, a phrasal verb that is normally separable has to stay together.

NOW YOU CAN Describe the impact of foreign imports

A NOTEPADDING

Suggested teaching time:	5 minutes	Your actual teaching time:

- Review that in Exercise A on the previous page, the various people gave their opinions on the impact of foreign imports. Explain that here students will voice their opinions on foreign imports.
- Have students work individually to list examples on their notepad. Then ask *Who wrote something in the other category? What categories did you add?* Tell students they can add any ideas if they come across these imports regularly.

B DISCUSSION ACTIVATOR

Suggested teaching time:	5–10 minutes	Your actual teaching time:

🎥 Discussion Activator Video

- Divide the class into pairs and have students use their descriptions from Exercise A, Notepadding, to discuss if the imports have had a positive or negative impact. Encourage the pairs to ask each other questions and provide details and examples. The goal is to say as much as they can about them.

For more support, play the Discussion Activator Video before students do this activity. After each video, ask if the students in the video included sufficient details. *Note:* You can print the script or you can view it on the video player on the ActiveTeach.

Option: [+5 minutes] Ask students to name products or traditions from their country that they think would have a positive impact on other countries.

C PAIR WORK

Suggested teaching time:	5–10 minutes	Your actual teaching time:

- Have students look at the photos. Call on volunteers to read the captions. Point out that *to go international* is an expression that means to become available and popular internationally.
- Have students read the model statements in pairs and respond, agreeing or disagreeing. Encourage students to provide examples and use phrasal verbs where possible.

D **UNDERSTAND THE GRAMMAR** Which phrasal verbs in the Grammar Spotlight are separable? Rewrite each of those sentences, with the direct object in a different position. See page T115 for answers.

E **GRAMMAR PRACTICE** Complete the sentences, using a form of the phrasal verb with the pronoun *it* or *them*. Pay attention to whether or not the phrasal verb is separable.

1 Yoga is really popular. Even my great-grandmother has (take up) taken it up.
2 Although only a small minority of the population can understand English, English words are visible everywhere. You often (come across) come across them on signs, product ads, and even clothing.
3 The workers who have been laid off have highly developed skills. It may not be so easy to (talk into) talk them into learning all new skills.
4 Because young adults are tech-savvy and have tremendous economic power, many Internet companies have developed marketing campaigns that (go after) go after them exclusively.
5 At the International Trade Fair, foreign companies offer samples of their products. People can (try out) try them out before deciding whether to buy them.
6 Once a foreign brand has become popular, it's hard to for people to (give up) to give them up.

NOW YOU CAN Describe the impact of foreign imports

A **NOTEPADDING** On your notepad, list examples of imports from foreign countries or cultures that you come across regularly.

Foods:	Entertainment:
Music:	Vehicles:
Products for your home:	Sports and games:
Clothing / personal accessories:	Other:

B **DISCUSSION ACTIVATOR** Have the imports you listed on your notepad had a positive or negative impact? Explain, providing examples. Say as much as you can.

C **PAIR WORK** Read the statements about foreign imports. Discuss whether you agree or disagree with them, providing examples. Use phrasal verbs when you can.

> There's a growing trend towards **giving up** local traditions and replacing them with imported things. But I question the wisdom of just **throwing away** our long-held traditions like that.

> Young people **are picking up** values from foreign media, so culturally we're becoming more and more alike. I wonder what would happen if we lose the things that make us different.

Hip-hop style has gone international.

Chinese restaurants are popular in Peru.

People dance salsa in Japan.

LESSON 3

GOAL Discuss the pros and cons of globalization

A **READING WARM-UP** Do people in your country generally view increased international trade positively or negatively? Explain.

B ▶ 5:23 **READING** Read the article on the effects of globalization. Do you share its concerns? Why or why not? See page T116 for answers.

GLOBALIZATION
DOES IT LIVE UP TO EXPECTATIONS?

Globalization and increased free trade in this century have brought the world's cultures and economies together. We depend more than ever on each other to thrive. Along with advances in technology and communication, we have become more interconnected as people, corporations, and brands travel across borders more easily than ever before. Nevertheless, most people agree that the social, economic, environmental, and political changes caused by globalization have brought both positive and negative results.

THE PROMISE
Advocates of globalization believed it would make the world smaller and bring diverse people and cultures closer. They were right. People in cities on opposite sides of the world can easily get in touch by phone, e-mail, instant messaging, or teleconference. Ease of communication and freer global trade have resulted in improved efficiency and competition. Companies are able to respond quickly to economic changes and market demands. As cooperation—and competition—have increased, new technologies are shared and developed.

Many countries have experienced improvements in their standard of living. For many people, an economic benefit of increased imports and exports has been an increase in income. Consumers enjoy a wider variety of choices when they shop. And as a result of increased prosperity, it has been possible to increase investment in new infrastructure—roads, bridges, and buildings.

THE OTHER SIDE OF THE STORY
While globalization promised to benefit everyone with an increase in worldwide wealth and prosperity, critics cite evidence of a widening gap between rich and poor. In developed countries, such as the U.S., corporations outsource both manufacturing and customer service jobs to developing countries in Asia and Latin America, where labor costs are lower. For example, India's economy benefits from the establishment of call centers, where English-speaking staff provide 24/7 technical support by phone and Internet to customers all over the world. Their technicians can do so at about one-fifth the cost of what companies would have to pay workers in developed economies for the same service. So while Indian workers benefit, workers in other countries complain that their jobs have been taken away.

Critics of globalization argue that free trade has made the world so competitive that criminal activities have flourished. For example, child labor, which is illegal in many countries, has increased to fill manufacturing demands for gold and textiles. Recent news reports have exposed the use of slavery on merchant ships, where workers are mistreated and forced to work without receiving any wages. Economic opportunities made possible by globalization have also encouraged corruption, in which government officials agree to ignore unethical business practices. Some argue that a global economy has helped drug cartels and terrorists move people and materials across borders more easily.

As internationally recognized fast-food chains have expanded throughout the world, critics complain that the fried foods and sugary drinks they serve have been replacing healthier local eating traditions and increasing the consumption of unhealthy junk food among young people. Some argue that globalization has led to a homogenization of culture in general—that local traditions are quickly being replaced by imported ones.

Even worse, without international regulation, developing countries such as Nigeria are becoming dumping grounds for hazardous industrial waste. In other countries such as China, increased development has brought with it uncontrolled pollution, reaching sky-high levels that threaten public health and contribute to global warming. And globalization has also been a strain on the environment as more and more natural resources are tapped for manufacturing.

Obviously, we can't turn back the clock on globalization. And we know that those countries that have embraced it have experienced increased economic growth. However, it is also clear that there are challenges to overcome despite globalization's many benefits.

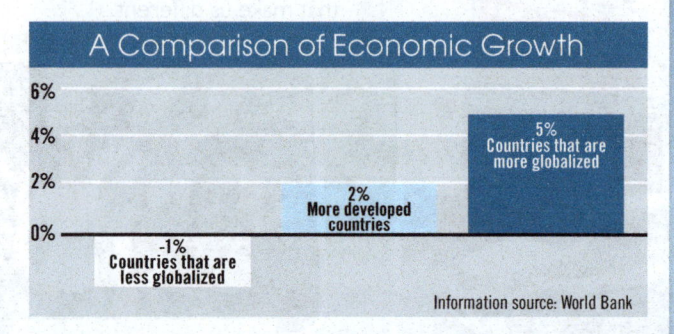

A Comparison of Economic Growth

- −1% Countries that are less globalized
- 2% More developed countries
- 5% Countries that are more globalized

Information source: World Bank

LESSON 3

GOAL Discuss the pros and cons of globalization

A READING WARM-UP

Suggested teaching time:	5 minutes	Your actual teaching time:

- To warm up, focus on the title of the lesson. Elicit that *globalization* refers to the process of extending something, for example a business, to other parts of the world.
- Ask a volunteer to read the question in the direction line. Call on students to answer.

B ▶ 5:23 READING

Suggested teaching time:	15–20 minutes	Your actual teaching time:

- Ask a student to read the title, including the question. Make sure students understand that *to live up to expectations* means that something is as good as one anticipates it will be. Ask *What do you think the expectations are?* (Possible answers: that the world will become smaller, people will become more aware, societies will become more developed, equality will increase) Ask *Do you think globalization lives up to expectations?*
- As students read and listen, tell them to underline information in the article that will help them answer the focus questions in the direction line.
- Have volunteers share their answers to the focus question with the class.

Answers to Exercise A
Answers will vary but may include the following:
I share the concerns related to globalization. There is a widening gap between the rich and the poor, giving an advantage to more developed and more globalized countries. Poorer countries can't be left behind, and the environment needs to be given more attention.

Challenge: [+5 minutes] On the board, write *Do you think that it is possible for everyone to benefit in the competitive global world? Why? Why not?* Have students discuss. Then have students speculate about what can be done to ensure that globalization works for the benefit of the most people possible.

⭐ 🖨 Reading Strategies

C UNDERSTAND MEANING FROM CONTEXT

| Suggested teaching time: | 5–10 minutes | Your actual teaching time: |

- Before doing the exercise, have students number the paragraphs in the article, 1 to 8.
- Have students work individually or in pairs to complete the exercise. Encourage them to utilize context to help determine the meanings.
- Circulate and assist as needed. Assist if students need help finding the words (*globalization* is in paragraph 1, *exports* is in paragraph 3, *investment* is in paragraph 3, *infrastructure* is in paragraph 3, *prosperity* is in paragraphs 3 and 5, *outsource* is in paragraph 4, *homogenization* is in paragraph 6).

🖨 **Extra Reading Comprehension Questions**

D IDENTIFY SUPPORTING IDEAS

| Suggested teaching time: | 5–10 minutes | Your actual teaching time: |

- Students will likely need assistance navigating the article. Note that answers to individual questions often appear in different paragraphs (1. improved standard of living in paragraph 3, decreased standard of living in paragraph 4; 2. paragraph 5; 3. workers who lose income in paragraph 3, workers who are denied income in paragraph 5; 4. pros of foreign imports in paragraph 2, cons of foreign imports in paragraph 6).
- Go over the answers as a class.

E INTERPRET INFORMATION IN A GRAPH

| Suggested teaching time: | 5 minutes | Your actual teaching time: |

- Have students study the graph in pairs and answer the questions.
- Bring the class together to discuss. Invite students to discuss which countries mentioned in the article would fall into the categories less globalized, more developed, and more globalized.

⭐🖨 **Extra Challenge Reading Activity**

NOW YOU CAN Discuss the pros and cons of globalization

A NOTEPADDING

| Suggested teaching time: | 5 minutes | Your actual teaching time: |

- Call on volunteers to read the heads on the notepad. Point out that the word *impact* can be positive or negative. For example, a company could be very environmentally conscious (positive impact) or carelessly pollute the environment (negative impact). Tell students be specific with details.
- Have a volunteer read the list of international companies. Ask *Are there any companies you've never heard of?* Have students explain what each company does.
- Then have students list companies that have had a specific impact on their country. If students don't know, tell them they can look up companies online.

CULTURE NOTE Apple™ is a prominent American hardware and software company headquartered in the United States. British Petroleum (BP™) is one of the top four oil companies in the world. IKEA™ is a Swedish retailer that specializes in affordable home furnishings. Nestle™, headquartered in Switzerland, is the world's largest food and beverage company. Samsung™, headquartered in South Korea, manufactures mobile phones and related devices, in addition to other electronics. The Gap™ is a popular U.S. clothing store.

B DISCUSSION

| Suggested teaching time: | 5 minutes | Your actual teaching time: |

- Ask a student to read the direction line. Then call on a volunteer to read the model answer.
- Have students discuss in pairs or small groups.
- Poll the class by asking *Overall, do you think globalization is good or bad for your country?*

Option: [+5 minutes] Have students think of the most popular foreign product or company in their country. Tell them to write a paragraph describing the impact it has had on the country's economy. Then have students read their paragraphs to the class. On the board, write the name of each product or company that students discuss. Encourage students to comment on each other's choices. Then take a vote to see which is the most popular product or company.

Challenge: [+5 minutes] Conduct a globalization debate. Divide the class in half. Assign one group to be for globalization and the other group to be against globalization. Tell groups to compile their arguments, referring to the article on page 116 as well as to Exercise A, Notepadding, and the discussion they had in Exercise B. Give each group an opportunity to present their argument. Then give groups an opportunity to rebut the opposing argument and defend their point of view. Judge the most solid argument and declare the winner of the debate.

⭐🖨 **Discussion: Speaking Booster**

C **UNDERSTAND MEANING FROM CONTEXT** Match each word from the article with its definition.

b 1 globalization   **a** money put into a company or business to encourage growth and make a profit
c 2 exports   **b** the act of making it easier to produce products and trade them internationally
a 3 investment   **c** products sold to other countries
f 4 infrastructure   **d** use other countries' services rather than one's own
e 5 prosperity   **e** financial success
d 6 outsource   **f** things that make transport of products efficient
g 7 homogenization   **g** causing things to become more similar

D **IDENTIFY SUPPORTING IDEAS** Answer the questions, supporting your answers with information in the article.

1 What are some specific examples of both improved and decreased standard of living, caused by globalization? Improved: increased number of available products; improvement in the infrastructure.
Decreased: many workers have lost jobs because workers in countries like China and India are cheaper.
2 What are some areas where businesses or governments could make investments that might address some of the challenges of globalization? Refuse to use unpaid or child workers in their companies.
Greater legislation and crack down on child labor and terrorism.
3 What are two examples given that describe workers who lose or are denied income? Manufacturing and customer service jobs and workers on merchant ships.
4 What examples are given to illustrate the pros and cons of availability of foreign imports? Pros: greater choice; cons less diversity.

E **INTERPRET INFORMATION IN A GRAPH** According to the graph, who benefits the most from globalization? Who benefits the least? Explain.
Answers will vary but may include the following:
According to the graph, countries that are more globalized enjoy the most economic growth. Countries that are less globalized suffer from economic decline.

Increased imports and exports have led to economic growth in many countries.

NOW YOU CAN   Discuss the pros and cons of globalization

A **NOTEPADDING** On your notepad, write the names of international companies that have had an economic, social, environmental, or political impact in your country.

B **DISCUSSION** What benefits or problems have these companies brought to your country? Overall, do you think globalization is good or bad for your country? Explain.

have had an economic impact	have had a social impact
have had an environmental impact	have had a political impact

❝ Toyota's investment in local factories has been good for the country. It provides employment and pays good wages, raising the standard of living for a lot of people. ❞

Some well-known international companies
Apple   Nestle
British Petroleum (BP)   Samsung
IKEA   The Gap

LESSON 4

GOAL Suggest ways to avoid culture shock

A **LISTENING WARM-UP** **DISCUSSION** Read the definition of culture shock. What feelings of anxiety or confusion might someone experiencing culture shock have? Give some examples of situations that might cause culture shock.

> **culture shock** n. the feelings of anxiety and confusion that people have when they visit a foreign country and experience a new culture for the first time

B ▶ 5:24 **LISTEN TO SUMMARIZE** Listen to the radio program. In your own words, summarize the characteristics of each of the four stages of culture shock.

Susan Cahill

Stage one: The honeymoon stage. Everything is new and exciting.

Stage two: The frustration stage. Things about the new culture start to bother you, especially things that are very different from your home country. You realize how different you are from the people in the new country. This is the frustration stage.

Stage three: The depression stage. The third stage is the hardest. You don't know if you can actually adjust to the new culture. You may feel sad a lot of the time. Some people can't sleep and feel lonely and even angry.

Stage four: The acceptance stage. You accept the differences in the culture, weather, people, and language. You've probably made some friends and learned the language.

Berat Yildiz

C ▶ 5:25 **LISTEN TO CONFIRM INFORMATION** Listen again. Check the correct answers, according to the program.

1 Which of the following disorienting experiences did not cause negative feelings for Berat in London?
   - ☑ the traffic
   - ☑ the money
   - ☐ the weather
   - ☐ the food
   - ☐ people's behavior

2 Which symptoms of culture shock did Berat experience?
   - ☐ headaches
   - ☑ disappointment
   - ☑ sadness
   - ☐ lack of sleep
   - ☑ loneliness

3 Which of the following were mentioned as signs that Berat was in the final stage of culture shock?
   - ☑ dressing right for cold weather
   - ☑ making friends
   - ☐ calling home
   - ☑ appreciating cultural differences
   - ☐ finding Turkish restaurants

118   UNIT 10

LESSON 4

GOAL Suggest ways to avoid culture shock

A LISTENING WARM-UP

Suggested teaching time:	5 minutes	Your actual teaching time:

- Write *culture shock* on the board. Invite a volunteer to read the definition in the book. Say *I had major culture shock when I moved to New York from a small town in Maine. There was so much noise and activity! I couldn't hear myself think.* Then invite students to share how someone with culture shock might feel and also if they or someone they know has experienced culture shock.

B ▶5:24 LISTEN TO SUMMARIZE

Suggested teaching time:	15–20 minutes	Your actual teaching time:

- **Pre-listening:** Have students look at the two photos. Ask *What will the format of this conversation be?* (a radio interview) *Where do you think Berat is from?* Tell students they will hear about the four stages of culture shock. Ask students if they can guess what these might be. Write student guesses on the board.
- **First listening:** Have students listen once to the interview, writing down the names of the stages as they hear them.
- **Second listening:** Have students listen again and then summarize each stage.

Option: [+5 minutes] Ask students to name topics that contributed to Berat's culture shock. (Possible answers: weather, food, money, people's behavior, traffic) Tell students to imagine they are moving to London for a year to study. With a partner, have them discuss which things they think would be hardest to get used to.

Challenge: [+5 minutes] In pairs, have students role-play a radio interview following the model in the listening. One student will play the role of the interviewer, and the other student will play the role of the person who experienced culture shock. Have students prepare scenarios related to the various stages of culture shock, referring to the notes they took in Exercise B. Invite students to use a culture they know something about and to be creative about what caused the culture shock.

⭐ 🖨 Listening Strategies

C ▶5:25 LISTEN TO CONFIRM INFORMATION

Suggested teaching time:	10 minutes	Your actual teaching time:

- **Pre-listening:** Have volunteers read each question thinking carefully about meaning.
- **Listening:** Have students listen and adjust any answers.
- Go over the answers as a class.

Option: [+5 minutes] In pairs, have students look at the topics in items 1 and 2. Ask *Which disorienting experiences from item 1 have you experienced or do you think you might experience in a foreign culture? Which symptoms of culture shock from item 2 have you experienced or do you think you might experience if you traveled to a foreign culture?*

D ▶ 5:26 LISTEN TO UNDERSTAND MEANING FROM CONTEXT

| Suggested teaching time | 5–10 minutes | Your actual teaching time |

- Have students listen to the excerpts. Stop after each one to let them answer the questions.
- Go over the answers as a class. For each item, ask *What in the context helped direct your answer?* (1. *Let's listen as Berat describes what it was like during his first month here*; 2. *it had long been a dream of mine to study here*; 3. *In Turkey we drive on the right, but as everyone knows drivers in London drive on the left*; In item 4, various negative symptoms are listed, followed by *Fortunately* which introduces an improvement; 5. *I had gotten used to the weather . . . crossing the street was a piece of cake by then . . . I made friends.*)

NOW YOU CAN Suggest ways to avoid culture shock

A NOTEPADDING

| Suggested teaching time | 5–10 minutes | Your actual teaching time |

- Bring students' attention to the cartoon at the bottom of the page. Ask *Do you know a country where people eat frogs?* (Frog legs are delicacies in French and Chinese cuisine.) *How would you feel if you were that man?*
- Call on students to read the topics in the list. Explain and provide or elicit examples as needed. For example, for traditional leisure activities, in a country that has beautiful mountains and a lot of snow in the winter, it could be common to go skiing every chance one gets. If a visitor to this country doesn't know how to ski, or does not enjoy winter sports, it could lead to culture shock.
- Then have students work individually to check off the topics that could cause culture shock to a visitor in their country. Have students add to the other category if they have other ideas.
- Next, have students choose three of the checked topics that they think might be the most surprising and write notes suggesting ways to avoid surprise and culture shock. (Possible answers: for formality and informality: In the United States children often call adults by their first names; for public transportation: A young person might not give up a seat to an elderly person)
- Point out that often there isn't something one can physically do to avoid culture shock related to a particular topic. However, being informed can help prevent surprise and helps a person to fit in faster and avoid making cultural mistakes.

B PAIR WORK

| Suggested teaching time | 5 minutes | Your actual teaching time |

- Divide the class into pairs. If a class consists of students of different cultures, you can pair up students from the same cultures to allow comparison, but this is not necessary. Have pairs discuss the topics presented in the direction line.
- Then bring the class together and call on pairs to share. Which topics were mentioned the most?

OPTIONAL WRITING [+15–20 minutes]

- Students can do this assignment individually or in pairs if they are from the same culture. Have them refer to ideas on their notepads and then write the article.
- Offer an opportunity for peer review in class, or collect students' work and provide individual feedback.

D ▶ 5:26 **LISTEN TO UNDERSTAND MEANING FROM CONTEXT** Listen to the excerpts from the radio program. Use the context to help you complete each statement.

1. When Susan Cahill says that Berat Yildiz knows about culture shock "firsthand," she means he knows it from …… .
   - **(a)** experience
   - **b** his studies
   - **c** his culture
2. When Berat says he felt like he was "in heaven," he means he felt …… .
   - **a** worried
   - **b** shocked
   - **(c)** great
3. When Berat says he found some things "disorienting," he means he felt …… .
   - **a** comfortable
   - **(b)** confused
   - **c** angry
4. When Susan says there is "a light at the end of the tunnel," she means that things will …… .
   - **(a)** get better
   - **b** get worse
   - **c** stay the same
5. When Berat says he got his "feet back on the ground," he means he stopped …… .
   - **(a)** feeling confused
   - **b** feeling happy
   - **c** thinking about Turkish food

NOW YOU CAN Suggest ways to avoid culture shock

A **NOTEPADDING** Check the aspects of your culture you think might cause culture shock to a visitor to your country. Add others. Then choose the three from the list you think are the most difficult to deal with. Write notes suggesting ways to avoid the negative effects of each one.

- ☐ local dishes
- ☐ eating and drinking customs
- ☐ the way people act at work
- ☐ greeting customs
- ☐ the way people socialize
- ☐ local holidays
- ☐ sense of humor
- ☐ formality and informality
- ☐ traditional leisure activities
- ☐ apologizing
- ☐ the do's and don'ts for clothing
- ☐ treatment of children
- ☐ customs for keeping pets
- ☐ how people shop
- ☐ public transportation
- ☐ driving or walking in traffic
- ☐ other ……………………

1 ……………………

2 ……………………

3 ……………………

B **PAIR WORK** Tell your partner why you chose the three topics. Describe your ideas for helping a visitor avoid the worst symptoms of culture shock.

OPTIONAL WRITING Write an article for visitors to this country, suggesting ways to be prepared for culture shock and avoid the most negative symptoms.

Try it. It's delicious!

WRITING Rebutting an opposing point of view

A WRITING SKILL Study the rules.

When writing a rebuttal to an opposing argument or point of view, support your ideas by presenting them one by one. Following is an outline to organize your essay effectively.

I. Introductory paragraph

Explain the issue and summarize the opposing point of view. Include a thesis statement stating your own point of view.

II. Supporting paragraphs

In each paragraph, state one aspect of the point of view you are rebutting. Use details and examples to support your own point of view.

III. Concluding paragraph

Summarize your point of view.

Expressions for introducing others' arguments:
According to [Bill Gates], …
[Some people] say / think / feel that …
[Many experts] argue / believe that …
It may be true that …
It has been argued / said / pointed out that …

Transitions and subordinating conjunctions for your rebuttal:
However, …   All the same, …
Nevertheless, …   In spite of this, …
Even so, …

WRITING MODEL

I There are many people who feel that globalization is causing more problems than it is solving. **Nevertheless, it is my opinion that, overall, globalization has contributed to a better world.** We need to accept it as a reality of today's world and do what we can to make it work for everyone.

II **Critics argue that** many countries have not benefited as much as others. **All the same,** we shouldn't assume that all countries will benefit at the same speed or time. It is a fact that free trade has been a tremendous benefit to nations in East and Southeast Asia. Their economies have grown substantially in this century and their standard of living has greatly improved. There's no reason to believe this won't happen elsewhere, for example in West Africa.

It has been argued that globalization has increased the spread of disease, worsened pollution, and made it easier for criminals to cross borders. **In spite of this,** I believe that free trade and increased international cooperation have also made it easier for nations to fight these problems more effectively. With attention, these are problems that can be solved.

III Clearly, globalization has areas for improvement. **Even so, I believe the advantages of globalization far outweigh the problems.**

B PRACTICE On a separate sheet of paper, write five sentences that introduce arguments for or against globalization. Paraphrase—using your own words—arguments from the article on page 116. Use the expressions for introducing others' arguments.

> *People who defend globalization argue that the standard of living has improved in many countries.*

See page T120 for answers.

C PRACTICE Now write statements to rebut each of the arguments opposing globalization that you introduced in Exercise B. Use the suggested transitions and subordinating conjunctions.

> *Even so, it can be argued that too many countries have not enjoyed the benefits.*

See page T120 for answers.

D APPLY THE WRITING SKILL Write an essay of at least four paragraphs in which you present your point of view about globalization and rebut the opposing point of view.

SELF-CHECK

☐ Did I summarize the point of view I want to rebut in my introduction?

☐ Did I rebut each argument by providing details and examples to support my own?

☐ Did I use the suggested expressions and transitions or subordinating conjunctions to link my ideas clearly?

☐ Did I summarize my point of view in my conclusion?

WRITING: Rebutting an opposing point of view

A WRITING SKILL

Suggested teaching time: 10–15 minutes
Your actual teaching time: _____

- Elicit that *to rebut* an argument means to prove that an argument someone else has made is false.
- Ask a student to read the writing skill introduction. Explain that *opposing argument or point of view* refers to someone else's "take," or opinion, on a topic that is different from what you believe.
- Call on a volunteer to read the introductory paragraph in the writing model. Ask *What is the thesis statement?* (Overall, globalization has contributed to a better world.) *What is the opposing view?* (Globalization is causing more problems than it is solving.) Bring students' attention to the expressions for introducing others' arguments. Invite students to experiment restating the first sentence of the writing model using a different expression. (Possible answer: It has been argued that globalization is causing more problems than it is solving.) Then bring students' attention to the transitions and subordinating conjunctions. Ask *Which one is used in the thesis statement?* (Nevertheless) *What other transition could be used here?* (In spite of this)
- Have students work in pairs to read about supporting and concluding paragraphs and analyze them in the writing model. Ask students to notice transitions used in the supporting and concluding paragraphs (All the same; In spite of this) and to suggest other ones from the box to replace them. (*Even so* to replace *All the same*; *Nevertheless,* to replace *In spite of this*)

B PRACTICE

Suggested teaching time: 5 minutes
Your actual teaching time: _____

- Have students refer to the expressions for introducing others' arguments to make five statements that introduce arguments supporting or opposing globalization. Tell students they can refer to the article on page 116 and other exercises, notes, and discussions from the unit for ideas.
- You may want to tell students to fold a piece of paper vertically and write each argument in this exercise and rebuttal in the next exercise side by side.

Answers to Exercise B

Answers will vary but may include the following:
1. According to the article, globalization has brought the world's cultures and economies together.
2. People on opposites sides of the world can easily get in touch via phone or internet.
3. It may be true that increased imports and exports have brought about economic benefits.
4. It has been argued that the developed countries enjoy the most benefits of globalization.
5. Critics complain that globalization has led to a homogenization of culture.

C PRACTICE

Suggested teaching time: 5 minutes
Your actual teaching time: _____

- Tell students they will now rebut the arguments from Exercise B, using the transitions and subordinating conjunctions from the box.
- If students wrote the initial arguments in Exercise B on a folded piece of paper, encourage students to use the space on the other side of the fold to write the counterargument.

Answers to Exercise C

Answers will vary but may include the following:
1. All the same, not all cultures and economies enjoyed the same growth and benefits.
2. However, not all people have access to this technology.
3. In spite of this, criminal activities have flourished as free trade has made the world so competitive.
4. Nevertheless, even in developed countries workers suffer as their jobs get outsourced to other countries where the jobs will be performed for a fraction of the cost.
5. Even so, people appear to enjoy the wider variety of choices available to them when they shop.

D APPLY THE WRITING SKILL

Suggested teaching time: 10–15 minutes
Your actual teaching time: _____

- Tell students to use their notes from Exercises B and C to write an essay. Tell them that the essay should have an introduction, a conclusion, and two supporting paragraphs. Tell students to follow the model to present their point of view and rebut the opposing point of view. Remind students to use the expressions for introducing others' arguments and the transitions and subordinating conjunctions for rebuttal.
- Refer students to the Writing Process Worksheet in ActiveTeach for guidance with pre-writing and peer feedback.
- Encourage students to use the Self-Check in the Student's Book to go over the essays they wrote.

Option: [+5 minutes] Time permitting, students can exchange papers with a partner and offer feedback using the topics in the Self-Check list. Encourage partners to also check for examples.

⭐ 🖨 Writing Process

REVIEW

🎮 **Digital Game**

A ▶ 5:27

Suggested teaching time:	5–10 minutes	Your actual teaching time:

- Have students listen to the three reports. Then have students listen again. Stop after each report and have students complete the statement.
- Tell pairs to compare answers. Then bring the class together and ask individual students *Do you think that improving living standards in developing countries will cause natural resources to run out? Why? Why not? Do you think globalization is causing social and economic problems? Why? Why not? What is your opinion of Starbucks stores?*

B

Suggested teaching time:	5 minutes	Your actual teaching time:

- Have students review the phrasal verbs in the grammar box on page 112 and in the vocabulary on page 114. Then have students work individually to complete the sentences with the correct particles. For less advanced classes you may opt to put a word bank on the board: *about, off, on, out, up*. Some particles are used more than once. You may want to hint that *out* is used four times.
- Go over the answers as a class.

Option: [+5 minutes] Invite students to determine if the phrasal verbs are separable. (All are separable except for the second verb in item 4 (catch on).) In pairs, have students experiment restating the sentences with verbs separated. For example, *A lot of families have been putting large purchases off.* Tell students to shorten sentences or use pronouns to avoid having long phrases break up the phrasal words

C

Suggested teaching time:	5 minutes	Your actual teaching time:

- Tell students to circle the phrasal verb in each sentence. (1. check out; 2. go without; 3. give up; 4. lay off; 5. turn on; 6. talk into; 7. Cater to; 8. Take up) Then tell them to identify which phrasal verbs are separable and which are inseparable (separable: 1, 3, 4, 5, 8; inseparable: 2, 6, and 7). Remind students that with separable phrasal verbs, the direct object pronoun must come before the particle.
- Have students complete the exercise individually and then compare answers with a partner.
- Go over any outstanding questions as a class.

Answers to Exercise C

2. We're trying to go without them.
3. They voted to give them up.
4. Falling profits forced the factory owner to lay them off.
5. Just turn it on and you'll see news and films from all over the world.
6. I talked them into buying tickets for the U2 concert.
7. Manufacturers of luxury products cater to them.
8. If you take it up, you'll probably be in great shape.

Option: TEST-TAKING SKILLS BOOSTER (p. 160)

EXTRA

- Workbook
- MyEnglishLab
- Online Student Resources (www.english.com/summit3e)
  - Classroom Audio Program
  - Extra Practice Activities
  - *Summit GO* App
  - Web Projects
- ActiveTeach
  - Assessment
  - Additional Printable Resources
    - Audioscripts and Answer Keys
    - "Can-Do" Self-Assessment Charts
    - Conversation and Discussion Activator Video Scripts
    - Oral Progress Assessment Charts
    - Reading Speed Calculator
  - Summit TV Video Program
    - Activity Worksheets
    - Teaching Notes
    - Video Scripts

REVIEW

A ▶ 5:27 Listen to three news reports on globalization-related topics. After each report, complete each statement so that it is true, according to the information presented in the report. Listen again if necessary.

Report 1: WorldWatch is concerned that improving living standards in developing countries ……… .
  (a) will cause natural resources to run out
  b will bring about an increase in prices for luxury goods

Report 2: According to the report, most people think that globalization ……… .
  a is causing social and economic problems
  (b) is not causing social and economic problems

Report 3: The chairman of Starbucks believes that his customers appreciate ……… .
  a the convenience of having Starbucks stores in so many locations
  (b) both the coffee and the experience of being in the store

B Complete each phrasal verb with the correct particle. Use the phrasal verb list on pages 124–126 if necessary.
1. The island voted to carry **out** the governor's plan to find foreign investors to develop the island into a tourist resort.
2. Technological advances such as social media have brought **about** great changes in the way people communicate.
3. The president is determined to figure **out** how to increase trade with other countries without causing a rise in unemployment.
4. Clerks were handing **out** free cups of Colombian coffee at a Tokyo supermarket in the hopes that it would catch **on** with local shoppers.
5. I picked **up** a little French when I visited my uncle in Paris last summer, but I wouldn't say that I'm fluent.
6. A lot of families have been putting **off** large purchases because they're afraid they may soon be out of work if the economy doesn't improve.
7. To be honest, I'm worried that the cultures of wealthier nations will one day wipe **out** the traditional cultures of poorer nations.
8. Asian martial arts have become really popular recently. I know so many people who have taken **up** tae kwon do, karate, or judo.

C On a separate sheet of paper, rewrite each sentence, replacing the underlined phrase with the pronoun it or them.
1. We should check out that new French film. | *We should check it out.*
2. We're trying to go without imported products.
3. They voted to give up protections against imports.
4. Falling profits forced the factory owner to lay off the workers.
5. Just turn on your TV and you'll see news and films from all over the world.
6. I talked my friends into buying tickets for the U2 concert.
7. Manufacturers of luxury products cater to wealthier consumers.
8. If you take up karate, you'll probably be in great shape.
See page T121 for answers.

TEST-TAKING SKILLS BOOSTER p. 160

Web Project: Global Warming
www.english.com/summit3e

121

Reference Charts

IRREGULAR VERBS

base form	simple past	past participle	base form	simple past	past participle
be	was / were	been	mean	meant	meant
beat	beat	beaten	meet	met	met
become	became	become	mistake	mistook	mistaken
begin	began	begun	pay	paid	paid
bend	bent	bent	put	put	put
bet	bet	bet	quit	quit	quit
bite	bit	bitten	read /rid/	read /rɛd/	read /rɛd/
bleed	bled	bled	ride	rode	ridden
blow	blew	blown	ring	rang	rung
break	broke	broken	rise	rose	risen
breed	bred	bred	run	ran	run
bring	brought	brought	say	said	said
build	built	built	see	saw	seen
burn	burned / burnt	burned / burnt	sell	sold	sold
burst	burst	burst	send	sent	sent
buy	bought	bought	set	set	set
catch	caught	caught	shake	shook	shaken
choose	chose	chosen	shed	shed	shed
come	came	come	shine	shone	shone
cost	cost	cost	shoot	shot	shot
creep	crept	crept	show	showed	shown
cut	cut	cut	shrink	shrank	shrunk
deal	dealt	dealt	shut	shut	shut
dig	dug	dug	sing	sang	sung
do	did	done	sink	sank	sunk
draw	drew	drawn	sit	sat	sat
dream	dreamed / dreamt	dreamed / dreamt	sleep	slept	slept
drink	drank	drunk	slide	slid	slid
drive	drove	driven	smell	smelled / smelt	smelled / smelt
eat	ate	eaten	speak	spoke	spoken
fall	fell	fallen	speed	sped / speeded	sped / speeded
feed	fed	fed	spell	spelled / spelt	spelled / spelt
feel	felt	felt	spend	spent	spent
fight	fought	fought	spill	spilled / spilt	spilled / spilt
find	found	found	spin	spun	spun
fit	fit	fit	spit	spit / spat	spit / spat
fly	flew	flown	spoil	spoiled / spoilt	spoiled / spoilt
forbid	forbade	forbidden	spread	spread	spread
forget	forgot	forgotten	spring	sprang / sprung	sprang / sprung
forgive	forgave	forgiven	stand	stood	stood
freeze	froze	frozen	steal	stole	stolen
get	got	gotten	stick	stuck	stuck
give	gave	given	sting	stung	stung
go	went	gone	stink	stank / stunk	stunk
grow	grew	grown	strike	struck	struck / stricken
hang	hung	hung	string	strung	strung
have	had	had	swear	swore	sworn
hear	heard	heard	sweep	swept	swept
hide	hid	hidden	swim	swam	swum
hit	hit	hit	swing	swung	swung
hold	held	held	take	took	taken
hurt	hurt	hurt	teach	taught	taught
keep	kept	kept	tear	tore	torn
know	knew	known	tell	told	told
lay	laid	laid	think	thought	thought
lead	led	led	throw	threw	thrown
leap	leaped / leapt	leaped / leapt	understand	understood	understood
learn	learned / learnt	learned / learnt	upset	upset	upset
leave	left	left	wake	woke / waked	woken / waked
lend	lent	lent	wear	wore	worn
let	let	let	weave	wove	woven
lie	lay	lain	weep	wept	wept
light	lit	lit	win	won	won
lose	lost	lost	wind	wound	wound
make	made	made	write	wrote	written

VERBS FOLLOWED BY A GERUND

acknowledge	celebrate	discontinue	escape	imagine	postpone	recall	risk
admit	complete	discuss	explain	justify	practice	recommend	suggest
advise	consider	dislike	feel like	keep	prevent	report	support
appreciate	delay	don't mind	finish	mention	prohibit	resent	tolerate
avoid	deny	endure	forgive	mind	propose	resist	undestand
can't help	detest	enjoy	give up	miss	quit		

EXPRESSIONS THAT CAN BE FOLLOWED BY A GERUND

be excited about	be committed to	make an excuse for	look forward to
be worried about	be opposed to	have a reason for	blame [someone or something] for
be responsible for	be used to	believe in	forgive [someone or something] for
be interested in	complain about	participate in	thank [someone or something] for
be accused of	dream about / of	succeed in	keep [someone or something] from
be capable of	talk about / of	take advantage of	prevent [someone or something] from
be tired of	think about / of	take care of	stop [someone or something] from
be accustomed to	apologize for	insist on	

VERBS FOLLOWED DIRECTLY BY AN INFINITIVE

afford	can't wait	demand	hope	need	pretend	swear	want
agree	care	deserve	hurry	neglect	promise	threaten	wish
appear	choose	expect	intend	offer	refuse	volunteer	would like
arrange	claim	fail	learn	pay	request	wait	yearn
ask	consent	grow	manage	plan	seem		
attempt	decide	hesitate	mean	prepare	struggle		

VERBS FOLLOWED BY AN OBJECT BEFORE AN INFINITIVE*

advise	cause	enable	force	need*	persuade	require	want*
allow	challenge	encourage	hire	order	promise*	teach	warn
ask*	choose*	expect*	instruct	pay*	remind	tell	wish*
beg	convince	forbid	invite	permit	request*	urge	would like*

*In the active voice, these verbs can be followed by the infinitive without an object (example: *want to speak* or *want someone to speak*).

VERBS THAT CAN BE FOLLOWED BY A GERUND OR AN INFINITIVE

with a change in meaning		without a change in meaning					
forget	remember	begin	continue	like	prefer	try	
regret	stop	can't stand	hate	love	start		

ADJECTIVES FOLLOWED BY AN INFINITIVE*

afraid	ashamed	depressed	eager	fortunate	lucky	relieved	surprised
alarmed	certain	determined	easy	glad	pleased	reluctant	touched
amazed	content	disappointed	embarrased	happy	prepared	sad	upset
angry	curious	distressed	encouraged	hesitant	proud	shocked	willing
anxious	delighted	disturbed	excited	likely	ready	sorry	

*Example: *I'm willing **to accept** that.*

PARTICIPIAL ADJECTIVES*

alarming	–	alarmed	embarrassing	–	embarrassed	paralyzing	–	paralyzed		
amazing	–	amazed	enlightening	–	enlightened	pleasing	–	pleased		
amusing	–	amused	entertaining	–	entertained	relaxing	–	relaxed		
annoying	–	annoyed	exciting	–	excited	satisfying	–	satisfied		
astonishing	–	astonished	exhausting	–	exhausted	shocking	–	shocked		
boring	–	bored	fascinating	–	fascinated	soothing	–	soothed		
confusing	–	confused	frightening	–	frightened	startling	–	startled		
depressing	–	depressed	horrifying	–	horrified	stimulating	–	stimulated		
disappointing	–	disappointed	inspiring	–	inspired	surprising	–	surprised		
disgusting	–	disgusted	interesting	–	interested	terrifying	–	terrified		
distressing	–	distressed	irritating	–	irritated	tiring	–	tired		
disturbing	–	disturbed	moving	–	moved	touching	–	touched		

STATIVE VERBS

amaze	contain	feel*	look like	please	smell*
appear*	cost	forget	look*	possess	sound
appreciate	desire	hate	love	prefer	suppose
astonish	dislike	have*	matter	realize	surprise
be*	doubt	hear	mean	recognize	taste*
believe	envy	imagine	mind	remember*	think*
belong	equal	include*	need	resemble	understand
care	exist	know	owe	see*	want*
consist of	fear	like	own	seem	weigh*

*These verbs also have action meanings. Example: *I see a tree.* (non-action) *I'm seeing her tomorrow.* (action)

TRANSITIVE PHRASAL VERBS

Some transitive phrasal verbs have more than one meaning. Not all are included here.

Abbreviations
s.o. = someone
sth. = something
e.g. = for example
inf. = informal

SEPARABLE

blow sth. **out**	stop a flame by blowing on it
blow sth. **up**	1 make sth. explode 2 fill sth. with air, e.g., a balloon 3 make sth. larger, e.g., a photo
bring sth. **about**	make sth. happen
bring sth. **back**	1 return sth. to a store 2 revive or renew sth., e.g., a custom or tradition
bring sth. **out**	1 introduce a new product 2 make a quality more noticeable
bring s.o. **up**	raise a child
bring sth. **up**	start to talk about an issue
burn sth. **down**	burn a structure completely
call s.o. **back**	return a phone call
call sth. **off**	cancel sth.
call s.o. **up**	call s.o. on the phone
carry sth. **out**	conduct a plan
check s.o./sth. **out**	look at s.o. or sth. more closely
cheer s.o. **up**	make s.o. feel happier
clean s.o./sth. **up**	clean s.o. or sth. completely
clear sth. **up**	clarify sth.
close sth. **down**	force a business or institution to close
cover sth. **up**	1 cover sth. completely 2 change facts to avoid responsibility
cross sth. **out**	draw a line through sth.
cut sth. **down**	make sth. fall by cutting, e.g., a tree
cut sth. **off**	1 remove sth. by cutting 2 stop the supply of sth.
cut s.o. **off**	interrupt s.o who is speaking
dream sth. **up**	invent or think of a new idea
drink sth. **up**	drink a beverage completely
drop s.o./sth. **off**	leave s.o. or sth. somewhere
empty sth. **out**	empty sth. completely
figure s.o./sth. **out**	understand s.o. or sth. after some thought
fill s.o. **in**	tell s.o. about recent events
fill sth. **out**	complete a form
fill sth. **up**	fill a container completely
find sth. **out**	learn new information
follow sth. **through**	do everything to complete a task
get sth. **across**	help s.o. understand an idea
give sth. **away**	give sth. you do not need or want
give sth. **back**	return sth. to its owner
give sth. **out**	distribute sth.
give sth. **up**	quit doing sth.
hand sth. **in**	submit work, e.g., to a boss or a teacher
hand sth. **out**	distribute sth.
hang sth. **up**	put sth. on a hanger or hook, e.g., clothes
help s.o. **out**	assist s.o.
keep s.o./sth. **away**	cause s.o. or sth. to stay at a distance
lay s.o. **off**	fire s.o. because of economic conditions
leave sth. **on**	1 not turn sth. off, e.g., an appliance 2 not remove sth. such as clothing or jewelry
leave sth. **out**	omit sth.
let s.o. **down**	disappoint s.o.
let s.o./sth. **in**	allow s.o. or sth. to enter
let s.o. **off**	allow s.o. to leave a bus, car, taxi, etc.
let s.o./sth. **out**	allow s.o. or sth. to leave
light sth. **up**	illuminate sth.
look s.o./sth. **over**	examine s.o. or sth.
look s.o./sth. **up**	1 try to find s.o. 2 try to find sth. in a book, the Internet, etc.
make sth. **up**	create a fictional story
pass sth. **out**	distribute sth.
pass sth. **up**	decide not to take an opportunity
pay s.o. **off**	bribe s.o.
pay sth. **off**	pay back money one owes
pick s.o./sth. **out**	identify or choose s.o. or sth.
pick s.o. **up**	stop a vehicle so s.o. can get in
pick s.o./sth. **up**	lift s.o. or sth.
pick sth. **up**	1 get or buy sth. from somewhere 2 learn sth. new 3 get an infectious disease
point s.o./sth. **out**	show s.o or sth. to another person
put sth. **away**	put sth. in its appropriate place
put sth. **back**	return sth. to its original place
put s.o./sth. **down**	1 stop holding or lifting s.o. or sth. 2 insult s.o.
put sth. **off**	delay or postpone sth.
put sth. **on**	get dressed or place sth. on one's body
put sth. **together**	1 put sth. on a wall 2 build sth.
put sth. **up**	build or erect sth.
set sth. **off**	cause sth. to explode
set sth. **up**	1 establish a new business, organization, etc. 2 prepare equipment for use
show s.o./sth. **off**	display the best qualities of s.o. or sth.
shut sth. **off**	stop a machine or supply
straighten sth. **up**	make sth. neat
switch sth. **on**	start a machine, turn on a light, etc.
take sth. **away**	remove sth.
take sth. **back**	1 return sth. to a store 2 accept sth. returned by another person
take sth. **down**	remove sth. that is hanging
take sth. **in**	1 notice and remember sth. 2 make a clothing item smaller
take sth. **off**	remove clothing, jewelry, etc.
take s.o. **on**	hire s.o.
take sth. **on**	agree to do a task
take s.o. **out**	invite s.o. somewhere and pay for his/her meal, show, etc.
take sth. **up**	start doing an activity habitually
talk sth. **over**	discuss sth.
tear sth. **down**	destroy sth.

tear sth. up	tear sth. into small pieces
think sth. over	consider sth.
think sth. up	invent or think of a new idea
throw sth. away	put sth. in the garbage
throw sth. out	put sth. in the garbage
touch sth. up	improve sth. with very small changes
try sth. on	try clothing to see if it fits
try sth. out	use sth. to see if one likes it or if it works
turn sth. around	1 turn so the front is at the back 2 cause things to get better
turn s.o./sth. down	reject s.o. or sth.
turn sth. down	lower the volume, heat, etc.
turn sth. in	submit a paper, application, etc.
turn sth. off	stop a machine, light, etc.
turn s.o. off	cause s.o. to lose interest (inf.)
turn sth. on	start a machine, light, etc.
turn sth. out	make or manufacture sth.
turn sth. over	turn sth. so the bottom is at the top
turn sth. up	raise the volume, heat, etc.
use sth. up	use sth. completely
wake s.o. up	cause s.o. to stop sleeping
wipe sth. out	remove or destroy sth.
work sth. out	1 resolve a problem 2 calculate a math problem
write sth. down	write sth. to have a record of it

ALWAYS SEPARATED

ask s.o. over	invite s.o. to one's home
bring s.o./sth. down	remove a ruler or government from power
do sth. over	do sth. again
keep sth. on	not remove sth. such as clothing or jewelry
see sth. through	complete a task
start sth. over	begin sth. again
talk s.o. into sth.	persuade s.o. to do sth.

INSEPARABLE

cater to s.o.	provide what s.o. wants or needs
carry on sth.	continue sth. another person has started
come across s.o./sth.	find s.o. or sth. unexpectedly
count on s.o./sth.	depend on s.o. or sth.
do without s.o./sth.	live without s.o. or sth. one needs or wants
go after s.o./sth.	pursue s.o. or sth.
go over sth.	examine sth. carefully
go without sth.	live without sth. one needs or wants
run into s.o.	meet s.o. unexpectedly
run into sth.	accidentally hit or crash into sth.
stick with s.o.	stay close to s.o.
stick with sth.	continue doing sth. as before

INTRANSITIVE PHRASAL VERBS

Some intransitive phrasal verbs have more than one meaning. Not all are included here.

blow up	1 explode 2 suddenly become very angry
break down	stop functioning
break out	start suddenly, e.g., a war, disease, or fire
burn down	burn completely
call back	return a phone call
carry on	1 continue doing sth. 2 behave in a silly or emotional way
catch on	become popular
check in	report one's arrival at an airport or hotel
check out	pay one's bill and leave a hotel
cheer up	become happier
clear up	become better, e.g., a rash or the weather
close down	stop operating, e.g., a factory or a school
come along	accompany s.o.
come back	return
come in	enter
come off	become unattached
come out	1 appear, e.g., the sun 2 be removed, e.g., a stain
dress up	wear more formal clothes or a costume
drop in	visit unexpectedly
drop out	quit a class, school, or program
eat out	eat in a restaurant
empty out	empty completely
fall off	become unattached
fill out	become bigger
fill up	become completely full
find out	learn new information
follow through	continue working on sth. until it is completed
fool around	have fun or not be serious
get ahead	make progress or succeed
get along	to not argue
get back	return from a place
get together	meet somewhere with a friend or acquaintance
get up	get out of bed
give up	quit
go along	1 accompany s.o. 2 agree
go back	return
go off	explode; make a sudden noise
go on	continue to talk about or describe sth.
go out	1 leave a building 2 leave one's home to meet people, enjoy entertainment, etc.
go up	be built
grow up	become an adult
help out	do sth. helpful
hang up	end a phone call
hold on	wait during a phone call
keep away	stay at a distance
keep on	continue
keep up	go or think as fast as another person
lie down	rest on a bed
light up	1 begin to shine brightly 2 look pleased or happy
make up	end an argument and reestablish a friendly relationship
pass out	become unconscious
pay off	be worthwhile
pick up	improve, e.g., the economy
play around	have fun or not be serious
run out	no longer in supply
show up	appear
sign up	register
sit down	sit
slip up	make a mistake
stand up	rise to one's feet
start over	begin again
stay up	not go to bed
straighten up	make neat
take off	depart by plane
turn in	go to bed (inf.)
turn out	have a particular result
turn up	appear
wake up	stop sleeping
watch out	be careful
work out	1 exercise 2 be resolved; end successfully

THREE-WORD PHRASAL VERBS

Some three-word phrasal verbs have more than one meaning. Not all are included here.

catch up on sth.	1 do sth. one didn't have time to do earlier 2 get the most recent information	give up on sth.	stop trying to make sth. happen
catch up with s.o.	exchange information about recent activities	go along with sth.	agree to do sth.
check up on s.o.	make sure s.o. is OK	go through with sth.	do sth. difficult or painful
come away with sth.	learn sth. useful from s.o. or sth.	grow out of sth.	stop doing sth. as one becomes an adult
come down to sth.	be the most important point or idea	keep up with s.o.	stay in regular contact
come down with sth.	get an illness	look down on s.o.	think one is better than another person
come up against s.o./sth.	be faced with a difficult person or situation	look out for s.o.	protect s.o.
		look up to s.o.	admire or respect s.o.
come up with sth.	think of an idea, plan, or solution	make up for sth.	do sth. to apologize
face up to sth.	accept an unpleasant truth	put up with s.o./sth.	accept s.o. or sth. without complaining
fall back on sth.	use an old idea because new ideas have failed	run out of sth.	no longer have enough of sth.
follow through on sth.	continue doing sth. until it is completed	stand up for sth.	support an idea or a principle
get around to sth.	finally do sth.	stand up to s.o.	refuse to let s.o. treat anyone badly
get away with sth.	avoid the consequences of a wrong act	team up with s.o.	do a task together
get back at s.o.	harm s.o. because he / she harmed you	think back on s.o./sth.	think about and remember s.o. or sth.
give up on s.o.	stop hoping that s.o. will change	walk out on s.o.	end a relationship with a wife, boyfriend, etc.
		watch out for s.o./sth.	protect s.o. or sth.

Verb forms: overview

SUMMARY OF VERB FORMS

	Present time	Past time	Future time
Simple	Simple present walk / walks	Simple past walked	Simple future will walk
Continuous	Present continuous am walking / is walking / are walking	Past continuous was walking / were walking	Future continuous will be walking
Perfect	Present perfect have walked / has walked	Past perfect had walked	Future perfect will have walked
Perfect continuous	Present perfect continuous have been walking / has been walking	Past perfect continuous had been walking	Future perfect continuous will have been walking

SIMPLE VERB FORMS: USAGE

	Present time	Past time	Future time
Simple verb forms describe habitual actions or events that occur at a definite time.	Simple present[1] **Habitual action** The department **meets** once a month to review the status of projects. **Facts and generalizations** The Earth **rotates** around the sun every 365 days.	Simple past **Completed action that occurred at a definite time in the past** Last year researchers **discovered** a new cancer treatment. **Habitual action in the past**[2] When I was young we **visited** my grandparents every week.	Simple future[3] **Action that will occur at a definite time in the future** Next year they **will offer** a course on global trade. **Habitual action in the future** Next month I**'ll go** to the gym three times a week.

[1] The simple present tense can also express a future action: *Her flight arrives this evening at eight.*
[2] <u>Used to</u> and <u>would</u> also express habitual actions in the past: *When I was a child, we used to spend the summer in the mountains. In the mornings we would go hiking and in the afternoons we would swim in a nearby lake.*
[3] <u>Be going to</u> can also express a future action: *Next year they are going to offer a course on global trade.*

CONTINUOUS VERB FORMS: USAGE

	Present time	Past time	Future time
Continuous verb forms describe continuous actions or events that occur at a definite time.	**Present continuous*** Action in progress now *The business managers are discussing next year's budget right now.*	**Past continuous** Action in progress at a definite time in the past *None of the computers were working when I came in this morning.*	**Future continuous** Action that will be in progress during a definite time in the future *We'll be listening to the speech when you arrive.*

*The present continuous can also express a future plan: *They're getting married next month.*

PERFECT VERB FORMS: USAGE

	Present time	Past time	Future time
Perfect verb forms describe actions or events in relation to other time frames.	**Present perfect*** Completed action that occurred at an indefinite time before the present *She has made many contributions to the field.* Recently completed action *He has just published an article about his findings.* Uncompleted action (action that began in the past, continues into the present, and may continue into the future) *They have studied ancient cultures for many years.*	**Past perfect** Action that occurred at some point before a definite time in the past *By 2016, he had started a new business.* Action that occurred before another past action *They had already finished medical school when the war broke out.*	**Future perfect** Action that will be completed by some point at a definite time in the future *By this time next year, I will have completed my research.*

*Many statements in the present perfect can also be stated correctly using the simple past tense, depending on the speaker's perspective: *She made many contributions to the field.*

PERFECT CONTINUOUS VERB FORMS: USAGE

	Present time	Past time	Future time
Perfect continuous verb forms describe continuous actions or events in relation to other time frames.	**Present perfect continuous** Uncompleted continuous action (action that began in the past, continues into the present, and may continue into the future) *She has been lecturing about that topic since 2015.* Very recently completed action *The workers have been protesting. They're finished now.*	**Past perfect continuous** Continuous action that occurred before another past action or time *By 2015, researchers had been seeking a cure for AIDS for more than thirty years.*	**Future perfect continuous** Continuous action that occurred before another action or time in the future *When the new director takes over, I will have been working at this company for ten years.*

Grammar Booster and Pronunciation Booster

Grammar Booster

The Grammar Booster is optional. It provides more explanation and practice, as well as additional related grammar concepts and review.

UNIT 1

Describing past actions and events: review

The past of be and the simple past tense
Use for completed actions and states that occurred at a specific time in the past.
 He **was** here at 10:00 and **left** this message.

The past continuous
Use for one or more recurring actions or actions in progress at a specific time in the past.
 Steven **was** always **talking** in class.
 The baby **was sleeping** and the older children **were eating** dinner when we arrived.

The present perfect
Use for actions completed at an unspecified time in the past.
 She **has** already **informed** her manager about the problem.
 New York **has been called** the capital of the world.

The past perfect
Use for an action that occurred before another past action.
 They **had** already **made** a decision when we called.

The past perfect continuous
Use for a continuing action that was occurring before another past action.
 We **had been working** for two hours when the storm began.

Used to / would
Use **used to** for past situations and habits that no longer exist. Use **would** or **used to** for actions that were repeated regularly in the past.
 When she was younger, she never **used to be** afraid of anything.
 In those days, we **would** (or **used to**) **take** a long walk every evening.

The future as seen from the past
Use **was** / **were going to** + the base form of a verb to express future plans someone had in the past.
 He **was going to start** his own business, but he couldn't get a loan.

Would + the base form of the verb can also express the future as seen from the past, but only after statements of knowledge or belief.
 We always thought that she **would become** an actor, but she decided to study law.

A Correct the errors with past forms.

1 Florence ~~has~~ *had* been walking for several hours before she realized that her wallet was missing.
2 As a child, he ~~was practicing~~ *would practice / used to practice* the piano for hours every day. Then he stopped taking lessons.
3 "I ~~have seen~~ *saw* that movie last year, and I thought it was great," Frank exclaimed.
4 Before this morning, I ~~never took~~ *had never taken* a yoga class.
5 He ~~was working~~ *had been working* on the problem all morning when he finally found the solution.
6 My husband believed he ~~will~~ *would* never get married, but then he met me.

Stative verbs

Stative (non-action) verbs express mental states, emotions, perceptions, descriptions, relationships, possession, measurements, and other conditions, rather than actions. They are not usually used in continuous verb forms, even when they describe a situation in progress.
 Many people **believe** the environment should be our top priority. NOT Many people ~~are believing~~ the environment should be our top priority.
 She **has** always **understood** that job satisfaction was important. NOT She ~~has always been understanding~~ that job satisfaction was important.

Some stative verbs have both non-action and action meanings. A stative verb that has an action meaning may be used in the continuous.

Non-action meaning	Action meaning
That**'s** ridiculous! (description)	You**'re being** ridiculous! (act in a ridiculous way)
She **has** two children. (possession)	She**'s having** another baby soon. (act of giving birth)
We **think** these laws are unfair. (mental state: opinion)	We**'re thinking** of organizing a protest. (act of planning)
How does the soup **taste**? (perception)	I**'m tasting** the soup to see if it needs salt. (act of tasting)
This garden **looks** neglected. (description)	The child **is looking** at the flowers. (act of looking)

NOTE: In informal spoken English, certain stative verbs, especially **want**, **need**, and **have to**, are becoming common in the continuous:
 I**'m** really **wanting** a cup of good coffee. Let's go into that coffee bar.

For a complete list of stative verbs, see the Reference Charts, page 124.

Grammar Booster

> **Note about the Grammar Booster**
> Many will elect to do the Grammar Booster as self-study. However, if you choose to use the Grammar Booster with the classroom activity instead, teaching notes are included here.

Unit 1
Describing past actions and events: review

- Give students a few minutes to read the seven headings and explanations in the review.
- Focus on *Used to / would*. Explain that it is common in writing to use *used to* at the beginning of a paragraph and then continue with *would* in the following sentences that provide further details. Write the first sentence on the board *When she was younger, she never used to be afraid of anything*—and have students suggest additional details. (Possible answers: She would pick up insects and mice. She would tell ghost stories at sleepovers.)
- Ask students to look at the head *The future as seen from the past*. Call on a volunteer to read the first explanation and example sentence. Have students suggest additional sentences describing things they had planned to do but didn't for some reason. (Possible answer: I was going to take a translating course, but it wasn't offered in the spring.)
- Then have a student read the second explanation and example sentence under *The future as seen from the past*. Point out that statements of knowledge or belief include verbs such as *understood, believed*, and *claimed*. Write these verbs on the board for reference, and have students suggest sentences using them. (Possible answer: She claimed that she would learn how to drive, but she never did.)

Challenge: [+15–20 minutes] Have students write a paragraph describing five activities they used to do regularly. Instruct students to use *used to* and *would* appropriately in their paragraph. Collect the papers and give feedback.

A Correct the errors . . .

- Have students do the exercise individually. Refer them to the review of past actions and events in the section above if they need help.
- Bring the class together and go over the answers. Call on students to explain each error and the best way to correct it. Note that for item 2 there are two possible corrections.

Stative verbs

- On the board, write 1. *I love chocolate!* 2. *I am loving chocolate!* To check student knowledge, ask *Which sentence is preferred?* (1) *Why?* (*Love* is a stative or non-action verb and is not usually used in the continuous.)
- Have a volunteer read the first explanation and example sentences in the Grammar box. Write on the board *believe, understand*. Ask *What does each stative verb express?* (They both express a mental state.) Then elicit additional stative verbs and what they express. (Possible answers: **amaze:** emotion or mental state; **exist:** description; **please:** emotion or mental state; **suppose:** mental state)
- Call on a student to read the second explanation. Then have pairs take turns reading the sets of example sentences with Non-action and Action meanings.
- Read the Note, and call on volunteers to read the example sentences. Stress that continuous forms of certain stative verbs are common in spoken English but should not be used in formal writing.

Option: [+15–20 minutes] Write the following sentences on the board, or photocopy and distribute them. Tell pairs to decide if the stative verb in each sentence shows a non-action or an action meaning.

1. I have been seeing John for over a year now.
2. We have a problem with flooding in our basement.
3. This material feels nice and soft.
4. You look really good in that jacket.
5. Kerry is appearing in a new feature film.
6. The kids are looking at the elephants in the zoo.

(Answers: 1. action, 2. non-action, 3. non-action, 4. non-action, 5. action, 6. action) Then have students use the verbs to write sentences that depict the alternate meaning. Have students share their sentences with the class. (Possible answers: 1. I saw John yesterday. 2. They're having a discussion about which course to sign up for. 3. I'm feeling the sweater to see if it's dry. 4. She was looking for a way to realize her childhood dream. 5. Jim's long-term goal appeared difficult to achieve. 6. The weather for tomorrow looks cold and windy.)

Challenge: [+15–20 minutes] Have students reread the second explanation. Then refer students to the list of stative verbs in the Reference Charts, page 124, and have them choose three starred verbs. Have students work together to write three pairs of sentences—one using the verb with a non-action meaning and one using the verb with an action meaning. Circulate and assist as needed.

B Decide if each stative verb . . .

- Have students check the correct boxes and complete the sentences individually.
- Then have students compare answers with a partner.
- Bring the class together and ask:

  Which non-action verbs express a mental state?
  (1. doubts, 5. doesn't remember)

  Which non-action verb expresses possession? (2. have)

- Go over any questions. You may wish to point out that spoken usage is changing, with stative verbs such as *want, like, need* and *have* being used in the continuous aspect more and more. *Remember* is occasionally used in the present continuous as well.

Note: If students are unsure which stative verbs have an action meaning, have them consult the list in the Reference Charts, page 124.

Challenge: [+15–20 minutes] Have students use the stative verbs to create sentences with the alternate action or non-action meaning. Have students share sentences with a partner. (Possible answers: 1. We were doubting her ability to get the job done on time. 2. They're not having lunch at home today. 3. Philip thinks the rule will be hard to enforce. 5. The bookstore has two copies of the book you ordered. 6. I was remembering the old songs I used to sing as a child. 7. I included my cell phone number on the application. 8. Ellen saw immediately how the movie would end.)

Unit 2

Adjective clauses: overview

- Have students skim the information in the first column of the chart to review the purposes of adjective clauses.
- Focus on each horizontal section of the chart. Have volunteers read the example sentences. Elicit additional example sentences for each section.
- After the class has gone through each section, point out that adjective clauses can be divided into restrictive and non-restrictive clauses. (Note that restrictive and non-restrictive clauses are taught on the Writing page.) Ask *What does a restrictive clause do?* (It gives information that is needed to identify the noun or pronoun it modifies.) *What does a non-restrictive clause do?* (It gives additional information that is not necessary to identify the noun or pronoun it modifies.) *Which of the two types of clauses can be omitted from a sentence without affecting its meaning?* (a non-restrictive clause)
- Have students skim the example sentences in the chart and note the restrictive clauses and nonrestrictive clauses. (Only the example sentence in section 3—to show possession—that begins *Paris . . .* is non-restrictive.) Remind students that the relative pronoun *that* cannot be used with a non-restrictive clause. Also remind students that a non-restrictive clause requires a comma before and after (or a comma before and a period after when the clause comes at the end of the sentence).

- Write the following on the board and have students note the commas in sentence 1 and the comma and period in sentence 2: *1. Tom, who has worked for our company for eight years, lied to his boss. 2. Tom lied to his boss, which was a serious mistake.*

Option: [+15–20 minutes] Write the following sentences on the board. Call on students to add commas to the sentences where they are necessary.

1. The person that we are talking about is standing over there.
2. My mother who had never used a computer learned to surf the Internet.
3. The bench that is in front of the library was donated by the class of 1987.
4. Tabor whose town square is 100 years old is a popular tourist destination.
5. This summer, we are going to Vienna which is where my husband was born.

(Answers: 2. My mother, who had never used a computer, learned to surf the Internet. 4. Tabor, whose town square is 100 years old, is a popular tourist destination. 5. This summer, we are going to Vienna, which is where my husband was born.)

Challenge: [+15–20 minutes] Have pairs write five sentences with adjective clauses, one for each category in the chart. Tell students to include both restrictive and non-restrictive clauses. Circulate and check as students work. Then have pairs swap sentences and identify the restrictive and non-restrictive clauses.

A Underline the best word . . .

- Have students look at the noun before each parenthetical choice of words. Have pairs decide whether the noun is a person, place, or thing. (1. person, 2. place, 3. person, 4. person, 5. thing [time], 6. person, 7. thing) To review, ask:

  Which words introduce an adjective clause about people? (who, whom, that, whose)

  Which words introduce an adjective clause about place? (which, that, where, in which)

  Which words introduce an adjective clause about things? (which, that)

  Which words introduce an adjective clause about time? (when, that, in which)

- Have students complete the exercise individually and then compare answers with a partner.
- Bring the class together and go over any questions. Then ask *How is the adjective clause used in each sentence?* (1. to identify people; 2. to identify a place; 3. to give additional information about people; 4. to give additional information about a person; 5. to identify a period in time; 6. to identify a person; 7. to give additional information about a thing)

B Decide if each stative verb in parentheses has an action or a non-action meaning. Then complete each sentence with the simple present tense or the present continuous.

	action	non-action	
1	☐	☑	Sara **doubts** (doubt) that she'll get a promotion at her job.
2	☐	☑	Our skills are excellent, and we **have** (have) experience in the field.
3	☑	☐	Philip **is thinking** (think) about moving abroad to teach for a year.
4	☑	☐	We **are having** (have) dinner at 6:00 today so we can go to the lecture on climate change.
5	☐	☑	Michael **doesn't remember** (not remember) where the meeting will take place.
6	☐	☑	The book **includes** (include) some diagrams to support the hypothesis.
7	☑	☐	The doctor **is seeing** (see) another patient now.

UNIT 2

Adjective clauses: overview

Purpose	Examples
To identify or give additional information about a person • relative pronoun can be subject or object of clause	The physicist { who / that } **made that discovery** teaches at my university. The psychologist { whom / that / who } **he interviewed** did a study about lying.
To identify or give additional information about a place or thing • relative pronoun can be subject or object of clause	The building { that / which } **is on your left** was formerly a bank. The article { (that)* / (which)* } **I read yesterday** is fascinating.
To show possession	The woman **whose house you admired** is a famous author. Paris, **whose museums hold so many treasures**, is a favorite destination for tourists.
To modify a noun of place	The town { where they live / in which they live / that they live in / which they live in } has many beautiful parks and squares.
To modify a noun of time	I can't remember the year { (when)* / (that)* / (in which)* } **we visited them for the first time**.

*Note: These relative pronouns may be omitted.

A Underline the best word or words to complete each sentence.

1 Parents (<u>who</u> / which) spend time with their children give them a sense of security.
2 The city (that / <u>in which</u>) my father grew up was destroyed during the war.
3 The Miller family, (<u>whose</u> / who) house is for sale, hopes to find a buyer soon.
4 The star of the film, (<u>whom</u> / which) we had hoped to meet, didn't come to the reception.
5 I will never forget the time (<u>when</u> / who) I told the truth and was punished for it.
6 The woman (<u>who</u> / which) used to teach English at my school is now the director there.
7 The *Sun Times*, (whose / <u>which</u>) is the best newspaper in town, recently published an article about the social uses of lying.

GRAMMAR BOOSTER

Grammar for Writing: adjective clauses with quantifiers

Some adjective clauses may include a quantifier that refers to a previously mentioned noun or noun phrase. These clauses are constructed as follows: quantifier + of + relative pronoun (whom, which, or whose).

He consulted three doctors, **all of whom** confirmed the original diagnosis.
I can think of several possible explanations, **none of which** justifies their behavior.
The reporters questioned the president, **one of whose** strengths is his ability to remain calm under pressure.

Adjective clauses that include quantifiers appear more often in written than spoken English.

Some expressions of quantity used with of

a few of	half of	none of
all of	little of	one of
a number of	many of	several of
both of	most of	some of
each of	neither of	

B Complete each sentence with a quantifier from the box and the correct relative pronoun. Use each quantifier only once.

| all of | each of | neither of | one of | both of |

1. I've bought several of the company's products, only **one of which** works.
2. He's upset with all three of his children, **each of whom** makes up a different excuse to avoid sharing chores at home.
3. The teacher sent six of her students to speak with the director, **all of whom** were caught cheating on the test.
4. The two articles, **both of which** deal with the issue of honesty in the workplace, should be required reading for everyone in the company.
5. My parents, **neither of whom** has ever told a lie, are the most honest people I know.

Grammar for Writing: reduced adjective clauses

Adjective clauses can be reduced to adjective phrases.
clause: Hawaii, **which is known for its beautiful topography and climate**, lies in the middle of the Pacific Ocean.
phrase: Hawaii, **known for its beautiful topography and climate**, lies in the middle of the Pacific Ocean.

There are two ways to reduce an adjective clause to an adjective phrase:
1. When the adjective clause contains a form of the verb <u>be</u>, drop the relative pronoun and the verb <u>be</u>.
   Herodotus, **who was the first Greek historian**, wrote about the wars between ancient Greece and Persia. →
   Herodotus, **the first Greek historian**, wrote about the wars between ancient Greece and Persia.
2. When the adjective clause does not contain a form of the verb <u>be</u>, drop the relative pronoun and use the present participle of the verb.
   The human skeleton, **which contains** 206 separate bones, is a strong and flexible structure. →
   The human skeleton, **containing** 206 separate bones, is a strong and flexible structure.

   Those **who tamper** with the smoke detector will be prosecuted. →
   Those **tampering** with the smoke detector will be prosecuted.

Adjective phrases often begin with an article or <u>one</u>, <u>a type of</u>, or <u>a kind of</u>.
My grandmother, **a very practical and hardworking woman**, made clothes for the entire family.
The largest city in Turkey, Istanbul is at the point where Europe joins Asia.
They're looking for a quiet place to live, preferably **one in the suburbs**.
Chanterelles, **a type of edible mushroom with a rich yellow color**, are very expensive.
The llama and alpaca are camelids, **a kind of mammal native to South America**.

Remember
A <u>clause</u> is a group of words that has both a subject and a verb.
A <u>phrase</u> is a group of words that doesn't have both a subject and a verb.

The use of commas in reduced adjective clauses follows the same rules as those for full adjective clauses. See page 24 for the use of commas in restrictive and non-restrictive adjective clauses.

C Reduce the adjective clause in each sentence to an adjective phrase.

1. Daniel Craig and Rachel Weisz, ~~who are~~ two of the U.K.'s best-known movie actors, do charity work with underprivileged teens.
2. Philanthropy, ~~which is~~ the act of giving time and money to help others, can be very time-consuming.
3. Executives ~~who fail~~ *failing* to accept responsibility for their mistakes risk losing the trust of their employees.
4. The United Nations, ~~which hosts~~ *hosting* a number of humanitarian organizations, invited Angelina Jolie to be a goodwill ambassador to countries in need of assistance.
5. Truthfulness, ~~which is~~ believed to be taught to us by our parents, develops in children from a very young age.

Grammar for Writing: adjective clauses with quantifiers

- Have a volunteer read the explanation in the Grammar box. Then have students read the example sentences to themselves. Ask:

    In the first sentence, what does all of whom *refer to?* (three doctors)

    In the second sentence, what does none of which *refer to?* (several possible explanations)

    In the third sentence, what does one of whose *refer to?* (the president)

- Ask *Are the adjective clauses in these sentences restrictive or non-restrictive?* (non-restrictive) Point out that quantifiers can be used only with non-restrictive clauses.

- Have students skim Some expressions of quantity used with *of*. Elicit additional example sentences. (Possible answer: I spoke to both managers, *neither of whom* was willing to take responsibility for the mistake.)

- Read aloud the last explanation about adjective clauses with quantifiers. Add that students might also hear quantifiers used in formal spoken contexts.

B Complete each sentence . . .

- Have students decide whether each adjective clause refers to a person or a thing. (1. thing: products; 2. person: children; 3. person: students; 4. thing: articles; 5. person: parents) Review the construction quantifier + *of* + *whom*, *which*, or *whose*. Then ask:

    Which relative pronoun can you use with a quantifier that refers to things? (which)

    Which relative pronouns can you use with a quantifier that refers to people? (whom, whose)

- Have students do the exercise in pairs. Circulate and assist as needed. If students have difficulty, tell them to make sure the verb in the sentence agrees with the quantifier. Explain that *both of* and *neither of* are used when talking about two people or things.

- Bring the class together and go over the answers.

Challenge: [+15–20 minutes] Have pairs rewrite items 1, 2, and 4, using different expressions of quantity from the list on the top right of the page / (In items 3 and 5, no other quantifier retains the same meaning.) Tell students to make any necessary changes. Ask volunteers to read their sentences to the class. (Possible answers: 1. . . . only some of / half of which work. 2. . . . all of / some of whom always make . . . 4. . . . each of which deals . . .)

Grammar for Writing: reduced adjective clauses

- Read the first explanation in the Grammar box. Then have students review the definitions of a clause and a phrase in the Remember note. Focus on the example sentences. Ask:

    In the clause in the first sentence, what is the subject?

    What is the verb? (The subject is the relative pronoun *which*. The verb is *is*.)

    Does the phrase in the second sentence have a subject and a verb? (No. A phrase doesn't have both a subject and a verb.)

- Tell students that there are two ways to reduce an adjective clause to an adjective phrase. Ask a volunteer to read the first way. Then have students look at the example sentences and notice that the relative pronoun *who* and the verb *was* were dropped. Tell students that this kind of adjective phrase can also start a sentence: *The first Greek historian, Herodotus wrote about the wars between ancient Greece and Persia.*

- Write on the board *Rome, which is the capital of Italy, is one of the world's oldest cities.* Have students identify the adjective clause. (which is the capital of Italy) Tell the class to rewrite the sentence, changing the clause to a phrase. (Rome, the capital of Italy, is one of the world's oldest cities.) Write the sentence on the board for confirmation.

- Ask a volunteer to read the second way to reduce an adjective clause to an adjective phrase. Review that a present participle is the base form of a verb + *-ing*. Have students study the two pairs of sentences and notice that the relative pronouns (which, who) and verbs (contains, tamper) were replaced by present participles (containing, tampering). Tell students that this type of adjective clause can be placed at the beginning or end of a sentence as well as in the middle: *Containing 206 separate bones, the human skeleton is a strong and flexible structure. The human skeleton is a strong and flexible structure, containing 206 separate bones.*

- Ask a volunteer to read the last explanation in the Grammar box. Point out that when an adjective phrase such as *a very practical and hardworking woman* appears in the middle of the sentence, it must follow the noun or pronoun it gives additional information about—in this case, *My grandmother*.

- Call on volunteers to change each adjective phrase in the examples to a clause. (My grandmother, who is a very practical and hardworking woman, . . . ; Istanbul, which is the largest city in Turkey, . . . ; . . . a quiet place to live, preferably one that is in the suburbs; Chanterelles, which are a type of edible mushroom with a rich yellow color, . . . ; The llama and alpaca are camelids, which is a kind of mammal . . .)

C Reduce the adjective clause . . .

- To introduce the exercise, ask *In which sentences does the adjective clause include a relative pronoun and a form of the verb* be? (1. who are; 2. which is; 5. which is) *How can these adjective clauses be reduced to adjective phrases?* (Drop the relative pronoun and the verb *be*.) *How can the adjective clauses in the other sentences be reduced to adjective phrases?* (Drop the relative pronoun and use the present participle of the verb.)

- After students complete the exercise individually, have them compare answers with a partner.

D On a separate sheet of paper...

- Ask a volunteer to read the pair of sentences in item 1. Then ask students to focus on the sample answer.
- Have students scan the rest of the sentences. Tell them to note the noun phrase that each adjective phrase will modify. (2. Telling a white lie; 3. My mother; 4. My brother; 5. last night's concert)
- Have students do the exercise in pairs. Then go over any questions as a class.

Option: [+15–20 minutes] Have pairs take turns reading the sentences, changing the adjective phrases to adjective clauses. Remind students to choose the correct relative pronoun. (2. Telling a white lie, which is the type of lie we tell to protect others, can still get us in trouble; 3. My mother, who is the only person I know who is unable to tell a lie, taught me a lot about how to be honest; 4. My brother, who is a man of great compassion, frequently volunteers at the hospital; 5. A lot of money was raised at last night's concert, which was the biggest charity event of the year.)

Unit 3

Embedded questions: review and common errors

- Read the title of the chart. Elicit that the word *embed* means to put something firmly into something else. Explain that an embedded question is a question that is included inside another question or statement.
- Ask a student to read the first explanation. Have students compare the example yes / no questions and embedded yes / no questions. On the board, write

    Does she get fed up?

    Let's ask whether she gets fed up.

    Ask how the word order changed. (It changed from question to statement order.)

    Tell students to skim the phrases that are often followed by embedded questions. Call on volunteers to use different phrases to embed the example yes / no questions (For example: Don't tell them if you've ever asked your boss for a raise.)

- Point out that yes / no questions embed differently than information questions. Call on a student to read the second explanation. Tell students to read the example information questions and embedded information questions to themselves. On the board, write

    What's she afraid of?

    I can't remember what she's afraid of.

    Ask how has the word order changed. (The position of the verb changed.)

- Call on volunteers to use different phrases to embed the example information questions. (For example: Tell me when it was found.)
- Bring students' attention to the question words and phrases in the box.

- To go over punctuation, ask students to read the third explanation and example sentence. Then look back at the Phrases that are often followed by embedded questions in the box. Have students note which introduce statements and which ones are questions. Then have students skim the punctuation in the example statements and questions throughout the chart.
- Focus on the fourth explanation and example sentences. On the board, write

    Where is everyone?

    I wonder where everyone is.

    Ask *Which sentence is softer?* (the second) Elicit additional examples.

- Finally have students look at the Remember note to review the word order of embedded questions. Read the explanation and call on students to read the example sentences.

A On a separate sheet of paper...

- Have students skim the exercise items. Ask *Are we going to be embedding yes / no or information questions?* (yes / no questions) Then have students study the phrases that will introduce each embedded question. Ask *Which items will be questions and which will be statements?* (3, 5, 6, are questions; 1, 2, 4 are statements)
- Have students work individually to write the sentences. Circulate and assist as needed.
- Ask them to compare answers with a partner. Go over any questions as a class. Ask *Could whether be replaced by if in items 1, 2, and 6?* (yes) *Could if be replaced by whether in items 3, 4, 5?* (yes). Invite students to restate the sentence with the alternate word. Stress that *if* and *whether* have the same meaning.

D On a separate sheet of paper, combine each pair of sentences. Use the second sentence as an adjective phrase.

1 Amal Hijazi is also known for her humanitarian work. (Hijazi is a Lebanese pop singer currently living in Beirut.)

> Amal Hijazi, a Lebanese pop singer currently living in Beirut, is also known for her humanitarian work.

2 Telling a white lie can still get us into big trouble. (A white lie is the type of lie we tell to protect others.)
Telling a white lie, the type of lie we tell to proect others, can still get us into big trouble.
3 My mother taught me a lot about how to be honest. (My mother is the only person I know who is unable to tell a lie.)
My mother, the only person I know who is unable to tell a lie, taught me a lot about how to be honest.
4 My brother frequently volunteers in a hospital. (My brother is a man of great compassion.)
My brother, a man of great compassion, frequently volunteers in a hospital.
5 A lot of money was raised at last night's concert. (Last night's concert was the biggest charity event of the year.)
A lot of money was raised at last night's concert, the biggest charity event of the year.

UNIT 3

Embedded questions: review and common errors

Remember: A question can be embedded in a noun clause.
Use **if** or **whether** to begin an embedded **yes / no** question.
If and **whether** have the same meaning.

Yes / no questions	Embedded yes / no questions
Does she get fed up when she's frustrated?	Let's ask **whether she gets fed up when she's frustrated**.
Do you know what I mean?	I'd like to know **if you know what I mean**.
Have you ever asked your boss for a raise?	Could you tell me **if you've ever asked your boss for a raise**?

Phrases that are often followed by embedded questions

Ask …	I'd like to know …
Tell me …	Don't tell them …
I wonder …	I can't remember …
Let's ask …	Do you know …?
Don't say …	Can you tell me …?
I don't know …	Can you remember …?
Let me know …	Could you explain …?

Use a question word to begin embedded information questions.

Information questions	Embedded information questions
What's she afraid of?	I can't remember **what she's afraid of**.
Why have you decided to stay home?	I don't understand **why you've decided to stay home**.
When was it found?	Do you know **when it was found**?

Question words and phrases

how	what color	which
how many	what day	who
how much	when	whom
what	where	why

Punctuation of embedded questions
Use a period with an embedded question within a statement.
Use a question mark with an embedded question within a question.

I don't know who is singing.   **Would you mind telling me** who is singing?

Social use of embedded questions
You can use an embedded question to soften a direct question.
Why isn't this printer working? → Can you tell me **why this printer isn't working**?
Where's the bathroom? → Do you know **where the bathroom is**?

Embedded questions: common errors
Remember: Use regular statement word order, not inverted (question) word order, in embedded questions.
Do you know **why your parents won't** fly? NOT Do you know why ~~won't they~~ fly?
Can you tell me **whether this bus runs** express? NOT Can you tell me ~~does this bus run~~ express?

A On a separate sheet of paper, combine the two parts of each item to write an embedded question, using **if** or **whether**, as indicated. Punctuate each sentence correctly.

1 I can't remember (Is there going to be a late show?) [whether] *I can't remember whether there is going to be a late show.*
2 We're not sure (Was it John or Bill who found the wallet?) [whether] *We're not sure whether it was John or Bill who found the wallet.*
3 Could you tell me (Is the movie going to start soon?) [if] *Could you tell me if the movie is going to start soon?*
4 I wonder (Will the traffic be bad at this hour?) [if] *I wonder if the traffic will be bad at this hour.*
5 Would she like to know (Is there a possibility of getting a seat on the plane?) [if] *Would she like to know if there is a possibility of getting a seat on the plane?*
6 Do you know (Does this movie have a good cast?) [whether] *Do you know whether this movie has a good cast?*

B On a separate sheet of paper, combine the two parts of each item to write an embedded question. Punctuate each sentence correctly.

1 Please let me know (When do you expect to arrive?) *Please let me know when you expect to arrive.*
2 I wonder (Where were your parents when the earthquake occurred?) *I wonder where your parents were when the earthquake occurred.*
3 Can you tell me (How do you know that?) *Can you tell me how you know that?*
4 We're not sure (Where can we buy flowers to take to the hostess of the dinner party?) *We're not sure where we can buy flowers to take to the hostess of the dinner party.*
5 They'd like to understand (Why don't you just call the restaurant for reservations?) *They'd like to understand why you don't just call the restaurant for reservations.*
6 Please tell us (What time does the performance begin?) *Please tell us what time the performance begins.*

C On a separate sheet of paper, rewrite the sentences, correcting errors, including punctuation errors.

1 Please tell me what do you usually say when you feel frustrated. *Please tell me what you usually say when you feel frustrated.*
2 Can you remind me what day is the party? *Can you remind me what day the party is?*
3 Could you explain how did you make this omelet? *Could you explain how you made this omelet?*
4 Tell me what is your favorite color? *Tell me what your favorite color is.*
5 I wonder what should they do. *I wonder what they should do.*
6 Do you think is something wrong? *Do you think something is wrong?*

Count and non-count nouns

Non-count nouns made countable
A non-count noun is neither singular nor plural. Except in certain circumstances, it is not preceded by an article.
A non-count noun can be preceded by certain quantifiers such as much, **a lot of**, **a little**, and **some**.
   I always like **a little** sugar in my oatmeal. NOT I like a sugar in my oatmeal. OR Sugar are good in oatmeal.

Many non-count nouns can be made countable by using a phrase to limit them or give them a form.
   If you want to serve fruit for dessert, serve each person **two pieces of** fruit instead of one. One piece might not be enough.
   They got scared when they heard **a clap of** thunder.

Some phrases to make non-count nouns countable
The following phrases are used to make non-count nouns countable. The list includes abstract ideas, natural phenomena, foods, drinks and liquids, and household products. Many phrases are used in more than one category.

an article of (clothing)	**a cloud of** (smoke)	**a liter of** (gasoline / oil)
a bar of (chocolate / soap)	**a cup of** (sugar / rice / coffee / tea)	**a loaf of** (bread)
a bottle of (water)	**a drop of** (rain / water)	**a piece of** (fruit / paper / wood / metal / advice)
a bowl of (rice / soup / cereal)	**a game of** (tennis / soccer / chess)	**a teaspoon of** (salt / sugar)
a box of (rice / pasta)	**a glass of** (juice / milk)	**a type (or kind) of** (energy / behavior / music)
a carton of (milk / juice)	**a grain of** (sand / salt / rice)	

Phrases that are used to make a number of non-count nouns countable
Here are four common phrases that are used to make a number of non-count nouns countable.

a piece of { advice, equipment, furniture, gossip, information, news, paper }

a sense of { achievement, community, confidence, control, humor, heroism, identity }

an act of { anger, defiance, generosity, insanity, justice, kindness }

a state of { confusion, disrepair, emergency, mind, war }

Nouns used in both countable and uncountable sense
Some nouns can be used in both a countable and an uncountable sense.

a chance	=	a possibility	a coffee	=	a cup of coffee
chance	=	luck	coffee	=	a type of beverage
a light	=	a light source, such as a light bulb, lamp, etc.	a hair	=	a single hair
light	=	a type of energy	hair	=	all the hair on the head
a metal	=	a specific substance, such as gold or steel	a shampoo	=	a brand of shampoo
metal	=	a type of substance	shampoo	=	soap for your hair

B **On a separate sheet of paper . . .**

- Have students skim the exercise items. Ask *Are we going to be embedding yes / no or information questions?* (information questions) Then have students study the phrases that will introduce each embedded question. Ask *Which items will be questions and which will be statements?* (1, 2, 4, 5, 6 are statements; 3 is a question).
- Have students work individually to write the sentences. Circulate and assist as needed.
- Ask them to compare answers with a partner. Go over any questions as a class.

C **On a separate sheet of paper . . .**

- Tell students they will be looking for errors in each sentence: specifically, errors in word order and punctuation. Model the first item on the board. Write the statement and call on a student to make the correction (word order: . . . what you usually say . . .). Ask *Is the punctuation correct?* (yes)
- Have students work individually to correct the sentences.

Count and non-count nouns

- Write *chocolate, water, advice.* Ask *Are these count or non-count nouns?* (non-count) Explain that non-count nouns can be made countable by placing certain words before them. Ask a student to read the first explanation and example sentence. Call on volunteers to attach quantifiers to the words on the board and make sentences (Possible answers: I drank a little water. Can I have some chocolate? I got a lot of advice from Gerald).
- Read the second explanation. Have students read the example sentences. Write on the board *fruit, bread, thunder.* For comparison, ask students to suggest sentences with those words as non-count nouns. (Possible answers: Fruit is good for you; I don't eat bread; I'm scared of thunder.)
- Have students skim the phrases. With a partner, have students create pairs of sentences—one sentence using a phrase + non-count noun, and another sentence using just the non-count noun. (For example, I would like to order a cup of coffee. If I drink coffee after dinner, I can't sleep.) Have groups share their sentences.
- Read the fourth explanation in the Grammar box. Have students skim the phrases and nouns. Elicit an example sentence for each phrase and write them on the board. (Possible answers: He gave his son a piece of advice about paying his bills on time. I think it's important to have a sense of humor, don't you? His offer was an act of kindness. The country is in a state of confusion.) Next, have students suggest sentences using the same noun in an uncountable sense. Write them on the board to compare. (Possible answers: It's easy to give advice and hard to follow. Humor has health benefits. The whole town talks about his kindness. The doctor said I might experience confusion after taking the medication.)

- Read the last explanation in the Grammar box. Have students read the nouns used in both a countable and an uncountable sense. Elicit an example sentence for each noun used in a countable sense and uncountable sense and write these on the board. Answer any remaining questions students have.

Option: [+15–20 minutes] Tell students to keep their books closed. Divide the class into two teams. Alternate giving teams a non-count noun from one of the charts. Have students use the noun with a phrase to make it countable. (Possible answer: sugar; a box of sugar) Use a selection of 15 to 25 nouns, depending on available time. Give one point for each correct phrase + noun. The team with the most points wins.

D On a separate sheet of paper . . .

- Have students skim the underlined non-count nouns in each sentence. Tell them to think about meaning. Then have them rewrite the statements using phrases to make the nouns countable. Circulate and assist, referring students to the grammar chart as needed.
- Have students compare answers with a partner. Then go over any questions as a class.

E Choose the best word . . .

- Have students cover the sentences with a piece of paper and scan the list of words in the box. Ask *Which non-count nouns might these words be combined with?* (Possible answers: an act of insanity; a bar of chocolate; a glass of water; a piece of candy; a sense of danger; a state of innocence)
- Then have students complete the exercise individually. Have them compare answers with a partner.

Challenge: [+15–20 minutes] Elicit sentences using the phrases from the exercise with other nouns. (Possible answer: Jan helped me move the heavy piece of furniture.)

Unit 4

Grammar for Writing: more conjunctions and transitions

- Have students read the Remember note to review the uses and punctuation of coordinating conjunctions, subordinating conjunctions, and transitions. Have students scan the chart vertically to see examples of each conjunction or transition.
- Then tell pairs to read through the chart horizontally and create example sentences with the conjunctions and transitions that are not already used in the examples in the chart. If students have difficulty, suggest example sentences on the board for reference.
- Note that *As a consequence* (under To express cause or result, Transitions) is taught in U8 Writing; *All the same* and *On the other hand* (under To show contrast, Transitions) are taught in U10 Writing section.

T133

D On a separate sheet of paper, rewrite the statements, using a phrase to make each underlined non-count noun countable.

1. If you're going to play <u>tennis</u> tomorrow morning, give me a call. *a game of tennis*
2. When I plant my garden in April, I wait eagerly for the first <u>rain</u> to make sure the plants grow. *drops of rain*
3. If you sew or repair <u>clothing</u> yourself instead of taking it to someone else, you will save a lot of money in the long run. *pieces of clothing*
4. They say that turning <u>bread</u> upside down after a slice has been cut from it will keep it fresh. *a loaf of bread*
5. When I make chicken soup, I like to serve <u>rice</u> on the side. *a bowl of rice*

E Choose the best word from the box to complete each sentence.

| act | bar | glass | piece | sense | state |

1. The group's donation was a true ...*act*... of generosity.
2. My sister has an amazing ...*sense*... of humor.
3. The woman slipped on a ...*piece /bar*... of soap in the shower.
4. Our town has been in a ...*state*... of emergency since the hurricane.
5. The park just installed a new ...*piece*... of equipment in the playground.
6. I asked the server for a ...*glass*... of orange juice.

UNIT 4

Grammar for Writing: more conjunctions and transitions

Purpose	Coordinating conjunctions	Subordinating conjunctions	Transitions
To add information Marc is working as a photographer, **and** he has experience in graphic design. **In addition to** working as a photographer, Marc has experience in graphic design.	and	in addition to besides	In addition, Furthermore, Moreover, Besides, More importantly,
To clarify information Smaller cars are more efficient; **in other words,** they use less fuel.			That is, In other words, In fact,
To illustrate or exemplify information Many European cities are found along waterways. **For example,** London, Paris, Vienna, and Budapest all lie on major rivers.			For instance, For example, To illustrate,
To show contrast Meg does not usually perform well under pressure, **but** she gave a brilliant recital. Meg does not usually perform well under pressure. **Despite this,** she gave a brilliant recital.	but yet	even though although though while whereas despite the fact that	However, Nevertheless, Nonetheless, In contrast, Even so, Still, Despite [this / that], In spite of [this / that], All the same, On the other hand,
To express cause or result They have a new baby, **so** they rarely get a good night's sleep! **Now that** they have a new baby, they rarely get a good night's sleep!	so for	because since due to the fact that now that so that	Therefore, Consequently, Accordingly, As a consequence, As a result,

Remember
- A <u>coordinating conjunction</u> links two independent clauses in a sentence. It is preceded by a comma.
- A <u>subordinating conjunction</u> introduces a dependent clause in a sentence. When a dependent clause starts a sentence, the clause is followed by a comma.
- A <u>transition</u> links ideas between sentences or paragraphs. It usually begins a sentence and is followed by a comma. A transition can be preceded by a semicolon.

GRAMMAR BOOSTER

To express a condition	or (else)	(only) if	Otherwise,
Pollution can be reduced **provided that** car manufacturers mass-produce cars with greater fuel efficiency. Car manufacturers should mass-produce cars with greater fuel efficiency. **Otherwise,** pollution will not be reduced.		provided that as long as unless even if whether (or not)	
To show similarity Water is necessary for life. **Similarly,** oxygen is required by all living things.			Similarly, Likewise,

A On a separate sheet of paper, combine each pair of sentences two ways: once with the connecting word(s) in **a** and once with the connecting words in **b**. Use a semicolon before a transition. Change the wording as necessary to retain the meaning. See page T134 for answers.

1. John is a bit of a perfectionist. His brothers are pretty easygoing. (**a** while **b** in contrast)
2. Nicole has always struggled with being disorganized. She has made a lot of progress recently. (**a** although **b** despite that)
3. My boss tends to be very negative. He gets angry too quickly. (**a** in addition to **b** furthermore)
4. I need to stop procrastinating. I won't ever finish the class assignment on time. (**a** unless **b** otherwise)
5. Carla has been trying not to be so controlling at work. She gets along better with her colleagues. (**a** now that **b** as a result)

Cleft sentences: more on meaning and use

Cleft sentences with What
Cleft sentences with What are often used to clarify what someone said, thought, or meant.

   A: Do you think Gail would like to go somewhere for her birthday?
   B: Actually, **what she'd really like is** for us to take her out to a nice restaurant.

   A: Were you surprised that Rob called you after your argument?
   B: Actually, **what surprised me was** that he was even willing to talk to me!

Cleft sentences with It
Cleft sentences with It are used to clarify who, what, when, where, or why.

   A: Did you try calling me a few minutes ago? Your number popped up in my missed calls.
   B: Actually, **it was my sister** who called you. She was using my phone. (clarifies who)

   A: Our neighbor had a great party last night. But I have to say, the noise really got to me.
   B: Well, **it was not getting an invitation** that really bugged me. (clarifies what)

   A: Don't I see you in the computer lab on Mondays?
   B: I doubt it. **It's usually on Tuesdays and Thursdays** that I go to the lab. (clarifies when)

   A: Did you hear about the bus accident this morning?
   B: Yeah. And **it was just down the street from me** where it happened! (clarifies where)

   A: Thanks for helping me with the homework.
   B: Well, **it's because you're always so nice** that I did it. (clarifies why)

B Clarify what B said, thought, or meant. Complete each cleft sentence using the underlined information.

1. A: <u>Are you excited about</u> going on vacation next week?
   B: Actually, **what I'm excited about is** getting to see my aunt and uncle again.
2. A: <u>Did you think</u> your boss was going to lose her temper?
   B: On the contrary. **what I thought was** that she was going to give me a promotion.
3. A: It's 6:15. I thought <u>you said</u> you'd be here at 6:00.
   B: **What I said was that** we should plan to meet at 6:00, but that I might be a little late.

134 GRAMMAR BOOSTER

A On a separate sheet of paper...

- Have students scan the connecting words in the exercise and identify which are subordinating conjunctions and which are transitions. (1. while: SC, in contrast: T; 2. although: SC, despite that: T; 3. in addition to: SC, furthermore: T; 4. unless: SC, otherwise: T; 5. now that: SC, as a result: T)
- To review, ask *What punctuation is used with subordinating conjunctions?* (When a subordinating conjunction introduces a dependent clause that starts a sentence, the clause is followed by a comma.) *What punctuation is used with transitions?* (A transition is followed by a comma. It can be preceded by a semicolon.)
- Have students rewrite the sentences individually. Then have them compare answers with a partner.

Cleft sentences: more on meaning and use

- Read the first explanation under Cleft sentences with What. Call on volunteers to read the example exchanges. Point out how in each second sentence the original verb is repeated with a clarification. Ask a student *Would you like to go to a museum this weekend?* If necessary, write the sentence on the board. Invite the student to clarify what he or she would actually like. (Possible answer: Actually, what I'd really like is to go to a concert this weekend.)
- Read the second explanation under Cleft sentences with It. Call on two volunteers to read the first example exchange. Then, in pairs, have students read each exchange to each other, focusing on who, what, when, where, why. Point out that even though the third exchange clarifies *when* something happened, you use *that*.

Answers to Exercise A

Answers will vary but may include the following:

1. a. While John is a bit of a perfectionist, his brothers are pretty easygoing.
   b. John is a bit of a perfectionist; in contrast, his brothers are pretty easygoing.
2. a. Although Nicole has always struggled with being disorganized, she has made a lot of progress recently.
   b. Nicole has always struggled with being disorganized; despite that, she has made a lot of progress recently.
3. a. My boss tends to be very negative in addition to getting angry too quickly.
   b. My boss tends to be very negative; furthermore, he gets angry too quickly.
4. a. Unless I stop procrastinating, I won't ever finish the class assignment on time.
   b. I need to stop procrastinating; otherwise, I won't ever finish the class assignment on time.
5. a. Now that Carla has been trying not to be so controlling at work, she gets along better with her colleagues.
   b. Carla has been trying not to be so controlling at work; as a result, she gets along better with her colleagues.

B Clarify what B said...

- Have students skim the statements and identify the tense of each verb phrase (1. simple present; 2. simple past; 3. simple past; 4. simple past; 5. modal + continuous). Tell students to be careful to maintain the same tense when creating the cleft. If necessary, model the first item. Ask *What pronoun do we need in B's answer?* (I) Write on the board *What I'm excited about is . . .*
- Have students work in pairs to complete B's responses.
- Go over the answers as a class. Call on pairs to role-play the conversations.

C Write cleft sentences . . .

- Have students skim the statements and determine if the sentence clarifies *who, what, when, where,* or *why* (1. what; 2. who; 3. that; 4. why; 5. where). Tell students to also identify the tense of each verb phrase (1. simple present; 2. simple past; 3. simple future; 4. simple present; 5. simple present). Remind them to maintain the same tense when creating the cleft.
- Have students work in pairs to complete B's responses.
- Go over the answers as a class. Call on pairs to role-play the conversations.

Unit 5

Indirect speech: review and expansion

- Have a volunteer read the first explanation. Then have pairs take turns reading each example, first in direct speech and then in indirect speech.
- Elicit additional affirmative and negative examples of the imperative in direct speech. Write these on the board. Then call on volunteers to put these into indirect speech. Listen for correct changes to the infinitive as well as *not* + infinitive for negative statements.
- Finally, call on a student to read aloud the information in the Remember note.
- Have students read the second explanation and then study the pairs of sentences, focusing on the pronouns.
- Write the following chart and sentences on the board:

Direct Speech	Indirect Speech
1. Nancy said, "I'm never too busy to complain to you about how busy I am."	
2.	He said he hoped I understood and that he didn't want to repeat the assignment.

Have students change the first sentence from direct to indirect speech, and the second from indirect to direct speech. (1. Nancy said she's never too busy to complain to me about how busy she is. 2. He said, "I hope you understand. I don't want to repeat the assignment.")

A On a separate sheet of paper . . .

- Ask students *What type of statements are the sentences in quotation?* (imperative) Elicit that these need to be changed to the infinitive in indirect speech. Hint to students to be careful of pronouns and possessives.
- After students do the exercise individually, have them compare answers with a partner.
- Then bring the class together and go over any questions.

Answers to Exercise A

1. Marian advised Claire to turn the TV on at 9:00 because there was a funny movie on.
2. Dr. Baker advised his patient not to let emotional tension make him sick.
3. She told me to be a good sport and laugh about it.
4. Fred instructed his son not to laugh at that joke because it was disgusting.
5. An old saying advises us to laugh first, cry later.
6. Lucas told us to never touch the green button on the printer.
7. Mr. Franklln's neighbor told him to take the penguin to the zoo the next day.
8. Nick said not to ask how the meeting had gone.

4 A: What did Gary mean when he said his tablet cost an arm and a leg?
    B: What he meant was that .... it was a lot more expensive than he thought it would be.
5 A: Should you be eating that cake?
    B: According to my doctor, what I should be eating is .... nothing but healthy food. But I don't care!

C Write cleft sentences with It to clarify who, what, when, where, or why. Use the prompts.
  1 A: Is feeding a parrot a lot of work?
      B: Are you kidding? It's cleaning the cage that's a lot of work. (clean the cage)
  2 A: Did Gina write that song?
      B: No. It was her sister who wrote the song. (her sister)
  3 A: Will the traffic be really bad at this time?
      B: I don't think so. It's usually at 5:00 that it's bad. (at 5:00)
  4 A: These cookies are so good!
      B: Thanks. It's because I added nuts that they're so good. (because / I add / nuts)
  5 A: Aren't we supposed to meet Jason at the coffee shop?
      B: No. It's at the bus stop where we're supposed to meet him. (at the bus stop)

UNIT 5

Indirect speech: review and expansion

Imperatives in indirect speech
When imperatives are used to report commands, requests, instructions, and invitations, the imperative form changes to the infinitive. The negative infinitive is used for negative commands, requests, and instructions.

Direct speech	Indirect speech
"Could you please **go** to the store?"	She asked me **to go** to the store.
The chef said, "**Add** two eggs and stir the mixture."	The chef said **to add** two eggs and stir the mixture.
"Please **have** dinner with us," he said.	He invited me **to have** dinner with them.
She told the child, "**Don't cross** the street."	She told the child **not to cross** the street.

Changes to pronouns and possessives
Remember: In indirect speech, pronouns and possessives change to reflect the point of view of the reporter rather than the original speaker.

My manager said, "**You** have to finish **your** report and give it to **me** as soon as possible."	→	My manager said (that) **I** had to finish **my** report and give it to **her** as soon as possible.
I told her, "**You'll** have **this** report on **your** desk by noon."	→	I told her (that) **she** would have **that** report on **her** desk by noon.
Peter asked them, "Are **these** coats **yours**?"	→	Peter asked them if **those** coats were **theirs**.

Remember
Indirect questions end with a period, not a question mark. Like in embedded questions, verbs in indirect questions follow the same changes as the verbs in indirect statements.

A On a separate sheet of paper, write each sentence in indirect speech. See page T135 for answers.
  1 Marian advised Claire, "Turn on the TV at 9:00 because there's a funny movie on."
  2 Dr. Baker advised his patient, "Don't let emotional tension make you sick."
  3 She told me, "Be a good sport and laugh about it."
  4 "Don't laugh at that joke," Fred instructed his son. "It's disgusting."
  5 "Laugh first, cry later," an old saying advises us.
  6 Lucas told us, "Never touch the green button on the printer."
  7 "Take the penguin to the zoo tomorrow," Mr. Franklin's neighbor told him.
  8 Nick said, "Please don't ask how the meeting went."

B On a separate sheet of paper, write these conversations in indirect speech, using correct pronouns and possessives.

1. **MARIA:** Your cartoon is great. Your drawing is so funny.
   JACK: Yours is hilarious, too! It really cracked me up!
2. **KATHERINE:** Allison, I'm not sure if this tablet is yours.
   ALLISON: It's definitely mine. Thanks!
3. **RICHARD:** My paper on the health benefits of humor has just been published in a medical journal.
   ME: I'm happy for you! I'd appreciate it if you could give me a copy.
4. **KIM:** I bought a new MP3 player last week.
   BEN: I know. I saw it on your desk. It looks much better than your old one.
5. **SAM:** I got all these articles about humor on the Internet last weekend.
   PIRI: That's great. Would you let me read them when you've finished them?

Maria said Jack's cartoon was great and that...
Jack answered that...

Say, tell, and ask

Remember: Use **tell** when you mention the listener. You can use **say** in indirect speech when you mention the listener, but you must use the preposition **to** and introduce the indirect speech with **that**.

Marie **told** Dr. Barton she had to change the time of her appointment. (listener mentioned)
Dr. Barton **said** that wouldn't be a problem. (listener not mentioned)
Dr. Barton **said to** the nurse that it wouldn't be a problem. (listener mentioned)

Use **ask** either with or without mentioning the listener. Don't use **to** after **ask** when you mention the listener.

Marie **asked** if she could make an appointment later in the week. OR Marie **asked** Dr. Barton if she could make an appointment later in the week.

BE CAREFUL!
DON'T SAY: He ~~said the manager~~ that he completely disagreed with her.
DON'T SAY: He ~~told~~ that he completely disagreed with the manager.
DON'T SAY: He ~~told to the manager~~ that he completely disagreed with her.
DON'T SAY: He ~~asked to the manager~~ if she agreed.

C Complete the sentences with a form of *say*, *tell*, or *ask*.

1. She ..**asked**.. the server if she could pay with a credit card.
2. We ..**said**.. that we would come back later when they were less busy.
3. He ..**told**.. his friends that he would be a few minutes late.
4. She ..**said**.. to her teacher that she needed a bit more time.
5. They ..**told**.. the reporter that they were ready to provide information about the case.
6. I ..**asked**.. them if they enjoyed the movie.

Grammar for Writing: other reporting verbs

Writers use a variety of reporting verbs to describe actions more specifically and accurately.

claim
"Things are definitely getting better," **claims** Charles Wilder, a patient trying out humor therapy for the first time.
Charles Wilder, a patient trying out humor therapy for the first time, **claims** that things are definitely getting better.

declare
"The nursing staff has been doing a brilliant job!" **declared** the head doctor on Tuesday.
On Tuesday, the head doctor **declared** that the nursing staff had been doing a brilliant job.

explain
"You should always discuss dieting with your doctor," Dr. Fish **explained**.
Dr. Fish **explained** that people should always discuss dieting with their doctors.

report
The New York Times **reports**, "Obesity is a growing problem in Asia."
Last year, the New York Times **reported** that obesity was a growing problem in Asia.

state
The new CEO **stated**, "Things are going to change around here."
The new CEO **stated** that things were going to change at the company.

More reporting verbs
add	maintain
announce	mention
answer	promise
comment	remark
complain	reply
exclaim	reveal
imply	write

B On a separate sheet of paper...

- Have volunteers read the conversations. Ask *What changes will you need to make when you write these conversations in indirect speech?* (There will be changes in verb forms, pronouns, and possessives.)
- Have students rewrite the conversations individually. Then have students compare answers with a partner.
- Bring the class together and go over any questions.

Challenge: [+15–20 minutes] Have pairs write their own short conversations. Then combine pairs into groups of four and have each pair read their conversation. Have the pair that is listening restate what the other pair said to each other.

Say, tell, and ask

- Call on a student to read the Remember note. Focus in on the two example sentences with *said*. Stress that when a listener is mentioned, *to* must be used. On the board, write:

    Lina said to us that she is very grateful.

    Lina said that she was very grateful.

- Ask *What is the difference between these sentences?* (in the first sentence the listener is mentioned—*us*; in the second sentence the listener is not mentioned)
- Focus on the Be careful! note. Elicit the possible corrections to the sentences. (He said told the manager...; He said to the manager...; He said that he completely...; He told us that he completely...; He told the manager...; He said to the manger...; He asked the manager if...; He asked if...)

Answers to Exercise B

1. Maria said Jack's cartoon was great and that his drawing was so funny. Jack answered that Maria's was hilarious, too, and that it really cracked him up.
2. Katherine said that she was not sure if that tablet was Allison's. Allison replied that it was definitely hers and thanked Katherine.
3. Richard said that his paper on the health benefits of humor had just been published in a medical journal. I told him that I was happy for him and would appreciate it if he could give me a copy.
4. Kim told Ben that she had bought a new MP3 player last week. Ben said that he knew because he had seen it on her desk. He thought it looked much better than her old one.
5. Sam said that he had gotten a lot of articles about humor on the Internet last weekend. Piri said that that was great. He asked Sam if he would let him read them when he had finished with them.

C Complete the sentences with...

- Tell students to skim the statements and have them note in which ones there is a listener mentioned. Remind students that *said* requires *to* when a listener is mentioned; *told* is just followed by the listener. Review that *ask* is followed by *if*.
- After students do the exercise individually, have them compare answers with a partner.
- Then bring the class together and go over any questions.

Grammar for Writing: other reporting verbs

- In pairs, have students study the variety of reporting verbs and the example sentences.
- Then tell them to test out other words from the list of More reporting verbs in place of the highlighted verbs. (For example: *Charles Wilder... remarks that things are definitely getting better.*)

D On a separate sheet of paper...

- Encourage students to look up verbs. Then have them work in pairs to rewrite the sentences.
- Bring the class together and have students share verbs they used to replace those in the exercise.

Challenge: [+15–20 minutes] Have students work in pairs to change the statements to direct speech. Remind students to pay attention to shifts in verb tenses and changes to pronouns and possessives.

1. "The president of Chile will be visiting Thailand next month." says the *Bangkok Post*.
2. "Major improvements have been made in schools across the country," said the minister of education yesterday.
3. "More should be done to alleviate world hunger," says the secretary of the United Nations.
4. "More research will have to be conducted," said the scientists who conducted the study.
5. "We won't do it again," said the children who wrote on the walls
6. "We will increase our coverage of the news in the Middle East," the BBC said.

Unit 6

The conditional: summary and extension

- Have students scan the first column to review the different types of conditionals.
- Focus on the factual conditional. Tell students to read the explanation about factual conditions that express a general or scientific fact. Elicit additional examples. (Possible answers: Classes are canceled if it snows heavily. If a pot is made of aluminum, a magnet doesn't stick to its surface.) Check that students use the simple present in both the *if* clause and the result clause. Then have students restate these sentences, replacing *if* with *when* or *whenever*. (... when OR whenever it snows heavily. When OR Whenever a pot is made ...)
- Have a volunteer read the explanation for the second use of the factual conditional. On the board, write *If you will help me study, I will pass the exam.* Ask *Is this sentence correct?* (no) Have students correct the mistake. (If you help me study ...) Point out that you cannot use a future form in the *if* clause.
- Next write on the board:

    If I knew the answer, I would help you.

    If I had known the answer, I would have helped you.

    Ask: *Are these sentences examples of the factual or the unreal conditional?* (unreal)

    Which sentence contains the present unreal conditional? (the first one) Keep the sentences on the board for use with discussion of the past unreal conditional.

- Tell students to read the explanation and example sentences for the present unreal conditional. Refer students to the first example sentence and ask:

    Do I have the time to explain the problem to you? (no)

    Under what condition would I explain the problem to you? (if I had the time)

- Continue referring to the two sentences on the board.

    Ask *Which sentence contains the past unreal conditional?* (the second one)

- Tell students to read the explanation and example sentences for the past unreal conditional. Refer students to the first example sentence and ask:

    Did they know about the storm? (no)

    Under what condition would they have taken a different flight? (if they had known about the storm)

- Finally, have students read the explanations for the mixed time frames. Ask students to create statements using the mixed conditional in relation to the present or to the past. (Possible answers: If I had understood the directions, I might not be lost now. If I knew how to repair my car, I wouldn't have called the service station.)
- Focus on Extension: other uses. Ask a student to read the first explanation. On the board, write *If Natalie calls, tell her the good news.* Have volunteers restate the *if* clause three different ways. (If Natalie should call; If Natalie happens to call; If Natalie should happen to call)
- Read the second explanation and example sentences to the class. Make sure students understand that inferences are deductions. Discuss the context of each situation. (Possible answers: Julie probably went to the party, so she saw what happened. Since you don't know the answer, I can tell you didn't do the homework. The results didn't come out yesterday, so they'll come out today. Since you haven't finished packing, you're going to miss your flight.)

Option: [+15–20 minutes] Write the following *if* clauses on the board. To review the factual, present unreal, and past unreal conditional, have students write a result clause for each clause. Then have them identify the type of conditional.

1. *If Phil leaves at 11:00, ...*
2. *If I were you, ...*
3. *If you put sugar in water, ...*
4. *If they had called us, ...*

(Possible answers: 1. he will come to class on time—factual; 2. I wouldn't buy that coat—present unreal; 3. the sugar dissolves—factual; 4. we would have picked them up—past unreal)

D On a separate sheet of paper, restate each sentence with a different reporting verb. Use a dictionary if necessary.
Answers will vary but may include the following:
1 The Bangkok Post says that the president of Chile will be visiting Thailand next month.
   The Bangkok Post reports that the president of Chile will be visiting Thailand next month.
2 The minister of education said yesterday that major improvements had been made in schools across the country.
   The minister of education stated yesterday that major improvements had been made in schools across the country.
3 The secretary of the United Nations says that more should be done to alleviate world hunger.
   The secretary of the UN claims that more should be done to alleviate world hunger.
4 The scientists who conducted the study said that more research would have to be conducted.
   The scientists who conducted the study implied that more research would have to be conducted.
5 The children who wrote on the walls said that they wouldn't do it again.
   The children who wrote on the walls promised that they wouldn't do it again.
6 The BBC said that it would increase its coverage of the news in the Middle East.
   The BBC mentioned that it would increase its coverage of the news in the Middle East.

UNIT 6

The conditional: summary and extension

Type	Use	If clause (states the condition)	Result clause (states the result)	Examples
Factual conditional	To express a general or scientific fact	simple present Note: In this type of conditional, if can be replaced by when or whenever.	simple present	If it **rains**, the gardens **close** early. Water **freezes** if the temperature **falls** below zero degrees Celsius.
	To talk about what will happen in the future under certain conditions	simple present Note: Don't use a future form in the if clause.	will / be going to + base form of the verb Note: Use can, may, might, should if the result is not certain.	If you **plan** your trip carefully, things **will go** smoothly. If we **arrive** late, they're **going to start** without us. If we **hurry**, we **may be able to catch** the train.
Present unreal conditional	To talk about present unreal or untrue conditions	simple past or were Note: Don't use would in the if clause.	would + base form of the verb Note: Use could or might if the result is not certain.	If I **had** the time, I **would explain** the problem to you. If he **were** here, he **might make** a lot of changes.
Past unreal conditional	To talk about past unreal or untrue conditions	past perfect Note: Don't use would have in the if clause.	would have + past participle Note: Use could have or might have if the result is not certain.	If they **had known** about the storm, they **would have taken** a different flight. If you **had told** us about the delay, we **could have made** other arrangements.
Mixed time frames	To talk about past unreal or untrue conditions in relation to the present	past perfect Note: Don't use would in the if clause.	would + base form of the verb Note: Use could or might if the result is not certain.	If I **had prepared** for the interview, I **wouldn't be** so nervous. If we **had left** earlier, we **might be** on time now.
	To talk about present unreal or untrue conditions in relation to the past	simple past or were Note: Don't use would have in the if clause.	would have + past participle Note: Use could have or might have if the result is not certain.	If she **were** honest, she **would have told** us the truth. If I **spoke** Russian, I **might have understood** the guide.

Extension: other uses

Use should, happen to, or should happen to in the if clause in factual conditionals when the condition is less likely.

If you { should / happen to / should happen to } see Peter, tell him to call me.

To express inferences in conditional sentences, different combinations of tenses can be used.
   If Julie **went** to the party last night, she definitely **saw** what happened.
   If you **don't know** the answer to this question, you **didn't do** your homework.
   If the results **didn't come out** yesterday, they**'ll** definitely **come out** today.
   If you still **haven't finished** packing by now, you**'re not going to catch** your flight.

GRAMMAR BOOSTER 137

A Circle the correct word or words to complete each sentence.
1. If Sam (**does**/ will do) well this year, he will apply to medical school.
2. Water (**boils**/ is going to boil) when the temperature reaches 100 degrees Celsius.
3. If you (will /**should**) find my scarf, please hold it for me.
4. If you (happen /**happen to**) see a good camera at the market, please buy it for me.
5. If it (wouldn't have been /**hadn't been**) for her savings, Anna wouldn't have been able to attend university.
6. If we (would have known /**had known**) that car insurance was so expensive, we would not have bought a car.
7. If you didn't get a reply today, you (would definitely hear /**will definitely hear**) from us tomorrow.
8. If I (**had**/ would have) a garden, I would grow several types of flowers.
9. If I (would have practiced /**had practiced**) my speech a bit more, I might not be so worried now.
10. If I (**should happen to**/ will) see John, I'll tell him to call you.

UNIT 7

Article usage: summary

Note where indefinite or definite articles are used or omitted.

	Indefinite article	Definite article	No article
General statement	Use with singular count nouns: **A cat** may symbolize good fortune.	Use with singular count nouns: **The cat** may symbolize good fortune. Use with non-count nouns: Freud called attention to **the importance** of dreams.	With plural count nouns: **Cats** may symbolize good fortune. With non-count nouns: **Misfortune** may strike at any time.
First mention	Use with singular count nouns: I found **a lucky charm**.		With plural count nouns: I have (some) lucky **charms**. With non-count nouns: I bought (some) **shampoo**.
Second mention		Use with singular count nouns: **The** lucky **charm** was in a box. Use with plural count nouns: **The** lucky **charms** were in a box. Use with non-count nouns: **The shampoo** is in the closet.	

A On a separate sheet of paper, rewrite the paragraph, correcting eleven errors and making any necessary changes.
See page T138 for answers.
    The homes are expensive these days, but Peter got lucky and bought small house last week. A house has two bedrooms and one bathroom. It also has large kitchen and the living room. Peter will use a living room as his home office. Bedrooms are in bad condition, and Peter will need a help painting them. Then he wants to have the party so his friends can admire a house. Later Peter will buy a furniture—when he saves some money!

Definite article: additional uses

When a noun represents a unique thing	Use with singular count nouns: **The sun** rises in the east.
With a comparative or superlative adjective to make a noun unique (or with <u>right</u>, <u>wrong</u>, <u>first</u>, <u>only</u>, <u>same</u>)	Use with singular count nouns: Telling the truth is **the best course** of action. It's always **the right thing** to do. The robin is **the first sign** of spring. Use with plural count nouns: People in different places often have **the same superstitions**. Use with non-count nouns: That's **the only information** I was able to find on the Internet.

138 GRAMMAR BOOSTER

A Circle the correct word...

- Have students scan the if clauses and think about the possible verb forms that could be used in the result clauses. Then have students complete the exercise individually. Refer them to the chart on page 137 if they have difficulty.
- Have students compare answers with a partner. Bring the class together and have students identify each type of conditional sentence. (1. factual; 2. factual—scientific fact; 3. factual—the condition is less likely; 4. factual—the condition is less likely; 5. past unreal—to express relief; 6. past unreal; 7. conditional expressing inference; 8. present unreal; 9. mixed; 10. factual—the condition is less likely)

Challenge: [+15–20 minutes] For more practice, have pairs make up different result clauses for the if clauses in the exercise, and different if clauses for the result clauses. Have students share their sentences with the class.

Unit 7

Article usage: summary

- Before students open their books, ask:
  What is the definite article? (the)
  What are the indefinite articles? (a, an)
- Focus on the use of articles in General statement. Call on a volunteer to read the explanation and example sentence under the heading Indefinite article. Then have another student read the explanations and the example sentences under the heading Definite article. Point out that, unlike the indefinite article, the definite article can be used with both count and non-count nouns. Finally, read aloud the explanations and example sentences under the heading No article.
- Have students look at the second row of the chart. Then ask *Would you use the indefinite article, the definite article, or no article for the first mention of a noun?* (the indefinite article or no article)
- On the board, create a chart like the following.

Singular count nouns	Plural count nouns	Non-count nouns
I found a lucky charm.	I have lucky charms.	I bought shampoo.
The lucky charm was in a box.	The lucky charms were in a box.	The shampoo is in the closet.

Have a student read aloud the explanations and example sentences, and write the example sentences in the first row on the board.

- Have students look at the third row of the chart in their book. Then ask *Would you use the indefinite article, the definite article, or no article for the second mention of a noun?* (the definite article) Ask a student to read the explanations and example sentences aloud, and write the example sentences in the second row on the board.
- Pointing to the chart on the board, review that singular count nouns use *a* for the first mention and *the* for the second mention. Plural count nouns use no article for the first mention and *the* for the second mention. Non-count nouns use no article for the first mention and *the* for the second mention.

Challenge: [+15–20 minutes] Bring English-language magazines to class (or print out appropriate materials from the Internet) and have pairs choose one article to focus on. Tell students to find examples of the article usage outlined in the chart. Have them highlight the examples and then share them with the class.

A On a separate sheet of paper...

- Tell students to read the paragraph through once before making the corrections. Then have them complete the exercise.
- Ask students to compare answers with a partner.
- Bring the class together, and have students explain the reasons for the corrections. (*Homes*: no article, general statement, plural count noun; *a small house*: article *a*, first mention, singular count noun; *The house*: article *the*, second mention, singular count noun; *a large kitchen, a living room*: article *a*, first mention, singular count nouns; *the living room*: article *the*, second mention, singular count noun; *The bedrooms*: article *the*, second mention, plural count noun; *help*: no article, general statement, non-count noun; *a party*: article *a*, first mention, singular count noun; *the house*: article *the*, second mention, singular count noun; *furniture*: no article, general statement, non-count noun)

Answers to Exercise A

Homes are expensive these days, but Peter got lucky and bought a small house last week. The house has two bedrooms and one bathroom.
It also has a large kitchen and a living room. Peter will use the living room as his home office. The bedrooms are in bad condition, and Peter will need help painting them. Then he wants to have a party so his friends can admire the house. Later Peter will buy furniture—when he saves some money!

Definite article: additional uses

- Have pairs read through the chart of additional uses of the definite article and the example sentences. Circulate and answer questions as needed.
- Then bring the class together. Elicit examples as follows: *Give some other examples of a noun that represents a unique thing.* (Possible answers: the equator; the universe; the sky; the president) *Give some other examples of a superlative adjective that makes a noun unique.* (Possible answers: the funniest joke; the oldest person; the most advanced computer) *Give some other examples of a context that makes a noun specific.* (Possible answers: the ideas in this essay; the food on this table)
- Continue eliciting examples from the class, as follows: *Give some other examples in which an adjective clause makes a noun specific.* (Possible answers: the report that's on the copier; the woman who came to the door)
- Have students suggest example sentences for the adjectives in the chart that represent a certain group of people. Remind them to use the definite article. (Possible answer: The poor in this city are eligible for food stamps.)

B Complete the paragraphs . . .
- After students complete the exercise individually, have them compare answers with a partner.
- Then bring the class together and go over the uses of the definite article. (1. the first men: adjective makes a noun unique; 2. the world: unique thing; 5. the wealthy: adjective represents a certain group of people; 7. The view: context makes the noun specific; 8. the sky: unique thing)

More non-count nouns with both a countable . . .
- Read the explanation in the Grammar box aloud. Then have partners take turns reading the pairs of example sentences.
- Elicit other non-count nouns that have both a countable and an uncountable sense, such as *noise*, *room*, and *work*. Ask partners to create sentences for each sense. (Possible answers: 1. A noise from the kitchen interrupted my studying. Too much noise can lead to hearing damage. 2. It's relaxing to sit in a room with a view of the ocean. There's no more room in this closet. 3. The museum has many works of art. Work takes up most of my day.)
- Bring the class together and have students share their sentences.

Option: [+15–20 minutes] Write these sentences on the board, and have students indicate whether the underlined non-count noun has a countable or an uncountable sense.

1. The team celebrated *victory* over its opponents.
2. I remember a *time* when I had fewer worries.
3. It's very difficult to overcome *fear*.
4. A *college education* was once more affordable.
5. *Superstition* used to be more common.

(Answers: 1. uncountable, 2. countable, 3. uncountable, 4. countable, 5. uncountable)

C Write a before a noun . . .
- After students complete the exercise individually, have them compare answers with a partner.
- Bring the class together and go over any questions.

Challenge: [+15–20 minutes] For more practice, have pairs write one sentence for each non-count noun in the Grammar box. Have them use either a countable or an uncountable sense and leave a space before the noun. Then have pairs swap papers and add articles where needed. Circulate and assist as needed.

T139

When context makes a noun specific	Use with singular count nouns: **The hospital** in this town has an excellent emergency room. Use with plural count nouns: **The buildings** in this town are no higher than ten stories. Use with non-count nouns: **The air** in this city is polluted.
When an adjective clause makes a noun specific	Use with singular count nouns: **The mirror that you broke** will bring you bad luck. Use with plural count nouns: **The mirrors that you broke** will bring you bad luck. Use with non-count nouns: **The progress that she made** was due not to good luck but to hard work.
When an adjective represents a certain group of people	Use with a noun derived from an adjective, such as the blind, the deaf, the dead, the living, the young, the old, the poor, the rich, the unemployed, the privileged, the underprivileged: **The unemployed** must often learn new job skills.

B Complete the paragraphs with words from the box. Use a definite article when appropriate.

tourists	gasoline	view	world	wealthy	sky	ballooning	first men

On March 20, 1999, Bertrand Piccard of Switzerland and Brian Jones of Britain were ..the first men..
                                                                                    1
to travel around ..the world... in a balloon. The numerous balloonists who had been attempting this
                    2
journey for decades beforehand ran into various problems with weather and equipment.

In the past several years, ..ballooning.. has become a popular adventure sport. Due to the high cost of balloons
                              3
and ..gasoline...., however, it is a sport reserved for ..the wealthy.. ..Tourists...... can get a taste of ballooning during
       4   5   6
their travels. ..The view... of a city or landscape from ....the sky..... is always breathtaking.
                  7   8

More non-count nouns with both a countable and an uncountable sense

With some non-count nouns, the change in meaning is subtle: The countable meaning refers to something specific and the uncountable meaning refers to something general.

a fear = the anticipation of a specific danger; a phobia He had **a fear** of heights.	fear = a general anticipation of danger Irrational **fear** can lead to anxiety.
a victory = a specific event in which mastery or success is achieved The battle of Waterloo was **a great victory** for the English.	victory = the phenomenon of winning She led her party to **victory**.
a time = a specific moment in the past or future; a specific occasion There was **a time** when food was much cheaper. How **many times** did you read it?	time = the general concept; clock time **Time** passes so quickly! What **time** did you arrange to meet?
a superstition = a specific belief or practice **A** common **superstition** is that a black cat brings bad luck.	superstition = a general attitude The prevalence of **superstition** today is surprising.

C Write *a* before a noun where necessary. Write *X* if a noun should not have an article.

1 a Will people ever learn to control their phobias? Only ...X..... time can tell.
  b There has never been ...a..... time when people didn't try to interpret their dreams.
2 a If you have ...a..... fear of flying, you shouldn't take a job that requires overseas travel.
  b Psychologists agree that ....X.... fear is a universal emotion.

3 a Ignorance and fear may sometimes lead to ...X.... superstition.
   b There is ...a.... widely held superstition that knocking on wood brings good luck.
4 a The coach's tactics helped the team win ...a.... major victory in last night's game.
   b Everyone cannot always experience the joy of ....X.... victory; someone has to lose.

Grammar for Writing: indirect speech with passive reporting verbs

A passive reporting verb can be followed by an infinitive phrase.
   Most superstitions are believed **to be** false.

The infinitive phrase reflects the time of the reporting verb. It can be simple, continuous, perfect, or perfect continuous.
   This book is said **to be** excellent.
   The robber was reported **to be running away** from the scene of the crime.
   The car is believed **never to have been** in an accident before.
   She was thought **to have been preparing** dinner when she got sick.

D On a separate sheet of paper, change each of the following sentences from the active voice to the passive voice.

1 Many people believe that flying isn't as safe as driving. *Flying isn't believed to be as safe as driving.*
2 They reported the driver was talking on his phone when he crashed into the back of that van. *The driver was reported to be talking on his phone when he crashed into the back of that van.*
3 Everyone says the tour was overpriced, but others think the price was very fair.
The tour is said to be overpriced by everyone, but it was thought to be very fair by others.
4 People have said the article was a lie, but it turned out to be perfectly true.
The article was said to be a lie, but it turned out to be perfectly true.

UNIT 8

Grammar for Writing: emphatic stress

In informal writing, you can underline the verb *be*, a modal, or an auxiliary verb to indicate emphatic stress. The addition of *do* for emphatic stress does not require underlining. In more formal writing, with the exception of adding the auxiliary *do*, emphatic stress is avoided.
   She <u>is</u> good at math, isn't she?
   Even though it was getting late, I <u>would</u> have liked to stay longer.
   I suddenly realized that I <u>had</u> been there before.
   BUT She didn't answer her phone, but she did text me.

> In the modal-like expression <u>had better</u>, underline <u>better</u>, not <u>had</u>.
>   He'd <u>better</u> pay attention in class!

A Use the prompts to write B's response with emphatic stress. Add the auxiliary *do* if possible, and underline stressed verb *be*, modal, or other auxiliary verb.

1 A: Do you worry much about global warming?
   B: *I do think about it* (I think about it) from time to time.
2 A: Would you say you have a way with words?
   B: *I do express myself* (I express myself) clearly.
3 A: I'm thinking of applying to medical school, but I haven't made up my mind yet.
   B: Well, *you <u>should</u> apply* (you should apply).
4 A: Do you have to pass any kind of tests to get a job at the Mason Corporation?
   B: *You do have to take* (you have to take) an EQ test.
5 A: Shouldn't Jamie hurry if she wants to catch the 3:00 bus?
   B: *She'd <u>better</u> hurry.* (She'd better hurry). That's the last bus.
6 A: Would you like me to introduce you to my brother?
   B: *I <u>would</u> like to meet* (I'd like to meet) him.
7 A: Would you like to grab dinner somewhere together?
   B: *I've <u>already</u> had* (I've already had) dinner.

140 GRAMMAR BOOSTER

Grammar for writing: Indirect speech with passive reporting verbs

- Read the explanation and focus on the first example sentence. Ask *What is the passive reporting verb* (are believed). *What is the infinitive phrase?* (to be false) Elicit the sentence in the active voice (People believe that most superstitions are false).
- Ask students to read the rest of the example sentences, noting the reporting verb and infinitive phrase.

D On a separate sheet of paper . . .

- Model item 1. Ask *Who or what is the receiver of the action?* (flying) *What is the reporting verb?* (believe) *What is it in the passive?* (isn't believed) Then elicit the full sentence and write it on the board: *Flying isn't believed to be as safe as driving.*
- Have students change the remaining exercise items in the passive. Circulate and assist as needed. Go over the answers as class.

Unit 8

Grammar for writing: emphatic stress

- Review that emphatic stress refers to drawing attention to a particular action or a verb in a sentence. Write *I do hope you can come* to review the structure from the unit. Then have a student read the explanation for another way to show emphatic stress. Read the example sentence for students to repeat after you. Put appropriate emphasis on the underlined word. Have students notice which parts of the auxiliary is underlined in each sentence.
- Write the following sentences on the board, and have volunteers come to the board and underline an auxiliary to show emphatic stress. Then have the student read the statement.

    I would like a new smart phone, but I can't afford it.
    (underline *would*)

    They hadn't told us they were coming for a visit.
    (underline *hadn't*)

    I am going to the concert. Jack got me a ticket.
    (underline *am*)

- Bring students' attention to the information and example sentence in the box. Review that *had better* is used to demonstrate urgency. Elicit additional examples with *had better* and write these on the board. Have students read the examples putting appropriate stress on *better*.

A Use the prompts . . .

- Tell students to first skim the items in parentheses and decide which ones can have the *do* auxiliary (1, 2, 4) Then have students complete the exercise.
- Bring the class together and go over the answer. Time permitting students can write the sentences with auxiliaries on the board. Point out that for item 4 both adding *do* or underlining *have* are possible answers.

Infinitive and gerunds . . .

- Have students read the first explanation in the Grammar box and the example sentences. Ask:

  Which sentence includes the subjunctive form? (the second one)

  What is the expression of urgency, obligation, or advisability? (It is essential)

  What is the verb? (find)

  What is the infinitive phrase in the first sentence? (to find)

- Write the following sentences on the board. Have students rewrite them, using an infinitive phrase instead of the subjunctive.

  1. It is crucial that Sarah not forget the concert tickets.
  2. It is necessary that we arrive at the airport two hours before our flight.
  3. It is desirable that you bring a gift to the party.

  (Answers: 1. It is crucial for Sarah not to forget . . . ; 2. It is necessary for us to arrive . . . ; 3. It is desirable for you to bring . . .)

- Have students read the second explanation and the example sentence. Return to sentences 1, 2, and 3 on the board and have students use an infinitive phrase without *for*, referring to people in general. This will require eliminating the specific people mentioned in the sentences: *Sarah, we, you* (1. It is crucial not to forget the concert tickets; 2. It is necessary to arrive at the airport two hours before our flight; 3. It is desirable to bring a gift to the party).

- Read aloud the final explanation, and have students skim the example sentence. Then write the following sentences on the board. Have students rewrite them, using a gerund phrase instead of the subjunctive.

  1. The directors proposed that the city build a new stadium.
  2. The professor suggests that students not postpone studying for the exam.
  3. He recommends that you meditate at least four hours a week.

  (Answers: 1. The directors proposed building . . . ; 2. The professor suggests not postponing . . . ; 3. He recommends meditating . . .)

B Rewrite each sentence . . .

- Have students scan the verbs and adjectives of urgency, obligation, and advisability and determine which ones will be followed by a gerund and which will be followed by an infinitive. (1. infinitive, 2. gerund, 3. gerund, 4. infinitive, 5. object before an infinitive OR gerund, 6. infinitive) If necessary, refer students to page 123 in the Reference Charts to review which verbs can be followed by a gerund or an infinitive.

- Then have students rewrite the sentences. Have students focus on items 4 and 6, and remind the class to change the pronoun as appropriate. (4. for us; 6. for her)

- Go over the answers as a class. Point out that items 1, 4, and 6 can be rewritten both with and without a pronoun.

Remind students that infinitive or gerund phrases used without a pronoun refer to people in general. Note that it is also correct to use a possessive pronoun before a gerund phrase. See items 2, 3, and 5.

Unit 9

Grammar for Writing: when to use . . .

- Read the introduction in the Grammar box. Then divide the class into five groups. Assign each group one of the first five situations. Have groups read the situations in which the passive voice is preferred and the example(s).

- Invite groups to present their situation and the example(s) to the rest of the class.

- Finally, read the last situation and example to the class. Write two more example sentences on the board.

  1. Harriet King, who has also published four books on nutrition, wrote the article "Eating Less."
  2. The dealership, which has been getting numerous complaints about faulty seatbelts, recalled the new SUV model.

  Ask students to change the sentences to the passive voice to avoid clumsy sentence constructions. (1. The article "Eating Less" was written by Harriet King, who has also published four books on nutrition. 2. The new SUV model was recalled by the dealership, which has been getting numerous complaints about faulty seatbelts.)

Option: [+15–20 minutes] Have students look for examples of the passive voice in English-language magazines and newspapers or in Internet articles. Tell students to copy down or bring to class three examples and to note the situation in which the passive voice is used. (Possible answer: The museum tour has been canceled and rescheduled for next week. Situation 3)

A On a separate sheet of paper . . .

- To warm up, have students underline the agent in each sentence. (1. Construction workers; 2. People; 3. engineers, workers, engineers, engineers, factory; 4. We; 5. The reporter). Remind students that the agent is often unknown or unimportant. In these cases, it is not necessary to include the agent in the sentence in the passive voice.

- After students complete the exercise, bring the class together and call on volunteers for answers. Ask *In which sentence is an agent necessary? Why?* (Sentence 5 is the only sentence in which the agent is necessary. It is necessary because the agent has a long modifier: *whose investigation uncovered many shocking facts and a pattern of corrupt behavior.*)

Option: [+15–20 minutes] Ask students to skim the situations again and match each sentence in the exercise to the appropriate situation. (sentence 1: situation 1; sentence 2: situation 5; sentence 3: situation 2; sentence 4: situation 3; sentence 5: situation 6) Go over the answers as a class and review as necessary.

Infinitives and gerunds in place of the subjunctive

Certain statements in the subjunctive can be rephrased less formally by changing <u>that</u> to <u>for</u> and using an infinitive.
  It is essential **for** John **to find** the time each day to relax. (= It is essential that John **find** the time each day to relax.)

An infinitive can also be used without a <u>for</u> phrase. It usually refers to "people in general."
  It is essential **to find** the time each day to relax.

Certain statements in the subjunctive can be rephrased using a gerund if it refers to "people in general."
  Dr. Sharpe recommends **spending** a few moments relaxing. (= Dr. Sharpe recommends that people **spend** a few moments relaxing.)

B Rewrite each sentence less formally, using infinitives and gerunds. Make any necessary changes.

1 It is crucial that you practice feng shui.
  It's crucial for you to practice feng shui.
2 The article suggests that you carry lucky charms.
  The article suggests carrying lucky charms.
3 The manager recommended that they finish the project fast.
  The manager recommended finishing the project fast.
4 It is important that we get enough sleep every night.
  It's important for us to get enough sleep every night.
5 The directions advise that you add salt.
  The directions advise you to add salt.
6 It is necessary that she arrive at the theater by 4:00 P.M.
  It's necessary for her to arrive at the theater by 4:00 p.m.

UNIT 9

Grammar for Writing: when to use the passive voice

Passive sentences focus attention on the result of an action rather than on the performer (agent) of the action. Writers prefer the passive voice in the following situations:

1 **To emphasize the result of an action, or if the agent is unimportant or unknown. This use is common in academic writing, scientific articles, and news reports.**
  Some sophisticated treatments **have been developed**. (emphasizes the treatments, not the people who developed them)
  Hundreds of people **were made** homeless by yesterday's floods. (emphasizes the result, not the floods themselves)

2 **To describe a process. This use is found in technical and scientific writing.**
  There are four basic steps in the commercial production of orange juice. First the oranges **are unloaded** from trucks and **placed** on a conveyor belt. Then they **are washed** and **sorted**. Next they **are put** into machines that remove the juice and put it into cartons.

3 **To use an impersonal or indirect tone, which suggests formality, impartiality, or objectivity. This use is favored in official documents, formal announcements, and signs, or to avoid placing blame.**
  Walking on the grass **is prohibited**.
  An error **has been made** in your account. It **will be corrected** on next month's statement. (The writer avoids mentioning who made the mistake and emphasizes the fact that it will be corrected, rather than who will do the correcting.)

4 **To keep the reader's attention focused on a previously mentioned noun, because it is the central topic of the paragraph.**
  They caught the thief later that evening. He **was placed** in jail and **was allowed** to call a lawyer. (The topic is the thief. By using the passive voice in the second sentence, the writer keeps the reader's attention focused on the thief.)

5 **To avoid using a "general subject." General subjects include the impersonal <u>you</u>, <u>we</u>, and <u>they</u>; <u>people</u>; <u>one</u>; <u>someone</u> / <u>somebody</u>; <u>anyone</u> / <u>anybody</u>. This use is common in formal documents, in official signs, and in newspaper editorials and other texts that express an opinion.**
  People must show their IDs before boarding. PREFERRED: IDs **must be shown** before boarding.
  Someone should inform consumers of their rights. PREFERRED: Consumers **should be informed** of their rights.

6 **To avoid awkward sentence constructions. This is a common solution when the agent has a long or complex modifier.**
  The Tigers, whose new strategy of offense and defense seemed to be working, defeated the Lions.
  PREFERRED: The Lions **were defeated** by the Tigers, whose new strategy of offense and defense seemed to be working.

A On a separate sheet of paper, write each sentence in the passive voice.

1 Construction workers built the museum in less than six months. The museum was built in less than six months.
2 People must present their passports at the border. Passports must be presented at the border.
3 First, engineers perfect the design for the new product. Then, workers build a prototype. Next, engineers test the prototype. After engineers approve the design, the factory begins production.
  First, the design for the new product is perfected. Then a prototype is built. Next, the prototype is tested. After the design is approved, production is begun.
4 We have credited the sum of eighty-five dollars to your VISTA account. The sum of eighty-five dollars has been credited to your VISTA account.
5 The reporter, whose investigation uncovered many shocking facts and a pattern of corrupt behavior, exposed the official for taking bribes.
  The official was exposed for taking bribes by a reporter, whose investigation uncovered many shocking facts and a pattern of corrupt behavior.

UNIT 10

Phrasal verbs: expansion

The passive form of phrasal verbs
Transitive phrasal verbs are always inseparable in the passive voice, even when they are separable or always separated in the active voice.

I couldn't **turn on** the TV (OR **turn** the TV **on**). → The TV couldn't be **turned on**.
They **turned** the empty lot **into** a beautiful garden. → The empty lot was **turned into** a beautiful garden.

> **Remember**
> Intransitive phrasal verbs are always inseparable. They can't be used in the passive voice since they don't have direct objects.

Transitive and intransitive meanings
Some phrasal verbs have both a transitive and an intransitive meaning.

He went to bed without **taking off** his clothes. (transitive meaning: remove)
What time does your plane **take off**? (intransitive meaning: leave)
She **broke in** the new employees by showing them the procedures. (transitive meaning: train someone)
Thieves **broke in** and stole her jewelry. (intransitive meaning: enter by force)

For a complete list of transitive and intransitive phrasal verbs, see the Reference Charts, pages 124–125.

Three-word phrasal verbs
A three-word phrasal verb consists of a verb, a particle, and a preposition that together have a specific meaning.
The verb, the particle, and the preposition in three-word phrasal verbs are inseparable.

As a result of his controversial ideas, the senator **came up against** members of his own party, who opposed him vigorously.
Does society have an obligation to **look out for** people who are disadvantaged?
Temper tantrums are not uncommon in young children. As they mature, they **grow out of** this behavior.
I'm going to close my door and not take any calls today; I've just got to **catch up on** my work.

For a complete list of three-word phrasal verbs, see the Reference Charts, page 126.

A On a separate sheet of paper, rewrite each sentence in the passive voice. Do not include a *by* phrase.

1. We have to call the meeting off.   The meeting has to be called off.
2. He talked the client into a better deal.   The client was talked into a better deal.
3. They covered the mistake up.   The mistake was covered up.
4. She dropped the children off in front of the school.   The children were dropped off in front of the school.
5. One of the applicants filled the form out incorrectly.   The form was filled out incorrectly.
6. I paid the balance off last month.   The balance was paid off last month.
7. Someone threw the document away.   The document was thrown away.
8. The speaker handed pamphlets out at the end of the presentation.   Pamphlets were handed out at the end of the presentation.

B Underline the phrasal verb in each sentence. Then decide if it has a transitive or an intransitive meaning.

	transitive	intransitive	
1	✓	☐	The photographer <u>blew up</u> the photo 200 percent so we could use it for the poster.
2	☐	✓	The plane <u>blew up</u> shortly before it was supposed to land.
3	☐	✓	The workers won't <u>give up</u> until they're paid fair wages.
4	✓	☐	She has tried to <u>give up</u> smoking several times, without success.
5	☐	✓	Phil has to <u>wake up</u> at 5:00 A.M. every morning to get to work on time.
6	✓	☐	The children played quietly in order not to <u>wake up</u> their parents.
7	☐	✓	He <u>works out</u> three or four times a week in order to stay healthy.
8	✓	☐	World leaders are meeting to <u>work out</u> a plan to eradicate poverty.

Unit 10

Phrasal verbs: expansion

- Review that a transitive verb is a verb that needs a direct object to complete its meaning. Ask a student to read the explanation in the Grammar box. Have students read the Remember note and study the pairs of example sentences.
- Write the following phrasal verbs on the board: *throw away, hand out, talk into, do over, cater to, count on*. Ask *Which phrasal verbs are always separated?* (talk into, do over) *Which phrasal verbs are separable, but don't have to be?* (throw away, hand out) *Which phrasal verbs are inseparable?* (cater to, count on) If necessary, refer students to the lists of transitive phrasal verbs on pages 124–125 in the Reference Charts.
- Have pairs use the phrasal verbs on the board in sentences in the passive voice. (Possible answers: The leftovers had to be thrown away because we forgot to put them in the fridge. Samples were handed out at the beginning of the presentation. I was talked into buying the product even though I didn't want it. The report had to be done over because the client was unhappy with it. The guests were catered to with great speed and care. I promised my employer that I could be counted on to complete the project on time.) Bring the class together and have pairs share sentences.
- To review transitive and intransitive meanings, point out that while a transitive verb needs a direct object to complete its meaning, an intransitive verb does *not* need a direct object.
- Have students read the explanation and the pairs of example sentences independently.
- On the board, write the phrasal verb *turn in*, and elicit sentences that show its transitive and intransitive meaning. (Possible answer: I turned in the application yesterday. Transitive meaning: submit. We're really tired, so we're going to turn in early. Intransitive meaning: go to bed.) If necessary, refer students to the lists of transitive and intransitive phrasal verbs on page 125 in the Reference Charts.
- Finally ask a volunteer to read the third explanation and have students study the example sentences. Have students name the direct object in each example. (1. members, 2. people, 3. this behavior, 4. my work)

Option: [+15–20 minutes] Have pairs look at the list of three-word phrasal verbs on page 126 in the Reference Charts and write two example sentences. Then have them share the sentences with the class. (Possible answers: Every evening, I sit down with the newspaper and try to catch up on the news. E-mail has made it easier to keep up with friends.)

Challenge: [+15–20 minutes] For more practice with transitive and intransitive meanings, write the following phrasal verbs on the board: 1. *give up*, 2. *work out*, 3. *make up*. Have partners write pairs of sentences to illustrate the transitive and intransitive meaning. (Possible answers: 1. Tanya gave up eating chocolate as part of her diet. Transitive meaning: quit doing something. I give up! Intransitive meaning: quit. 2. I can't work out this problem. Transitive meaning: resolve a problem. Peter works out every day. Transitive meaning: exercise. 3. Even though they fight a lot, they make up quickly. Intransitive meaning: end an argument and reestablish a friendly relationship. I made up an excuse about being stuck in traffic. Transitive meaning: create a fictional story.) Have students share their sentences with the class.

A On a separate sheet of paper . . .

- Have students underline the phrasal verb in each sentence. (1. call off; 2. talked into; 3. covered up; 4. dropped off; 5. filled out; 6. paid off; 7. threw away; 8. handed out)
- Before students complete the exercise, remind them that transitive phrasal verbs are always inseparable in the passive voice.
- Go over the answers as a class. Point out that only sentence 5 requires an agent. Tell students that sentences 3 and 8 are correct with or without an agent. In these two cases, the agent provides additional and more precise information.

Option: [+15–20 minutes] Have students look at the phrasal verbs they underlined in the exercise. Ask *Which phrasal verb is always separable?* (2. talk someone into) Call on volunteers to restate all the sentences except 2 with the phrasal verbs *not* separated. (1. We have to call off the meeting. 3. They covered up the mistake. 4. She dropped off the children in front of the school. 5. One of the applicants filled out the form incorrectly. 6. I paid off the balance last month. 7. Someone threw away the document. 8. The speaker handed out pamphlets at the end of the presentation.)

B Underline the phrasal verb . . .

- After students do the exercise, bring the class together and elicit the direct object for each phrasal verb with a transitive meaning. (1. the photo, 4. smoking, 6. their parents, 8. a plan)
- Go over any questions.

T142

Pronunciation Booster

Note about the Pronunciation Booster
Many will elect to do the Pronunciation Booster as self-study. If you choose to use the Pronunciation Booster as a classroom activity instead, included in these pages are teaching notes for the pronunciation presentations and exercises.

Unit 1

Sentence stress and intonation: review

- Have a student read the title of the box. Remind students that sentence stress refers to the words that are emphasized in a sentence. Intonation refers to the rising or falling tone the speaker uses.

Sentence stress

- Read aloud the first explanation about content words. Review that content words are words that carry the basic meaning of a sentence. Point out that capital letters are used to show which words are stressed.
- Have students read the categories and examples of content words in the Content words note. For further review, have students suggest additional words for each category.
- Read the first example sentence, putting stress on the capitalized content words, and have students repeat. Then ask volunteers to read the next two example sentences. Make necessary corrections, and have students repeat.
- Focus on the note about compound nouns. Make sure students understand that a compound noun is made up of two or more words. Have students read aloud the example sentences in the note, putting appropriate stress on the first word. Point out that the large dot above a capitalized word shows which syllable gets the most stress.
- Elicit additional compound nouns and write them on the board. (Possible answers: dream job, traffic jam, cell phone) Have volunteers say the compound nouns aloud, putting appropriate stress on the first word of each compound noun.

Intonation

- Have students read the first explanation. If necessary, review that pitch refers to how high or low a sound is.
- Point out that the last stressed word in a sentence is usually the last content word. Have students study the example sentences. Explain that a falling line indicates lower pitch. A rising line indicates higher pitch. Ask:

  What is the last stressed word in each sentence?
  (naturalist, experience, stopping, married)
  What type of sentence is each example?
  (statement, command, information question,
  yes / no question)

- Summarize on the board:

  statements ⎫
  commands ⎬ lower pitch falls after last stressed syllable
  information ⎪
  questions ⎭

  yes / no questions — raise pitch after last stressed syllable

Call on volunteers to read each example sentence, using the correct intonation.

- Have students read the second explanation to themselves. Explain that an arrow pointing downward indicates a lengthened vowel and lowered pitch. An arrow pointing upward indicates a lengthened vowel and rising pitch.
- Call on volunteers to read the example sentences. Offer corrections as needed, and have students repeat. Make sure students hear how the last syllable is stressed in each of the sentences.

Pronunciation table

These are the pronunciation symbols used in *Summit 2*.

Vowels

Symbol	Key Word	Symbol	Key Word
i	beat, feed	ə	banana, among
ɪ	bit, did	ɚ	shirt, murder
eɪ	date, paid	aɪ	bite, cry, buy, eye
ɛ	bet, bed	aʊ	about, how
æ	bat, bad	ɔɪ	voice, boy
ɑ	box, odd, father	ɪr	beer
ɔ	bought, dog	ɛr	bare
oʊ	boat, road	ɑr	bar
ʊ	book, good	ɔr	door
u	boot, food, student	ʊr	tour
ʌ	but, mud, mother		

Consonants

Symbol	Key Word	Symbol	Key Word
p	pack, happy	z	zip, please, goes
b	back, rubber	ʃ	ship, machine, station, special, discussion
t	tie	ʒ	measure, vision
d	die	h	hot, who
k	came, key, quick	m	men, some
g	game, guest	n	sun, know, pneumonia
tʃ	church, nature, watch	ŋ	sung, ringing
dʒ	judge, general, major	w	wet, white
f	fan, photograph	l	light, long
v	van	r	right, wrong
θ	thing, breath	y	yes, use, music
ð	then, breathe	t̬	butter, bottle
s	sip, city, psychology	tʔ	button

Pronunciation Booster

The Pronunciation Booster is optional. It provides a pronunciation lesson and practice to support speaking in each unit, making students' speech more comprehensible.

UNIT 1

Sentence stress and intonation: review

Sentence stress
Remember: Content words are generally stressed in a sentence.
 I've **ALWAYS DREAMED** about **BEING** a **PHOTOGRAPHER**.
 You've been **TALKING** about **DOING** that for **YEARS**!
 Have you **EVER THOUGHT** about a **CAREER** in **LAW**?

Intonation
Lower pitch after the stressed syllable in the last stressed word in statements, commands, and information questions. Raise pitch after the last stressed syllable in yes/no questions.

 I love the outdoors, so I've decided to become a naturalist.   What's stopping you?

 Tell me something about your experience.   Have you made plans to get married?

If the last syllable in the sentence is stressed, lengthen the vowel and lower pitch. In yes/no questions, lengthen the vowel and raise pitch.

 I just gave notice at the bank.   Have you decided on a career?

Content words

nouns	photographer, Robert, career
verbs	think, study, discuss
adjectives	important, young, successful
adverbs	carefully, ever, recently
possessive pronouns	ours, yours, theirs
demonstrative pronouns	this, that, these
reflexive pronouns	myself, yourself, ourselves
interrogative pronouns	who, what, why

In compound nouns, stress only the first word.

 She has just been accepted to a top **BUSINESS** school.

 Have you made any progress with your **JOB** search?

A ▶6:02 Listen and practice.
1 I've always dreamed about being a photographer.
2 You've been talking about doing that for years!
3 Have you ever thought about a career in law?

B ▶6:03 Listen and practice.
1 I love the outdoors, so I've decided to become a naturalist.
2 Tell me something about your experience.
3 What's stopping you?
4 Have you made plans to get married?
5 I just gave notice at the bank.
6 Have you decided on a career?

C Circle the content words.
1 It was (very) (difficult) for (Dan) to (hide) his (disappointment).
2 He was (rejected) by (two) (law) (schools).
3 (What) does he (plan) to (do) (now)?
4 He (just) (accepted) a (position) (teaching) (math) at the (university).
5 (MediLabs) has an (opening) for a (junior) (lab) (specialist).

▶6:04 Now practice reading each sentence aloud. Listen to compare.*

D Circle the last stressed content word in each sentence.
1 He wants to start his own (travel) agency.
2 I don't really know how to get (started).
3 Do I need to have experience in the (tourism) industry?
4 Why are you looking for a (change)?
5 Tell me about your plans for the coming (year).
6 Do you want to become a (flight) attendant?
7 Have you applied for that (job)?

▶6:05 Now practice reading each sentence aloud, using the intonation patterns you have learned. Listen to compare.*

UNIT 2

Emphatic stress and pitch to express emotion

Use emphatic stress and higher pitch on content words to indicate intensity of emotion.
I'm **SO SORRY**!
I'm **REALLY UPSET**!
What do you **MEAN**?
How could you **DO** that?
What **GREAT NEWS**!
Thank you **SO MUCH**!

A ▶6:06 Listen and practice.
1 I'm so sorry!
2 I'm really upset!
3 What do you mean?
4 How could you do that?
5 What great news!
6 Thank you so much!

B ▶6:07 Practice reading each sentence aloud, using intonation to express emotion. Listen to compare.*
1 **JOHN**, what **HAPPENED**?
2 You look **WORRIED**.
3 I feel **JUST TERRIBLE**!
4 How did **THAT** happen?
5 Why didn't you slow **DOWN**?
6 We could have been **KILLED**!
7 How could you **SAY** that?

*NOTE: Whenever you see a listening activity with an asterisk (*), say each word, phrase, or sentence in the pause *after* the number. Then listen for confirmation.

A ▶ 6:02 Listen and practice.

- First listening: Have students listen and study the examples.
- Second listening: Have students listen and repeat chorally.

Note: This procedure for first and second listening is repeated in each unit.

B ▶ 6:03 Listen and practice.

- First listening: Have students listen and study the examples.
- Second listening: Have students listen and repeat chorally.

C Circle the content words.

- Have pairs circle the content words. If necessary, remind students that content words are words that carry the basic meaning of a sentence. You may also want to review function words with your students: prepositions (in, to), conjunctions (and, but), determiners (an, some), personal pronouns (I, we), possessive adjectives (my, our), and auxiliary verbs (have + present or past participle, be + present or past participle). Function words are covered in *Summit 1,* page T141.
- Then have pairs take turns reading the sentences aloud.

▶ 6:04 Now practice reading . . .

- Have students read each sentence aloud and then listen for confirmation.

Note: To build students' confidence, make sure they have ample practice before reading. Students will say the item aloud when they hear the item number and then will hear the speaker say the same item immediately after.

D Circle the last stressed content word . . .

- Have students scan the sentences and underline the compound words. (1. travel agency; 3. tourism industry; 6. flight attendant) Then have students complete the exercise.
- Call on volunteers to identify each type of sentence as a statement, a command, an information question, or a yes / no question. (1. statement; 2. statement; 3. yes / no question; 4. information question; 5. command; 6. yes / no question; 7. yes / no question) Remind students that they will lower pitch after the last stressed syllable in statements, commands, and information questions, and raise pitch in yes / no questions.

▶ 6:05 Now practice reading . . .

- Have students read each sentence aloud and then listen for confirmation.

LANGUAGE NOTE In American English, it is common to hear neutral statements end with a rising intonation. For example,

A: *My son is studying to become a pilot.*
B: *Oh, yeah?*

▶ 1:03 Option: [+15–20 minutes] To provide more practice, refer students to the conversation in Exercise E, Spotlight, on page 3 in the Student's Book. Have pairs read the conversation aloud, paying attention to the content words and intonation patterns for the different sentence types. Then have students listen to the conversation to compare their reading.

⭐ 🖨 Pronunciation Pair Work

Unit 2

Emphatic stress and pitch to express emotion

- Read the explanation aloud. Elicit examples of emotions such as regret, happiness, anger, or confusion. Point out that the pitch used to express intensity of emotion varies with each individual speaker.
- Have students read the example sentences to themselves and identify the emotion each one expresses. (Possible answers: 1. regret; 2. distress; 3. anger or confusion; 4. disbelief or anger; 5. happiness; 6. gratitude)
- Call on volunteers to read the example sentences, using emphatic stress and higher pitch as appropriate. Make corrections as needed. Then call on different students to read the same sentences to show how individual pitch varies.

A ▶ 6:06 Listen and practice.

- Refer to the procedure for Exercise A on page T144.

B ▶ 6:07 Practice reading each sentence . . .

- First, have pairs read the sentences for content and identify the emotion each one expresses. (Possible answers: 1. concern or surprise; 2. concern; 3. regret or distress; 4. surprise or anger; 5. confusion; 6. anger or concern; 7. anger)
- Then have pairs take turns reading the sentences, using the appropriate intonation.
- Have students read each sentence aloud and then listen for confirmation.

Challenge: [+15–20 minutes] Write the following emotions on the board: *joy, disbelief, anger, gratitude, confusion.* Have pairs create sentences and read them aloud, using the appropriate intonation to express each emotion.

⭐ 🖨 Pronunciation Pair Work

T144

Unit 3
Vowel reduction to /ə/

- On the board, write /ə/. Explain that this is the schwa, or the pronunciation symbol for the sound *uh*. Have students repeat the sound after you. Point out that the schwa can be represented by any vowel. On the board, write the following words and underline the vowels as shown:

    a: <u>a</u>luminum
    e: th<u>e</u>
    i: dec<u>i</u>mal
    o: intr<u>o</u>duce
    u: medi<u>u</u>m
    y: s<u>y</u>ringe

    Read each word aloud with the appropriate schwa, and have the class repeat.

- Write /u/ on the board. Explain that this is the pronunciation symbol for the sound *ooh*. Have students repeat the sound after you.

- Read the first explanation in the box aloud. On the board, write /tu/ and /tə/. Have students practice both pronunciations. Then call on volunteers to read the example sentences. Make corrections as needed, and have students repeat.

- Have students study the second explanation and the example sentence. Point out the schwa in the word *a* (in the phrase *to a friend*). Have a student read the sentence aloud. Make any necessary corrections, and ask the class to repeat chorally.

- Tell students to study the third explanation and the example sentences. Have students practice reading the two sentences in pairs. Then bring the class together, and have volunteers read the sentence both ways. Make any necessary corrections, and ask the class to repeat chorally.

- Read the last explanation aloud. Review that *have to* and *ought to* are modals. *Have to* means need to, and *ought to* means should. *Be going to* is a future form. Have students study the example sentences, noting the reduction of /u/ to /ə/ and the additional sound changes. Then call on volunteers to read the sentences aloud. Make any necessary corrections, and ask the class to repeat chorally.

A ▶ 6:08 Listen and practice.

- Refer to the procedure for Exercise A on page T144.

B Circle the words . . .

- Have pairs circle the words that they think have sounds that will be reduced. Refer them to the explanations in the box if they need help.

- Then have pairs practice reading the sentences aloud.

▶ 6:09 Now practice reading . . .

- Have students read each sentence aloud and then listen for confirmation.

Option: [+15–20 minutes] Write the following sentences on the board:
1. He wants <u>to</u> give the tickets <u>to</u> us.
2. I forwarded the message <u>to</u> him yesterday.
3. The letter was addressed <u>to</u> me.
4. They ought <u>to</u> go <u>to</u> Rome for a vacation.
5. We have <u>to</u> finish the report by tomorrow.
6. Jerry sent the manuscript <u>to</u> her house.
7. I'm going <u>to</u> look up this word in a dictionary.

Have volunteers come to the board and write the appropriate /tu/ or /tə/ above each instance of the word *to* and then read the sentence to the class. Tell students to explain when there are two possible ways of pronouncing *to* and to discuss other pronunciation changes in the sentence. (1. /tə/, /tu/; 2. /tə/ + /h/ OR /tu/ + /ə/; 3. /tə/; 4. /tə/, /tə/; 5. /tə/; 6. /tə/ + /h/ OR /tu/ + /ə/; 7. /tə/) Offer feedback as needed.

⭐ 🖨 **Pronunciation Pair Work**

Unit 4
Shifting emphatic stress

- Ask a volunteer to read the explanation. Point out that the focus of a sentence can change depending on the emphatic stress you use.

- Invite a volunteer to read the first conversation with you. Have the student read Student A's line, and you read Student B's. Then have students repeat B's line chorally.

- Have pairs read the remaining conversations, alternating parts. Circulate and offer corrections as needed.

- Bring the class together and discuss the emphatic stress and its meaning in each conversation. (Conversations 1 and 2 focus on the adverbs *enough* and *too* to show how critical each person is of other people. Conversation 3 focuses on the pronoun *I'm* to emphasize which speaker is too critical. Conversation 4 focuses on the verb *think* to show that the person isn't sure whether he or she is too critical.)

UNIT 3

Vowel reduction to /ə/

Remember: The /u/ sound in the function word **to** is often reduced to /ə/ in spoken English.

    We tried **to** cheer him up. /tə/
    They were scared **to** death. /tə/
    It was starting **to** get me down. /tə/
    You just need **to** give it a little more time. /tə/

Do not reduce the /u/ sound when **to** comes before another /ə/ sound.
             /tə/   /tu/
    She was trying **to** e-mail a message **to** a friend.

When **to** occurs before **her** or **him**, you can say it two ways (Note the change in syllable stress, too):
    Use /tə/ and pronounce /h/ → I sent it **to her** yesterday. /tə'hər/
    Use /tu/ and drop /h/ → I sent it **to her** yesterday. /'tuər/

In the phrases **have to**, **ought to**, and **be going to**, /u/ generally reduces to /ə/, and there are often other sound changes.
    I didn't **have to** walk very far. /hæftə/
    You really **ought to** be careful next time. /ɔtə/
    We're definitely **going to** take a cell phone on our next trip. /gʌnə/

Function words
- **prepositions**: of, from, at, to
- **conjunctions**: and, but, or
- **determiners**: a, the, some
- **personal pronouns**: he, she, they
- **possessive adjectives**: my, her, their
- **auxiliary verbs**: have [+ past participle], be [+ present participle]

Be careful! When an auxiliary verb is negative or used in short answers, it is generally stressed.
I **CAN'T GO**.   He **WON'T LIKE** it.
No, they **DON'T**.   Yes, I **HAVE**.

A ▶ 6:08 Listen and practice.

1. We tried to cheer him up.
2. They were scared to death.
3. It was starting to get me down.
4. You just need to give it a little more time.
5. She was trying to e-mail a message to a friend.
6. I sent it to her yesterday.
7. I sent it to her yesterday.
8. I didn't have to walk very far.
9. You really ought to be careful next time.
10. We're definitely going to take a cell phone on our next trip.

B Circle the words in the following sentences that you think contain sounds that will be reduced, according to what you have learned about vowel reduction.

1. I'm learning (to) sail my ship.
2. They had sent (an) SOS text message from (a) cell phone (to) (a) friend in London.
3. They got several messages telling them (to) be strong.
4. The helicopters had been unable (to) take off because (of) the severe weather.
5. You ought (to) tell your brother that you can't talk (to) him right now.
6. Don't let it get (to) you.
7. I'm going (to) refuse (to) give up.
8. We have (to) keep trying, no matter how tired we are.

▶ 6:09 Now practice reading each sentence aloud and listen to compare.*

UNIT 4

Shifting emphatic stress

You can shift stress within a sentence to change emphasis. Place emphatic stress on key words to get your meaning across.

A: I think I'm too critical of other people.
B: Really? I don't think I'm critical **ENOUGH**.

A: I don't think I'm critical enough.
B: Really? I think I'm **TOO** critical.

A: I think I'm too critical of other people.
B: I don't see you that way at all. **I'M** too critical.

A: I think I'm too critical of other people.
B: Really? Not me ... At least I don't **THINK** I'm too critical.

A ▶ 6:10 Listen and practice.
1. I don't think I'm critical **ENOUGH**.
2. I think I'm **TOO** critical.
3. **I'M** too critical.
4. I don't **THINK** I'm too critical.

B Study each conversation, paying attention to emphatic stress.
1. "You know what my problem is? I'm a perfectionist."
   RESPONSE: Well, **I'M** just the opposite.
2. "You know what my problem is? I'm a perfectionist."
   RESPONSE: Not me. I'm just the **OPPOSITE**.
3. "What set Sam off this morning?"
   RESPONSE: I have no idea. But he's **ALWAYS** angry about **SOMETHING**.
4. "Why did Sam tell Paul off in front of everyone?"
   RESPONSE: It's just the way he is. He's always **ANGRY** about something.
5. "Why was Judy so angry this morning?"
   RESPONSE: I don't know. I've **NEVER** seen her lose her cool like that.
6. "Can you believe how angry Judy was this morning?"
   RESPONSE: Not really. I've never seen her lose her cool like **THAT**.

▶ 6:11 Now practice reading each response aloud, using emphatic stress as shown. Listen to compare.*

UNIT 5

Intonation of sarcasm

Saying the opposite of what you mean in order to show that you don't think a joke is funny is a type of sarcasm. When someone thinks a joke is funny, the response is usually said with raised pitch. The same response can convey sarcasm if it is said with flattened pitch and at a slower pace.

Pleasure
How funny! (= It's funny.)
That's hysterical! (= It's funny.)
That's terrific! (= It's great.)
I love it! (= It's great.)

Sarcasm
How funny. (= It's not funny.)
That's hysterical. (= It's not funny.)
That's terrific. (= It's not great.)
I love it. (= It's not great.)

A ▶ 6:12 Listen and practice.
1. How funny! / How funny.
2. That's hysterical! / That's hysterical.
3. That's terrific! / That's terrific.
4. I love it! / I love it.

B ▶ 6:13 Practice saying each statement two ways, first with intonation showing pleasure and then sarcasm. Listen to compare.* (Note that your choices may differ from what you hear on the audio.)
1. That's hilarious! / That's hilarious.
2. That's so funny! / That's so funny.
3. What a funny story! / What a funny story.
4. That's great! / That's great.
5. That's too much! / That's too much.
6. That really made me laugh! / That really made me laugh.

A ▶ 6:10 Listen and practice.
- Refer to the procedure for Exercise A on page T144.

B Study each conversation . . .
- Instruct pairs to read the conversations, alternating parts. Tell them to use emphatic stress as shown.

▶ 6:11 Now practice reading . . .
- Have students read each response aloud and then listen for confirmation.
- For further practice, call on volunteers to read the conversations again, placing emphatic stress on different key words. Discuss how the focus of a sentence shifts when the emphatic stress is changed.

▶ 2:16 **Option: [+15–20 minutes]** To provide more practice, refer students to the conversation in Exercise E, Spotlight, on page 39 in the Student's Book. Have pairs read the conversation aloud, placing emphatic stress on key words. Tell students to underline the words they put stress on. Then have them listen to the conversation to compare their reading.

⭐ 🖨 Pronunciation Pair Work

Unit 5
Intonation of sarcasm
- On the board, write *sarcasm*. Ask *What is the meaning of sarcasm?* (saying the opposite of what you mean)
- Write on the board *Nice shirt*. Read it aloud two ways, first with raised pitch to convey pleasure and then with flattened pitch and at a slower pace to convey sarcasm. Ask *How can you tell if a comment is sarcastic?* (Flattened pitch and a slower pace convey sarcasm.)
- Have a volunteer read the explanation aloud. Then have pairs practice reading the sets of example sentences, contrasting their pitch and pace to convey pleasure and sarcasm. Circulate and offer suggestions if students have difficulty.
- Ask pairs of volunteers to read their contrasting sentences to the class.

LANGUAGE NOTE Point out that, while there are tips for the intonation of sarcasm, there is no one correct way to communicate a sarcastic remark. While one person may be overtly sarcastic, another may be much more subtle, possibly to the point of leaving the listener uncertain whether or not the speaker is being serious.

CULTURE NOTE Body language, such as rolling one's eyes or making a facial expression, may also accompany a sarcastic remark. In addition to pitch, body language helps the listener interpret sarcasm.

A ▶ 6:12 Listen and practice.
- Refer to the procedure for Exercise A on page T144.

B ▶ 6:13 Practice saying each statement . . .
- Have partners practice reading the pairs of statements, using the appropriate intonation for pleasure and for sarcasm.
- Have students read each pair of statements aloud and then listen for confirmation.

Option: [+15–20 minutes] For more practice, have pairs tell each other jokes. Have students respond with one of the sentences from Exercise B. The intonation of the response should indicate whether the listener thought the joke was funny or not.

Challenge: [+15–20 minutes] Have pairs create short conversations using the intonation of sarcasm. For example,

A: *Nice job on that presentation.* [sarcastic tone]
B: *I know. It was horrible, wasn't it? I really had no time to prepare.*

Invite pairs to present their conversations to the class. After each presentation, ask students to use a different intonation to make the sarcastic remark express pleasure.

⭐ 🖨 Pronunciation Pair Work

Unit 6

Regular past participle endings

- Write the following on the board:

  zzzzzzz

  sssssss

  Tell students to put their fingers on their Adam's apple at the front of their throat and repeat the *zzzzzzz* and *sssssss* sounds after you. Ask *What difference do you notice between the two sounds?* (There is vibration with the *zzzzzzz* sound. There is no vibration with the *sssssss* sound.) Tell students that the *zzzzzzz* sound is called a voiced sound and the *sssssss* sound is called a voiceless sound. Clarify the difference between voiced and voiceless sounds: Your vocal cords vibrate for voiced sounds but don't vibrate for voiceless sounds.

- Read aloud the example verbs in the box whose base form ends with a voiced sound, and have the class repeat with their books closed. Make sure students hear the /d/ sound of the *-ed* ending and feel the vibration of the voiced sound. Then read aloud the example verbs whose base form ends with a voiceless sound, and have the class repeat. Make sure students hear the /t/ sound of the *-ed* ending and notice the absence of vibration with the unvoiced sound.

- Have students open their books and read the first explanation in the box. Then ask a volunteer to read the second explanation about voiced sounds. Call on students to pronounce the voiced sound at the end of each base form. Then have them repeat each verb after you.

- Ask a volunteer to read the third explanation about voiceless sounds. Call on students to pronounce the voiceless sound at the end of each base form. Then have them repeat each verb after you.

- Read the final explanation aloud. Have students repeat each word after you. Focus on the linking of the /t/ or /d/ sound with the *-ed* ending.

- Have students look at the chart of Voiced sounds and Voiceless sounds. Suggest or ask pairs to suggest a regular verb whose base form ends in each sound. Point out that the list of voiced vowel sounds does not include all the voiced vowel sounds. (voiced consonant sounds: rob, rig, breathe, love, raise, rouge, change, farm, clean, ring, fire, call; voiced vowel sounds: There are few high-frequency verbs that end in the short vowel sounds. /i/ ski, /eɪ/ play, /ɔ/ thaw, /oʊ/ veto, /u/ view; voiceless sounds: hop, like, tooth, roof, kiss, finish, match) Then have pairs say the past participles aloud to each other, making sure their partner can hear the difference between the voiced and voiceless sounds at the end of each base form.

- To check students' understanding, write the following words on the board:

  laughed, stated, yelled, tamed, missed, loaded

  Read the words with the correct pronunciation of the *-ed* ending, and have students repeat. (laughed: /t/, stated: /ɪd/, yelled: /d/, tamed: /d/, missed: /t/, loaded: /ɪd/) If students are unsure, have them focus on the final sound of each base form. Review that the final sounds in the base forms of *yelled* and *tamed* are voiced, and the *-ed* ending is pronounced /d/. The final sounds in the base forms of *laughed* and *missed* are unvoiced, and the *-ed* ending is pronounced /t/. The final sounds in the base forms of *stated* and *loaded* are pronounced /t/ and /d/, and the *-ed* ending is pronounced /ɪd/.

Reduction in perfect modals

- Have students study the explanation and the example sentences. Call on volunteers to read the sentences aloud, reducing the perfect modals. Tell students to pay attention to the pronunciation of the past participles as well, distinguishing among *-ed* endings pronounced as /d/, /t/, or /ɪd/. If necessary, review that the final sound in the base form of *renewed* is voiced, so the *-ed* ending is pronounced /d/. The final sound in the base form of *needed* is /d/, so the *-ed* ending is pronounced /ɪd/. The final sound in the base form of *missed* is voiceless, so the *-ed* ending is pronounced /t/. Make corrections as needed.

- Direct attention to the Perfect modals note. Read each perfect modal aloud to show reduction of the auxiliary *have*. Ask students to repeat.

- Elicit sentences using the perfect modals listed + a past participle. Encourage students to use regular past participles with *-ed* endings (rather than irregular verbs like *gone*) for additional pronunciation practice. As an example, write the following sentence on the board:

  I could have walked home, but I was too late.

A ▶ 6:14 Listen and practice.

- Refer to the procedure for Exercise A on page T144.

B ▶ 6:15 Listen and practice.

- Refer to the procedure for Exercise A on page T144.

C Circle the correct pronunciation . . .

- First, have students focus on the sound at the end of each base form. Then have them circle the correct pronunciation of the *-ed* ending.

- After pairs practice saying each word, bring the class together and answer any questions. If necessary, refer students to the first box on page 147. To review the pronunciation of the *-ed* ending following the sounds /t/ and /d/ and voiced and voiceless sounds.

▶ 6:16 Now practice saying . . .

- Have students say each word aloud and then listen for confirmation.

UNIT 6

Regular past participle endings

There are three pronunciations of the past participle ending -ed, depending on the final sound of the base form of the verb.

With voiced sounds (except /d/)
When the base form ends with a voiced sound, pronounce the -ed ending as /d/.
moved   canceled   described   stayed   agreed

With voiceless sounds (except /t/)
When the base form ends with a voiceless sound, pronounce the -ed ending as /t/.
helped   asked   crushed   watched

HOWEVER: When the base form ends with the sound /t/ or /d/, pronounce the -ed ending as a new syllable, /ɪd/ or /əd/. In American English, the final sound before the -ed ending is always /t̬/, no matter whether the base form ended in the sound /t/ or /d/. Link /t̬/ with the -ed ending.

| wai ted | → | /weɪt̬ɪd/ | nee ded | → | /niːt̬ɪd/ |
| re por ted | → | /rɪpɔrt̬ɪd/ | in clud ed | → | /ɪnklut̬ɪd/ |

Voiced sounds		Voiceless sounds
/b/	/i/	/p/
/g/	/ɪ/	/k/
/ð/	/eɪ/	/θ/
/v/	/ɛ/	/f/
/z/	/æ/	/s/
/ʒ/	/ɑ/	/ʃ/
/dʒ/	/ɔ/	/tʃ/
/m/	/oʊ/	/t/
/n/	/ʊ/	
/ŋ/	/u/	
/r/	/ʌ/	
/l/	/ə/	

Reduction in perfect modals

The auxiliary have in perfect modals is generally reduced. The /h/ is dropped and /æ/ is reduced to /ə/.

/wʊt̬əv/
If I'd looked at the expiration date, I **would have** renewed my passport.

/maɪt̬əv/
If I weren't Japanese, I **might have** needed a visa to enter the country.

/wʊt̬ənəv/
If we'd left on time, we **wouldn't have** missed our flight.

Perfect modals
would have
could have
should have } + [past participle]
might have
may have

A ▶ 6:14 Listen and practice.

1 moved	5 agreed	9 watched	12 needed
2 canceled	6 helped	10 waited	13 included
3 described	7 asked	11 reported	
4 stayed	8 crushed		

B ▶ 6:15 Listen and practice.

1 If I'd looked at the expiration date, I would have renewed my passport.
2 If I weren't Japanese, I might have needed a visa to enter the country.
3 If we'd left on time, we wouldn't have missed our flight.

C Circle the correct pronunciation of each -ed ending.

1 avoided	(/ɪd/)	/t/	/d/	9 promised	/ɪd/	(/t/)	/d/
2 looked	/ɪd/	(/t/)	/d/	10 covered	/ɪd/	/t/	(/d/)
3 summarized	/ɪd/	/t/	(/d/)	11 added	(/ɪd/)	/t/	/d/
4 arrived	/ɪd/	/t/	(/d/)	12 changed	/ɪd/	/t/	(/d/)
5 owed	/ɪd/	/t/	(/d/)	13 reported	(/ɪd/)	/t/	/d/
6 ruined	/ɪd/	/t/	(/d/)	14 discussed	/ɪd/	(/t/)	/d/
7 kicked	/ɪd/	(/t/)	/d/	15 investigated	(/ɪd/)	/t/	/d/
8 refunded	(/ɪd/)	/t/	/d/	16 enjoyed	/ɪd/	/t/	(/d/)

▶ 6:16 Now practice saying each word aloud and listen to compare.*

PRONUNCIATION BOOSTER

D ▶6:17 Practice saying each sentence aloud, paying attention to reductions. Listen to compare.*

1. If I'd put my passport in my briefcase, it wouldn't have gotten lost.
2. If you'd checked the luggage limits, you might have avoided extra charges.
3. If my friend's luggage hadn't gotten stolen, he could have gone on the sightseeing tour.
4. I probably wouldn't have missed my flight if I had come on time.
5. If they'd taken a few simple precautions, their luggage might not have gotten stolen.

UNIT 7

Linking sounds

Link plural noun endings to the first sound in the word that follows.
  Superstitions about animals are very common. /supərˈstɪʃənzəbout/
  Some say rats leaving a ship will cause it to sink. /ræt͡sˈlivɪŋ/

Link third-person singular endings to the first sound in the word that follows.
  A belief in a superstition often results in fear. /rɪˈzʌltsɪn/

Remember: There are three different sounds for the endings of plural nouns and third-person singular verbs.

/z/	/s/	/ɪz/
diamonds	results	promises
superstitions	sharks	noises
bottles	types	matches
believes	beliefs	wishes
dreams	sleeps	judges

A ▶6:18 Listen and practice.

1. Superstitions about animals are very common.
2. Some say rats leaving a ship will cause it to sink.
3. A belief in a superstition often results in fear.

B ▶6:19 Practice reading each sentence aloud, paying attention to the linking sounds you have learned. Listen to compare.* (Note that your choices may differ from what you hear on the audio.)

1. A frog brings good luck to the house it enters.
2. Babies born with teeth become extremely selfish.
3. An itchy nose means you'll have a fight.
4. A lucky charm protects against the evil eye.
5. She keeps a large bowl of water near the front door.
6. Superstitions can be found in every culture.
7. A company claims to have invented a machine that allows people to talk with their pets.
8. Some fears are hard to overcome.
9. My sister believes in ghosts, avoids black cats, and carries a lucky charm in her pocket.

UNIT 8

Emphatic stress with auxiliary verbs

Use emphatic stress on an auxiliary verb to confirm or contradict.
  A: Do you think Carrie Mulligan has a successful acting career?
  B: I think so. She **IS** getting a lot of lead roles these days.

  A: I wonder if I should take French lessons.
  B: Great idea! I think you **SHOULD** learn French.

  A: Have you eaten at the Blue Moon Café before?
  B: Actually, I think I **HAVE** eaten there before.

  A: Jan says you love coffee. Is that true?
  B: Not at all. I really **DON'T** like coffee.

Remember: The auxiliary do needs to be added for emphatic stress in affirmative statements in the simple present or past tense.
  A: Jan says you love coffee. Is that true?
  B: Yes, it is. I really **DO** like coffee.

A ▶6:20 Listen and practice.

1. She **IS** getting a lot of lead roles these days.
2. I think you **SHOULD** learn French.
3. Actually, I think I **HAVE** eaten there before.
4. I really **DON'T** like coffee.
5. I really **DO** like coffee.

148 PRONUNCIATION BOOSTER

D ▶6:17 **Practice saying each sentence . . .**

- Have students scan the sentences and underline the perfect modals. (1. wouldn't have; 2. might have; 3. could have; 4. wouldn't have; 5. might not have) Then have them look at the past participle that follows each perfect modal and circle the past participles that end in -ed. (2. avoided, 4. missed)
- Tell pairs to practice saying the sentences aloud, paying attention to the reductions and the pronunciation of the -ed endings.
- Have students read each sentence aloud and then listen for confirmation.

⭐ 🖨 Pronunciation Pair Work

Unit 7
Linking sounds

- On the board, write /z/, /s/, and /ɪz/. Elicit or produce the sound of each symbol. Then call on volunteers to read the words in each column of the Remember note. Correct pronunciation as needed. If necessary, have students repeat the final sound in each word to hear the difference in the endings. Then read the explanation in the Remember note aloud.
- Have students study the first explanation and the example sentences. Read each sentence aloud, and have students repeat chorally.
- Tell students to study the second explanation and the example sentences. Read each sentence aloud, and have students repeat chorally.

Option: [+15–20 minutes] For additional practice in linking the /z/ sound to the first sound in the word that follows, write on the board:

  Superstitions about animals are popular in this country.
  I recycled the bottles last night.

Have students repeat. For additional practice in linking the /s/ and /ɪz/ sounds to the first sound in the word that follows, write on the board:

  The dog sleeps on the kitchen floor.
  My shirt matches my shoes.

Have students repeat.

A ▶6:18 **Listen and practice.**

- Refer to the procedure for Exercise A on page T144.

B ▶6:19 **Practice reading each sentence . . .**

- First, have students scan the sentences and underline the plural nouns and third-person singular verbs. Tell students to circle the sounds in each sentence that should be linked and then practice reading the sentences with a partner. (Linking sounds are indicated by underlining. 1. brings good; 2. babies born; 3. means you; 4. protects against; 5. keeps a; 6. superstitions can; 7. claims to, allows people; 8. fears are; 9. believes in, avoids black, carries a)
- Have students read each sentence aloud and then listen for confirmation.

Challenge: [+15–20 minutes] On the board, draw the following chart:

/z/, /s/, /ɪz/ + vowel	/z/, /s/, /ɪz/ + consonant

First, have pairs find and circle examples of linking sounds in Exercise A. Then have students write the examples and the ones they circled in Exercise B in the chart.

⭐ 🖨 Pronunciation Pair Work

Unit 8
Emphatic stress with auxiliary verbs

- Read the first line. Then model the first conversation with a volunteer, the teacher reading A and the student reading B. If necessary, correct emphasis. Then read the B line again and have students repeat. Ask *Does the person confirm or contradict?* (The person confirms that Carrie Mulligan has a successful acting career.)
- Call on pairs to read the next three conversations. After each one, ask *Does the person confirm or contradict?* (Only the fourth conversation contradicts: *I really DON'T like coffee.*)
- Then read the Remember note and model the conversation with a volunteer. To illustrate adding the auxiliary *did* in the simple past tense, write on the board:

  A: You didn't like the movie, did you?
  B: Actually, I DID like it.

Option: [+15–20 minutes] Have students work in pairs to make up mini-conversations, following the models in the Pronunciation Chart. Then have them read the conversations to the class, using emphatic stress to confirm or contradict.

A ▶6:20 **Listen and practice.**

- Refer to the procedure for Exercise A on page T144.

T148

B ▶6:21 **Practice responding . . .**
- First, have students scan the sentences and underline the auxiliary verb in each response.
- Have students read each response and then listen for confirmation.

Option [+5 minutes] In pairs, have students read the dialogues using correct emphatic stress in the response.

⭐ 🖨 **Pronunciation Pair Work**

Unit 9
Reading aloud

- To introduce the topic, ask: *What's the difference between reading aloud to an audience and reading to oneself?* (Possible answer: When you read to yourself, you focus on understanding the text rather than on making sure others understand it.) *Do you prefer to read or listen to someone read? Why?*
- Read the explanation to the class. Then have students read it to themselves. Ask *Did you understand more when you read the explanation to yourselves or when I read it to you? Why do you think that is?*
- Have pairs practice reading the example selection to each other, using a regular rhythm, making fewer reductions, pausing at all punctuation, and separating thought groups. Point out that the single slash (/) in the selection indicates a pause within a sentence or between sentences.
- Bring the class together, and invite a volunteer to read the selection. Ask students to give feedback on the clarity of the reading. Suggest corrections, and have students repeat after you.

A ▶6:22 **Listen to the selection . . .**
- After listening to the selection, have pairs practice reading it to each other.

B ▶6:23 **Practice reading each selection . . .**
- First, have students use single slashes (/) to mark necessary pauses in the selections, following the example in the box.
- Then have pairs practice reading the selections to each other. Remind students to use a regular rhythm and to make appropriate pauses.
- Have students read the first selection aloud. Then play the selection so students can listen for confirmation. Repeat with the second selection.

Challenge: [+15–20 minutes] For more practice reading aloud, have pairs choose either the article "Envisioning the Future" on page 100 or "Ordinary People with Big Ideas" on page 104 in the Student's Book. Tell pairs to read the article aloud to each other, pausing at all punctuation and between thought groups. Remind students to state the title separately with falling intonation. Circulate and assist as needed. Then have students listen to each article, to compare with their reading. If there is time, create groups of four and have pairs read their articles to each other.

⭐ 🖨 **Pronunciation Pair Work**

T149

B ▶ 6:21 Practice responding to each speaker, using emphatic stress on the auxiliary verb. Listen to compare.*

1 "I think Olivia's a great cook."
RESPONSE: I agree. She does make great food.

2 "Your husband doesn't dance very well."
RESPONSE: That's true. He really doesn't dance well.

3 "Can you eat seafood?"
RESPONSE: Actually, I can't eat seafood. I'm allergic to it.

4 "Your cousins are hysterical!"
RESPONSE: I agree. They really do tell a lot of funny jokes.

5 "Ana's report is late again."
RESPONSE: Well, she does tend to procrastinate.

6 "Does Gary have a head for figures?"
RESPONSE: No. But he is taking a math class on Tuesday evenings.

7 "I think it's time to tell everyone you're going to quit."
RESPONSE: You're right. I should tell them sooner rather than later.

8 "Have you made up your mind yet?"
RESPONSE: No. But I have been thinking about it.

UNIT 9

Reading aloud

Because it's more difficult to understand language when it is read rather than spoken in conversation, read with a regular rhythm and use fewer sound reductions. If there's a title, state it separately with falling intonation. Pause at all punctuation. Separate sentences into thought groups, pausing after each. Pause slightly longer between sentences.

Envisioning the Future
In the 1960s, / only large institutions, / such as banks, / corporations, / and the military, / had computers. // They were expensive, / slow, / and very large— / requiring a special air-conditioned room— / and access to them was limited / to only a few people. // In the 1970s, / computer prices came down / and then small businesses began to use them. // Nevertheless, / in 1977, / the CEO and founder of Digital Equipment, / Kenneth Olsen, / predicted that computers would never be used in the home.

A ▶ 6:22 Listen to the selection. Then practice reading it aloud.

Envisioning the Future
In the 1960s, only large institutions, such as banks, corporations, and the military, had computers. They were expensive, slow, and very large—requiring a special air-conditioned room—and access to them was limited to only a few people. In the 1970s, computer prices came down and then small businesses began to use them. Nevertheless, in 1977, the CEO and founder of Digital Equipment, Kenneth Olsen, predicted that computers would never be used in the home.

B ▶ 6:23 Practice reading each selection aloud. Then listen to compare.* (Note that your choices may differ from what you hear on the audio.)

1 **Birth of the Personal Computer**
In the early 80s, Steve Jobs and Bill Gates introduced the personal computer—the Macintosh and the IBM PC, respectively—which made computing at home possible. In 1983, Jobs gave a speech about the future, in which he predicted that, for most people, a great deal of time would be spent interacting with personal computers. He also predicted that, within ten years, computers in the office and at home would be connected so people would be able to use them to communicate.

2 **Predicting Social Media**
In 1999, Gates predicted that small devices would be carried around by everyone so that they could get instant information and stay in touch with others. He also claimed that, by the early twenty-first century, Internet communities would have been formed, based on one's interests or to connect with friends and family.

UNIT 10

Intonation of tag questions

When a tag question follows a statement to which a speaker anticipates agreement, both the statement and the tag question are said with falling intonation. The main stress in the tag question falls on the auxiliary verb and not on the pronoun. Note that there is generally no pause at the comma.

It's really shocking, isn't it?

They'll come up with a solution, won't they?

It's not really surprising, is it?

She didn't speak out against that project, did she?

It really makes you feel angry, doesn't it?

When the tag question represents a genuine question to which the speaker expects an answer, the statement is said with falling intonation, but the tag question is said with rising intonation.

It's really shocking, isn't it?

They'll come up with a solution, won't they?

It's not really surprising, is it?

She didn't speak out against that project, did she?

It really makes you feel angry, doesn't it?

A ▶6:24 Listen and practice. (Each sentence is said two ways.)

1. It's really shocking, isn't it?
2. It's not really surprising, is it?
3. It really makes you feel angry, doesn't it?
4. They'll come up with a solution, won't they?
5. She didn't speak out against that project, did she?

B ▶6:25 Listen to the following tag questions. Check to indicate if each one anticipates agreement or expects an answer.

	Anticipates agreement	Expects an answer
1. That's really appalling, isn't it?	✓	
2. He's worried about his children, isn't he?	✓	
3. It really makes you feel good, doesn't it?	✓	
4. It wasn't really true, was it?		✓
5. They're going to do something about that problem, aren't they?		✓
6. It's not really important, is it?	✓	
7. You heard that on TV, didn't you?		✓
8. You'll support us, won't you?		✓

▶6:25 Now practice saying each tag question aloud and listen to compare.*

C ▶6:26 Practice saying each tag question two ways, first to express anticipated agreement and then to express a genuine question. Listen to compare.*

1. It really makes you stop and think, doesn't it?
2. They're concerned about global warming, aren't they?
3. The president's economic policy is effective, isn't it?
4. The benefits of globalization are very clear, aren't they?
5. The benefits of globalization aren't very clear, are they?
6. There's no turning back, is there?

DIGITAL PAIR WORK

150 PRONUNCIATION BOOSTER

Unit 10

Intonation of tag questions

- Tell students to study the first explanation and example sentences. Then have pairs practice reading the sentences to each other, using correct intonation. Explain that the falling arrow indicates falling intonation. Circulate and offer feedback as needed.
- Have students study the second explanation and example sentences. Then have pairs practice reading the sentences to each other, using correct intonation. Explain that the rising arrow indicates rising intonation. Circulate and offer feedback as needed.
- Write the following sentence on the board:

  That's really wonderful, isn't it?

  Read the sentence two ways: First, say both the statement and tag question with falling intonation, and then say the statement with falling intonation and the tag question with rising intonation. Ask *What does each intonation convey?* (The first intonation pattern anticipates agreement, and the second expects an answer.)
- To check understanding, read the example sentences to the class, varying intonation for anticipated agreement and for an expected answer. Have students identify the meaning each intonation expresses.

A ▶ 6:24 Listen and practice.

- Refer to the procedure for Exercise A on page T144.

B ▶ 6:25 Listen to the following tag questions . . .

- To review, ask:
  What intonation do you use in a tag question to anticipate agreement? (Both statement and tag question are said with falling intonation.)
  What intonation do you use when you expect an answer to a tag question? (The statement is said with falling intonation, and the tag question is said with rising intonation.)
- Before students listen, have them read the items and note the check boxes.
- Then have students listen to the tag questions and check the correct boxes.
- Tell students to compare answers with a partner. Then go over the answers as a class.

▶ 6:25 Now practice saying . . .

- Have students say each tag question aloud and then listen for confirmation.

C ▶ 6:26 Practice saying each tag question . . .

- Have pairs practice saying each tag question two ways, using appropriate intonation.
- Then have students read each tag question aloud two ways and then listen for confirmation.

⭐ 🖨 Pronunciation Pair Work

Test-Taking Skills Booster

Test-Taking Skills Booster

The Test-Taking Skills Booster is optional. It provides practice in applying some key logical thinking and comprehension skills typically included in reading and listening tasks on standardized proficiency tests. Each unit contains one Reading Completion activity and one or more Listening Completion activities.

*Note that the practice activities in the Booster are not intended to test student achievement after each unit. Complete Achievement Tests for *Summit* can be found in the *Summit* ActiveTeach.

UNIT 1

READING COMPLETION

Read the selection. Choose the word or phrase that best completes each statement.

Gender Roles

Until recently in the developed world, most married couples (1) ..... traditional roles, with the husband working outside the home and the wife taking care of the children and the house. Although many families still follow this tradition, those roles have become less iron-clad. A number of factors have contributed to this (2) ..... . (3) ..... , perhaps as a consequence of feminism, people have begun to believe that one's (4) ..... should not dictate one's role. (5) ..... , people feel they have "permission" to decide what they want to do in life. It's no longer (6) ..... for men to want to be the primary caregiver or homemaker. (7) ..... , many women would prefer to enter the working world instead of staying home. (8) ..... , a large number of women have achieved advanced academic and professional training, providing them with a significant earning potential.

On the other hand, factors other than personal choice have (9) ..... to the fluidity of gender roles. Life has become more expensive and it's (10) ..... for a family to exist on only one income, requiring married women to leave the home to earn money to help support the family. (11) ..... , the number of two-income households has grown exponentially. And despite the fact that women on average still earn less than men for the same job, their incomes have become an (12) ..... component of survival and prosperity in today's world. In similar fashion, a man's decision to stay home may not be voluntary. In the event he has lost his job, his decision to stay home might be one of necessity, not (13) ..... .

1	A rejected	**B adopted**	C gave	D needed
2	**A change**	B consequence	C continuation	D conflict
3	A Whereas	B While	**C On the one hand**	D On the other hand
4	A parents	B income	**C gender**	D age
5	A Despite this	**B As a result**	C Nevertheless	D Whereas
6	A beneficial	B advantageous	C harmful	**D shameful**
7	A Nevertheless	B Despite the fact	**C By the same token**	D First
8	A On the other hand	**B Moreover**	C For example	D Finally
9	A contradicted	**B contributed**	C coincided	D donated
10	A convenient	**B difficult**	C easy	D traditional
11	A Yet	B Even though	C Even if	**D Consequently**
12	A ordinary	B arbitrary	C unnecessary	**D essential**
13	A need	B habit	**C choice**	D logic

LISTENING COMPLETION

▶ 6:27 You will hear a conversation. Read the paragraph below. Then listen and complete each statement with the word or short phrase you hear in the conversation. Listen a second time to check your work.

The woman, Diane, is upset because she can't (1) **find her phone** . Her husband is trying to help her, and he asks her (2) **when** she saw it (3) **last** . She remembers that she used it (4) **to text** her friend Mark when she was (5) **in the car** . Her husband asks if she had been (6) **driving** when she texted Mark. Diane wants to know why that question is relevant, and her husband says that even though it's (7) **reckless** to text while driving, the main reason he asked was to help her figure out when she (8) **sent the text** . That question helps Diane remember that she had been downstairs (9) **in the parking garage** when she texted and that she had stuck (10) **the phone** in the grocery bag.

UNIT 2

READING COMPLETION
Read the selection. Choose the word or phrase that best completes each statement.

Where Values Come From

All of us live by a set of principles or beliefs that guide our actions and help us develop a sense of what is morally acceptable **(1)** ..... what is unacceptable behavior. But where do our values come from? According to psychologists, they develop throughout our lives and **(2)** ..... from a variety of sources, such as family, school, religious upbringing, the places we work in, **(3)** ..... as the media and music we watch and listen to.

For example, most of us learn from our parents to **(4)** ..... between right and wrong. When they read to us or tell us children's stories, we **(5)** ..... moral lessons about the consequences of good and bad behavior. **(6)** ..... we make mistakes or when we don't tell the truth, our parents correct us. Moreover, we learn from our parents' actions. Children **(7)** ..... how their parents relate to each other and handle social situations, and they always notice whether their parents are truthful or not.

(8) ..... , we are strongly affected by the views of our peers. Our friends, colleagues, and acquaintances "categorize" the people we know or who we hear about on the news—for example, who is unfriendly, who is generous, which politicians or celebrities are honest. Many people also believe their moral principles can be **(9)** ..... to their religious upbringing. Religion can provide a clear set of guidelines to live by that make it easier to distinguish between right and wrong.

1	A between	**B from**	C to	D about
2	**A originate**	B learn	C match	D populate
3	A known	B such	**C as well**	D as far
4	A activate	**B distinguish**	C enter	D educate
5	**A absorb**	B calculate	C inspire	D encourage
6	A Therefore	B Although	C Even if	**D When**
7	**A observe**	B disagree	C ignore	D compete
8	A Consequently	B As a result	C For instance	**D Similarly**
9	A described	B contributed	**C attributed**	D celebrated

LISTENING COMPLETION

▶ 6:28 You will hear part of a report. Read the paragraph below. Then listen and complete each statement with the word or short phrase you hear in the report. Listen a second time to check your work.

In the report, the speaker notes that celebrity philanthropists get lots of attention but also have their (1) ...**critics**... . For example, an aid worker complains that bringing celebrities in to do humanitarian work is more (2) ...**trouble**... it's worth. Why? Because celebrity philanthropists can be (3) ...**self-centered**... and demanding. They also often do little to (4) ...**learn about**... the people they came to help. On the other hand, supporters note that some celebrity philanthropists (5) ...**pay their own**... way and don't ask for special (6) ...**treatment**... . Another criticism of celebrity philanthropists, however, is that they sometimes spread a (7) ...**false impression**... that places like Africa are hopeless and (8) ...**helpless**... . Finally, some critics say celebrities (9) ...**ignore**... local humanitarian efforts and provide increased opportunities for (10) ...**corruption**... .

152 TEST-TAKING SKILLS BOOSTER

UNIT 3

READING COMPLETION

Read the selection. Choose the word or phrase that best completes each statement.

Avoiding Hearing Loss

Hearing plays a crucial role in all aspects of communication and learning. (1) ..... does even a small amount of hearing loss have a profound, negative effect on language development and comprehension, it (2) ..... affects the classroom learning of students who have difficulty hearing. (3) ..... deafness that occurs at birth or because of disease or injury, permanent (4) ..... to hearing can result from excessive exposure to noise. In fact, millions of people (5) ..... from this sort of hearing loss, called "noise-induced hearing loss." It is (6) ..... by damage to structures and / or nerve fibers in the inner ear. It can result from a one-time exposure to a very loud sound or from listening to loud sounds over an extended period of time. Unfortunately, noise-induced hearing loss cannot be medically or surgically (7) ..... .

So how can noise-induced hearing loss be (8) ..... ? In some cases it's impossible to avoid the (9) ..... exposure to one very loud sound, and some work environments are noisy. Nevertheless, there are many cases in which people can avoid voluntary exposure to loud sounds, and they (10) ..... . What are some steps anyone can take? Most importantly, identify the (11) ..... of loud sounds, such as lawnmowers, power tools, and music in your life. Next, adopt behaviors to protect hearing, such as avoiding or (12) ..... exposure to the loud sounds as much as you can. After that, make it a practice to automatically turn down the volume of music systems. Finally, when it's not feasible to avoid or (13) ..... loud sounds, use hearing protection devices. Such devices can reduce the noise to a safe level.

1	A Even though	**B Not only**	C If only	D Therefore
2	A yet	B in spite of this	C even if	**D also**
3	A Whenever	B Whereas	C Before	**D Unlike**
4	A aid	**B damage**	C benefits	D symptoms
5	A enjoy	B are helped	C result	**D suffer**
6	A aided	**B caused**	C benefitted	D cured
7	A caused	**B corrected**	C heard	D possible
8	A improved	**B prevented**	C treated	D confirmed
9	A fortunate	**B accidental**	C intentional	D obvious
10	A can	B might	**C should**	D do not
11	A effects	**B sources**	C problems	D consequences
12	**A limiting**	B combining	C making	D causing
13	A increase	B hope for	C create	**D reduce**

LISTENING COMPLETION

▶ 6:29 You will hear a report. Read the paragraph below. Then listen and complete each statement with the word or short phrase you hear in the report. Listen a second time to check your work.

Seol Ik Soo, a Korean (1) ...tour guide... who was a passenger on a flight returning (2) ...home to... South Korea (3) ...from a trip to... China, was daydreaming about his wife as the plane prepared (4) ...to land... . He and his wife had been married only (5) ...one month... before and this was the first time they had been (6) ...apart... . Suddenly, he saw a ball of (7) ...fire... in the cabin of the plane and the plane (8) ...crashed... . Luckily, Seol escaped through a hole in the crashed plane. From outside of the plane he could hear other passengers calling (9) ...for help... . Instead of running away, Seol went back in to rescue others. No one knows exactly how many passengers Seol managed to carry out of the plane. There may have been (10) ...as many as... ten. After it was all over, Seol was asked how he had managed to behave so heroically and he responded that he's sure he couldn't have done it in his (11) ...right mind... .

UNIT 4

READING COMPLETION
Read the selection. Choose the word or phrase that best completes each statement.

Friendship

In the words of a famous song, friendship is "like a bridge over troubled water." In other words, you can always count on your friends' support when you need it the (1) ..... . Friends can tell when you're feeling (2) ....., and they know whether or not you want to talk about it. They are thoughtful when it comes to your well-being, and they can (3) ..... according to your needs.

The truth is we need our friends to be dependable—through thick and thin. (4) ..... constantly trying to change you, good friends accept you as you are. And good friends roll with the punches. They get it that inside you're a good person with flaws, and that those shortcomings are part of who you are. (5) ....., they know you make mistakes, and they forgive you for them, knowing you'll try to do better next time. And when people criticize you, friends stick up for you because even (6) ..... you're being difficult, friends are patient.

While you and your friends may have disagreements, you (7) ..... respect each other's opinions. Above all, you need to know that you can (8) ..... your friends with your secrets. If there's a problem between you, a friend will talk to you (9) ..... and not gossip about you with others. We can always count on our friends to be honest with us when others aren't. Friends don't keep things bottled up inside. Whenever there's an (10) ....., they work things out together and move on.

1	A heaviest	**B most**	C least	D nearest
2	A ready	B cold	C energetic	**D blue**
3	A criticize	B argue	**C adjust**	D learn
4	**A Rather than**	B Whereas	C Despite	D Before
5	**A Moreover**	B Otherwise	C Whether or not	D Unfortunately
6	A despite	B especially	**C when**	D so
7	**A should**	B never	C don't	D might
8	A help	B save	**C trust**	D lend
9	A formally	B casually	C importantly	**D directly**
10	A accident	**B issue**	C attribute	D examination

LISTENING COMPLETION

A ▶6:30 You will hear a description. Read the paragraph below. Then listen and complete each statement with the word or short phrase you hear in the description. Listen a second time to check your work.

The woman says she sometimes feels (1) ...overwhelmed... because she's so (2) ...disorganized... . She says that when she puts things away, she then can't (3) ...find them... . She feels embarrassed to (4) ...have anyone over... because there's such a mess. So she asked her friend Alicia for help because Alicia's so (5) ...organized... . Alicia helped her (6) ...go through... all her stuff to decide what was important and what she could (7) ...throw away... .

B ▶6:31 You will hear a description. Read the paragraph below. Then listen and complete each statement with the word or short phrase you hear in the description. Listen a second time to check your work.

The woman is concerned about what she calls a problem with her (8) ...temper... . It's not a problem at (9) ...work..., but she worries when she gets really angry at her (10) ...kids... and starts (11) ...yelling... at them. She believes that, after a bad day at work, she's just (12) ...taking... it out on them. As a result, she took a workshop on (13) ...anger management..., where she learned that it's important to let off a little steam. So she took up (14) ...aerobics... three days a week. When she feels angry, exercising helps her (15) ...let go of... what's making her mad.

UNIT 5

READING COMPLETION

Read the selection. Choose the word or phrase that best completes each statement.

Laughter Yoga

The principle of Laughter Yoga is that you cannot be physically stressed and mentally relaxed at the same time. (1) ..... most forms of Yoga include body positions and exercises, Laughter Yoga is based on the physical activity of laughing, which relaxes the body and mind. Proponents of Laughter Yoga (2) ..... that it permits us to be more aware of the present (3) ..... dwelling on the past or worrying about the future. In short, it enables us to simply *be*.

Some (4) ..... that Laughter Yoga can be considered a new form of exercise. (5) ..... its proponents, it's a kind of internal jogging. Anyone can do it because, they say, everybody knows how to laugh. It is not necessary to tell jokes, have a sense of (6) ..... , or be happy in order to laugh. In fact, practitioners of Laughter Yoga are invited to "laugh for no reason," faking the laughter until it becomes real. It is (7) ..... that the physical action of laughing brings oxygen and certain body chemicals such as hormones to the body and the brain, thus fostering (8) ..... feelings and improving interpersonal skills. (9) ..... Laughter Yoga is practiced in groups, people leave each session laughing and feeling (10) ..... to each other. Believers in Laughter Yoga (11) ..... contend it can contribute to world peace. They say, "World peace first starts inside every one of us. We don't laugh because we are happy. We are happy because we laugh."

1	A Until	(B) While	C Whether	D If
2	A continue	B complain	(C) assert	D admit
3	A in addition to	(B) instead of	C in favor of	D along with
4	A tell	B ask	(C) claim	D wonder
5	A Even if	B Whenever	C Although	(D) According to
6	A anger	(B) humor	C happiness	D knowledge
7	A argued	B disputed	C required	D intended
8	A negative	B hopeless	C lucky	(D) positive
9	A Since	B All the same	C Even if	D Until
10	A separate	(B) connected	C different	D annoyed
11	A however	B nevertheless	(C) therefore	D besides

LISTENING COMPLETION

▶ 6:32 You will hear a story. Read the paragraph below. Then listen and complete each statement with the word or short phrase you hear in the story. Listen a second time to check your work.

The woman tells a story about her friend Mark, who loves to (1) ...play practical jokes... . Mark decided to play a joke on his friend John, who was very (2) ...cheap... and was always looking for (3) ...a bargain... . One day, Mark spoke to (4) ...the manager... of the Bargain Burger restaurant and asked her if she would (5) ...prepare... two very large burgers. The manager said "Sure," and Mark paid her for them (6) ...in advance... . Mark explained that he would bring (7) ...a friend... for lunch and that the manager should (8) ...serve... the huge burgers and put the regular low price on the check. When Mark and John finished eating, (9) ...the check came... and John was pleasantly surprised at the low price of the burgers. So the (10) ...next day... John invited a couple of his friends to Bargain Burger for the huge hamburgers. But when the burgers came to the table, they were the ordinary tiny little ones, which made John (11) ...look really stupid... in front of his friends.

TEST-TAKING SKILLS BOOSTER 155

UNIT 6

READING COMPLETION
Read the selection. Choose the word or phrase that best completes each statement.

Wi-Fi Safety

Staying connected anywhere is relatively easy today. We almost always have smartphones, tablets, or laptops at the ready. And **(1)** ..... the availability of free Wi-Fi everywhere—in hotels, cafés, stores, even in parks—we feel empowered to act as we do at home. For instance, we can do our online banking and make online purchases anywhere with **(2)** ..... . On the one hand, easy connectivity is a great **(3)** ..... . But on the other, wishful thinking can lull us into a false sense of **(4)** ..... . It's important to remember that **(5)** ..... at home, where our Internet connections are securely encrypted, free public Wi-Fi away from home is not.

What are some of the possible **(6)** ..... of using unencrypted Wi-Fi? First, a thief might be able to access your credit card information and make online or in-store purchases, leaving you to pay the bill. Many such purchases, however, especially if they don't conform to your usual buying pattern, **(7)** ..... the credit card company that the purchaser isn't you. Luckily, the company can cancel your card to stop any further **(8)** ..... from being made. **(9)** ..... , but perhaps more importantly, thieves can **(10)** ..... your usernames and passwords, enabling them to access your bank accounts and withdraw money. Finally, in the worst-case scenario, they can steal your identity, leaving you to **(11)** ..... it at great trouble to you. So how can you **(12)** ..... yourself? In summary, although free public Wi-Fi seems convenient, send personal information only to sites that are fully encrypted, and avoid using any mobile apps that **(13)** ..... personal or financial information.

1	A in spite of	B since	C in addition to	**D due to**
2	A aggravation	B difficulty	C cash	**D ease**
3	**A advantage**	B disadvantage	C importance	D problem
4	A disadvantage	B the future	**C security**	D anxiety
5	A like	B similarly	**C unlike**	D as well
6	A reasons	**B consequences**	C points of view	D possibilities
7	A indicate	B avoid	**C alert**	D accuse
8	**A purchases**	B decisions	C claims	D conflicts
9	**A Secondly**	B By the same token	C After	D Before
10	A provide	B recover	C return	**D steal**
11	**A recover**	B relate	C return	D resist
12	A affect	B promote	C remove	**D protect**
13	A provide	**B require**	C resist	D donate

LISTENING COMPLETION

▶ 6:33 You will hear part of a report. Read the paragraph below. Then listen and complete each statement with the word or short phrase you hear in the report. Listen a second time to check your work.

Consider this situation: You are waiting patiently for your bags at (1) _the baggage carousel_ . You see other travelers pick up their bags, but still yours are nowhere in sight. There are fewer and fewer bags until finally (2) _the carousel stops_ . You wonder what happened to your bags and think perhaps they weren't transferred to your (3) _connecting flight_ when you changed planes. Or maybe the missing luggage was sent to (4) _the wrong destination_ . You go to the airline's (5) _missing luggage counter_ to file a claim and hope the bags will (6) _arrive on the next flight_ and be delivered to (7) _your local address_ within a short time. If, on the other hand, the bags are permanently (8) _lost_ or completely (9) _destroyed_ , you will want to file a claim for damages. If you can document what you have lost, you will probably be reimbursed. But be aware that even if you have (10) _sales receipts_ to prove the value of items in your luggage, you won't receive (11) _the full amount_ you originally paid for your property. But you will definitely receive something.

UNIT 7

READING COMPLETION
Read the selection. Choose the word or phrase that best completes each statement.

Coping with Phobias

According to recent research, one in ten people worldwide has some kind of phobia or overwhelming (1) ..... . And even though phobias are (2) ..... , they are much more severe than the common garden-variety fear. But in what way?

For one thing, while most people can (3) ..... with most normal fears, a full-blown phobia is something people can't just put out of their mind. (4) ..... , phobics don't have much control over their phobias. As a result, they suffer from unpleasant physical and mental (5) ..... when confronted with what they fear. Such symptoms are similar to ones people experience when faced with real physical (6) ..... . (7) ..... , their heartbeat gets rapid, their throat goes dry, and their sweating increases. These unpleasant physical symptoms are intended to prepare people to (8) ..... harm in the face of real danger. However, the phobic, who isn't in any real physical danger, reacts in the same way. (9) ..... , phobics will go to great lengths to avoid what they fear and these extremely unpleasant physical responses. (10) ..... , there is hope for people with phobias despite their severity. In "cognitive behavioral therapy," or CBT, phobics are repeatedly (11) ..... to what causes the fear, which desensitizes them to it because nothing bad happens. If CBT doesn't work, "counter-conditioning" can teach patients to substitute a physical relaxation response when in the presence of what (12) ..... them. In summary, there is hope for phobics who get (13) ..... . The success rate of therapy is excellent.

#	A	B	C	D
1	danger	anxiety	relaxation	need
2	talents	harmful	**(C) fears**	certain
3	appreciate	come down	**(C) cope**	notice
4	Fortunately	**(B) In other words**	Similarly	Even so
5	**(A) symptoms**	fears	benefits	emotions
6	relief	pleasure	**(C) danger**	symptoms
7	Even so	**(B) For example**	However	Moreover
8	undergo	**(B) avoid**	cause	receive
9	However	Because	In contrast	**(D) Consequently**
10	For example	While	Unfortunately	**(D) Fortunately**
11	**(A) exposed**	allowed	reduced	increased
12	relaxes	helps	angers	**(D) frightens**
13	success	failure	**(C) treatment**	ready

LISTENING COMPLETION

A ▶ 6:34 You will hear a conversation. Read the paragraph below. Then listen and complete each statement with the word or short phrase you hear in the conversation. Listen a second time to check your work.

The man is reading about a way (1) __to make big money__ in a short time. But the woman is doubtful and says it sounds (2) __too good to be true__ . He disagrees and explains the scheme: You get a list of (3) __names and addresses__ and then send (4) __ten dollars__ to the last person on the list. Then you add (5) __your name__ to the list. When someone else gets that list, the money (6) __starts__ rolling in. The woman says that this is such an (7) __obvious__ get-rich-quick scam.

B ▶ 6:35 You will hear a conversation. Read the paragraph below. Then listen and complete each statement with a word or short phrase you hear in the conversation. Listen a second time to check your work.

The woman says there's a company that has (8) __a method__ for people to learn to speak a new language during the time when they're (9) __sleeping / asleep__ . She thinks it's absolutely (10) __impossible__ . The man, on the other hand, says he wouldn't (11) __be so sure__ that it's impossible. He says he heard that some (12) __students__ in a sleep-learning lab had (13) __learned__ the basics of Russian in only one week.

UNIT 8

READING COMPLETION

Read the selection. Choose the word or phrase that best completes each statement.

Can We Increase Our Intelligence?

In a general sense, intelligence can be defined as the ability to learn, understand, and apply knowledge or skills. While many experts have argued that one's IQ score simply cannot be (1) ....., others claim that these abilities can be maximized by exercising the brain. In their opinion, certain activities, (2) ..... reading regularly, doing puzzles daily, or learning a new language, may in fact improve our thinking skills, capacity to remember, and general knowledge. Furthermore, they make the point that IQ tests don't provide an adequate (3) ..... of real intelligence. In fact, they measure how one's level of academic achievement can be predicted but do not measure creativity or "street smarts"—the ability to (4) ..... with everyday life. Likewise, they are (5) ..... to measure one's potential for growth. Some experts suggest that other aspects of intelligence be considered as well—emotional intelligence being one example.

Moreover, Harvard University's Howard Gardner proposed that psychologists and educators (6) ..... the existence of at least seven distinct areas of intelligence. Two of these, linguistic and mathematical, are currently measured to some degrees by IQ tests. (7) ....., another two, interpersonal and intrapersonal, are measured by EQ tests. He also proposed including visual-spatial intelligence. In addition, Gardner recommended that two other aspects of intelligence be (8) ..... : musical and physical. Gardner considers each of these intelligences to be areas of human potential; (9) ....., they can be developed and increased.

1. A believed   **B increased**   C provided   D genetic
2. A such as   B from   **C for instance** D to
3. A tool   **B measurement**   C improvement   D completion
4. A measure   B encounter   C face   **D deal**
5. **A unable**   B equipped   C incomplete   D designed
6. A contribute   B criticize   **C acknowledge** D change
7. **A Similarly**   B As a result   C Because of this D For instance
8. **A recognized** B removed   C presented   D altered
9. A otherwise   **B that is**   C even so   D besides

LISTENING COMPLETION

▶ 6:36 You will hear part of a lecture. Read the paragraph below. Then listen and complete each statement with the word or short phrase you hear in the lecture. Listen a second time to check your work.

The lecturer says that a key argument in favor of (1) ...the environment... being the source of extreme intelligence is that most geniuses don't have extremely (2) ...gifted... ancestors. However, an argument in favor of the (3) ...opposite... view is that talented families do (4) ...exist.... They believe it shows that talent is (5) ...passed on... through genes. One living example that supports this (6) ...theory... is the story of the (7) ...mathematical genius... Srinivasa Ramanujan, who was raised in a (8) ...poor village... in India and had almost (9) ...no training... in mathematics. In other words, he was (10) ...born with... talent.

158 TEST-TAKING SKILLS BOOSTER

UNIT 9

READING COMPLETION

Read the selection. Choose the word or phrase that best completes each statement.

Protecting Wildlife and People's Livelihoods

Due to its **(1)** ..... rising population as well as unregulated development, Cambodia's wildlife habitats have been at risk. **(2)** ..... more and more poor, uneducated, and inexperienced farmers have taken up agriculture near the edges of Cambodia's shrinking forests, conflicts with Cambodia's wild Asian elephants have increased. An increasing number of hungry elephants have been searching for food near the edges of the forests. As a consequence, they have **(3)** ..... crops severely, forcing the farmers to kill the elephants in order to protect their livelihoods.

Tuy Sereivathana (known as Vathana), who grew up in the countryside, learned to respect both nature and the elephants. After choosing to study forestry at his university, he committed himself to the **(4)** ..... of Cambodia's natural resources and began working for the protection of the country's national parks. To begin with, Vathana focused his attention on understanding the **(5)** ..... the Cambodian farmers were facing. As a result, he came to the **(6)** ..... that the farmers needed to know more about the elephants' migration patterns and how to apply practical solutions for protecting their farms.

First, he helped them build electric fences. Then, he **(7)** ..... them how to use hot chili peppers and other native plants that elephants don't like in order to discourage the animals from eating their crops. Moreover, he **(8)** ..... the farmers to organize themselves to help each other guard their farms at night and to use fireworks and make other loud noises to scare the elephants off. Most **(9)** ..... , he helped farmers improve their farming techniques so they would have no reason to go farther into the elephants' habitat.

1	A simply	B respectfully	**C rapidly**	D likely
2	**A As**	B Provided that	C Unless	D Whether or not
3	A lost	B gathered	**C damaged**	D planted
4	A ecology	**B conservation**	C habitat	D education
5	A opportunities	**B challenges**	C tools	D families
6	**A realization**	B education	C occupation	D notification
7	A asked	**B showed**	C indicated	D developed
8	A ordered	B changed	C corrected	**D advised**
9	**A importantly**	B truthfully	C quickly	D interestingly

LISTENING COMPLETION

▶ 6:37 You will hear part of a report. Read the paragraph below. Then listen and complete each statement with the word or short phrase you hear in the report. Listen a second time to check your work.

Some experts believe the world's total population will increase through 2070. However, it will stabilize and will have (1) ..... stabilized ..... by that time. They also predict an (2) ..... increased ..... life expectancy and (3) ..... falling ..... birthrates. This will contribute to a (4) ..... continuing shift ..... toward aging populations worldwide, particularly in (5) ..... high-income ..... developed countries. According to newsweek.com, one in every six people will be (6) ..... seniors ..... over sixty-five by 2050. In fact, there will be (7) ..... twice as many ..... seniors as children. However, in Africa, the population of children under eighteen years old will (8) ..... increase by two-thirds ..... . These challenges will require more funding for children's (9) ..... education ..... and (10) ..... health care ..... resources for seniors. In addition, more (11) ..... food ..... will have to be produced for a growing population.

TEST-TAKING SKILLS BOOSTER

UNIT 10

READING COMPLETION

Read the selection. Choose the word or phrase that best completes each statement.

The Other Side of the Story

Although globalization has promised to benefit everyone with an increase in worldwide wealth and prosperity, critics argue that there is (1) ..... a widening gap between the rich and the poor. While corporations in some developed countries have outsourced both manufacturing and customer service jobs to developing countries overseas, workers who have lost those jobs (2) ..... to make ends meet. On the other hand, India's economy has reaped the (3) ..... of globalization with the establishment of call centers, where English-speaking staff provide 24/7 technical support by phone and Internet to customers all over the world. So, more people in India have (4) ..... good jobs and a steady income.

Even so, critics of globalization argue that (5) ..... free trade has made the world so competitive that criminal activities have flourished. While child labor is illegal in many countries, its practice has increased to fill manufacturing (6) ..... for gold and textiles. Recent news reports have exposed the use of slavery on merchant ships, where workers are mistreated and forced to work without receiving any wages. Even worse, due to the fact that there is little international (7) ..... regulation, some developing countries are becoming dumping grounds for hazardous industrial waste. In other countries, increased development has brought with it uncontrolled pollution, (8) ..... threatens public health and contributes to global warming.

(9) ....., economic opportunities made possible by globalization have also encouraged government corruption. Some argue that a global economy has helped drug cartels and terrorists move people and materials across borders more easily.

1 A either   **B instead**   C contrast   D neither
2 **A struggle**   B demonstrate   C apply   D interview
3 A changes   B unemployment   C challenges   **D benefits**
4 **A obtained**   B lost   C searched   D desired
5 A unwanted   **B unregulated**   C inadequate   D decreased
6 A locations   B resources   C opportunities   **D demands**
7 **A environmental** B illegal   C recognized   D agreement
8 **A which**   B so that it   C since it   D and
9 A For instance   B Even so   C As a result   **D Unfortunately**

LISTENING COMPLETION

A ▶6:38 You will hear a report. Read the paragraph below. Then listen and complete each statement with the word or short phrase you hear in the report. Listen a second time to check your work.

The woman says that consumers in (1) *developing countries* have been catching up with consumers in (2) *developed countries* in purchasing nonessential luxury goods. However, there is concern that the increase in (3) *consumption* of luxury goods will have a (4) *negative impact* on the environment. The director of research for Worldwatch warns that supplies of natural resources may (5) *be threatened* .

B ▶6:39 You will hear a report. Read the paragraph below. Then listen and complete each statement with the word or short phrase you hear in the report. Listen a second time to check your work.

The man reports that a recent survey conducted in more than (6) *44* countries shows that people continue to be concerned about (7) *social and economic* issues. Specifically, they worry about their country's (8) *standard of living* , deteriorating (9) *working conditions* , and the growing gap between the (10) *rich and the poor* . However, most respondents didn't blame these concerns on (11) *globalization* .

160 TEST-TAKING SKILLS BOOSTER

Student's Book Audioscript

UNIT 1
PAGE 5, EXERCISE D
Conversation 1
A: You'll never believe what I saw on my way to class today.
B: What?
A: Well, I was running to catch the bus when I saw a bear at the bus stop eating ice cream.
B: Come on!
A: No, seriously. They were shooting a video to promote some children's movie, and I guess they thought the bus stop would be a good location. In any case, by the time my bus came, they had finished the shoot.

Conversation 2 [A = teenage girl; B = mother]
A: Oh, no, Mom!
B: What happened?
A: That girl over there at the cashier. She's buying the sweater I was thinking of buying.
B: How did she get it?
A: She must have taken it when I was trying on this one. But I wanted that one.
B: Well, did you leave it on the table?
A: I must have. I tried it on and then I put it back on the table when I went into the dressing room to try *this* one on. I wanted to compare it with the first one. I could kick myself. I had my heart set on that sweater.
B: Well, there's no way she could have known you wanted it. I think you're out of luck, Lisa.

Conversation 3
A: Oh, no! I can't find my phone. Again.
B: Well, I'm sure it must be somewhere. When did you see it last?
A: Let me think. Well, I used it to text Mark.
B: Where were you when you texted him?
A: Hmm. I guess I was in the car.
B: No offense, Diane, but were you driving at the time?
A: What difference would that make?
B: Well, first, it's pretty reckless to text while driving. But the main reason I asked was to help you figure out when you sent the text.
A: Actually, I remember now. I had parked and I was in the parking garage downstairs when I texted him. Right after that, I came up here.
B: Did you have a lot of packages?
A: Yes, I did. Oh, now I remember! I stuck the phone into the bag from the supermarket. It must still be there. I haven't put the food away yet. Thanks!

PAGE 6, EXERCISE B
Conversation 1
A: What are Jan's plans for next year? I'll bet she'll be doing something with math—she's such a whiz.
B: As a matter of fact, she's starting engineering school in September.
A: No surprise there.
B: And three schools have already accepted her!
A: That's great.

Conversation 2 [B = French]
A: So, have you made up your mind about a career yet?
B: Pretty much. It's going to be something with either singing or dance. I'm really serious about a career in music.
A: Makes sense to me. You've always been the musical type.

Conversation 3
A: Bob seems a lot calmer than he used to. What's come over him?
B: I know—I've noticed it, too. I guess those meditation classes have really taught him how to relax.
A: So that's it.

Conversation 4
A: What's with Nina? Someone started talking about where we'd all be a year from now, and she just got up and walked out of the room.
B: Oh, she's a bit disappointed. She just heard from two of the three graduate programs she applied to. And she didn't get into either of them.
A: Wow. That's too bad.
B: Well, you can't blame her for feeling down.
A: Nope.

Conversation 5 [A = Australian English]
A: Did you hear about Tom? He just quit his job in accounting and accepted a position teaching math at the university.
B: That's quite a career change!
A: No kidding. But you know, I never thought he was really well suited for the business world.
B: Me neither. I think he'll make a great teacher, though.
A: Me too.

Conversation 6 [B = Japanese]
A: I hear you want to do something in medical research.
B: That's right.
A: Well, have you gone on any interviews yet?
B: Not yet. But I found out that MediLabs has an opening for a junior lab specialist.
A: Oh, great.
B: So I filled out an application, and I'm going for an interview on Monday.

PAGES 8–9, EXERCISES C, D, AND E
[A = Diana, U.S. standard; B = Dan, U.K. standard;
C = U.S. standard; D = U.S. standard]

A: Hello, hello, hello, and welcome to *Lifestyles*, the program that examines hot trends and other issues of interest to today's families. Today, we'll be talking about a growing trend—the stay-at-home dad. And to make this topic come alive, we've invited Dan, a real, live stay-at-home dad, who'll share his experiences with us. People here in the studio audience will have a chance to ask questions—and those of you watching at home can submit questions or comments online at #lifestyletalks.
Please join me in welcoming Dan Barton to today's show. Welcome, Dan. Please make yourself comfortable.
B: Thank you, Diana. I'm pleased to be here.
A: Dan, let's start with some definitions. The most general definition of a stay-at-home dad is a father who's the daily, primary caregiver of his children under the age of 18. Now, in some cases, a stay-at-home dad's a father who's at home out of necessity. In this case, a father loses his job and stays home to take care of the kids, while his wife takes a job to support the family—or, if she already works, she becomes the sole support of the family. This dad might continue to look for a job during the time he's out of work and at home.

STUDENT'S BOOK AUDIOSCRIPT 161

Another category of stay-at-home dad, which is growing exponentially, is the dad who *chooses* to be a stay-at-home parent, rather than one who has no other alternative. According to statistics, there's been a significant rise in men who fit this definition. In fact, in the U.S., in recent years, the number of fathers living with children younger than 18 and who do not work outside the home has more than doubled, from 1.1 million to more than 2 million.
I understand, Dan, that you fall into this last category. You've chosen to be the primary caregiver of your three children, and your wife is the primary breadwinner.

B: Yes, that's right. It may seem odd, but before my wife and I got married—long before we had children, of course—we had a heart-to-heart talk, and we decided that she would pursue her lifelong dream to be a surgeon and I would eventually stay at home, taking care of the household responsibilities, and if we had children, I would be the primary caregiver.

A: Dan, can you take a question from the gentleman there in the first row?

B: Sure.

C: Dan, what did your friends and family think of your plan? I mean, didn't they think it was a little strange?

B: Well, we did get some negative feedback. Some people thought it was completely unrealistic; some just couldn't accept it. I was amazed that so many people had feelings about this . . . that it was so controversial.

A: Well, it *is* a role reversal, isn't it? Traditionally, the husband's the breadwinner and the wife, even if she has a career, usually takes on the larger share of responsibilities of the household and the kids.

B: Right. People even asked whether there was something wrong with me. They said it was weird for a man not to have any career ambitions. All in all, it was just a lot of run-of-the-mill sexism. I mean, why automatically would a man *not* want to raise children and make a beautiful home for his family? What's so strange about that? And why would anyone think there was something wrong with a woman who had ambitious career goals?
In any case, we gave ourselves plenty of time. We decided to put off being parents for a few years, and I worked to support the two of us while Sarah completed her training. We were able to save up a nest egg, and during *that* time we shared all the household responsibilities—well, maybe not exactly 50-50, but close.

A: So when did that all change?

B: Well, our first daughter was born the year after Sarah began working at the hospital. As a surgeon, she was earning enough that I could afford to stay home, and we just started off our life in the way many couples do, with one parent at home and the other out in the workforce.

A: You worked from home?

B: No. Actually, I just stopped working altogether. I suppose we could have had a higher income if I had been working too, but our goal was for our kids to have one full-time parent at home if financially possible. We realize that not every couple is able to afford that, but in our case we've been lucky and we can. We're not rich, but we have enough, and we try to live within our means.

A: Tell us about your typical day.

B: Well, now that we have three girls at home . . .

A: Three girls! Wow. You must feel like an alien in your own family!

B: Well, what can I tell you? I don't think my day is much different from any mother who's a homemaker. I shop and I cook family meals, I help the girls with their homework, I take them to their music lessons—the whole kit and caboodle.

A: Dan, Here's something that's just come in. [*reads*] I'm more traditional. I would be upset if my son decided to stay home and expect his wife to be the breadwinner.

B: Well, many people hold on to traditions, and there's nothing wrong with that. But, to Sarah and me, we don't like the idea of a double standard for men and women. We want to raise our children so they can pursue their individual dreams and not have those dreams limited based on what sex they are.

A: Yes. I see we have a question from the audience. Yes, ma'am, in the third row.

D: Dan, I can understand how you do this, since your wife's a surgeon. She probably earns a lot of money. But what about the fact that most women earn so much less money than men for the same job? Isn't it unrealistic for most couples to depend on a wife's income, since for sure it's less than what her husband could earn?

B: What you're saying is true. You've put your finger on a large societal problem that we're all aware of and should try to change. Don't get me wrong. I'm not saying our arrangement's realistic for *all* families, just that we feel that people should have the right to set their own goals. And we hope that in the future, the next generation won't think it's weird to do what *we're* doing—if that's what they choose.

A: Well, that's all the time we have for today. Please stay tuned for this important message . . .

PAGE 13, EXERCISE A

Conversation 1 [B = Chinese (Mandarin)]

A: That's quite a stamp collection!

B: I guess. I've been collecting for over 30 years now.

A: Really? You must have started when you were really young.

B: When I was five, actually. And after all these years, I still dream about having the biggest collection in the world.

A: And do you think you ever will?

B: It's hard to tell. Some people have huge collections. To be honest, though, I don't think I'll ever really be able to outdo them.

Conversation 2

A: Have you found a house yet?

B: Nope. I've been looking for a year now, but no luck. Not even close. I'm starting to feel like maybe it's time to just give up.

A: What? Don't give up now! I'm sure something will turn up.

B: The thing is, I'm looking and looking and prices just keep going up. I'm really not sure I'll ever have a house of my own.

A: Look. Just be patient. Who ever said finding a house was going to be easy?

Conversation 3

A: I'm really fed up with working for a large corporation.

B: Huh? What are you all ticked off about?

A: I'm just tired of having to do what other people tell me to do. I want to be able to make my own decisions for a change.

B: OK. So, like, what are you going to do about it?

A: Start my own business.

B: Start your own business? You're dead serious, aren't you!

A: You bet I am. Don't tell anyone, but I've already applied for a loan.

B: Good for you!

Conversation 4 [A = Italian]

A: You know, I've always dreamed about being a flight attendant. I love traveling and meeting new people.
B: Why don't you apply for a job, then?
A: Well, I just don't think I have the right qualifications.
B: What do you mean? You speak three languages . . . and you've got some experience in the travel industry.
A: You mean the job I had as a tour guide?
B: That's right. I think they'd consider that to be related experience. Your qualifications are fine.
A: You're probably right.

UNIT 2

PAGE 18, EXERCISES A AND B

Conversation 1 [A = Portuguese]

A: I don't know how to tell you this, but I had a little accident with your bike.
B: Oh, no! Are you OK?
A: I'm fine. I'm fine.
B: Thank goodness.
A: But I'm afraid the bike got pretty badly damaged. Don't worry, though. The repair shop says they can fix it . . . and I will pay for the damage, of course.

Conversation 2

A: Uh, what happened to this suitcase? When I loaned it to you, it had two wheels.
B: Uh-oh. I guess they broke off when they were unloading the luggage. Those baggage guys are way too rough with people's bags.
A: Well, it's not going to be much use to me this way. Do you think you could get it repaired?
B: You know, it wasn't really my fault. Why don't you just call the airline and see if they'll take care of it?

Conversation 3

A: Frank! Why didn't you slow down? We could have been killed!
B: Didn't you see? That guy just cut me off!
A: What are you talking about? It was your fault. You were going too fast.
B: No way. If it hadn't been for him, we'd be fine.

Conversation 4

A: Pat, I was looking at this contract you completed. It's got June first as the due date. I'm sure it was supposed to be May first. I hope you didn't send it out like this.
B: I don't believe I missed that . . . I'm sorry. I just sent it out in the morning mail.
A: Well, we've got to do something about it.
B: I know. Look, it was totally my fault. I'll send out a revised contract right away.

Conversation 5

A: So, how'd the meeting go?
B: Not good. I was an hour late.
A: Uh-oh. They must have been pretty annoyed.
B: Well, I just told them the traffic was terrible.
A: Did they buy it?
B: Not really. I looked pretty bad.

Conversation 6 [A = Slovak]

A: Laura, this is for you.
B: What's this? My birthday isn't till next month!
A: Well, you know that scarf you loaned me? I'm afraid I lost it. Uh, I feel just terrible about it . . . so I got you this to replace it.
B: You didn't have to do that!
A: No, really. I want to do the right thing.

PAGES 22–23, EXERCISES D, E, AND F

Part 1

What would you do if you had achieved fame and celebrity and you were fabulously rich? Would you use your wealth to buy the things you've always wanted? Or would you give some of it away to help people who have nothing—and use your fame to speak out for those who don't have a voice?

Over the last few decades, we have seen a huge increase in celebrity philanthropy—actors, singers, and athletes—who have added to their fame by making donations of time and money to address some of the world's biggest problems. Angelina Jolie, the U.S. actress and film director, and the Irish superstar known as Bono, who sings with the band U2, are two of the best-known celebrity philanthropists today.

Angelina Jolie began doing philanthropic work after filming a movie in Cambodia in 2000. During her time there, she observed the effect of years of conflict on Cambodian children, and she remembered what her mother had taught her—to live a life of use to others.

Jolie began working with the United Nations as a special ambassador, visiting more than twenty-five countries, providing humanitarian support to refugees who had lost their homes because of war and conflict around the world. She has used her fame to raise awareness and call attention to various global causes and humanitarian issues, including sexual violence against women. Not only has she given her name and her time to these causes, but she and actor Brad Pitt have together been key donors, contributing more than thirteen million dollars to various causes, including the creation of new schools in developing countries to make education more accessible to more children. She has also become an environmental activist, working to help protect wildlife in Africa and Southeast Asia. Jolie encourages people to live a life of use to others too, saying, [read] "Get outside yourself. Get outside your environment. Do something for other people."

Bono, whose real name is Paul Hewson, has been working to fight poverty and hunger for more than twenty years. He is particularly skilled at bringing very different people together—politicians, business leaders, religious leaders, and other artists—to work together on solutions to important world problems. Bono has called attention to the fact that many African countries are having difficulty paying back their huge debts. He has worked with government leaders to get those debts forgiven, so those countries can focus more on economic development for the future. In addition, his activism has helped improve medical care in Africa and fight the AIDS epidemic there. Bono has also collaborated with other artists to organize benefit concerts in order to raise money for humanitarian causes. Bono explains, quote: As a rock star, I have two instincts—I want to have fun, and I want to change the world. I have a chance to do both. Unquote.

So what motivates celebrities to get involved in philanthropic activities? Well, Angelina Jolie is one of Hollywood's highest-paid actors, and Bono is one of the world's most successful musicians. For each of them, their philanthropic work is a way to express gratitude for their own success and a way to give back by doing something for those in need. Many celebrity philanthropists are also driven by their own passion for specific causes and their concerns about the future. It is clear that both Jolie and Bono care deeply about important causes such as human rights, education, and the environment.

Celebrity philanthropy may also be driven by simple human kindness—a compassion for those who are suffering and a desire to help end that suffering. We've seen Jolie deeply moved by her conversations with victims of war and conflict during her travels—calling their experiences horrific and heartbreaking. And Bono has talked about holding starving children in his arms during a famine.

Philanthropy can also greatly change a celebrity's life and help him or her develop new skills. When Jolie was younger, before her trip to Cambodia, she had a reputation as a "bad girl." The media would often report on her sometimes strange behavior as a Hollywood actress. And although she attended New York University, Jolie had never completed her college degree. As a philanthropist, Jolie has changed the public's perception of her and has become a leading expert on human rights and humanitarian causes.

PAGE 23, EXERCISES G AND H

Part 2

Celebrity philanthropists have gotten lots of attention, but they have also had their critics. One aid worker blogged to complain that using celebrities to do difficult humanitarian work is more trouble than it's worth. Many celebrities can be self-centered and demanding—for example, they may insist on having a constant supply of bottled water in places where there is little water. Or they simply fly in and fly out, at great cost, and do little to learn about the people they are supposed to be helping. In the case of Jolie and Bono, however, supporters point out that the actor and singer each pay their own way and ask for no special treatment. And both are well known for their careful preparation and knowledge.

Celebrities have also been criticized for spreading a false impression about poverty—particularly in the case of Africa—that Africa is a hopeless and helpless continent and that nothing can get done there without international celebrity help. Celebrities have been criticized for ignoring the efforts of local businesspeople and humanitarian organizations. And the unfortunate result is that the huge donations raised by celebrities are providing increased opportunities for corruption.

Writer Paul Theroux argues that celebrity philanthropists seem to be motivated mainly by their own fame—that they have a need to convince the world how important they are, that they crave the attention and recognition that comes from their humanitarian efforts. Other critics argue that celebrities are just interested in looking for photo ops—opportunities to be seen in photos and video clips in the media. The media loves all this because fans want to read about their favorite celebrities. And corporations love it too, competing with each other to use these celebrities' names in association with their products.

Clearly, Jolie's fame today is greatly enhanced by her reputation as an activist, humanitarian, and philanthropist. The fact that she pays someone to plan and organize her philanthropic work and photo ops seems to support this view. In the case of Bono, some journalists have pointed out that, while some of Bono's concerts had raised charitable donations, they also resulted in greater publicity and income for his band U2 at the same time.

While the criticisms may hold some truths, supporters argue that both Jolie and Bono have demonstrated long-term commitment and deep knowledge of the issues. As some have pointed out, if Jolie's activism and passion for her philanthropic work weren't sincere, it is unlikely that she would have been able to do as much as she has while building her film career and raising a family. And they argue that Bono has focused on using his fame to pressure politicians to do the right thing. It would be hard to argue that these two celebrities aren't dedicated to their work.

PAGE 25, EXERCISE A

Conversation 1 [A = Spanish]

A: You know Allan, that new guy at the office I was telling you about?
B: I think so. What about him?
A: Well, I hate to complain, but . . . he's always borrowing money from me.
B: You mean he doesn't pay you back?
A: No . . . no. He always pays me back. But the truth is, I really don't like being put in the position of lending people money. I don't even like borrowing money myself.
B: Oh, I see.
A: I'm wondering if maybe I should just tell him the truth next time he tries to borrow money from me.
B: Hmmm. Tough call. Why don't you just tell him you're short of cash?
A: I don't know . . . I really hate to tell lies.
B: Yeah, but you also don't want to offend him, right?
A: I suppose. Maybe I'll try that next time he asks.

Conversation 2 [A = Chinese (Mandarin)]

A: I'm in an embarrassing situation.
B: What happened?
A: Well, last week I borrowed this beautiful silk jacket from Mary.
B: So?
A: I lost it.
B: Uh-oh. Not good.
A: I know. I feel just terrible. I think I left it on the train.
B: Did you check the lost-and-found?
A: Of course. Twice. But no one's returned it.
B: Yikes. So what are you going to do now?
A: Well, I can't shift the blame to anyone else. It was my fault.
B: Why don't you just get her a new one?
A: I would, but the thing is, she bought it in one of those out-of-the-way places she always goes to on vacation.
B: So much for buying a new one, I guess.
A: I'm just going to have to tell her what happened. Since I can't replace the jacket, I'll just ask her what she'd like me to buy her instead.

UNIT 3

PAGE 28, EXERCISE B

Conversation 1 [A and B = U.S. regional]

A: No way!
B: What's wrong?
A: I just weighed myself. No matter how little I eat, I just can't lose weight.

Conversation 2 [A = Brazilian]

A: Oh, my goodness! Look at your car!
B: No way! I just had my car washed!
A: I guess you shouldn't have parked under that tree. There are like a million birds in it!
B: Can you believe this is the second time this has happened this week? It's really frustrating.

Conversation 3 [B = Chinese]

A: So what happened when you asked your boss if you could take the day off on Friday?
B: I never got a chance to ask.
A: You're kidding. Why's that?

B: He said he was too busy to talk. I think he knows I'd like the day off and he's just avoiding the conversation.

Conversation 4

A: You know what?
B: What?
A: I just failed the exam again.
B: Oh, no. That must be so disappointing. I know you really studied.
A: I did. It seems that no matter how hard I study, I just can't pass that thing. I can't believe I'll have to study for it *again*. There goes my vacation!

Conversation 5

A: I don't believe it! I forgot the fish! I must have left it in the supermarket.
B: Well, that's not the end of the world. I'll just hop in the car and go back and pick it up. It won't take long.
A: There won't be enough time. The guests are coming in a half hour. You have to be here. This is just incredible! No matter how careful I am, I always forget something.

PAGES 34–35, EXERCISES B, C, AND D

You're watching **30 Minutes**. And I'm Katie Fleming. And do we have a story for you tonight—a terrible tragedy and an amazing heroic act.

The desire to save one's own life is an extremely powerful instinct in all of us. It takes tremendous courage to be able to act against such a powerful instinct,
to risk one's own life to save the life of another person.

Twenty-five-year-old tour guide Seol Ik Soo was returning home with a group of South Korean tourists from a trip to Beijing, China. As the plane prepared to land at Kimhae Airport in South Korea, Seol was thinking about his wife. They'd been married one month earlier, and it was their first time apart.

Suddenly, the airplane started shaking, and he heard a crashing sound. The lights went out, and a ball of fire ran up and down the cabin. The plane crashed into a mountaintop, killing more than a hundred twenty of the passengers on board.

Somehow Seol managed to crawl through a hole in the side of the plane and escape. Seol feared an explosion, so his first thought was to run to save his own life. But he could hear the other passengers inside the plane calling for help. He went back and lifted a survivor onto his back, carrying him away from the plane to safety. Seol remembers carrying at least three or four injured people from the plane—but in fact there may have been as many as ten. When asked about it later, he said, "I don't know where the energy came from. It felt like I wasn't carrying anything at all."

Seol tore his shirt into bandages for the wounded and used his belt to bind up a man's badly bleeding leg. It wasn't until he stopped and sat down to smoke a cigarette that he realized his own face was covered in blood. When asked how he managed to perform so heroically, Seol replied, "I couldn't have done it in my right mind."

Everyone who knows Seol describes him as an ordinary guy. His boss describes him this way: "I know Seol as cheerful and hardworking, but just a normal young man. Now I have a new view of him. He's a remarkable person. We're all very proud."

Where does this kind of courage come from? How does a normal person manage to act so fearlessly? Seol says, "My parents always brought me up to believe people and life are very precious." It was this belief that enabled Seol, an ordinary person, to do something truly extraordinary and heroic.

PAGE 37, EXERCISE A

1
Felix Tan is putting in very long hours on a big project he's been assigned at work. Felix has been working nights and weekends to finish the project on time, but it doesn't look like he'll make it. He has been telling his boss that he needs help in order to meet the project deadline, but his boss ignores his requests.

2
Robert Reston has been struggling with high blood pressure since he was a child. His doctors have tried everything they can to help him lower it, from diet to exercise and now drugs, but his blood pressure just doesn't come down.

3
Eva García's husband is turning 30 next week, and Eva would like to get him something special to mark the occasion. She's spent a lot of time and energy going from store to store in her search for the "perfect" gift, but she just can't find the right thing.

UNIT 4

PAGE 42, EXERCISE C

Conversation 1 [A = Spanish]

A: Hey, Katy. I need to bring something up.
B: Of course, Jorge. Is there anything wrong?
A: Well, you were supposed to be at the meeting this morning. We were counting on you for an update on the project.
B: Oh no. I completely forgot! I'm so sorry. I really messed up.
A: I don't want to make an issue out of it, but it's the third time.
B: You're right. It was my bad. I promise to make up for it.

Conversation 2

A: Sorry I'm late. I just had a long talk with Simon.
B: About what happened yesterday?
A: Yeah. I'm still angry about it.
B: Well, as far as I'm concerned, it was all his fault.
A: I suppose. But I just wanted him to know how I felt about it.
B: I think he should have apologized.
A: Well, he did. He knows he's too hot-tempered. He admitted that he shouldn't have lost his cool.

Conversation 3

A: Excuse me, Evan?
B: Hi, Cynthia. What's up?
A: There's something I need to bring up with you.
B: Uh-oh. What's wrong?
A: It's not a big deal. But yesterday, remember when you came by my office when I was talking with Judy?
B: Yeah?
A: Well, we were in the middle of something, but you just barged in and started talking about something else. I'd really appreciate it if you could at least ask if I was busy first.
B: Gee, I'm sorry. You're right. I guess I wasn't thinking.
A: Like I said, no huge deal. Thanks for understanding.

Conversation 4 [A = eastern European]

A: Rilla, are you OK? You look upset about something.
B: Me? Oh . . . I guess I am.

A: What happened?
B: It's Janis. We had a bit of an argument this morning. She's not talking to me now.
A: What? I thought you two were such great friends.
B: It was my fault. I said something I shouldn't have.
A: Well, good friends should be able to work things out, don't you think?
B: I know. I'm going to call her right now and say I'm sorry.

Conversation 5
A: Brian, have you got a minute? I have something I need to bring up.
B: Sure. Have a seat.
A: Well, I hope you don't mind my pointing this out, but you've been really negative this past week. I mean, no matter how much work I've gotten done, you've been super critical about everything.
B: I didn't realize I was doing that. I'm so sorry.
A: I mean I don't want to make a big issue out of it, but it's been bothering me all week.
B: Well, I apologize. I certainly didn't mean to be so critical. It's no excuse, but I've been under a lot of pressure lately. I want you to know how much I appreciate the quality of your work.
A: Thanks. I didn't want to just say nothing about it.
B: Well, I'm glad you did. Thanks for bringing it up.

PAGE 44, EXERCISES C AND D

[A = Interviewer; B = Celina Gaspari, Argentinean Spanish; C = Joseph Chu, Taiwanese]

A: Good evening and welcome to our continuing discussion of cultural differences in how people express anger. On the line, I have Celina Gaspari, a sales manager calling in from the city of Rosario in Argentina. Good evening, Celina.
B: Good evening.
A: And Joseph Chu, a computer technician calling from the city of Tainan in Taiwan. Good morning to you, Joseph. Sorry to get you up so early over there.
C: No problem. I always get up at this time. Thanks for having me.
A: Joseph, is there any way to generalize about how people in Taiwan handle anger? I mean, I've heard that, culturally, it's unacceptable or inappropriate to express anger openly there. Is that true?
C: Well, it depends on the situation. But in Chinese culture, we're probably less inclined to lose our cool publicly.
A: And I imagine the opposite is true in Argentina, Celina?
B: Definitely. But Argentina is somewhat unique in that there are lots of people—myself included—whose background is Italian. I think the way people express anger in other Latin American countries may be somewhat different.
A: In what way?
B: Well, I used to live and work in Lima, the capital of Peru—for about seven years. Our boss—a guy named Alejandro—was, like me, from Argentina. But most of our colleagues were Peruvian. I remember one day having a loud disagreement about something with my boss—like any Argentinean might do. Alejandro and I were good friends and colleagues, so we didn't hold anything in. And all of a sudden this Peruvian woman, Amparo, leaves the room—but she has this funny look on her face. So I was concerned and stepped outside to see if everything was OK. It turns out she completely freaked out about our argument. She thought it was really serious. I had to calm her down and explain that was just how Argentineans talk to each other when they disagree about something. I'm sure that, to her, we sounded like we were really having a fit, but to us it was nothing.
A: That's really interesting. Reminds me of the many films depicting Italian families arguing over dinner.
B: Exactly.
A: So, Joseph, how are things different in Taiwan?
C: Well, generally speaking, I think it would be very unusual for someone to express anger at an authority figure, like in the case of Celina's story, a boss or a manager. That would just not be considered appropriate. Speaking for myself, if I were mad at my boss about something, I certainly wouldn't lose my temper—or even bring it up.
A: So what would you do instead?
C: I might let off a little steam by taking a walk or venting to a colleague about what happened. But I'd try not to let it show in any way—to my boss, I mean. I'd definitely keep it to myself.
A: What if one of your friends or colleagues did something that made you mad? Don't people in Taiwan ever go ballistic when they're angry about something?
C: Of course. People sometimes get really angry about politics, for example. And I wouldn't want to suggest that everyone is the same.
A: Of course not.
C: But you asked about generalizations. I would say we're a little slower to anger here than people in some other places. We tend to just let things go—you'd have to be pretty upset about something before you'd actually express any anger, much less lose your temper.
B: Excuse me for interrupting, but I just had to say . . . that's definitely not true in Argentina. I may be over-generalizing a bit, but I'd say people from Argentina don't usually hold things in.
A: Clearly two very different ways of handling anger. So Joseph, give us an example.
C: Let's say you're supposed to meet a friend for lunch and he makes you wait a long time before he finally shows up. Most people here wouldn't even bring it up with that friend. But if that happened all the time with the same friend—well, you'd probably finally say something. But you'd certainly not have an outburst of anger or anything like that.
A: So it sounds like people in Taiwan generally keep things inside rather than make an issue out of every little thing.
C: I'd say that, yeah.
A: And I guess things would have to get really bad before anyone actually had a total fit about something, right?
C: Right. But even then, losing your cool with a friend or colleague would be pretty unusual. As I mentioned before, people here are fairly reluctant to express their anger.
A: Celina, based on what you told us earlier about you and your boss, I would guess the total opposite is true for Argentineans.
B: That's right. Between friends, *not* getting angry *ever* would be pretty unusual. If your friend does something that makes you angry, you say something.
A: What about in Taiwan, Joseph?
C: You might raise your voice a little—but not as much as people probably do in other places. You might even bring something up that bothered you—but nicely. I can't imagine anyone actually going ballistic with a friend or colleague here. It would be really surprising.
A: What about people who don't know each other—people who are complete strangers? For example, what would happen if you were driving your car and someone just cut you off?
C: Ah, road rage. That's one situation that might set someone off. Some people might even open the window and say something to the other driver—loudly!
A: Even you?
C: Me? Well, I might get mad, but I probably wouldn't do or say anything about it. But that's just me.
A: And road rage in Argentina, Celina?

B: We tell bad drivers off whether the window is open or not. It's no big deal.
A: Well, thank you both for joining us.

PAGE 49, EXERCISE A

Speaker 1 [Speaker = Chinese]
So I'm a manager, and my job is telling people what to do. But some of my colleagues have told me they think I'm way too controlling. I didn't listen to them at first, but then I realized that I was feeling a lot of stress at work. It was like it all fell on *me*. If I didn't take care of everything . . . if I didn't watch what everyone was doing . . . it was my fault if there were any problems. That put a lot of pressure on me. Fortunately, my company offers professional training workshops, and I found out they're pretty good. They suggested that I ask my colleagues to share the responsibilities with me instead of always trying to manage *every*thing myself—and to allow them to make their own mistakes and learn from them. I still get a little nervous about it, but so far it's been great.

Speaker 2
Sometimes I feel a little overwhelmed. I mean, I know what's causing it. I'm totally disorganized. I put things away and then I can't find them. There's a mess all around my computer. I've got memos, bills, books, you name it, everywhere. I'm embarrassed to have anyone over. Last week, I decided to ask my friend Alicia for a hand. *she's* really organized, unlike me, and she's been a great friend. She helped me go through all my stuff to decide what was important and what I could throw away. I'm not sure what will happen in the future though. I may have to count on Alicia's help again.

Speaker 3 [Speaker = U.S. regional]
It's a little embarrassing to admit, but I have a bit of a problem with my temper. I mean, at work, I never show my feelings. If someone makes me angry, I usually just hold it in. But when I get home, that's another story. My kids are great kids, but when they do something wrong, I sometimes completely lose my temper and start yelling at them. The thing is, I know it's really about what happened at work. I'm just taking it out on them. Anyway, I wasn't happy about my behavior with my kids, so I went to a workshop on anger management—not that long ago, actually. I think it really helped. They suggested finding a way to let off a little steam when I'm angry. So I've taken up aerobics three times a week. It helps me think through what's been bugging me— and then I can just let it go. By the time I'm with my kids again, I have a whole new perspective on things.

UNIT 5

PAGE 54, EXERCISE B

Conversation 1

A: I saw this incredibly funny video someone posted on Facebook.
B: What was it about?
A: Well, these two guys wanted to have some fun. So they went out and bought one of those benches—you know, the kind they have in the park, where people sit and have their lunch, read the paper, whatever.
B: Yeah. A park bench.
A: Right. So the two guys carry the bench to the park and put it down, in a place where you'd see a park bench. And they sit down and take out some sandwiches they brought and sit there like they're just having lunch. Normal.
B: OK. So?
A: Well, they waited until they see a policeman walking in their direction. Then they pick up the bench and start running away with it, like they're stealing it, one guy at each end of the bench.
B: You're kidding. What happened?
A: So the cop sees them and yells, "Hey! Where do you guys think you're going with that bench?" One guy says, "It's our bench." The cop says, "You guys are under arrest."
B: No way!
A: No. Listen. At that point, the second guy takes the sales receipt for the bench out of his pocket. And of course, what could the cop do? Pretty funny, right? It really *was* their bench. Pretty funny, right?
B: I don't know. Maybe it went over my head.

Conversation 2 [B = Australian English]

A: Have you ever heard a knock knock joke?
B: A knock knock joke? What's that?
A: It's a typical American joke, kind of a play on words about a name.
B: OK. How do they go?
A: So one person is supposed to be knocking on the door. The jokes always start with one person saying, "Knock, knock." Then the other person answers "Who's there?" Then the first person gives a first name. And . . .
B: OK. I get it. Hit me.
A: OK. Knock, knock.
B: Who's there?
A: Banana. . . . Now you say, "Banana who?"
B: Banana who?
A: Knock, knock.
B: Who's there?
A: Banana.
B: Banana WHO!?
A: Knock, knock.
B: Who's there?
A: Orange.
B: OK. OK. Orange who?
A: Orange you glad I didn't say banana?
B: That's the joke?
A: Yeah. Isn't it funny? Get it? "Orange you glad I didn't say banana?"
B: No offense, but I think that's silly.

Conversation 3

A: Wanna hear a great joke?
B: Sure. Shoot.
A: A guy wants to park his car, so he drives up to a policeman and says, "I'm looking for a parking place. Can I park here?" The policeman says, "No." So the guy asks, "Well, what about all these other cars?" The cop says, "They didn't ask!"
B: They didn't ask? That's too much!

Conversation 4

A: Did you hear the one about the couple with the perfect marriage?
B: No.
A: Well, he's deaf and she's blind.
B: What's that supposed to mean?
A: Get it? He's deaf and she's blind.
B: Uh, that's really offensive.
A: Well, I guess it's a little politically incorrect.

Conversation 5 [B = U.S. regional]

A: Know any good jokes?
B: Umm . . . yeah. Here's a good one. An old man goes into a restaurant and orders some soup, and the waiter brings it to him.
A: And?

B: Well, after a minute the old man calls the waiter over and says, "I want you to taste my soup." The waiter says, "Is it cold?" The old man says, "No. It's fine. I just want you to taste it."
A: How weird.
B: So the waiter says, "Oh, I can't do that, sir. But I'd be happy to get you another bowl if there's something wrong." So again the old man says, "I said it's fine. I just want you to taste it."
A: So?
B: So finally the waiter says, "OK, OK. I'll taste your soup. Where's the spoon?" The old man says, "Aha!"
A: That's it?
B: Yeah.
A: I don't get it.
B: What do you mean you don't get it? "Aha!" He didn't have a spoon!
A: Oh . . . that's pretty silly, if you ask me. Sorry!

Conversation 6 [A = Australian English; B = Brazilian Portuguese]
A: You know the one about the woman who calls her lawyer?
B: No. How does it go?
A: She calls her lawyer and the man who answers says, "Smith, Smith, Smith, and Smith."
B: Smith, Smith, Smith, and Smith? That's so weird. What does that mean?
A: It's the name of the law firm. There are four lawyers named Smith. They're all partners.
B: OK. So?
A: So the woman says, "Let me talk to Mr. Smith." He says, "I'm sorry, he's on vacation." "Then let me talk to Mr. Smith." He says, "He's on a big case, not available for a week." "Then let me talk to Mr. Smith." He says, "He's away. He's playing golf today." "OK, then, let me talk to Mr. Smith." "Speaking."
B: Now that's funny!

PAGE 57, EXERCISE D

Joke 1

"How much do you charge?" a woman asks a lawyer.

"I get $50 for three questions," the lawyer answers.

"That's awfully steep, isn't it?" says the woman.

"Yes, it is," replies the lawyer. "Now what's your final question?"

Joke 2

A couple of dog owners are arguing about whose dog is smarter.

"My dog is so smart," says the first owner, "that every morning he waits for the paperboy to come around. He tips the kid and then brings the newspaper to me, along with my morning coffee."

"I know," says the second owner.

"How do you know?"

"My dog told me."

Joke 3

A man is hitting golf balls at a driving range with his nine-year-old son. Each time he hits the ball, his son cheers him on. "Great shot, Dad!" "Perfect!" "Way to go!" A woman hitting balls next to them watches as each of the man's shots flies farther and farther away.

After a few minutes, the woman walks over and asks, "Do you think I could borrow your son for a few minutes?"

PAGE 58, EXERCISES B AND C

A: I've got a good one. My dad was famous for playing jokes on people. Usually they were in pretty good taste, but this one may have crossed the line.
B: Really? What did he do?
A: Well, I'll tell you the whole story. My dad was the chief of staff at Claremont Hospital—you know, they have a huge psychiatric ward with patients who have to be kept under lock and key. Well, one day, this young doctor, Dr. Adams—the butt of the joke—asks my dad to arrange for him to visit the ward.
B: Uh-huh.
A: Well, my dad invites him to come to the ward at three. But before Adams gets there, my dad goes to the guard at the ward and tells him that he's going to admit a patient who thinks he's a doctor. My dad says to just go ahead and let this guy examine the other patients.
B: Oh, no. I can see what's coming!
A: Yeah. So, at three, my dad brings Dr. Adams to the ward and then leaves. Adams starts examining the patients, and at four o'clock he asks the guard to let him out.
B: Uh-oh!
A: Uh-oh is right. Adams tells the guard, "OK. I'm ready to go now." And the guard says, "Sit down. You're not going anywhere." So Adams says, "But I'm Dr. Adams." And the guard says, "Yeah, right. And I'm Napoleon."
B: That's terrible!
A: Well, maybe so. Anyway, eventually my dad came back to the ward and straightened everything out. It's a good thing Adams could take a joke.
B: I would have killed him! Adams was a really good sport.

PAGE 58, EXERCISE D

Speaker 1 [Speaker = Spanish]

You won't believe what my friends did to me last night. You know, I just got a new car, and I was so excited. I invited a couple of friends out to dinner to celebrate. So when we get to the restaurant, they tell me to park in the lot instead of on the street. The car will be safer there, they said. Well, you know how it is with a new car. You really don't want anything to happen to it. So we finish dinner and when we get to the car, there's this note from some woman apologizing for scratching my car. I couldn't believe it. So I start walking around the car looking for the damage, but I can't see anything wrong. Then my friends all start cracking up. It turns out they had left the note on the car as a joke. It was all made up. Boy, did I feel dumb. But no harm done. Once I got over the shock, I was fine. Those guys! Don't worry. I'll get even with them some day.

Speaker 2 [Speaker = U.S. regional]

A couple of years ago, my friend Alex helped me get a job as a salesperson where she worked—over at Lakeside Department Store. Well, on my first day on the job, Alex was showing me the ropes, and she asked me if I'd been told yet about the "first year reward" program. I said no. And she seemed kind of surprised. So she tells me that on your first day, new employees get to pick out something from the store worth up to $500, and at the end of the year, if you make your sales quota, you get to keep it—for free—as a sort of reward. So Alex tells me I'm supposed to walk around and choose something and then let the manager know what it is. It was still early and the store was pretty empty, so I figured it'd be a good time to browse. All of a sudden, the manager shows up and asks me what I'm doing walking around looking at everything. Why aren't I at my counter waiting for customers? I wasn't sure what to say. I mean, it dawned on me that this was some big joke—on me—so I figured I'd better say something. I just told him

I wanted to get familiar with what the store was selling so I could do a good job. But inside, I was pretty ticked off at Alex. I could have gotten fired! Oh . . . did I mention that Alex is my ex-friend?

Speaker 3

Someone actually played a practical joke on me in the office about a month ago. Because I'd gotten some long e-mail attachments I needed to print out for the General Manager, I had come in super early. She was going to make some big PowerPoint presentation that morning and I wanted to be sure the printer was free. So I turn on the computer and I can't get any of the files to open. I'm about to panic when all of a sudden this message pops up on the screen saying, "I'm taking a break. I'll be back in a half an hour." I thought, "What? The computer's telling me it's taking a break?!" And then I totally freaked. How am I going to get this done in time? I get up to ask this guy who sits right across from me and who always comes in early if he could give me a hand, when all of a sudden he starts laughing his head off. It seems the jerk had turned off my keyboard and connected his wireless keyboard to my computer and programmed the message onto my screen as some kind of practical joke. I should have known—he's always doing this sort of thing. I have to admit, it was pretty clever. And in retrospect, it was pretty funny. And P.S.: It turned out he took pity on me and helped me get all the printing in time.

PAGE 61, EXERCISE A

1

So I have this friend Mark who loves to play practical jokes. He had a friend named John, who was very cheap. I mean John *hated* to spend money, and he was always looking for a bargain. Well, there's this hamburger restaurant—it's called Bargain Burger—that's very, very inexpensive. The burgers cost almost nothing, but, of course, they're tiny little things.

So Mark wanted to play a joke on John. Mark went to the Bargain Burger and told the manager he wanted to play a joke on a friend and asked the manager if she could prepare two special *huge* hamburgers if Mark paid for them in advance. The manager said, "Sure." Then Mark paid the manager and said he was coming in for lunch with a friend and that the manager should just serve them the huge burgers and bring them a check at the regular low price. That afternoon, Mark and John had the two large hamburgers for lunch. When the check came, John was very surprised at how cheap the hamburgers were. In fact, he was so happy about the bargain that he told two other friends about the great bargains on huge hamburgers at Bargain Burger, and they all went there for lunch the next day. Well, of course, the burgers they ordered were tiny little things, which made John look really stupid in front of his friends. I think it was mean, but it was kind of funny.

2

A: Did you hear the one about the intelligence test?
B: No. How does it go?
A: One day this guy comes home and his wife says, "Wasn't today the day everyone at the company was supposed to take an intelligence test?" He says, "Yes, that's right." "Well," she says, "did you take the test, too?" "Absolutely," he says. So she asks him, "How'd you do?" So he says, "Well, let me put it to you this way. It's a good thing I own the company!"

3 [A = French]

A: How many letters are in "the alphabet"?
B: Twenty-six.
A: Wrong! There are eleven letters in "the alphabet."
B: I don't get it.
A: Eleven letters! T – H – E – A – L – P – H – A – B – E – T.

UNIT 6

PAGE 66, EXERCISES C AND D

Conversation 1

A: What happened to you? You look like you fell in the river!
B: Very funny! I got caught in the rain. I didn't have an umbrella and the bus was late.
A: Couldn't you get a ride with someone?
B: Actually, I finally did. Ben drove by and saw me standing at the bus stop and gave me a lift, but I was already drenched. You know what, though? I'd still be standing there if it hadn't been for him.
A: Let me make you a hot cup of tea.

Conversation 2

A: Wow, that was a close one!
B: Yeah! Did you see that guy? He went right through the red light. I think he was speeding too!
A: It's a good thing I looked that way when the light changed to green. If it hadn't been for that, we might have had a terrible accident.
B: I don't want to even think about it. Thank goodness we didn't!
A: I guess that's a lesson for everyone. Don't count on other drivers' observing the law!

Conversation 3

A: Hey, Millie. I know it's really short notice, but I have an extra ticket for the Martha's Vineyard sightseeing boat. Stan has to work and can't use it. I'd really love you to come. What do you say?
B: Gee, thanks, Iris. I'd love to, but I can't. If it weren't for this cold, I'd definitely accept that invitation. I hear the tour is spectacular, and I've been wanting to take it myself.
A: Oh, no. Do you have that awful cold that's been going around?
B: I do.
A: I guess an open boat isn't a good place to be if you have a cold. I'm so sorry to hear you're sick.
B: Thanks so much for thinking of me.

Conversation 4 [A = Spanish]

A: Oh, my gosh. This line is so long.
B: Well, it's to be expected. There were five international flights that landed at the same time. Immigration can't handle so many people at once.
A: Do you think we'll ever get out of here?
C: Could we please have your attention? Is there a Spanish speaker here? We need assistance translating for a traveler.
A: I'm going to raise my hand.
C: Excuse me, ma'am. Do you speak Spanish?
A: I do. Yes.
C: Do you think you could step to the head of the line with me? We need your help translating for a Spanish-speaking traveler. She doesn't speak any English.
A: Sure. But can I bring my friend with me? We're traveling together.
C: Of course. Please step this way.
B: Wow. What a lucky break. If it weren't for the fact that you speak Spanish, we'd be standing in line until 8:00 tonight!

Conversation 5

A: Can you believe this?! A flat tire.
B: Oh no! Now what?
A: What do you mean? We'll have to change the tire.

STUDENT'S BOOK AUDIOSCRIPT 169

B: We? You mean you.
A: We. Are. So. Late.
B: True. It looks like we won't make the play. What a shame! And it was so hard to get these tickets.
A: And we left plenty early.
B: I still can't believe it. I really wanted to see it. If it weren't for this flat tire, we'd be arriving about now.

Conversation 6

A: Sam! What a surprise. This cruise is fantastic, isn't it?
B: It's really great, Joanne, I was so sorry to hear about your divorce.
A: Thanks, Sam. I appreciate it. It's been a hard few months. But I'll get through it.
B: How long were you and Jeremy married?
A: Almost five years. And you know, looking back, I can see why our marriage fell apart. I actually blame myself.
B: What do you mean? It's never only one person's fault.
A: Well, in this case, to be honest, I think it pretty much was. I acted more interested in my career than in my husband. I was a regular workaholic, and Jeremy had to spend so many evenings alone.
B: Can't you patch things up?
A: No. It's over. Time to move on. This trip has given me some time to focus on the future. But I can't help thinking that Jeremy and I would still be married if it hadn't been for my thoughtlessness.

PAGES 70–71, EXERCISES D, E, AND F

Part 1

This is Tina Traveler, your travel advisor with your travel tips of the day. Listen every day, and learn something new and interesting every time. So, nothing can ruin a vacation or business trip faster than not having the clothing and other belongings you shopped for and packed thoughtfully in anticipation of your trip. As we all know, baggage can be delayed, stolen, and damaged as you make your way from home to your destination. But today, we'll be talking about the worst: baggage that is simply lost, most often by an airline.

Here's the scenario: You've arrived at your final destination and waited patiently for what seems like forever at the baggage carousel as other bags roll by, picked up one-by-one by other travelers. The bags slow to a trickle until finally the carousel stops. Your bags are nowhere in sight. If you had to change planes, you wonder whether the bags were transferred to your connecting flight or whether they simply were sent to the wrong destination. You take your luggage checks to the airline's missing luggage counter and file a claim. You're optimistic. The majority of bags that don't arrive with you will usually arrive on the next flight and will be delivered to your local address within a few hours, or, if they were sent to the wrong airport, within a day or two. If you're lucky, you aren't planning to fly on to another destination, because in that case getting your bags to you can get quite complicated.

Many airlines will reimburse you for any unexpected expenses caused by the delay, such as the need to replace underwear or cosmetics and other toiletries. Ask your airline to do this and keep your receipts. And if the worst happens, and your bags are permanently lost or completely destroyed, be sure to file a claim for damages, meaning the cost you will incur to replace what you have lost. The maximum amount you can receive differs from country to country and airline to airline, but one thing is certain: you won't receive anything if you are unable to document what you lost. You may need to produce sales receipts to prove the value of the items you had in your suitcase. If you have them, include them with your claim. Don't expect to receive the full amount you originally paid for your things. The airline will pay you for the depreciated value of your items if they aren't new.

Here are some tips to prevent the loss of your airline baggage: Put your name on the outside and inside of every bag. Put a copy of your itinerary inside the bag, especially if you're traveling to more than one destination. That way the airline can locate you. Avoid checking in to your flight late and avoid tight connections where your bag has to be transferred. These two situations are the cause of most lost or delayed bags. Don't put expensive valuables in checked bags: computers, cameras, wallets, and jewelry should go with you in your carry-on baggage. Airlines almost never reimburse you if those items are lost. Keep an itemized list of what you have in your bag for the unlikely event that you'll have to tell the airline what you've lost. And finally, be sure to look at the destination label the airline puts on your bag to be sure it's the destination you're traveling to. Mistakes happen and when they do, your bag will go where the label sends it. And be sure to hold on to the luggage checks you are given when you check in. In tomorrow's show, I'll tell you where bags lost in the United States often end up.

PAGE 71, EXERCISE G

Part 2

Tina Traveler here again with today's travel tip of the day—still on the subject of lost luggage, but from a very different angle. Yesterday we discussed how to avoid having the airlines lose your luggage. But let's say that happens. And let's say you've agreed to be reimbursed for your loss and you have moved on. But here's an interesting twist: today, we're at the Unclaimed Baggage Center, a one-of-a-kind store in the U.S., and a major tourist attraction here in the state of Alabama in the U.S. South. Over a million people visit it each year from the U.S. and over 40 other countries. The Unclaimed Baggage Center's motto is "You never know what you'll find!" This unusual business buys bags left behind by passengers—from airlines, bus companies, and railways. I know what you're thinking, but yes, some people just don't pick up their bags. They buy them sight unseen, and one company executive says, "We have no idea what's in the bags when we purchase them." The company says it sorts the contents of the luggage and only puts the best merchandise out for sale. All clothes are dry-cleaned and laundered. Fine jewelry is cleaned and priced. All electronic equipment is tested and cleared of data. What they can't sell they donate or recycle.

The Unclaimed Baggage Center feels more like a department store than the typical lost and found department you can find at any train or bus station. Here you can find top brands with some items that still have their original store price tags attached to them. Many high-end electronic products are, in spite of all advice, packed in checked luggage. In a recent year the Unclaimed Baggage Center sold over 3,000 iPads, as well as thousands of smartphones, headphones, cameras, laptops, and their accessories. It is said that the Center puts out more than 5,000 items a day and the price is right. Many are discounted as much as 80% below their original selling prices.

You might ask why these items hadn't been returned to their original owners. The owner of the Unclaimed Baggage Center says that it has contracts with airlines and other companies who have already settled and paid claims to customers. Sometimes, however, the items couldn't be returned because they had no identification on them.

Before you get mad, however, it's important to note that airlines say that only half of 1% of checked bags are lost, and of those, 98% are eventually returned to their owners.

PAGE 73, EXERCISE A

Conversation 1 [A = security woman at security checkpoint]

A: Please remove all electronic devices and laptops and place them in the container on the belt. Remove all metal items such as belts, coins, and cell phones and place them in the container.
A: Excuse me, sir. Would you mind opening your bag?
B: Sure.
A: I'm sorry, sir, but I'll have to take your shampoo and aftershave.
B: But, there's just a little shampoo left in the bottle. And the aftershave is almost empty.
A: I'm sorry sir. It's the size of the container that counts. And, besides, liquids and gels have to be in a plastic ziplock bag.
B: OK. Sorry!
B: By the way, can I get reimbursed for the confiscated items?
A: No, sir. There are no reimbursements. It's your responsibility to know the rules and follow them.
B: Just asking . . .

Conversation 2

A: You'll never believe what happened to me. Or actually, to my suitcase.
B: What happened?
A: Well, I took the airport bus out to the airport. They have those big spaces to put your luggage in under the bus?
B: Ri-ight . . .
A: Well, my bag somehow got left in the street and the driver backed up over it! Everyone on the bus heard the noise. The driver got out and called me outside—my name was on the bag.
B: So was the bag crushed?
A: Totally.
B: So what did you do?
A: Well, luckily I was really early for my flight, and there was a luggage store right there on the same street. The driver was very apologetic. He gave me a form saying the company was responsible for the damage and showing me how to submit a receipt for a replacement bag. So I went into the luggage store and got a really nice bag.
B: And what about your clothes?
A: Unbelievably, they were OK. I just moved them into the new suitcase and left the old one there. I caught the next bus and made my flight. When I get home, I'll file a claim.
B: All's well that ends well.

Conversation 3

A: How can I help you?
B: My bag was damaged. One of the wheels is broken. It was fine when I checked it in Saigon. But when I got it from the carousel, I found it like this.
A: Can I see the bag, please?
B: Sure. Here you go.
A: Well, I'm sorry. But there's no way to know if we were responsible for the damage. It's possible the wheel was in bad shape before you checked it in.
B: Actually, the suitcase was new. I got it in Saigon. Just yesterday.
A: Well, ma'am, if you wish, you can file a claim. Do you have the sales receipt for the bag? The airline'll want to see that to determine if it was new.
B: Yes, I do. By the way, what's the airline's policy on reimbursement?
A: Well, you file your claim and if it meets the requirements, you will be reimbursed for the price of the bag. It generally takes 6 to 8 weeks.
B: OK. How do I file the claim?
A: Here's the form.
B: Thanks.

UNIT 7

PAGES 82–83, EXERCISES C AND D

[B = South African]

A: I'm Timothy Allen for It's *All in Your Mind*. Are you so terrified of getting on a plane that you avoid traveling? Does seeing a spider in the sink make your blood run cold? When you go to the doctor for a shot, does the sight of the needle make you want to run the other way? If these situations—or the sight of blood, standing at the top of a mountain, going to the dentist, or being in enclosed spaces—fill you with fear, even dread, then you may have a phobia. Today we're interviewing Dr. Karen Nordlinger of the Cape Town Psychological Association in Cape Town, South Africa. Dr. Nordlinger is a noted specialist in the treatment of phobias. Dr. Nordlinger, welcome.
B: Thank you, Tim. Thank you for inviting me.
A: Dr. Nordlinger, why do movies and TV programs often make fun of people with phobias, and why are there so many jokes about them?
B: I think that's because phobias are often laughed off. People see them as totally irrational—essentially without reason. And people who don't suffer from extreme irrational fears find them difficult to understand. If someone they know develops a phobia, their response is "It's all in your mind," suggesting that the phobia isn't real. But to the person with the phobia, the fear is real, even if they understand that it's irrational. To them, it's no joke.
A: How many people suffer from phobias?
B: It's estimated that approximately 10% of the population worldwide has some kind of phobia or overwhelming anxiety. And their fears aren't something they can just put out of their mind. People with phobias—or "phobics"—don't have much control over their phobias. They cause them both physical and mental symptoms.
A: It's interesting that they cause physical symptoms as well as mental ones. Can you elaborate?
B: Sure. We all have a built-in defense system to protect ourselves from physical danger. When we are faced with danger, our heartbeat gets faster, our throat goes dry, our sweating increases. These unpleasant physical symptoms are referred to as the fight-or-flight response and prepare us either to protect ourselves or to run away to avoid harm. However, a person with a phobia of something that doesn't present a real danger reacts in the same way—as if the danger were real. In fact, that's the distinction between a run-of-the-mill fear and a true phobia. Phobics will go to great lengths to avoid being confronted with what they fear and the unpleasant fear responses they cause. Their efforts to avoid situations that scare them can lead to difficulties at work and in everyday life. I mean, imagine you have a phobia of being on a high floor in a tall building, and one day you have to attend a meeting on the top floor. Your extreme fear response will be embarrassing and may be harmful to you in your work. People will think you're out of your mind—and they might laugh about it behind your back.
A: What are some of the most common phobias?
B: The list of recognized phobias is enormous. Two of the most common ones, though, are arachnophobia . . .
A: Arachnophobia! That's fear of spiders, right?
B: Right! . . . And claustrophobia: the fear of being in an enclosed space, such as a subway car, or even an elevator, for example.

A: Well, it would be pretty hard to avoid elevators, wouldn't it? That could be really limiting.

B: Keep in mind that people can develop fears of almost anything. For some, just being in social situations such as meetings and parties fills them with dread. They plan to go to a social event, and then suddenly at the last minute, they change their mind and call and make up an excuse, such as an illness or some other problem. Think of it. It's embarrassing to be afraid of something that no one recognizes as a real danger.

A: So, Dr. Nordlinger, tell us: can people with phobias be helped?

B: Definitely! As with other problems that can be treated, the first step is to make up your mind that you want to be free of your phobia. When you're totally sick and tired of your anxiety taking over your life—and are willing to do something about it—there are a number of effective treatments. The most popular one is cognitive behavioral therapy, or CBT.

A: What does that therapy consist of?

B: So, in CBT, the patient is exposed repeatedly to whatever causes the fear. In fact, this therapy is sometimes called "exposure therapy" for that reason. But some patients can't tolerate exposure therapy. For those patients, another treatment, called "counter conditioning," often works.

A: How is counter conditioning different from exposure therapy?

B: In counter conditioning, patients are trained to substitute a physical relaxation response for the unpleasant fight-or-flight symptoms. It can be very effective.

A: So what thought would you leave us with today?

B: I think I'd say to people with phobias: you're not alone. Lots of people have phobias, and if you make up your mind to overcome them, good treatment options exist, and the success rate is excellent.

A: Thank you, Dr. Nordlinger, for an interesting and informative interview.

PAGE 85, EXERCISE A

Conversation 1

A: Listen to this—a way to make big money in just two weeks.

B: Uh . . . that sounds too good to be true.

A: No, really. They send you a list of names and addresses. You just send the last person on the list ten dollars and then add your name to the list.

B: And . . .

A: And then someone gets your list and the money starts rolling in.

B: That's such an obvious get-rich-quick scam. You're not going to fall for that, are you?

A: Well, I suppose you're right—it's just wishful thinking on my part.

Conversation 2 [A = Portuguese]

A: Honestly, they must think people will believe anything!

B: What are you talking about?

A: This company has a method for learning a language while you sleep. That's impossible!

B: I wouldn't be so sure. Actually, it's very possible. There was something on the news just the other day. A group of students learned the basics of Russian in just one week, in a sleep-learning lab.

A: For real? Maybe we should get some more information. Might be a fun way to learn French!

Conversation 3 [B = Punjabi]

A: Here's something I'd really like to try!

B: What is that?

A: A speed-reading course. They can train you to read a 200-page book in an hour!

B: I don't know. I find that kind of hard to believe. I mean, I've heard of improving your reading speed, but 200 pages in one hour—it just doesn't seem likely that anyone could do that.

A: Yeah . . . it does sound a bit much.

UNIT 8

PAGE 94, EXERCISES B AND C

Part 1

So we've been discussing some views on intelligence, including Gardner's theory of multiple intelligences . . . but today I'd like to shift the discussion to the idea of genius. When I say the word "genius," who comes to mind? Albert Einstein, definitely. The composer Ludwig von Beethoven? Probably. So what is genius? In fact, there's a fair amount of disagreement on what it means.

To a lot of people, a genius is simply a person with an extremely high IQ. We know that most average people have an IQ score that can range from about eighty-five to one fifteen. A genius is commonly defined as a person with an IQ score of over one forty-five. I just mentioned Albert Einstein—the famous scientist who most people would agree was definitely a genius. Well, he was estimated to have had an IQ of one sixty. And his intellectual achievements clearly earned him the label of genius.

But many people disagree with a definition of genius based on IQ scores alone. They would argue that merely having a high IQ doesn't make someone a genius. At the beginning of the twentieth century, American psychologist Lewis Terman selected fifteen hundred gifted children—children with high IQ scores—who were then followed by researchers as they grew up, for a period of more than twenty years. None of these people stood out; none went on to become great inventors or brilliant thinkers. To the psychologists who studied them, this was proof that a person may have a high IQ but still not be a genius. They concluded that there is something special and unique about genius—perhaps in how that person chooses to use his or her high IQ.

PAGE 94, EXERCISE D

Part 2

So scientists have long argued about where genius comes from. And just as they've argued about where one's personality comes from, they argue about whether extreme intelligence is genetic—or inherited—in other words, passed down to us from our parents through their genes, or whether it is determined by the environment we grow up in—that is, our education, our families, our life experiences.

To get at the answer, we need to look at the origins of intelligence itself. Many researchers rely on studies of identical and fraternal twins to learn more about where intelligence, as well as other characteristics, come from. This is because identical twins—those that develop from the same egg—share the same genes. But fraternal twins come from two different eggs and therefore don't share as many genes.

Interestingly, between identical twins, in about 85% of all cases, IQ scores are fairly close. However, between fraternal twins—those who do not share all the same genes—only about 60% have similar IQ scores, even though they grew up in the same environment. This data is a strong argument in favor of the genetics argument.

But according to some experts, it could just as easily be argued that it's the shared environment that twins experience that determines their IQ scores. In fact, even though identical twins may have the same genes, they don't necessarily have the same talents and abilities.

One of the key arguments in favor of the environment being the primary factor in someone's developing extreme intelligence is this: if intelligence were inherited, every genius in history would have had extremely gifted ancestors—his or her parents, grandparents, great-grandparents—they would all have been geniuses or near-geniuses too. And this—we all know—is far from true.

Arguing in favor of the opposite view, however, supporters of the genetics explanation would say that talented families do exist—families of successful scientists or musicians, for example—and this is precisely because talent is passed on through genes. A living example in support of the theory that genius is genetically determined is the mathematical genius Srinivasa Ramanujan, from India. Ramanujan was raised in a poor village and had almost no training in mathematics. Scientists who argue against an environmental explanation note that, if genius were a product of the environment, Ramanujan's genius would be impossible to explain—except through genetics. In other words, he was born with the talent.

Now scientists have proposed other explanations of the origin of genius, but these are the two main theories—greatly simplified, of course.

PAGE 97, EXERCISE A

1: Liza
Well, unfortunately, Liza is really struggling in French and Italian. She clearly does not have a knack for languages. But she is wonderfully imaginative! And she shows a real flair for creating stories and writing poetry.

2: Ben
Ben needs to pay more attention to his academic subjects, especially math and science. He's not doing well in those areas, I'm sorry to say. However, he does show real artistic talent, especially with crafts and design. He's been making beautiful sculptures and jewelry, and his woodwork is very skilled.

3: Stella
I'm happy to tell you Stella is a very strong student, and she's doing well in all her subjects, especially German. After only two years of German, she speaks it quite fluently! Her only weakness is in music. Her lack of interest in this area really surprises me, because she has such a good ear for languages.

4: Steven
Steven is really smart in math. He understands the concepts immediately, and he's comfortable with numbers in a very practical sense: His ability to solve problems in his head is extraordinary. He's a bit shy, though, and is having trouble making friends and working with his classmates.

5: Sophie
Sophie really shines in her music and art classes. She shows a natural ability in both these areas. As I'm sure you've noticed, even though she just started piano classes, she's able to play pieces easily and with great skill. It's amazing how sometimes she can play a piece after hearing it only once or twice.

6: Dan
Well, no surprise here. What Dan seems to enjoy most is working with cars and engines . . . figuring out how they work. The only problem I see is that he often works too quickly and doesn't pay enough attention to the little things. That can really create problems when you're trying to repair a machine!

7: Karen
Karen's power of observation is really well developed for a child of her age. She notices every single detail. Karen really stands out in that area. Where she has difficulty is in communicating her ideas. Her written work could be a bit stronger.

8: Sam
I find it fascinating how Sam seems to be able to know what other students are thinking before they even speak. But I'd like to see him develop his social skills more. Sometimes he gets a little impatient when one of his classmates needs him to explain something. He's great when he's on his own, but he's having trouble working well with the other students.

UNIT 9

PAGE 102, EXERCISES B AND C

Conversation 1
A: It sounds like scientists are getting pretty close to being able to use someone's genes in order to create an identical genetic copy of that person.
B: I've read that. But I think it's a crazy thing to do with humans.
A: Really? I mean, imagine if you couldn't have kids of your own. Scientists could take your genes and create an embryo that would develop into a baby. Wouldn't that be great?
B: What if they started to create designer babies, using genes from people who are celebrities or athletes . . . or only the wealthy . . . or geniuses . . . people who scientists have decided are superior to everyone else? To me, it'll just open a can of worms.
A: Well, I think the good far outweighs the bad.

Conversation 2 [B = Turkish]
A: Can you believe all these stories in the news about people's identities getting stolen?
B: I know. It's kind of scary. I've heard that once someone gets a hold of enough of your personal information, they can pass themselves off as you and spend all your money. And trying to fix it is almost impossible. Too bad they can't prevent it from happening in the first place.
A: Actually, there's a way to prevent it, but it's kind of weird. They say you can put a tracking device under your skin, and then no one can get away with trying to be you.
B: What? Would you have one of those things implanted under your skin?
A: Me? That's going too far.

Conversation 3 [B = Italian]
A: Don't you think putting animal genes into plants is kind of questionable morally?
B: Not really. Why do you think that?
A: Well, for example, I read that scientists are putting the genes of fish into tomatoes, which is something that would never happen in nature. It just doesn't seem right to me.
B: That's true, but that kind of technology can do a lot of good, too.
A: Like what?
B: Well, something like that could increase a plant's ability to survive cold temperatures or resist insects. That could be a really important agricultural development.
A: Well, it still sounds kind of fishy to me.

Conversation 4 [B = U.S. regional]
A: I just read that a Japanese doctor working in a Los Angeles hospital operated on a patient in a hospital in Tokyo.
B: How did he do that?
A: With some high-tech videoconferencing. The surgeon in Los Angeles used the technology to guide the surgical instruments electronically . . . in Tokyo.
B: That sounds like something out of a horror movie!
A: Well, I guess he must have been really skilled. Otherwise, why wouldn't they have just used a local surgeon?
B: I suppose. But it just doesn't sound very safe to me.

Conversation 5 [A = Korean]
A: I just got one of those digital chess games that you play against your computer.
B: Really? How does that work?
A: Well, the software program makes chess moves based on your moves. They say it's a lot more challenging than playing against a human.
B: You mean the computer actually thinks?
A: That's probably not true. But it does figure out the best move based on hundreds of thousands of potential moves—and it does it almost instantaneously.
B: That sounds amazing.

Conversation 6
A: Whoa! This is awesome! I feel like I'm actually walking on Mars.
B: Me too! It's unbelievable.
A: Hey, can you see a small mountain behind the spaceship?
B: Yeah.
A: Well, I'm going to walk toward it and see what it feels like to try and climb it.
B: OK. Listen, I'm going to quit for now. I've got some homework to do. But let me know how that works out.
A: OK. You can just leave your headset on the desk. Talk to you later.

Conversation 7
A: I just read about something amazing doctors are doing now to help cancer patients.
B: Oh yeah? What's that?
A: They've created these tiny capsules that can be introduced into your arteries where they can deliver medication to exactly where it's needed.
B: Actually, I heard that someday they might be able to create tiny molecular machines that can produce the medication inside your body.
A: It's incredible the things they talk about doing now.

PAGE 106, EXERCISE C

Conversation 1 [A = Indian]
A: You know, in this country, there is a falling fertility rate.
B: What exactly is a fertility rate?
A: It's the number of children per family. Fifty years ago, the average family had 3.2 children. Today, the rate is only 1.9.
B: What do they think is the reason for that change?
A: Apparently there are a number of factors. But the most important is that the country has changed from a mostly rural farm economy to a mostly urban technological one. Farm families need a lot of kids to help out. But children are just an added expense for urban families.

Conversation 2
A: Can you believe that Rongovia has only a 20% literacy rate?
B: That's horrendous. No wonder they've got so many problems. There's no way to improve the situation if so many people can't read or write.

A: True. But this article says the rate's been increasing. Five years ago it was just 10%. And it's going up at a rate of 2% a year.
B: At least the trend's in the right direction.

Conversation 3 [A = British English]
A: Just look at this statistic! There were over a thousand assaults in the city this year. That's an increase of 50% over last year.
B: That is pretty steep. Does the article say why they think the crime rate is rising?
A: They think it has something to do with the changing demographics in the area.
B: What's that supposed to mean?
A: Well, lots and lots of young men have moved here to work at the chemical factory that opened this year. The percentage of young men in the population has risen over 100% in just one year. And since the crime rate is generally higher among young men that seems to account for it.

Conversation 4
A: This country's going to the dogs!
B: Why? I don't think it's so bad.
A: Well, have you read this morning's paper?
B: What are you talking about?
A: They say the divorce rate's rising and the birthrate's declining. If this keeps up, there won't be enough people around to keep things going.
B: Oh, lose the gloom and doom, would you? Tomorrow there'll be another study that says we're overpopulated.

PAGES 106–107, EXERCISES D AND E

Following are some population growth trends into the second half of this century.

The United Nations reports that the world's population is growing at a rate of approximately 74 million people per year. Based on this growth rate, it is estimated that the world's population will have increased to 9 billion people by 2040. As a comparison, the world's population hit 7.3 billion in 2015. That's an increase of more than 30% by 2040. This rate of increase, however, assumes that the world's fertility rate and infant mortality rates in developing countries will decrease at the same time, controlling the rate of growth worldwide. However, some more pessimistic experts predict an increase in the world's population growth rate, with the world's total population hitting 11 billion by 2050.

Twelve countries currently account for half the world's total population and will continue to do so this century. These, in order by size, are China, India, the United States, Indonesia, Nigeria, Pakistan, Brazil, the Democratic Republic of the Congo, Ethiopia, the Philippines, Mexico, and Egypt. Before 2050, a United Nations report predicts that China will have been surpassed by India as the world's most populous country. In fact, more than 95% of the increase in the world's population will be found in developing countries like China, India, and Brazil, and nearly all in rapidly expanding urban areas.

In contrast, populations in most developed countries—like those of Western Europe— will not grow significantly. And in other developed countries, such as Japan, Russia, and Germany, populations will actually decrease. Some experts predict that the world's total population will continue to grow through 2070, but will have stabilized by then and will have stopped growing.

Increased life expectancy and falling birthrates will contribute to a continuing shift toward aging populations worldwide, especially in high-income developed countries.

Worldwide, the number of people 65 or older will triple in size. Newsweek.com reports that, by 2050, one in every six people in the world will be seniors over the age of 65. In fact, there will be twice as many seniors as children—with the exception of Africa. According to a UN report, the number of children under 18 years old in Africa will increase by two thirds—representing 40% of all children worldwide. In 1950, they only represented 10%.

These demographic trends will present challenges in the countries that experience them. For countries with younger populations, more funding for education will be required. For an aging population, health care resources will need to be increased. And for a growing total population, more food will have to be produced.

PAGE 109, EXERCISE A

Conversation 1
A: Isn't it amazing how smart computers are getting? I've heard that one thing programmers would like to be able to do is to help doctors by getting computers to perform all the steps of diagnosing patient health—without human help.
B: That sounds a little scary to me. Can we really trust a computer to do something like that?
A: Well, computers already do things with a high level of accuracy, so I don't see why not. They're already taking over all kinds of human activities.
B: But it still sounds weird to me. I mean, you'd have to really trust the computer to do everything a doctor would normally do.
A: I think it would be a huge advance for medicine to have computers that can do things to reduce the chance of human errors.

Conversation 2
A: You know I love to travel, but I worry a lot about all the things that could go wrong. Like what if something happened when I was overseas and I needed surgery?
B: Uh . . . they have doctors in other countries, you know. Very good doctors.
A: I know. But I really trust my doctor.
B: Well, one day doctors are going to be able to operate on you from anywhere. The doctor won't have to be in the operating room with you to perform surgeries.
A: I've read about that, but I just don't think I'd feel comfortable about it.

Conversation 3 [A = Spanish]
A: Did you hear they found that little boy who'd been lost since this morning?
B: That's fantastic. How did they find him?
A: He had one of those things under his skin, you know? The police department was able to pick up his signal and they were able to locate him at Smith Park.
B: Is he OK?
A: Yeah. They said he was tired and hungry, but he was fine. He'd just wandered off while his father was reading a magazine.
B: You know, I have mixed feelings about putting one of those things under a kid's skin. They say it's the wave of the future, but I think it's a slippery slope.
A: Really? This has totally convinced me it's a great thing.

Conversation 4 [B = Australian English]
A: Are you really going to drink that milk?
B: I was planning to. Shouldn't I?
A: Don't you know what they do to prepare that brand?
B: Not really.

A: Well, they use the latest dairy technology to mix the genes of their cows with those from a variety of reptiles. And that's how they make that milk. It's supposed to prevent it from going bad without refrigeration.
B: What's wrong with that? That's progress. It's great that they can improve animals so they produce better milk.

UNIT 10

PAGE 112, EXERCISE B

Conversation 1
A: Have you been following the news about the refugees?
B: I have been. It's really distressing, isn't it? I can't imagine what it must be like for them to suddenly become homeless.
A: Apparently they have nothing—just the clothes on their backs.
B: Terrible. It's bad enough that they have lost their homes, but I heard that relief groups are running out of food for them. The situation must be just awful.
A: It's really a crisis. The government has got to come up with an effective emergency plan or it's going to be a catastrophe—thousands of people are going to die.

Conversation 2
A: Have you heard about the polio epidemic in Afghanistan?
B: What? I thought polio had been wiped out years ago.
A: It was in a lot of places, but apparently not everywhere.
B: That's too bad. I wonder why it hasn't been wiped out there.
A: Well, they've been trying to wipe out polio once and for all by convincing more people to get vaccinated. It hasn't been a problem in urban areas. But in some more rural places a lot of people feel it's against their religion. So they've just refused to get vaccinated.
B: That's really a shame. Sounds like a losing battle.
A: Maybe so.

Conversation 3
A: Have you been following the story about the economic crisis?
B: Yeah. It's unbelievable. They say workers are getting laid off left and right.
A: It makes you realize how lucky we are, doesn't it? I feel really bad for those people who lost their jobs.
B: Well, the good news is a group of super wealthy celebrities have been pressuring the president to come up with a plan to turn things around. And the president has actually been paying attention.
A: How do you like that! It just goes to show you, money talks.
B: Hey, as long as it gets the ball rolling to end the crisis, I'm all for it. But get this . . . the president has come up with a plan. But the liberals and the conservatives haven't been able to agree on how to pay for it.
A: Well, this is no time for them to be sitting on the fence.
B: I totally agree.

PAGE 118, EXERCISES B AND C

[A, radio announcer; B, Susan Cahill = British; C, Berat Yildiz = Turkish]

A: You're listening to WKBC. And this is *Road Runner*, with Susan Cahill.
B: Culture shock. Anyone who has spent more than a day or two in another country has experienced some degree of it—that disorientation you experience when you are in an unfamiliar culture. If you haven't yet spent

STUDENT'S BOOK AUDIOSCRIPT 175

time in another country, experts say it can help to be aware—before you go—of the kinds of feelings you might experience as a result of culture shock. Well, today's program is going to help you do just that.

When you're traveling or living in a new culture, everything is unfamiliar to you—the way the food smells and tastes, the weather, how people act socially, the daily customs . . . In other words, everything you're used to suddenly seems so different. Even if you're traveling on business, you may discover that the rules you've been familiar with are not the same—for example, what you can talk about during a business lunch, or how to address a manager . . . At first, it's fascinating and you enjoy all the new sights and sounds. Berat Yildiz, an exchange student from Istanbul, Turkey, who has spent two years studying in London, knows culture shock firsthand, and we spoke with him earlier today. Let's listen as Berat describes what it was like during his first month here.

C: I was really excited to be in London. It had long been a dream of mine to study here, and it had finally come true. I mean, this is such a famous place . . . There were so many things to do. And people were really nice. I just felt like I was in heaven. Everything was interesting to me . . . even ridiculous things like counting out money when I had to pay for things. I felt like a kid. I had to ask for help all the time because I couldn't tell the coins apart. And the most disorienting thing was the traffic. In Turkey we drive on the right, but as everyone knows, drivers in London drive on the left. So I had to be extra careful when I crossed the street. But it was all fun and new. I really loved being here.

B: Sociologists say culture shock has four stages to it, and they call what Berat is describing the honeymoon stage—like newlyweds on a honeymoon, everything seems great. But it doesn't last forever. After a while the new culture becomes a bit overwhelming and you start wishing you were back at home again where everything is comfortable and familiar. Listen as Berat describes what came next.

C: After a couple of months, things seemed to change for me. The London weather started to really get to me—it seemed like it was cold and rainy all the time. For someone like me—from Turkey, where it's warm and sunny—well, I felt like a fish out of water. It was hard to take. And I was finding it difficult to make friends. British people seemed a bit cold to me, which is very different from the way people act in my country. The food was also a problem. I got really tired of it and dreamt of the food back home. Thank goodness there are some good Turkish restaurants in London.

B: Here Berat was experiencing what experts call the frustration stage of culture shock. You start to feel negative about the new culture and everything about your own culture, which right now is very far away, seems wonderful. Listen as Berat continues.

C: After a while, everything about London began to really get to me. It was bad enough that Londoners seemed so formal all the time. But even worse, they were constantly apologizing—always saying, "Sorry!" It really seemed insincere to me, and it got on my nerves. I felt really homesick. I missed my family and friends back home, so I would call them and complain about my life in London. I also just felt sad a lot of the time, though I wasn't really sure why. It was actually affecting my studies. I still had over a year to go and I really wondered at that time if maybe my decision to come here had been a mistake.

B: This is the hardest stage of culture shock—what some experts call the depression or distress stage. Some people have strong feelings of sadness or loneliness—even anger, or they don't sleep well. Some actually experience physical symptoms such as headaches. Fortunately there's a light at the end of the tunnel. Berat describes what came next.

C: It took about a year for me to get my feet back on the ground again. But by that time I had gotten used to the weather—I learned that it's all about dressing right. And crossing the street was a piece of cake by then—you just have to remember to look both ways. But most importantly I made friends in my classes, both Brits and other foreigners like me. What a difference that made! I started to feel like I had a place where I belonged. And I was really able to appreciate some of the things that made British and Turkish culture different. I still prefer Turkish food, but I've come to appreciate what they call a full English breakfast. My cousin Orhan is coming to visit next week, and I'm looking forward to showing him around my adopted city.

B: In the end, Berat finally experienced the acceptance stage of culture shock. He learned to appreciate the differences from his own culture and to find his own place in the culture he was living in. Culture shock is something everyone goes through when they travel overseas—the important thing is to be aware of what's happening to you. For those who will be staying in an unfamiliar culture for an extended period of time, we also have these suggestions: Even though you might feel strange, don't avoid people. Get out and be social. Meeting new people can help you manage any negative feelings. Wherever you're staying, take some time to settle in and make it feel like home. Put up your own decorations. Walk around your new neighborhood and get to know it well. Identify some favorite places and visit them often so people get to know you too. Get into the habit of greeting people. And get to know the city you're living in. Learn about its history and culture.

I'm Susan Cahill, and good night.

PAGE 119, EXERCISE D

1

Berat Yildiz, an exchange student from Istanbul, Turkey, who has spent two years studying in London, knows culture shock firsthand, and we spoke with him earlier today. Let's listen as Berat describes what it was like during his first month here.

2

I was really excited to be in London. It had long been a dream of mine to study here, and it had finally come true. I mean, this is such a famous place . . . There were so many things to do. And people were really nice. I just felt like I was in heaven. Everything was interesting to me . . .

3

I had to ask for help all the time because I couldn't tell the coins apart. And the most disorienting thing was the traffic. In Turkey we drive on the right, but as everyone knows, drivers in London drive on the left. So I had to be extra careful when I crossed the street.

4

Some people have strong feelings of sadness or loneliness—even anger, or they don't sleep well. Some actually experience physical symptoms such as headaches. Fortunately there's a light at the end of the tunnel. Berat describes what came next.

5

It took about a year for me to get my feet back on the ground again. But by that time I had gotten used to the weather—I learned that it's all about dressing right. And crossing the street was a piece of cake by then—you just have to remember to look both ways. But most importantly I made friends in my classes, both Brits and other foreigners like me. What a difference that made!

PAGE 121, EXERCISE A

Report 1
According to an annual report prepared by the Worldwatch Institute, consumers in developing countries have been catching up with those in developed countries in the purchase of nonessential luxury goods such as electronic gadgets and entertainment systems. And they warn that this increase in consumption of luxury goods will have a negative impact on the environment as the production of these goods puts more pressure on the Earth's supplies of water and other natural resources. Gary Gardner, director of research for Worldwatch, believes we need to figure out how we can provide people all over the world with an adequate standard of living, using the lowest amount of resources. If we fail to do this, he warns, supplies of natural resources may be threatened.

Report 2
A new report is available from the Pew Global Attitudes Project, which conducts extensive research on attitudes about globalization around the world. A recent survey conducted among respondents from over 44 countries has revealed that, people continue to be concerned about social and economic issues—their country's standard of living, deteriorating working conditions, and the growing gap between the rich and the poor. Yet, despite that, the majority of respondents were not inclined to blame these concerns on globalization. Their attitudes about globalization remain positive.

Report 3 [Speaker = British English]
Did you know that the Starbucks Coffee Company, the U.S.-based company that has opened its highly recognizable coffee shops worldwide, opened its first shop in the city of Seattle in 1971? Since then, the company has opened more than twenty-one thousand stores in 65 countries on six continents. From Peru to Saudi Arabia to Korea, Starbucks has changed the way the world sees coffee. Starbucks CEO Howard Schultz describes their success this way: "Starbucks has a universal language because of the quality of the coffee, the social atmosphere, the romance—all of these things are as relevant in Singapore and China as they are in Zurich or Seattle." Starbucks also presents itself as a socially conscious company, giving to local charities and working to preserve the environment.

TEST-TAKING SKILLS BOOSTER

UNIT 1

PAGE 151, LISTENING COMPLETION
A: Oh, no! I can't find my phone. Again.
B: Well, I'm sure it must be somewhere. When did you see it last?
A: Let me think . . . well, I used it to text Mark.
B: Where were you when you texted him?
A: Hmm. I guess I was in the car.
B: No offense, Diane, but were you driving at the time?
A: What difference would that make?
B: Well, first, it's pretty reckless to text while driving. But the main reason I asked was to help you figure out when you sent the text.
A: Actually, I remember now. I had parked and I was in the parking garage downstairs when I texted him. Right after that, I came up here.
B: Did you have a lot of packages?
A: Yes, I did. Oh, now I remember! I stuck the phone into the bag from the supermarket. It must still be there. I haven't put the food away yet. Thanks!

UNIT 2

PAGE 152, LISTENING COMPLETION
Celebrity philanthropists have gotten lots of attention, but they have also had their critics. One aid worker blogged to complain that using celebrities to do difficult humanitarian work is more trouble than it's worth. Many celebrities can be self-centered and demanding—for example, they may insist on having a constant supply of bottled water in places where there is little water. Or they simply fly in and fly out, at great cost, and do little to learn about the people they are supposed to be helping. In the case of Jolie and Bono, however, supporters point out that the actor and singer each pay their own way and ask for no special treatment. And both are well known for their careful preparation and knowledge.

Celebrities have also been criticized for spreading a false impression about poverty—particularly in the case of Africa—that Africa is a hopeless and helpless continent and that nothing can get done there without international celebrity help. Celebrities have been criticized for ignoring the efforts of local businesspeople and humanitarian organizations. And the unfortunate result is that the huge donations raised by celebrities are providing increased opportunities for corruption.

UNIT 3

PAGE 153, LISTENING COMPLETION
Twenty-five-year-old tour guide Seol Ik Soo was returning home with a group of South Korean tourists from a trip to Beijing, China. As the plane prepared to land at Kimhae Airport in South Korea, Seol was thinking about his wife. They'd been married one month earlier, and it was their first time apart. Suddenly, the airplane started shaking, and he heard a crashing sound. The lights went out, and a ball of fire ran up and down the cabin. The plane crashed into a mountaintop, killing more than a hundred twenty of the passengers on board.

Somehow Seol managed to crawl through a hole in the side of the plane and escape. Seol feared an explosion, so his first thought was to run to save his own life. But he could hear the other passengers inside the plane calling for help. He went back and lifted a survivor onto his back, carrying him away from the plane to safety. Seol remembers carrying at least three or four injured people from the plane—but in fact there may have been as many as ten. When asked about it later, he said, "I don't know where the energy came from. It felt like I wasn't carrying anything at all."

Seol tore his shirt into bandages for the wounded and used his belt to bind up a man's badly bleeding leg. It wasn't until he stopped and sat down to smoke a cigarette that he realized his own face was covered in blood. When asked how he managed to perform so heroically, Seol replied, "I couldn't have done it in my right mind."

Everyone who knows Seol describes him as an ordinary guy. His boss describes him this way: "I know Seol as cheerful and hardworking, but just a normal young man. Now I have a new view of him. He's a remarkable person. We're all very proud."

UNIT 4

PAGE 154, LISTENING COMPLETION, EXERCISE A
Sometimes I feel a little overwhelmed. I mean, I know what's causing it. I'm totally disorganized. I put things

away and then I can't find them. There's a mess all around my computer. I've got memos, bills, books, you name it, everywhere. I'm embarrassed to have anyone over. Last week, I decided to ask my friend Alicia for a hand. *She's* really organized, unlike me, and she's been a great friend. She helped me go through all my stuff to decide what was important and what I could throw away. I'm not sure what will happen in the future though. I may have to count on Alicia's help again.

PAGE 154, LISTENING COMPLETION, EXERCISE B

It's a little embarrassing to admit, but I have a bit of a problem with my temper. I mean, at work, I never show my feelings. If someone makes me angry, I usually just hold it in. But when I get home, that's another story. My kids are great kids, but when they do something wrong, I sometimes completely lose my temper and start yelling at them. The thing is, I know it's really about what happened at work. I'm just taking it out on them. Anyway, I wasn't happy about my behavior with my kids, so I went to a workshop on anger management—not that long ago, actually. I think it really helped. They suggested finding a way to let off a little steam when I'm angry. So I've taken up aerobics three times a week. It helps me think through what's been bugging me—and then I can just let it go. By the time I'm with my kids again, I have a whole new perspective on things.

UNIT 5
PAGE 155, LISTENING COMPLETION

So I have this friend Mark who loves to play practical jokes. He had a friend named John, who was very cheap. I mean John *hated* to spend money, and he was always looking for a bargain. Well, there's this hamburger restaurant—it's called Bargain Burger—that's very, very inexpensive. The burgers cost almost nothing, but, of course, they're tiny little things.

So Mark wanted to play a joke on John. Mark went to Bargain Burger and told the manager he wanted to play a joke on a friend and asked the manager if she would prepare two special *huge* hamburgers if Mark paid for them in advance. The manager said, "Sure." Then Mark paid the manager and said he was coming in for lunch with a friend and that the manager should just serve them the huge burgers and bring them a check at the regular low price. That afternoon, Mark and John had the two large hamburgers for lunch. When the check came, John was very surprised at how cheap the hamburgers were. In fact, he was so happy about the bargain that he told two other friends about the great bargains on huge hamburgers at Bargain Burger, and they all went there for lunch the next day. Well, of course, the burgers they ordered were tiny little things, which made John look really stupid in front of his friends. I think it was mean, but it was kind of funny.

UNIT 6
PAGE 156, LISTENING COMPLETION

Here's the scenario. You've arrived at your final destination and waited patiently for what seems like forever at the baggage carousel as other bags roll by, picked up one by one by other travelers. The bags slow to a trickle until finally the carousel stops. Your bags are nowhere in sight. If you had to change planes, you wonder whether the bags were transferred to your connecting flight or whether they simply were sent to the wrong destination. You take your luggage checks to the airline's missing luggage counter and file a claim. You're optimistic. The majority of bags that don't arrive with you will usually arrive on the next flight and will be delivered to your local address within a few hours, or, if they were sent to the wrong airport, within a day or two. If you're lucky, you aren't planning to fly on to another destination, because in that case getting your bags to you can get quite complicated.

Many airlines will reimburse you for any unexpected expenses caused by the delay, such as the need to replace underwear or cosmetics and other toiletries. Ask your airline to do this and keep your receipts. And if the worst happens, and your bags are permanently lost or completely destroyed, be sure to file a claim for damages, meaning the cost you will incur to replace what you have lost. The maximum amount you can receive differs from country to country and airline to airline, but one thing is certain: you won't receive anything if you are unable to document what you lost. You may need to produce sales receipts to prove the value of items you had in your suitcase. If you have them, include them with your claim. Don't expect to receive the full amount you originally paid for your things. The airline will pay you for the depreciated value of your items if they aren't new.

UNIT 7
PAGE 157, LISTENING COMPLETION, EXERCISE A

A: Listen to this—a way to make big money in just two weeks.
B: Uh . . . that sounds too good to be true.
A: No, really. They send you a list of names and addresses. You just send the last person on the list ten dollars and then add your name to the list.
B: And . . .
A: And then someone gets your list and the money starts rolling in.
B: That's such an obvious get-rich-quick scam. You're not going to fall for that, are you?
A: Well, I suppose you're right—it's just wishful thinking on my part.

PAGE 157, LISTENING COMPLETION, EXERCISE B

A: Honestly, they must think people will believe anything!
B: What are you talking about?
A: This company has a method for learning a language while you sleep. That's impossible!
B: I wouldn't be so sure. Actually, it's very possible. There was something on the news just the other day . . . a group of students learned the basics of Russian in just one week, in a sleep-learning lab.
A: For real? Maybe we should get some more information. Might be a fun way to learn French!

UNIT 8
PAGE 158, LISTENING COMPLETION

One of the key arguments in favor of the environment being the primary factor in someone's developing extreme intelligence is this: if intelligence were inherited, every genius in history would have had extremely gifted ancestors—his or her parents, grandparents, great-grandparents—they would all have been geniuses or near-geniuses too. And this—we all know—is far from true.

Arguing in favor of the opposite view, however, supporters of the genetics explanation would say that talented families do exist—families of successful scientists or musicians, for example—and this is precisely because talent is passed on through genes. A living example in support of the theory that genius is genetically determined is the mathematical genius Srinivasa Ramanujan, from India. Ramanujan was raised in a poor village and had almost no training in mathematics. Scientists who argue against an environmental explanation note that, if genius were a product of the environment, Ramanujan's genius would be impossible to explain—except through genetics. In other words, he was born with the talent.

Now scientists have proposed other explanations of the origin of genius, but these are the two main theories—greatly simplified, of course.

UNIT 9
PAGE 159, LISTENING COMPLETION

Some experts predict that the world's total population will continue to grow through 2070, but will have stabilized by then and will have stopped growing.

Increased life expectancy and falling birthrates will contribute to a continuing shift toward aging populations worldwide, especially in high-income developed countries. Worldwide, the number of people 65 or older will triple in size. Newsweek.com reports that, by 2050, one in every six people in the world will be seniors over the age of 65. In fact, there will be twice as many seniors as children—with the exception of in Africa. According to a UN report, the number of children under 18 years old in Africa will increase by two thirds—representing 40% of all children worldwide. In 1950, they only represented 10%.

These demographic trends will present challenges in the countries that experience them. For countries with younger populations, more funding for education will be required. For an aging population, health care resources will need to be increased. And for a growing total population, more food will have to be produced.

UNIT 10
PAGE 160, LISTENING COMPLETION, EXERCISE A

According to an annual report prepared by the Worldwatch Institute, consumers in developing countries have been catching up with those in developed countries in the purchase of nonessential luxury goods, such as electronic gadgets and entertainment systems. And they warn that this increase in consumption of luxury goods will have a negative impact on the environment as the production of these goods puts more pressure on the Earth's supplies of water and other natural resources. Gary Gardner, director of research for Worldwatch, believes we need to figure out how we can provide people all over the world with an adequate standard of living, using the lowest amount of resources. If we fail to do this, he warns, supplies of natural resources may be threatened.

PAGE 160, LISTENING COMPLETION, EXERCISE B

A new report is available from the Pew Global Attitudes Project, which conducts extensive research on attitudes about globalization around the world. A recent survey conducted among respondents from over 44 countries has revealed that, people continue to be concerned about social and economic issues—their country's standard of living, deteriorating working conditions, and the growing gap between the rich and the poor. Yet, despite that, the majority of respondents were not inclined to blame these concerns on globalization. Their attitudes about globalization remain positive.

Summit TV Teaching Notes

For some general guidelines on using the *Summit TV* interviews and documentaries, see the Teaching Ideas document in the *Summit TV* Activity Worksheets folder on the ActiveTeach. **Note**: The Answer Keys provide answers to the Activity Worksheets exercises from the ActiveTeach. Printable unit video scripts are also available on the ActiveTeach.

UNIT 1
Dreams and Goals

On-the-Street Interviews:
I have a couple of dreams ...

PREVIEW

- Ask students the following questions:
    What are some of your short-term goals?
    What are some of your long-term goals?
    What life goals have you already achieved?
  Write students' answers on the board.

VIEW

Ask students to focus on a different topic each time they view. Some ideas:

- Write on the board, in three columns: *Career, Family, Other*. Ask students to listen for the types of goals each interviewee talks about.
- Ask students to listen for specific details about career goals.
- Ask students to listen for specific details about family or other goals.

If you decide to use the optional Activity Worksheet, ask students to read each activity before viewing.

REVIEW

- Ask comprehension questions. Play the video segment again if necessary. (Answers may vary—some possible answers are included here.)
    Why does Vanessa want to run the New York City marathon? (to be able to say she completed it)
    Is running the marathon a short-term or long-term goal? (a short-term goal)
    What is Vanessa's long-term goal? (to open an agency for special-education children)
    What kind of a career is Rob considering changing to? (landscape architecture)
    What is he doing to make that dream happen? (taking a class)
    What other dream does he have? (to be an opera singer)
    How does he plan to follow that dream? (He plans to take a voice lesson.)
    Is Joe satisfied with the goals he has achieved in his life? (Yes. He has moved to the city, has a good job, and he's comfortable with his life.)
    What other goal does he have? (to find someone to share his life with him)
    What is Jessica's career goal? (to open her own restaurant)
    What are her personal goals? (to be happy and have a family, to be tolerant and honest, to listen to people, and to be someone people can rely on)
    What does Lorayn say about having a family and parenthood? (that she would like to have a family and that she hopes to be as good a parent as her parents were)
    What is Alvino's long-term goal? (to own his own clothing line)
    How does Alvino plan to attain this goal? (by developing marketing skills, doing research, and saving money)
    Does Alvino think he will be successful? (Yes. In ten years he plans to be opening his fifteenth shop in the New York area.)

EXTENSION

Oral work

- Discussion. On the board, write: *Future Goals*. Then have students recall the goals mentioned in the interviews. Write them on the board. Have students compare their own goals with those in the interviews.
- Pair work: role play. Have pairs of students choose one of the following interviewees from the video segment: Rob, Alvino, Jessica, or Vanessa. Tell them to role-play the short conversation between the interviewer and the interviewee and to extend the conversation with more detailed questions about career goals. For example, *What type of restaurant would you like to own, Jessica?* or *How did you become interested in landscape architecture, Rob?*

Written work

- As a class, summarize Lorayn's comments regarding children and parenthood. Then tell students to write a paragraph describing the influence their own parents had on their lives. Invite volunteers to read their paragraphs to the class.
- Pair work. Replay Alvino's comments. Then ask *Do you think it's likely that Alvino will be opening his fifteenth store in ten years? Why?* Have students work with a partner to write up a detailed plan for Alvino's long-term goal. Write the following questions on the board to help them:

What can Alvino do to develop his skills?
What kind of research does he have to do?
How much money does he need to save? How can he do this?

Invite students to share their plans for Alvino with the class.

- Have students write a paragraph describing their own short- and long-term goals. They should include what they can do or intend to do to achieve those goals and, if applicable, the time frame in which they hope to do so.

LANGUAGE NOTE: When Rob says *I don't know how far I can take that* when talking about his dream of becoming an opera singer, he means that he isn't sure how successful he'll be in achieving this goal.

VIDEO SCRIPT

Interviewer: Could you tell me something, a dream or a future goal that you have for yourself?

Vanessa: I want to run the New York City marathon. I want to be able to, maybe not come in first, but at least be able to say that I completed twenty-six point one miles in a certain time, so that's my goal for the future. That's my, I would say, my short-term goal. My future goal would be to open up an agency of my own, for children, special-education children. That's my long-term goal.

Rob: I have a couple of dreams that I'm pursuing. One of them is to look into a different career, possibly landscape architecture. So I'm taking a class at the New School to explore that. Another dream of mine is to be an opera singer. I don't know how far I can take that, but I plan to take a voice lesson very soon.

Joe: I have to say that I think I have succeeded in a lot of goals that I've set for myself to this point in my life. I . . . since I was very young, I always wanted to move closer and closer to a city. And now I've done that and I live in a city. I have a great job and I'm very comfortable in my life. As for goals, I'd like to continue with that. I wouldn't mind finding someone to share that life with me. But as for attaining any goal, I think that's possible as long as you set your mind to it and that's what you really want.

Jessica: My goal in life is to be happy and to have a family, to have two kids. And my other goal, like career-wise, is to have my own restaurant. That might be a little difficult to combine, but I think I can make it, and it's . . . yeah, that's . . . these are my, like my first-priority goals. And also one of my first-priority goals is to make like, to try to make everybody else happy, like to be tolerant, to listen to people, to be honest and, yeah, to be somebody who people can rely on. So I think that's the most important thing.

Interviewer: How about family or other goals besides work?

Lorayn: Family, like I said, I would love to have a family one day. When that's going to happen, I don't know. I don't think a person is ever fully ready to commit to having a baby. I think it's something that you have to work through as you go through it. But I would love to have a family one day. And I would . . . I hope that I could be a parent as good as m y parents have been to me. If I'm half as good, I think I succeeded.

Alvino: I would like to own my own clothing line and to attain it I think I would develop my marketing skills and research . . . and save money.

Interviewer: So what do you think you'll be doing in ten years?

Alvino: Ten years? Opening my fifteenth shop in the New York area.

ANSWER KEY

A. 1. c 2. a 3. b 4. d
B. 1. False 2. False 3. True 4. False 5. False 6. True 7. True 8. False
C. *Individual responses should include variations on the following:*
Jessica: Jessica wants to have a family and two kids. She thinks this might be difficult to balance with her other long-term goal of having her own restaurant, but she thinks she could make it work.
Lorayn: Lorayn wants to have a family one day, though she doesn't know when. She's not yet ready to commit to having a baby. She hopes to be as good a parent as her parents were to her.
D. *Answers will vary.*

UNIT 2
Character and Responsibility

TV Documentary: *White Lies*

PART 1

PREVIEW

- Write *white lie* on the board and elicit the meaning (a harmless lie that you tell someone to avoid hurting their feelings). Elicit examples of white lies (Possible answers: You look great! This meal is delicious! Of course you don't look fat!)

- Poll the class *Do you think there is any harm in telling a white lie?*

VIEW

Ask students to focus on a different topic each time they view. Some ideas:

- Ask students to listen for white lies often used with women.
- Ask students to listen for excuses for being late.
- Ask students to listen for statistics about lying.
- Ask students to listen for workplace lies.

If you decide to use the optional Activity Worksheet, ask students to read each activity before viewing.

REVIEW

Ask comprehension questions. Play the video segment again if necessary.

> Who does the first woman on the street say she lies to most? (other women)
> What examples of excuses for being late does the second man on the street give? (doctor's appointments, taking care of kids, car breaking down, dog eating homework)
> What example of a personal lie does the second woman on the street give? (her weight)
> Does the reporter admit to having lied? (yes, he does)
> What percentage of people have been caught in a lie? (15%)
> What percentage of managers have fired someone for lying? (24%)
> According to the social psychologist, how often do people lie? (a couple times per day)
> What are some examples of workplace lies? (I don't know how that happened.; I have another call to take.; I didn't get your email.; I like your outfit.)
> Whom are we most likely to lie to? (a coworker)
> Why are we not likely to lie to a perfect stranger? (perfect strangers don't know us and they're not judging us on so many different levels)
> What leads to white lies? (wanting to avoid a conflict, fit in, have smooth relationships)

EXTENSION

Oral work

- Discussion. Say *This segment gives opinions from American culture. Is white lying as prominent in your culture(s)*. Ask students to share and encourage them to compare. Return to details in the documentary as necessary.
- Group work. Write these questions on the board for students to discuss in groups:
  > Why do you think the woman says "When you work with all women, you have to lie?"
  > Do you agree with that statement?
  > Do you think white lies are less necessary for men?
  > What are things men might lie to each other about?
  > When do you think women might prefer to hear the truth?
  > What other examples of lies said to women can you think of?

- Pair work: role play. Have pairs role-play white lying. Tell them they can use scenarios from the interviews (e.g., workplace lies, excuses, lies about appearance, weight, etc.). Then bring the class together and have students share the role-plays with the class. After each presentation ask, *Has anyone ever used this lie? Do you think it's believable? What do you think the person actually means?* At the very end, ask *Did you get any ideas of new lies to use? If yes, which ones?*
- Pair work. Ask *What personal lie does the second woman on the street mention?* (lying about her weight) In pairs, have students write a list of lies people say about themselves (Possible answers: grades, salary, where they live, job history, workout routines, hobbies, items they own, etc.) Bring the class together and have pairs share. Then, as a class, discuss why people lie about these things. (Possible answers: to impress others, to feel better about themselves, to fit in)

Written work

- Have students write a paragraph about being caught in a lie. It can be a situation from any stage in life: childhood, adolescence, adulthood, etc. Tell students to provide details of the lie and the consequences that followed. Time permitting, have students share the paragraph with a partner or the class. If students claim to have never lied, or don't feel comfortable writing about themselves, tell them they can write about someone they know.
- Ask students to write a short essay titled *Reasons Why We Lie*. Instruct them to choose three reasons and develop each reason into a paragraph. Tell students they can use ideas from the last line of the segment. Remind them to include an introduction, where they list their reasons, and a conclusion where they make a general statement about lying.
- On the board, write *Do people lie on social media? What kinds of lies do they tell? How do these lies affect other people?* Invite students to think about these questions and respond to them on paper. Then have them share with the class.
- Have students work in pairs to compile a list of advice to someone who has been caught in a lie at work. On the board, write *If you are caught in a lie, you should . . .* (Possible answers: apologize, admit the truth, explain yourself; OR try to cover up the lie, blame someone else, do what it takes to stay out of trouble) Have pairs combine into groups of four to share ideas. Tell students they can discuss how being caught in different lies may require a variety of actions. They can also discuss which actions they think are right and which are wrong.

LANGUAGE NOTES: *To bend the truth* means to say something that is not completely true.

To be caught in a lie means that someone finds out that you are lying.

VIDEO SCRIPT

Jeff Glor: Alright. Do you tell little white lies? Most of us do. But why? Ben Tracy of WCCO TV of Minneapolis hit the streets to get some answers.

Ben Tracy: Our parents told us never to tell a lie, but it's pretty hard to get through the day without bending the truth a little bit. We generally don't lie about the big things. They're those little white lies. So why do we lie about little things. That's Saturday's question.

Ben Tracy: Today we're talking about lying.

Man on the Street: [*laughs*] OK

Ben Tracy: Do you ever tell little lies?

Man on the Street (1): Yes.

Woman on the Street (1): When you work with all women you have to lie. You look really good in that skirt. You know that kind of thing.

Ben Tracy: From our excuses for being late…

Man on the Street (2): Doctor's appointments, had to take care of your kids, car broke down, dog ate my homework…

Man on the Street (1): Those are little lies.

Ben Tracy: To the more personal.

Woman on the Street (2): My weight for one.

Ben Tracy: We lie a lot.

Woman on the Street (1): You've even lied.

Ben Tracy: I think I probably have lied.

Woman on the Street (1): I'm sure you've lied.

Ben Tracy: In fact 19% of us admit we lie at work at least once a week. 15% have been caught in a lie. And 24% of managers have fired someone for lying.

John Tauer: Virtually no one will say, yes it's a good thing to lie.

Ben Tracy: John Tauer is a social psychologist.

John Tauer: The research indicates that people lie far more often than most of us would like to admit. Most people lie, on average a couple times a day. We say, "Great to see you. We'll have to get together some time." I have no intention of giving the person a call. It means OK, enough of the conversation, have a good day.

Ben Tracy: Top workplace lies are: "I don't know how that happened," "I have another call to take," "I didn't get your email," and of course "I like your outfit," or "You look great!"

Ben Tracy: Have you ever told anybody that they look nice when they really don't?

Man on the Street (3): Definitely.

Woman on the Street (1): Do we look nice?

Ben Tracy: You guys, well, you all look very nice.

Women: [*laughing*]

Ben Tracy: Why do we lie about little things?

John Tauer: We have competing goals: the need to be liked and then the need to be accurate or right.

Ben Tracy: Studies show we are more likely to lie to a co-worker than to a stranger.

Woman on the Street (3): Perfect strangers don't know you and they're not judging you on so many different levels.

John Tauer: Avoiding that conflict, wanting to fit in, wanting to have smooth relationships oftentimes leads to white lies.

ANSWER KEY

A. 1. b   2. a   3. c   4. b

B. I don't know how that happened.; I have another call to take.; I didn't get your e-mail.; I like your outfit.; You look great.

C. 1. c   2. b   3. a   4. c

D. *Possible answers*
1. We have competing goals, the need to be liked and then the need to be accurate or right.
2. It is less likely to lie to a stranger because a stranger doesn't know you and won't judge you.

PART 2

TV Documentary:
Lying on a Resume

PREVIEW

- Ask students *What do you think are the consequences of lying on a resume?* (Possible answers: You could lose your job, face legal action, lose the respect of your colleagues, be reprimanded, etc.)

- Poll the class *Do you know anyone who has lied on a resume? Did he or she get caught?*

VIEW

Ask students to focus on a different topic each time they view. Some ideas:

- Ask students to listen for the reason why Andrea Stanfield lied on her resume.

- Ask students to listen for the consequences of Andrea lying on her resume.

- Ask students to listen for information about screening resumes.

- Ask students to listen for where Andrea is now.

If you decide to use the optional Activity Worksheet, ask students to read each activity before viewing.

REVIEW

Ask comprehension questions. Play the video segment again if necessary.

What is Angela Stanfield's current job?
(She works at an animal rescue company.)
Why did she need a well-paying job ten years ago?
(She had growing legal bills because she was fighting for custody of her daughter.)
Why did she have a hard time finding a well-paying job? (She didn't have a bachelor's degree.)
What did Angela do to solve this problem?
(She lied that she was a graduate of Akron University.)
What type of jobs and salary did this lie lead to?
(two high-level financial jobs and a six-figure salary)
What were the negative consequences of this lie?
(She suffered from severe guilt, anxiety attacks, and a second divorce.)
According to statistics, how many people lie on resumes? (three out of ten)
What does Greg Slamowitz's firm do?
(counsels businesses on the importance of screening resumes)
What percent of companies do background checks? (96%)
What did Andrea Stanfield end up doing?
(eventually after ten years she quit her job)
Did she ever get caught? (no)
What did she do as a result of her experience?
(She wrote a book.)
What does she mean when she says she's still trying to earn back her integrity? (She's still trying to earn people's trust.)

EXTENSION
Oral work

- Group work. Divide the class into groups of three or four. Say *Andrea Stanfield needed a well-paying job to have enough money to secure custody of her daughter.* On the board, write:

    Do you think there are desperate situations when lying on a résumé or doing something similarly dishonest is OK? Why? Why not?
    Would you have done the same in her situation? What else could a person in her situation do?

- Pair work: role play. Invite students to role-play a scenario where Angela Stanfield is called to her boss's office, because he has found out her lie. Tell students to use detail from the segment like the university she claimed to have graduated from, the types of jobs she had, the salary, etc. Have pairs decide how the situation is resolved—whether she would be fired or not. Then have pairs share the role-plays with the class.

- Discussion. Discuss the negative consequences of Andrea's lie (e.g., guilt, anxiety attacks, divorce, a decade spent looking over her shoulder, costing her her integrity). On the board, write:

    Do you think some people would be able to handle such a lie if it brought such great success? Would you?

Have students discuss in pairs or small groups. Then discuss as a class.

Written work

- On the board, write: *Phony: How I Faked My Way Through Life*. Make sure students know that this is the title of the book that Angela wrote, which is briefly shown in the segment. Elicit that *to fake your way through something* means to pretend that you know what you are doing. On the board write the following questions for students to respond to in writing. Hint to students how in the segment, this book was referred to as a cautionary tale.

1. What do you think this book is about?
2. How could her story deter someone from making the same mistake?
3. Would you buy this book?
4. Do you think by buying this book you are financially rewarding her for her lie?

Bring the class together and have students exchange papers and share.

- Have students work in pairs. Tell them to imagine that they are employees at Greg Salmowitz's security firm. They have been asked to run an in-depth background check on Angela Stanfield who has recently applied for a job. Tell them to write a letter with their results. Instruct them to include details from the segment and make up their own information. On the board, write:

X Financial
10 Mountain Ave
Springfield, MA 01101

Dear Mr. Carson,
We are writing regarding your requested background check on job applicant Angela Stanfield . . .

Sincerely,

LANGUAGE NOTES: *To dog someone* means to cause problems for an extended time.

Mounting means increasing.

Custody is the right to take care of a child that is awarded one or both parents when they get a divorce.

To claim something means to state that something is true, even though no proof has been given.

To deceive means to make someone believe something that is not true.

A six-figure salary is a yearly income that contains six numbers, for example $100,000.

To stretch the truth means to say something that is not fully true, usually to make something appear better than it is in reality.

Fraudulent means fake, something that intends to deceive people.

To screen something means to check if it is acceptable. To screen a résumé means to make sure that all the information on it is true.

A degree mill is a fake higher-educational institution that sells diplomas.

To look over one's shoulder means to be worried that something bad is going to happen to you. The expression reflects literally looking over your shoulder to make sure isn't following you.

A cautionary tale is a story that gives a warning.

To pull something off means to succeed in doing something.

Integrity refers to the quality of being honest and strong about what you believe is right. When something *costs* your integrity it means you give up your integrity and you don't live up to what you believe is right.

CULTURE NOTES: Typically, a university or college diploma is signed by any combination of a college president, the chair of the board of trustees, a dean, or a department head. In some cases, even the governor of the state. A lot depends on the size of the educational institution. When Kelly Wallace says *Edmund Brown wasn't even governor at the time,* she refers to the name appearing on a diploma even though he was not in office when the diploma was claimed to have been signed.

Edmund Brown (also known as Edmund Gerald "Jerry" Brown Jr.) has been serving as the 39th Governor of California since 2011. His father Edmund Brown (also known as Edmund Gerald "Pat" Brown Sr. served as the 32nd Governor of California from 1959 to 1967.

VIDEO SCRIPT

Kelly Wallace: Ten years ago, Andrea Standfield, who now runs an animal rescue company, was dogged by mounting legal bills as she fought for custody of her daughter. She needed a well-paying job.

Andrea Standfield: I would do anything, anything. You know. What's the fastest way to get there before I lose my daughter or lose everything that I have?

Kelly Wallace: But most well-paying jobs required a bachelor's degree. Andrea only had a high-school diploma. So the Ohio native lied on her résumé, claiming to be a graduate of Akron University, which is actually called the University of Akron.

Kelly Wallace: Did you think about the consequences when you lied?

Andrea Standfield: Not really. I really worked very hard at putting the consequences out of my head.

Kelly Wallace: The lie led to two high-level financial jobs and a six figure salary, but it also caused severe guilt, anxiety attacks, and a second divorce.

Andrea Standfield: I did lose part of myself, you know, part of my life, and you can't get that back, you just can't. You know. I lived ten years of my life deceiving everyone I knew.

Kelly Wallace: Three out of 10 people lie on their résumés, according to experts, and in a tight economy with unemployment close to 10%, more jobseekers may be feeling desperate enough to stretch the truth.

Greg Slamowitz: We have seen a substantial increase in fraudulent résumés over the last 12–24 months.

Kelly Wallace: Greg Slamowitz's firm counsels businesses on the importance of screening resumes, but even his company was almost fooled last year until a background check raised suspicions about a candidate's degree and her diploma.

Greg Slamowitz: At first glance, it looked good.

Kelly Wallace: On closer examination, ninety was misspelled and Edmund Brown wasn't even governor at the time.

Greg Slamowitz: You are foolish if you do not do a thorough background check on every one.

Ben Allen: Hamilton University and Vanderbilt College are what we call well-known degree mills. These are fictitious institutions.

Kelly Wallace: Ben Allen says clients at his security firm are requesting more in-depth background checks than ever before. 96% of companies nationwide do background checks, up from 66% more than 10 years ago.

Ben Allen: People are asking us to check more things than they have historically. So it would suggest that they're more concerned about it.

Kelly Wallace: As for Andrea, after spending a decade looking over her shoulder, she quit her job before getting caught and turned her past into a cautionary tale.

Andrea Standfield: You might be able to pull it off for years, but it's just gonna get worse and worse and worse. It's not worth it.

Kelly Wallace: Andrea says her actions cost her her integrity, and 10 years later she's still trying to earn it back.

ANSWER KEY

A. Most well-paying jobs require a bachelor's degree.; The number of people who lie on résumés has increased over the past ten years.; After lying, it can be difficult to earn one's integrity back.

B. 1. b 2. d 3. a 4. c

C. 1. True 2. False 3. False 4. True

D. *Possible answers*
  1. Degree mill means they don't really provide an education, they just give people diplomas for money. Hamilton University and Vanderbilt College are two schools mentioned.
  2. The job applicant lied about the school she graduated from. They found out because she misspelled the word *ninety* in the graduation year and the signature on the diploma was not the person who was governor at that time.

UNIT 3
Fears, Hardships, and Heroism

On-the-Street Interviews:
I could have died ...

PREVIEW

• Ask students to brainstorm dangerous things people do—for example, rock climbing or racing cars. Write student responses on the board. Then ask *Has anyone done any of these things? Why did you do it? Would you do it again?*

VIEW

Ask students to focus on a different topic each time they view. Some ideas:

• Ask students to listen for what activity the interviewee was doing in each story.

• Ask students to listen for what made each experience dangerous.

• Ask students to listen for specific details that describe each story.

If you decide to use the optional Activity Worksheet, ask students to read each activity before viewing.

REVIEW

• Ask comprehension questions. Play the video segment again if necessary.
  What dangerous thing did Catherine and her husband do? (They explored an area in Hawaii where a volcano had just erupted.)
  What happened to Catherine and her husband? (They watched the volcano while standing on a cliff made of lava. Nothing hit them, but they were very nervous.)
  How does Catherine describe the experience? (as dangerous but incredible)
  What dangerous thing did Christine do? (She went skydiving.)
  What did she think the experience would be like? (She thought it would be fun and exciting; she did not think it was dangerous.)
  What does go tandem *mean when referring to skydiving?* (to strap yourself to your instructor and jump out of the plane together)
  What happened to Christine and her instructor? (They started to spin uncontrollably; they needed to use the reserve parachute; they crashed; the instructor disappeared.)
  How did Christine feel? (She was in shock.)
  What dangerous thing did Angelique do? (She jumped onto train tracks to pick up money that had fallen out of her bag.)
  What happened next? (Two men pulled her up from the tracks before the train came.)
  What did Angelique learn from this experience? (to stuff her money deep in her bag)

EXTENSION
Oral work

• Pair work: role play. Have students take turns role-playing the conversation between the interviewer and one of the interviewees. Tell students to include as many details of the story as they can remember.

• Discussion. Ask:
  Which of the three experiences do you think was the most dangerous? Why?
  Who has had a similar experience?
  Were these dangerous experiences avoidable?
  Why do you think some people put themselves in dangerous situations?
  Do you ever put yourself in dangerous situations? Why?

Written work

- On the board, write: *Which of the people do you think might repeat the dangerous activity? Explain*. Have students write a paragraph responding to the question. Then call on students to share their paragraphs with the class.

- Tell students to write about a dangerous experience that they or someone they know has had. Ask them to include as many details as possible.

OOPS! Angelique says that the wind *threw* her envelope *into* the train tracks. She means to say that the wind *blew* her envelope *onto* the train tracks.

VIDEO SCRIPT

Interviewer: Have you ever done anything that was genuinely dangerous? What happened? What were the consequences?

Catherine: OK.

Interviewer: And how did you feel about it? Was it a positive or a negative experience?

Catherine: I . . . I did do something that was genuinely dangerous once. I look back at it and I think, yeah I could have died, but the experience was incredible. My husband and I, just before we got married, went to Hawaii and we rented a car and we went out into this area where the volcano had taken out a whole neighborhood. So we hiked out there at night. There's no lights. It's just black. To the edge of this cliff and watched . . . it was incredible, watched the lava just coming out. But we're standing on a cliff that's made of lava, and lava's very unstable and there's no warning. It breaks off. It falls into the ocean. We were, it felt like we were close. You could see the smoke. The sulfur was coming towards us but the ocean kind of, the waves kind of pushed everything up. So it didn't really hit us. I heard, I kept hearing popping noises. I was getting nervous. My husband was definitely nervous. That's probably the most dangerous thing I've ever done. But it was incredible. Incredible experience.

Christine: Well, I went . . . I went skydiving a few years ago. I actually did not think it was insane. I did not think that it was dangerous or anything. I went because I thought that it would be fun and exciting and I almost died. I went tandem, so that means that you have to actually strap yourself into your instructor and you jump out of the plane and dive with them. And we were supposed to have a thirty-five second free fall, and which basically means that you, you know, kind of enjoy the fall for thirty-five seconds before you have to release the chute. So when we jumped out of the plane, we started spinning uncontrollably for twenty-eight seconds. After twenty-eight seconds, he released the parachute and we jerked up into the air, and we thought everything was fine, and all of a sudden we started crashing to the ground again at a rapid speed. So he had to use his reserve parachute. So he opened up the reserve parachute just in time for us to go crashing into a cornfield, miles from where we were supposed to be. When I finally came to—I didn't pass out or anything, but I think I was just over-stricken with shock—I realized that my instructor was gone, and he was nowhere to be found. So I had to find my way out of the cornfield. It felt like it took hours. I don't actually know how long I was in there for, but when I finally found my way out, a Jeep came and found me, and it ended up being people from the sky-diving school.

Angelique: I was on the subway . . . I was in the subway, and I had picked up my money from work. And so I had my money in a little envelope, and I was walking down on the tracks, and da, da, da, da, da, and a gush of wind came, and it threw my envelope into the train tracks. So against my complete better judgment, and it was a horrible idea, but I jumped down on the tracks, got the envelope, and then had two men pull me up before the train got here. It's a bad mistake. Never, never do it again but I got my sixty dollars so, I don't know. And what I learned was to stuff my money deep in my bag, as opposed to right outside of my bag so it could fall out. But I'm safe 'cause it worked out.

ANSWER KEY

A. 1. Hawaii 2. died 3. volcano 4. lava
   5. nervous 6. incredible

B. 5, 2, 7, 9, 3, 4, 1, 8, 6

C. *Individual responses should include variations on the following*:
   Angelique was in the subway, and the wind blew an envelope with money out of her bag and onto the train tracks. Against her better judgment, she jumped on the tracks to get the envelope. Two men pulled her up before the train arrived. She said she would never do such a thing again. The experience taught her to stuff her money deep in her bag so it doesn't fall out.

D. *Answers will vary*.

UNIT 4
Getting Along with Others

TV Documentary:
Why We Explode

PREVIEW

- On the board, write *explode* and elicit the meaning (to explode means to burst or fly into pieces or break up violently). Then add the words *Why we* and *?* to write *Why we explode?* Ask *How can people explode?* (in laughter, in anger, in tears). Point out that this segment will focus on why people explode in anger.

VIEW

Ask students to focus on a different topic each time they view. Some ideas:

- Ask students to listen for mental disorders in which anger is a common symptom.
- Ask students to listen for reasons why people without mental disorders might explode in anger.
- Ask students to listen for ways to manage anger.

If you decide to use the optional Activity Worksheet, ask students to read each activity before viewing.

REVIEW

Ask comprehension questions. Play the video segment again if necessary.
> *Do people ever explode over small things?* (Yes, but it doesn't feel like a small thing at the time.)
> *What caused Dr. Lieberman to almost lose it?* (the TSA line)
> *What do Rebecca and Anthony suggest about the TSA line?* (that it is a stressor for all people)
> *Which mental disorders have emotional volatility and irritability?* (PTSD, depression, bipolar disorder, intermittent explosive disorder)
> *What are the symptoms of intermittent explosive disorder?* (losing your temper violently, excessively, too frequently)
> *How do apparently normal people in everyday life lose it?* (they overreact or they do something they are embarrassed about)
> *Are people losing it more often?* (yes)
> *What is causing this?* (it is probably related to socio-cultural factors; people have a lower threshold before they explode)

EXTENSION

Oral work

- Discussion. Elicit the ideas for controlling emotions and managing anger that Rebecca Jarvis mentions in the segment, and write these on the board:
  Best ways to manage anger
  Recognize your hot button issues
  Don't be reactive
  Think before you speak
  Take a time out and walk away
  Use humor to diffuse the situation

Then ask, what does Dr. Lieberman add to the list? Add these to the tips the board:
  Exercise
  Meditation
  Therapy

Group work. Divide the class into groups and have students discuss the various ways for managing anger. Invite students to share what works and what doesn't work for them. Tell them to add to the list if they have other ideas. Then bring the class together and call on volunteers to share.

- Write the following vocabulary from the segment on the board:
  The breaking point for me is…
  I lose it when …
  … is the end for me
  …is a trigger for me
  …pushes my buttons
  …sends me over the top
  I become unhinged when…
  A hot button for me is…

In groups of three or four have students use expressions from the list to discuss what situations and scenarios make them "explode".

- Pair work: role play. Ask students to prepare two role-plays: one where a person overreacts to a situation and explodes, and another role-play where a person manages anger (for example by walking away, diffusing the situation with humor, etc). After each one, invite students to respond. If students need ideas, invite them to role-play a scenario in a TSA line at the airport, which according to Dr. Lieberman and the reporters, is a common stressor.

Written work

- Have students recall a scenario when they flew off the handle. Write the following instructions on the board:
  Write a paragraph describing when and where you exploded and details about how you felt and how you and people around you reacted.
  Then write a paragraph describing how you could have handled the situation better.

- Ask students to summarize the segment. Tell them to start like this:

According to Dr. Lieberman, everyone explodes once in a while… Tell them to include as many details as they can. If necessary, let students watch the segment again and encourage them to take notes to then use in their summary.

LANGUAGE NOTES: *Breaking point* refers to the point at which a person can no longer handle stress.

The straw that breaks the camel's back is an idiom referring to the final limit of what a person can handle. It goes back to an anecdote about a camel that was loaded with an extraordinary amount of straw to carry. Then one more piece of straw was put on it. That proved to be just too much, and the animal fell and broke its back. The idiom is used to describe the times a person is loaded or annoyed by something until he or she can't take it anymore.

The drop that overfills the cup is similar to the above idiom. It refers to that added element of something that makes a person unable to handle a situation any more.

To lose it refers to suddenly being unable to control your emotions.

To be the end means to be the limit of what a person can take.

To cross the line means to start behaving in an unacceptable manner.

To precipitate means to make something happen quickly.

Volatility is the state of suddenly becoming angry or violent.

Irritability is the state of being annoyed quickly and easily.

Ostensibly means supposedly.

Threshold refers to the level at which something starts to have an effect on a person.

An epidemiologist studies the way diseases spread, and how to control them.

Comorbidity refers to concurrent medical conditions that are present in a patient.

A trigger is the thing that causes something to happen, like a problem or a bad reaction.

To push someone's button means to aggravate someone.

Send (someone) over the top means to make someone overreact.

To come unhinged means to make someone become upset.

A hot button is a subject that causes a strong reaction in a person.

CULTURE NOTES: The TSA is the Transportation Security Administration. It is an agency of the U.S. Department of Homeland security. It oversees the security of travelers in the United States. It focuses on air travel and has officials screen travelers in airports. The screening process is known to cause delays and stress for travelers.

PTSD is the abbreviation for Post Traumatic Stress Disorder, which is a disorder that develops in some people who have experienced an overwhelming or difficult event. Anxiety, agitation, and irritability are some symptoms.

VIDEO SCRIPT

Rebecca Jarvis: Dr. Jeffrey Lieberman, Chief of Psychiatry at New York Presbyterian/Columbia Medical Center is here with his insights. Great to have you. Good morning.

Dr. Lieberman: Thank you.

Rebecca Jarvis: So we never really feel when we explode that it's over a small thing. But sometimes it really is.

Dr. Lieberman: Well, first, everybody has their breaking point. I mean whether it's the straw that breaks the camel's back or the cup that over… the drop that overfills the cup. It can happen to anybody. I flew up here yesterday from being out of town, and the TSA line, I almost lost it. But…

Rebecca Jarvis: I don't think anybody has ever not lost it at the TSA line.

Anthony Mason: No, that's, that's, that's gonna be the end for me. Where I cross the line.

Dr. Lieberman: But the question is sort of what is precipitating these reactions and are they occurring more frequently than they have in the past. It's a little bit complicated. I'm gonna try and break it down. First, oftentimes in the context of real mental disorders people have emotional volatility and irritability; it's the signature symptom of PTSD. It occurs in depression or bipolar disorder. There's even a disorder that has a name for losing your temper violently, excessively, too frequently: it's called intermittent explosive disorder, very strict criteria. But what we're talking about here is when ostensibly normal people in everyday life just lose it. They overreact. They do something that they are either embarrassed for or they can actually incur legal consequences about. And it happens to everybody. The question is: is it happening more often? And why? To some extent, it's probably related to socio-cultural factors. There was a survey that was done by a noted Harvard epidemiologist in 1990—the national comorbidity survey. He repeated it 15 years later in 2005. He found that the biggest increase of any disorder was intermittent explosive disorder. So people do seem to be having a lower threshold…

Anthony Mason: Right.

Dr. Lieberman: ... before they explode.

Anthony Mason: And, so ultimately, there, it's, there, frequently, they're not really angry about, you know, people cutting in line. It's a cumulative thing, yes?

Dr. Lieberman: That's the trigger. That's the trigger that sort of pushes their button or sends them over the top. And, as I said, it can happen to everybody. When it happens to people that don't have some preexisting disorder, it seems to be the accumulation of a number of stresses and slights and things that have happened in the course of our life. And now we're in a culture where never in human history have people haven't been having to deal so much. Information...

Rebecca Jarvis: So what do people do if they're coming unhinged?

Dr. Lieberman: Well, the first thing, having a mental melt meltdown or emotional meltdown is a sign or a signal that you're having difficulty with emotional control. People should be able to control their emotions, behave appropriately, and also be able to conduct themselves in an appropriate way. If they lose that, then they have to be able to understand why.

Rebecca Jarvis: So you have some some great ideas for people to think about their hot button issues, not be reactive, think before you speak, take time and walk away, and I like this one use humor to diffuse the situation.

Dr. Lieberman: These are little devices that you can use, but anything to diffuse stress: exercise, meditation, or therapy to gain insights into what's stimulating you in this way.

Rebecca Jarvis: Thank you, Dr. Jeffrey Lieberman. Have a great one.

ANSWER KEY

A. 1. True 2. False 3. True 4. True
B. 1. mental 2. PTSD 3. Depression 4. Violently 5. Explosive 6. normal 7. legal
C. Choose 3: not be reactive, think before you speak, take time, walk away, and use humor to diffuse the situation.
D. *Possible answer*
The expression *straw that breaks the camel's back* means that someone can carry a very heavy burden, but if one more tiny thing is added, it is too much to handle. Similarly, *the drop that overflows the cup* means that someone can handle a certain amount, but if a small drop more is added, it is too much to handle. These are used to explain why someone may lose their temper over a minor issue. The tensions and stresses build up over time and they are able to handle them, but the addition of one more small thing is enough to make them explode.

UNIT 5
Humor

TV Documentary:
Laughter is Contagious

PREVIEW

- Ask students *Have you ever started laughing just because you saw someone else laughing?*
- Write *Laughter is contagious* and elicit that when something is contagious it causes another person to feel or act the same way.

VIEW

Ask students to focus on a different topic each time they view. Some ideas:

- Ask students to listen for what researchers in England did to find out why laughter is contagious.
- Ask students to listen for what happened to people when they heard sounds of joy.
- Ask students to listen for the results of the experiment.

If you decide to use the optional Activity Worksheet, ask students to read each activity before viewing.

REVIEW

Ask comprehension questions. Play the video segment again if necessary.

How did researchers in England conduct their experiment on laughter? (by playing different sounds to people)
What did the sounds monitor? (what the people's facial expressions were doing)
What conclusions did the experiments make? (that sounds of joy activated facial muscles)
What did people participating in the study think was being researched? (facial perspiration)
What did sounds of laughter and joy evoke in the participants? (laughter)
Does the experiment conclude that laughter is contagious? (Yes, it does.)
Are we more likely to laugh alone or in a group? (in a group)
What does a sense of humor help with? (to get along and be healthy)
The article quotes the line 'Laugh and the whole world laughs with you.' What happens when you cry? (you cry alone)

EXTENSION

Oral work

- Discussion. Ask *Did you find yourself smiling while watching this segment?* Time permitting, have students watch the segment again, being aware how they react to the discussion of laughter, the sounds of laughter, etc. Then let students discuss their reactions in groups. Invite students to share stories where laughter sounds have made them laugh as well.

- Discussion. On the board, write *Laugh, and the whole world laughs with you. / Weep, and you weep alone.* In groups have students respond to these lines (which come from a 19th century poem, Solitude by Ella Wheeler Wilcox). Invite students to share related situations where, when things were well, they were surrounded by many friends; when all wasn't well, this wasn't the case.

- Pair or group work. In pairs have students try to replicate the experiment described in the segment. Tell them to think up four sounds to evoke various reactions from other groups. If technology like phones or computers are available, allow students to use them to find these sounds. Then combine pairs into groups of four and have them test the sounds on each other and monitor the reactions. Tell students to be mindful not to laugh at every sound.

- Discussion. Harry Smith says *If you really want to get along and be healthy it doesn't hurt to have a sense of humor*. In groups, have students discuss if a sense of humor is something you can work on and develop, or if it is something a person is born with. Then bring the class together and have students share opinions.

Written work

- On the board, write *Are other emotions contagious, too?* Review Dr. Senay's comments that part of interacting in a group is responding and reacting to the way other people are responding and reacting. Ask *Does this apply to other emotions too, for example anger, sadness, fear?* Invite students to respond in writing, giving specific examples.

- On the board, write: *People who live alone, don't live as long as others with better social relationships.* Have students write a paragraph speculating why this is true.

- Invite students to write down the funniest jokes they know which they will then read to the class. As the joke is read, tell students to be aware if they are laughing because the joke is actually funny, or because other people are laughing.

LANGUAGE NOTES: *Contagious* is an adjective used to describe an action or attitude (e.g., enthusiasm, laughter) that affects other people and they begin to have it, too. The word is also commonly used for illness, describing that it can be passed on from person to person.

A skeptic is a person who disagrees with statements that are generally believed to be true.

To be predisposed means someone to be made more likely to behave or think in a particular way.

To mislead means to make someone believe something is not true by giving them false information.

To hang together means something is well-organized and the different parts go well together.

CULTURE NOTES: The lines *Laugh, and the world laughs with you* and *Weep, and you weep alone* come from 19th century poet's Ella Wheeler Wilcox's poem Solitude.

VIDEO SCRIPT

Harry Smith: This morning in Health Watch it's time for a good laugh. And if these people leave you smiling or maybe even laughing, a new medical study can explain it, and our doctor Emily Senay is here with details. I was hoping you would come on with a little red rubber nose this morning.

Dr. Senay: I'm funny enough without that. I don't need that.

Harry Smith: That's right. Now what is it, there's a serious study...

Dr. Senay: Yes.

Harry Smith: ...about laughter. And what does it find?

Dr. Senay: There is. There is. Well obviously we know that laughter can be contagious. But researchers in England wanted to know why this is. What is it about laughter that we just, you know, can't stop being infected by it? So they actually took 20 volunteers, hooked 'em up to MRI machines, hooked 'em up to devices, electrodes, that measured their facial muscles...

Harry Smith: Right.

Dr. Senay: ...and then they played for them a variety of different sounds. Some of it was like triumphal sounds, like, "Woo hoo!"

Harry Smith: Right.

Dr. Senay: Some of it was laughter. Some of it was sounds that are like fear and disgust. No words just sounds.

Harry Smith: Right.

Dr. Senay: And then monitored what was going on inside their brains and what their facial muscles were doing.

Harry Smith: Right. And what'd they, what'd, what'd kind of conclusions did they come to?

Dr. Senay: Well what they found that was when people heard amusement or sounds of joy, parts of the brain that were activated were those parts of the brain that control the facial muscles. And they were much more likely to be activated when they heard those sounds like laughter or amusement or joy than they, than they were when they heard sounds like fear or disgust.

Harry Smith: Right.
Dr. Senay: So there's something involuntary going on inside the brain that's actually greater with those kind of sounds than fear or disgust.
Harry Smith: Yeah, alright, alright, let me play the skeptic, because in any kind of research methodology, you're thinking, okay, well, they're predisposed because they know what the deal is here. So they're going to help laugh…
Dr. Senay: Sure.
Harry Smith: … because it's a laughter study.
Dr. Senay: Well they got around that by tricking the participants. They didn't tell them…
Harry Smith: OK.
Dr. Senay: … what the study was about. In fact, they mislead them a little bit and told them it was about facial perspiration. But… [laughter]
Harry Smith: How pleasant.
Dr. Senay: I know. But at the end of the study, when they revealed to the participants what it was that they were actually looking for, they, the participants all said, as anybody would, well I couldn't help it. When I heard the laughter, when I heard the sounds of joy, I just had to laugh.
Harry Smith: Wow.
Dr. Senay: So it's actually something deep inside our brain that makes us respond to other people's laughter.
Harry Smith: So, so, so laughter is contagious?
Dr. Senay: It is contagious, and it's a good thing because we're social animals and part of interacting in a group is responding, ah, responding and reacting to the way other people are responding and reacting and laughter is one way that we sort of are altogether. We are much more likely to laugh in a group than we are alone, for example. When you're in a theater and people are laughing around you, I mean it all sort of make sense and hangs together.
Harry Smith: Exactly. Because we've been talking about some studies about people who live alone and that they don't live as long as others with better social relationships.
Dr. Senay: That's right.
Harry Smith: And if you really want to get along and be healthy it doesn't hurt to have a sense of humor.
Dr. Senay: That's right. And it also proves, "Laugh and the whole world laughs with you. Weep and you weep alone."
Dr. Senay and Harry Smith: Alone.
Harry Smith: Wow, you are the best. Gimme some of that. Alright, Emily Senay.

ANSWER KEY

A. A sense of humor helps people stay healthy; Researchers told participants the study was about facial perspiration; People who live alone don't live as long as others with better social relationships; People are more likely to laugh in a movie theater than when watching something alone.
B. 1. True 2. False 3. True 4. False 5. True
C. 1. activated 2. disgust 3. involuntary 4. skeptic 5. laughter
D. *Possible answer*
The expression means that when you are happy and laughing, it is contagious and people around you are more likely to be happy and laughing. Facial muscles were more likely to be activated when people heard sounds like laughter or amusement or joy then they were when they heard fear or disgust.

UNIT 6
Troubles While Traveling

TV Documentary:
Inside Hotel Security

PART 1
PREVIEW

- On the board, write *Hotel Security*. Elicit that this refers to things that are done to keep people safe in a hotel. Ask *What kinds of things are done to ensure hotel security?* (extra locks on doors, safes in rooms and in hotel lobbies, key cards that change codes after use, etc.)

- Poll the class *How many of you have stayed at hotels? Did you feel that the hotel security was sufficient in those hotels? Why? Why not?*

VIEW

Ask students to focus on a different topic each time they view. Some ideas:

- Ask students to listen for the steps Bill Stanton takes to rob the first would-be hotel guest.
- Ask students to listen for the steps Bill Stanton take to rob the second would-be hotel guest.
- Ask students to listen for security glitches in each hotel.

If you decide to use the optional Activity Worksheet, ask students to read each activity before viewing.

REVIEW

Ask comprehension questions. Play the video segment again if necessary.

What is the first step Bill Stanton takes in robbing a hotel? (He waits, looking at the would-be guest's car, checking out what watch he's wearing and what luggage he has.)

What key information does he collect about the would-be guest right away? (his name and room number, as he gives it at the front desk)

When does would-be thief Bill Stanton "attack"? (when the guest goes to the gym to work out)

What does he mean when he says "the clock starts now"? (that the limited time he has to complete his task of robbing the room starts the minute that the would-be guest leaves and goes to the gym)

What is the first step? (The would-be thief calls housekeeping to clean the room he wants to rob.)

What does he do next? (He walks into the room like it is his own and asks housekeeping to give him a few minutes, and he takes all the valuables in sight and the guest's suitcase, as well as the valet ticket for the car. He goes on to call the valet to bring up his car.)

Does the would-be thief need the valet ticket? Why or why not? (no he does not, the name on the stolen suitcase suffices)

How is the burglary at the second hotel similar? (The would-be thief gets the name and room number in the same way during check in. He calls housekeeping to clean the room like in the other hotel and then robs it.)

What is different about the second robbery? (He tells housekeeping to leave and goes on to call the front desk to open the room safe for him.)

EXTENSION
Oral work

- Pair work: role play. In pairs have students role-play the parts in the second robbery when the would-be thief calls the front desk about the combo to the safe. Have students decide how the conversation should have gone, had the hotel had better security. Then bring the class together and have pairs share role plays.

- Pair work. On the board, write *Mandatory Security Seminar for Hotel Personnel.* Elicit that hotel personnel refers to people who work for a company. In pairs, have students prepare a security seminar for hotel personnel in light of recent multiple robberies. Encourage students to address issues that were viewed in the video (for example, housekeeping should get instructions about not just letting anyone in the room; rooms requested to be cleaned should be monitored carefully, etc.). Tell pairs to write up several points to address various hotel personnel.

Students can then present their seminars to the class or share with another group.

- Discussion. Invite students to share hotel security stories they have experienced or heard of. Discuss various classes of hotels. Ask *Do you think better hotels are necessarily more secure?* Draw five stars on the board to indicate how hotels are often rated. Ask *What additional measures might a 5-star hotel have compared to a 2-star hotel? How might a smaller, less fancy hotel with fewer amenities and rooms have better security?*

Written work

- On the board, write: *Write down each security flaw as it appears in the video.* Have students view the segment again and take notes, adding lines between notes. Then instruct students to return to each note and indicate what should have happened differently

- Have students imagine they are one of the would-be victims of the hotel robberies. Instruct them to write a letter of complaint to the hotel about their flawed security. Tell students they can write as forcefully as they wish, making any references to police reports that may have followed the robberies, or still may follow. Invite students to be creative.

Time permitting, pairs can swap letters and role-play hotel management responding to the complaint letters.

LANGUAGE NOTES: *On the lookout* means watching for danger.

To heat up means to become more active or extreme.

Brazen means not embarrassed about behaving in a wrong or immoral manner.

Lo and behold is a colloquial expression use to mention something surprising.

The clock starts right now means that the time I have to complete a task begins at this moment.

Let's roll is an expression used to suggest starting to do something or to go somewhere.

To work up a sweat means to do physical exercise that makes you sweat; it can also mean to put a lot of effort into something.

Would-be is an adjective that means wanting or trying to be something.

To be off the hook means to let someone get out of having to do something.

Combo is an abbreviation for *combination* used in this segment to refer to the series of numbers or letters that open a lock or safe.

CULTURE NOTES: GMA refers to Good Morning America, which is an American morning television show. Set in New York's Time square, co-anchors report on the day's news, give interviews, share reports on a variety of topics, and give the weather forecast. *GMA on the Lookout* is a recurring topic on Good Morning America which covers various topics like burglaries, crime, security, and related topics.

VIDEO SCRIPT

Lara Spencer: And we are back now with "GMA on the Lookout." And as summer travel season heats up, we are investigating just how secure you and your valuables are at a hotel. Check out what our hidden cameras uncovered and how you can avoid becoming a victim after you check in. Watch as this brazen thief walks into a hotel last month as a couple is sleeping. Moments later, he flees. Police say he stole more than $4,000 worth of items. So, how to prevent that from happening to you? To see how safe your belongings are during a hotel stay, we conduct an experiment. A guest arrives at a downtown Richmond, Virginia hotel. But this guest is actually a "GMA" producer. Approximately 20 minutes prior, with three undercover cameras rolling, safety and security expert Bill Stanton shows up at the same hotel, but he's not here to check in.

Bill Stanton: I'm waiting, looking at his car, what watch he's wearing, the luggage he has.

Lara Spencer: Stanton is playing the role of would-be thief.

Bill Stanton: When I see an opening that's when I approach and that's when I hear the magic words.

Wynn: Hi, I'm Wynn. W-Y-N-N.

Bill Stanton: I follow him right to his door. So now I have his name, now I have his door number.

Lara Spencer: Armed with just two pieces of information, Stanton is about to show us how vulnerable we can be during a hotel stay. The waiting game ends the very next morning while our producer goes to the gym to work out.

Bill Stanton: Lo and behold, he comes with his workout outfit. He comes down to the lobby for a bottle of water. As far as I'm concerned, the clock to me to get in that room starts right now. Let's roll. I figure I got at least 30 minutes to do what I need to do.

Lara Spencer: His plan, so bold it seems almost ridiculous. Stanton goes to the front desk and asks for housekeeping to clean our producer's room.

Bill Stanton: Room 1112, Wynn. Thank you.

Lara Spencer: Stanton simply walks in as if it's his own room. He has our producer's permission. Otherwise this could be the beginning of a crime.

Bill Stanton: Hello.

Housekeeper (female): Hi.

Bill Stanton: I am so sorry, can you give me two minutes? It doesn't take long for me to find everything, Rolex, right by the phone and what is it? It's an expensive watch and a valet ticket to his car. Yes, I'm in room 1112. Can you please bring up my car right now?

Lara Spencer: We are just 15 minutes into our experiment. Our producer is working up quite a sweat, but Stanton not so much.

Bill Stanton: Where's my car coming?

Valet Parking Attendant (male): It's coming right there.

Bill Stanton: Ah, there we go.

Lara Spencer: They asked for the ticket, which Stanton claims he doesn't have. But they look at the name on stolen luggage and off he goes.

Bill Stanton: And it's as easy as that.

Lara Spencer: Later that day, at a nearby hotel, Stanton tracks another "GMA" producer.

Ferguson: Ferguson. F-E-R-...

Bill Stanton: So once again, right to the front desk, listening to the name, room exchange.

Lara Spencer: When our producer leaves the hotel, Stanton sees his opening, and our would-be thief springs into action, again pretending to be someone he's not.

Bill Stanton: I'm in room 711.

Lara Spencer: From a house phone, Stanton calls to have housekeeping sent to our producer's room. With undercover cameras rolling, he walks right in. But instead of letting housekeeping do their job, he sends them away.

Bill Stanton: You're off the hook.

Housekeeper (female): I'm off the hook?

Bill Stanton: You're off the hook. I'm gonna jump in the shower.

Lara Spencer: Now, with the room to himself, Stanton has his mind set on a bold and nearly unthinkable scenario.

Bill Stanton: I'm in the room. I forgot the combo to the safe.

Hotel Employee: Okay, I'll have them come and open it.

Bill Stanton: Thank you so much.

Lara Spencer: You heard right, a hotel room safe. And moments later, a gentleman from security arrives to help.

Security Employee: All right, she's wide open for you.

Bill Stanton: Perfect. As soon as that security guy is out, I'm dressed, I got his cash, I got his credit card, and I took his laptop. Oh, and by the way, I put it all in his luggage.

ANSWER KEY

A. watch; luggage; car
B. His plan was so bold it seemed almost ridiculous; This experiment is the beginning of a crime; The hotels are in Ridgefield, Virginia.
C. 1. b 2. d 3. c 4. a
D. *Possible answer*
   Magic words are the ones that give him the information he needs to steal things from his victims. The person's name and room number are two examples.

TV Documentary: *Inside Hotel Security*

PART 2
PREVIEW

- Ask volunteers *How do you think the two hotels reacted when they were approached by Bill Stanton and his team? Do you think they minded the in-depth undercover experiment with video surveillance?*

VIEW

Ask students to focus on a different topic each time they view. Some ideas:

- Ask students to listen for each hotel's response to the allegation of security problems.
- Ask students to listen for what Bill Stanton thinks tends to be top priority for people in hotels.
- Ask students to listen for tips for staying secure.

If you decide to use the optional Activity Worksheet, ask students to read each activity before viewing.

REVIEW

Ask comprehension questions. Play the video segment again if necessary.

How did the hotels respond to allegations that they have problems with security? (The first hotel took steps to correct shortfalls; The second hotel admitted that security did fall short—they also addressed the situation.)
What was Bill Stanton's reaction to the results of his experiment? (He was not surprised.)
What did Bill Stanton say is the top priority at hotels? (comfort and service, not security)
Which most important tip does he leave the viewer with? (Not saying your name, but taking out your ID to check in)
What does the viewer learn about hotel safes? (That they are not failsafe and they don't usually insure you for more than a thousand dollars.)
Based on the video, which is suggested to be safer—a room safe or a hotel safe at the front desk? (hotel safe at the front desk)
What might be the safest thing to do with your personal belongings? (keep them with you)
Whom does Bill Stanton suggest counting on when traveling? (yourself, not the hotel)

EXTENSION
Oral work

- Group work. In groups of three of four, have students discuss personal experience with hotel security. Invite students to share things they always do when staying in hotels. Ask one person in each group to take notes. Bring the class together and write student tips on the board. For example, *I tell the front desk I don't want housekeeping to come to my room. I make my own bed.*

- Pair work: role play. In pairs, have students role-play phone conversations between Bill Stanton and a manager or one of the two would-be burglarized hotel managers, where the information of failed security is relayed. On the board, write:

  A: Hello, this is Bill Stanton from Good Morning America. I . . .

  B: . . .

  Encourage pairs to be creative in their conversations. Tell them the hotel managers can voice surprise, or be reluctant to speak with Bill Stanton. Considering the factual information in the segment, however, they should, in the end, be willing to address the problem.

- Discussion. Both hotels, claimed that they took steps to address the security situation, upon learning of security shortfalls. As a class, brainstorm how this may have been done (better training of employees, stricter rules about opening safes for guests, etc.)

Written work

- Lara Spencer ends the show saying *All right, everybody go to goodmorningamerica.com on Yahoo for Bill's top five tips*. In pairs, have students compile the five tips they think appear on this list. Then invite them to try to locate the tips online and compare their list with his (If students need help finding the website, hint that they should put the following words in their search engine: *good morning america bill stanton five tips*)

- On the board, write *"Well, security is a priority, but it's not the top priority. It's more about comfort and service."* Ask students to respond agreeing or disagreeing to Bill Stanton's statement. Tell students to indicate what the top priority is for them when choosing a hotel.

LANGUAGE NOTES: The noun *a shortfall* is an amount that is less than what is needed or expected. The verb variation *to fall short* means to have less than what is needed or expected.

To go undercover means to use a fake appearance or identity to get information.

The number one takeaway is the most important piece of information that you learn from something.

Zip your lips is a colloquial way to say be quiet.

Fail safe means not likely to fail.

Be all, end all means the most important part of something; in referring to a safe in a hotel room not being a *be all end all* the speaker suggests it is not completely reliable.

CULTURE NOTES: The website goodmorningamerica.com is related to the American morning television show Good Morning America set in New York's Time square, co-anchors report on the day's news, give interviews, share reports on a variety of topics, and give the weather forecast. The website supplements the show.

VIDEO SCRIPT

Lara Spencer: All right, so the first hotel you saw in the piece says they have already taken steps to correct any shortfalls in security. The second hotel, where they opened that safe, they told us that the standards they set for security did fall short. They immediately addressed the situation as well. We wanna bring in safety and security expert Bill Stanton, who you just saw going undercover for us in that piece. Oh, my goodness.

Bill Stanton: Yes, yes.

Lara Spencer: I mean, obviously, you are not surprised?

Bill Stanton: Well, security is a priority, it's not the top priority. It's more about comfort and service. The tips that you should do when you approach the front desk is take out your ID, do not say the name out loud because they'll hear, someone could hear you.

Lara Spencer: So, so, show your ID, but don't necessarily, I always am careful with that if they ask you for a phone number. But you got, you say the number one takeaway is...

Bill Stanton: Yeah, don't say, zip your lip, push your license forward, let them read it and then check you in that way.

Lara Spencer: All right. What are some other great tips that people could take away from this?

Bill Stanton: Well, as you saw with the safe, it's anything but fail safe. You know, put your valuables in, but they won't insure you up to $1,000 in most hotels.

Lara Spencer: And that's really maybe what people are gonna have with them.

Bill Stanton: That's right. So if you have those expensive family heirloom items, go to the front desk, ask if they have a safe behind that desk or just wear them on your person.

Lara Spencer: All right, so don't trust that that room's safe is necessarily a be-all, end-all.

Bill Stanton: Don't count on the hotel. Count on yourself.

Lara Spencer: All right, everybody, go to goodmorningamerica.com on Yahoo for Bill's top five tips. Those, I mean, it's pretty surprising. And there's more to come tomorrow, Robin and George, wait 'til you see.

George Stephanpoulus: Okay, looking forward to it, Lara. Thanks very much.

ANSWER KEY

A. security; comfort; service; name; ID; number
B. 1. True 2. False, The second hotel said that the standards they set fell short. 3. False, Bill Stanton advises you to put your family heirlooms in the safe at the front desk or wear them. 4. False, Most hotels will insure you for up to $1,000.
C. 1. L 2. B 3. B 4. N 5. L
D. *Possible answer*
Bill Stanton means that even though people may believe they are safe in hotels because of security, they should take responsibility for keeping themselves safe. Ask to use the hotel safe instead of a room safe for very valuable items. Don't say your name out loud when checking in.

UNIT 7
Mind Over Matter

On-the-Street Interviews: *I'm afraid of falling...*

PREVIEW

• Write on the board: *Phobias and Superstitions.* Have students brainstorm examples and write them on the board. Then invite students to share phobias and superstitions they have. (See Language Notes for definitions of *phobia* and *superstition*.)

VIEW

Ask students to focus on a different topic each time they view. Some ideas:

- Ask students to listen for the kind of fear or phobia each interviewee describes.
- Ask students to listen for the interviewees who describe how the fears or phobias affect their actions.
- Ask students to listen for the interviewees who describe how they deal with their fears or phobias.

If you decide to use the optional Activity Worksheet, ask students to read each activity before viewing.

REVIEW

- Ask comprehension questions. Play the video segment again if necessary.
    What is Deepti's superstition? (She has to wear her socks on the correct feet. If she doesn't, she believes something bad will happen.)
    What does she realize about her belief? (that it is irrational, but she still can't help it)
    What is Dan afraid of? (closed spaces)
    What is the scientific term for this phobia? (claustrophobia)
    What does he avoid? (tight spaces; even going so far as to keep from covering his face and mouth when in bed)
    What does he love? (open spaces)
    What is San's phobia? (She is afraid of water and of drowning.)
    Why does she get nervous when she is flying? (Because if a plane were to crash when flying over water, she could drown.)
    What is Christiane afraid of? (heights, falling from high places)
    What does she do to deal with her fear? (She makes sure to have things to hold onto and tries not to go to high places.)
    Why does Ian avoid touching doorknobs? (for health reasons)
    Why does he avoid walking under ladders? (Because he is superstitious.)

EXTENSION

Oral work

- Discussion. On the board, write the interview question: *Do you have any unreasonable fears, phobias, or superstitions?* (See Language Notes.) Have students discuss the interviewees' answers. Then ask:
    Which people talk about fears and phobias? (Dan, San, and Christiane)
    Which people talk about superstitions? (Deepti and Ian)
    Who has similar fears, phobias, or superstitions to those mentioned in the interviews?
    How do you deal with them?
- Replay Dan's comments on his claustrophobia. Ask *What does Dan do to avoid feeling claustrophobic?* (He tries to be in large open spaces.) Have students brainstorm different phobias and discuss what people with these phobias might do to avoid them. For example, a person who has a fear of water prefers to be on land and might prefer to travel by car rather than by boat. Or a person who is afraid of the dark might avoid the dark and sleep with the lights on. Write student ideas on the board. Then invite students to respond to the following question: *Do you think it is OK to simply avoid one's fear, or should a person face a fear and try to overcome it?*

Written work

- Have students choose one of the following interviewees: Dan, San, or Christiane. Tell them to pretend they are that person and write a letter to a friend asking for advice on how to deal with their phobia. Encourage students to use the information from the interview as well as their own details in the letter. Then have students swap letters and write letters in response.
- Have students write a paragraph describing a fear, phobia, or superstition that they have. They should include its origins, if possible, and what they do to deal with it.

LANGUAGE NOTES: A *phobia* is a strong, usually unreasonable, fear of something.

A *superstition* is a belief that some objects or actions are lucky and some are unlucky.

When Dan says not being able to move really *freaks him out*, he means that it makes him very uncomfortable.

It's not my thing means It's not something I like to do or that I do well.

OOPS! Deepti says *I don't know to call it phobia or superstition . . .* She means to say *I don't know whether to call it a phobia or a superstition.*

VIDEO SCRIPT

Interviewer: Do you have any unreasonable fears, phobias, or superstitions?

Deepti: Yes, I do have this, I don't know to call it phobia or superstition, but it's with socks. My left sock has to go on my left foot and my right sock has to go on my right foot. I fear that if it gets switched, that my day would go wrong and I would step into a huge mess or something horrible will happen. I learned these things when I was a kid, and there is no reason . . . I mean, really rationally, there is no reason to believe in this, but I do because . . . I don't know why.

Dan: I have a fear of closed spaces, claustrophobia. I can't, I don't really know how to surpass it. I have . . . I can't even have the blanket or the sheet covering my mouth or nose when I'm in bed. The idea, the sheer idea of being in a very, very tight space and not being able to move, really freaks me out, even when I'm not in that kind of situation. And conversely, I really have a love of large open spaces. I like to be in very large open spaces to sort of counteract all of that.

San: I can't think of any off . . . oh, I do have a fear. I have a fear of water. Even though I can swim, my biggest fear is drowning. I don't know why, I just, you know, I'm always . . . that's why I think why I kind of get nervous when I fly, 'cause we're gonna go into the water if we crash, so my biggest fear is drowning. I don't go too far into the ocean, basically.

Christiane: I am afraid of falling—falling from higher places, from windows, or even from diving boards in the swimming pool. I am not very good with heights. Jumping off or falling down somewhere is a big fear of mine. So I try to always have something to hold onto or places where I don't have to go very much downhill, things like that. I don't like that, going down. It's not my thing.

Ian: I really don't have . . . you know, I'm not really too superstitious. I may be conscious not really to touch a lot of doorknobs, but that's, that's more of a health thing than anything else. I'm not really superstitious. I don't walk under ladders. That's something I'm conscious of. I don't walk under a ladder.

Interviewer: So is that for safety or just 'cause it's . . .

Ian: No. I'd say that's a superstition. I don't want to walk under a ladder. They always say don't walk under a ladder; it's bad luck. So I don't want bad luck.

ANSWER KEY

A. 1. b 2. a 3. c 4. e 5. d
B. 1. b 2. a 3. b 4. c 5. a 6. c
C. *Individual responses should include variations on the following:*
   1. To deal with her fear of heights, Christiane tries to always have something to hold onto. She avoids high places. 2. To deal with her fear of drowning, San doesn't go too far into the ocean. 3. To deal with his claustrophobia, Dan doesn't have a blanket or a sheet covering his mouth or nose when he's in bed; he also avoids tight spaces whenever he can and tries to be in large, open spaces.
D. *Answers will vary.*

UNIT 8
Performing At Your Best

On-the-Street Interviews:
I'm really good at multi-tasking...

PREVIEW

- Call on individual students to name strengths that they have. Write these on the board. Note if any students have similar strengths. Then ask individual students to name their weaknesses and write these on the board. Ask *What can you do to overcome your weakness?*

VIEW

Ask students to focus on a different topic each time they view. Some ideas:

- Write on the board: *Strengths.* Ask students to listen for the strengths the interviewees mention.
- Write on the board: *Weaknesses.* Ask students to listen for the weaknesses the interviewees mention.

If you decide to use the optional Activity Worksheet, ask students to read each activity before viewing.

REVIEW

- Ask comprehension questions. Play the video segment again if necessary.
   What are some of Emma's strengths? (She is very helpful; she works well under pressure; she's good at multi-tasking and getting things done; she deals well with people; she doesn't let her emotions get in the way of her work; and she is good with children.)
   What is Emma's weakness? (She is sometimes bad at listening.)
   What are James's strengths and weaknesses? (His strengths include patience and attention to detail; his weaknesses are that he is sometimes a bit too slow and painstaking.)
   What skills and abilities does Martin have? (He is an amateur photographer.)
   Does he consider himself a good photographer? (He says he is working on it.)
   What does it take to be an excellent photographer? (You have to really work at it; in addition to developing technique, you have to have a vision.)
   How can a person learn to be a good photographer? (by taking a lot of pictures, going to a lot of exhibits, looking at other photographers' work to get inspired)
   What are Angelique's strengths? (singing, dancing, and acting)

How did she become interested in the arts? (She grew up singing in a church, at school, and in competition; she grew up with art around her.)
What weaknesses does Angelique have? (She's bad at math, cleaning, taking care of her roommate's dog, and keeping in contact with people.)

EXTENSION

Oral work

- Discussion. Replay Emma's description of her strengths and weakness. Ask students:
    Do you think that Emma has a way with people?
    Do you think her difficulty listening to others could negatively affect her relationships with people? How?
    Based on Emma's response, what type of job do you think she has?
    What other kinds of jobs do you think she would be good at? Explain your answer.

- Pair work: role play. Have pairs role-play the conversation between the interviewer and Martin. Tell students to try to include all the information they discussed. Then have students take turns interviewing each other about a strength or ability they have. Tell them they can use the interviewer's questions below and/or make up their own.
    I want to ask you about some skills or abilities you might have. I hear you _____. Is that true?
    Are you good at it?
    Is it hard?
    So, how do you learn to _____?

Written work

- Have students write a paragraph describing the strengths and weaknesses of themselves or someone they know. They should provide examples.
- Have students imagine they are Emma's supervisor at work. The supervisor is concerned that Emma has difficulty listening to other people during meetings. Tell students to write an e-mail to Emma pointing out this weakness and offering her suggestions on how to overcome it. Tell students to use information from the interview to help them. Encourage them to keep the tone of the e-mail friendly and helpful.

LANGUAGE NOTES: *Multi-tasking* means doing many different things at one time.

To *get fired up* means to get passionate about something.

Painstaking means very careful and meticulous.

OOPS! Angelique says . . . *so I'm a singer and dance and theater* . . . She means to say that she is a singer, a dancer, and an actress.

James says *Weaknesses might be sometimes a little bit too slow and painstaking.* He means to say <u>My</u> weaknesses might be <u>that I am</u> sometimes a little bit too slow and painstaking.

Martin says . . . *if you want to be very good and excellent photographer* . . . He means to say . . . *if you want to be <u>a</u> very good and excellent photographer* . . .

VIDEO SCRIPT

Interviewer: Tell us a little bit about some of your strengths, your talents, your abilities.

Emma: I'm very helpful. I believe I work really well under pressure. Sometimes when I'm working, the phones are ringing and somebody wants a copy of this, so I'm really good at multi-tasking and getting things done, and just handling people and the way they speak to me. And sometimes it's not nice, but you know, you take it, and I think I'm good at holding back how I feel so that I can get the job done. What else am I good at? I'm good at taking care of people's kids. Like children, I love being around children and they love being around me. And I enjoy doing that.

Emma: What am I bad at? I'm bad at listening sometimes. That's not really good, but I tend to go on and the person that's talking with me sometimes, and I'm just not paying attention. And it's because sometimes I get so fired up, and I have a point, and I just, I just look right past what they're saying, and that's not a good thing. I like to . . . like, let's say, we're having a conversation, sometimes I'll just cut them off. That's not good.

James: Probably patience and attention to detail are my strengths. Weaknesses might be sometimes a little bit too slow and painstaking.

Interviewer: You know, I want to ask you about some skills or abilities you might have. I hear you're a photographer. Is that true?

Martin: Yes, I'm an amateur photographer.

Interviewer: And are you good at it?

Martin: I'm working on it.

Interviewer: Is it hard?

Martin: Depends. You can get to a certain level, but if you want to be very good and excellent photographer, then you really need to work on it. It's not just, you know, techniques. You also need to have a vision, also.

Interviewer: So how do you learn to be a good photographer?

Martin: I think you have to take a lot of pictures, and you have to go to a lot of exhibits, look at other photographers' work. That might inspire you, and I think that's actually very important.

Angelique: Well, I grew up singing in the church and at school and in competition so I'm a singer and dance and theater and all those things and art as well. But . . . yeah, probably just those. Probably just the whole artistic thing. I mean, my mother's an artist so it's kind of always been around me.

I am bad at math. I'm bad at cleaning. I'm bad at tons of things. I'm bad at taking care of my roommate's dog, very bad at that. I'm bad at keeping in contact with people I should keep in contact with, but it's just, I mean, just silly things like that.

ANSWER KEY

A. 1. Angelique 2. Emma 3. James 4. Emma
5. Martin 6. Angelique 7. James 8. Angelique

B. *Individual responses should include variations on the following:*
Strengths: Emma is very helpful. She works well under pressure and is good at multi-tasking and getting things done. She deals well with people and doesn't let her emotions get in the way of her work. She is very good with children.
Weaknesses: Emma is sometimes bad at listening. She often doesn't pay attention to what another person is saying to her, and she cuts people off in conversation.

C. *Individual responses should include variations on the following:*
Martin explains that to be a good photographer you have to really work at it. Not only do you have to learn techniques, but you also have to have a vision. He says that you learn to be a good photographer by taking a lot of pictures, attending exhibits, and looking at other photographers' work for inspiration.

D. *Answers will vary.*

UNIT 9
What Lies Ahead?

TV Documentary:
Mirror Technology

PREVIEW

- Then poll the class *Do you spend a lot of time clothes shopping in stores?*
- Then ask students *How do you think mirrors in dressing rooms could be improved to enhance the shopping experience?* Write student ideas on the board. Then write *mirror technology* on the board, and tell students they will learn about an interesting new mirror.

VIEW

Ask students to focus on a different topic each time they view. Some ideas:

- Ask students to listen for the reason it's called the memory mirror.
- Ask students to listen for functions of the mirror.
- Ask students to listen for the shopper's reaction to the new technology.
- Ask students to listen for other innovations being created for shoppers.

If you decide to use the optional Activity Worksheet, ask students to read each activity before viewing.

REVIEW

Ask comprehension questions. Play the video segment again if necessary.

What is the segment about? (a high-tech dressing room mirror)
How do you start recording what you see in the mirror? (by looking into your own eyes)
What does Ben Tracey mean when he says this is not your mama's mirror? (This isn't just some regular old-fashioned mirror.)
What is the mirror actually? (a giant video screen and camera)
What functions did it offer the shopper? (She got to see her outfit from 360 degrees and compare clothing options side-by-side; It remembered what she tried on.)
Why is it called the memory mirror? (because it remembers what you tried on)
What is the shopper's reaction to the memory mirror? (She loves it. She wants one for her room.)
According to Tracey, what is the drawback of a regular mirror when you are shopping? (If you try on a lot of stuff, you might forget what you put on in the first place.)
How does the memory mirror incorporate other people into the shopping experience? (It lets you email people pictures and get their opinions.)
What other innovations are being created for shoppers? (interactive tablets that work like a giant iPad; 3D scans of brides that can be printed in an actual dress; full color figurines; printing dresses as flower vases; ceramic figurines as brides)
What important question does the mirror eliminate for shoppers? (if the woman's butt looks big)

EXTENSION

Oral work

- Discussion. Tell students they will be preparing advertisements for the memory mirror. First tell students to write down all the unusual facts about the mirror. Then have them prepare a commercial to present to the class. If students need help recalling the facts, have them view the segment once more time to listen for functions of the mirror (e.g., look into your own eyes to start recording; do a 360, compare clothing side-by-side, etc.). Hint to students to listen for why it's called a memory mirror.

- Discussion. On the board, write *drawback*. Ask *What might be some drawbacks to the mirror?* (Possible answers: too expensive to have in stores; too honest, people might not like what they see from every detailed angle and therefore not buy a product; people might delay buying a product, as they send pictures and wait for feedback from friends) Poll the class *Do you think mirrors like these will become the norm? Would you want one of these mirrors in your house?*

Written work

- Tell students they will imagine they are the young woman who enthusiastically used the mirror for the first time at Neiman Marcus. She is so excited by it that she decides to send several pictures from her shopping experience to a bunch of girlfriends, describing how the mirror works and how great the experience was. Tell them to include details about how it remembers everything you try on, let's you see yourself from many angles, pulls up images side-by-side, etc.
- Divide the class into pairs. Tell students they will write up a survey to gather feedback on the memory mirror. Tell them to include eight questions in the survey, starting with where they first used the mirror. Have pairs swap surveys and write answers, deciding in pairs if they want to give positive or negative feedback about it. If members of a pair have differing views, they can answer questions on the survey individually.

LANGUAGE NOTES: *Strike a pose* means to stand or sit in a specific position.

To blow one's mind means to make you feel surprised and/or excited about something.

To do a 360 means to turn around completely.

A bevy is a large group of people of the same kind—for example women or girls…

To beam in means to emit or transmit a message.

CULTURE NOTES: The two questions *How does my butt look?* and *Does this make my butt look big?* refers to typical questions women or girls make when trying on clothes.

When Ben Tracey says *Any good man doesn't need a mirror on the wall to tell him the answer to that question is always no*, by "mirror on the wall" he refers to the story of Snow White where a magic mirror responded to the Evil Queen's question as to who is the most beautiful. By saying that the answer is always no, he is referring to the question women often ask *Does this make my butt look big?* He is joking that the correct answer to this question is always no, so as not to insult a woman.

VIDEO SCRIPT
Gayle King: Strike a pose in your dressing room mirror. Your next trip to the mall could really blow your mind. First on CBS This Morning, Ben Tracy reveals the technology behind a high-tech mirror that could transform your shopping experience.
Employee: And look into your own eyes to start recording…
Ben Tracy: This is not your mama's mirror.
Employee: So you can do a 360… Check how you look in the back…
Ben Tracy: It's actually a giant video screen and camera. The shopper we asked to try it out got to see her outfit from 360 degrees and compare clothing options side by side. It also remembers what you've already tried on. That's why it's called the memory mirror.
Ben Tracy: So you tried out the memory mirror. What'd ya think?
Shopper: I think I need one of those in my room. That's what I think. I loved the memory mirror.
Ben Tracy: Get dressed every morning with that.
Shopper: Yes.
Karen Katz: Technology has changed everything in terms of the shopping experience.
Ben Tracy: Karen Katz is president and CEO of Neiman Marcus. 80% of its customers are women, which is why the company is embracing the future by testing these very modern mirrors in their San Francisco stores.
Ben Tracy: Somebody could come in and have to try on five outfits. They get to the fifth outfit and then they say, "I forget what the first outfit looked like." Is that, kind of, you're short circuiting that process?
Karen Katz: Yeah, exactly. To save the, you know, the customer that time of having to retry on outfits and equally important is that ability to share the outfits with friends and family. I think that that social part of it is as important as the editing part of it.
Employee: Start your personal try on…
Ben Tracy: The mirror records an eight-second video. It's password protected and can be emailed, allowing you to instantly share and solve any shopping situation with the help of your friends and family.

Ben Tracy: So basically you can still go shopping with your friends even if your friends don't have time to go shopping.

Karen Katz: Exactly. And for those really important decisions in women's lives—buying a mother of the bride dress or an outfit for a special event—she can have her entire, you know, bevy of girlfriends right around her even if they're not there physically.

Ben Tracy: The mirror was created in Neiman's top secret innovation lab in Dallas. Our cameras are the first to be allowed in. This is where the company is experimenting with the future of retail.

Man in the lab: You can get a 360 view of by simply dragging this icon to rotate the product.

Neiman Marcus representative: We are constantly looking for new innovations that would appeal to our customers and really make the store come to life in a different way.

Ben Tracy: It's blending the virtual world with the real one. From displays that are activated when a customer picks up a product to interactive tables that work like a giant iPad.

Scott Emmons: We 3-D scanned a bride, and we printed her in the actual dress.

Ben Tracy: Scott Emmons, who runs the innovation lab, beamed in remotely to explain a project for the bridal salon.

Scott Emmons: We did some full-color figurines that Michael's holding now. We printed the dress as a flower vase.

Ben Tracy: They created ceramic figurines of actual brides. But back in the store, the memory mirror is solving one of shopping's most important questions.

Ben Tracy: So this allows you to cut out the question of, "How does my butt look?" Is that what we're talking about?

Karen Katz: You asked it. I won't answer that.

Ben Tracy: However, this shopper did not have to be asked. What's the best part of this for you?

Shopper: The best part is being able to see the full 360, you know, like every girl really does want to know, "Does this make my butt look big?" So…

Ben Tracy: Any good man doesn't need a mirror on the wall to tell him the answer to that question is always no. For CBS This Morning, Ben Tracy, San Francisco.

ANSWER KEY
A. shows how the outfit looks from all angles; shows how the outfit looks in different colors; allows you to compare two outfits side by side; allows you to send a video recording of the outfit to friends
B. 1. c 2. b 3. d 4. a
C. 1. printed 2. innovation 3. project 4. flower vase 5. brides
D. *Possible answer*
Not your mama's mirror means that this is something new and different not the same ordinary mirror.

UNIT 10
An Interconnected World

TV Documentary:
Sonic Booms Bright Future

PREVIEW
• Ask students *What positive predictions can you make about the future?* Write students' ideas on the board. If students need direction, suggest they can make predictions about education, wars, or jobs.

VIEW
Ask students to focus on a different topic each time they view. Some ideas:
• Ask students to listen for Gregg Easterbrook's predictions for women.
• Ask students to listen for Gregg Easterbrook's thoughts on war.
• Ask students to listen for Gregg Easterbrook's ideas on manufacturing.
• Ask students to listen for Gregg Easterbrook's comments on white-collar professions.

If you decide to use the optional Activity Worksheet, ask students to read each activity before viewing.

REVIEW
Ask comprehension questions. Play the video segment again if necessary.
  What does Gregg Easterbrook predict for the developing world? (an increase in prosperity)
  What does Diane Sawyer mean when she says the new ideas made the sun shine for one brief second in her afternoon? (The ideas made her happy.)
  Why does Gregg Easterbrook think there will be double the ideas in the world? (because women will be participating in full force, and they haven't been)

In what areas will women be contributing full force? (science, engineering, business management, administration of governments)
What statement does Gregg Easterbrook make about people dying in battle? (in the last 20 years it is the lowest in human history)
What countries are exceptions to the rule? (Iraq, Afghanistan, and Sudan)
What are nations competing for these days? (market share)
According to Gregg Easterbrook, which is better—competition for market share or competition for territory? (competition for market share)
What statement does Gregg Easterbrook make about manufacturing? (manufacturing is up, but jobs in manufacturing are down)
What is the reason for this? (manufacturing is more efficient)
What does this shift in manufacturing compare to 100 years ago? (agriculture—fewer people work in manufacturing today than 100 years ago)
What statistics does he give? (100 years ago 70% of Americans worked in agriculture, today 2% do)
What jobs today are replacing manufacturing jobs? (white-collar jobs)
According to Gregg Easterbrook, what would our grandparents think about white-collar jobs? (they would think they are great)
What drawbacks of white-collar jobs does Easterbrook mention? (stressful relationships with bosses)

EXTENSION
Oral work
- Discussion. Invite students to respond to Gregg Easterbrook's thoughts on manufacturing. On the board, write:
    What do you think of his comparison of manufacturing jobs disappearing to what happened in agriculture 100 years ago?
    How do you predict white-collar jobs will change or evolve as more people will be available to do them?

- Pair work. Tell students to make their own positive prediction for a bright future. In pairs, have them discuss topics like technology, education, and the environment. Have them make one hopeful prediction, providing as much detail as they can. Then invite pairs to present their prediction to the class.

Written work
Write the following statement from Gregg Easterbrook on the board: *Nations are now competing for market share more than they're competing for territory. And there's lots of things wrong with that...but it's so much better than military competition.* Ask students to respond to this statement in writing. Encourage students to indicate what he means when he says that there's lots of things wrong with that.

- Write ... *one to two generations down the road twice as many people in the world will be contributing to the global supply of ideas and I think that they will lead to a flowering of more progress.* Ask students to say if they agree that progress at such a rapid pace is a good thing.

LANGUAGE NOTES: *Sonic boom* is the explosive sound made by something traveling faster than the speed of sound.

An exception to the rule is when a rule does not apply in a special case or circumstance.

Market share is the percentage of sales in a market that a company or product has.

To have a banana peel in the economy means that a problem exists in an economy that could cause major problems at any time and unexpectedly.

VIDEO SCRIPT
Diane Sawyer: Sonic Boom. What's the boom you hear? What's the sound you hear?
Gregg Easterbrook: The last two years I've worked on this book, predicting a major global economic boom, my wife thought I was crazy, my editor thought I was crazy, I hope I'm not crazy. Obviously there are many problems in the world economically, but I think a global increase of prosperity is about to happen. I think the developing world especially which needs it the most is going to become much better off in the near future.
Diane Sawyer: I couldn't get over the fact that you were bringing us these new ideas that actually made the sun shine for one brief second in my afternoon.
Diane Sawyer: You said that there's no question that there will be double the ideas in the world because women will be participating in full force.
Gregg Easterbrook: As recently as the last generation most of the world's women have very little ability to participate in science, engineering, business management, the administration of governments. That hasn't changed everywhere now, but it is in the process of changing. So this means one to two generations down the road twice as many people in the world will be contributing to the global supply of ideas, and I think that will lead to a flowering of more progress.
Diane Sawyer: You also had a sentence which really struck me: "Fewer people are dying in battle than any time in the history of the planet."
Gregg Easterbrook: Your chance of dying in battle in the last 20 years has been the lowest in human history. Iraq and Afghanistan and the Sudan are terrible exceptions to an overall rule of less combat, fewer deaths from combat, less global military spending. It's been going down

for 20 years. The end of the Cold War is one factor, but I think economic interconnectedness is another factor. Nations are now competing for market share more than they're competing for territory. And there's lots of things wrong with that. I mean obviously our relationship with the Chinese drives us crazy. But it's so much better than military competition that there's just no comparison.

Diane Sawyer: You say that the manufacturing drought, the manufacturing collapse that is hitting America is also hitting China and that we don't take that into account. That they've got a banana peel in their economy too?

Gregg Easterbrook: Well you see, it's not manufacturing. Manufacturing's up everywhere. It's jobs in manufacturing that are down.

Diane Sawyer: Ah ha.

Gregg Easterbrook: And I think this would have happened regardless of the financial panic of recent years. United States has lost 6 million manufacturing jobs in the last decade. In the same period China's lost 28 million because of more efficient forms of manufacturing. More efficient forms of manufacturing are good news for most people: they keep prices down, improve products. They're real bad news if you're a factory worker. So we see this transition away from lots of jobs in factories. It would have happened regardless. The same thing happened in agriculture 100 years ago. 100 years ago 70% of Americans worked in agriculture. Today it's 2%. If you'd told somebody 100 years ago that in the year 2010 2% of Americans would work in agriculture, they would have said, "Oh my god, it's going to be the end of the world."

Diane Sawyer: If those manufacturing jobs are shrinking, where do the jobs surface? What's the new…?

Gregg Easterbrook: 60% of Americans now work in white-collar professions. White-collar professions are far from ideal. Many of them are very stressful. Some people don't like to be in cubicles, like the people behind you at ABC News. Well, maybe, maybe they like it.

Diane Sawyer: They love it.

Gregg Easterbrook: They love it. OK, they're very happy. If you'd told your great-grandparents, look most of your great-grandchildren are going to work in air-conditioned offices, they will not do anything back breaking or physically dangerous, they will have stressful relationships with their bosses, but they're not going to be working in mines or cutting down trees, your great-grandparents would have said, "That's great."

Diane Sawyer: Gregg Easterbrook, thank you so much. Good to talk to you.

Gregg Easterbrook: Thank you, Diane.

ANSWER KEY
A. less military spending; fewer people dying in battle; women will be more involved
B. 1. Iraq 2. Afghanistan 3. Sudan
C. 1. False 2. True 3. True 4. False
D. 1. six 2. twenty-eight 3. seventy 4. two
E. *Possible answers*
   1. More women will be working in technical fields and in business so that twice as many people will be able to contribute to the global supply of ideas. 2. Manufacturing is more efficient and it takes fewer people to produce the same number of goods.

Conversation Activator Video Script

Unit 1, Lesson 2

F1: So, have you decided on a graduate program yet?
F2: Actually I have. I've decided on a career in psychology.
F1: How terrific!
F2: I agree. It's very exciting.
F1: Correct me if I'm wrong, but haven't you been volunteering at the community center after your classes lately?
F2: Yes, I have. I've been helping the social worker there. And I think that's what got me interested in psychology. Originally, I thought I'd take up law.
F1: So, have you applied to any graduate schools yet?
F2: Not yet. I was hoping you could steer me in the right direction.
F1: Well, I know a little about your background, but tell me something about your interests. Is there a particular specialty you'd like to take up in psychology?
F2: Yes, there is. I love working with children. I think I'd like to be a child psychologist.
F1: Well, in that case, I'd suggest Simpson University. They have a wonderful child psychology program.
F2: That sounds like good advice.
F1: You'll make a great psychologist. I'd be happy to write you a recommendation.
F2: Thanks so much. I really appreciate your support.

Unit 2, Lesson 2

M: I'm sorry, but I have some bad news. I really messed up. You know that flash drive you lent me yesterday? I'm afraid I lost it.
F: Oh, no. How did that happen?
M: Well, I'm not sure. I know I used it yesterday in the computer lab, and I was pretty certain I put it in my backpack. But this morning I couldn't find it.
F: Are you sure you didn't leave it in the computer?
M: Well, I went back to the lab and checked, but it wasn't there. I really should have been more careful.
F: It's not a big deal. They're not that expensive. And I don't think there was anything on there that I can't replace.
M: Well, I'm going to get you a new one, if that's OK. I feel terrible.
F: That's really not necessary.
M: No, I insist. And please accept my apology.
F: Look, I appreciate your taking responsibility—which is very nice—but it's really OK. You don't need to get carried away.
M: Well, I'll go to the office and check if anyone found it and brought it there.
F: That's a good idea.
M: And let me at least buy you lunch. OK?
F: If you insist.
M: I do! 12:30 at the front entrance?
F: OK. I'll see you there. And please don't worry about losing the flash drive. It's fine.

Unit 3, Lesson 1

F: Is something wrong? You look upset.
M: Well, it's nothing serious, but I've been having a bit of trouble with something lately.
F: Oh, I'm sorry. Would it help to talk about it?

M: Maybe. Here goes: Basically, no matter how much exercise I get, I can't gain any weight.

F: That must be disappointing. How much weight do you want to gain?

M: I'm not sure. Maybe a couple of kilos.

F: But you don't look skinny to me. Are you sure you want to gain weight?

M: Well, I think I'd feel better if I did. I think I'd have a lot more energy. I feel tired all the time now.

F: Have you thought of going to one of those diet doctors? Sometimes they can help.

M: Hmm. That's not a bad idea. I think I will see a doctor. Thanks!

F: Anytime. And my advice is: Don't freak out about a few kilos. It's not the end of the world to be a little underweight.

M: That's true, but in addition to having more energy, I WOULD like to look a little better in my clothes. In any case, thanks for listening. Wish me luck!

F: OK. I'll keep my fingers crossed for you! Just hang in there, OK?

M: I'll try.

Unit 4, Lesson 2

M1: Luke, there's something I need to bring up.

M2: Really? What's wrong?

M1: Well, yesterday during lunch, when you asked me to pay back the money you lent me you really made a big issue out of it.

M2: I did?

M1: Yeah. What bothered me was that it felt like you were telling me off in front of everyone else at the table. It was kind of embarrassing.

M2: I'm so sorry. I didn't realize that! I really didn't mean to be rude!

M1: Well, it's not a huge deal. But it's been kind of bugging me, so I thought I should say something.

M2: Well, I totally see your point. It's no excuse, but the truth is I had had an argument with my brother that morning and I guess I was just taking it out on you. Otherwise I would never have lost my cool like that. I'm really sorry.

M1: Well, I hope you don't mind my bringing it up. I don't want you to feel like you have to walk on eggshells around me.

M2: On the contrary. I appreciate your pointing it out. I just hope we can pick up the pieces.

M1: Of course. And thanks for listening and taking it so well.

Unit 5, Lesson 2

F: Hey, you've got to see this! I just can't tell you how hysterical it is.

M: What is it?

F: Here. Look at this cartoon. Isn't it hilarious? Seriously, what do you think?

M: Oh, that's too much. Look at the passengers just sitting there not saying anything. They're not even surprised that the airline would charge them money for oxygen! What magazine is this anyway?

F: Chicago Week.

M: This week's issue?

F: Yup.

M: Great! We have that at home. I can't wait to show it to my wife. By the way, have you seen this funny video clip of the cat flushing the toilet?

F: Let me see. That's priceless. You know, I saw another one of a cat that cracked me up.

M: What was it doing?

F: Actually it was a commercial for energy conservation. Someone had trained a cat to jump up on the wall and hit the light switch to turn off the lights. Can you believe that?

M: That's funny. And I didn't realize you could train cats to *do* things.
F: Neither did I! I could just watch that clip over and over. I guess I find it funny when animals do things you expect *people* to do.
M: Totally.

Unit 6, Lesson 2

F: Excuse me. I wonder if you could do me a favor.
M: I'd be happy to. How can I help?
F: This bag is so heavy and I can't lift it. Do you think you could help me put it in the overhead rack? I had shoulder surgery a couple of weeks ago.
M: No problem.
F: Thanks so much. If it hadn't been for you, I don't know what I would have done. It's terrible, but other people saw me struggling and no one offered to help. It's a good thing you were here.
F: By the way, I'm Lisa Barton.
M: And I'm Dan Sims. Nice to meet you.
F: It's a beautiful day for flying, isn't it?
M: It really is. Where are you from?
F: Actually, I live in Miami now, but I've been up here in New York for a few days.
M: On business? Or was this a pleasure trip?
F: A little bit of both. My parents live here, so I figured I could mix a little business and pleasure. What about you?
M: I live here. I'm on my way to spend a few days in Miami. My girlfriend lives there. How long have *you* been living there?
F: Not very long. My company moved its main office from New York and they offered to move me, so I accepted. I actually like it a lot. I hate the cold winters in New York.
M: You can say that again.
F: Well, thanks again.
M: Anytime.

Unit 7, Lesson 1

M1: Can you believe this?
M2: What?
M1: This book. Look at the title! *Rich Quick* Turn garden dirt into genuine diamonds in just one month.
M2: Oh, come on! You don't buy that, do you?
M1: Absolutely not. But I'll bet lots of people *do*.
M2: You think so? Who'd fall for that? It's just too crazy.
M1: You and I know that, but lots of people are gullible. They believe what they want to be true.
M2: You're right, I guess. It's just wishful thinking. Everybody wants to get rich quick. And, I suppose one of the things they like is that all they have to do is get some soil from their garden.
M1: Right? It's free.
M2: But you'll have to buy the book. And you'll definitely have to buy the 4D printer.
M1: True.
M2: But, you know. That's not the worst scam I've ever seen. Yesterday, my wife showed me a flyer that came in the mail. It said that if you invested $5,000 in this gold mine in Kazakhstan, you would earn $25,000 in six weeks. They say gold has just been discovered there.
M1: That's got to be a total scam.
M2: You can say that again.

Unit 8, Lesson 1

F: Guess what?
M: I'm all ears.
F: I've decided to sign up for some university classes.

CONVERSATION ACTIVATOR VIDEO SCRIPT 207

M: Hey, that's great!
F: I figure it's now or never.
M: What are you going to be studying?
F: I'm not sure yet. I can't make up my mind between business administration and marketing.
M: Which subject do you think you have the most talent for?
F: Well, I do have lots of experience in business finance.
M: So business administration would be a good fit.
F: On the other hand, I wouldn't say I'm particularly creative, but I've been told that I do have a way with people. My gut feeling is that could be helpful in marketing.
M: I think you're right. But to tell you the truth, I don't think you can go wrong. Either choice sounds really good. Besides, you could always switch subjects down the road if you want.
F: Good point. If only I could make up my mind.
M: You know, my sister is working in marketing right now. She's really good at what she does, and I'm sure she'd be happy to talk with you if you want. Would you like her number?
F: Are you sure she wouldn't mind my calling her out of the blue?
M: Not at all. Besides, I'll talk to her first.
F: Thanks so much. That would be great.
M: And taking classes is a great idea.
F: I'm just hoping to be able to do something I really love.
M: Well, I wish you luck!

Unit 9, Lesson 2

M: I've been thinking about it and computer chip implants sound like a bad idea to me. For one thing, I'm against putting anything unnatural like that into the human body. But more importantly, it just seems to me like another way to control people.
F: I see your point but, if you ask me I think the good outweighs the bad. Imagine the technology from the point of view of a family that's lost someone they love in a disaster. A computer chip would help identify the victim quickly and efficiently. That's a pretty important benefit, isn't it?
M: Maybe. But it just seems to me that science and technology are going in the wrong direction. And computer chip implants? It's like opening Pandora's box. I mean, who's to say it wouldn't then be used for something bad?
F: But people have always said that about new things.
M: Mark my words. Before you know it, we're all going to be required to get chip implants.
F: Come on. That's never going to happen.
M: Don't be so sure. In my opinion, it isn't a question of if, but when.
F: Wow. That's a pretty pessimistic view. What about a technology like remote surgery? Don't you think that'll be used for good purposes?
M: I guess.
F: There are people who'll be able to get medical care that wouldn't have been available otherwise.
M: That's true.
F: And nanotechnology could lead to all kinds of important inventions that could change people's lives for the better.
M: Probably.
F: Medical treatments will be improved and lives will be saved.

They're already talking about using nanotechnology to fight cancer. And I'll bet that what they're planning is just scratching the surface.

M: Those are all good points. But I guess what I worry about is that all these technologies can have unintended consequences.

F: Maybe so. But I guess I'm more optimistic than you about the future. I think people's lives will be improved with these technologies. In my view, the good far outweighs the bad.

Unit 10, Lesson 1

F: Can you believe all these recent terrorist attacks?

M: You mean what happened in Beirut?

F: Yeah. It's really shocking, isn't it?

M: Terrible. I feel sorry for the victims and their families.

F: It's bad enough that people get hurt, but they say that tourism's really going to be affected. And if tourism's affected, the economic impact will be huge.

M: Well, that's another story . . . But anyway, it makes you feel kind of helpless, doesn't it?

F: Totally. Don't get me wrong, but . . . you'd think in this day and age people would be able to solve their problems without killing each other.

M: Well, my gut feeling is it's a losing battle.

F: I think you're right.

M: But on the bright side, have you heard about that businesswoman in Colombia?

F: No. What's that about?

M: Well, her husband was killed years ago in a bombing, and today she helps raise money to help other bombing victims pay their medical costs. It makes you stop and think, doesn't it? If only more people were like her.

M: How do you like that? She sounds like a very special person. It just goes to show you how people can do good things if they put their minds to it.

M: I have to say though, what I find interesting about the Colombian woman is this: When some people are at their worst, someone like her does something really good.

F: That's really true.

Discussion Activator Video Script

Unit 1, Lesson 1

M1: So tell me something about yourself. Let's start with where you were born, OK?

M2: I was born right here. I grew up here and have never lived anywhere else.

M1: Really? Have you ever thought about moving away?

M2: Actually, I thought about it several years ago, but I decided to finish my studies before leaving.

M1: So, have you always lived at the same address?

M2: No. I lived with my parents until I got married and then my wife moved in with us. About a year later my father got a job closer to the center of town so my parents moved out. The apartment was way too big for just us, so we got our *own* place. That's where we're living now.

M1: How long have you been married?

M2: Let me think ... oh, three and a half years.

M1: And do you have children?

M2: Not yet. We had been thinking of starting a family right away after we got married, but then my wife decided to go back to school so we've postponed that for a few years. But we definitely plan to have children when she completes her degree.

M1: What's she studying?

M2: Architecture.

M1: Architecture! That's terrific. And what about you? Do you have a career?

M2: Yes, I do. I'm a graphic designer for a hotel chain.

M1: How long have you been doing graphic design?

M2: Well, to tell you the truth, I've been doing it all my life. When I was a student, I liked to design my essays as if they were real magazine articles. Later, when I was working as a restaurant manager, I began designing menus and advertisements freelance at night to make a little extra money. All of a sudden I realized I could make a career out of it. So I enrolled in a graphic design course and got my certificate about four years ago.

M1: That's great. So all in all you're doing what you've always liked to do.

M2: Totally ... So what about you? Where were *you* born?

Unit 2, Lesson 1

F: So what are some situations in which you think we shouldn't tell lies?

M: Well, I think if you tell a lie to shift the blame to someone else, or to avoid taking responsibility for your own actions—then I think it's just dishonest.

F: Can you give me a specific example?

M: OK. This is a little personal, but as long as we're being truthful here ... when I was about ten years old, I accidently broke one of my mom's plates. She was really upset and she asked me if I knew how it happened. So I blamed it on our cat.

F: And of course if you had told the truth you would have gotten into trouble with your mom.

M: Right. But I was too scared to tell the truth. It's understandable why a ten-year-old would lie in such a situation, but as an adult I wouldn't want to act like a ten-year-old. I think it's important to admit making a mistake and take responsibility for it.

F: So do you think there are situations in which telling a lie is the best solution?

M: The *best* solution? Let me think . . . well, actually there are times when you just *can't* tell the truth . . . like when my girlfriend asks me if I like her dress, or her hair, or her jewelry. I tell the truth if I do, and I lie if I don't. I can't help it.

F: I suppose that's because you know you'll get into trouble with her if you do tell the truth, right?

M: Totally. Believe me, I don't want to get into trouble with my girlfriend. But more importantly I don't want her to feel bad. Let's just say I'm protecting her feelings. And I don't think there's any harm done.

F: So you lied to your mother as a kid, and now you lie to your girlfriend. Hmm . . .

M: Oh, come on.

F: So is there anyone in your life who you'd never tell a lie to?

M: Not really. I believe you have to tell people white lies. It's just a part of life.

F: I suppose that's true.

M: Hey, what about you? Is there anyone you'd never lie to?

F: Well, my best friend Greta is someone who I'd never tell a lie to. Ever. I wouldn't want to destroy her trust in me—and that's what telling a lie would do to our friendship.

M: Wow, you must be really close friends. And you'd never tell her a white lie to protect her?

F: I don't think so. She knows I'll always give her an honest answer. A few years ago, when Greta and I first became friends, she said . . .

Unit 3, Lesson 2

M: So, when I was in secondary school, I was in the drama club. We were going to put on a play.

F: That sounds like fun. What happened?

M: Well, I was pretty shy, so I liked to work backstage helping the other kids with their makeup and costumes—rather than performing on stage. That was fun for me. But everyone in the club had to learn a part in case one of the actors got sick. So this was the second night of the play and all the parents and teachers were in the audience.

F: OK . . .

M: Well, of course you can guess that the boy who had the leading role got sick and couldn't act, so I had to play his role.

F: No way! So did you totally freak out?

M: Well, my classmates could tell right away that I was going to have a problem. They tried to encourage me, but when the curtain went up, I went on stage and tried to say my lines, but I had totally lost my voice! No matter how hard I tried to say my lines no one could hear me.

F: That's awful! What happened?

M: Well, actually, when I think about it today, it seems pretty funny. One of the other actors thought fast and said: Wow, you must have a terrible cold. Why don't you sit down and I'll get you a glass of water.

F: Wow. That was some quick thinking. What finally happened?

M: Well, everyone kind of laughed, and that gave me the time I needed to calm down. The fear just disappeared and I played the part. I guess it wasn't the end of the world, after all!

F: Well, there was a time I got really scared too. When I was . . .

Unit 4, Lesson 1

F: The guy who says he wishes he weren't so disorganized really reminds me of my sister.

M: How so?

F: Well, her apartment's always a mess, and she can never find the things she needs.

M: Really?

F: Yeah. And when she needs to find something in her purse . . . forget it! Unless she puts something in one of the pockets, it takes her forever to find it.

M: Wow. Maybe she needs a bigger purse.

F: Are you kidding? She needs a *smaller* one. Otherwise she'll just put more in it.

M: Sometimes it helps to make an effort to throw away things you don't really need. But I think for some people it's just hard to do.

F: I've suggested that to her, but— between you and me—she's a little oversensitive. I feel like I have to walk on eggshells around her because, no matter what I suggest, she thinks it's a criticism.

M: I see what you mean. My brother's kind of like that too.

F: The truth is, she'll change her habits only if she's ready to. I can't make her change.

M: True.

F: So what about this woman here? She says she thinks she's a procrastinator.

M: Uh-oh. Sounds like me.

F: You?

M: Yeah. I tend to put things off. Even if there's plenty of time to do something, I'll wait till the last minute before I start.

F: Well, I have to admit I do that too. Sometimes I worry whether it'll cause problems for me professionally.

M: I worry about that too.

F: You know, I've heard there are tons of websites that give advice about overcoming procrastination.

M: I know. I was planning to do a search . . . but I keep putting it off.

F: Are you serious?

M: Just kidding!

F: That's funny! So what about the woman who says she's too negative? . . .

Unit 5, Lesson 1

F: You know, I really believe that laughter can be good medicine.

M: How?

F: Well, it just makes sense to me. I've read that negative emotions like anger and depression can actually make you sick.

M: That's pretty well known. But how does it follow that laughing can make you well?

F: Well, if being sad can make you sick, why wouldn't laughing and happiness make you better?

M: Is there any scientific *proof* of that?

F: I'm not sure it's actually been proven, but scientists have believed for hundreds of years that laughing increases your breathing rate—I guess sort of like exercise does, right? And it uses your muscles, which is also healthy. I mean, sick people usually just sit around or lie in bed and not do much. That can't be good for their health.

M: So you're saying that in a strictly physical sense laughing is good for our health?

F: Well, in any case, it couldn't hurt. And then we read about

Norman Cousins and his personal experience. He was totally sick and he decided to watch hundreds of hours of funny movies and TV.

M: Right. And he had his friends tell him jokes.

F: M-hmm. And he got better. And you know—I believe it was the laughing that cured him.

M: So what would you do if you had a friend or a relative who was sick?

F: Well, if the person were well enough to go out, I would take him or her to see funny movies. If not, there's always a bunch of hysterical stuff on YouTube. I actually stream funny video clips when I'm feeling down. It cheers me up. So I would encourage my sick friend or relative to watch those. It couldn't hurt.

M: True, but have you ever tried to recover from a real physical *illness* by watching funny videos?

F: Actually no. But you can be sure that next time I get a bad flu, I'm going to park myself in front of my tablet and watch tons of funny movies. We'll see what happens!

M: That'll be your research. Should be interesting.

Unit 6, Lesson 2

F: I had a terrible experience on a business trip. I missed my connection, and I had to spend 8 hours in the airport waiting for another connecting flight. It was a pretty nice airport, but what a hassle!

M: Where were you going?

F: To Toronto, and there are only two flights a day: one in the morning and the other one at night. I had to take the night flight so I got to Toronto pretty late.

M: That's too bad. So what happened that made you miss the connection?

F: Well, to tell you the truth, I think my travel agent made a mistake.

M: How?

F: There was only one hour to connect with my Toronto flight, but I was changing airlines and had to check in again.

M: Uh-oh.

F: The travel agent should have realized that there wouldn't have been enough time—especially if my first flight arrived late, which of course it did . . .

M: That's awful.

F: You know, it's my own fault, though. If I had checked the itinerary, I would have noticed the problem right away. And I would have asked the travel agent to book me on an earlier flight.

M: Right.

F: And it turns out there *was* a flight that arrived an hour earlier. If I had taken that one I would have made the connection.

M: Don't blame yourself. It's really the travel agent's responsibility to prevent those problems. But at least you got to Toronto the same day. One time I had almost the same problem, but it was a little more complicated.

F: What do you mean?

M: Well, last month I had to go to Korea from Chicago. Unfortunately the non-stop flight was full so I had to connect in Los Angeles.

F: That's inconvenient. It can make the trip so much longer.

M: You can say that again. But that's actually not the problem I had. My flight to Los Angeles had a weather delay and I arrived there late. *I* made the connection, but my checked bag didn't. So when I arrived in Seoul, no bag.

F: Oh, no. That's really a hassle. What did you do?

M: Well, they told me the bag would be on the next flight, but I was only staying in Seoul for eight hours, and then I was going to Pusan. And the worst thing is I had a quick business meeting in Seoul. I was wearing jeans and a sweatshirt for the flight—totally inappropriate for the meeting.

F: That's pretty bad, but what about the luggage? Did you ever get it?

M: Actually, I did—a day later in Pusan. But I felt really uncomfortable at that meeting in Seoul. In the end, though, everyone understood. And you know, lots of people had a story to tell about a similar thing.

F: Really? But it still must have been embarrassing.

M: You know, I could kick myself. My bag was small enough to carry onto the plane. If I'd been thinking, I would never have checked it.

F: Right.

M: I should have taken it as a carry-on.

F: You've hit the nail on the head there!

M: Totally. If I'd done that, this wouldn't have happened.

F: Yup. Always better safe than sorry. Actually, I just remembered another time when I was flying from . . .

Unit 7, Lesson 2

F1: I believe in the superstition that if you break a mirror you'll have 7 years bad luck.

F2: You do?

F1: Actually, I do. Well, maybe not *7 years* of bad luck. But I do believe it's bad luck to break a mirror.

F2: Why?

F1: Well, in the first place, the mirror's broken and you'll have to buy another one.

F2: True.

F1: And you might cut yourself on the broken glass.

F2: Oh, come on. That's ridiculous.

F1: OK. I'm kidding. But there's something about it that freaks me out—It makes me feel like something bad is going to happen to my face or something.

F2: What gives you that impression?

F1: Well, this is kind of embarrassing, but when I was about 12, I did break a mirror and soon after that I started getting terrible skin problems. I've always thought it had something to do with breaking the mirror.

F2: Really?

F1: Well, on the other hand, maybe the two things weren't connected. After all, 12-year-olds tend to get skin problems, right?

F2: No offense, but no way could the broken mirror be connected to the skin problems. So any other superstitions you or someone you know believes in?

F1: Well, my grandpa believes that the number 13 is unlucky. I mean he *really* believes that. I actually think he's even a little paranoid about it.

F2: What do you mean?

F1: So you know that lots of people won't rent an apartment or a hotel room on the 13th floor, right? Well, he of course wouldn't. But keep in mind that lots of buildings don't even have a 13th floor, so that's not a big problem.

F2: So what *is* the big problem?

F1: Well, my grandpa is so afraid of the number 13 that if he goes to the movies, he looks at the row numbers on the arm of the aisle seats. If it's a 13, he just doesn't sit there.

F2: That is kind of crazy. I mean, what could happen to someone sitting in the 13th row that wouldn't happen to someone in the 12th or the 14th?

F1: And the same thing goes for airplane flights. He'd rather take a more expensive flight than one with a 13 in the flight number. And of course he'd *never* sit in the 13th row on a plane. He says, "Why take chances? Better safe than sorry."

F2: Well, I guess it's harmless.

F1: You're probably right. The worst thing is that it embarrasses him. He's sure people talk about him behind his back because he knows the superstition is ridiculous. So, do YOU think people who believe in superstitions are gullible?

F2: Well, maybe . . . I'm a realist. For me, seeing is believing. I don't believe something just because it's *claimed* to be true by a lot of people. I need evidence. Don't get me wrong. I . . .

Unit 8, Lesson 2

F1: So, do you think it's possible to boost someone's intelligence?

M: In my opinion, it is.

F2: Actually, I'm not so sure. I mean, the experts say you're born with your level of intelligence.

M: But that's for only one kind of intelligence. We can all boost our intelligence in *some* way.

F1: I agree. After all, that's what education is for, isn't it?

F2: I suppose that's true. Lots of people do improve themselves through education.

M: I mean, just taking a class is one way to boost your intelligence. It's important to always be learning something new, right?

F2: Definitely.

F1: Or here's another example. My fifteen-year-old nephew plays video games all the time. His dad thinks it's a waste of time, but—I hate to admit it—I think it's making him smarter.

M: Really?

F1: Yeah. He suggests I try playing some of the games too, and I'm thinking about it. It's like exercising your brain.

F2: I guess it couldn't hurt! Hey . . . do you think there are any brain-healthy foods?

M: I've heard that it's essential to eat fish on a regular basis if you want to keep your brain healthy.

F1: I've heard that too. Or you can take pills with fish oil every day.

F2: Oh, come on. Do you really believe that?

M: Why not? If the experts recommend we do that, I think it's a good idea to try it.

F2: Well, how about getting enough sleep? They say it's important that we get at least eight hours.

F1: I think that's true too. Lack of sleep can't be good for the brain.

M: So it sounds like there are plenty of things we can do to boost our intelligence. I'm going to try taking fish oil every day. What about you?

Unit 9, Lesson 1

F: So, do you have any wild predictions for the future?

M: Don't laugh, OK?

F: I won't.

M: I think that by 2050 we'll be driving flying cars.

F: Flying cars by 2050? Sorry, but that sounds a bit far-fetched to me.

M: It may sound far-fetched, but I think it's possible. They've already been invented. Do an Internet search and you'll see.

F: You're right. But there are a lot of things they'll have to figure out first before everyone can actually own one.

M: Of course . . . like the astronomical price, to begin with. But I think by that time a lot of the problems will have been addressed. And at that point, flying cars could really catch on.

F: But what about driving—I mean flying—one of those things? Not only would it be confusing for most people, but it would be more dangerous than a conventional car.

M: True. But I think people are fast learners—they'll learn to operate them in no time.

F: Do you think so?

M: I do. And besides, other technological advances will make a difference; for example, cars that drive themselves. They've already invented that. And it could be applied to flying cars.

F: I suppose you may be right.

M: So what about you? What's your wild prediction?

F: Robots.

M: What about robots?

F: In ten years, robots will have been designed to do most household chores.

M: Well, that's pretty believable, depending on what you mean by robots.

F: I don't understand.

M: Well, there are robots that look like humans. I don't think that's going to happen so quickly. And there are robots that look like machines—a robot vacuum cleaner, for instance. They already exist.

F: I see your point. I guess I was thinking about robot *machines*. But you know, I recently saw a show on TV about robots and they've been some amazing things. . . .

Unit 10, Lesson 2

M: I would say that imports have generally had a positive impact here, wouldn't you?

F: I'm not sure. Why would you say that?

M: Well, for one thing, consumers have more choices.

F: I'm not so sure that's always true. For example, we've always had so many varieties of local corn to choose from. But people seem to prefer the sweeter imported corn, and more and more food stores are now only selling that type. Seems like less consumer choice to me. I'm worried that imported corn is having a negative economic impact and might even wipe out our local varieties.

M: That may be true, but if we look at foreign imports in general, I think the good outweighs the bad. Just walk into any department store. There are many more choices today than there were years ago.

F: But on the other hand, the more we depend on imports, the more problems there are. It's a slippery slope. For example, we'll have to put up with astronomical prices for imports—Let's face it, they generally cost more than local products do.

M: Good point. But I still think having the choice is a positive thing.

F: So what imported products would you never be willing to give up?

M: My car, of course! I love my imported car.

F: Me too. I couldn't give up mine either. What else?

M: My smart phone. I couldn't live without it!

F: Me neither. And I couldn't live without my tablet.

M: I don't have a tablet, but I feel the same way about my laptop. So what do we export from here that you think would have a positive impact overseas?

F: Well, we're already pretty well-known for our silver jewelry. That's been a successful export business for decades.

M: Right. You know, I think people in other countries would really love our traditional music if they were more familiar with it.

F: Good point. But you know what? I'd like to see our country offer more services. We have a growing number of talented people who can speak English. I think call centers could be a successful business model.

M: Well, that's another story. And an interesting idea.

F: I actually have a friend who's been thinking about starting a business in that area . . .